FEB.-27-2021

Professional Comments about
Glimpses of Other Realities – Vol. II: High Strangeness

"In July 1997 at Roswell, New Mexico, I had the honor and privilege of meeting Linda Moulton Howe. She commented that it took courage for me to write *The Day After Roswell.* However, it took a much greater courage for her to write *An Alien Harvest* and *Glimpses of Other Realities, Vol. I and II.* I was a soldier all my life and here she has 'guts' unparalleled in my experience. She took the difficult subjects of animal mutilations, human abductions and a non-human intelligence, withstood all the resistance and criticism, and moved ahead. I salute her."

– Lt. Col. Philip J. Corso (U.S. Army, Ret.), Former Chief, U. S. Army's Foreign Technology Division and best selling author, *The Day After Roswell*

"Emmy-award winner Linda Moulton Howe's *Volume II: High Strangeness* blends her unique, meticulous research, fascinating true-life stories and a thought-provoking analysis of what may ultimately lie behind the UFO contact/abduction phenomenon, alleged government cover-ups and the human body-soul connection. Linda has produced a brilliant contribution to our understanding of who we are, where we come from and where we may be heading as we approach the Millennium. I highly recommend it."

– Chet B. Snow, Ph. D., Author, *Mass Dreams of the Future*

"In *High Strangeness,* the second volume of her *Glimpses of Other Realities,* Linda Moulton Howe again demonstrates why she is one of the best researchers in this or any other field. Like her first volume and *An Alien Harvest,* this book maintains both objectivity and fascination in a way that reminds readers what journalism should be. Linda Howe looks with a dispassionate eye and writes with a passion for truth that draws readers in and yet allows them to weigh the evidence for themselves. This book would be a remarkable achievement in any field. In this one, it's a wonder."

– Denise Breton & Christopher Largent, Authors of *The Soul of Economies* and *The Paradigm Conspiracy*

"With the analytic curiosity of a scientist, the fearless courage of a warrior, and the gentle compassion of a therapist, Linda Moulton Howe applies her skills as an investigative reporter as she delves into many modern mysteries. Her writing reflects not only what she has learned from witnesses to these anomalies, but also her own reflections on the political, military, and scientific implications for humankind. The writer is to be commended for her efforts to explore these mysteries and her dedication in sharing her findings."

– R. Leo Sprinkle, Ph. D., Psychologist

Also by Linda Moulton Howe

An Alien Harvest

Glimpses of Other Realities - Volume 1: Facts & Eyewitnesses

Front Cover Photograph: *The Hourglass Nebula (MyCn18) is 8,000 light years from earth and surrounds a dying star in the central "blue eye." This photograph was taken with the Wide Field and Planetary Camera 2 (WFPC2) aboard NASA's Hubble Space Telescope by Raghvendra Sahai and John Trauger. Planetary nebulae are formed when some stars age, become red giants and eject all of their outer layers. The ultraviolet radiation from the exposed hot stellar core makes the surrounding cloud of matter glow. But how planetary nebulae evolve into such complex shapes from originally round suns and gas clouds is still a mystery.*

Back Cover Photograph: *A sunrise from one hundred fifty-five nautical miles above Pecos, Texas. The thin blue and white band extending across the image is light scattered back through the earth's upper atmosphere into space. Photograph STS-029-06-020 by NASA crewmembers onboard Discovery, Orbiter Vehicle 103, March 18, 1989.*

GLIMPSES OF THER REALITIES

NATIONAL GEOGRAPHIC SOCIETY
1999 Member

GREGORY B HYDE
Member No. 594619HDEKO263G96
Valid 1/1/99 - 12/31/99

Signature

WAS-ON-P.41

To Greg-
All the best,
Linda Moulton Howe
9/98

LINDA MOULTON HOWE

First published 1998

First Edition, First Printing, 1998

Printed in the United States of America at
Paper Chase Press
5721 Magazine Street, Ste. 152
New Orleans, Louisiana 70115

Library of Congress Catalog Card Number: 93-91681

ISBN 1-879706-78-4

PAPER
CHASE
PRESS

To those who struggle toward truths beyond high strangeness. And to my parents in another reality.

IV

" In the field of UFOs, deeper acquaintance reveals a subject that has not only potentially important scientific aspects, but sociological, psychological, and even theological aspects as well. ...More and more high strangeness cases are surfacing (which) outrage our common sense and constitute a challenge to our present belief systems."

J. ALLEN HYNEK
ASTRONOMER
1979 PREFACE, *THE ANDREASSON AFFAIR*

CONTENTS

VOLUME II: HIGH STRANGENESS

ACKNOWLEDGMENTS

Many people have contributed their firsthand experiences to this Volume II about incidents of high strangeness which challenge our understanding and belief systems. Some can be named; others cannot, but they know who they are. The patterns of events in these encounters are often similar and perhaps give some insight into the non-human intelligences which interact with animal, plant and human life on earth.

I am very grateful to the following people, in alphabetical order: John J. Andrews, "Axle," Art Bell, "Steve Bismarck," Ray Boeche, Peter A. Bostrom, Chris Carey, Lt. Col. Philip J. Corso, U. S. Army (Ret.), Wes Crum, Paul Davids, Timothy J. Fint, Josie Galante, Victor Golubic, David Huggins, Benton Jamison, "Joe," Steven Kaeser, Andrew Kissner, Bill LaParl, "Wanna Lawson," Bob and Betty Andreasson Luca, Debbie Pagliughi, Staff Sergeant Jim Penniston, USAF (Ret.), Beau Peterson, Linda Porter, "Reed," "Ken Rose," 1st Lt. Robert Salas, USAF (Ret.), Ray Santilli, Bob Shell, "Sherman," "Derek Smith," Jim Sparks, Lt. Col. Wendelle Stevens, USAF (Ret.), Sgt. Clifford Stone, U. S. Army (Ret.), and Dwain Wright.

I also want to thank Andy Abercrombie, Thomas Adams, Denise Breton, Vincent and Barbara Creevy, Darryl Diamond, M. D., Bob Durant, Raymond Fowler, Ron Garner, Andy Hauck, Anna Hayes, Chris Largent, Michael Lindemann, Mario Pazzaglini, Ph.D., Bruce Ratcliff, Kenneth Ring, Ph.D., Chet Snow, Ph.D. and Leo Sprinkle, Ph.D. for reading, editing and offering their own insights into high strangeness and other realities. And a special thanks to Colin Wilson who wrote the Foreword. He has had the courage to explore unusual phenomena most of his life and to share his insights in remarkable works of fiction and non-fiction.

I am also deeply grateful for the friendship and help of Michael Pill, Massachusetts attorney and fellow researcher of unexplained phenomena, whose research into ancient mysteries and insightful responses to my evolving manuscript were so valuable.

Others who have helped with the challenge of producing *Glimpses of Other Realities, Volumes I and II* are Ann Douden who designed its format and covers, Pioneer Printing, Attorney Robert Dorr, Emilie Springfield, Kate Blizzard, Paper Chase Press and Aware Book Group.

A special thanks to Lynda and Bill Beierwaltes and John St. Clair for their friendship and support. Without them, I could not have done this two-volume book.

FOREWORD

BY COLIN WILSON
AUTHOR, *MYSTERIES* AND *THE OUTSIDER*

As I read *Glimpses of Other Realities, Volume II: High Strangeness,* I found myself in an almost permanent state of excitement. It was all so incredible that it sounded like fiction. Yet, I knew enough about Linda Moulton Howe to know that it was not. She is a hard-working journalist and a good researcher and her synthesis of patterns in high strangeness are based on a vast amount of field work.

My first surprise came at the beginning of the first chapter. Major Donald Keyhoe (U. S. Marine Corps, Ret.) was one of the original writers on unidentified flying objects, and *The Flying Saucers Are Real* (1950) was one of the first books to make an impact on the public at large. I had read two of his books, but not the fourth, *Flying Saucers: Top Secret* (1960). And I was amazed to read that Major Keyhoe had been approached by a U. S. Air Force broadcasting unit and asked to cooperate on a program in which the Air Force admitted that all members of the Defense Department had been muzzled when it came to reports on flying saucers and that there is "a blackout on UFO reports by the Federal Government." I must admit that I had always been vaguely incredulous about allegations of massive government cover-ups about UFOs. But Major Keyhoe said there was "prolonged secrecy and censorship imposed by the United States Air Force on all authentic UFO information."

It was only the first of a number of such shocks in *Glimpses of Other Realities.* I have never read a book that excited such a powerful series of reactions in me. Again and again, I found myself thinking: "If this is true, then we are all asleep. Something tremendous is going on, something that is going to affect every human being on this planet sooner or later, and we still go on living as if we were in the comfortable security of the Victorian age."

The question that keeps returning to me is: Why, if all this is true — or only half true — can so many people ignore it? Why have skeptics such as writer Philip Klass and the late astronomer Carl Sagan asserted that UFOs are some kind of hysterical delusion?

The answer to that question, I have concluded, is that we all need a sense of security, the feeling that we can get on with our lives without too much anxiety. So, we tend to ignore things that do not immediately affect us.

If you take the cases in this book individually, each one can be subjected to skeptical analysis and, if not dismissed, at least reduced to a minus on the credibility scale. Various military personnel speak off the record, various abductees describe their experiences under hypnosis — or in one case a man recalls his experiences consciously. Each might be regarded as less than reliable. But once the total picture is grasped, it is overwhelming. Nitpicking criticism leaves it unaffected. And that total picture tells us that something very strange is going on, and very important.

The next chapter "Light Beams, Discs and Animal Deaths" underlines and expands points Linda Howe has already made in the previous two volumes:[1] that there is overwhelming circumstantial evidence of eyewitness tales about little silver-suited men who can levitate animals in a beam of light, who paralyze human beings who try to interfere, and who commandeer the help of large, shaggy creatures that sound like the traditional Bigfoot. (Are the aliens deliberately making these stories so preposterous that any normal person would refuse to take them seriously? I suspect this has always been a part of the alien strategy.)

But it is in the next two chapters that I really began to feel the full meaning of her title "High Strangeness." The experiences of Jim Sparks, Linda Porter and Wanna Lawson seem like science fiction. If I had encountered them in another context, I would have applied a very high degree of critical skepticism. But, accounts from abductees are also cited by historian David Jacobs and researchers such as Raymond Fowler, Budd Hopkins and many others.

There are certain things that I find very hard to accept. For example, the notion that the aliens can travel backwards in time. It has always seemed to me that time travel is an impossibility. It would involve obvious paradoxes, such as being able to go back to the "you" of five minutes ago — or even five seconds ago — and bring that "previous-time-you" to the present so there were two "yous." Time has always struck me as a misconception anyway. When we say time passes, we actually mean things change. As I look out of my window, I see trees swaying in the wind and clouds moving across the sky. To make time go backwards, I would have to reverse these movements, as I can put back my clock. But even if I were God, and could make the whole universe go backwards, would that be time travel?

Then I realize that, as a writer on psychical research, I have accepted for nearly three decades the reality of precognition — people who see, with

[1] An Alien Harvest - Further Evidence Linking Animal Mutilations and Human Abductions To Alien Life Forms © *1989 and* Glimpses of Other Realities, Vol. I - Facts & Eyewitnesses © *1994 by Linda Moulton Howe, LMH Productions.*

complete accuracy, something that has not yet happened. But chaos theory tells us that there is no scientific way of predicting what will happen in a few days time. So I am forced to suppress my grumbling objections to beings traveling from the future — even if not convinced.

Like Linda Moulton Howe, Jacques Vallee and John Keel and everyone else who has studied the UFO phenomenon, I find myself trying to formulate a general theory that encompasses a mass of utterly confusing and contradictory information. Certain things seem obvious. When Kenneth Arnold saw unidentified flying objects, or "flying saucers," in June 1947 at the beginning of a major UFO flap, many people felt they were visitors from Mars. Then writers like the Englishman Harold Wilkins pointed out ancient accounts that sound very like UFOs and many came to accept that the earth might have been visited for thousands of years. That, in a way, was comforting: if They — whoever They are — had been around that long, then They certainly intended no harm.

In 1961 came the first abduction story of Betty and Barney Hill. Betty Hill was convinced that UFO occupants are benevolent and described their presence in her excellent book *A Common Sense Approach to UFOs.*

Animal mutilations were reported in the 1960s as well and abduction reports became more frequent. *Missing Time* (1981) and *Intruders* (1987) by Budd Hopkins made it clear that people were reporting missing time linked to alleged non-human contact more often than anyone had supposed.

John Mack, M. D., a Harvard University psychiatrist, wrote *Abduction: Human Encounters With Aliens* in which he left no doubt that he had come to accept the abduction phenomenon. Another large work called *Alien Discussions* provided a transcript of a conference held on the grounds of MIT in 1992 which swung the balance heavily in favor of the credibility of the phenomenon. It looks as if, without landing on the White House lawn or otherwise violently interfering with our normal way of life, that the "aliens" are slowly convincing us that they are real. It also begins to look as if the millennium is, indeed, going to bring one of the great changes in human history.

But what change? Do they intend to hybridize the human race? Or take us over? What is their purpose?

When I try to look at the whole phenomenon, I come back to my most basic intuition which has been at the heart of all my work since *The Outsider* in 1956: that there is something oddly wrong with human consciousness. Although we have evolved further than any other animal on the face of the earth, it is at the cost of an absurd narrowness which means that we look at reality through the long end of a telescope, failing to see the wood or even leaves because we can only focus on individual trees. Our evolution in the past twenty-five thousand years has been incredible, yet it has been largely wasted in the sense that we take it for granted and go plodding on dully. We see the world from a worm's eye view, when we urgently need a bird's eye view.

It seems to me that the aliens might be the instrument of some bigger purpose, environmental or other, and might not have all the answers themselves. Linda Moulton Howe came close to one major answer, I think, with her spiritual experiences in Idaho and Peru described in her Prologues for this two-volume work.

Studying the UFO phenomenon, particularly as it is expressed in Linda's books, has made me clearly aware of one thing that I had formerly grasped only vaguely: that, far from being the most intelligent species in the universe, human beings are not really so far ahead of the cows who graze in our meadows. We eat animals without feeling guilt-stricken because we feel that they are so much less intelligent than ourselves. Yet anyone who reads Howe's book will end by being fairly certain that we are equally unintelligent compared to the aliens who abducted Jim Sparks and Linda Porter.

But *is* our intelligence really so low? I only have to think of Linda Howe's experience in Idaho to see that this is untrue. We simply suffer from a kind of tunnel vision. Our greatest need at this point in our evolution is to change our intellectual viewpoint — to recognize that we are not alone in the universe and that we ought to be making far more vigorous use of the intelligence we possess. Our narrowness *hypnotizes* us into passivity.

The astronomer Fred Hoyle has been convinced for decades that life, far from being rare, is a universal norm. He even believes that life might have come to earth originally from outer space and that the sudden and simultaneous appearance of outbreaks of worldwide plagues like the Black Death and the 1918 flu epidemic prove that space might be responsible for unpleasant surprises on our planet.

It seems to me that what is now being forced upon us, whether we like it or not, is a more universalist point of view. I do not know whether the "aliens" are trying to tell us this, or whether it is something altogether bigger. But we are certainly being told that we have to wake up. The UFO phenomenon — or many-related phenomena – are gradually forcing us to accept that there *are* "other realities and dimensions," and that we cannot continue living like cows ruminating in a field.

In the 19th Century, the rise of spiritualism did its best to convince us that although our reality *looks* logical and complete, it doesn't really add up. But it didn't work. Those who studied the subject *knew* it had to be real, but not enough people studied it. They didn't have to, so they yawned and went back to sleep. I, myself, didn't take it seriously until I was asked to write a book about the occult and went into it with my tongue in my cheek, convinced it would all turn out to be nonsense. I ended by recognizing that phenomena such as ghosts, poltergeists and precognition are as real as the world studied by science.

But it doesn't really matter a damn whether you believe in ghosts or not — they aren't likely to impinge on your life. And even if they do, you can ignore and forget it. Yet, what is now happening is demanding our attention with a persistence that cannot be ignored and will become more persistent until it gets our full attention.

For anyone who has so far managed to sleep through the increasing furor about UFOs, I cannot recommend a better alarm clock than Linda Moulton Howe's book.

COLIN WILSON
GORRAN HAVEN, CORNWALL, ENGLAND
JULY 17, 1997

AUTHOR'S INTRODUCTION

"Recent decades have taught us that physics is a magic window. It shows us the illusion that lies behind reality — and the reality that lies behind illusion. Its scope is immensely greater than we once realized. We are no longer satisfied with insights only into particles, or fields of force, or geometry, or even space and time. Today we demand of physics some understanding of existence itself."

JOHN WHEELER [1]
QUANTUM PHYSICIST

[1] Quantum Theory and Measurement *by John Archibald Wheeler and Wojciech Hubert Zurek, Editors, © 1983 Princeton University Press.*

An Air Force intelligence officer once told me about an elderly colleague, a Colonel, who supposedly spent time with an extraterrestrial biological entity retrieved from a crashed silver disc in New Mexico. The Colonel said the being explained telepathically that this is not the only universe. He said, "Imagine a large island of white sand and that each sand grain is a different universe separated from the others by an electromagnetic membrane. And surrounding the island is a cold, dark sea."

I asked the intelligence officer what the dark sea was and he answered, "You don't want to know. It would change you forever."

I argued that I wanted to know the truth no matter what it was. But he refused to talk further. His silence, like that of the larger government he worked for, has evolved from a policy of and reverence for secret knowledge — secrets hidden and protected by the overriding authority and power of "national security" interests.

Some of the most highly strange, and often contradictory, information about the UFO phenomenon has come to me from active or retired military and intelligence operatives who ask to remain anonymous. Their communications are about alleged government knowledge and cover-up of contact with one or more non-human intelligences since at least the 1940s. One exception to the anonymity was my radio interview in July 1997 with Lt. Col. Philip J. Corso (Ret.) in Roswell, New Mexico at the time his book *The Day After Roswell* was published and became a best-seller. We met at the 50th Anniversary commemoration of the alleged crash of a disc, or two discs, between Corona and Roswell in the first week of July 1947. As the Colonel and I shook hands, he said, "Linda Howe, I have your book *(Glimpses, Vol. I)* and want to know how you got so much classified information?" The Colonel told me that he had read highly classified documents about extraterrestrials mutilating animals and abducting humans as early as the 1950s.

Lt. Colonel Corso's book reveals his assignment in 1961-1963 to work for General Arthur Trudeau, head of Army Research and Development in the Pentagon in Washington, D. C. where pieces of extraterrestrial biological entity (EBEs) technologies retrieved from downed alien craft were stored in a file cabinet. Col. Corso's task, as head of General Trudeau's Foreign Technology desk, was "to filter the Roswell (disc) technology into the mainstream of industrial development through the military defense contracting programs. Today, items such as lasers, integrated circuits, fiber-optics networks, accelerated particle-beam devices, and even the Kevlar material in bulletproof vests are all commonplace. Yet the seeds for their development of all of them were found in the crash of the alien craft at Roswell and turned up in my (Pentagon) files fourteen years later."

I had the Colonel's book with me and had underlined pages 267-268 concerning the Strategic Defense Initiative, or "Star Wars," program launched in the early 1980s by the Ronald Reagan Administration. The Colonel wrote:[2]

> "We knew who the real targets of the SDI were, and it wasn't a bunch of ICBM warheads. It was the UFOs, alien spacecraft thinking themselves invulnerable and invisible as they soared around the edges of our atmosphere, swooping down at will to destroy our communications with EMP bursts (electromagnetic pulse), buzz our spacecraft, colonize our lunar surface, mutilate cattle in their own horrendous biological experiments, and even abduct human beings for their medical tests and hybridization of the species. And what was worse, we had to let them do it because we had no weapon to defend ourselves."

[2] *Reprinted with the permission of Pocket Books, a Division of Simon & Schuster from* The Day After Roswell *by Lt. Col. Philip J. Corso (Army Ret.) with William J. Birnes, © 1997 Rosewood Woods Productions, Inc.*

I asked the Colonel if he thought the U. S. was in a secret war with one extraterrestrial group and allied with another. He said he no longer had inside information, but assumed that not much had changed since his Pentagon days working for General Trudeau when the general considered the EBEs to be a potential threat to national and world security. I told him I thought the whole truth of the situation was so complex that it couldn't be easily categorized. He responded enigmatically, "Linda, there's a new world coming if we can take it."

The Colonel admitted that no one knew exactly all the motives of the different EBEs and their androids, but they were real and they were here whether the government denied or the general media ignored.

Glimpses of Other Realities, Volume I grew out of my efforts to investigate the worldwide crop circle, animal mutilation and human abduction mysteries through hard physical evidence and firsthand eyewitness testimony. This *Volume II* has evolved from human testimony that often cannot be proved and is so highly strange that the content can easily be rejected as "too weird to be real." Astronomer J. Allen Hynek in fact devised a "Strangeness Rating" in his 1972 ground-breaking book *The UFO Experience, A Scientific Inquiry* [3] which introduced the concept of Encounters of the First, Second and Third Kind ranging from distant lights to actual occupant sightings. Dr. Hynek wrote: "Each report that has satisfied the definition of UFO used in this book can be assigned two numbers: its Strangeness Rating and its Probability Rating. The Strangeness Rating is, to express it loosely, a measure of how 'oddball' a report is within its particular broad classification. More precisely, it can be taken as a measure of the number of information bits the report contains, each of which is difficult to explain in common-sense terms."

[3] The UFO Experience, A Scientific Inquiry © *1972 by Dr. J. Allen Hynek, Ballantine Books. Hynek was former Chairman of Northwestern University's Department of Astronomy, former Assoc. Director of the Smithsonian Astrophysical Observatory in Cambridge, Massachusetts; former head of the Observatory's NASA-sponsored satellite tracking program; scientific consultant to the U. S. Air Force Project Blue Book 1952-1969; established the Center for UFO Studies in 1972; deceased 1986.*

In Chapter 1, the military sources are haunted by secret knowledge of government projects related to extraterrestrials and/or other-dimensional intelligences which could include time travelers. Insiders say there are well-defined procedures for debriefings and field operations to learn as much as possible about non-human intelligences and their technologies while keeping the public ignorant. Their insider goals are to prevent public panic, to gain technology for military, space and civilian use, and to sustain the current socio-economic-religious status quo for as long as possible.

Some contend that the "big picture" involves the manipulation of past and present time lines by other life forms trying to survive a dead end future. The origins of those other life forms might be from earth's future, or even from an unimaginable place outside this visible universe. But whatever their origins, one of their goals might be to influence human genetic development and to access information from human genes, minds and souls.

Manipulation of minds, bodies and animals by another intelligence and its sophisticated beam and craft technologies are also issues for civilian eyewitnesses in Chapter 2. Soil indentations, biochemical and biophysical changes in plants, and the dead and surgically cut bodies of animals are physical residues of some kind of technology and intense energies. Eyewitnesses have even seen animals, and possibly a human body, rise up inside beams into disc-shaped aerial craft.

In Chapter 3, Florida real estate developer Jim Sparks describes conscious interactions with grey beings who showed him a series of holographic images. Sparks understood the images to be his ancestors' bloodline back to a primate species. "The aliens made us," Sparks said, "but we're now like parasites destroying the garden and it has to stop, or we humans are going to be stopped. The alien technologies are so advanced they could move us to another dimension in a second. They can change matter into energy and back like it's nothing."

In fact, current earth physicists are redefining the relationship between mass and energy. In *The Sciences,* November/December 1994,[4] Bernhard Haisch, Alfonso Rueda and H. E. Puthoff outlined a new physics "in which mass, inertia and gravity arise from underlying electromagnetic processes" in an article entitled "Beyond $E=mc^2$." Bernhard Haisch is a staff scientist at the Lockheed Palo Alto Research Laboratory in California and a regular visiting fellow at the Max Planck Institut fur Extraterrestrische Physik in Garching, Germany. Alfonso Rueda is a Professor of Electrical Engineering at California State University in Long Beach. H. E. Puthoff is Director of the Institute for Advanced Studies in Austin, Texas.

[4] *"Beyond $E=mc^2$,"* The Sciences, *November/December 1994, Pages 26-31.*

The three scientists wrote, "Recent work by us and others now appears to offer a radically different insight into the relation $E=mc^2$, as well as into the very idea of mass itself. To put it simply, the concept of mass may be neither fundamental nor necessary in physics. In the view we will present, Einstein's formula is even more significant than physicists have realized. It is actually a statement about how much energy is required to give the appearance of a certain amount of mass, rather than about the conversion of one fundamental thing, energy, into another fundamental thing, mass.

"Indeed, if that view is correct, there is no such thing as mass — only electric charge and energy, which together create the illusion of mass."

Three-dimensional illusions and other mind manipulations are common to non-human encounter experiences, as computer scientist Jacques Vallee and writer John Keel both pointed out in their early 1960s investigations. Later Vallee would write, "I believe that the UFO phenomenon is one of the ways through which an alien form of intelligence of incredible complexity is communicating with us symbolically. ...I believe that the UFO phenomenon represents evidence for other dimensions beyond space-time; the UFOs may not come from ordinary space, but from a multiverse which is all around us, and of which we have stubbornly refused to consider the disturbing reality in spite of the evidence available to us for centuries. ...What we see here is not an alien invasion. It is a spiritual system that acts on humans and uses humans."[5]

[5] Dimensions: A Casebook of Alien Contact © *1988 by Jacques Vallee, Contemporary Books.*

Chapter 4 concerns another technology in which humanoid bodies are cloned and even life force appears to be transferred from one body container to another. "The aliens seemed very surprised that I was upset, that the body was just going to be tossed overboard," said Linda Porter after a medical encounter with large-headed, grey-skinned beings. "They told me my body was just a container for the soul and of no other value. They think our concept of funerals is barbarous. To them, there is no difference between an empty beer can and an empty body." Also in Chapter 4, Wanna Lawson says there is an argument between two main groups of advanced intelligences about the artificial manipulation of DNA in already-evolving life forms to produce creatures such as *Homo sapiens,* the one and only living species of the primate genus Homo which comprises modern humankind.

One possible motive that an advanced intelligence might have for creating *Homo sapiens* could be the production of a sophisticated android to do work on this planet. An android is a synthetic humanoid created from biological materials. If an advanced intelligence engineered life-seeding projects on planets throughout this and other galaxies, "caretakers" specifically designed to live in a particular atmosphere and environment would be needed to tend and harvest the planetary "gardens." Humans might be someone else's android worker whose genetic material is harvested periodically for other android productions. Android caretakers might also be used to tend wide varieties of life forms on planets designed to be living libraries, zoos or museums. Perhaps the most challenging concept of all might involve access and perpetuation of souls in specific life forms for yet unknown reasons.

Each year the Big Picture has become more complicated, multiplying into more and more mysteries. Once upon a time, people argued about whether "strange lights in the sky" really were metal discs with extraterrestrial beings in them. The discussion has now evolved to men, women and children who describe interactions with entities whose motives remain hidden or confusing, but which demonstrate an ability to control human minds and bodies with ease. Humans have returned from alleged alien abduction experiences with descriptions of other realities and a different cosmology — one that includes parallel universes, missing time or time expansions and compressions, different time lines and time travellers, multiple dimensions and energy beings. The longer I have tried to study and analyze the various physical and anecdotal residues of the UFO phenomenon, the deeper I have found myself in a hall of mirrors with a quicksand floor.

My hope is that the reader of this high strangeness volume will absorb the chapters in the frame of mind in which I wrote the prologues for Volume I and Volume II — that good and bad characterizations might be too simple for the enormity of a Control System that seems to be involved with our planet, galaxy and universe. Perhaps the main issue is survival and experimentation to accomplish genetic goals that were begun thousands of years ago in earth time. But to the Control System, earth's past, present and future might be simultaneous. The genetic challenge might also involve a dispute among higher forces about what is allowable to do with DNA manipulation and artificial creation of life.

I suspect there is truth to the controversial assertion that a non-earth intelligence interfered genetically with primate evolution on this planet. So, efforts to understand the modern day non-human presence is a challenge inextricably bound up with the origin of our species and what seems to be the forbidden history of humankind. This quest spirals back to ancient wisdom which long ago tried to explain who we are and why we are here by pointing to the stars. There, in the gigantic cosmic theater, it was said that God-made souls entered different forms to learn and grow in migrations from one reality to another.

LINDA MOULTON HOWE
JAMISON, PENNSYLVANIA
NOVEMBER 10, 1997

PROLOGUE

"Mass is a phenomenon of connecting light rays which go back and forth, sort of freezing them into a pattern.

So matter, as it were, is condensed or frozen light. Light is not merely electromagnetic waves but in a sense other kinds of waves that go at that speed. Therefore, all matter is a condensation of light into patterns moving back and forth at average speeds which are less than the speed of light. Even Einstein had some hint of that idea. You could say that when we come to light we are coming to the fundamental activity in which existence has its ground, or at least coming close to it."

DAVID BOHM, THEORETICAL PHYSICIST
FROM RENEE WEBER'S
DIALOGUES WITH SCIENTISTS AND SAGES[1]

[1] Dialogues with Scientists and Sages *© 1986 by Renee Weber, Routledge & Kegan Paul, London.*

My dad always said God was the breeze and sun and cold water coming out of the hose when he washed the car. My mother said all life was precious and always carried bugs and spiders out of the house in dust rags. Those two philosophies were as close as our family ever got to religion.

When I was nineteen, I went on a camping trip with my younger brother and cousin into the remote Salmon River country of Idaho. Each day, to explore and exercise, I hiked up a mountain near our camp site. Late one afternoon as I was walking back down, I saw orange-gold shafts of light shining through thick stands of lodgepole pine. The sun was setting and the low angle cast beams that shimmered with forest dust. I was stunned by the beauty as if I had never before seen light. I began to walk toward the rays. I can clearly remember my legs and arms moving, but something changed as if I were motion picture film suddenly switched from normal speed to slow motion.

My next memory is being further down the mountain. Near my feet was a small, blooming wildflower. The petals were pulsing with an intense white light edged with an orchid glow. Confused and wanting everything to go back to normal, I ran several yards. When I stopped, the pulsing light had spread to all the blooming wildflowers as far as I could see. Behind me, the mountain was a dark shadow with the setting sun to its back. The silhouette seemed to move slowly up and down against the twilight sky as if the mountain were breathing. A few first stars pulsated with the same orchid-white light that was shining from the wildflowers.

Then as if an unseen force gently took hold of my arms, I watched as my hands came together palms up in front of my face. I heard a thought-voice in my mind say, "You are one with the light. The light is one with you. And you are in the hands of God."

Then the flowers, stars and mountain stopped pulsing. Below me in the distance near the river, I could see a fire. My brother and cousin were cooking dinner, black shadows outlined by the firelight. It was as though someone had lifted up the surface around me for awhile to let me see what was underneath.

Since then, I have been convinced that a common source of energy pervades all there is and can be an ally to living life. That energy, I think, moves in cycles like the spiral on the next page found carved in rock all over this planet. Part of the old symbol's meaning is that the machinery of the universe involves the evolution of souls. The spirals are not static and not two-dimensional. The symbol is a slice. A larger reality can be imagined as a spiral upward and downward through innumerable other frequencies or dimensions. Ancient wisdom understood that the moment of death was simply a transition into another frequency on the spiral. So all lines in all directions are simultaneous and filled with life forms ebbing and flowing, supported by a singular force, an invisible matrix of energy from which everything emerges and to which everything returns.

The spiral labyrinth representing the cyclic renewal of life, the great round of death and rebirth, the journey of the soul in and out of past, present and future forms. These labyrinths have been found carved on ancient rocks in England, Ireland, the Adriatic Sea region, Hopi Indian lands, Greece and the island of Crete dating at least 4,000 years before Christ.

CHAPTER 1

MILITARY VOICES

"The alien technology is so advanced and the beings are so strange that no one would believe it. Keeping the public and media away from what's really happening isn't difficult. It's a story that no one wants to tell, that no one knows how to tell. The truth is stranger than fiction."

RETIRED U. S. MILITARY OFFICER, 1991

In addition to my work as a TV producer, documentary filmmaker and writer, I have reported news about science, the environment and unexplained phenomena since 1993 on the nationally syndicated radio program *Dreamland* hosted by Art Bell. The title is slang used at Nellis AFB, Nevada to describe the top secret Area 51 where highly classified technology and craft have been stored and tested. Some say there are "extraterrestrial" craft there hidden behind and below the Papoose Mountain range.

Several of my radio interviews have concerned research about alleged extraterrestrial vehicles that had crashed near Roswell, Capitan Mountain and Socorro, New Mexico in 1947. Some of those reports I did from England and Italy in the fall of 1995. That's when scenes of a six-fingered and six-toed humanoid dissection and craft debris were broadcast in the U. K. and United States amid intense controversy about whether or not the film was actually historic.

A few months later, Bell and I received a series of letters, each postmarked from South Carolina and signed only "A Friend." The first letter was dated April 10, 1996 and included several metal pieces:

> "I've followed your broadcasts over the last year or so and have been considering whether or not to share with you and your listeners some information related to the Roswell (New Mexico) UFO crash.

"My grandfather was a member of the Retrieval Team sent to the crash site just after the incident was reported. He died in 1974, but not before he had sat down with some of us and talked about the incident. I am currently serving in the (United States) military and hold a Security Clearance and do NOT wish to 'go public' and risk losing my career and commission.

"Nonetheless, I would like to briefly tell you what my own grandfather told me about Roswell. In fact, I enclose for your safekeeping 'samples' that were in the possession of my grandfather until he died (in 1974), and which I have had since his own estate was settled. As I understand it, they came from the UFO debris and were among a large batch subsequently sent to Wright-Patterson AFB in Ohio from New Mexico."

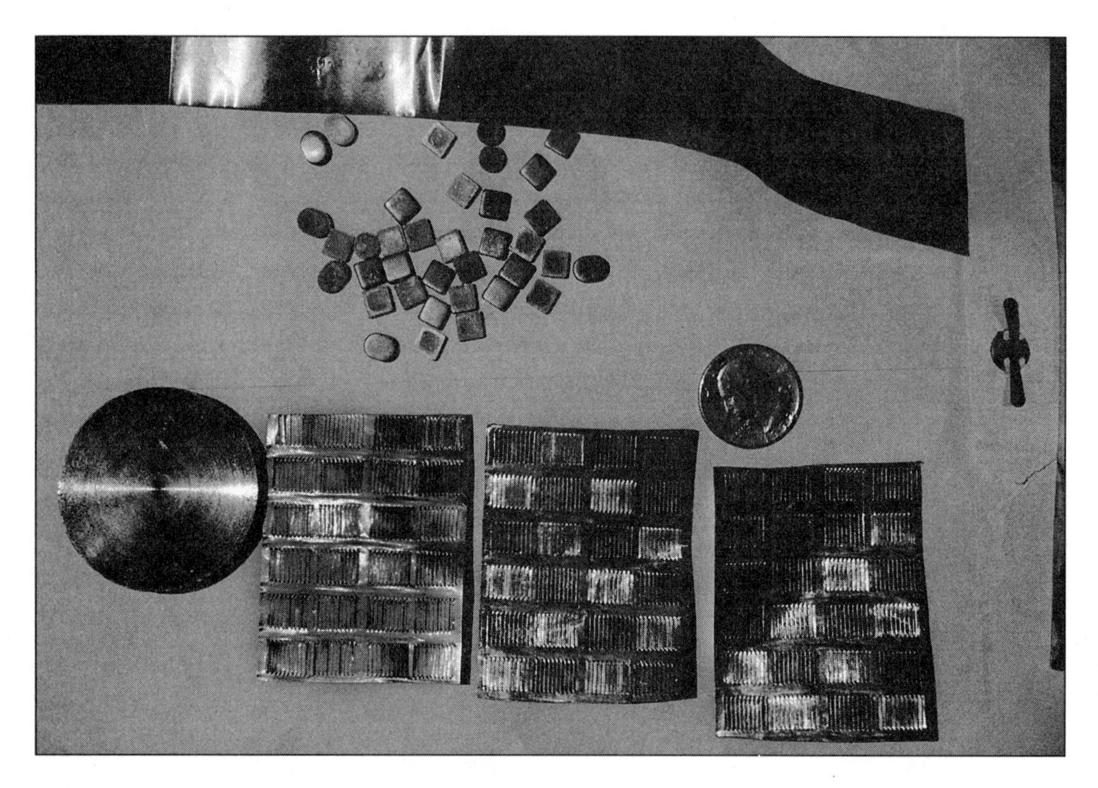

Plate 1 - *Aluminum pieces sent by anonymous South Carolina source with his first April 10, 1996 letter allegedly "appropriated" by his grandfather as samples from a wedge-shaped vehicle that crashed "between San Mateo Mountains and Sierra Blanca" west of Roswell. Date not given by source. Photograph by Art Bell © 1996.*

The writer did not give a specific crash date or location in that first letter. Bell and I repeatedly asked during radio broadcasts for those facts because several different testimonies have emerged the past few years about crashed or landed discs in different locations and different time periods. If true, the incident that made newspaper headlines about a "flying saucer" crashing on the Foster Ranch between Corona and Roswell the first week of July 1947 was not unique.

In his fifth and final letter received July 5, 1996, the writer finally quoted notes "from Grandad's journal" that placed the impact site "between San Mateo Mountains and Sierra Blanca" west of Roswell, but did not give a date. Sierra Blanca peak is about seventy miles straight west of Roswell. San Mateo Peak is another eighty miles west of Sierra Blanca. Between those two mountain regions is the White Sands Missile Range. Magdalena and Socorro are at the northeastern edge of the Plains of San Agustin and north of the San Mateo Mountains. (See New Mexico maps, pp 4-5.)

The source also clarified in another letter that the vehicle was a "*Wedge-shaped Disc.*" (Howe's emphasis.) A wedge could be shaped like a piece of pie or perhaps a curved crescent, but a disc is round. So, we assumed the grandfather was using "disc" generically for UFO.

The South Carolina writer included the following highly strange description — based, he said, on conversations with his grandfather — about the security team's efforts to retrieve the wedge-shaped "Disc" and three non-human bodies, two dead and one alive:

> "...the Team arrived at the crash site just after the AAF/USAF reported the ground zero location. (Howe's Note: Army Air Force was splitting into Air Force and Army during the summer of 1947.) They found two dead occupants, hurled free of the Disc. A lone surviving occupant was found within the Disc and it was apparent its left leg was broken. There was a minimal radiation contamination and it was quickly dispersed with a water/solvent wash, and soon the occupant was dispatched for medical assistance and isolation. The bodies were sent to the Wright-Patterson AFB for dispersal. The debris was also loaded onto three trucks which finished the on-load just before the sunset.
>
> "Grandad was part of the Team that went with the surviving occupant. The occupant communicated via telepathic means. It spoke (transmitted) perfect English and communicated the following: The Disc was a 'probeship' dispatched from a 'launchship' that was stationed at the dimensional gateway to the Terran Solar System. The occupants were part of a race of explorers from a Solar System 32 Light Years from Terra. They had been conducting operations on Terra for over 100 years. Another group (sic) were exploring Mars, and Io (Martian moon). Each 'probeship' carried a crew of three. A 'launchship' had a crew of (100) One-Hundred.
>
> "The Disc that crashed had collided with a meteor in orbit of Terra and was attempting to compensate its flight vector, but

Plate 2 - *Map of New Mexico.*

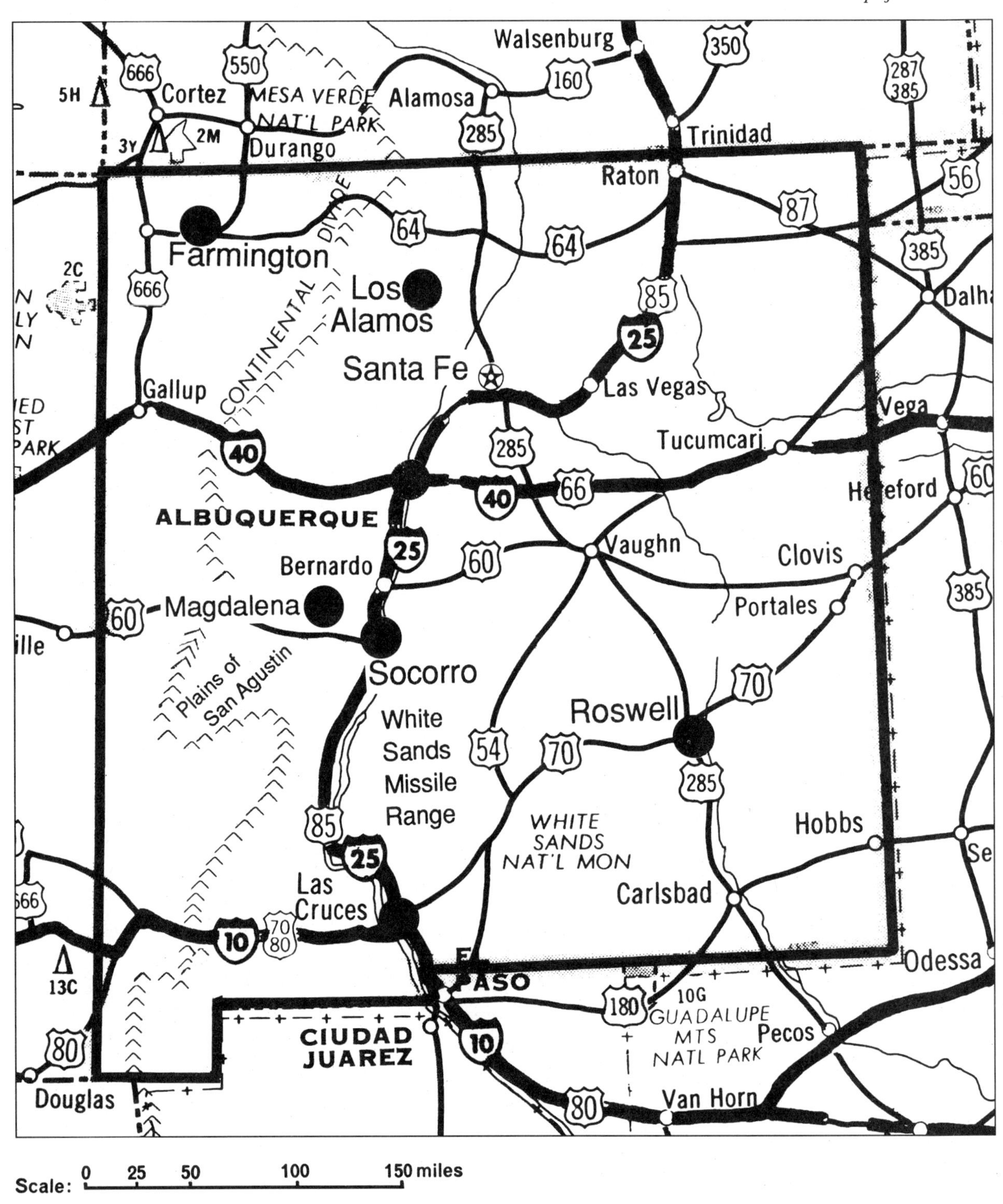

Plate 3 - *Roswell and White Sands Missile Range to Socorro and Plains of San Agustin, New Mexico.*

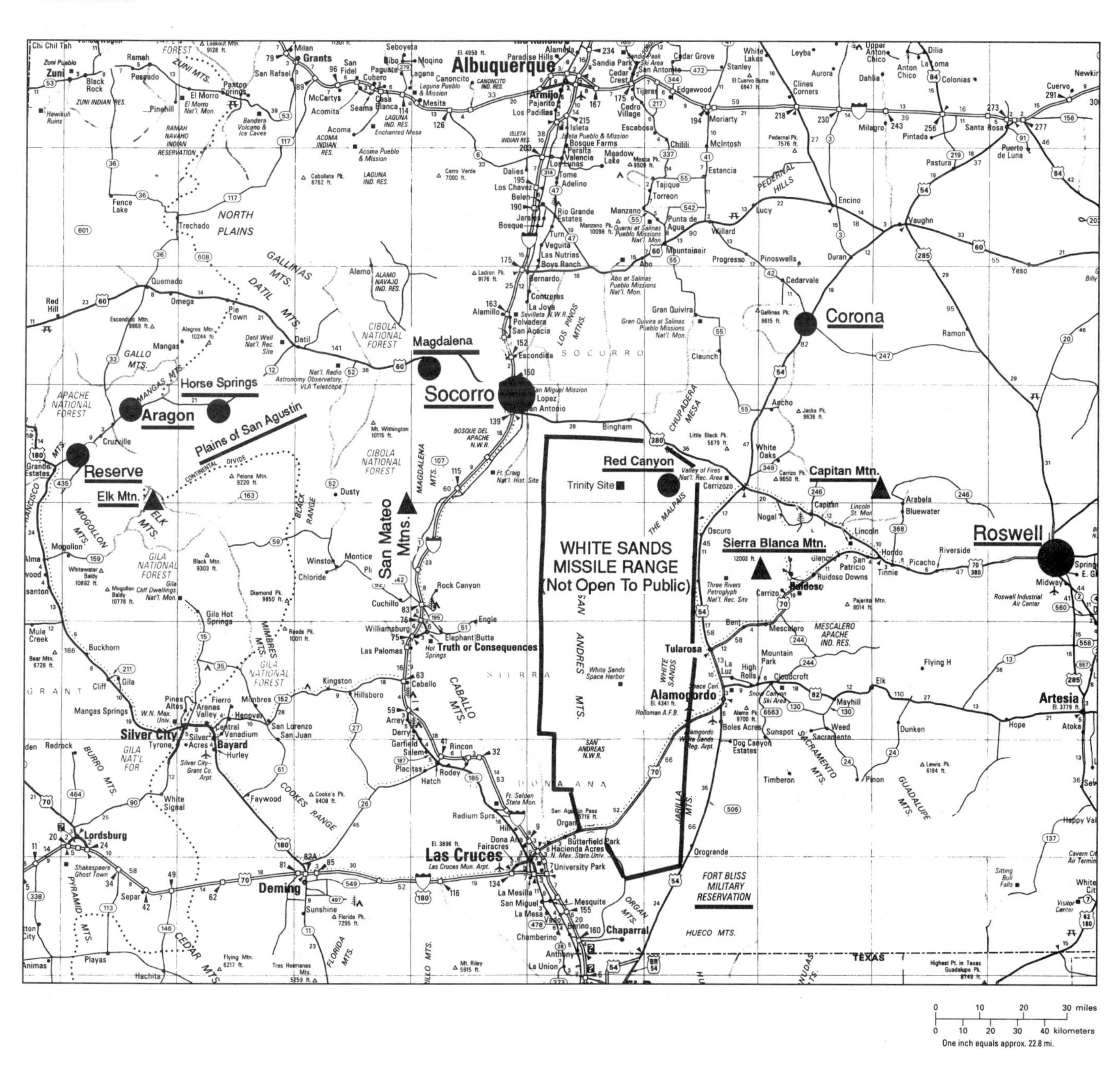

because of the collision, the inter-atmospheric propulsion system malfunctioned..."

The letter writer also listed some of the institutions his grandfather said were involved in research on the craft and its occupant. Included were the University of Colorado; Office of Naval Research; the Army/Air Force which were splitting into separate military divisions the summer of 1947; University of California, Los Angeles; Atomic Energy Commission; National Advisory Committee on Aeronautics; and Office of Scientific Research and Development.

"Grandad spent a total of 26 weeks in the Team that examined and debriefed the lone survivor of the Roswell crash. Grandad's affiliation with the 'project' ended when the occupant was to be transported to a long-term facility. He was placed on-board a USAF Transport aircraft that was to be sent to Washington, D. C."

The statement that a meteor impact disabled the extraterrestrial craft was curious. One would assume that space travellers, or time and dimension skippers,[1] would have sensors and deflection shields for all sorts of intruders in their space and around their remote-controlled explorer craft. Some government insiders said microwave radar experiments conducted at White Sands Missile Range in the 1940s might have interfered with the extraterrestrial craft guidance systems. (See Plate 14, Memo to FBI.)

[1] *To pass from point to point omitting or disregarding what intervenes.*

At least the metal pieces sent by the South Carolina writer were hard physical facts that could be tested. I contacted a scientist in a major Midwestern university who has helped me analyze unusual materials. He used a scanning electron microscope to examine structure and energy dispersive spectroscopy (EDS) to analyze element composition. He confirmed that the metal was greater than ninety-nine percent aluminum of normal density.

After I reported those findings on the radio, we received a second letter dated April 22, 1996. The source said that "based on past conversations on the subject (of a Roswell crash) with Grandad," he understood that the aluminum provided "a conductor for the electromagnetic fields created in the propulsion systems." This letter also elaborated about the "occupant-survivor."

"... critically-needed data was 'eliminated' by the self-destruct mechanisms on the disc vehicle itself. Furthermore, the occupant-survivor of the crash refused to disclose technical information, despite a series of interrogative attempts to extract technological data. No means could be found to secure the information. There were always two Security Team members present at every face-to-face meeting with the survivor. The survivor had the ability to deduce thoughts and questions prior to them being asked. Sometimes it became frustrating.

"The Disc itself was literally dissected and it was discovered that the propulsion system had actually fused together the many interior components. There were *control-type devises forged in the shape of the alien hand,* which were assumed as controls and activation surfaces. (Howe's emphasis.)

"What is today fiber-optic technology was part and parcel of the alien technology within the control panels, albeit fused and melted when the self-destruct mechanism was activated. There were Westinghouse-affiliated persons on the Team, and Grandad always thought some of them had gone back with the knowledge and incorporated it into the future research with the phone systems."

Back-engineering extraterrestrial technology for American military and commercial development was well known to retired U. S. Army Lt. Colonel Philip J. Corso, former Chief of the Army's Foreign Technology Division in the early 1960s. In *The Day After Roswell,* his 1997 ground-breaking and best-selling book, Colonel Corso described his assignment in 1961 to 1963 to get extraterrestrial technology out of Pentagon storage into the hands of defense contractors. His boss was General Arthur Trudeau, then head of Army Research and Development. The Colonel's list of back-engineered extraterrestrial technologies included night vision image intensifiers, fiber optics, supertenacity fibers, lasers, molecularly aligned metallic alloys, integrated circuits, microminiaturization of logic boards, particle beams, electromagnetic propulsion systems — and hand imprinted control panels.

This is what Col. Corso wrote about panels retrieved from a "crescent-shaped" extraterrestrial vehicle that crashed in New Mexico and which sounds similar to the South Carolina writer's description:

"...the series of raised deck panels where there were indentations for the creatures' hands. The indentations on these panels, as the Roswell field reports described them, looked like the handprints pressed into the concrete at the old Grauman's Chinese Theater in Hollywood. Were the directional commands a series of electronic instructions transmitted directly from the creatures' brains along their bodies and through the panels into the ship itself as if the ship were only an extension of the creature's body?"[2]

[2] *Reprinted with the permission of Pocket Books, a Division of Simon & Schuster from* The Day After Roswell *by Lt. Col. Philip J. Corso (Army Ret.) with William J. Birnes, © 1997 Rosewood Woods Productions, Inc.*

Colonel Corso said that extraterrestrial bodies first went to Wright Field in Cincinnati, Ohio, but after the USAF became its own separate branch of the service, "the remaining bodies stored at Wright along with the spacecraft were sent to Norton Air Force Base in California. Experiments were carried out at Norton and ultimately at Nellis Air Force Base in Nevada at the famous Groom Lake site (Area 51 known as Dreamland) where the Stealth technology was developed." The Colonel said that the USAF and CIA "maintained a kind of alien technology museum" at Norton Air Force Base near San Bernardino, California, "the final resting place of the Roswell spacecraft" — at least one of them. Norton AFB was closed down in the 1990s and one wonders where the "alien technology museum" went? Or if it's still there, is it underground or disguised in some way?

Col. Corso said the motives of the extraterrestrials were puzzling and of great concern to government insiders when he worked in the White House National Security Staff under President Dwight Eisenhower and later in the Pentagon under General Arthur Trudeau. The priority of the U. S. government was to get as much advanced extraterrestrial technology as possible, keep it out of the hands of Cold War enemies, while "pushing through weapons development that might reduce the advantage" of the advanced and potentially threatening non-human intelligence. He wrote on pages 180-182 in his book:

> "In the Pentagon from 1961 to 1963, I reviewed field reports from local and state police agencies about the discoveries of dead cattle whose carcasses looked as though they had been systematically mutilated and reports from people who claimed to have been abducted by aliens and experimented on. One of the common threads in these stories were reports by the self-described abductees of being subjected to some sort of probing or even a form of surgery with controlled, intense, pencil-thin beams of light" which Col. Corso associated with a laser instrument retrieved from downed spacecraft.
>
> "...Local police reported that when veterinarians were called to the scene to examine the dead cattle left in fields, they often found evidence not just that the animal's blood had been drained but that entire organs were removed with such surgical skill that it couldn't have been the work of predators or vandals removing the organs for some depraved ritual.
>
> "...I also remembered that both civilian and military intelligence personnel attached to the staffs of individuals who worked for the Hillenkoetter and Twining[3] working group on UFOs in the 1950s were actively engaging in research into the kinds of surgical methods

[3] *Roscoe Henry Hillenkoetter, U.S. Navy Admiral, first Director of the Central Intelligence Agency and member of the MJ-12 Special Studies Group appointed in 1947 by President Harry S. Truman; Nathan Farragut Twining, Chairman of the Joint Chiefs of Staff 1957-1960 and member of the MJ-12 Special Studies Group.*

> that would produce 'crime scene evidence' like this.
>
> "...Although the first public reports of cattle mutilations surfaced around 1967 in Colorado, at the White House we were reading about the mutilation stories that had been kept out of press as far back as the middle 1950s, especially in the area around Colorado. ...Our intelligence organizations and especially the working group believed that the cattle mutilations that could not be obviously explained away as pranks, predators, or ritual slaughter were the results of interventions by extraterrestrials who were harvesting specific organs for experimentation.
>
> "...We had irrefutable evidence that EBEs were landing on farms, harvesting vital organs from livestock, and then just leaving the carcasses on the ground because they knew we couldn't do anything about it."

The Colonel agreed the government had extraterrestrial artifacts from more than one spacecraft. He said that during the Norton AFB testing it was discovered that "the entire vehicle functioned just like a giant capacitor...the craft itself stored the energy necessary to propagate the magnetic wave that elevated it ... as if gravity was being folded around the outside of the wave that enveloped the craft. ...Somehow the pilots became part of the electrical circuitry of the vehicle, vectoring it in a way similar to the way you order a voluntary muscle to move." The Colonel told me how amazed military and science investigators were about the spacecraft functioning as an extension of the beings' neurological systems, including their molecularly aligned and strengthened flight suits and hand imprinted control panels.

The 6-fingered hand imprinted panels in Plate 4 were filmed by a former U.S. Air Force cameraman who said those panels were retrieved from a vehicle that crashed on May 31, 1947. Another May 31st date associated with a crash was described to me by a New Mexico resident. He said he has talked to a ranch family in the Plains of San Agustin who wanted to remain anonymous. Their story is that the former ranch owner, his teenage son, and a hired hand heard a loud explosion near their property on the evening of May 31, 1947. The father was outside on a tractor and saw something crash on a mesa a few miles north of Elk Mountain at the southern end of the Plains and southeast of Aragon.

In the next two days, the rancher asked a Magdalena doctor who had surveying equipment to help survey some property above his ranch. The rancher, his teenage son, hired hand and doctor rode horseback up to about 4,000 feet toward Elk Mountain. There they saw an Army helicopter hovering over what they first assumed was a crashed airplane. Very thin, silver ma-

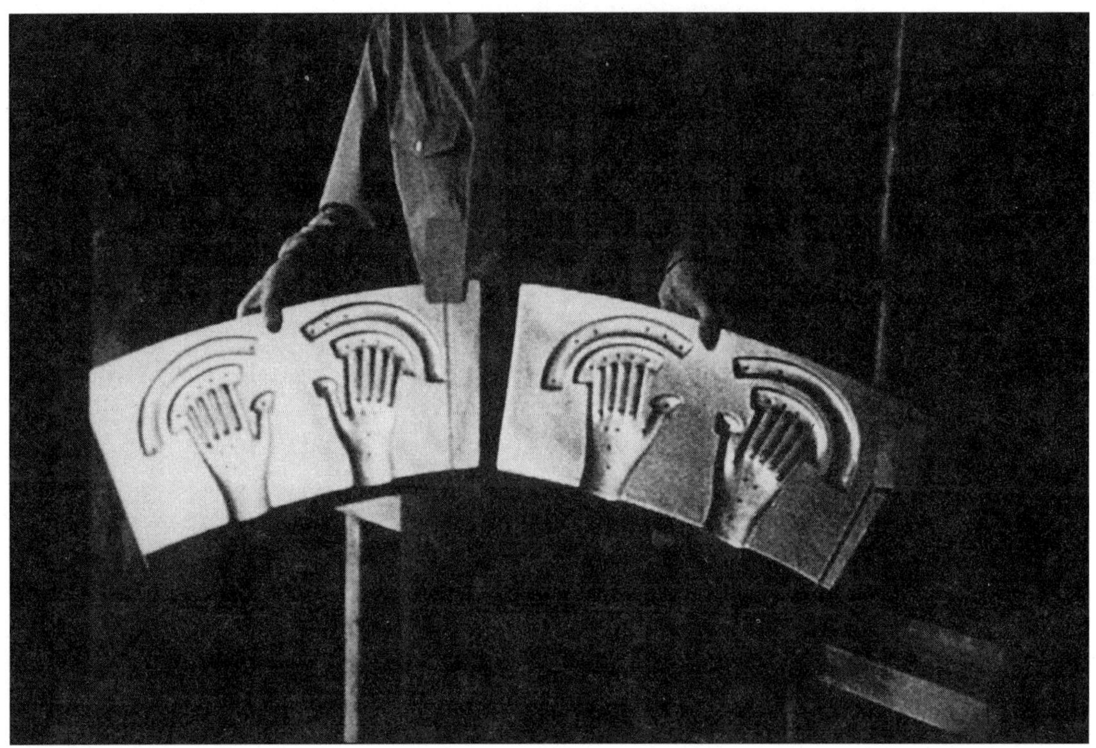

Plate 4 - *Panels with six-fingered hand depressions allegedly found with six-fingered humanoids at UFO crash site a few miles from Socorro, New Mexico. First broadcast on U.K. and U.S.A. television September 28, 1995. Photograph from 16mm film © 1996 Orbital Media Ltd., U.K.*

terial was torn and scattered on the ground and military personnel were picking it up. While the ranch owner talked to a military man about who was going to clean up his land and pay for any damage to it, the doctor got off his horse and walked through some of the debris. Then a military policeman and an Army officer approached and told the rancher he could not go further because it was an off limits "military zone." So the four left.

The son said later he heard the doctor tell his dad that before the Army kicked them out, he found a body "that wasn't human. It had real big eyes and real strange looking arms and hands."

The rancher's son also remembered seeing a tent set up around tables covered with pieces of crash debris and one big piece that looked "like a seat from a ferris wheel with a curved top."

A few days later two Army officers and a civilian brought U. S. Army damage claim forms to the ranch. The son was asked to read and fill them out for his father who did not read and write. When the father asked about the "ship from Mars" and the "Martian laying on the ground," the civilian said it was "a chimpanzee inside an experimental plane." When the father challenged that explanation, the civilian offered to bypass the paper work and pay him cash then and there if the rancher would sign a statement relinquishing any claims against the U. S. government and promising to turn over to the Army anything else found at the crash site.

The rancher and doctor, now deceased, were certain there was a cover-up about a crashed flying saucer, but the only thing they heard in public after that was a military plane had crashed near Reserve, New Mexico.

Long time residents in the Horse Springs, Magdalena, Socorro and Elk Mountain areas do remember airplane crashes through the years, but cannot corroborate a "flying saucer" crash. In research I did for the *UFO Report: Sightings* special I created and produced for the FOX network in 1991, I talked with Socorro resident Harold Baca. He had helped an elderly and sick man named Barney Barnett who lived across the street until Barnett died in 1969. Barnett had been a field engineer for the U. S. Soil Conservation Service and worked throughout the Plains. Stanton Friedman, nuclear physicist and long time researcher of crashed discs and government cover-up, had reported in his 1992 book *Crash At Corona*[4] that Barnett's close friend Vern Maltais and Barnett's niece, Alice Knight, remembered Barney saying he had come upon a silver disc and small, dead non-humans wearing one piece, grey body suits somewhere in the Plains of San Agustin.

[4] Crash At Corona, The U. S. Military Retrieval and Cover-up of a UFO © *1992 by Stanton T. Friedman and Don Berliner, Paragon House.*

Baca said Barnett suspected his throat cancer was caused from bending down over the strange bodies. But no one remembered an exact date and specific location. Arizona researcher Victor Golubic thinks there is other evidence to support a crash location about ten miles south of Horse Springs.

Unfortunately, the South Carolina writer never gave a definite date either and the reference to "Between Sierra Blanca and the San Mateo Mountains" is too broad. If the grandfather meant the Tula Rosa Mountains instead, it might match the rancher's location. Or the Barnett story. Or the military cameraman's alleged May 31st crash southwest of Socorro. Perhaps the grandfather stood guard over bodies and debris at yet a different crash site closer to the White Sands Missile Range. Part of the problem is that government efforts to deliberately suppress or mix up dates have been a good way to cover-up history with confusion. For an example, see Jim Penniston's experience beginning on page 99.

I continued to investigate the possibility that the aluminum pieces might be "punch outs" from terrestrial machining operations since they measured in common terrestrial quarter-inch and inch sizes. However, Alcoa Aluminum engineers thought that the purity of the aluminum was not typical of industrial machining which usually involves harder alloys. So, there was speculation that if the South Carolina writer's story were true, the military handlers might have had samples from the alleged extraterrestrial craft punched out to distribute to American scientists for study.

On May 27, 1996, a third letter arrived containing a surprise — six more pieces of metal that were very different from the aluminum. The letter said:

"I have listened with interest to the ongoing reports on the samples I sent your way. I noted that the Researcher (Linda Moulton Howe) discussing the testing of the samples noted that basically it is merely Aluminum. Slight variations on the testing, but indistinguishable from 'normal' Aluminum.

"Actually this is precisely the same initial findings of Grandad's Team. However, I neglected to include metallic samples of the exterior of the crashed Roswell disc. I now include the enclosed, and can only say that these scrapings came from the exterior underside of the Disc itself. It literally was a 'shell-like' shielding of the Disc. Brittle and layered, almost with a pre-fabricated design and placing. Keep in mind that these are the last of Grandad's samples. They have sat for years inside a closet with his personal effects.

"Because of certain concerns, I will not be contacting you on this matter. Perhaps I am a bit paranoid, but I do have a family & career to think about. I hope you understand. Hope these last samples are helpful. Of course, I will be listening."

Plate 5 - *Photograph of two metal pieces from the South Carolina writer's second shipment May 27, 1996. Each piece had a dark side and a shiny silver side. On the left, the dark side is up; on the right, the silver side is up. An inch diameter quarter coin is for size comparison. Photograph by university professor © 1996.*

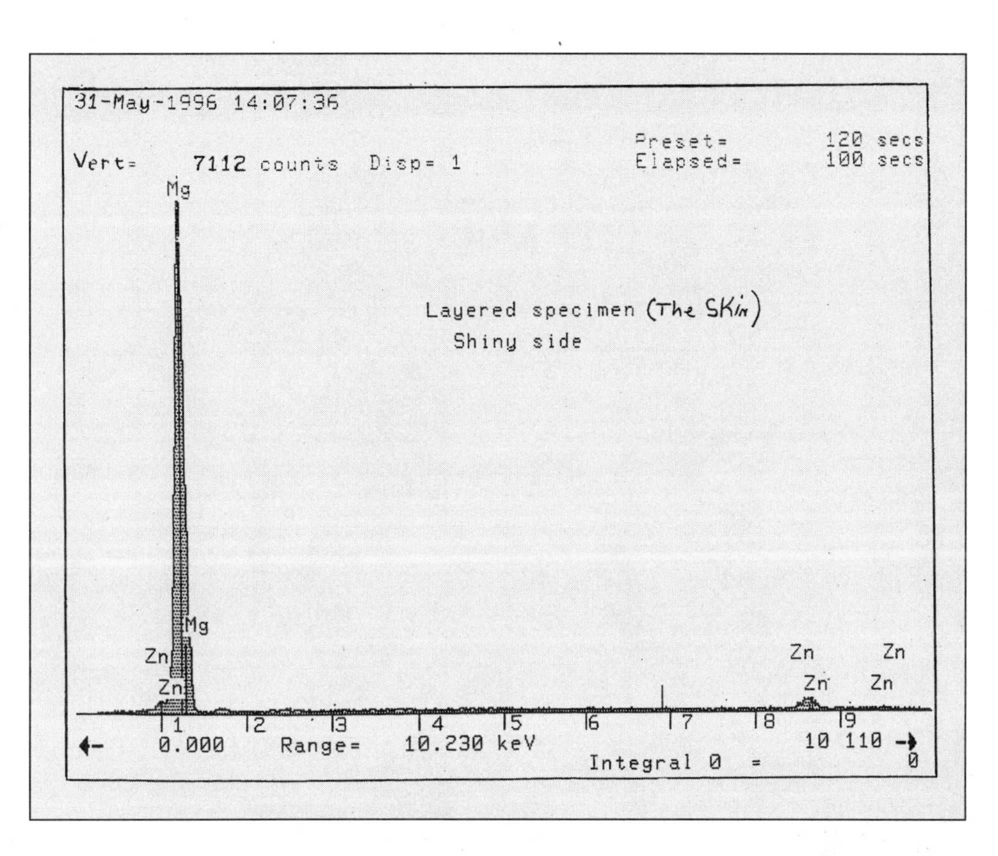

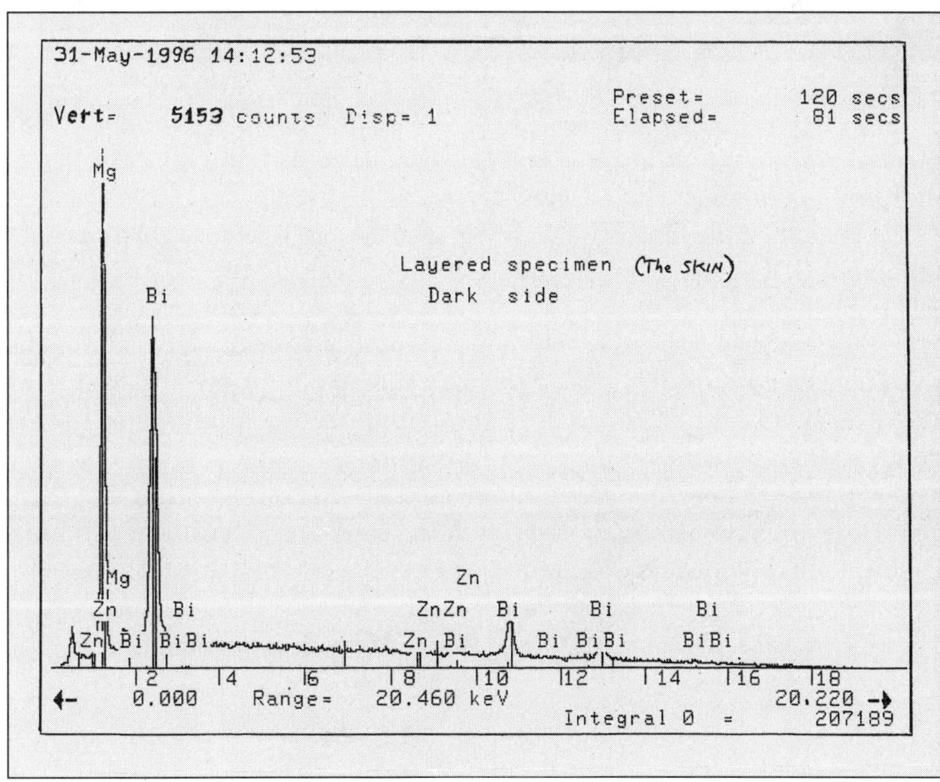

Plates 6 & 7 - *Energy dispersive spectroscopy (EDS) spectra. The top spectrum is focused on the shiny side of the layered metal which showed primarily Magnesium (Mg) and a small amount of Zinc (Zn). The bottom spectrum is focused on the dark side which revealed only Bismuth (Bi).*

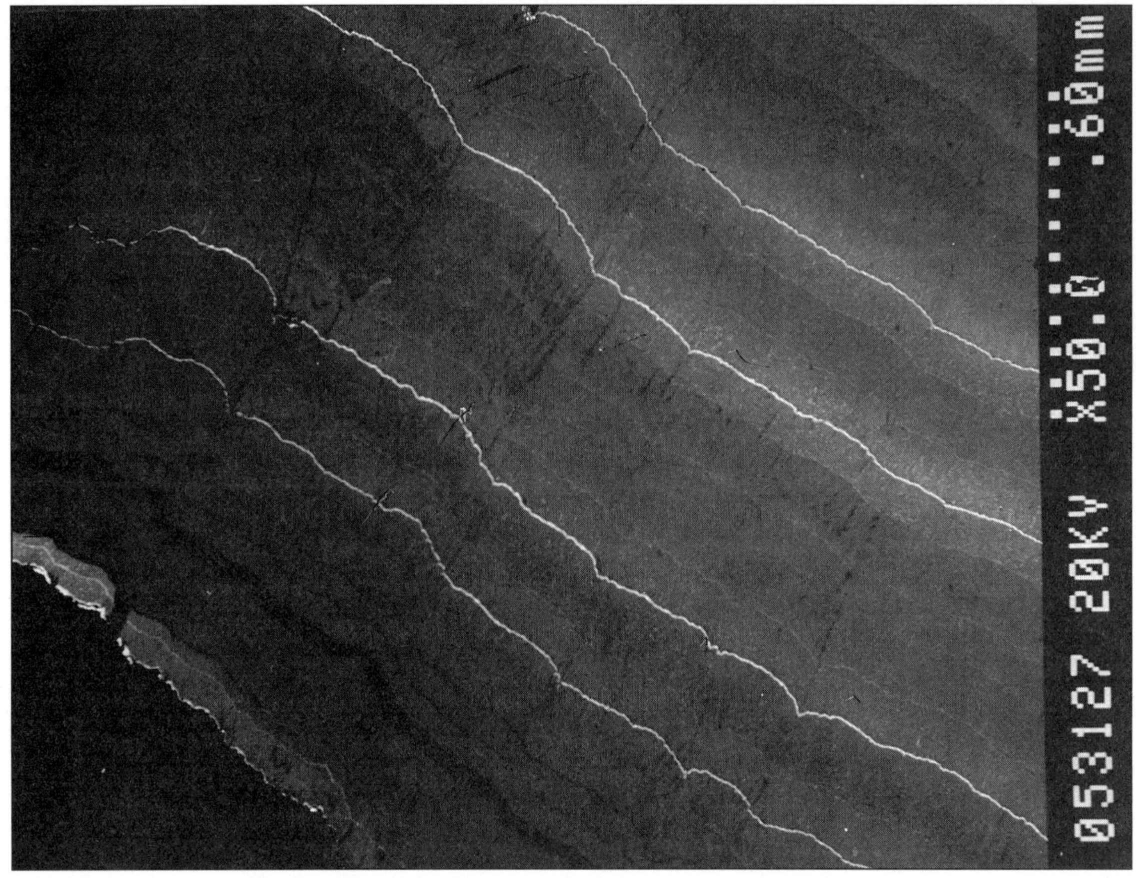

Plate 8 - *Scanning electron microscope photograph at 50 times magnification of the alternating layers of bismuth and magnesium/zinc. Photograph by professor © 1996.*

Art Bell called me and said there were half a dozen pieces about two inches long, an inch wide and about a quarter of an inch thick. One side was dark and the other side was a shiny silver.

I contacted the university professor who agreed to analyze the new material and Bell shipped two fragments to him, keeping the other four in a safe deposit box.

The professor's first step was to photograph the metal pieces as they arrived at his laboratory. He placed the dark side of one piece on the left and the silver side of the other on the right, both next to a quarter coin that is about an inch in diameter for size comparison.

On June 8, 1996, the professor released his first report about the material. He had examined a cut and polished cross-section with the scanning electron microscope and energy dispersive spectroscopy (EDS). He stated:

> "Each sample had a 'silvery,' shiny side with a rough (granular) appearance. The other side was blackish-gray. Looking at the

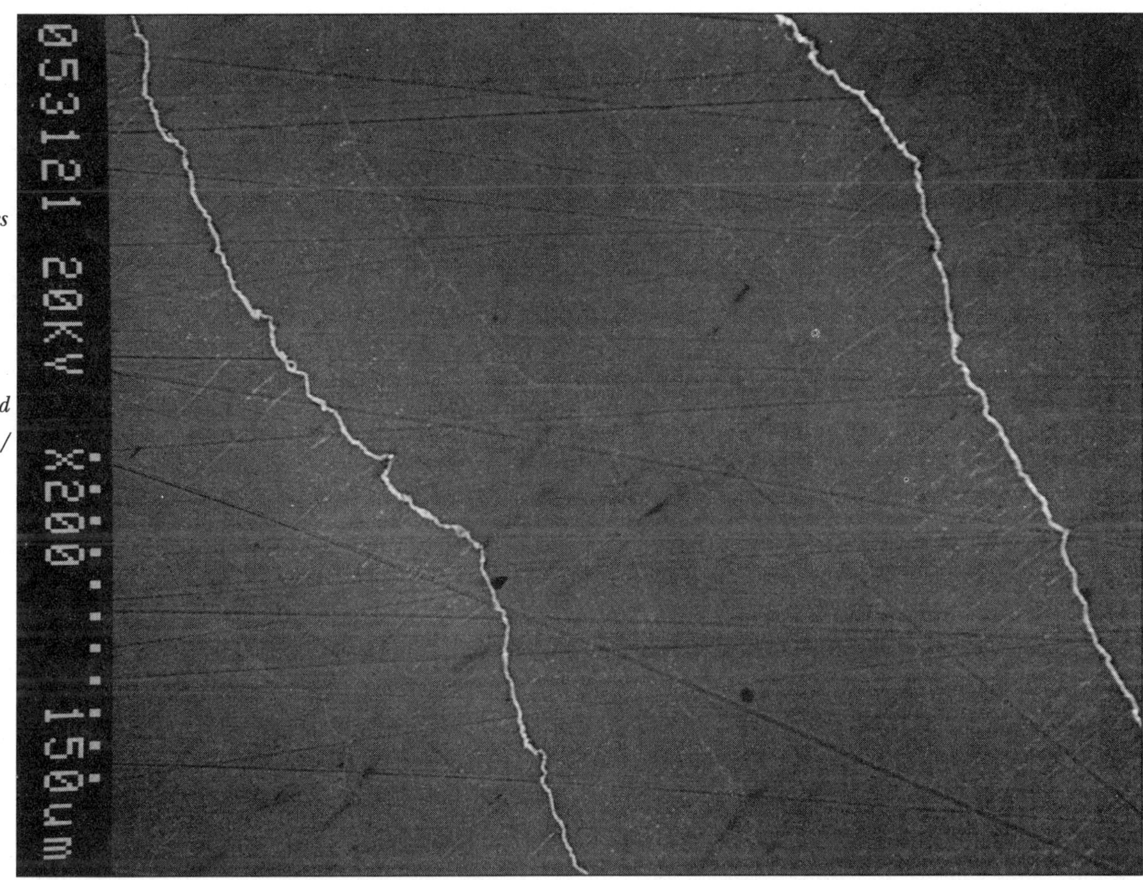

Plate 9 - *Scanning electron microscope photograph at 200 times magnification of the alternating layers of bismuth and magnesium/zinc. Photograph by professor © 1996.*

samples edge-on, numerous layers can be seen. The samples were hard but brittle, and a few small pieces could be broken off using a small hand vice and manual pressure.

"...Energy dispersive spectroscopy (EDS) revealed that the shiny side contained more than 95% magnesium (Mg) and a small amount (2-3%) of zinc (Zn). The dark side contained a significant amount of bismuth (Bi)."

"...the material appears to represent layers ... consisting mainly of magnesium and a small amount of zinc separated by thin layers containing a high bismuth content."

The SEM was set in a "back-scattering" configuration so that heavier elements show up brighter. Therefore, the dark bismuth appears as thin white lines and the much lighter magnesium/zinc shows as darker shades of grey. The professor measured the layers and found that the thin, wavy lines of bismuth varied from one to four microns, about half the diameter of a human blood cell, and the magnesium/zinc varied from one hundred to two hundred microns. One scientist thought the waviness might be a fractal wave pattern calculated in the layered material's construction, perhaps to better resonate with a specific frequency. Or, the waviness might be the result of heat absorbed in the metal's production or function.

Later the professor did more refined analysis with Wavelength Dispersive Spectroscopy (WDS) and said:

> "The material corresponds to layers of Bi and Mg/Zn with the weight percent of the Zn varying slightly from about 2.4% to 2.9% between Bi layers. No Zirconium (Zr) could be detected with the Mg/Zn area which is frequently found in magnesium/zinc alloys."

In summary, the metal fragments allegedly from the "central underside of a wedge-shaped" spacecraft found in New Mexico have about twenty-five alternating layers. The bismuth layers average one to four microns and the magnesium/zinc layers average 100 to 200 microns.

Bismuth is a hard, brittle metallic element that is greyish-white with a tinge of red. That pink color in the stomach medicine, Pepto-Bismal, comes from a bismuth ingredient.

Plate 10 - *A pure, man-made bismuth crystal. Photograph by Linda Moulton Howe © 1996.*

Bismuth's atomic number on the Periodic Table of Elements is 83. Lead is 82, so bismuth is heavier than lead. Bismuth is frequently found in ores of tin, lead, copper and cobalt. Bismuth is not attacked by hydrochloric acid, and only slightly by hot sulfuric acid. But the element is rapidly dissolved by either dilute or concentrated nitric acid.

Further, the *Guide to Uncommon Metals* says, "Bismuth is one of the few metals that expands when cooled, like water does when it turns to ice, and that makes bismuth valuable for detailed metal castings. Bismuth also has a low melting point, but its thermal conductivity is lower than that of perhaps every other metal with the exception of mercury, and its electrical resistance is high. A modern use is as a coolant for nuclear power reactors."

Bismuth is the most diamagnetic of the elements — meaning it resists penetration by magnetic fields more strongly than any other element. Magnetic field lines tend to be displaced around bismuth, rather than passing through it. Bismuth also has the greatest Hall Effect. That means if a voltage is placed on bismuth while the metal is in a magnetic field, a current flow will be induced that is ninety degrees to the voltage. Bismuth is an efficient absorber of infra red energy and researchers are experimenting with bismuth coatings that will convert heat to electricity. Bismuth is also added to metal mixtures in superconducting research.

On July 5, 1996, the fifth and final letter from the South Carolina source added a few more comments about the layered fragments, supposedly copied verbatim "from Grandad's journal:"

> "Sample extraction radiated light for a full (3) hours. Originally located on central underside of Wedge-shaped Disc. Speculate some type of Shielding to enable Craft & Crew to survive accelerated entry into atmosphere, when Craft was experiencing uncontrolled descent. Pile of blackened ash was analyzed and ash was confirmed of same elements of layering. Ash consisted of (sic) fiberous dust & residue. Ash & all debris swept into bagging. Bags placed in tagged boxes. Boxes placed into Metal Footlockers. Initial examination (offsite) conducted at New Mexico Institute of Mining & Technology. Secondary examinations at Los Alamos Facility. Footlockers subsequently airlifted by Courier to Wright Field, Ohio."

In addition to the unfamiliar combination of bismuth and magnesium/zinc, there were questions about the isotope ratios in the magnesium. Isotope refers to the number of protons and neutrons in the nucleus of each atom. For example, magnesium on earth is made up of about eighty percent ^{24}Magnesium. That means there are twelve protons and twelve neutrons at

the center of each ^{24}Magnesium atom.

The other twenty percent is equally divided between ^{25}Mg, which has one additional neutron compared to ^{24}Mg, and ^{26}Mg, which has two additional neutrons compared to ^{24}Mg. If the layered metal were truly extraterrestrial in origin, some wondered if anomalies might be detected in those ratios, or percentages, of isotopes.

One such anomaly was reported in 1957 when a metal fragment allegedly from a UFO in Ubatuba, Sau Palo, Brazil was analyzed by the Brazilian government in laboratory tests. The fragment was found on September 14, 1957 after eyewitnesses saw a "flying disc" explode into thousands of fiery fragments which fell onto the beach and sea. The metal tested to be nearly 100 percent pure magnesium and was 6.7 percent heavier than ordinary pure magnesium. Former NASA scientist Paul Hill[5] calculated that the density anomaly could be explained if the metal were the pure isotope ^{26}Magnesium not found naturally on earth. Supposedly, that Brazil metal no longer exists to test further.

I learned that an ion microprobe which could analyze magnesium isotopes was newly installed at the Carnegie Institution of Washington, D. C. After discussions with Dr. Erik Hauri in the Department of Terrestrial Magnetism who agreed to analyze the layered Bi/Mg metal, I drove to Washington on July 20, 1996 with a cut and polished slice of the layered material. Dr. Hauri found about eleven percent more ^{26}Mg in our mysterious sample, but still not outside terrestrial ranges for magnesium metal.

[5] Unconventional Flying Objects - A Scientific Analysis *© 1995 by Paul R. Hill, Hampton Roads Publishing Co., Inc, Charlottesville, Va.*

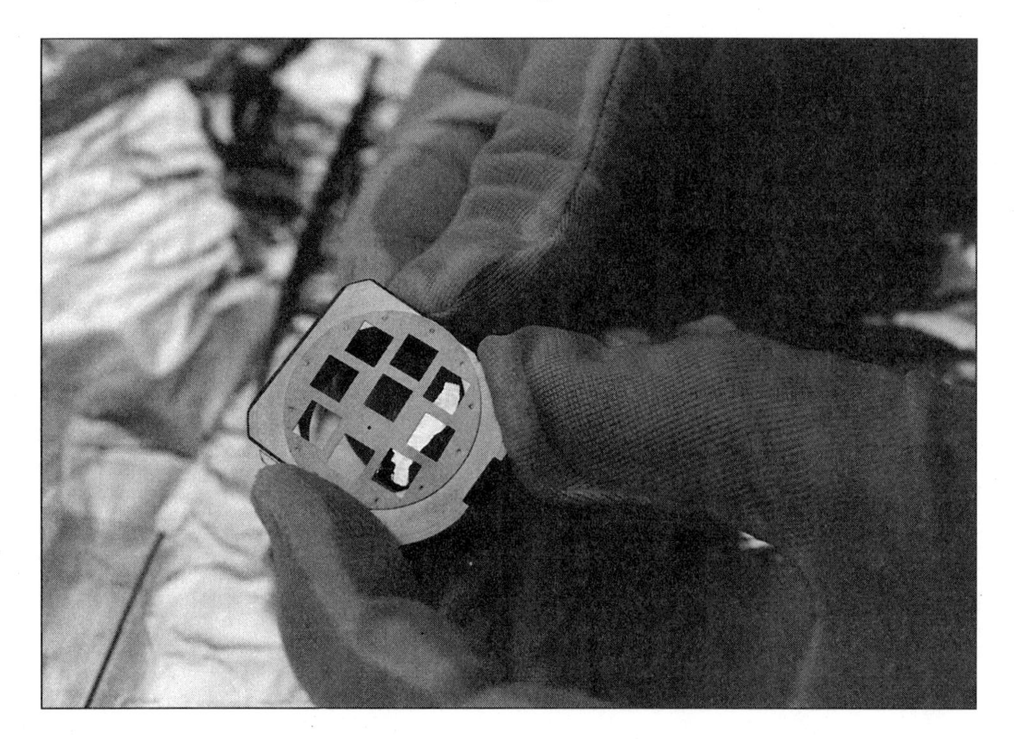

Plate 11 - *Slice of bismuth and magnesium/zinc layered metal being placed by Dr. Erik Hauri, operator of the ion microprobe, into container for magnesium isotope ratio analysis July 20, 1996 at Carnegie Institution of Washington, D. C. Photographs by Linda Moulton Howe © 1996.*

Plate 12 - *Ion microprobe at Carnegie Institution of Washington, D. C., July 20, 1996, during magnesium isotope ratio analysis of bismuth and magnesium/zinc layered metal.*

One anomaly was that the bismuth/magnesium layered material emitted more positive ions than the pure magnesium metal being used for standard comparison. Hauri wrote in his report to me:

> "The Bi-Mg sample gave count rates of Mg+ ions which were enhanced *sixty times* more than in the pure Mg metal standard."
> (Howe's emphasis.)

Dr. Hauri suggested three possible reasons for the difference. First, he explained that the zinc might act as a catalyst for Mg ionization. Second, that catalytic process might be enhanced if there were a distinctive arrangement in the Mg crystal structure which related to how the material was originally constructed. Third, if oxygen were somewhere in the sample it could enhance Mg ionization. However, Hauri acknowledged that none of the ion microprobe spectra showed any oxygen.

Another scientist, Nick Reiter, who is an expert with solar cell manufacturing, agreed to try to make a bismuth and magnesium/zinc layered material that matched the fragments sent by the South Carolina source. Reiter tried several methods including vacuum vapor deposition. After slowing down the vacuum process to building a layer per week, Reiter produced one four-layer sample that was mostly white, not alternating silver and black.

Plate 13 - *Ion Microprobe graph comparing layered metal in dotted line to pure magnesium metal standard in solid line for* ^{26}*Magnesium isotope. The layered metal had about 11% more* ^{26}*Mg than Mg metal standard, but not outside terrestrial magnesium ranges. Ion Microprobe analysis by Dr. Erik Hauri, Department of Terrestrial Magnetism, Carnegie Institution of Washington, D. C., July 20, 1996.*

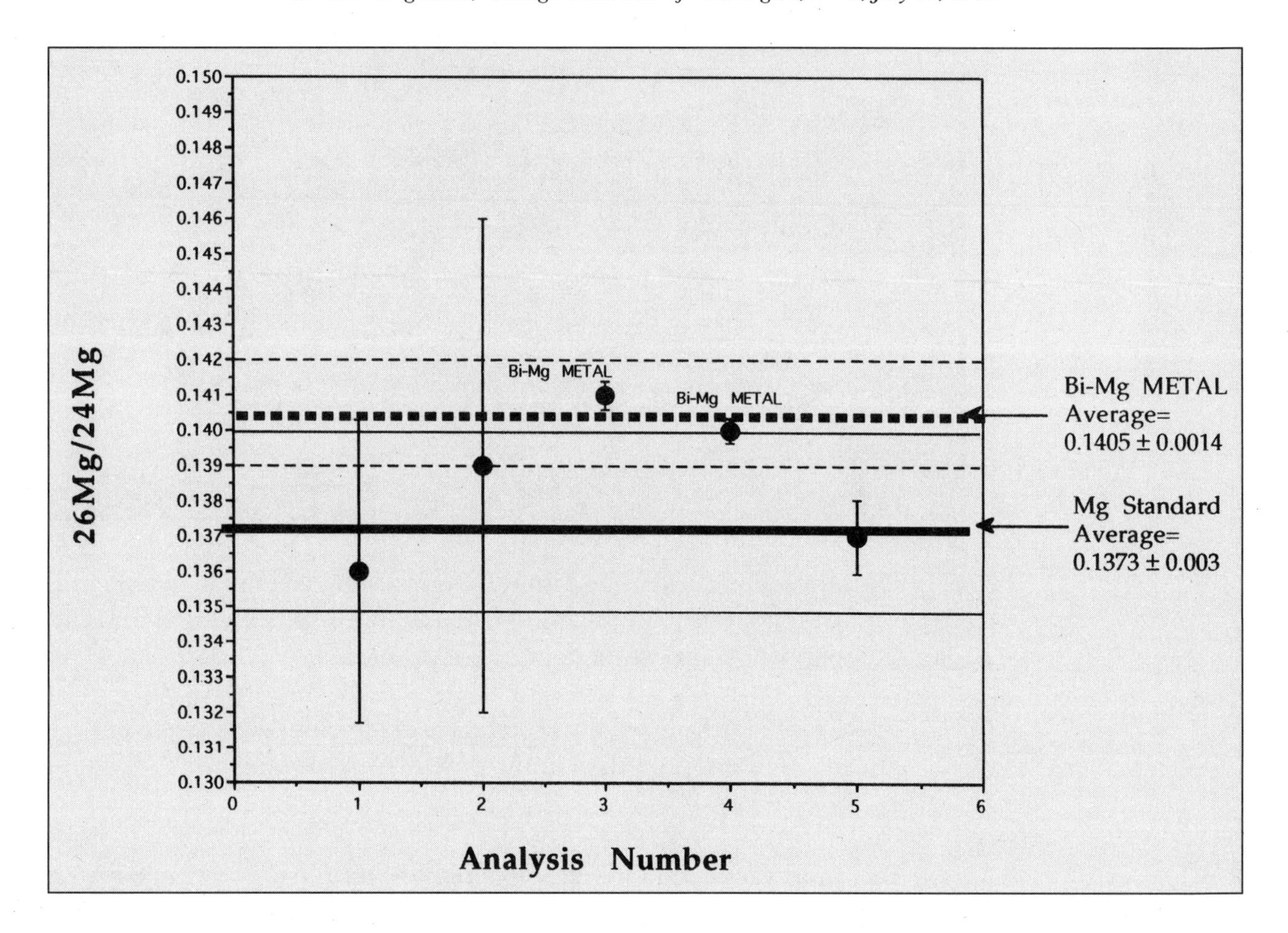

Further, all the bismuth deteriorated into small grains like black pepper within a few months leaving two delaminated magnesium/zinc layers.

I kept reporting the research findings on *Dreamland* and asked if anyone listening had any information about the construction or function of the layered Bi/Mg. I also contacted dozens of people in the scientific and industrial community to see if I could find anyone who had worked with bismuth and magnesium/zinc layered together in the alternating and wavy micron thicknesses. Those inquiries ranged from the Director of Material Sciences at the Massachusetts Institute of Technology (MIT) in Cambridge, Massachusetts and the National Science Foundation to metallurgists at Sandia National Laboratory in Albuquerque, New Mexico, and aerospace and exotic metals manufacturers to military labs and intelligence agencies. But no one had any knowledge of such layered material.

Speculation about the metal's possible function included resisting or detecting magnetic fields. Another suggestion came from a man who claimed to have worked on back-engineering technology retrieved from the Soviet Union and other sources during the Cold War in the 1970s. He said metal made out of bismuth and magnesium layers came into a lab at Edwards AFB, California as an "unknown" and left as an "unknown."

He said later he learned the material might "turn into a lifting body" if placed in a million volt electrostatic field augmented by an unspecified frequency of a "Class C RF signal."

On the radio, I asked for research help. Electrical engineer and physicist Travis Taylor at the Army's Redstone Arsenal in Huntsville, Alabama volunteered to try the experiment. But first, he asked his superiors and contacts at the Defense Intelligence Agency (DIA) if it was all right to work with me on the Bi/Mg. Taylor told me the DIA officials approved as long as he kept them informed about what we learned.

First, I asked Travis if he would do a literature search in scientific and military channels to see if he could find any references to bismuth and magnesium in thin micron layers. After several weeks, he told me:

> "I have basically exhausted every resource that I have ever tried to use in the past from about 1940 to now. I have found no reference, even in government research, for bismuth/magnesium layers. This material didn't just make itself. It had to come from somewhere. And that's one of the things about it that excites me — somebody had to build it and no one has reported building it. It's a very high tech piece of material, so if they didn't report it, why did they build it? That's what we do in science. We do some research and then we tell everyone about it. And nobody's told anyone about this material!"

Then he tried 500,000 volts produced by a Van de Graaff generator with the Bi/Mg on a plastic insulator. The layered metal at one point moved sideways through the electric field so energetically that it fell off the insulator.

After that, Taylor built a Van de Graaff generator big enough to produce 1.2 million volts. Nick Reiter made a control that matched the magnesium and zinc percentages without bismuth and without the wavy pattern peculiar to the layered metal. Insulation from the electrostatic field was a thin piece of paper suspended above the generator. The layered bismuth/magnesium metal and the control were placed on the paper.

To Taylor's surprise, the Bi/Mg tended again to move sideways in the electrostatic field while the control did not. When a tunable 1 to 20 MHz radio signal was added, the Bi/Mg seemed to have a more energetic reaction to *back away* from the direction of the RF signal when it was tuned to about 7MHz. Taylor wondered if there might be a connection to the nuclear magnetic resonance frequency of bismuth which is about 7 MHz, the same as the stimulating RF signal. Nuclear magnetic resonance occurs at the subatomic level under certain conditions when a substance is placed in an external static magnetic field.

Research continued with tests of the metal in static and oscillating magnetic fields by a scientist working on "electro-gravitic" research. That scientist had already narrowed his interest to two elements most likely to influence gravity: mercury and bismuth. So far, the Bi/Mg was "dead," not moving, in the magnetic fields tried. The researcher wondered if the large positive ion emission discovered during the Carnegie test might relate to an ion generation function for an unconventional craft propulsion system.

Col. Corso told me he had not heard of layered bismuth and magnesium, but described his understanding of one extraterrestrial spacecraft propulsion: "The craft was able to displace gravity through the propagation of magnetic waves, controlled by shifting the magnetic poles around the craft so as to control, or vector, not a propulsion system but the repulsion force of like charges."[6]

[6] *Reprinted with the permission of Pocket Books, a Division of Simon & Schuster from* The Day After Roswell *by Lt. Col. Philip J. Corso (Army Ret.) with William J. Birnes, © 1997 Rosewood Woods Productions, Inc.*

Government Knowledge and Cover-Up

Whatever the layered bismuth and magnesium/zinc's function might be, it remains a mystery. The information from the South Carolina source could be a controlled government release into public consciousness without the political commitment of official sanction. If government insiders do know about layered Bi/Mg and the extraterrestrial wedge-shaped craft it is supposed to have come from, their silence is consistent with a policy of cover-up since at least the early 1940s.

Since I began investigating unusual animal deaths in 1979 and their link to a non-human intelligence interacting with our planet, I have been contacted by several people actively employed by, or retired from, the U. S. military or intelligence. Some contacts have been face-to-face meetings, always off-the-record. Other communications have come by anonymous mail or through Federal Express intermediaries.

In this chapter, I have selected excerpts from a variety of such contacts which all relate to alleged government knowledge and cover-up about one or more non-human intelligences that interact with this planet.

What has impressed me over time are details which are similar from case to case. Examples are matching descriptions of symbols and structural details seen on disc-shaped craft and the use of drugs and hypnosis to debrief military and intelligence personnel exposed to close encounters with the UFO phenomenon. I am also confused by the contradictions. Some insiders insist the phenomenon does not pose a threat to humanity or national security; others hint of a secret war around us between adversaries both biological and other-dimensional. Whatever the whole truth is, these military voices imply considerable government knowledge and cover-up about non-human entities, their aerial vehicles and the high strangeness of their interactions with earth life.

This chapter's military voices also remind me of a Greek chorus which has more knowledge about the action in the play than the civilian audience, but does not have all the plot lines and does not know how the revolutionary drama will unfold as the whole world learns we are not alone in this universe. Military eyewitnesses struggle with security oaths and government reprisals if they talk. Equally repressive to civilians are the social ridicule and uninformed media skepticism heaped upon people who try to describe a UFO or non-human entity encounter. Government insiders, under ordered policy, have inspired and fueled ridicule of witnesses with weather balloon, Venus, flares and swamp gas explanations to make sure that the public and media stayed away from the bodies, craft and technologies.

A good example of early military thinking is stated in a November 8, 1948 SECRET memo to the U. S. Air Force's Chief of Staff in Washington, D. C. from USAF Colonel H. M. McCoy, Chief, T-2, Intelligence Department, Air Material Command (AMC) at Wright Field, Ohio, later known as Wright-Patterson AFB. This memo was released under a Freedom of Information Act request by investigator William LaParl in 1996. (See Appendix XI for complete text.)

McCoy stated: "Although it is obvious that some types of flying objects have been sighted, the exact nature of those objects cannot be established until physical evidence, such as that which would result from a crash, has been obtained. It is not considered advisable to present to the press information on those objects which we cannot yet identify or about which we cannot present any reasonable conclusions."

Colonel Corso stressed the military's concern about a hostile threat and Cold War spies while trying to sustain the status quo. But, the Colonel told his story because he thinks the policy of silence, lies, misinformation and intimidation after fifty years needs to end. Even if there is hostility, it is not clearly defined. General statements such as "there are bad, grey guys who lie and want to use earth for themselves versus good, grey guys who want to help humans survive" might be the bottom line, but we all need more details about who and why. The "Joe" story in this chapter implies at least one non-human being in the jungles of Cambodia in 1971 showed restraint when attacked by human gunfire.

Before 1971, government insiders produced training manuals about recovering extraterrestrial entities and their technology from downed craft, which in some instances were shot down by "direct military action." One such document is the "Restricted SOM1-01 Majestic-12[7] Group Special Operations Manual – Extraterrestrial Entities and Technology, Recovery and Disposal, TOP SECRET/MAJIC EYES ONLY" discussed on pages 71-78 and shown more completely in Appendix I.

The training manual clearly defined the United States government's denial and cover-up strategy about extraterrestrial recovery operations:

> "The official government policy is that such creatures do not exist, and that no agency of the federal government is now engaged in any study of extraterrestrials or their artifacts. *Any deviation from this stated policy is absolutely forbidden.*" (Howe's emphasis.)

I would like to add some insights about the government's position in all this from one of the best behind-the-scenes chroniclers of U. S. government response to the UFO situation in the 1940s through the 1950s. That was the work of Major Donald E. Keyhoe, U. S. Marine Corps, and former Director of the National Investigations Committee on Aerial Phenomena (NICAP), an organization whose director at one time was Navy Vice Admiral Roscoe Hillenkoetter, first head of the Central Intelligence Agency. Hillenkoetter was also at the top of the Majestic-12 Special Studies Group list appointed by President Harry S. Truman in 1947 to oversee matters concerning the UFO phenomenon.

From Major Keyhoe's first book in 1950 through his next four,[8] there was an evolution from open inquiry to an environment so suppressed that research became dangerous and even life-threatening. In the beginning, Major Keyhoe asserted that flying saucers were real, were from outer space and that the government was trying to find out what the extraterrestrials wanted and whether their intentions were hostile or peaceful.

By 1960 when Keyhoe wrote *Flying Saucers: Top Secret,* he was frustrated by the ever-tightening censorship and outright lies that had become the strictly enforced policy of what Keyhoe called the "Silence Group."

Keyhoe described his surprise when in June 1958 he received a formal request on official letterhead from Lackland Air Force Base, Texas by Robert C. Balsey, then director of Lackland AFB's closed-circuit programs.

[7] *See* SOM1-01 *in Appendix 1. For more information about Majestic-12 (MJ-12), also see Appendices VI, VII and X; and* An Alien Harvest, *Chapter 7 and Appendices, © 1989 by Linda Moulton Howe.*

[8] *Books by Major Donald E. Keyhoe (USMC Ret.):* The Flying Saucers Are Real *© 1950, Henry Holt & Co.;* Flying Saucers From Outer Space *© 1953, Henry Holt & Co.;* The Flying Saucer Conspiracy *© 1955, Henry Holt & Co.;* Flying Saucers, Top Secret *© 1960, G. P. Putnam's Sons;* Aliens From Space *© 1973, Doubleday & Co.*

Balsey wanted permission to use information and quotations from Keyhoe's earlier book *The Flying Saucer Conspiracy* for closed-circuit radio broadcast at the base. Balsey said he would send a copy of the script to Major Keyhoe for approval before it was used.

A month later Balsey sent Keyhoe a 17-page script entitled "Look To The Skies" to be broadcast first on the Lackland Air Force Base Hospital closed-circuit radio station KLRH and taped simultaneously for post release. The scripted program had been approved by the hospital's Assistant Adjutant. When Keyhoe read it, he realized "the script completely reversed all the (previous) Air Force (denial) claims." Since both the Lackland AFB Office of Public Information and the hospital Adjutant's Office were involved, "it must have been okayed higher up." He guessed it might be "a private test to see how some people will react to the facts."

The following text from the 1958 Air Force script is excerpted from Keyhoe's 1960 book *Flying Saucers: Top Secret* [9] and his comments are in italics.

[9] Flying Saucers, Top Secret © *1960 by Major Donald E. Keyhoe (USMC Ret.), G. P. Putnam's Sons.*

USAF Script for Lackland AFB, Texas
Closed-Circuit Radio Broadcast
Summer of 1958

LOOK TO THE SKIES

U. S. Air Force: "What you are about to hear is based on documented fact."

Major Keyhoe: *(After reference to AFR 200-2* [10] *which stressed that unsolved UFO sightings are kept from the public, the Air Force statement continued:)*

[10] AFR 200-2 - *See Appendix II.*

Air Force: "The question now is not 'IF' but 'WHY' and 'WHERE DO THEY COME FROM?'"

Major Keyhoe: *(After comparing refusals to accept UFO reality with earlier refusals to accept the possibility of telephones, automobiles, aircraft and television, the script led into excerpts from* The Flying Saucer Conspiracy *with this unqualified endorsement:)*

Air Force: "All sightings mentioned are authenticated as described in the broadcast."

Major Keyhoe: *(With this official confirmation, the Air Force script cited one of the most disturbing cases ever to leak out — the mysterious loss of an F-89 interceptor during a UFO pursuit):*

Air Force: "It was the evening of November 23, 1953 and wintry darkness had settled over Michigan. At an isolated radar station, Air Defense operators were watching their scope in a routine guard against possible enemy attack..."

Major Keyhoe: *(With full details, this official report then showed how the Air Force radar operators had picked up the blip of an unknown object over the Soo Locks. Since this was a restricted area, an F-89 jet from Kinross Air Force Base in Michigan was immediately sent to investigate. At the controls was Lieutenant Felix Moncla, Jr. In the rear cockpit was Lieutenant R. R. Wilson, the radar observer.)*

Air Force: "The UFO, flying as fast as a jet airliner, was heading toward Lake Superior. At over 500 m.p.h. the F-89 raced after it, out across Whitefish Bay. Nine minutes ticked by. Slowly the jet cut down the gap. By now, Wilson should have spotted their quarry on the fighter's short-range radar..."

Major Keyhoe: *(Then the closed-circuit documentary (script), in a dramatic statement, revealed the sudden merging of the UFO's blip with that of the F-89, as seen by Air Force ground radarmen. Quoting a stunned radar officer, it went on:)*

Air Force: "It seems incredible, but the blip apparently just swallowed our F-89. ... No trace was ever found of the missing men, the F-89 or the UFO."

Major Keyhoe: *(In quick succession, the script disclosed official Air Force confirmation of the F-89's disappearance by Lieutenant Robert C. White of the Air Force Press Desk. Then a Truax Air Force Base statement to the Associated Press headlined 'JET, TWO ABOARD, VANISHES OVER LAKE SUPERIOR,' appeared in the* Chicago Tribune *— deleted from later issues — which read:)*

Air Force: "The plane was followed by radar until it merged with an object 70 miles off Keweenaw Point in upper Michigan. Kinross Air Force Base spokesmen said the missing plane was equipped with two rubber rafts and that each officer wore a life jacket."

Major Keyhoe: *(Continuing with the F-89 case, the Lackland script candidly showed an Air Force attempt to explain away the UFO as a Canadian DC-3 airliner which had strayed off course. It also included a statement that the Canadian pilots denied this. This was followed by an evaluation proving that a DC-3, with an average cruising speed of 165 m.p.h. and a maximum of about 215 m.p.h., could not possibly have been the UFO tracked at over 500 m.p.h.*

Whether or not this was a deliberate audience-reaction test, the Air Force treatment continued on a sober note. Steadily, it piled up proof that the flying saucers were outer space machines. Halfway through, the script repeated the opening statement:)

Air Force: "All accounts given on this program are authenticated fact."

Major Keyhoe: *(Then it launched into the details of a jet chase in 1954.)*

Air Force: "At 8:30 PM on August 28, 1954, a formation of fifteen flying saucers approached Oklahoma City. Picked up by radar, the strange machines were spotted from Tinker Air Force Base. Within seconds, by standing orders of the Air Defense Command, a flight of jets was dispatched.

"Under AFR 200-2, emergency teletype messages were flashed to ADC (Air Defense Command) Headquarters, to ATIC (Air Technical Intelligence Command) and the Pentagon. At the same time, warning alerts were phoned to Will Rogers Airport, the Oklahoma State Police and to GOC (a Ground Observer Corps) posts in a radius of 200 miles.

"Meanwhile, in precision triangular formation, the fifteen saucers had raced over the edge of the city. The jets, guns set to fire, hurtled after them at full power. Abruptly the formation broke and, changing into a semicircle, the saucers speeded up and vanished into the west."

Major Keyhoe: *(Emphasizing that the UFO surveillance was global, the Air Force-approved script stated:)*

Air Force: "Since the fall of 1954, secret investigations have been made in twenty-one countries, including England, France, Italy, Brazil, Venezuela and South Africa ..."

Major Keyhoe: *(Then, once again, fear of the UFOs was dramatized.)*

Air Force: "On the night of November 21, 1954, a Brazilian airliner was bound for Rio de Janeiro. Flying at 8,000 feet, the plane was over the Paraiba River when a strange glow suddenly appeared ahead. In a moment, a weird formation of nineteen round machines took shape — each machine more than one hundred feet in diameter. Glowing like hot metal, the mysterious craft approached at supersonic speed. Before the pilot could move his controls, the saucers were flashing past and beneath his wings.

"As several machines streaked by the cabin, the thirteen passengers stampeded. One woman, screaming, ran into the pilots' compartment. Another passenger, battling a crewman, tried to reach the main exit. But the frightened passengers finally were subdued, and the plane landed safely. The Brazilian Air Force is badly worried. The Government wants all countries to pool their secret UFO information so that each country will know what it's up against."

Major Keyhoe: *(Then there was an Air Force scripted comment on JANAP 146:)* [11]

[11] JANAP 146, *See Appendix III re: Security Regulations.*

Air Force: "This order is backed by threats of fines and imprisonment and applies to military, naval and airline pilots making reports on UFOs. It also muzzles all members of the Defense Department, the CAA, the Civil Aeronautics Board and any other agency involved with CIRVIS reports (CIRVIS: Communications Instructions for Reporting Vital Intelligence Sightings.) Even a private citizen could be prosecuted for disclosing a saucer sighting if in some way he had learned the details from a CIRVIS message.

"JANAP 146 and AFR 200-2 are official proof of the blackout on UFO reports by the Federal Government, indicating that the United States of America is very much concerned with the flying saucers and also, in spite of denials, that the Air Force has kept information from the public.

"But because of the prolonged secrecy and censorship imposed by the United States Air Force on all authentic UFO information and the flippant attitude of the general public concerning the possibility of life on other planets, the American people had not been prepared for an admission about space visitors.

"And so the Silence Group was now forced by their own policy to continue with the elaborate and detailed censorship which had been thrown around the real facts. Now it was not a question of how to keep it from the public, but how to let the public know in such a way that panic, fear and mass hysteria would not result and cause an economic crisis."

Major Keyhoe: *(Going back to official UFO sightings, the script described a formation of six flying discs seen over Port Townsend, Washington, May 1, 1954:)*

Air Force: "Glowing a bright yellow, the round machines circled in echelon. Sheriff Peter J. Naughton, who first observed the discs, phoned to Payne Air Force Base near Tacoma. Minutes later he received an urgent call from Payne Field operations.

'Ground all planes at Port Townsend! Interceptors are coming in with live ammunition.'

"For at least two years there had been a standing order that pilots could not fire on UFOs unless the saucers proved hostile. Jet pilots would not be preparing to fire rockets at reflections or hallucinations. Few people ever learned of this significant affair."

Major Keyhoe: *(Then leading back to the question, 'Where do they come from?' the Air Force-approved script gave the answer which all the censors had hotly and repeatedly denied:)*

Air Force: "The most logical explanation is that the sau-

> cers are interplanetary. This is the ONLY answer which meets all the known criteria."
>
> Major Keyhoe: *(In the last part of the Air Force script ... here are their own conclusions, summed up separately from mine.)*
>
> Air Force: "The earth and its inhabitants are at this very moment under careful study by living intelligences far surpassing our own. ...Evidence indicates that they come from Mars.
>
> "They have undoubtedly examined our atmospheric conditions, our terrain, our vegetable and animal life ... in fact, all things which might in any way help them in their eventual progress.
>
> "Acting in the best interest of the public of the United States of America, the Federal Government in conjunction with the U. S. Air Force has carefully concealed information which was thought to be of danger, because of the impending possibility of hysteria and panic which could result in an economic collapse and dissipation of our social structure."

End of 1958 Lackland AFB Radio Script
with comments by Marine Major Donald Keyhoe.

Major Keyhoe approved the script, but there never was a broadcast. In fact, the program rehearsals were stopped and within six months, the base radio station KLRH was completely dismantled.

The rest of this book is about high strangeness linked to non-human intelligences which the "Silence Group" or MJ-12 enforcers never wanted the media and public to know. But information has leaked out anyway from people frustrated by their own firsthand knowledge of a non-human presence in a world where denial has become a substitution for truth.

What do other intelligences want from humans and our planet? One government agent told me his superiors hoped to be dead before the "true story" erupted, while others such as those behind the 1958 Lackland AFB radio script apparently wanted the public to know long ago that we aren't alone in this universe. Those who want the story opened up insist that citizens have a right and need to know about the interactions of other life forms with our planet, whether benign, neutral or hostile.

Reprinted with the permission of Pocket Books, a Division of Simon & Schuster from The Day After Roswell *by Lt. Col. Philip J. Corso (Army Ret.) with William J. Birnes, © 1997 Rosewood Woods Productions, Inc.*

While some government insiders say "there is no threat to national security," Lt. Col. Corso has a Cold War military officer's perspective and wrote in his book on page 267: "These creatures weren't benevolent aliens who had come to enlighten human beings. They were genetically altered humanoid automatons, cloned biological entities, actually, (working for someone else) who were harvesting biological specimens on earth for their own experimentation."

Perhaps the truth has a complex range because several non-human intelligences have different vested interests in earth life.

A Crash Near Farmington and Aztec, New Mexico — March 1948

I begin this section of military voices with a crashed disc story that is different in place and date from the alleged Roswell or Soccoro, New Mexico incidents. More than one crashed "flying saucer" was also referenced in a Federal Bureau of Investigation (FBI) Memorandum dated March 22, 1950 from Guy Hottel, Special Agent In Charge in Washington, D. C. to the Director of the Federal Bureau of Investigation who was then J. Edgar Hoover. (Plate 14)

The memo even admitted that each disc was "occupied by three bodies of human shape, but only 3 feet tall." (See EBE Type II, Page 72.) The memo also indicated "high-powered radar" interfered with the "controlling mechanism of the saucers" which were described as "circular" in shape.

In my book *An Alien Harvest,*[12] I also discussed an alleged briefing paper for the President of the United States shown to me on April 9, 1983 at Kirtland AFB in Albuquerque which listed U. S. government retrieval operations of downed aerial vehicles. Locations included Aztec, Roswell and Magdalena, New Mexico; Kingman, Arizona; and northern Mexico south of Laredo.

According to other sources, a disc was discovered pretty much intact near Aztec and Farmington, New Mexico in March 1948. Those two towns are only a few miles apart. The incident was discussed in detail by William J. Steinman in *UFO Crash At Aztec.*[13] Steinman summarized from his unnamed sources that "three separate radar units" tracked an unidentified flying object to an "area of impact calculated to be in the vicinity of Aztec, New Mexico." The object appeared to be circular in shape, domed on top, and roughly one hundred feet in diameter." Steinman placed the date at March 28, 1948 while other information to follow suggests it might have been March 17, 1948.

[12] *Chapter 7,* An Alien Harvest – Further Evidence Linking Animal Mutilations and Human Abductions to Alien Life Forms © *1989 Linda Moulton Howe.*

[13] UFO Crash At Aztec – A Well Kept Secret © *1986 by William J. Steinman and USAF Lt. Col. (Ret.) Wendelle C. Stevens, America West Publishers.*

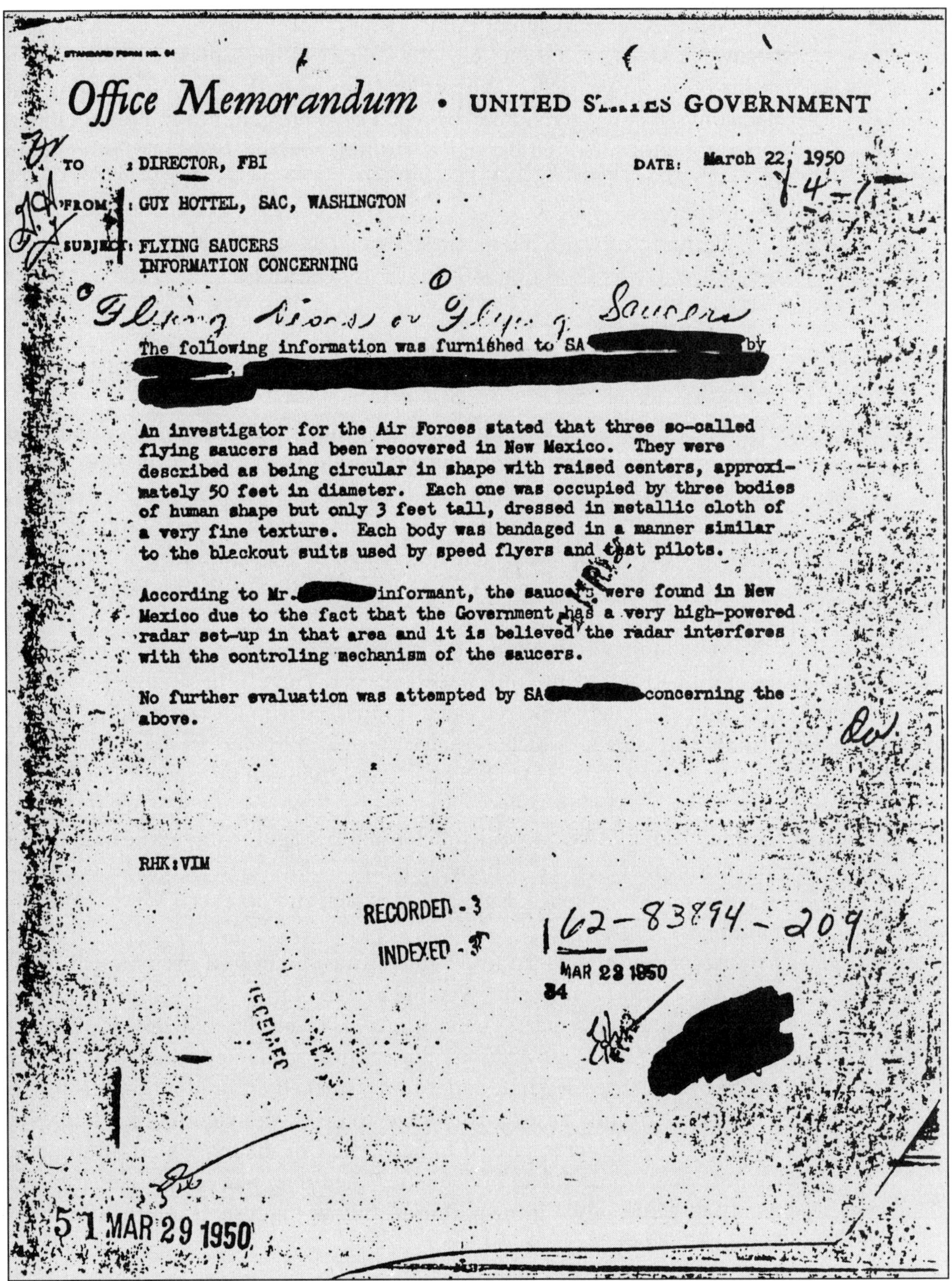
STANDARD FORM NO. 64

Office Memorandum • UNITED STATES GOVERNMENT

TO : DIRECTOR, FBI DATE: March 22, 1950

FROM : GUY HOTTEL, SAC, WASHINGTON

SUBJECT: FLYING SAUCERS
INFORMATION CONCERNING

Flying Discs or Flying Saucers

The following information was furnished to SA [redacted] by [redacted]

An investigator for the Air Forces stated that three so-called flying saucers had been recovered in New Mexico. They were described as being circular in shape with raised centers, approximately 50 feet in diameter. Each one was occupied by three bodies of human shape but only 3 feet tall, dressed in metallic cloth of a very fine texture. Each body was bandaged in a manner similar to the blackout suits used by speed flyers and test pilots.

According to Mr. [redacted] informant, the saucers were found in New Mexico due to the fact that the Government has a very high-powered radar set-up in that area and it is believed the radar interferes with the controling mechanism of the saucers.

No further evaluation was attempted by SA [redacted] concerning the above.

RHK:VIM

RECORDED - 3
INDEXED - 3

62-83894-209

MAR 23 1950

51 MAR 29 1950

Plate 14 - *A Federal Bureau of Investigation Special Agent In Charge Memorandum dated March 22, 1950 first released with other UFO-related papers in response to a mid-1970s Freedom of Information Act request to the FBI by Navy Physicist Bruce Maccabee.*

In 1991, I received eighteen pages loosely bound and entitled "The Report on the Crash at Farmington" about the discovery of a crashed silver disc containing dead non-human beings near Farmington, New Mexico. In 1948, Farmington was a larger town than the rural farming community of Aztec. So, it is logical that in the 1940s Farmington would have been the geographical reference point. Therefore, Steinman's Aztec account and the reference I saw at Kirtland AFB and this Farmington report could all concern the same crashed disc.

The authors of the report are two investigators whom I know and they told me that "as independent researchers with limited time and funds, we were not able to validate the claims of this individual" and emphasized that perhaps the story was made-up. But they wanted me to see a computer-generated drawing based on a photograph the alleged eyewitness said he had seen during a military assignment. The image depicted a disc shaped like two smooth saucers glued edge-to-edge and topped by a shallow dome. The caption read: "A computer simulates the disc-shaped craft as it was seen intact on the ground in the actual photograph." (Plate 15)

Plate 15 - *A computer simulation of a photograph allegedly seen by former military officer. Source said silver-colored disc was found near Farmington, New Mexico prior to 1950.*

I agreed not to identify the authors at their request and they gave me permission to excerpt from their discussions with a "witness who was a former military officer. While serving, he said he had a special security clearance that enabled him to access a restricted library (prior to 1970). Due to the highly sensitive nature of the information, and possible risk to this individual, no information is provided which could be used to identify him or the location of the base."

The following excerpts are not verbatim, but were compiled from notes after four separate conversations.

"Q: What was the occasion in which you viewed documents concerning crashed saucers?

A: While I was stationed at this particular base, ...the materials library was available to those officers with a designated security clearance and I had the appropriate clearance. I was passing time in the library and I discovered a file on the subject of an alien craft and its dead occupants that had been retrieved. The file contained a report, a separate black and white photograph, and a book by Major Donald Keyhoe.[14]

Q: What did you see in the photograph?

A: There was a perfectly intact, circular-shaped craft and it was lying somewhat tilted to one side on the ground in the desert. There did not appear to be a crater or other ground-surface disturbance in the photograph that would indicate a crash, but I could not tell for sure. ...it was stated that the craft was retrieved somewhere near the town of Farmington, New Mexico, prior to 1950. As I could see in the photograph, the material of which the craft was composed was metallic, and resembled brushed aluminum. The report noted this also.

Q: Could you make out any identifying markings or symbols on the craft as it appeared in the photograph?

A: No, and there was nothing mentioned about it.

Q: Were there any surface features on the craft at all?

A: It was stated in the report that there were portholes on the cabin part of the craft, but they were not made of any type of glass. I couldn't make out this feature in the photograph.[15]

Q: Did the information reveal what that material could have been?

A: Well, this porthole had a puncture that was the diameter of a pencil; that was the only defect discovered on the entire ship. Our people tried diamond drills, an acetylene torch — everything they could come up with on the porthole where this opening was located,

[14] *Books by Major Donald E. Keyhoe (USMC Ret.) listed on Page 24.*

[15] *Other sources report that extraterrestrial craft can appear to be a solid, opaque silver until a certain electrical connection is activated. Then window-like "panels suddenly emerge in the craft's crystal metallic hull."*

but nothing would break through it. They couldn't enlarge the hole, either. The material was tougher than anything we were familiar with on earth. But they eventually got into the cabin.

Q: Did the report say how they accessed it?

A: Yes, it was described as a chance opening. They had gone over the outside of the craft and could not even find a seam or crack that might indicate the location of a door or other entrance. This led them to focus on the small opening in the porthole. As I mentioned earlier, they used everything they could think of to enlarge this hole, and nothing worked. It was concluded that they would have to somehow gain access through this hole and they eventually did because a door popped open. It appeared from a place where there were no obvious seams or other indications of a door. The report said (referring to the opening and closing of the door) that it was 'almost as if the material of the craft had liquefied and then solidified again,' leaving no clue of the door's location upon closing. If there was a seam, it was so tight it couldn't be observed.

Q: Was there anything in the report that indicated the weight of the craft?

A: Yes, it was apparently composed of a very lightweight material. The report stated that two average men could lift or move the entire ship.

Q: Did you ever see anything about the ability of these ships to become invisible, like the cloaking idea presented on *Star Trek*?

A: It was indicated that there was no way of telling whether they got out of sight so fast that your eyes couldn't follow them, or if they actually had cloaking or light-bending ability.

Q: I am especially interested in what these dead occupants were like. Were they described as biological extraterrestrials?

A: They didn't use that terminology that I can remember, but they were described as being like us, but smaller — two arms, two legs, a head, feet and hands.

Q: Were they all alike in appearance?

A: Well, it said that the two bodies were badly charred. So was the interior of the cockpit of the craft. The report also said that they were about four feet in height. There was no description of their features beyond that.

Q: So, there was no mention of sexual difference?

A: No, no mention of that. But it's interesting that the report said that the clothing wasn't burned at all.

Q: So, there was a description of the fabric?

A: Yes, it was some type of woven fabric and the report said that it had a tensile strength of 800 pounds.

Q: Was the color of the fabric mentioned?

A: No, there was no reference to it.

Q: How about the style of the clothing? Did they both wear the same thing?

A: It was only described as being like a one-piece flight suit. And yes, it was the same on each one.

Q: Was there any mention of craft propulsion systems? Anything involving jet, nuclear, or anti-matter driven engines?

A: There was no mention of a propulsion system other than the idea that their technology utilized magnetic or gravitational fields of the planets to travel in space. It was speculated that they were able to cross greater distances of space within a much shorter time than we thought possible. For instance, based on our present day technology, it would take us years to get very far in space; to them, it would only be a matter of days, or even hours.

Q: How could the military figure this out?

A: The report didn't go into depth on this, but part of the conclusion was based upon the fact that there was no food or bathroom facility found within the cabin of the craft.[16]

Q: Was there anything in the report that indicated the reason for the craft coming down? For example, there have been rumored reports that our military was under orders to intercept and shoot them down. Is it possible that we shot this one down?

A: According to the report, we were not responsible for bringing this craft down. There was mention of a magnetic fault, or opening, or something like that, located in the area where the craft came down. There were three of these faults or openings located in North America: one was located in the Southwest, around the Texas/New Mexico area; one was somewhere in the Carolinas; and one was somewhere in the Northeast sector, but I can't remember exactly where.

Q: Have there been more than one crash?

A: Yes, the report referred to 'crashes' and the Farmington crash information was used to relate general information on similarities with other crashes.

Q: Are you saying that these aliens are not able to control their craft in certain areas?

A: From the report, I learned these areas occur naturally and could possibly interfere with the navigation of these craft. The way I

[16] *An odd logic since small airplanes don't have bathroom facilities either. Further, a non-human species — especially if android drones — might metabolize photons or aerosols or fluids and not need kitchen and toilet facilities. Lt. Col. Philip J. Corso wrote in his book on Page 97: "...the skin analysis that I was reading sounded more akin to the skin of a houseplant ... (and could explain) the lack of food or waste facilities" — implying chlorophyll and metabolism of light. See page 116 this chapter. Other government sources say there are alien bases beneath the earth's land and oceans which allow a constant presence without long distance space travel.*

understand it, they use the natural magnetic lines of a planet and a gravity field to move their ships from one place to another. That's how they are able to make near-right angle turns which our jets are incapable of doing. They can fly circles around any of our aircraft.

Q: Was there anything in the report that suggested where the craft and little beings originated, or why they are coming here?

A: No, nothing ... but the report did say that hundreds of alien craft flew over the town of Farmington, New Mexico on the anniversary of this crash. That also corresponded with the celebration of some national holiday. It said that may have been a tribute to the beings that were killed, or they were letting us know by a show of force they had overcome the factor that caused their ships to crash.

Q: Why do you feel that the military or the government is withholding this information from the public?

A: They felt that only people in professional levels were capable of dealing with this information. Based on what occurred with the Orson Welles *War of the Worlds*[17] radio presentation, this information could create panic. Then it threatens to break down the industrial complex that supports the military complex; it would obviously undermine it. And it could possibly reduce our ability to counter an attack by a hostile alien culture. But it was also clear that the intent of these particular beings was not known.

While our technicians worked on the craft out in the desert (trying to gain access), other alien ships would from time to time fly by the site, pausing momentarily to view the scene, perhaps to see if there were any survivors. At no time did they attempt to harm our people.

Q: Do you have any other comments you would like to make about this?

A: I think I've covered everything. All the information on this subject was removed from the library in the late 1960s. One thing I can say is that I would sure like to know what's going on now."

It is a fact that on Friday, March 17, 1950, hundreds of people in Farmington reported seeing "saucers" in the sky. The *Farmington Daily Times* topped its front page with this headline and story:

"HUGE 'SAUCER' ARMADA JOLTS FARMINGTON
Crafts Seen By (sic) Hudreds
Speed Estimated at 1000 M.P.H.
Altitude 20,000 Feet"

[17] *Film director and actor Orson Welles adapted the novel* The War of the Worlds *by H. G. Wells for a radio play that was broadcast on Halloween night in 1938. The drama was presented as a series of realistic news bulletins and interviews. The program began with a disclaimer that the story was fictional, but hundreds of thousands of listeners who tuned in later were startled to hear the details of what they assumed was an invasion of New Jersey by monsters from Mars. Many New Jersey residents left their homes, suicides were reported, and telephone lines and highways were blocked for hours before the public hysteria subsided.*

Plate 16 -
Microfilmed front page headline and article in Farmington Daily Times, *March 18, 1950, Farmington, New Mexico. See Appendix XII for complete text.*

FARMINGTON DAILY TIMES

Our Faith—New Mexico

VOL. 61—NO. 194 Formerly the Farmington Times-Hustler—established 1884 Published Daily Except Sunday at Farmington, New Mexico SATURDAY, MARCH 18, 1950 Five Cents

HUGE 'SAUCER' ARMADA JOLTS FARMINGTON

Crafts Seen By Hudreds

Speed Estimated At 1000 M.P.H. Altitude 20.000 Feet

For the third consecutive day flying saucers have been reported over Farmington. And on each of the three days their arrival here was reported between 11 and noon.

Three persons called the Daily Times office to report seeing strange objects in the air just before noon.

Persons along Main street once again could be seen looking skyward and pointing.

High winds and a dust storm prevented clear vision.

Fully half of this town's population still is certain today that it saw space ships or some strange aircraft—hundreds of them—zooming through the skies yesterday.

Estimates of the number ranged from "several" to more than 500. Whatever they were, they caused a major sensation in this community, which lies only 110 air miles northwest of the huge Los Alamos atomic installation.

The objects appeared to play tag high in the air. At times they streaked away at almost unbelievable speeds. One witness who took a triangulation sighting on one of the objects estimated its speed at about 1,000 miles an hour, and estimated its size as approximately twice that of a B-29.

Farmington citizens stood in the streets yesterday watching the first reported mass "flying saucer" flight ever sighted. Traffic was slowed to avoid hitting sky gazers. The office of the Farmington Daily Times was deluged with calls from persons who saw the objects.

A Red Leader

Scores described the objects as silvery discs. A number agreed they saw one that was red in color – bigger and faster, and apparently the leader.

Clayton J. Boddy, 32, business manager of the Farmington Times and former Army Engineers captain in Italy, was one of those who saw the startling objects.

Boddy was on Broadway when "all of a sudden I noticed a few moving objects high in the sky."

"Moments later there appeared what seemed to be about 500 of them," Boddy continued. He could not estimate their size or speed, but said they appeared to be about 15,000 feet high.

Boddy's account was confirmed by Joseph C. and Francis C. Kalloff, retail grocers from Antonito, Colo., who were in Farmington to inspect the site of a proposed new store, and by Bob Foutz and John Burrell of Farmington. The Kelloffs said the objects appeared to be fly-

Jury Gets Bribe Case; Heard Denies Charges

Veracity of Negro Attacked

TRUMAN STEPS ASHORE — President Truman followed by his military aide, Maj. Gen. Harry H. Vaughan, steps ashore from the presidential yacht Williamsburg at Key West, Fla., to spend a three-week vacation. They were glad to hit dry land for it had been a rough voyage from Washington. (AP Wirephoto)

Moscow Press Attacks U.S. Indian Treatment

'Blackout' Game Preceded Slaying Of Pretty Coed

SUNKEN SUB SURFACED — Held by lifting gear of two salvage vessels, the British submarine, Truculent, is beached in the Thames River estuary, England. Multiple nine-inch hawsers of the salvage vessels lifted the sub 54 feet from the Thames bottom where she had rested since her sinking by a Swedish tanker, Divina, Jan. 12, with a loss of 64 men. (AP Wirephoto)

Man Seeks Wife, $2,000 In Cash

Newsman Writes Letter To Flying Saucer Pilot

Drafting Reply To Commie Charge

Entire Crew Rescued From Exploded Ship

Along The Way

With Orval Ricketts

Ingalls Appointed

Mule, Camel Steaks

Shades of the Green

Belgium Splits Over Leopold III

Johnson Denounces CD

Plate 17 -
The Denver
Post,
March 18, 1950,
Denver, Colorado.

Mass 'Saucer' Flight Reported Over N. M. City

Denver Post Special.

FARMINGTON, N. M., March 18.—Most people in this northwestern New Mexico oil boom town were convinced Saturday that "flying saucers" exist and that a mass flight of the strange objects hovered over the city for twenty minutes late Friday.

All of the 250 persons interviewed by Walt Rogal, editor of the Farmington Daily Times, insisted they had seen the flying disks. Rogal estimated that 85 per cent of this town's population of 6,100 saw the objects.

Opinion was divided as to what the objects were. Some said they were a new secret weapon. Many favored the "space ship from Mars" theory advanced recently by a naval officer stationed at the White Sands, N. M., proving grounds.

REPORTS SEEING 100.

Clayton Boddy, advertising manager of the Farmington paper, said he was with a group of five businessmen who first sighted the disks. He estimated that more than 100 of the objects appeared. He and other witnesses said they maneuvered over the town at high altitude, appearing in group waves, then streaked out of sight.

Most witnesses agreed all of the objects were of a silvery color except for one red-hued saucer which descended to a lower altitude than the others.

Business was brought to a standstill in Farmington as the report of flying saucers spread over the town. Persons crammed the streets by the hundreds to crane their necks at the sky.

'Not True,' Avers A. F. On Disks

WASHINGTON, March 18.—(UP)—The air force said Saturday that, despite a flood of new reports to the contrary, it still believes there is no such thing as a "flying saucer."

A spokesman said that air force intelligence and technical officers are not impressed by any of the latest accounts of flying disks.

The spokesman also categorically denied that the air force was denying the existence of flying saucers to cover up some of its own experiments in space ships and similar air machines.

375 INVESTIGATIONS.

The air force position, he said, still is that reports of unidentified flying objects result from "misinterpretation of various conventional objects, a mild form of mass hysteria or hoaxes."

"For the (sic) third consecutive day[18] flying saucers have been reported over Farmington. And on each of the three days their arrival here was reported between 11 and noon. ...Fully half of this town's population still is certain today that it saw space ships or some strange aircraft — hundreds of them — zooming through the skies yesterday.

"Estimates of the number ranged from 'several' to more than 500. Whatever they were, they caused a major sensation in this community, which lies only 110 air miles northwest of the huge Los Alamos atomic installation. (See Appendix XII for whole article.)

[18] *Inconsistency with later sentence in whole story Appendix XII, Page 432: "The first reports of flying saucers were noted a few minutes before 11 AM yesterday" (Friday, March 17, 1950).*

An Eyewitness Account of 16mm Film Labelled "Roswell," Pre-1960

Peter A. Bostrom is a Vietnam veteran who served on active duty in the United States military from 1969 to 1971. He owns an Illinois farm and operates a unique business of making molds and casting highly detailed replicas of stone age artifacts from archaeological sites around the world. He also does large negative photography and has printed several posters showing rare stone age artifacts that have been displayed in university collections and museums such as the Smithsonian Institution.

Bostrom has long had an interest in unusual phenomena and has wondered how the ever-increasing awareness of a more technologically advanced intelligence will change humanity. He thinks modern day eyewitnesses of the UFO phenomenon can be compared to a primitive culture that sees an airplane for the first time without comprehension.

The following is a transcribed conversation Bostrom audiotaped in February 1996 with the permission of a former U. S. Army soldier I will call "Reed." Reed said he viewed more than a dozen 16mm films that were stored in a highly secure vault contained within a larger vault for double security at the Army's Fort Richardson in Anchorage, Alaska in either 1960 or 1961. According to Reed, the several film rolls were stored in one container box marked "Roswell." The films showed *two distinct crash sites.* (Howe's emphasis.) One was a large debris field with a portion of a disc. The other site was a smaller disc that had evidently impacted into an embankment. The film did not specify with titles or any other way the difference between the two apparent crash sites.

But by 1996, there was increasing speculation based on circumstantial eyewitness testimonies that at least two different craft came down in two different locations in the first week of July 1947 not far from Roswell, New

Mexico. The Roswell UFO Museum published a small book[19] about a man named James Ragsdale who signed a notarized death bed statement on April 15, 1995 that "about 11:30 PM the night of July 4, 1947 ... there was a big flash, an intense, bright explosion, and then, shortly thereafter, with a noise like thunder, this thing came plowing through the trees, shearing off the tops, and then stopped between two huge rocks."

[19] The Jim Ragsdale Story - A Closer Look at the Roswell Incident *© 1996 by Ragsdale Productions Inc., Roswell, New Mexico.*

Jim Ragsdale said he was with his girl friend in the Capitan Mountain forest northwest of Roswell about thirty-two miles from the J. B. Foster ranch operated by Mac Brazel now well-established as the site of some kind of crash or explosion that created an enormous debris field also around July 4, 1947.[20]

[20] Crash At Corona, The U. S. Military Retrieval and Cover-up of a UFO © *1992 by Stanton T. Friedman and Don Berliner, Paragon House.*

Ragsdale's statement said: "We went down to the crash of this disc-like thing. It was propped up against one rock. It was about twenty feet around. ... There were also the little people, four of them. They looked like midgets, about four feet long." This sounds like the little human-like bodies mentioned in the memo to the FBI on page 32 which also match the EBE Type II heights described on Page 72 in the SOM1-01 Training Manual.

The "midgets" seem different from the alien bodies described to me in 1984 as the type found between Corona and Roswell, New Mexico in July 1947. Those bodies, my source said, were about five feet tall with large heads reminiscent of Oriental features, cat eyes with vertical pupils, and four long fingers with dark nails. (See Plates 34-35.) This description matches the EBE Type I on pages 71-72.

The Reed experience might involve yet another type. Reed said the film he viewed in Alaska showed three body bags that held small bodies. There was a fourth partially covered up by debris, but a *six-fingered hand* was clearly visible. (Howe's emphasis.) [21]

[21] *Different types of entities and craft have been described in alleged recovery operations for different dates from the 1940s into the 1980s, including controversial dissection film of 6-fingered and 6-toed humanoids also discussed in this chapter.*

The military might have used the name "Roswell" as a catchall label for a series of craft and body retrievals in New Mexico from 1947 onward.

The following February 1996 interview by Pete Bostrom is reprinted with his permission and an assurance of anonymity for his military contact.

TRANSCRIBED INTERVIEW ABOUT U. S. ARMY SIGNAL CORP FILM LABELLED "ROSWELL":

BOSTROM: "Please start at the beginning. How did you come to be in a position to view the films?"

REED: "I was sent to Anchorage, Alaska in 1959. What I did up there was I operated high frequency radio equipment. Our principle item that we put across tape or across radio was cryptographic work. Of course, we handled regular communications, too — you know, radios, telephones and just standard military communications. To do this, we all had security clearances of one type or another. We would spend most of our winters in various sites around the state furnishing communications for whoever needed it. Periodically, people in our group who had security clearances would be used for other assignments, especially in the spring time and in the summer because they (higher command) didn't have much demand for the communications we did then. They used other methods.

"One time, for instance, we had a large vault which had been welded shut at the end of World War II. We spent two weeks cleaning that vault out and burning all the security papers that were in there from all the time that World War II was going. We had other times when they were putting in the satellite tracking stations, the early ones. We furnished communications for them because of our security clearances. All of that was Top Secret. They had a hangar over on Elmendorf Air Force Base (near Ft. Richardson) where they were flying the U-2s out of and we occasionally worked over there, usually as security guards.

"Anyway, one day we had several fellows sent for us to do a job. They just told us, 'Go report to such and such an officer at such and such a building.' This was there at Fort Richardson.

"We went over there to this building that had a vault in the basement. They had bricked up the windows and installed security doors. They put us in there and the idea was that they had a tremendous amount of film stored there. Most of it was classified for one reason or another. We were there to inventory it. They had an officer there. If I remember right, he was a captain. He was in charge and so we went to work cataloging and inventorying all the film.

"There was an awful lot of it and we'd been there several days. They had a small viewing room where certain films were not allowed outside the vault and people who needed to know what was on that film would come in there and view them. After several days, we had worked our way to the back of the vault and inside this main vault there was a smaller vault.

"About the time that we were ready to start on this (smaller vault), the captain opened it for us. There was probably, I would guess, twenty five hundred rolls of film in there. This vault was big enough so you could walk in it with a couple of fellows.

"Anyway, about that time the captain announced that he had something he had to do that day. He just up and left. He didn't give us any explanation and I think probably he had some kind of a personal matter he wanted to take care of, probably a lady friend or something. Everything had been going smooth so I'm sure he wasn't afraid that anything would go wrong and he just left. It was obvious he didn't know what was in this vault. There were just numbers on the outside of the cans. And a box marked 'Roswell.'"

BOSTROM: "And that's how you were inventorying all this film? Only by the numbers on the outside of the cans?"

REED: "Well, I think it was (one larger) container marked 'Roswell' that had several cans in it. I had no idea what this stuff was. (In 1960, Reed was 20 years old.)

"We finished the vault out in probably two hours. Basically we were done and we didn't want to go back to our company area because if we did, we'd just end up doing something else for the rest of the day. Basically, we also knew the captain had to sign us off. So, one of the guys grabbed a can of this film (from the container labelled 'Roswell') and we walked into the viewing room and looked at it through a projector. All of it was 16mm film as far as I can remember.

"They were all ten to fifteen minute rolls.[22] It was pretty obvious these things had all been shot with hand-held type cameras. I can remember the quality of the film. They were all black and white."

[22] *Standard 400-foot rolls of 16mm film at 24 frames per second ran twelve minutes; 100-foot rolls ran three minutes.*

CRASH AREA # 1

Debris with Broken Piece of Disc

REED: "One of the first rolls had a — it looked like a chunk of a — it kind of reminded me of a greenhouse. It looked like a frame with windows in it. It was basically in a partial circle. You couldn't tell how big the circle had been. There was a big chunk of it laying there against a kind of little rise in the ground. It wasn't a big rise. You could see a long line of debris of small pieces of metal and items and there were some larger items laying around."

BOSTROM: "Did it look like anything you were familiar with like parts of an airplane propeller or wheels? Were they easy to identify, or was it something that looked a little exotic?"

REED: "Well, first off, I never saw any wheels of any kind. Never saw any propellers. Never saw any jet engines. This thing was mainly just chunks of metal. It had obviously been a hell of a crash. There was burning on the ground. You could see the ground was scorched.

"In the film, you could see a lot of Army GIs. They were out there picking this stuff up."

BOSTROM: "How many people do you think there were?"

REED: "In the film that I saw, there was a lot of people."

BOSTROM: "Several dozen?"

REED: "Oh, at least, if not more. They had some vehicles you could see in the background and they were loading some of this stuff on it. ...This film was silent, all of it. There was no sound and there was never any lead-ins on it (titles and explanations). Normally, military film has got some kind of a nomenclature on the front of it and none of this did and there was numerous rolls of it."

BOSTROM: "OK. And that was in that one canister marked 'Roswell?'"

REED: "It wasn't a canister. It was a container of some kind. I've forgotten if it was a wooden box or if it was cardboard or canvas or what, but it was a container and all these rolls were in it together, consecutively numbered.... Each roll seemed to sort of point at one particular thing. The one that was marked 'First Roll' showed an overall crash site. At one time, the cameraman backed up far enough to where you could see probably a forty acre area. This entire area was covered with debris.

"One of the later films showed some of the guys were out there playing with some of this material. It was obviously very light and it was very strong. I remember one portion, there was some GIs that had laid a piece of this thin material that looked like paper, literally, from the edge. And they were jumping on it. And they were having a real tough time bending it."

CRASH AREA # 2:
Small Disc and 6-Fingered Hand

REED: "In the last two or three rolls, they showed another area. I'm guessing — because it didn't say and it didn't show you — but it appeared from the way people were interacting that this area was not too far from the first area we had seen. It looked like people were going back and forth even though you didn't actually see that. And this was the area where they had a small, circular object that was kind of buried halfway into an embankment. It was a small embankment and there were people out there with body bags. It looked like they had four bodies. The cameraman stayed back far enough to where you couldn't really see.

[23] *(Footnote for Page 45) On September 28, 1995, Channel 4 in London, England and the Fox Network in the United States broadcast scenes from an alleged 1947 non-human dissection filmed by a former U. S. Air Force intelligence cameraman who worked sensitive missions between 1942 and 1952. The story and film were provided by Ray Santilli, owner of Merlin Productions, a small music video company in London. Santilli said the cameraman sold him the film which contained a dissection of two humanoids. Each had six fingers and six toes and allegedly were two of four such humanoids found at a crash site in New Mexico on May 31, 1947.*

"The one thing that I remember was I saw a hand that was sticking up and it was silhouetted against something light in the background."

BOSTROM: "This was at a distance or close up?"

REED: "The hand, I'm guessing from the camera, was probably twenty or twenty-five feet away. ... Close enough that *I could count six fingers*. I can remember that clearly." (Howe's emphasis.)

BOSTROM: "Like that (6-fingered) dissection hand?"[23]

REED: "Very similar."

BOSTROM: "Could you tell by the size of the body bags if these were large or small?"

REED: "They were small."

BOSTROM: "And where these body bags were, was it close to the disc?"

REED: "Very close. As a matter of fact, one of them appeared to be right up under the edge of it. And there were two (more) ...probably ten or fifteen feet from it and the other one was like thirty feet and one that had the hand sticking was probably a hundred feet away. These are just guesses."

Plate 18 - *Military source's drawing of 6-fingered hand he saw on 16mm black and white film labelled "Roswell" while assigned to inventory film inside a vault at the Army's Anchorage, Alaska Fort Richardson in 1960 or 1961.*

BOSTROM: "The hand, was that sticking out of the body bag?"

REED: "I couldn't tell. There was some debris laying there and they could have had a body bag with the hand sticking out of it or it could have been laying behind some of this debris."

BOSTROM: "But it wasn't moving? It was just sticking up in the air?"

REED: "Sticking up in the air. I got the distinct impression from watching this film that there had already been some other activity there just from what I saw. One of the guys made the comment that he wondered if one of them was alive. And I asked him, 'Why would you ask that?' And he said, 'Well, notice that they're putting the body bags in the back of a truck.' And I said, 'Yeah.'

"Then we went back to the front of the film and you saw an ambulance driving off. And he said, 'They don't put (dead) bodies in ambulances. They put (dead) bodies in the backs of trucks.'"

BOSTROM: "But you actually saw three body bags and one that probably wasn't in a body bag? Is that what you counted?"

REED: "Yes. ...Unfortunately, the cameraman never got near enough to give us any real close views, but you could ascertain a few things. One, that they were small. Two, some were real dead. And we could see that one hand with six fingers on it silhouetted well enough to where you could see it. And the quality of the film wasn't half bad."

BOSTROM: "And were the small canisters of film marked?

REED: "The film cans themselves said right on the outside: 'U.S. Army Signal Corp.' And then it had a serial number. ... It was all just raw footage and none of it had been edited. There was numerous places in several of the films where the cameraman had screwed up. You know, took pictures of the ground, took pictures of the sky." [24]

BOSTROM: "How many different cameramen do you think you saw?"

REED: "There was at least two or three other cameramen using cameras that we actually saw on the film."

BOSTROM: "Did you see anybody using any other equipment out there besides...?"

REED: "Yes. I saw one guy with a Geiger counter. ...There was a number of people who had firearms. There was trucks, of course, and we saw one ambulance and we saw numerous trucks and jeeps. Several vehicles. They were obviously there to stay for awhile. They were busy picking everything up. You saw that in every roll of film.

[24] *The standard, commercially available 16mm film camera in 1947 was the Filmo Automatic Cine Camera, a registered trademark by the Bell & Howell Co. in Chicago, Illinois. The magazine held 100-foot reels (3 minutes) which had to be wound by hand. Each wind lasted about forty seconds before having to be wound again. During rewind, the room, floor, sky or ground might be exposed to the film as the cameraman hurried. Electric motor attachments with accessory magazines were also available for the Filmo that could hold 400 to 1200 feet of film, depending upon special needs such as high speed to record slow motion. Bell & Howell introduced the 16mm Filmo in 1923 and continued to manufacture the same camera with minor modifications until a new 1974 model called the Bell & Howell 70-DR.*

They were just very busy picking up everything. And most of it was being done on foot by hand."

BOSTROM: "Did it look like a southwestern scene? Or heavily forested?"

REED: "I never saw a tree except down in that gully where the small craft was. I would call it a small craft (compared to) where I saw it (because) there was a couple of small bushes that would look like maybe junipers or something like that nearby. But the areas where the main crash was, it was virtually devoid of any kind of vegetation that would stick up more than a few inches. ...It was obviously in the southwest somewhere."

BOSTROM: "So how many complete rolls of film did you actually get a chance to look at?"

REED: "We did look at every one in that box." (12 to 20 reels)

BOSTROM: "You thought there were two scenes of crashes? There was a large circular chunk with windows in the forty acres of debris and a smaller disc buried in an embankment (next to small bushes)."

REED: "It looked like two distinct different locations. But from the terrain, it was obvious they were very close together and I saw some of the same people in both films."[25]

BOSTROM: "Now the disc. Did it show any outline of a door or window or anything other than just a smooth surface?"

REED: "The edge of it was stuck into the ground and I didn't see any doors or windows. It was in broad daylight, too."

BOSTROM: "There was no appendages or anything on it?"

REED: "Never saw anything. No legs, no wheels, no propellers, no engines."

BOSTROM: "And the captain finally came back at the end of the day and you just left from there and that was the end of the project of the cataloguing of the film?"

REED: "Yes. And all of us were smart enough to keep our mouths shut because we realized we'd have been in big trouble if anybody had said anything about seeing it. The guys didn't want to jeopardize themselves. They kept their mouths shut."

[25] *On Page 51 in this chapter, the alleged cameraman of the six-fingered dissection film said there was a smaller disc that had broken from struts attached to a larger disc. The circular chunk Reed described as looking like a greenhouse could be part of a shattered large disc from which a smaller craft broke off and embedded in the hillside.*

Six-Fingered, Six-Toed Dissection Autopsy Film – 1995 TV Broadcast

On Friday, May 5, 1995, about one hundred people gathered at a small cinema in the Museum of London. Their invitations had come from Merlin Productions owner Ray Santilli who operated a small music video business on Balcombe Street in England's capital. Santilli screened videotape which he said contained several minutes of black and white 16mm film that had been transferred from old and deteriorated original celluloid.

The photographer was described as a former U. S. Air Force cameraman, "JB," who said he filmed a "flying saucer" that had crashed May 31st in New Mexico and three subsequent dissections of six-fingered, six-toed humanoids retrieved from the crash site southwest of Socorro. The year, he said, was 1947. May 31st was also remembered by the Plains of San Agustin ranchers who heard a loud explosion, encountered Army personnel and a strange humanoid body with big eyes.

Santilli said he first saw the film in 1994 while negotiating the purchase of Elvis Presley footage that showed the singer when he was in the U.S. Army. Santilli said he bought the Presley film in Cleveland, Ohio for a music video and was surprised when the elderly retired cameraman told him about other old film he had that contained "flying saucer" crash debris and autopsies of strange bodies. JB said that film was not stored in Cleveland, but could be seen at his Florida home. So, Santilli flew with the cameraman to Florida to see a few film reels projected on a wall and decided to buy the film for broadcast and video distribution.

On September 28, 1995, Channel 4 in London and the Fox Network in the United States broadcast documentaries which included excerpts of the dissection and debris footage. Critics were angry that the film was presented without the cameraman's presence and firsthand testimony. Santilli explained that the cameraman, referred to as Jack Barrett or Barnett, wanted to remain anonymous to protect his family. "JB" also wanted his granddaughter to have the money (est. $150,000) paid him by Merlin Productions and its German financier, Volker Spielberg.

Controversy raged about the truth of the story. Some insisted that the six-fingered, six-toed humanoid cut by a surgeon's scalpel and bleeding in the film was a Hollywood special effects production. Others argued it was a genetically abnormal human in a real autopsy. Medical doctors who saw the footage generally agreed that the tissue separated around the scalpel the way actual skin would and at least some of the internal organs were not recognizable as human.

By the end of July 1995, Santilli announced that he had been allowed to tape record the cameraman's statement about the film. Santilli produced a transcript which began "Operation: ANVIL — Now known as the Roswell Incident." Santilli told me in London that the contradiction between his reference to Roswell and the cameraman's reference to Socorro was due to Santilli's ignorance about New Mexico geography and knowing Roswell had something to do with a UFO crash.

After *Shutterbug* magazine editor Bob Shell and New Jersey researcher Joe Stefula studied Santilli's transcript of his conversation with the cameraman, Shell released another "exact transcription of tape recorded statement" with his and Stefula's notes added in *square* brackets. The cameraman's statement by Santilli's office already included parentheses. The following is a verbatim copy of Shell's August 1995 release.

> The Cameraman's Story
>
> I joined the forces in March of 1942 and left in 1952. The ten years I spent serving my country were some of the best years of my life.
>
> My father was in the movie business, which meant he had good knowledge about the workings of cameras and photography. For this reason, I believe I passed a medical that would not normally allow me in, due to polio as a child.
>
> After my enrollment and training, I was able to use my camera skills and became one of the few dedicated cameramen in the forces. I was sent to many places, and as it was war time, I fast learned the ability of filming under difficult circumstances.
>
> I will not give more detail on my background, only to say that in the fall of 1944 I was assigned to Intelligence, reporting to the Assistant Chief of Air Staff. I was moved around depending on the assignment. During my time I filmed a great deal, including the tests at White Sands (Manhattan Project/Trinity).
>
> I remember very clearly receiving the call to go to White Sands (Roswell). I had not long returned from St. Louis, Missouri where I had filmed the new Ramjet ("Little Henry"). [According to official records, "Little Henry" was a helicopter project. This discrepancy is resolved by referring to Janes' *All The World's Aircraft* for 1949, which mentions that McDonnell, located in St. Louis, had a project at this time called J-1, which was a one-man ramjet powered helicopter, with a small ramjet engine on the tip of each rotor blade.] It was June 1st when McDonnell [George C. McDonnell was the first Air Force Chief of Staff for Intelligence. He was most likely Assistant Air Chief of Staff for Intelligence in June of 1947] asked me to report to General McMullen [Major General Clements M. McMullen, Deputy Commander of the Strategic Air Command in Washington] for a special assign-

ment. I had had no experience working with General McMullen, but after talking with him for a few minutes I knew that I would never wish to be his enemy. McMullen was straight to the point, no messing.

I was ordered to a crash site just southwest of Socorro [this could be the Plains of San Agustin]. It was urgent and my brief was to film everything in sight, not to leave the debris until it had been removed and I was to have access to all areas of the site. If the commander in charge [at the site] had a problem with that, I was told to get them to call McMullen. A few minutes after my orders from McMullen, I received the same instructions from "Tooey"[26] [nickname for General Carl Spaatz, supposedly on vacation in Washington State at the time], saying it was the crash of a Russian spy plane. Two generals in one day, this job was important.

I flew out from Andrews with sixteen other officers and personnel, mostly medical. We arrived at Wright Patterson and collected more men and equipment. From there we flew to Roswell on a C54.

When we got to Roswell we were transported by road to the site. When we arrived, the site had already been cordoned off. From the start, it was plain to see this was no Russian spy plane. It was a large disc "Flying Saucer" on its back, with heat still radiating from the ground around it.

The commander on site handed over [command] to the SAC medical team who were still waiting for Kenney [General George C. Kenney[27] was SAC Commander at the time. He was supposedly away on an inspection at the time.] to arrive. However, nothing had been done as everyone was just waiting for orders.

It was decided to wait until the heat subsided before moving in as fire was a significant risk. This was made all the worse by the screams of the Freak creatures that were lying by the vehicle. What in God's name they were no one could tell, but one thing's for sure, they were Circus Freaks, creatures with no business here. Each had hold of a box which they kept hold of in both arms close to their chests. They just lay there crying, holding the boxes.[28] [This implies that all four creatures were still alive at this time.]

Once my tent had been set up, I started filming immediately, first the vehicle, then the site and debris. [The sun would not yet have been up, so this filming must have been done under artificial light.] At around 06:00, it was deemed safe to move in. (Howe's Note: 6AM MST, June 1? or 2? 1947) Again, the Freaks were still crying and when approached they screamed even louder. They were protective of their boxes, but we managed to get one loose with a firm strike at the head of a Freak with the butt of a rifle.

[26] General Carl "Tooey" Spaatz was Commander of the U. S. Strategic Air Forces in Europe in 1944; moved to the Pacific theater in July 1945 and under orders of President Harry S. Truman dropped the atomic bombs on Hiroshima and Nagasaki; became Chief of Staff of the newly independent U. S. Air Force after its creation in September 1947 and retired in 1948.

[27] General George C. Kenney was Commander of the Strategic Air Command (SAC) in June 1947.

[28] It is not clear if the "boxes" the cameraman referred to are the panels with 6-fingered hands depressed in them as shown in "the debris film." See Plates 4 and 25. At least one government-employed scientist has stated off-the-record that the panels are extremely advanced computers.

The three Freaks were dragged away, and secured with rope and tape. The other one was already dead. The medical team were reluctant at first to go near these Freaks, but as some were injured, they had no choice. [Unless this is a mistake or poor choice of words, it means that only some of them were injured.] Once the creatures were collected, the priority was to collect all debris that could be removed easily, as there was still a risk of fire. This debris seemed to come from exterior struts which were supporting a very small disc on the underside of the craft which must have snapped off when the disc flipped over. The debris was taken to tent stations for logging, then loaded onto trucks. [In verbal statements he mentions a truck full of ice into which the dead alien is placed. The trucks were heavy duty Diamond trucks used by the military.] After three days, a full team from Washington came down and the decision was taken to move the craft. Inside it, the atmosphere was very heavy. It was impossible to stay in longer than a few seconds without feeling very sick. Therefore, it was decided to analyze it back at base, so it was loaded onto a flattop and taken to Wright Patterson where I joined it.

I stayed at Wright Patterson for a further three weeks working on the debris. I was then told to report to Fort Worth (Dallas) for the filming of an autopsy. Normally I would not have a problem with this, but it was *discovered that the Freaks may be a medical threat.* (Howe's emphasis.) Therefore, I was required to wear the same protective suits as the doctors. It was impossible to handle the camera properly, loading and focusing was very difficult. In fact, against orders, I removed my suit during the filming. The first two autopsies took place in July 1947.

After filming, I had several hundred reels. I separated problem reels which required special attention in processing (these I would do later). The first batch was [processed and] sent through to Washington, and I processed the remainder a few days later. Once the remaining reels had been processed, I contacted Washington to arrange collection of the final batch. Incredibly, they never came to collect or arrange transportation for them. I called many times and then just gave up. The footage has remained with me ever since. [This may not be as incredible as it seems. At this time, the Army and the Air Force were being separated into two new agencies, and there was much confusion as "turf" was sorted out.]

In May of 1949, I was asked to film the third autopsy.[29]

[This amazing statement suggests that one of the aliens, probably the uninjured one, lived in 'custody' for nearly two years. The cameraman did not have any of the film from this autopsy.]

[29] *The cameraman used the word "autopsy" which medically is the procedure to determine cause of death. A dissection is to cut apart or separate tissue especially for anatomical study. Bob Shell learned in a May 1996 conversation with Ray Santilli in London that the third 1949 dissection was performed before a gallery of observers at a large operating theater in Washington, D. C. and that U. S. President Harry S. Truman might have secretly attended.*

After the August 28, 1995 broadcasts of brief dissection and debris excerpts on Channel 4 in England and the Fox network in the United States, I saw unedited versions of the footage at conferences the first week of September in Leeds, England and the Republic of San Marino, Italy. Viewers with us who were medical doctors seemed generally to agree the surgery was consistent with a dissection procedure on a real body and that the oozing blood along the cut lines indicated the body was either fresh or had been kept very cold immediately upon death. When the cameraman was asked what the blood color was, he told Santilli it was red and that the skin was pinkish-colored in the live beings and grey in death. Another source said the skin was lightly mottled in overlapping pink and brown areas that looked slightly orange.

Medical doctors did not recognize the large, round mass in the abdomen on top of other internal organs and agreed that the dark-colored tissue removed from inside the head did not resemble normal human brain.

Other unusual features were dark membranes on each humanoid eye that the surgeon removed with a tweezer-like instrument and placed in containers of fluid, most likely for preservation and later examination under a microscope. Inside the chest, one puzzling scene showed the surgeon cutting and pulling from tissue what looked like half of a quail's egg[30] and putting his gloved index finger inside as a seamstress would put on a thimble.

The humanoid did not have breasts, a belly button, penis or testicles. However, there was an orifice in the pubic area which humans associate with the female gender, while others pointed out that the absence of a belly button suggested a clone. I learned in Italy that the dissection film of a second, nearly identical, humanoid — not yet seen and under the control of German financier Volker Spielberg — had more details of an internal examination of the pubic orifice and a clearer image of another thimble-like object also found in the second humanoid's chest.

Back in London on Tuesday, September 12, I went to see Ray Santilli at his Balcombe Street office for Merlin Productions. Red-colored CD labels and posters about Elvis Presley were on the walls and desks related to four Elvis music videos Santilli had produced by then.

Ray Santilli had a warm, engaging smile and polite English manner. His thin body seemed carved by a fast metabolism that ran on nervous energy. He talked rapidly about meeting the elderly retired cameraman in Cincinnati, screening the old Army footage of Elvis Presley, and being surprised when the cameraman said he also had about two hundred three-minute canisters of old black and white 16mm film of a crashed disc and humanoid dissections.

[30] *Some chest and heart surgeons have identified the object removed from the heart as a prosthetic heart valve. But there is no surgery scar visible on the chest. If this film proves to be 1940s vintage of a non-human, it raises a question: Did the government discover the unusual prosthetic device and then back-engineer it for application in human medicine?*

"I didn't know what I was getting into!" Ray Santilli told me. "I had no experience dealing with the UFO community. I come from the very commercial world of music and video. I didn't know what Sir Occo was," he said, mispronouncing Socorro, New Mexico. "All I had heard about was Roswell and that's what I thought he was talking about. And that's what I later told people I had, with Truman in the window at the autopsy because that's who he said was definitely there for one of the autopsies. In fact, one of the canisters we have we can see the name 'Truman' and a reel number. (Plate 19) [31] But unfortunately we weren't able to process that piece of film because it was all stuck together and deteriorated too much."

On the film cannister label containing the word "Truman," there is also a stamped eagle holding spears inside a circle that is similar to the current logo for the Central Intelligence Agency (CIA) which evolved from WWII's Office of Strategic Services (OSS). In September 1947, President Truman signed the National Security Act that produced the National Security Council (NSC) and the Central Intelligence Agency to advise the NSC on intelligence matters pertinent to national security. The first CIA director, Navy Admiral Roscoe Hillenkoetter, was also head of the alleged MJ-12 Special Studies Group assigned by Truman to analyze the UFO phenomenon.[32]

Santilli showed me black and white still photographs reproduced from the dissection film already released to the media. Copies of those photographs are on the following pages along with photographs of other alleged

[31] *If there was a 1949 dissection procedure before a gallery of observers at a large operating theater in Washington, D. C., as the cameraman allegedly told Santilli, President Truman might secretly have attended.*

[32] *See Appendices I, VI, VII, X. Also see Chapter 7 and Appendices in* An Alien Harvest *© 1989 by Linda Moulton Howe ; and* TOP SECRET/ MAGIC *© 1996 by Stanton T. Friedman, Marlowe & Company.*

Plate 19 - *16mm film canister label provided by Ray Santilli which shows a handwritten notation "Reel #52, Truman's..." Santilli said the rest of the label is torn off.*

non-human bodies which have been circulated on the computer World Wide Web since the summer of 1995.

"You've seen both autopsies, Ray. How would you describe the differences between the humanoid we've all seen on TV and the other one (in Volker Spielberg's possession)?"

"I think the only way you could describe it without being an expert on what these creatures are is to say the other creature, the one you haven't seen, looks slightly blemished and wrinkled. You can't see any wounds on it, either. There was no visible sign of damage to that creature. But then if you look at the cameraman's statement, he was quite certain that three of the creatures were alive and that apart from the dead one and an injured one, the other two were in reasonably good shape."

"Do you see more cutting, more organs, in the second dissection?"

"It's a similar type of procedure, although the doctors spend a great deal of time examining the (pubic orifice) and we don't have the full (dissection) procedure as much as we do on the one you've already seen. They examine the orifice more and turn the creature up and fiddle around with the limbs and then you see them cut the chest open and start work on the organs. You can see the (thimble-like) object inside the chest cavity more clearly. The cameraman told me it was like a crystal, but he did not know anything more about it. And there is a head shot and they do remove the membranes on the eyes. That's one of the very first things they do in the other dissection, like they already know how to do it."

"When they examine the orifice, is it any different from the dissection we've already seen?"

"No, it's the same, except it's a little more graphic and a little more unpleasant for the squeamish, I'm afraid. It's the full pull-the-legs-apart-and-look and the surgeon sticks almost his entire gloved hand and arm up inside."

"Like a gynecological exam?"

"Yes, exactly. That's what it looks like. And a small, white thing of some kind with strings or tendrils was removed, but I couldn't tell you what it is."

"How many dissections did the cameraman say he filmed?"

"He filmed three. He says he did not film the creature that was already dead at the site (and was put on ice and transported away in a large truck.) And it's not clear which of the creatures are in the two dissections that we have. We know we have the two that were conducted in July 1947, but we don't have the 1949 footage."

"Which leaves one humanoid unaccounted for, doesn't it?"

"Yes."

Plate 20 - *Unidentified humanoid allegedly filmed by U. S. military cameraman after retrieval from disc that crashed May 31, 1947. Photographs provided by Ray Santilli of Merlin Productions, London, England © 1996 Orbital Media Ltd.*

During my travels in Europe, I transmitted interviews with researchers about the humanoid autopsy controversy back to the United States for my weekly news segment on *Dreamland.* My interview with Ray Santilli was one of those programs. Contrary to what Santilli remembered from the cameraman, I speculated that perhaps the shrivelled and blemished, or perhaps mottled, body was in fact the first dead alien at the scene which had been put on ice, that the humanoid with the large wound in its right leg was the one wounded at the crash site and that those were the two bodies dissected first. The third dissection in 1949 implied that humanoid had survived for two years after the crash and the fourth might have survived even longer.

As if someone had been listening to my radio report and decided to respond, I discovered that an anonymous voice message had been left on my answering machine by a man with a slow and deliberate Texas accent : *"The government made contact in 1949 when they returned the alien that survived."*

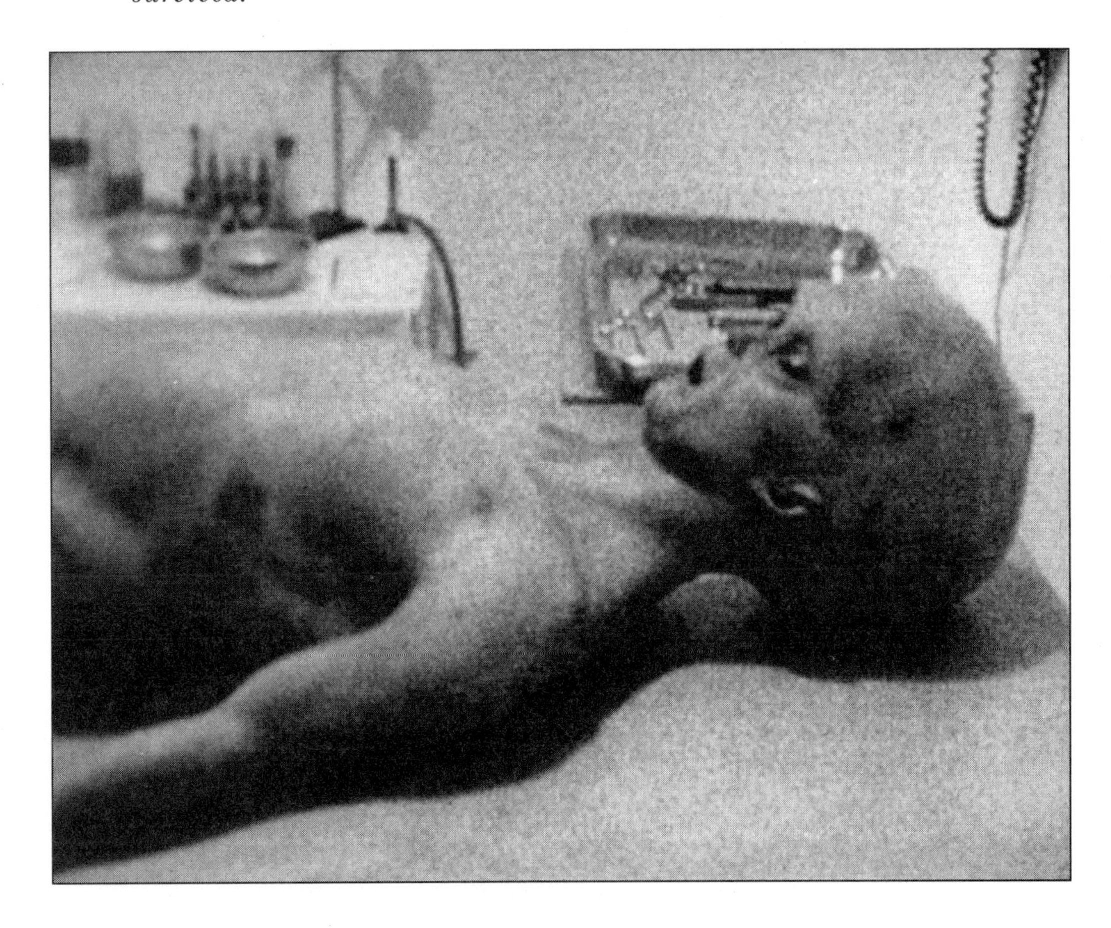

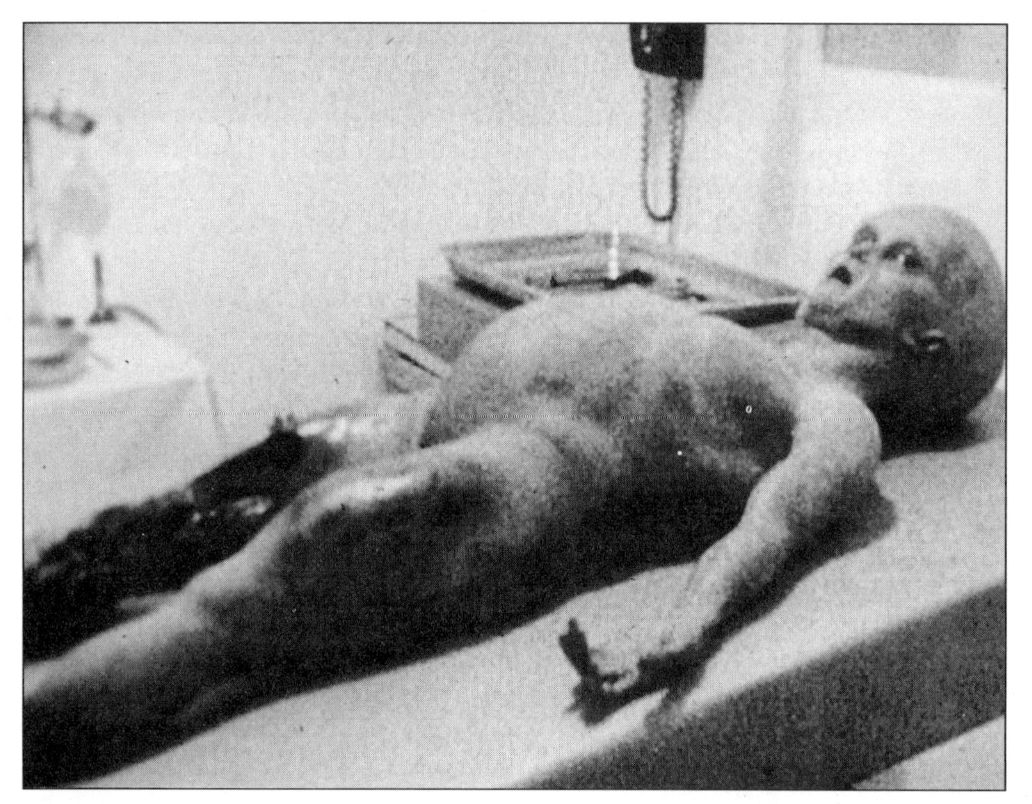

Plate 21 - *One of two humanoids with six fingers and six toes seen in dissection film. The cause of the large leg gash is unknown. The second humanoid did not have a leg wound, according to Ray Santilli.*

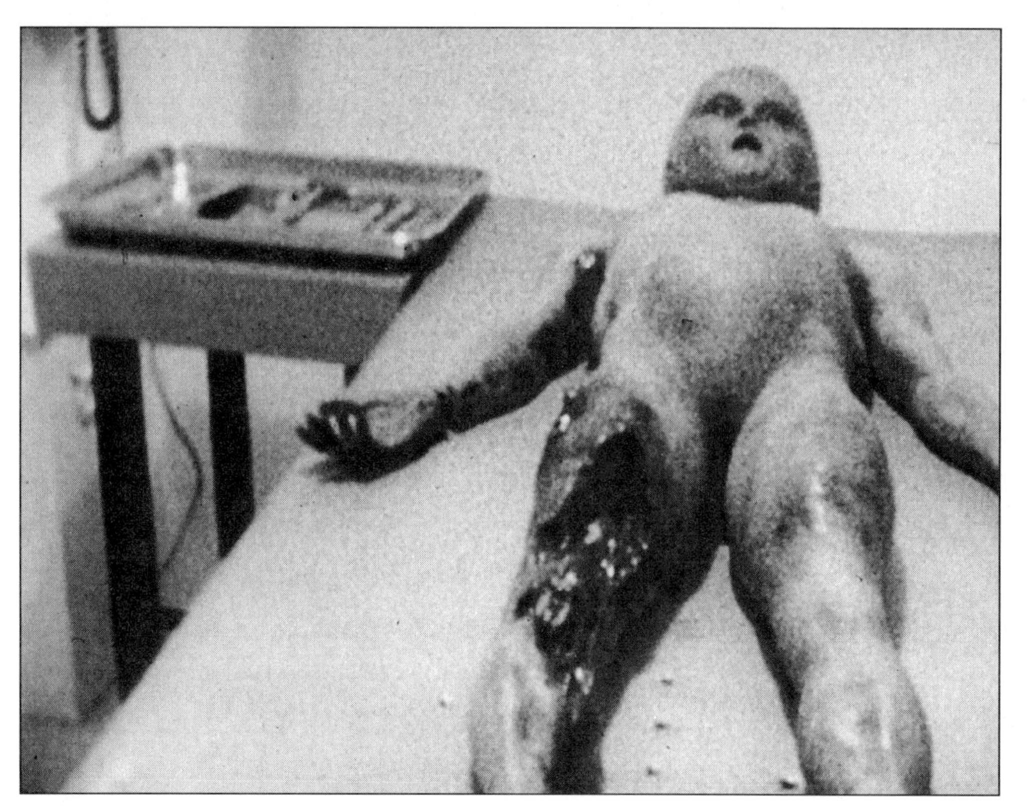

Plate 22 - *Humanoid has large wound in right leg. The right hand appears cut off, or nearly so, at the end of the right arm. The arm appears to have several more wounds.*

Plate 23-
Humanoid's six-fingered hand examined by white-gloved surgeon.

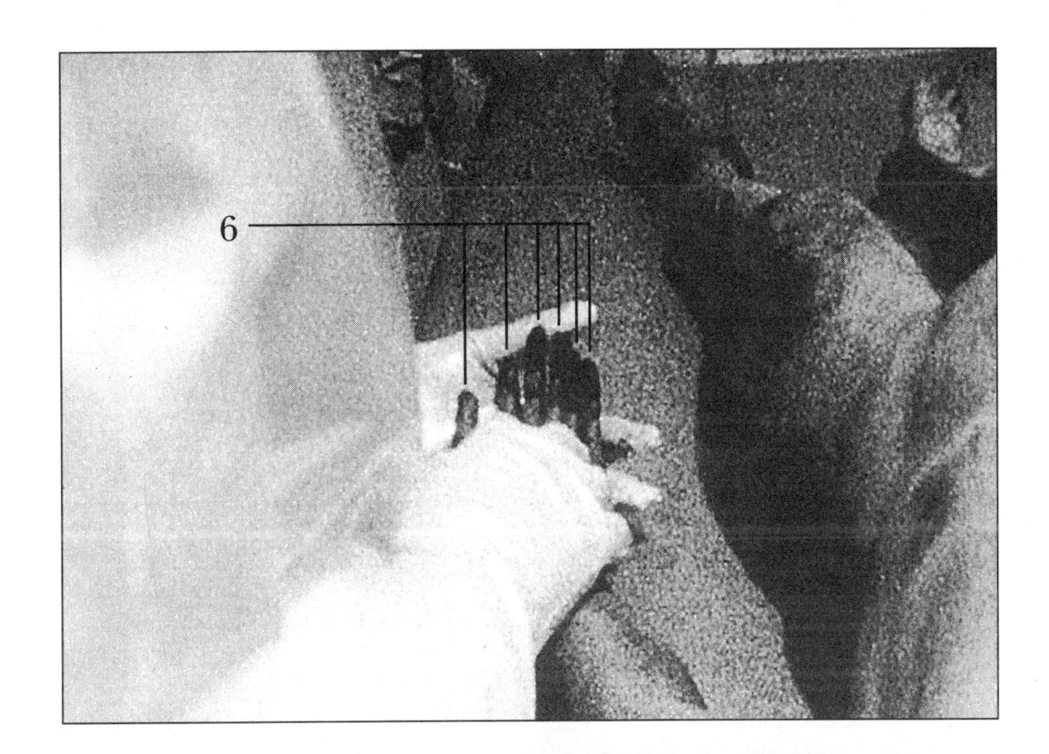

Plate 24 -
Humanoid's six-toed foot next to surgeon's gloved hand.

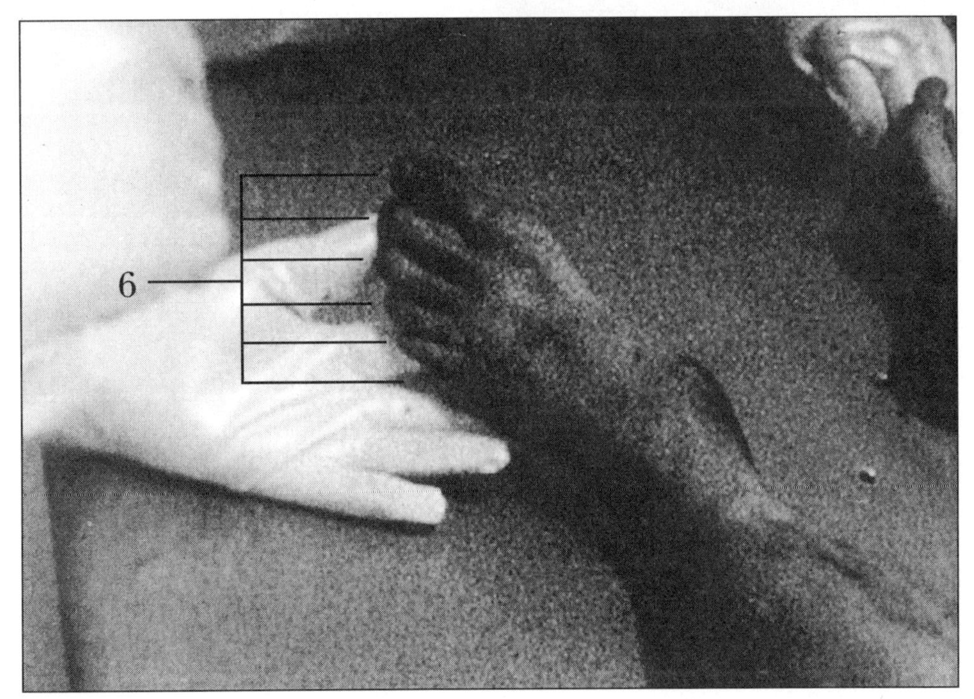

Plate 25 - *Panels with depressions of six-fingered hand prints allegedly found with the six-fingered humanoids in May 31 to June 2, 1947 recovery operation at crash site southwest of Socorro. Photograph from 16mm film © 1996 Orbital Media Ltd.*

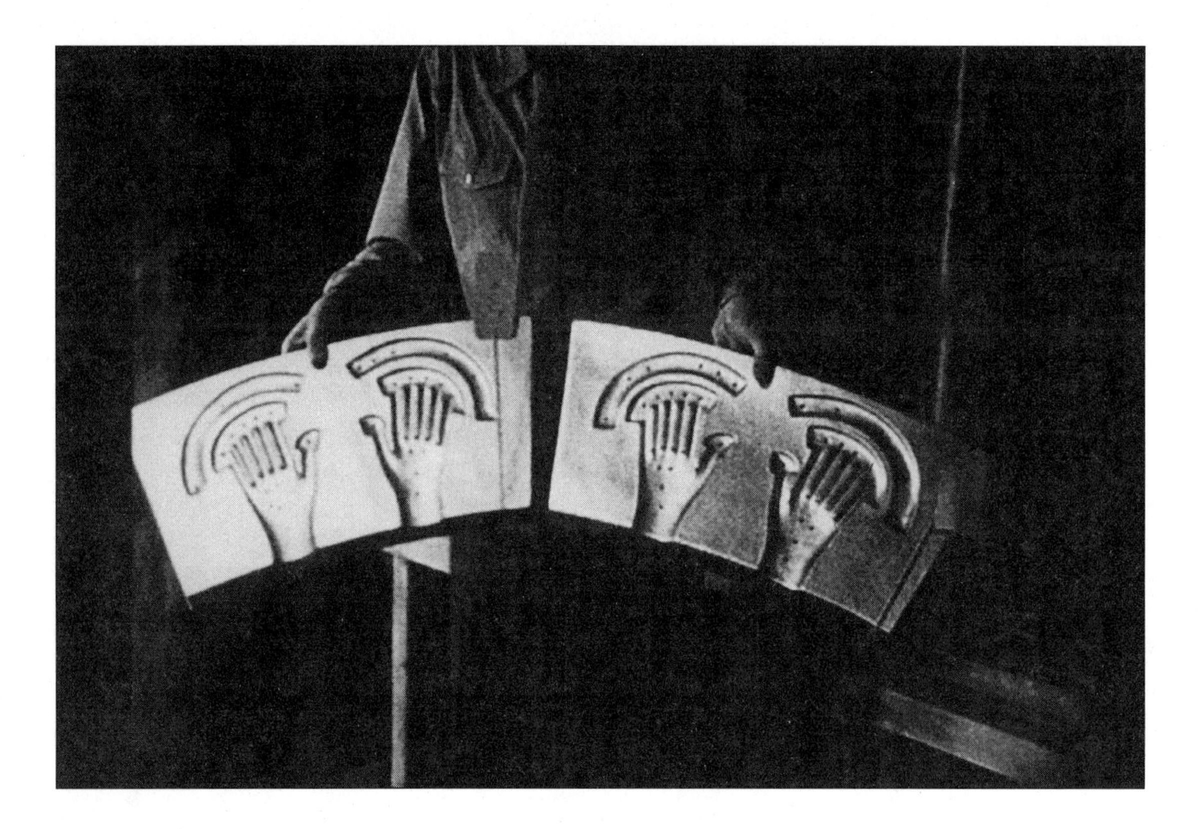

Plate 26 - *In the film of crash debris, there is an I-beam which reflects like shiny metal as it is turned in the hands of an unidentified person who seems to be showing the camera different angles and orientations without knowing precisely what is top or bottom. In this orientation, the imprinted symbols resemble early and classic Greek shown below.*

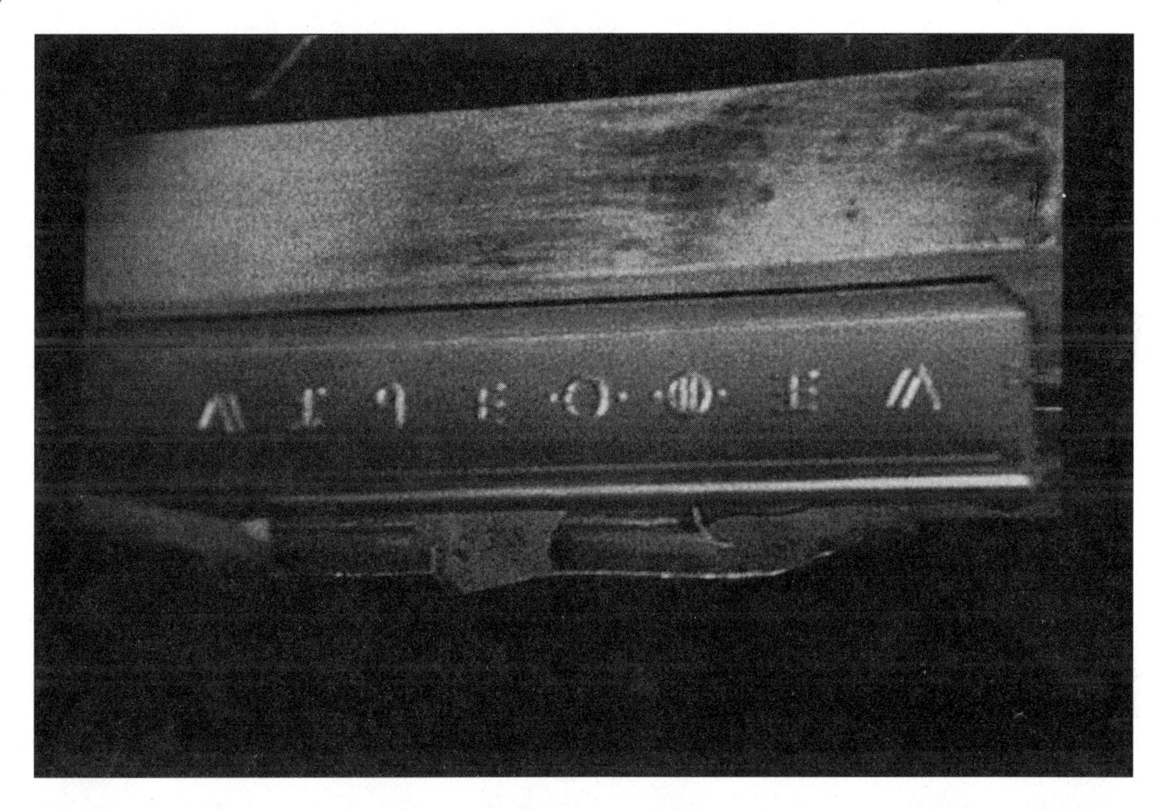

Plate 27 - *Comparison of I-beam symbols to Early and Classic Greek letters.*

Λ λ	Γ γ	ᒣ ᒣ	Ξ	Θ θ	Φ ϕ	Ξ	Λ λ
Lambda	*Gamma*	*Rho*	*Xi*	*Theta*	*Phi*	*Xi*	*Lambda*
Classic Greek	*Classic Greek*	*Early Greek*	*Early Greek*	*Classic Greek*	*Classic Greek*	*Early Greek*	*Classic Greek*

Plate 28 - *Photograph from another film segment of I-beam debris showing more symbols.*

I ι	E ϵ	H η	Θ θ
Iota *Classic Greek*	*Sigma* *Classic Greek*	*Eta* *Classic Greek*	*Theta* *Classic Greek*

Plate 29 - *Comparison of I-beam symbols to Classic Greek.*

Plate 30 - *This 1960s sketch by Aerial Phenomenon Research Organization artist Norm Duke depicts the alien beings described by Betty Hill after an abduction with her husband in New Hampshire in 1961. From* UFOs: A Pictorial History from Antiquity to the Present © *1979 by David Knight, McGraw-Hill Books. There is some resemblance to six-fingered humanoids pictured below.*

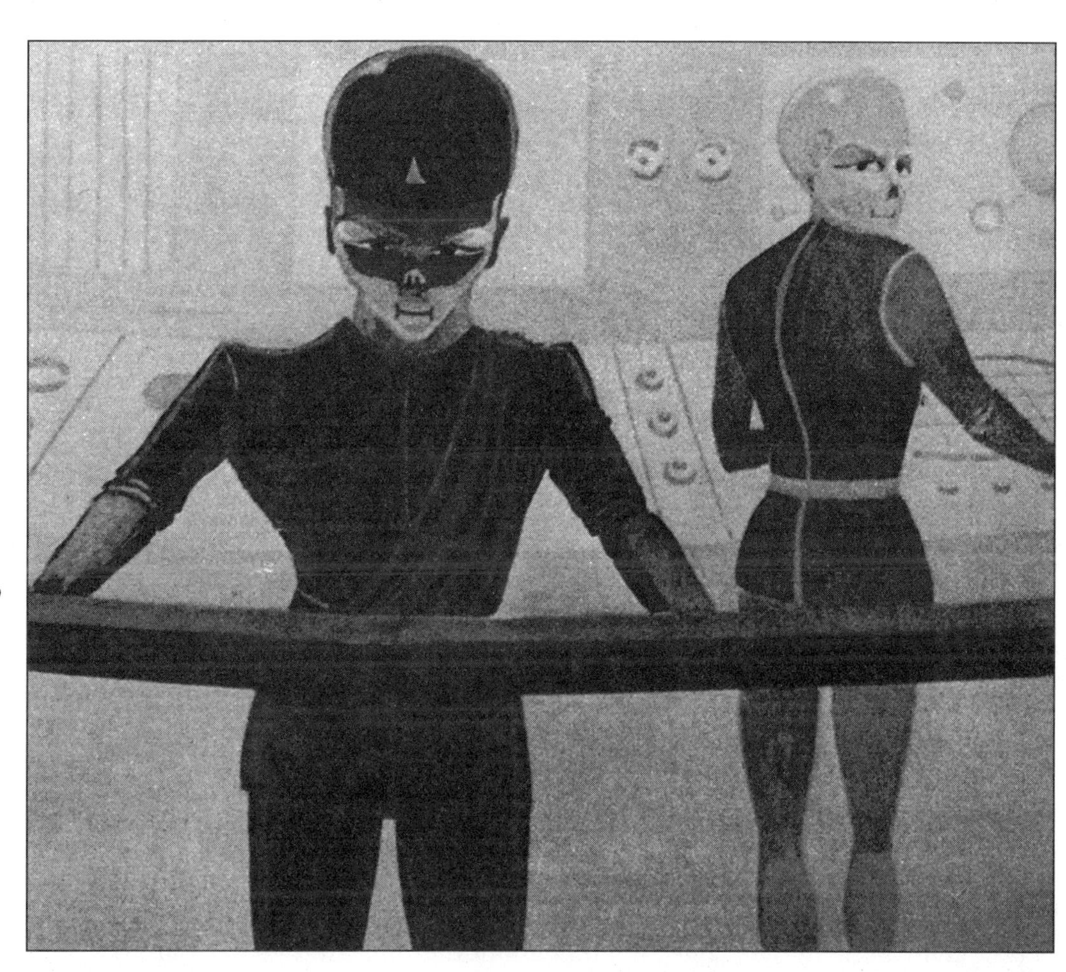

Plate 31

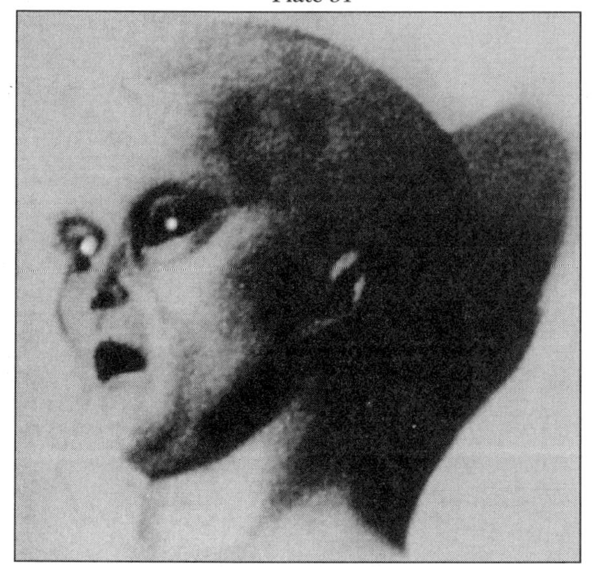

Plate 32

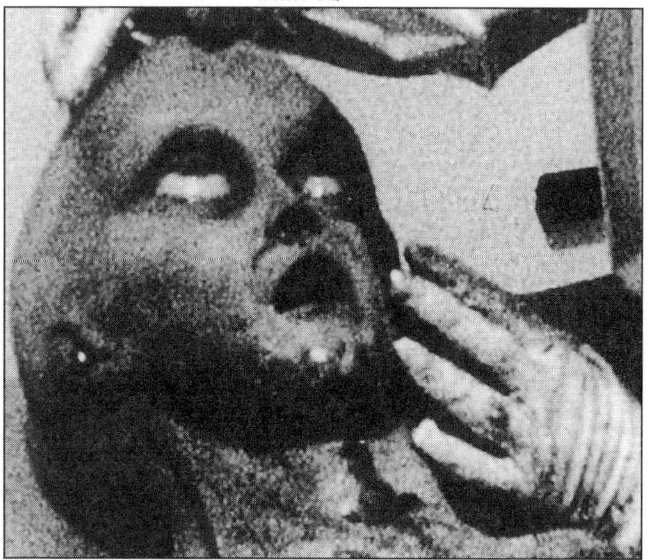

By the summer of 1995, *Shutterbug* editor Bob Shell in Radford, Virginia was seriously investigating the humanoid autopsy film. Shell had a longtime professional interest in and knowledge of film and cameras. He also had a biology/zoology degree and had applied that knowledge in work for the Central Intelligence Agency in Washington, D. C. in the mid-1960s.

In an interview for the record on October 5, 1995, I asked him, "They say once in the CIA, you're never out. What about you?"

"That's not really true," Shell answered. "I wasn't a spook. I was just a biologist and zoologist. I stayed in touch with some of my friends who are members of the intelligence community in the intervening years. I talk to one of them quite frequently. But I am no longer in the employment of the Agency and no longer do any work for them."

"Have you talked with anybody in the inner sanctum at all off the record about the dissection film?"

"Linda, it's *only* off the record to talk to those people! Let me tell you what I did first when I was approached about this whole project."

"And who approached you first?"

"Ray Santilli. In early 1995, and he told me what the film was supposed to be."

"What did he say then?"

"He said it was film of an alien autopsy from Roswell, New Mexico in 1947. And, of course, I knew generally about the Roswell story. I had read a couple of the books. I knew what was supposed to have happened. So, I called up my friend who is in intelligence, officially retired, and said, 'Jim, let me tell you this story.' And I tell him about the film. And — pardon my language — but I'll quote him precisely. He said: 'Holy shit, you mean it's finally out!'"

"And I said, 'Maybe it is.'"

"And he said, 'I figured it was only a matter of time.'"

"And I said, 'Jim, am I getting myself into any personal danger by getting involved in this?'"

"And he said, 'Let me get back to you on that.'"

"So he called me back three days later after talking to some of his friends and said, 'Bob, I don't think you have anything to worry about because if they had wanted this hushed up, Santilli and the cameraman both would have been dead a week ago.'

" So, based on that assurance from him, I went ahead and got involved in it. And I have had no sign that anybody is monitoring me, following me, nobody has threatened me. I see no intelligence involvement at all, which really surprises the hell out of me!"

"Bob, I'd say the government has been too silent in all this."

"Yes, and it's very puzzling. It either means this is the real thing and they have just decided to let it run its course. Or maybe they did it themselves."

"To test public reaction?"

"Yeah. Or it's a hoax and they know it's going to come out in time."

"But given your retired friend's first reaction, and assuming that the film is real, maybe this is not the ET film the inner sanctum expected to come out first?"

"I think possibly the release is an accident. But maybe they were close to releasing stuff anyway."

"Or, Bob, they are over a barrel and the silence is related to the fact that the film is real and there's nothing they can say, so they are using this opportunity to judge public reaction."

"Yeah, could be."

"Any other information that has come to you from sources verifying the film in some way?"

"Only that I talked to one man who was referred to me by my other friend (who said 'Holy shit!'). This man is an active intelligence officer at a very high level who says that he personally has seen one of those control panels — the things with the hand prints — years ago back in the early 1960s. He said he was partially involved in a project that was attempting to reverse engineer them and that they are very advanced computers. And he said that after all the years of research that they have done on them, they were no closer to understanding them now than the first day they laid eyes on them."

"Bob, don't the knobs placed in the palm at the ridges of the largest knuckles and at the tips of the fingers suggest a connection to whatever electrical field or nerve impulses there are in the humanoids?"

"He said what those panels are — the way he put it to me is: 'Neuron-based computers.'"

"Neuron-based?"

"Not electronic, but biological in base. Which is very curious because there is an article in the October 1995 *Discover Magazine* talking about building such a thing, that computer scientists are working in that direction. Maybe when a creature's hands were placed in its matching panel depressions, a closed computer system was created between the humanoid and its panel."

"Meaning that the panels responded to the *thought processes* of the humanoids?"

"Something like that, maybe."

"Did he elaborate on how it could be neuron-based?"

"He didn't. Probably the computer itself would be inside those panels. The one that is broken in half — if you look at it carefully on the film you can sort of see that there is a bunch of stuff hanging out where it's broken. I don't know what it is."

"Could it be fiber optics?"

"Could be."

"Bob, did either of the men you talked to indicate whether he had seen film from the crash site on the early morning of June 1 or 2, 1947 in which the creatures were alive and screaming, according to the cameraman?"

"No. In fact, so far there is no evidence that there is film of that. The whole thing is peculiar. There are pieces that seem to fit and other pieces that don't fit. I don't know if we will ever know exactly what happened."

I explained to Bob Shell that one of the hypotheses about the alleged Roswell UFO crash was that two discs collided above the Foster ranch between Corona and Roswell, New Mexico around July 4, 1947. In that scenario, the two discs came down at two different sites. One blew to smithereens and fell on the ranch. The other went further toward Capitan Mountain and crashed pretty much intact. There was the July 4, 1947 Capitan Mountain crash site described in the deathbed testimony of Jim Ragsdale.[33]

[33] The Jim Ragsdale Story – A Closer Look at the Roswell Incident © *1996 by Ragsdale Productions, Inc., Roswell, New Mexico.*

Whatever actual incidents there have been, the Santilli cameraman's May 31st crash date matched the 1947 Memorial Day explosion heard by the ranchers in the Plains of San Agustin.

Concerning the confusion between the names Roswell and Socorro, Santilli told me he wondered if the cameraman originally told him "Roswell" because it was the only name the public generally knew about UFO crashes. The cameraman might have felt more comfortable showing Santilli the film reels without too much explanation.

In August 1995, Bob Shell did a preliminary visual inspection and chemical "taste test" on a few frames of the cameraman's film which Ray Santilli released to him, pending further analyses by Kodak in Rochester, New York. By 1997, Kodak testing was still pending. Shell issued a report entitled "Summary of Points In Physical Research On Film Dating" © August 31, 1995 which said:

> "The edge code markings on the film, a square followed by a triangle, immediately following the word KODAK, indicate film manufactured in 1927, 1947 and 1967. Kodak changed the system to a three-symbol code in the early 1970s, so this code was not used in 1987.

> "Film is made of a light sensitive photographic emulsion coated onto a flexible film base. In 1927, the film base was cellulose nitrate, a highly flammable material which was discontinued and replaced with acetate. All film coated onto acetate base is referred to as 'safety film' because it does not spontaneously combust. In 1947, the film base used was acetate propionate, one of the original safety film base materials. By 1967 acetate propionate was no longer in use and had been replaced with triacetate. The 'Roswell film' has (an) acetate propionate base.
>
> "The 'Roswell film' is on Cine Kodak Super XX High Speed Panchromatic Safety Film, a film type introduced in the early 1940s (Kodak doesn't know exact year) and discontinued in 1956-57 when all film types were discontinued and replaced with new types which were processed in new high temperature, more caustic chemicals. Film made prior to 1957 cannot be properly processed in later chemicals.
>
> "Super XX film was a high speed film designed for photography indoors or outdoors in dim light. Because of its high sensitivity, it had a very short shelf life and deteriorated rapidly prior to processing. Based on the stated very short shelf life and the high quality of the images on the 'Roswell (dissection) film,' it is my conclusion that the film was exposed and processed while still quite fresh. My educated guess is within two years of manufacture.
>
> "It would be impossible to take unexposed Super XX film from 1947 and expose it today and get any sort of usable image. The film would be heavily fogged from cosmic radiation by now. High speed (high sensitivity) films are much more sensitive to cosmic rays than slow (low sensitivity) films.
>
> "I find the physical characteristics of the 'Roswell film' and the characteristics of the images on the film to be totally consistent with film manufactured, exposed and processed in 1947."

Bob Shell later added the following information to his statement: "In 1927, 35mm motion picture film had a cellulose nitrate base, while 16mm motion picture film had a cellulose acetate propionate base for consumer sales. Cellulose nitrate was used in 16mm made only for the newsreel services and might have been supplied to the U. S. government on special order. Also, my first statement was written when I was still under the impression that what Ray Santilli had was original camera film. I learned later in subsequent research that he has mostly, if not entirely, copy film."

If Santilli has mostly copy film, who has the original 16mm B&W film? The cameraman? Volcker Spielberg? Or someone else? And why hasn't that original 16mm film been tested by Kodak straightforwardly in a timely and professional manner with a formal report for the public to see? Shell said one of the reasons might be that collector and financier Spielberg doesn't want to risk finding out. If the film genuinely dated to the 1947 period, it is extremely valuable. If not, his investment could be useless. Not confirming the film's age has helped to sustain its mystery and value.

A problem that Bob Shell also acknowledged is that the film frames Santilli gave him to test do not show dissection images. The frames he was given possibly show stairs and could have come from any film.

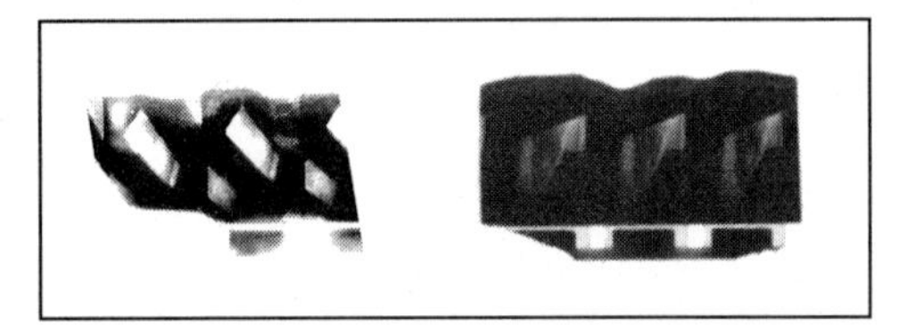

Plate 33 - *Photograph of 16mm film frames that Bob Shell inspected and discussed in his August 1995 report that suggested the frames are "consistent with film manufactured, exposed and processed in 1947."*

Also in September 1995, while controversy was raging about the six-fingered humanoids, bluish-colored images of yet another humanoid type with four fingers were circulated as the "Hong Kong Alien" on the World Wide Web.

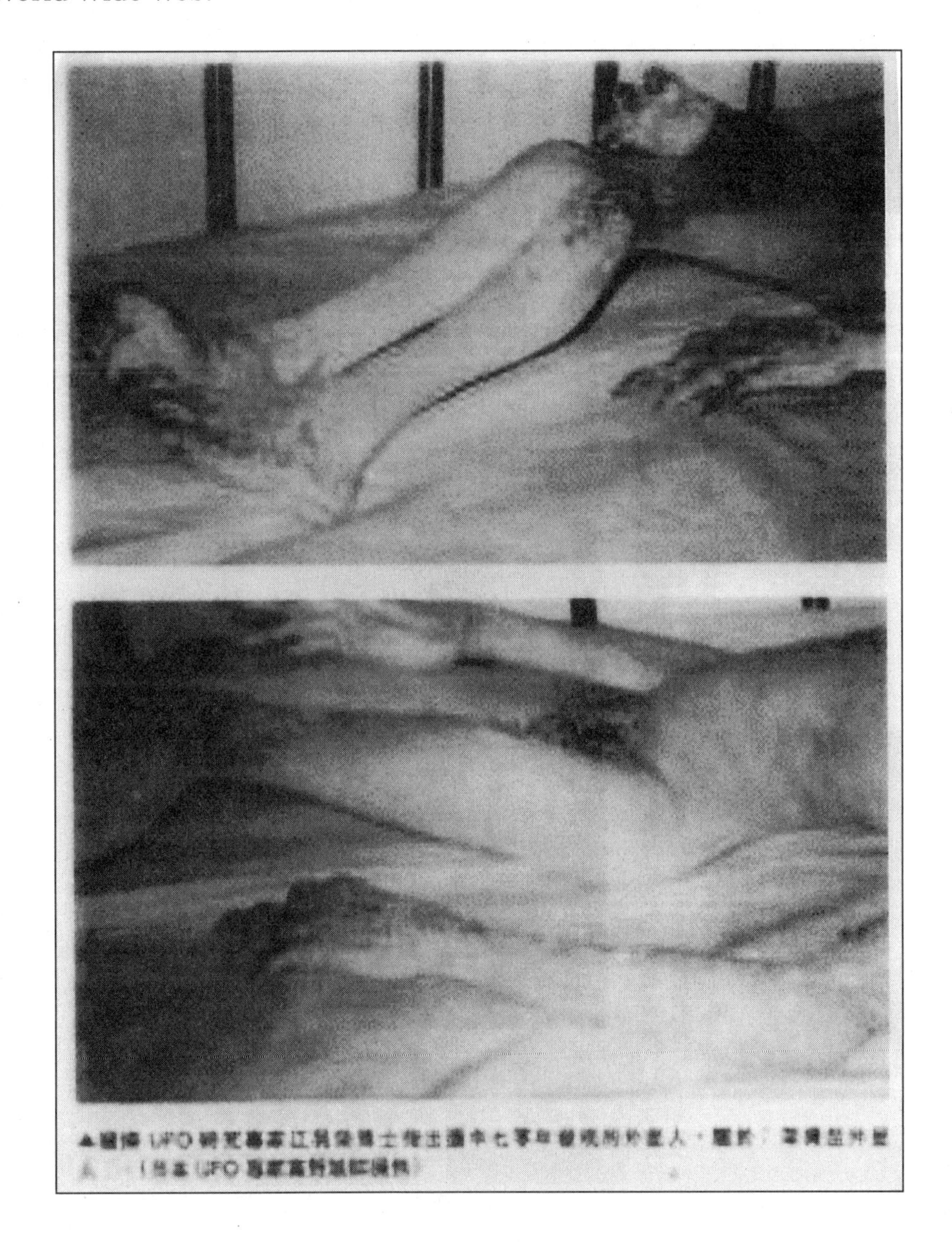

Plate 34 - *"Hong Kong Alien" computer images of non-human feet, legs and hands distributed on the Internet in 1995. The Chinese text supposedly says: "Based on a source from the Japanese UFO Institute, the picture or photograph shows the 1970 alien incident." Spelling of location was not clear, but could be Gongzui on Dadu River southwest of Leshan, China.*

Compare to Plate 37, dummy alien created by Hollywood special effects artist Steve Johnson for the television docudrama "Roswell." These "Hong Kong Alien" photographs were also published in the September 1996 issue of Penthouse *magazine.*

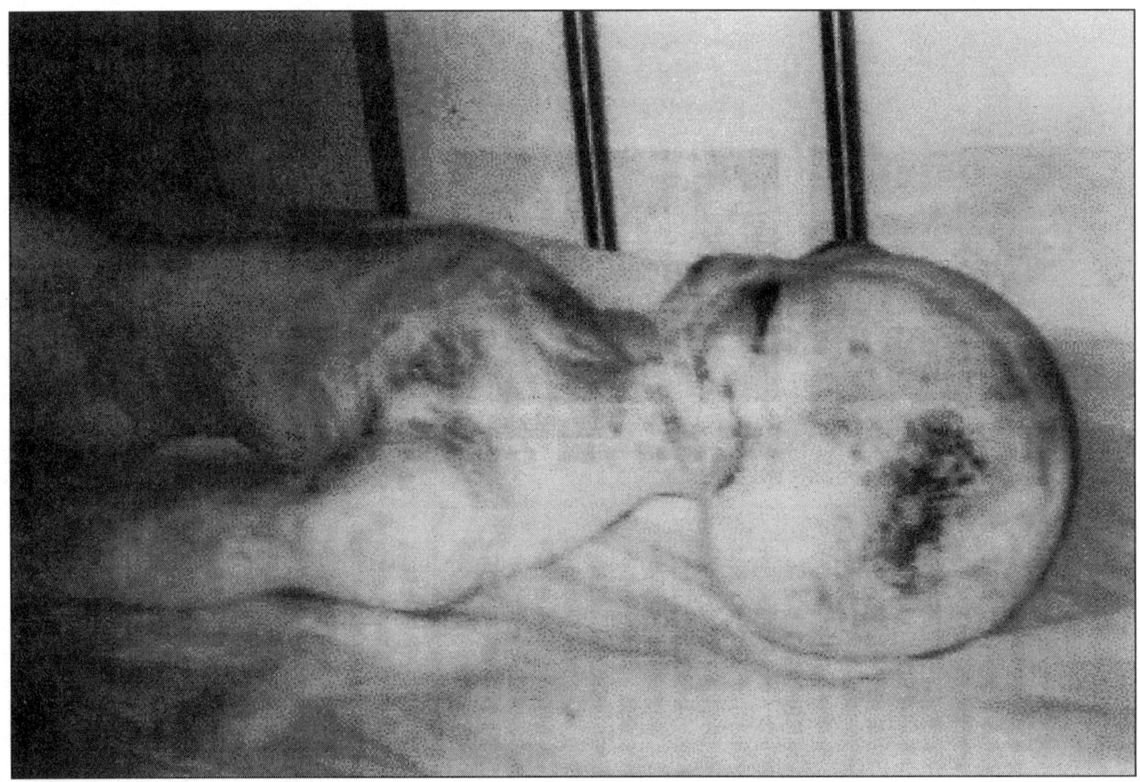

Plate 35 - *"Hong Kong Alien" image of alleged non-human head and torso.*

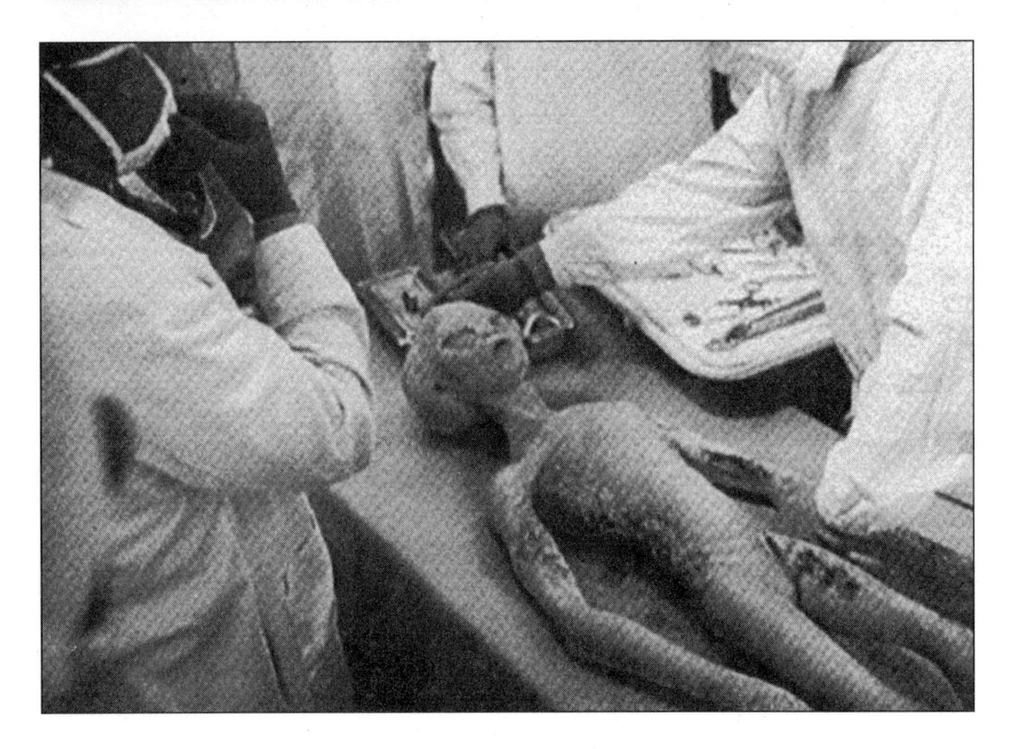

Plate 36 - *Dummy alien created by Hollywood special effects artist Steve Johnson and his company XFX for the television docudrama "Roswell" produced by Paul Davids for Showtime cable broadcast in 1995.*

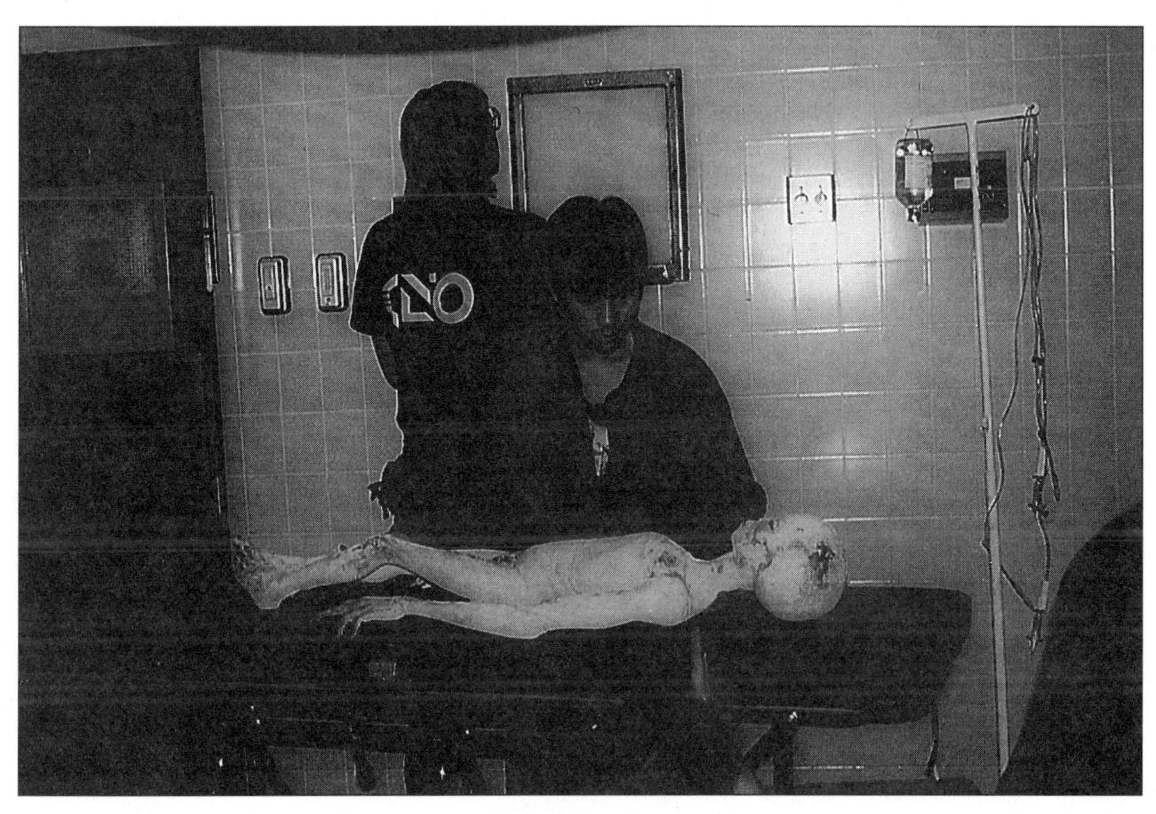

Plate 37 - *XFX special effects and props team working on "Roswell" produced by Paul Davids for Showtime cable network. Originally broadcast July 31, 1994. Photograph provided by Paul Davids.*

Television producer Paul Davids explained to me the origin of the alien dummies used in his television special *Roswell.*

"Director Jeremy Kagan and I had no access to any 'real' photographic evidence to share with our effects specialist, Steve Johnson of XFX. We did, however, give Johnson drawings from UFO researcher Leonard Stringfield's files based on eyewitness testimony of the 1947 Roswell, New Mexico UFO crash. One unique feature we gave our alien was a head with a rear section that inflates and deflates like a bladder. In the film, the living alien seems to be breathing through lungs in the back of its head.

"In the case of the Hong Kong photos and the Guccione *Penthouse* magazine photos, there's no doubt that my own movie has been used by pranksters to create confusion. A full-scale model of one of our four props (the one that was 'alive') has been for sale since the fall of 1995 through the *Sharper Image Holiday Catalogue.*

"I do not know the true story behind the 'Santilli autopsy' film. As far as I can tell, one year after its release, no one yet has identified its actual origin or found a conclusive 'smoking gun' to prove or disprove it."

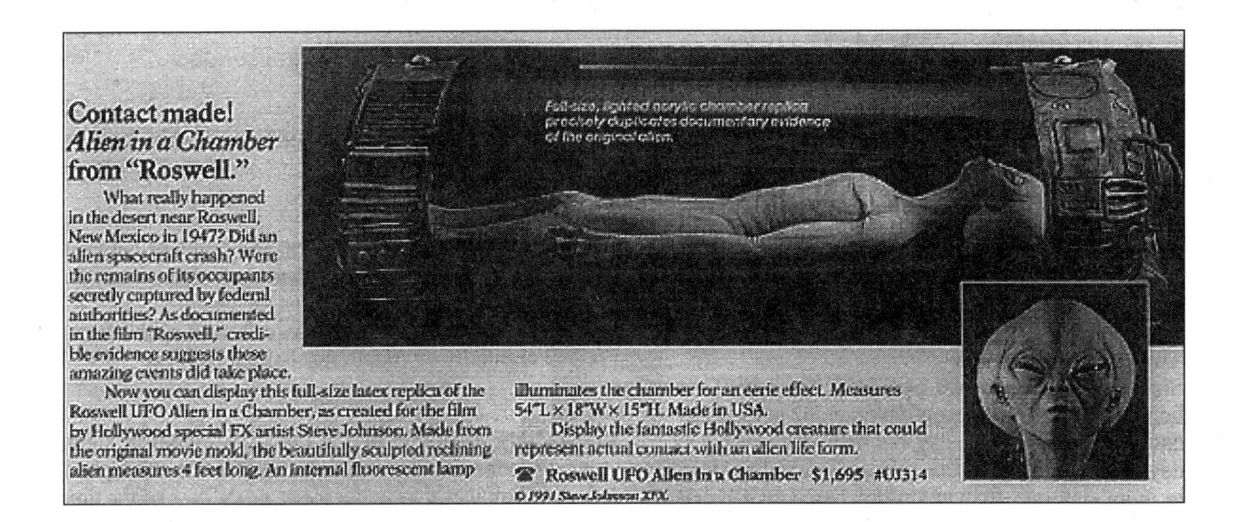

Plate 38 - *"Roswell UFO Alien in a Chamber" advertised in the December 1995* Holiday Catalogue *distributed by The Sharper Image Company. Model created by Steve Johnson of XFX, a special effects company in Sun Valley, California.*

This advertisement appeared in the December 1995 *Holiday Catalogue* distributed by The Sharper Image company. For $1,695, you could purchase a full-scale model of an alien being created for the 1995 Showtime cable television docudrama *Roswell* produced by Paul Davids about the alleged crash of a UFO in July 1947. The creator was Steve Johnson's XFX office in Sun Valley, California north of Burbank. I called the office and talked to his assistant, Joe Fordham.

I asked him what photographs or drawings Steve Johnson had to work from and Fordham said, "We worked with the director of the Showtime project, Jeremy Kagan. He came to us because we do creature effects and prosthetics. He told us he was doing a movie about the Roswell incident and gave us some books and artwork from an artist he liked. He asked us to come up with creatures based on factual reports and eyewitness sketches from Roswell. So, Steve made a couple of small-scale clay sculptures, one head and shoulders and one full body, showing two different directions we could go and we ended up combining both. He made a full sculpture in clay of the best looking grey alien he could that would look real. Later, we were contacted by Morris Costumes who licensed from us our creature sculpture, mass produced and sold it through various outlets, Sharper Image being one of them."

In early August 1995, I received a plain manila envelope with only a San Francisco terminal annex postal stamp to indicate its origin. Inside were several pages and a title sheet that said, "Restricted SOM1-01 Majestic-12 Group Special Operations Manual – Extraterrestrial Entities and Technology, Recovery and Disposal, TOP SECRET/MAJIC EYES ONLY, Warning! This is a TOP SECRET-MAJIC EYES ONLY document containing compartmentalized information essential to the national security of the United States. EYES ONLY ACCESS to the material herein is strictly limited to personnel possessing MAJIC-12 CLEARANCE LEVEL. Examination or use by unauthorized personnel is strictly forbidden and is punishable by federal law. Majestic-12 Group, April 1954." A War Department Logo position was indicated at the bottom of the cover page.

J. Andrew Kissner, New Mexico House Representative for District 37 in Las Cruces, researched early United States efforts to collect and analyze flying discs. He has contributed information which suggests that as RADAR is a word formed from Radio Detecting And Ranging, the terms MAJIC and MJ-12 were acronyms formed from Manhattan (Engineering District) Joint Chiefs of Staff) Integrated Command - (Z Division, Group) 12. (See Z Division in Appendix VI.) The mysterious and highly classified Project Y and Z Divisions were established at Sandia Base in Albuquerque, New Mexico in September 1947. The Z Division Leader was Jerrold R. Zacharias and the activities were administered through presidential invitation by AT&T Bell Telephone beginning in March 1948. MAJIC's function and purpose was still classified in 1995. Originally, Project Y and Division Z were involved in nuclear weapons development.

In Appendix I, I have re-printed the entire MJ-12 SOM1-01 training manual as it was sent to me by the anonymous source. But here I would like to share the portion specifically about non-human types so that this alleged historic government information about extraterrestrials can be compared to the preceding images of aliens which have been emerging in the 1990s.

Page 6 of the SOM1-01 Operations Manual states:

> **"10. Description of Extraterrestrial Biological Entities (EBEs):**
>
> Examination of remains recovered from wreckage of UFOBs [34] indicates that Extraterrestrial Biological Entities may be classified into two distinct categories as follows:
>
> a) EBE Type I. These entities are humanoid and might be mistaken for human beings of the Oriental race if seen from a distance. They are bipedal, 5 to 5 feet 4 inches in height and weigh 80 to 100 pounds. Proportionally they are similar to humans, although the

[34] *The acronym UFOB for Unidentified Flying Objects was used instead of UFOs in official government documents in the early 1950s. See 1954 UFOBs reporting guideline entitled "AFR200-2 Intelligence Report" in Appendix II.*

> cranium is somewhat larger and more rounded. The skin is a pale, chalky-yellow in color, thick, and slightly pebbled in appearance.
>
> Their eyes are small, wide-set, almond-shaped, with brownish-black irises with very large pupils.[35] The whites of the eyes are not like that of humans, but have a pale grey cast. The ears are small and *not low on the skull.* The nose is thin and long, and the mouth is wider than in humans, and nearly lipless. (Howe's emphasis.)
>
> There is no apparent facial hair and very little body hair, that being very fine and confined to the underarm and the groin area. The body is thin and without apparent body fat, but *the muscles are well-developed. The hands are small, with four long digits but no opposable thumb.* The outside digit is jointed in a manner as to be nearly opposable, and there is no webbing between the fingers as in humans. The legs are slightly but noticeably bowed, and the *feet are somewhat splayed and proportionally large.*" (Howe's emphasis.)

This description of EBE Type I matches closely Plates 34-35 of the "Hong Kong Alien" and the beings at the Snohomish, Washington daylight encounter in Chapter 2. It is this EBE Type I that I understand was found at one July 1947 crash site and another in 1949, both in the Roswell area.

> b) EBE Type II. These entities are humanoid but differ from Type I in many respects. They are bi-pedal, 3 feet 5 inches to 4 feet 2 inches in height and weigh 25-50 pounds. Proportionally, the head is much larger than humans or Type I EBEs, the cranium being much larger and elongated. The eyes are very large, slanted, and nearly wrap around the side of the skull. They are black with no whites showing. There is no noticeable brow ridge, and the skull has a slight peak that runs over the crown. The nose consists of two small slits which sit high above the slit-like mouth. There are no external ears. The skin is a pale bluish-grey color, being somewhat darker on the back of the creature, and is very smooth and fine-celled. There is no hair on either the face or the body, and these creatures do not appear to be mammalian. The arms are long in proportion to the legs, and the hands have three long, tapering fingers and a thumb which is nearly as long as the fingers. The second finger is thicker than the others, but not as long as the index finger. The feet are small and narrow, and four toes are joined together with a membrane."

The memo to the FBI in Plate 14 which described "bodies of human shape, but only 3 feet tall" might be a reference to EBE Type IIs. This type might also relate to the "grey androids" or "worker bees" often described and sketched after human abduction experiences.

[35] *See* Glimpses of Other Realities, Vol. I, *Page 267, drawing in Plate 19 © 1994 by Linda Moulton Howe. Also, reference to ears "not low on the skull" implies contrast to another EBE type with low set ears. The six-fingered humanoid has small, low set ears. Dade County, Florida resident and wildlife film producer K. T. Frankovich reported in* Unknown *Magazine, Issue No. 1, December 1997, her May 1992 face-to-face encounter with a six-fingered humanoid nearly identical, she said, to the being in the dissection film, including small, low-set ears.*

Plate 39 - *EBE Type II: Small, grey, earless being with three long fingers and opposable thumb, long arms, large black eyes, and nose slits described by Paula Watson, Mt. Vernon, Missouri. Watson has had repeated abductions since 1983. Artist's rendering by Hingwah Hatch, August 1990, Springfield, Missouri.*

The SOM1-01 Training Manual concluded about EBE Types I and II:

> "It is not definitely known where either type of creature originated, but *it seems certain that they did not evolve on earth.* (Howe's emphasis.) It is further evident, although not certain, that they may have originated on two different planets."

Whoever the anonymous source was, the copy sent to me could only have originated with an aerospace engineer named Bob Wood in California.

At the top of each page in small type were these words:

> "This unclassified copy is for research purposes. Rev. 6: 3/5/95; Helvetica headers, Times New Roman text 10/12 pts. The Government has declared that such a classification (TOP SECRET/MAJIC EYES ONLY) does not exist."

Bob Wood wrote those words at the top of each page he reproduced on his computer from photographic prints of the SOM1-01 Operations Manual from another investigator, Don Berliner at the Fund for UFO Research in Mt. Rainier, Maryland. Berliner said that in January 1993, an employee of NASA obtained a copy of the actual 1954 training manual allegedly by mail postmarked in Wisconsin and took 35mm photographs of it. Then the NASA source sent Berliner 35mm negatives of the pages. Berliner had prints made which were not very clear. Berliner went to Bob Wood for help and Wood took on the chore of studying the photographic prints and reconstituting the text clearly so it could be studied. It was a copy of his Revision Number 6 dated March 5, 1995 which reached me by mail in early August 1995 with only a San Francisco terminal annex postmark. Wood and I have talked about what could have happened. He said he mailed his son, Ryan Wood, a copy of this same Revision 6 sometime in mid-1995 which his son in San Francisco never received. Perhaps I received that copy, but it means it was somehow diverted in the United States Postal Service by unknown hands for unknown purposes.

Since receiving the SOM1-01 manual, I have talked with another former CIA employee who said he saw a very similar manual during his intelligence career, but that it was a 1970s version. If the training manual is real and is a true insight into government knowledge and cover-up, insiders knew long ago that EBE Type II "little guys," EBE Type I and others were being described and sketched by men, women and children in the human abduction syndrome after reports of disc encounters and missing time. From the Betty and Barney Hill case of 1961 onward, people all over the planet have reported being taken up in beams of light, subjected to physical examinations by non-humans often described as three and a half to four foot tall grey-colored humanoids with huge, black, slanted eyes. Frequently, sperm is mechanically removed from men and ova removed from women. Humans are then returned in an altered state back to their cars, bedrooms or backyards where they are haunted by the nagging eeriness of a too-real nightmare and the hard, cold facts of scars, clocks and missing time.

People in the abduction syndrome have also contributed their own insights about the non-human beings. One of the most commonly expressed is that the small, grey "things" with the big, black eyes — EBE Type II? — are not independently functioning intelligences. "They are like bellhops," the Navy man named Axle says later in this chapter. "They come to take you where you're supposed to go and then they bring you back."

Some government insiders have said that EBE Type II's might be biological androids created by another more advanced intelligence to do work on this planet. If so, who or what is the intelligence behind them? Is the confusion compounded if the "master" grey intelligences deliberately make androids in their image?

And what is the relationship to the EBE Type I's who have an Oriental appearance? Do the EBE-IIs work for EBE-Is? EBE Type I fits Steve Bismarck's description in Chapter 2 about his experiences at his wilderness home in Snohomish, Washington in 1977. At that time, there were mutilations of cattle, deer and other animals, sightings of Bigfoot that left huge tracks in the mud and were associated with horrible, high-pitched howling at night, orange, glowing balls of light and silver discs. At the same time, Bismarck had a firsthand, broad daylight encounter with two "men" who looked to him like very thin "Filipinos." But they came straight down out of the sky in egg-shaped machines.

Such interactions with human and animal life were not mentioned in 1954 when the SOM1-01 Training Manual was written. In fact, the manual concluded:

> "...there are few indications that these objects and their builders pose a direct threat to the security of the United States, despite the uncertainty as to their ultimate motives in coming here."

Did the Eben activity change after 1954 and become more intrusive with animal mutilations and human abductions? Or is there another "grey troublemaker" species or renegade faction that has its own agenda outside Eben and government control? The following paragraph explains MJ-12's "reason that the recovery and study" of craft be "given such a high priority."

> "Certainly the technology possessed by these beings far surpasses anything known to modern science, yet their presence here seems to be benign, and they seem to be avoiding contact with our species, at least for the present.
>
> "Several dead entities have been recovered along with a substantial amount of wreckage and devices from downed craft, all of which are now under study at various locations. No attempt has been made by extraterrestrial entities either to contact authorities or to recover their dead counterparts of the downed craft, even though one of the crashes was the result of direct military action. The greatest threat at this time

> *arises from the acquisition and study of such advanced technology by foreign powers unfriendly to the United States. It is for this reason that the recovery and study of this type of material by the United States has been given such a high priority."* (Howe's emphasis.)

The training manual specified that "encounters with living Extraterrestrial Biological Entities (EBEs)... fall under the jurisdiction of MJ-12 OPNAC BBS-01." For similar, but not identical acronym, see Appendix IV regarding 1954 guidance procedures to be followed for reporting unidentified flying objects from the Potomac River Naval Command, Washington, D. C. in OPNAV Notice 3820 dated September 26, 1952.

There is no further clarification about OPNAC BBS-01 except that "this special unit only" will handle EBE encounters. Here is where MJ-12 asserts an Orwellian policy in which lies are ordered to become official truth.

> "Any encounter with entities known to be of extraterrestrial origin is to be considered a matter of national security and therefore classified TOP SECRET. Under no circumstance is the general public or the public press to learn of the existence of these entities. *The official government policy is that such creatures do not exist, and that no agency of the federal government is now engaged in any study of extraterrestrials or their artifacts. Any deviation from this stated policy is absolutely forbidden.* (Howe's emphasis.)
>
> "...Possible contact may take place as a result of overtures by the entities themselves. In these instances, it is anticipated that encounters will take place at military installations or other obscure locations selected by mutual agreement. Such meeting would have the advantage of being limited to personnel with appropriate clearance away from public scrutiny. Although it is not considered very probable, there also exists the possibility that EBEs may land in public places without prior notice. In this case the OPNAC Team will formulate cover stories for the press and prepare briefings for the President and the Chiefs of Staff.
>
> "Contact with survivors of accidents or craft downed by natural events or military action may occur with little or no warning. In these cases, it is important that the initial contact be limited to military personnel to preserve security. Civilian witnesses to the area will be detained and debriefed by MJ-12. Contact with EBEs by military personnel not having MJ-12 or OPNAC clearance is to be strictly limited to action necessary to ensure the availability of the EBEs for study by the OPNAC Team.
>
> "... EBEs will be detained by whatever means are necessary and removed to a secure location as soon as possible. Precautions will be taken by personnel coming in contact with EBEs to minimize the risk

of disease as a result of contamination by unknown organisms.[36] If the entities are wearing space suits or breathing apparatus of some kind, care should be exercised to prevent damage to these devices. While all efforts should be taken to assure the well-being of the EBEs, they must be isolated from any contact with unauthorized personnel. While it is not clear what provisions or amenities might be required by non-human entities, they should be provided if possible. The officer in charge of the operation will make these determinations, as no guidelines now exist to cover this area.

"... Injured or wounded entities will be treated by medical personnel assigned to the OPNAC Team. If the team medical personnel are not immediately available, First Aid will be administered by Medical Corps personnel at the initial site. Since little is known about EBE biological functions, aid will be confined to the stopping of bleeding, bandaging of wounds and splinting of broken limbs. No medications of any kind are to be administered as the effect of terrestrial medications on non-human biological systems are impossible to predict. As soon as the injuries are considered stabilized, the EBEs will be moved by closed ambulance or other suitable conveyance to a secure location.

"... In dealing with any living Extraterrestrial Biological Entity, security is of paramount importance. All other considerations are secondary. Although it is preferable to maintain the physical well-being of any entity, *the loss of EBE life is considered acceptable if conditions or delays to preserve that life in any way compromises the security of the operations.*

"... Once the OPNAC Team has taken custody of the EBEs, their care and transportation to designated facilities become the responsibility of OPNAC personnel. Every cooperation will be extended to the team in carrying out duties. OPNAC Team personnel will be given TOP PRIORITY at all times regardless of their apparent rank or status. *No person has the authority to interfere with the OPNAC Team in the performance of its duties by special direction of the President of the United States.*" (Howe's emphasis.)

The last emphasized sentence sounds like the OPNAC Team is not accountable to anyone and has complete autonomy in its actions with extraterrestrials and its counterintelligence strategies to keep the general public and the media away from the truth that other intelligences *are* interacting with our planet while our government has been trying to obtain and back-engineer their advanced technologies.[37] That overriding power and authority of OPNAC personnel might explain their detached, cold arrogance described

[36] *The Cameraman on Page 51 stated, "... it was discovered that the Freaks may be a medical threat. Therefore, I was required to wear the same protective suits as the doctors."*

[37] The Day After Roswell *authored by Lt. Col. Philip J. Corso (Army Ret.) with William J. Birnes © 1997 by Rosewood Woods Productions, Inc., Pocket Books, Simon & Schuster.*

by military personnel in debriefings about non-human encounters.

The OPNAC Team might also be part of the answer to the Men In Black[38] appearances in the 1950s and 1960s when eyewitnesses were threatened at their homes with bodily and financial harm if they talked publicly about what they had seen and heard.

Later in this chapter's 1971 close encounter in Cambodia, the source specifically mentions MJ-12 and its "grey flannel suits" who were "overly concerned about enemy aircraft" during the Vietnam war and especially concerned about any GI experience with UFOs or alien beings. If there is an OPNAC Team as described in the S0M1-01 Training Manual, the debriefers from the "Firm" in Cambodia were likely part of the OPNAC team.

[38] They Knew Too Much About Flying Saucers © *1956 by Gray Barker and* Flying Saucers and The Three Men © *1962 by Albert K. Bender, Saucerian Books.*

Nuclear Missiles Disabled at Malmstrom AFB — March 16, 1967

In the fall of 1996, I received a newspaper article from the Great Falls, Montana *Tribune* headlined "1967 UFO Incident Still Mystifies Man." The article read: "(Robert) Salas, a former Air Force officer, detailed his role in an incident when an unidentified flying object reportedly hovered above a central Montana missile launch control center and shut down its electronic systems in 1967."

I called Bob Salas on November 23, 1996 and asked him if I could tape record an interview for radio and this book about what he did in the United States Air Force in 1967 and details about the March 16, 1967 incident. Salas agreed and the following are excerpts from that taped interview.

EXCERPTS OF NOVEMBER 23, 1996 INTERVIEW WITH FORMER USAF 1ST LT. ROBERT SALAS:

SALAS: "In 1967, I was a 1st Lieutenant stationed at Malmstrom AFB. I was on missile crew duty at November Flight. We monitored and were prepared to launch strategic nuclear missiles — the Minuteman missile system — in the event of war. So that was our primary duty: to monitor and report any security incursions, monitor the maintenance of the missiles themselves, and to be prepared to launch if necessary."

HOWE: "How did the March 16, 1967 incident begin?"

SALAS: "I was on duty and my commander was taking a nap in a regularly scheduled rest period. We alternated because it was a 24-hour shift. It was early morning and we were below ground in what is called the Launch Control Center (LCC) about sixty to eighty feet down. In the early morning, I got a call from my security guard upstairs — we had guards stationed upside and others patrolling sites. But my main security guard upstairs called and said that he and others had been seeing UFOs flying over the launch control facility. He described them as bright lights flying very fast and making strange maneuvers so he didn't think they were airplanes."

HOWE: "Did he describe the maneuvers and any colors?"

SALAS: "He just said they were moving lights. Then about fifteen minutes later, the security guard called back and this time his voice was agitated and very frightened. He told me that a UFO was hovering right outside the front gate. It was silent, it was glowing red and it appeared to be saucer-shaped. I told him to make sure the outer fence was secure with guards. I was kind of in shock myself that he would tell me this and the way he told it, very frightened and agitated.

"Then about that time, he said he had to go because one of the guards had become injured and he hung up abruptly."

HOWE: "Was the implication that the object had some how injured the security guard?"

SALAS: "Well, that was the first thing that came to my mind. Later on I talked to him about it and he told me the guard had been injured in some way trying to approach or avoid the object."

HOWE: "Was the injury in the nature of a burn?"

SALAS: "I'm not sure, but I seem to remember he was helicoptered off the site back to the base."

HOWE: "Is that guard available now for more follow up?"

SALAS: "No, we have not been able to locate any of the guards. I have located the other crews. But one of the reasons that I am going public with this now is to try to locate some of the other individuals who actually saw the UFOs."

HOWE: "Did you ever leave your position underground and go up and outside?"

SALAS: "No. We weren't allowed to leave our capsule until we were relieved. So after that second call, I woke my commander and started telling him the story of the two phone calls. Then at that point, our missiles started shutting down. And when that happens, we get a lot of bells going off and lights flashing on our panels. We had no-go. Our missiles went off alert status and therefore, we couldn't launch them."

HOWE: "All the missiles were shutting down?"

SALAS: "My recollection was that most of our missiles shut down. Now in speaking with my commander thirty years later, he recalls that something like five shut down. But either way, we lost somewhere between five and ten nuclear missiles in this unusual circumstance. And even if we lost more than one, it would have been a very unusual thing to happen because these missiles were very reliable."

HOWE: "You mean you would have electronic monitoring systems that would be able to check that everything was normal and when this red light object was at the front gate, something interfered electronically with your entire monitoring system?"

SALAS: "It was more than that. We did have a monitoring system. But those missiles were unlaunchable. The monitoring system clearly indicated that we could *not launch* those missiles."

HOWE: "And the implication was that there was some connection between the red UFO at the gate and an interruption with the missiles?"

SALAS: "Yes. The UFO was right there hovering outside the front gate and within minutes our missiles started shutting down. The UFO departed right after the missiles shut down. We got a call from the top side guard who said, 'The UFO is gone.'

HOWE: "What happened then?"

SALAS: "We followed our procedures. We reported back to the base and we got maintenance crews to come out. We also sent out security patrols. And while on patrol, one of our security teams reported back another siting of a UFO over one of our launch facilities.

"Then we got another call from another launch control center saying the same thing had happened to them — and *all ten* of their missiles shut down. That was Echo Flight. I was in November Flight at least ten miles away. So that morning of March 16, 1967, both Flights had missiles shut down by a UFO."

HOWE: "The newspaper article only mentioned Echo Flight?"

SALAS: "The time I gave the interview to the (Great Falls, Montana) *Tribune* in August 1996, we had asked through the Freedom of Information Act (FOIA) to send us information about the March 1967 incident. And they sent us the information about Echo Flight. So when I got the documents, I assumed I was there. But in fact, I was not in Echo. I was in November Flight." (See Appendix V.)

HOWE: "And why didn't you also get back FOIA information about the November Flight shut down as well?"

SALAS: "Good question. We still don't know."

HOWE: "So you are saying that at least five Minutemen nuclear missiles in your November Flight and ten in Echo Flight all went down that same morning of March 16, 1967?"

SALAS: "Yes. After my commander and I got relieved, we went upstairs and talked to the security guard. I looked him in the eye and asked, 'Are you telling me the absolute truth about these UFOs?' He assured me that he was. And I believed him. He had fear in his voice. And the missiles shutting down was highly unusual. The system was not designed for anything remotely like that to happen. Whenever we lost a missile off alert status, it was a very rare occasion. And that would happen only to an individual missile, not to a *whole flight* of missiles."

HOWE: "So having five or ten nuclear missiles all go down at the same time had never happened before?"

SALAS: "Never *ever* happened before! The missiles themselves were not interconnected. If one failed, it would not affect the other missiles. So this system was designed to prevent all ten missiles going down at once. In fact, the Air Force did studies, brought in contractors and tried to describe or define what could have done this and they were not able to come up with a definitive explanation."

HOWE: "Did the manufacturer of the missiles have any explanation for what could have happened?"

SALAS: "No. We've been able to contact two of the engineers who worked for Boeing at the time and who investigated the incident. Both told us that they were never able to determine a definitive cause."

HOWE: "Did they think it was actually impossible for all the missiles to shut down as they did?"

SALAS: "I don't know if they would have used the word 'impossible,' but the Air Force considered this a very critical incident. I have one of the documents received under FOIA request. It's a telegram that was sent, I believe, from 15th Air Force Headquarters to Boeing asking for assistance on an evaluation. To use words from the document, it said it '*is cause for grave concern to this headquarters.'* And I don't think they would have used that terminology if they had any ideas about how this could have happened." (See Plate 41 and Appendix V for documents.)

"And the Air Force has been on record and I have copies of what they have stated that no UFO incident has ever had any impact on the national security of the United States."

HOWE: "And that is false?"

SALAS: "That is false, absolutely. And that statement was made by the U. S. Air Force in 1969, *two years after* the incident in 1967."

HOWE: "What was your reaction when you heard the Air Force essentially lie?"

SALAS: "Well, our incident and the Echo Flight incident were classified. We were not supposed to talk about it and we didn't. None of us even talked about it among ourselves. But certainly we weren't supposed to tell the public any of this happened. It was not until a couple of years ago when a friend of mine submitted the FOIA request that we were able to get the incident declassified. And we're looking for others now who were there to come forward and tell their experiences.[39] I know there were at least three guards upstairs and other guards out in the field who saw UFOs. At the Echo Flight there were also guards and maintenance personnel who saw UFOs over those launch facilities."

[39] *Contact: Robert Salas, P. O Box 52721, Bellevue, Washington 98015-2721.*

HOWE: "Why do you think the Air Force chose a policy to lie about it?"

SALAS: "That's a good question. And I can't answer it. I would like to have the Air Force answer it. Why are they covering these incidents up? In the history about the investigation we got under FOIA, it stated there was even an *earlier* strange missile shut down at Alpha Flight on December 16, 1966. I think the public has a right to know that there are some very strange and unexplained things that have happened involving UFOs which are obviously not from this planet."

HOWE: "Were you ever debriefed? Did anyone ever try to tell you what they thought was in that red glowing object and how it had the ability to bring the missiles down off alert status?"

SALAS: "No. I was there from 1966-1969 and during that time period after this incident, we were never told anything about what happened, why it might have happened, or the results of any investigations or anything like that.

Plate 40 - Great Falls Tribune, *March 25, 1967, Great Falls, Montana.*

Great Falls Tribune Saturday, March 25, 1967

Officers Sight UFO at Belt

The latest episode in a series of recent unidentified flying object sightings in the Great Falls area Friday night sent a large number of law enforcement officers, reporters and photographers to the Belt area.

One Highway Patrol officer late Friday night was quoted as saying he saw a lighted object hovering low in a gulch in the vicinity of the Belt Hill.

Other Great Falls sheriff's officers and members of The Tribune staff rushed to the area to check out the report and remained on the scene at Tribune press time.

"I was going up the hill toward Great Falls when off to the left I saw this dome-shaped light —pure white— land in a gully about three-fourths of a mile off the highway."

This is the way Ken Williams, Laurel truck driver, described an unidentifiedobject he saw late Friday as

Saucer

Continued from page 1

he was bringing a fully loaded car carrier from Laurel into Great Falls.

"It was a blinding light. It was like looking into a searchlight. The first time I saw it, the closer it got to the ground, the brighter the light got," Williams said.

"I flagged down a car coming from Great Falls and asked the two in it to get to the nearest phone and call the highway patrol Bud Natter, the patrolman, got there just after I spotted it the second time. I had been watching it for maybe 30 seconds."

"This second time it was farther away. It started up into the air. Then it seemed to drop right back down. I couldn't tell if it landed or not.

"I'm sure glad the patrolman saw it, too," Williams said. He added, "I wish it would take off again so more could see it. Estimate the size? Gosh, I don't know what to say to that."

Air Force personnel were being dispatched to the scene at midnight and sheriff's officers were advised that amilitary helicopter would search the area t daybreak.

Advised of the incident here a member of The Associated Press staff in Helena responded that UFO sightings were coming in from all sections of the state Friday night.

SECRET

VZCZCNIA278
PTTS JAW RUCSAAA0196 0762315-SSSS--RUWMBOA.
ZNY SSSSS
P 172250Z MAR 67
FM SAC
TO RUWMMBA/OOAMA HILL AFB UTAH
INFO RUWBKNA/15AF
RUWMBOA/341SMW MALMSTROM AFB MONT
RUWMBAA/AFPRO BOEING CO SEATTLE WASH
RUWJABA/BSD NORTON AFB CALIF
BT
SECRET DM 02752 MAR 67.
ACTION: OOAMA (OONCT/OONE-COL DAVENPORT). INFO: 15AF
(DM4C), 341SMW (DCM), BOEING AFPRO (D.J. DOWNEY, MINUTEMAN
ENGINEERING) BSD (BSS, BSQR)
SUBJECT: LOSS OF STRATEGIC ALERT, ECHO FLIGHT, MALSTROM
AFB. (U)
REF: MY SECRET MESSAGE DM78 02751, 17 MAR 67, SAME SUBJECT.
ALL TEN MISSILES IN ECHO FLIGHT AT MALMSTROM LOST STRAT ALERT WITHIN
TEN SECONDS OF EACH OTHER. THIS INCIDENT OCCURRED AT 0845L ON
16 MARCH 67. AS OF THIS DATE, ASS MISSILES HAVE BEEN RETURNED TO STRAT

JJ 2342
17 C-208
DCM-1
WC-1
DCO-1

PAGE 2 RUCSAAA0196 SECRET
ALERT WITH NO APPARENT DIFFICULTY. INVESTIGATION AS TO THE CAUSE OF THE
INCIDENT IS BEING CONDUCTED BY MALMSTROM TEAT. TWO FITTS HAVE
BEEN RUN THROUGH TWO MISSILES THUS FAR. NO CONCLUSIONS HAVE BEEN
DRAWN. THERE ARE INDICATIONS THAT BOTH COMPUTERS IN BOTH G&C'S
WERE UPSET MOMENTARILY. CAUSE OF THE UPSET IS NOT KNOWN AT THIS
TIME. ALL OTHER SIGNIFICANT INFORMATION AT THIS TIME IS CONTAINED IN
ABOVE REFERENCED MESSAGE.
FOR OOAMA. THE FACT THAT NO APPARENT REASON FOR THE LOSS OF TEN
MISSILES CAN BE READILY IDENTIFIED IS CAUSE FOR GRAVE CONCERN TO THIS
HEADQUARTERS. WE MUST HAVE AN IN-DEPTH ANALYSIS TO DETERMINE CAUSE
AND CORRECTIVE ACTION AND WE MUST KNOW AS QUICKLY AS POSSIBLE WHAT
THE IMPACT IS TO THE FLEET, IF ANY. REQUEST YOUR RESPONSE BE IN KEEP-
ING WITH THE URGENCY OF THE PROBLEM. WE IN TURN WILL PROVIDE OUR
FULL COOPERATION AND SUPPORT.
FOR OOAMA AND 15AF WE HAVE CONCURRED IN A BOEING REQUEST TO SEND
TWO ENGINEERS, MR. R.E RIGERT AND MR. W. M. DUTTON TO MALMSTROM
TO COLLECT FIRST HAND KNOWLEDGE OF THE PROBLEM FOR POSSIBLE ASSISTANCE
IN LATER ANALYSIS. REQUEST COOPERATION OF ALL CONCERNED TO PROVIDE
THEM ACCESS TO AVAILABLE INFORMATION, I.E., CREW COMMANDERS LOG
ENTRIES, MAINTENANCE FORMS, INTERROGATION OF KNOWLEDGEABLE PEOPLE, ETC.

PAGE 3 RUCSAAA0196 SECRET
SECURITY CLEARANCES AND DATE AND TIME OF ARRIVAL WILL BE SENT FROM
THE AFPRO BY SEPARATE MESSAGE.
FOR 15AF. OOAMA HAS INDICATED BY TELECON THAT THEY ARE SENDING
ADDITIONAL ENGINEERING SUPPORT. REQUEST YOUR COOPERATION TO INSURE
MAXIMUM RESULTS ARE OBTAINED FROM THIS EFFORT. GP74. BCASMC-67-437
BT

SECRET GROUP 4
DOWNGRADED AT 3 YEAR INTERVALS;
DECLASSIFIED AFTER 12 YEARS

Plate 41 - *March 17, 1967 SECRET message from the Strategic Air Command (SAC) in Omaha, Nebraska to Air Material Center at Hill AFB, Utah which managed Minuteman missile repairs. Released through a Freedom of Information Act request filed in 1994 on behalf of Robert Salas, former U. S. Air Force 1st Lieutenant stationed at Malmstrom AFB, Great Falls, Montana from 1966 to 1969.*

SECRET

VZCZONIA278
FITTS JAW RUCSAAA 0196 (Message Reference Number) 0762315-SSSS--RUWMBOA.
ZNY
P 172250Z MAR 67 (17 of March 1967 at 2:25 ZULU Time)
FM SAC (From: Strategic Air Command Hdqts., Omaha, Nebraska)
TO RUWMMBA/OOAMA HILL AFB UTAH (To: Management Office for SAC's Minuteman Office, Air Material Center, Hill AFB at Provo, Utah.)
INFO RUW BKNA/15AF (15th Air Force)
RUWMBOA/341SMW MALMSTROM AFB MONT (341st Strategic Missile Wing)
RUWMBAA/AFPRO BOEING CO SEATTLE WASH (Boeing in Seattle, Washington was a principal contractor for Minuteman Missiles)
RUWJABA/BSD NORTON AFB CALIF (Ballistic Missile Systems Division was at Norton AFB while Hill AFB in Utah had management over Minuteman Missiles.)
BT
S E C R E T D 02752 MAR 67. (02752 is the Reference Number of this message.)
ACTION; OOAWA 9OONCT/OONE-COL DAVENPORT). IMFO: 15AF (This message is directed to Col. Davenport at Hill AFB, Utah) and
(DM4C), 341SMW (DCM) Deputy Chief of Maintenance at Malmstrom AFB, Montana and
BOEING AFPRO (D. J. DOWNEY, MINUTEMAN ENGINEERING) BSD (Office at Norton AFB) (BSS, BSQR)
SUBJECT; LOSS OF STRATEGIC ALERT, ECHO FLIGHT, MALMSTROM AFB. (U)
REF; MY SECRET MESSAGE DM73 02751, 17 MAR 67, SAME SUBJECT. (The sender of this message had sent a secret message Reference Number DM73 02751 earlier that day of March 17, 1967. According to Robert Salas, one of his colleagues saw that Secret Message and its specific reference to a UFO sighted over missile launch facilities.)
ALL TEN MISSILES IN ECHO FLIGHT AT MALMSTROM LOST STRAT ALERT WITHIN TEN SECONDS OF EACH OTHER. THIS INCIDENT OCCURRED AT 0845L ON 16 MARCH 67. AS OF THIS DATE, ASS (Typo - All) MISSILES HAVE BEEN RETURNED TO STRAT

PAGE 2 RUCSAAA0196 (Message Reference Number) S E C R E T
ALERT WITH NO APPARENT DIFFICULTY. INVESTIGATION AS TO THE CAUSE OF THE INCIDENT IS BEING CONDUCTED BY MALMSTROM TEAT. TWO FITTS (tests) HAVE BEEN RUN THROUGH TWO MISSILES THUS FAR. NO CONCLUSIONS HAVE BEEN DRAWN. THERE ARE INDICATIONS THAT BOTH COMPUTERS IN BOTH G &C's (Guidance and Control) WERE UPSET MOMENTARILY. CAUSE OF THE UPSET IS NOT KNOWN AT THIS TIME. ALL OTHER SIGNIFICANT INFORMATION AT THIS TIME IS CONTAINED IN ABOVE REFERENCED MESSAGE (Secret Message 02751)
FOR OOAMA. (Hill AFB, Utah) THE FACT THAT NO APPARENT REASON FOR THE LOSS OF TEN
MISSILES CAN BE READILY IDENTIFIED IS CAUSE FOR GRAVE CONCERN TO THIS HEADQUARTERS. WE MUST HAVE AN IN-DEPTH ANALYSIS TO DETERMINE CAUSE AND CORRECTIVE ACTION AND WE MUST KNOW AS QUICKLY AS POSSIBLE WHAT THE IMPACT IS TO THE FLEET, IF ANY. REQUEST YOUR RESPONSE BE IN KEEPING WITH THE URGENCY OF THE PROBLEM. WE IN TURN WILL PROVIDE OUR FULL COOPERATION AND SUPPORT.
FOR OOAMA AND 15AF WE HAVE CONCURRED IN A BOEING REQUEST TO SEND TWO ENGINEERS, MR. R. E. RIGERT AND MR. W. M. DUTTON TO MALMSTROM TO COLLECT FIRST HAND KNOWLEDGE OF THE PROBLEM FOR POSSIBLE ASSISTANCE IN LATER ANALYSIS. REQUEST COOPERATION OF ALL CONCERNED TO PROVIDE THEM ACCESS TO AVAILABLE INFORMATION, I.E., CREW COMMANDERS LOG ENTRIES, MAINTENANCE FORMS, INTERROGATION OF KNOWLEDGEABLE PEOPLE, ETC.

PAGE 3 RUCSAAA0196 (Message Reference Number) S E C R E T
SECURITY CLEARANCES AND DATE AND TIME OF ARRIVAL WILL BE SENT FROM THE AFPRO BY SEPARATE MESSAGE.
FOR 15AF. OOAMA (Air Material Center, Hill AFB, Provo, Utah) HAS INDICATED BY TELECON THAT THEY ARE SENDING ADDITIONAL ENGINEERING SUPPORT. REQUEST YOUR COOPERATION TO INSURE MAXIMUM RESULTS ARE OBTAINED FROM THIS EFFORT.
GP74. BCASMC-67-437.
BT

18 **Great Falls Tribune** Sunday, March 26, 1967

UFO Breaks Monotony of Run

This truck driver didn't have to blink running lights at oncoming rigs, adjust his seat or keep the radio going to break the monotony of a Laurel-to-Great Falls run Friday night.

An extremely bright UFO hovering over a gully near the crest of Belt Hill made Ken Williams, trailing a loaded car carrier Friday about 9 p.m., sit up and take notice.

"I was going up the hill toward Great Falls when off to the left I saw this dome-shaped light – pure white – land in a gully about three-fourths of a mile off the highway, he related.

Williams took his load to the top of the grade and then stopped to flag down a car. A passing motorist called the Cascade County sheriff and Highway Patrolman Bud Nader arrived at the spot just as Williams spotted the UFO a second time.

"I had been watching it for maybe thirty seconds," Williams said, when Nader arrived.

This second time it was farther away," Williams continued. "It started up into the air. Then it seemed to drop right back down. I couldn't tell if it landed or not."

Nader said Saturday morning: "I noticed a light off to the right as I approached the top of the Belt Hill and then it went down out of sight and I couldn't see it any more."

He said he and Williams walked back down the hill and saw a light at the head of a coulee.

Sheriff's deputies covered on foot the sighting area and found nothing unusual other than freshly broken twigs on bushes and branches as if cattle had wandered through. One of the deputies, however, was quick to point out that there were no cattle in the area and no cattle tracks on the ground.

Airmen at Malmstrom Air Force Base reported sighting a UFO about 5 to 10 miles northeast of the base at 3:30 a.m. Saturday.

FAA radar picked up the object at 3:42 a.m. to the northwest and reported it was off the radar at 4:26 a.m.

Airman 2C Richard Moore, a communicator-plotter at Malmstrom, observed the object and said it couldn't have been a satellite because of its jerky movements in crossing the sky.

An aviation weather forecaster on Gore Hill said the Weather Bureau radar didn't pick up anything, but noted their radar was adjusted to pick up mostly clouds and precipitation.

The Associated Press in Helena reported sightings from all parts of the state Friday night.

Plate 42 - Great Falls Tribune, *March 26, 1967, Great Falls, Montana. UFO sightings near Malmstrom AFB and areas east of Great Falls, Montana one week after the Echo and November Flight nuclear missiles at Malmstrom suddenly went off alert status in the presence of a red, glowing disc-shaped object.*

When we reported back to the base that morning and talked to our squadron commander, he was just as shocked and surprised at what we told him as we were. If it had been some kind of exercise, or if the Air Force had known about what had happened before hand, the commander would have known about it. The fact that we crews that were responsible for maintaining those missiles weren't updated in any way indicated either the government wasn't able to determine what had happened and couldn't give us any valid information, or they knew and just wanted to keep it covered up.

"We're talking about a time when the Cold War with the Soviet Union and the Vietnam War were going on. Losing strategic strike capability was very important to us. And we would not have been playing these kinds of games with those weapons. This was *not* an exercise. I'm convinced of that."

HOWE: "And the fact that more missile interrupts occurred in the fall of 1975 all along the Canadian and United States border[40] suggests that the U. S. government by then had a great deal of information about UFOs having the ability to intrude in our most sensitive missile sites without any problem and even could change target information on the missile's computer tapes."

[40] *Pages 23-26,* An Alien Harvest *© 1989 by Linda Moulton Howe.*

SALAS: "The government definitely knew that UFOs had the ability to bring missiles to no-go or non-alert status."

HOWE: "All those incidents in 1966, 1967 and 1975 contradicted the government's assertions that UFOs had never threatened national security."

SALAS: "Absolutely contradicts it. And I don't think this is something that only the military or government insiders should be able to decide because it affects all of us."

HOWE: "It's been suggested that whatever this alien presence is, it's motive is not evil hostility, but trying to save itself by preventing us from destroying ourselves and the earth. Earth's destruction would affect them, too, somehow."

SALAS: "I have no way of knowing what the military is thinking about this. All I can say is that our government has made an effort to get rid of nuclear weapons on a worldwide basis. I salute them for that and all the other countries that have cooperated in reducing the presence of nuclear weapons and testing and I think that is a worthy effort we have to continue."

Close Encounter In Cambodia — 1971

Allegedly the United States government has known about UFOs, their occupants, and their advanced technological ability to interrupt electronic equipment since at least the Truman Administration. According to some military insiders, the United States tried aggressively in the early 1950s to bring discs down. Retrievals of crashed discs and non-human beings have been described during the 1940s, 1950s and beyond. Evidence of retrieval operations were hidden from the public inside double vaults, behind "weather balloon" headlines and under a policy of silence in the interests of national security.

Leonard Stringfield, longtime UFO researcher since his days in the U. S. Air Force, told me before he died that no one would ever know how many of our own pilots we lost trying to carry out orders to bring down the discs. Was our initial aggression a provocation for alien retaliation? By the 1970s, it appears the aliens were interacting not only with nuclear missile sites, but with animals, plants and humans all over the world either with, or without, government knowledge and approval.

I learned about one extraordinary military interaction with grey-skinned, non-human entities from Pete Bostrom when I spoke at a Midwestern conference in 1990. Bostrom handed me several typed pages.

"Read this. It's one of the strangest conversations I've ever had with anyone in my life. If you want to use it in your work, you have my permission."

The subject was a close encounter during the Vietnam war. This is one of several eyewitness accounts I have received from men who describe having seen round, silver discs and grey beings during their respective tours in Southeast Asia. Some men claiming inside intelligence knowledge have suggested that extraterrestrials were covertly helping the United States during the war. Other men have implied that the non-humans used the war's violence to cover up an alien harvest of tissue and genetic material from animals and humans.

The following account describes a violent interaction between Vietnam GIs and non-human beings in which one human attacked and a non-human responded with restraint. This incident also indicates there is an immediate, aggressive, intimidating, and well-planned U. S. intelligence response to "handle" UFO eyewitnesses, especially those responsible enough to lead men in combat, but who are not included in the need-to-know agendas of government insiders who have knowledge about non-human entities.

PETER BOSTROM INTRODUCTION:

"The following is a conversation I audiotaped in the mid-1980s with the permission of a retired military Special Forces officer who served in Thailand during the Vietnam War. His special training was in electronics.

"At the time of this conversation, 'Joe' (at his request, his real name is not used) was retired and repairing television sets, VCR players and other electronic equipment in a Midwestern town. This is an account of his close encounter with several EBEs (extraterrestrial biological entities) and their space vehicle.

"Unlike other countless reports of similar 'high strangeness' meetings with extraterrestrials, this account is maybe even more interesting because it happened in wartime surroundings in Cambodia, a country supposedly out-of-bounds for U. S. troops then. Plus, there is mention of MJ-12 as a government entity who was involved with the gathering of information about Unidentified Objects in the airspace in and around Thailand and it shows how determined the government is to extract all information it can on the subject. Also, there is mention of another strange encounter in the same general area.

"I spoke with Joe off and on for several weeks. When he spoke about this encounter, he never changed his story and I believe he wants to give the true account as he himself saw it happen. As my conversations continued with Joe around 1985, he said he had been contacted by an officer friend still on active duty who told Joe that he could freely speak about the subject of his encounter with the extraterrestrials in Cambodia and anything else concerning the subject. He said the officer told him 'this information will be made public in the near future anyway.'

"But Joe was told not to specifically indicate the true reason why he was in Cambodia. This other officer also talked about the UFO subject in general and told Joe the Roswell crash really happened and described precise methods of how people who need to see the alien vehicle and bodies are transported in high security procedures. The officer also discussed two different alien beings. One name he used was the Greys and the other was the Nordics.

"Several months later, Joe said he was going back into government service. He still seemed to have government friends with high level security clearances."

TRANSCRIBED G.I. ENCOUNTER WITH NON-HUMAN BEINGS IN CAMBODIA — 1971

JOE: "In September 1971, I was stationed with the Army in Thailand. Originally it was a routine mission into Cambodia close to an area called Tonie Sap, just south of Angkor Wat, where the temples are. We had gone on a previous mission in answer to some problems and had gone back on a search and destroy mission. The area we were mainly concerned about was insurgents from the Khmer Rouge — Pol Pot's people. They were really causing havoc at the time with the local indigenous personnel. We were after one group and when going through the jungle, we heard some noises that sounded like generators or machinery. Something with a hum."

BOSTROM: "So, that's what attracted you?"

JOE: "Yes, we assumed they had some kind of refueling station or something out there. It was quite common for the Khmer Rouge and Phathet Lao to use a high place in the jungle to make an artificial clearing for refueling helicopters, things like that. Most of them were Russian-made and they could refuel them.

"When we came into the clearing we were quite surprised to find something quite unlike what I've ever seen before. At the time, I held the rank of Lieutenant. We had with us approximately fourteen Special Forces of our country (U.S.) and several dozen Thai arranged with us."

BOSTROM: "So you were in Special Forces?"

JOE: "Yes. I was originally with the 101st Airborne special tactical unit. We were reassigned 506th Air Cavalry sent to Thailand. They were with the auspices of a group we won't discuss for obvious reasons. During this time, there had been several reports of some strange incidents of things flying through trees. We more or less poo-pooed them, thinking they were people getting scared in combat.

"We entered the clearing. (What we saw) was almost spherical in shape and suspended close to the ground on four legs. And there were a number of, the best description I could say, were humanoids. There were at least as many of them as there were of us."

BOSTROM: "How many do you think?"

JOE: "I would say there was anywhere between sixteen to twenty-one. Their appearance was not that of any human being I'd ever seen on earth. Skin was a greyish-whitish color. They were wearing what appeared to be a one-piece jump suit which was silver in color, much like a metalized mylar heat suit. It didn't appear to be a pressure suit of any kind. We found out later that it was quite a strong material.

"When we approached, they really didn't notice us at first and when they did, they turned toward us. Some of the fellows (non-humans) were carrying some type of instruments. Didn't see any weapons anywhere. Made a quick judgement. It didn't look like any weapon I'd ever seen, so I thought it could be safe.

"We had a young corporal with us (George). Well, it was his second time in combat and he didn't react very well. These — I'll call them aliens — one of the aliens turned toward him with something in his hand which George evidently thought was a weapon of some type and felt threatened and let loose a short burst of fire from a Browning FNFAL which is literally a three-way Winchester. It has a 150 grain slug, the same hitting power as the 30-0-6 out to 150 yards. About the shortest burst you could fire one full auto is somewhere between 8 and 12 rounds. Which at the distance from 30 to 35 feet where it struck this fellow would devastate a normal human being.

"We were wearing flack jackets most of the time. The material (on the humanoid), whatever it was, is like the 'second chance' material we had which was a compact, lightweight bullet proof vest. I've been struck several times with slugs wearing those — rib cage broken, you get bruised very badly, you feel like you are going to die, but as a general rule, unless it's an armor piercing slug or some type of teflon sliding jacket, the slugs don't penetrate. I've seen 50 caliber shells go through, but nothing much smaller than that. Nothing except high caliber and high velocity will pierce it. Occasionally a tracer will burn a pretty good size hole in it.

"When it struck this fellow (humanoid), he went down, dropped like a stone, like he was dead. We assumed he was dead. In that humanoid group, most of them were all approximately the same height. I would say some were five-foot or less, maybe four-foot eight inches. In that range. (EBE Type I?) They were very small people. More like dwarfs and perfectly proportioned. Only one fellow was taller, about five-six or five-seven. He intervened at this point. I pushed the weapon down that George had in his hand. I thought, 'God, this (humanoid) guy is going to kill us!'

"At this point, I was terror-stricken. We didn't know who these guys were. Something like this happens — all the science fiction movies you've ever seen in your life run through your mind. You think, 'Oh, my God, are they going to pull out ray guns? Are they going to atomize us?'"

BOSTROM: "Did any of them ever say anything?"

JOE: "Never heard a single word. This fellow (taller humanoid) turned to me evidently knowing that I was platoon commander. He raised his hand with palm out and fingers up in just a peaceful gesture and stopped and walked over to George and struck him on the cheek. It wasn't a real heavy blow. It was something like you'd smack your child to get his attention, but the effect was devastating. George went down like a limp rag, just like an electric shock had gone through him. The only thing I could figure is either this (humanoid) fellow is a lot stronger than we imagined he was or he did something else. You've seen blows, even in martial arts, that don't appear to be very heavy but have a devastating effect. George went down like a stone, just a limp rag.

"About the time I was trying to pull him up, I didn't know what we were going to do at that point. I didn't want anybody else to fire because I figured if we open fire on these guys, we were dead. I was scared. I soiled my pants at that point, a nervous reaction. I didn't know quite what to do. With the exception of George, we were all veterans of at least twenty to twenty-five fire-fights. We were relatively well-seasoned combat veterans. It could have been George's third time out, but probably second, and he was green and he panicked and I thought, 'Well, he just paid the price for it. This (humanoid) fellow just killed him.' But George recovered quickly.

"I tried to pull George up and turned around about the time the fellow (humanoid) that was shot (by George) got up and brushed himself off. I thought, 'Oh, shit, these fellows are going to wipe us out! If an FNFAL didn't take him down in 8 to 12 shots, that is one tough little hombre.'

"The only thing I could figure is that the (body suit) material is tough enough that it acted as a cushion just like a vest. We spent many times picking slugs out of our flack jackets. It smarts. It will knock you out cold sometimes from the impact. It's like having a very large electric shock run through your body. What takes people out, knocks them out flat, is not the actual impact of the bullet but the nervous reaction of the impact and it will literally lay you out flat before you hit the ground. Every muscle in your body goes rigid. So, I guess they (aliens) have basically the same physiological reaction that we do.

"When he (taller humanoid) turned to me and placed his palm up toward me again to stop, I had a feeling that everything was OK. I'm not going to say that it was some kind of telepathic message. It didn't really seem like anything like that. It just seemed like 'Hey, it's cool. He panicked and I understand the situation.'

"At this point, the humanoids packed up all their little instruments, packed themselves back into the craft and left almost soundlessly. It sat there on the ground as the four legs resting on the ground with pads on them retracted back into the body of the craft, which was spheroid. Then it just lifted straight up off the ground. I didn't see any visible means of propulsion. There was a little noise. It was hard to tell if it was just the wind blowing through there or what. Then it was just like an instantaneous burst of speed."

BOSTROM: "What do you think the diameter was?"

JOE: "I would say that it was at a minimum of fifty feet. It could have been as far across as 150 feet. It was very difficult to judge. It was a *mirrored surface.* So you're looking at something and the jungle is being reflected and it's really hard to judge the size. I know it was at least as tall as a five story building. What didn't make any sense is why it should be spheroid. Whatever propulsion system it required, I don't know. Perhaps it's some type of anti-gravity drive and you'd have to have everything centered?"

BOSTROM: "Was it round like a ball?"

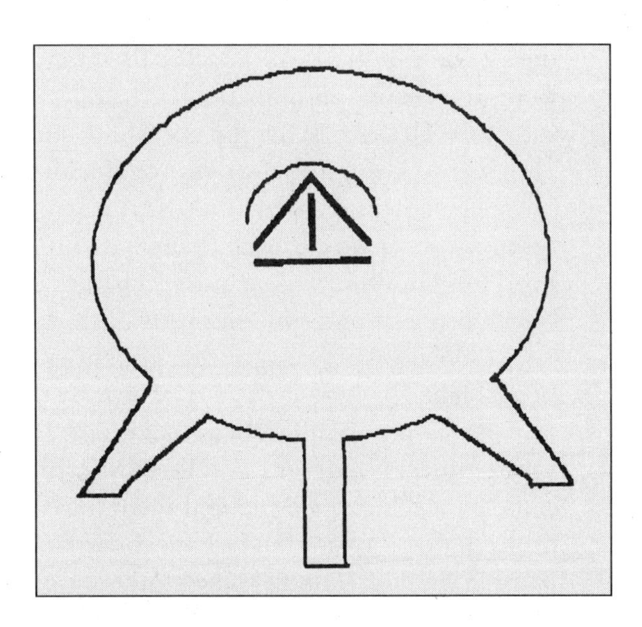

Plate 43 - *Spherical craft with symbol etched in mirrored surface that matches symbol drawn by Officer Lonnie Zamora in Socorro, New Mexico on April 24, 1964. Drawing by Joe from 1971 Cambodia encounter.*

JOE: "Round like a ball. Perfectly round as far as I could tell. There was one symbol on the side of what appeared to be, I would say, black paint. Either this, or there was just no coating on this area.

It was a simple symbol of an arc, almost like a pyramid, with a line drawn underneath it."[41]

Joe drew the round craft encountered during the military operation near Tong Li Sap, Cambodia in April 1972 and wrote:

"The craft was polished, highly reflective, mirrored in appearance. Spherical in shape, the craft appeared to be approximately 50 feet in diameter. Symbol on surface seemed to be ground and sandblasted as it was less reflective. No apparent opening or door was seen until just before departure. This was evidently due to an extremely precise fit and the nature of materials involved. Although armor was not readily apparent, the surface was impervious to small arms fire. (Howe: Implies that bullets were fired at the craft.) The craft emitted a high-pitched hum, even while motionless on the ground, and was otherwise nearly silent in its ascent. Legs appeared to be one contiguous piece with the body, but withdrew into the orb during take-off. The encounter and the description of the object were reported directly to civilians who identified themselves as representatives of 'MAJIC.'"

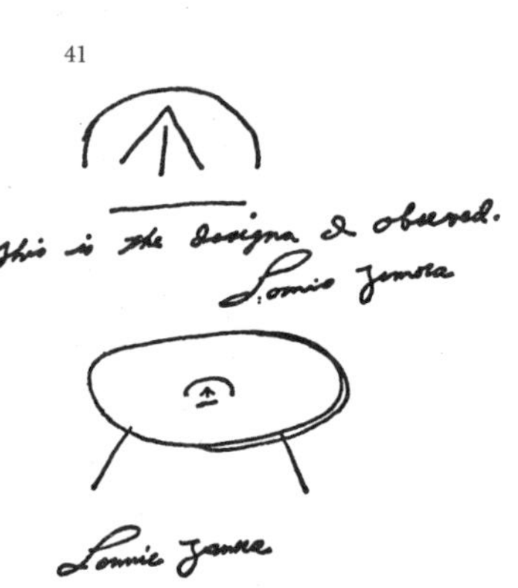

New Mexico State Highway Patrol Officer Lonnie Zamora described a symbol similar to Plate 43 located at the center of an egg-shaped object near U. S. Highway 85 outside Socorro, New Mexico on April 24, 1964 at approximately 5:45 PM. This is a copy of the insignia that Zamora drew in his police report, noting that it was colored red about 2 1/2 feet wide. From UFOs: A Pictorial History... *© 1979 by David Knight, McGraw-Hill.*

"JOE: We returned to base. The Thais, of course, weren't going to say anything to anybody. They 'saw nothing, heard nothing.' Just along for the ride. Which was typical reaction for the Thais. They didn't want to get involved. But they were quite shaken by it as we were. It took us approximately three days to get back to the border."

BOSTROM: "What did everybody talk about on the way back?"

JOE: "Absolutely nothing. We decided on the way back that nobody saw anything. We didn't hear anything. We didn't know anything about it. We got back to the base and the first thing we did was head for a hot shower because you had to pull all the lice off you and everything else and you felt pretty darn dirty."

BOSTROM: "The guy that got knocked down — George — was he all right?"

JOE: "He was all right at that point. He was a corporal and went to the officers' barracks. A fellow from the provost marshal's office came in and informed me that I had to report to the captain's office immediately. I said, 'Do I have time to rinse off?' He said, 'Just barely.' He said, 'Put on some clothes and get over there. They want to talk to you right now.' I asked him what it was about. He said, 'I don't know. They won't tell me. Just get your tail over there. It's something very heavy.' He said they were quite confused about something. I walked into the captain's office. We were met by the captain, a couple of majors, a colonel and some civilians. If you've ever worked with anybody with the 'Firm,' they reek of it. You generally expect them in grey flannel suits and white socks, but these fellows just reeked of the 'Firm.'"

BOSTROM: "What is the Firm?"

JOE: "When you hear people involved in security, they never call a certain agency of the government the 'Company.' (Central Intelligence Agency, CIA.) Insiders like to call it the Firm. Again, what we were with was literally a front for the CIA's military part which it's not supposed to have. Well, it had one. Recently there have been little leaks about that. Miller (real name withheld) rode with MJ, you know, Majestic 12."

BOSTROM: "MJ-12?"

JOE: "Right. The only way we ever heard Miller call it was MJ-12 or MJ. We knew he worked for that. We didn't know what the heck it was. The only thing we knew was that any enemy aircraft that was sighted had to be reported to him. Any photographs we took had to be given to him. He was overly concerned about enemy aircraft, unusual sightings, anything out of the ordinary.

"He'd call us in occasionally to look at photographs and say, 'What is this?' And we'd say, 'That's a Russian gun ship, it has so much armament.' He'd say, 'OK, that's what I want to know. Thank you very much. Discuss this with no one and have a nice day.' Miller was very single-sided with information. We gave him everything. He told us absolutely nothing."

"He was a cold-blooded man. I don't think I ever saw the man sweat. Most of the time he wore a black suit or a dark grey flannel suit. When you're in Thailand and it's at that point in the year when it's somewhere between 97 and 100 degrees, 100 to 110% relative humidity, it's so hot you get heat that's like fog. I don't think I ever saw him sweat except for this incident. But he had a cold sweat going into this. He ended up taking his jacket off and you never saw him outside of a jacket. Miller and these other guys sat us down and grilled us that day at least three and a half to four hours. And I was trying to find out who it was that told them because when we got back, nobody said anything. So something or somebody snitched."

BOSTROM: "Someone would have had to run in immediately and tell them?"

JOE: "We hadn't been back more than an hour. We usually took a shower, got cleaned up and got a little rest before we were debriefed because that could sometimes take many hours. It was very interesting. They even sequestered us in our quarters. We were told not to have any outside activities at all, and meals would be brought to us. We were not to talk to any unauthorized personnel. 'Authorized' meant them, or someone directly with authorization from the provost marshal's office.

"Then we spent the next three to three and a half weeks talking to various people, some of which I don't know who in the heck they were. Several were psychologists. It was very obvious by the kind of questions we were being asked and they started dragging out the ink blots. We went on with this for two weeks and then they started using *narco-hypnosis.*"[42]

BOSTROM: "How did that operate?"

JOE: "Essentially, they sit you in a chair. Hook up the sphygmomanometer, blood pressure tape, and get you highly relaxed using soothing music sometimes, and give you an injection of basically what is called a hypnotic drug. There were drugs like Seconal, Scopolamine, the type that have a tendency to reduce what they call psychic resistance. You get your body as relaxed as possible and you lose your will. They actually hypnotize you at that point. It's a combination of drugs and hypnosis. The only thing I can say that occurred during that time was that in one way or another, *they altered our memories.* (Howe's emphasis.)

"Now, I do not know whether we saw something else or they gave us a different memory and that's what we ended up with or what we saw was much worse than (what we thought had) occurred and I toned it down. I do know that every one of us still has occasional nightmares about it and we get flashes of things that are just an incredible bloodbath. George was reassigned from our unit after we had all cleared through medical and psychological. I was called into the captain's office approximately six or eight weeks after the incident to identify a body they told me was George. Now, I'd seen the man on the base a few days before. The body they showed me was far, far decomposed for even the jungle where you have rapid decomposition."

BOSTROM: "But you couldn't positively identify the body?"

JOE: "I couldn't identify it as George. The flesh was all liquefied."

BOSTROM: "So, it may have been someone else?"

JOE: "The only thing I can say is his tissue seemed to suffer from some kind of extreme disruption — like every cell wall had

[42] *Similar drug and hypnosis procedure described by Staff Sargeant James Penniston on* *Page 100.*

been broken. Like you see with a cold sore. I think whatever happened to him, they transferred him (so they could) show me the body and say that's George."

BOSTROM: "Then why would they show you a body you couldn't identify?"

JOE: "I don't know. The people we were dealing with (MJ-12) were very, very careful about covering all avenues. They never left a thread hanging. As far as I knew, he was dead. I was called in to identify the body and sign the papers. The only way I could identify was his dog tags. The usual thing was that during combat, because of the nature of our unit, dog tags were retrieved by a ranking officer and returned to you when you returned to base. We carried what was called T8407 -?-T101 which was a get-out-of-jail-free card. It was a cardboard card with two sides and department logo on one side to say the individual was allowed to be carrying strange and unusual weapons, may or may not be in uniform, and was not to be detained for any reason whatsoever. If this card is found on a body, it is to be burned with the body and reported to a telephone number and group stateside."

BOSTROM: "Is this all you can remember?"

JOE: "Well, that's the problem. If we really sit down and try to pressure us through it, I get confused. I talked to a couple of fellows that were involved in it and they have the same kind of problem. Slowly but surely, things emerged and over the years more and more has come up. It was years before I ever had a desire at all to talk about it — not because it was frightening, or because the Firm told us not to because they were going to place it under the national security end — but because I absolutely had no desire whatsoever to talk about it."

BOSTROM: "Do you remember any other details such as how the humanoids entered the craft?"

JOE: "It was like a section slid down. Like it just created itself on the side and slid down."

BOSTROM: "Do you remember a ramp?"

JOE: "It slid down and tilted to the ground and had a stair on it that formed a ramp for them to walk right up with steps on it."

BOSTROM: "Did it look like they were walking on steps?"

JOE: "It had steps on it because they were stepping and it wasn't like they shuffled up the ramp. Their gait was very smooth, almost unerring, and they covered a lot of ground in a little bit of time. But the main problem is like I said, if we sit down and try to really go through the details and think hard about it, I end up almost with anxiety attack. Whatever it was that they (MJ-12/CIA) did to bury those things is pretty permanent. Over the years, I still occasionally have nightmares about it. I wake up in a cold sweat and I'd remember for awhile. It's frustrating. I find myself angry because I don't know what the heck they (MJ-12/CIA) did to us.

"I did find out that a few weeks after we had our incident, there were at least two more. In one, some GIs were pinned down and two of those little (alien) fellows stepped out of the woods. One of the aliens threw a small object out between them and the Phaphet Lao that had the GIs pinned down. The men described it as a 'darkness' grenade instead of a smoke grenade. It put up enough of a partition of darkness that they were able to escape. These guys came back and others immediately came down saying, 'What the hell did they do to you guys when you saw that thing?!' And they said they went through the same debriefing procedure we had to go through."

BOSTROM: "What did the guys that saw the smoke bomb say about the craft?"

JOE: "They didn't see a craft. All they saw was the (alien) fellows that we had seen — some of the smaller ones."

BOSTROM: "They just appeared there?"

JOE: "The men heard a noise out in the jungle and these two aliens peeked out, looked at the men who could see them clearly. The aliens turned to each other and whatever discussion they had, one of them reached up and threw a small object and the guys there said it couldn't be any smaller than a tennis ball, and it went off with a loud pop. Not an explosion, but a pop. It's just like a dark gas. It came up like smoke does, but it was darkness and they looked at each other and said, 'WHAT THE HELL IS THIS?!' And one of them said, 'I don't care. Let's get out of here!' So, they high-tailed it out. It took the Phaphet Lao back far enough that they couldn't pursue the GIs. They'd never seen anything like that and neither did we.

BOSTROM: "Did they take their clothes to check for residue?"

JOE: "They'd done that several times. They took our fatigues. I know that up to that point in time, I've always been fascinated with the idea of other life in the universe, but never saw enough that really made me believe that there was any such things. But whoever or whatever those alien fellows were, I'm convinced that they're not present populace of this earth.[43]

[43] *Joe returned to active duty in 1983 for a period of time with the rank of Lieutenant Colonel.*

UFO Sightings At Bentwaters AFB, England
December 26-28, 1980

The use of drugs with hypnosis to learn information and alter memories also occurred after another military encounter with the UFO phenomenon, this time in England. Christmas week in December 1980 was a tense and confusing time for several dozen men at the joint United States and English Royal Air Force Base at Bentwaters near the southeastern coast of the British Isles. In the early morning hours of December 26, odd lights were seen moving in the Rendlesham forest and various security and military personnel investigated.

Two of the security men, Staff Sergeant James Penniston and Airman First Class John Smith (alias), had a close encounter with one of the lights. Penniston has had haunting memories and dreams of both the night in the forest and a follow-up debriefing session by intelligence agents who apparently used a drug and hypnosis combination to retrieve further information from Penniston and to possibly erase part of his memory, similar to the Cambodia officer's story.

On September 10, 1994, Jim Penniston volunteered to undergo hypnosis with a hypnotherapist to remember more details of the Bentwaters AFB incidents and his own involvement in them. The following is a summary with verbatim excerpts from that hypnosis session which I transcribed from an audiocassette recording provided by researcher Benton Jamison.

Penniston remembered having Christmas Day dinner (December 25, 1980) with his family and then went back to work that night at the base. The hypnosis session began with Penniston describing the appearance of blue and red lights moving in the forest at the East Gate of Bentwaters around 2 AM in the early morning of December 26, 1980. Afterward, there were a series of meetings and debriefings with superior officers.

Lt. Col. Charles I. Halt, Deputy Base Commander at Bentwaters, told Penniston, "The reports will remain confidential and we should treat the incident as Top Secret and not discuss it with anybody."

Penniston remembered being told there was radiation where the lights had been, a dosage equivalent to "five or ten x-rays."

After his encounter with lights, Penniston received a call to report on December 30, 1980 to the Orderly Room at the head of the 81st Security Police Squadron, Bentwaters. There Major Malcolm Zickler ordered Penniston to report to the Air Force Office of Special Investigations (AFOSI) for a meeting to tell his story to AFOSI Special Agent "G." Present also was Major "B." AFOSI's task is to investigate Air Force personnel crimes and other sensitive matters. Therefore, it is the only organization that can legally intrude into the command structure at any level without commanders having full knowledge.

Penniston knew he had purposely left out the most significant part of his encounter: approaching a white light, seeing a large disc-shaped craft with raised symbols on its surface, reaching out to touch the symbols and receiving binary code information.

Penniston was asked to wait while the officers talked outside in the hall with unidentified men. Through the wall, Penniston overheard the name "D.S.8 or A or D. C. 8 or A."[44] Agent G returned to introduce two more men who asked Penniston to repeat his story a second time. He did, but again left out touching the raised symbols on the craft's hull.

Then Agent G left to confer privately outside his office yet again and two other agents came back to tape record the third telling of Penniston's story.

[44] *Most likely DS8, Britain's Ministry of Defence Secretariat "responsible for dealing with complaints of low-flying aircraft," according to* Sky Crash *about the December 1980 Bentwaters mystery © 1984 by Brenda Butler, Jenny Randles & Dot Street, Neville Spearman Ltd., Sudbury, U.K..*

EXCERPTS FROM SEPTEMBER 1994 HYPNOSIS SESSION WITH FORMER USAF STAFF SERGEANT JAMES PENNISTON ABOUT UFO ENCOUNTER AT BENTWATERS AFB, ENGLAND, DECEMBER 26, 1980:

The agents asked Sgt. Penniston to sign a release so he could be given Sodium Pentothal[45] combined with hypnosis that would be recorded by two tape recorders. Penniston said he agreed "to get them off my back. They seemed a lot happier after I signed the release."

Penniston remembered that the agents at Bentwaters had him "lay down on a walnut table" and that a "British guy" got the needle ready. An American said the procedure would not hurt, that "it's standard procedure and not to worry about it. We've done it before."

The questions began about the lights that appeared at the Bentwaters AFB East Gate at zero, zero, zero, two hours (00:02 AM) on December 26, 1980.

[45] *Thiopental, a barbiturate, induces unconsciousness smoothly and rapidly and has been referred to colloquially as a "truth serum" when used with hypnosis techniques.*

> "WHAT'S HAPPENING?
>
> I see the craft. The lights dissipate. They want to know what symbols I'm seeing. I don't want to tell them, but I tell them. They want to know what I did next. *I said I felt the symbols because they were raised.* (Howe's emphasis.) Tell them about the lights. White light. They already know about the lights. They are asking me if I see binary code? I see the binary code. They are slowing me down.
>
> WHAT'S HAPPENING?

I understand.

WHAT DO YOU UNDERSTAND ABOUT THE CODE?

I'm the interpreter. They need interpreters. The lights.

THE LIGHTS. SO WHAT IS THE CODE SAYING?

You can't read these codes unless you have an interpreter. I understand what's going on now.

WHAT'S GOING ON?

The symbols.

THE SYMBOLS — WHAT DO THEY MEAN?

Oh, it's information being exchanged. That machine — that's for interpreters, there's lots of interpreters.

YOU ARE AN INTERPRETER?

Yes.

CAN YOU INTERPRET THAT CODE FOR ME?

Yes.

DO THAT NOW.

Explain. Mission. Purpose.

AND THE MISSION IS?

Contact.

DO THEY SAY CONTACT WITH WHAT?

Us.

PURPOSE?

Research.

FOR?

To help them.

TO HELP THEM WITH WHAT?

Themselves. *They are time travelers. They are us.*

(Howe's emphasis.)

THEY ARE US FROM?

The future.

HOW FAR IN THE FUTURE?

A long time. Very long time.

WHAT DO THEY NEED FROM HERE?

They need something from all interpreters.

WHAT DO THEY NEED?

Not sure, but it has to do with chromosomes?

Or something like that.

AND HOW DO THEY GET THAT?

They take it.

FROM WHERE?

From the other people's bodies.

FROM WHAT PART OF THE BODY?

Depends.

WHERE DID THEY TAKE IT FROM YOU?

Didn't.

BUT YOU WERE AN INTERPRETER.

We only interrupted. ...*They* (time travelers) were interrupted. They are having problems. The program's ... I understand what they are saying, but they weren't supposed to be there. They are having problems. The odds are against them.

YOU WEREN'T SUPPOSED TO UNDERSTAND THE PROGRAM?

No. By touching these things (raised symbols on surface of craft), I activated these things.

YOU TOUCHED THE SYMBOLS AND YOU SET OFF A PROGRAM?

Yes. It was repairing itself. All they wanted was a place to stay while it repaired itself.

AND BY TOUCHING THE SYMBOLS, YOU DISRUPTED THE REPAIR PROGRAM?

I activated a binary code. The two (govt.) men want to know why.

AND WHAT DO YOU ANSWER THEM?

They ask me if I ever had any other encounters with them (lights and time travelers)? I haven't. They are discussing it between themselves. The situation. They've got a problem.

WHAT'S THEIR PROBLEM?

Their (govt.'s) problem is because I can't tell anybody. They ask no more questions about the craft. And they want to know what to do with me."

Penniston explained chromosomes were gathered for different reasons, particularly to help the time travelers because they have a "physical problem" and he felt sympathy for them. Penniston said the time travelers have "been coming here for a long time, at least thirty or forty thousand years, trying to sustain their children in the future. He explained that the children have hairless, humanoid bodies with pale skin and very large eyes "to take in more light" because the future earth will be different.

"THEIR COMING AND GOING, IS IT GOING TO HAVE ANY NEGATIVE EFFECT ON US?

No. It won't hurt us at all.

WILL IT ALTER OUR FUTURE AT ALL?

Not sure.

IF FOR SOME REASON THEY CAN'T GET THESE CHROMOSOMES, WHAT WILL HAPPEN TO THEM?

They will die.

THE RACE WILL DIE. CAN THEY REPRODUCE?

This is a problem.

REPRODUCING IS A PROBLEM. DO OUR CHROMOSOMES HELP WITH THAT?

Apparently.

ARE THEY USING US SOMETHING LIKE BREEDING STOCK?

No. Like Band-Aids.

BAND-AIDS? BAND-AIDS FOR THEIR PROBLEM?

Increase ... they are going to be increasing. We haven't noticed them (before, but now) it's becoming more cumbersome.

THEY ARE GOING TO INCREASE THE AMOUNT OF WHAT?

Visits.

DO THEY EVER TAKE FETUSES?

If it's tasked, they do. There are different ships for tasking. Everyone (the govt. agents) knows about this.

HOW DO YOU KNOW THIS?

That's what they (agents) are talking about. That's why they want to contain the situation.

WHO WANTS TO CONTAIN THE SITUATION?

Damage control.

WHO HAS DAMAGE CONTROL?

The Americans and British.

THEY SEE YOU AS DAMAGE CONTROL?

They see me and John and they're worried about Col. Halt. They know all about us.

WHY ARE THEY WORRIED ABOUT COL. HALT?

He won't leave it alone.

WHAT DO THEY PLAN ON DOING ABOUT COL. HALT? DO THEY SAY?

They have options. They were going to discredit him, but the UFO story is fine." (Howe's Note: Implication is that perhaps an extraterrestrial UFO story is easier to handle publicly than the concept of time travelers from *our* future that are having survival problems.)

Penniston was frustrated that the time travelers would not answer his questions such as what year they came from in the future. He explained that the time travelers' communication was telepathic. "Their brains are very large. More importantly, they use more (brain) than we have. We have it, but it's not developed. We don't use everything."

"WHEN YOU WERE COMMUNICATING WITH THEM, DID THEY EVER SAY THEY COME IN PERSON?

Oh, yes.

THEY HAVE MANNED CRAFT?

They have different tasks. Initial tasks are to find interpreters.

DO THEY EVER TAKE CHROMOSOMES OR CELLS OR THINGS FROM ANIMALS?

They have, but not for them.

FOR WHOM?

Study. It doesn't help them. ... Sometimes they make different chemicals.

WHAT WOULD THEY MAKE DIFFERENT CHEMICALS FOR?

I don't know. They've had their problems, too. ...This time they were having problems, but they got it off. They have to be out in space to travel. I thought they just had to sit there. They've got to be in space. They need speed to travel.

TO TRAVEL THROUGH TIME?

To go backwards. They can't go forward.

THEY CAN'T GO INTO THEIR FUTURE? BUT THEY CAN GO BACK INTO THE PAST?

They go to their past. It's impossible to go into the future.

HOW FAR INTO THE PAST CAN THEY GO?

These ships can go forty or fifty thousand years. They can't go back much further. They might not be able to get back.

SO THEY DON'T HAVE THE CAPACITY TO GO BACK TO THE BEGINNING OF TIME?

No, they can't generate that kind of speed. It takes a lot of speed."

Penniston said that the U. S. government gained access to one of their craft because "they mess up some times," implying there was a crash.

"HAVE THEY HAD VERBAL CONTACT WITH THE GOVERNMENT TO EXPLAIN THIS SITUATION?

No. Only through interpreters.

ONLY THROUGH INTERPRETERS LIKE YOURSELF?

That makes it hard for our government. They're not sure what the problem is. That's why I am being debriefed.

DOES THE GOVERNMENT BELIEVE WHAT YOU ARE

SAYING ABOUT THEM COMING FROM THE FUTURE?

Oh, yes.

THEY BELIEVE THAT?

Oh, yes.

DOES THE GOVERNMENT FEEL THAT THEY POSE ANY THREAT?

No military threat.

WHAT OTHER TYPE OF THREAT WOULD THEY BE?

Sometimes they become impatient.

AND THEN WHAT?

They take what they want because it does help their study.

SO SOMETIMES THEY TAKE PEOPLE?

Sure.

SO IF THEY TOOK GENETIC MATERIAL FROM SOMEONE TODAY, THEN YOUR CHILDREN COULD BE BORN WAY IN THE FUTURE?

I play a very small part depending on the offspring. I might be responsible for their offspring, but it is thirty or forty generations down the road who is responsible for parenting. That's the person who could accept the time line.

WHY DO THEY COME BACK SO FAR?

So it doesn't affect the time line. The farther it is, the better, the least affect it has on changing the future. They don't want to change the future.

SO IT'S NOT THAT IT'S NOT POSSIBLE TO CHANGE THE FUTURE. THEY DON'T...

They can't control it. It's too cumbersome. They're not tampering with it. That's why they come back so far. Does that make sense?

YES. OK, LET'S MOVE FORWARD TO WHERE YOU HEAR THE AGENTS TALKING ABOUT WHAT THEY ARE GOING TO DO WITH YOU.

They are going through their check list. They have a scripted check list.

WHAT'S THE SCRIPT?

They tell me when I was at the East Gate with John, they have five different stories to tell. *Important to scramble dates.* That's the unique thing about this — all stories are the same. They just have different dates. (Howe's emphasis and note: Changing dates confuses and undermines consistency of eyewitness testimonies and thus confounds investigators.)

WHAT'S HAPPENING?

They are reading my story to me. The dates are just different. I'll remember. They're going to give me a warning.[46]

[46] *One possible consequence of a warning might be that Jim Penniston has had a peculiar nausea response to certain memories or efforts to recall memories. See Axle in next segment for similar nausea interference.*

WHAT'S THE WARNING? WHAT HAPPENS IF YOU DISOBEY THE WARNING?

There is nothing they can do. They tell me that I will hurt the world. It will breach national security and can destroy the system, cause wars, chaos in the streets. That's why it's important to keep it quiet. (But) ...it doesn't make any difference if I talk about the story. They could care less. It's too unbelievable."

Two weeks after Sgt. Jim Penniston's December 26, 1980 experience, USAF Lt. Col. Charles I. Halt who was Deputy Base Commander at Bentwaters in December 1980, wrote a report on official Air Force Headquarters letterhead to the Royal Air Force/CC dated January 13, 1981. The subject was "Unexplained Lights."

Col. Halt stated that "around 3 AM in the early morning of December 27, 1980, two USAF security police patrolmen saw unusual lights outside the back gate at RAF Woodbridge. (Howe's Note: Date discrepancy to confuse? Or a different night in a series of events?) Thinking an aircraft might have crashed or been forced down, they called for permission to go outside the gate to investigate. The on-duty flight chief responded and allowed three patrolmen to proceed on foot. The individuals reported seeing a strange glowing object in the forest.

The object was described as being metallic in appearance and *triangular in shape,* approximately two to three meters across the base and approximately two meters high. (Howe's emphasis) It illuminated the entire forest with a white light. The object itself had a pulsing red light on top and a bank of blue lights underneath. The object was hovering or on legs. As the patrolmen approached the object, it maneuvered through the trees and disappeared. At this time, the animals on a nearby farm went into a frenzy. The object was briefly sighted approximately an hour later near the back gate."

Col. Halt's January 13, 1981 report about the Bentwaters incident was not the only one to emerge. An alleged English Ministry of Defence letter in which the date, addressee and writer were blacked out specifically referenced "entities" that were small, "approximately 1 1/2 metres tall, wore what appeared to be nylon-coated pressure suits, but *no helmets.* Conditions on the night were misty, giving the appearance that the entities were hovering above ground level. ... According to OSI (Air Force Office of Special Investigations), entities had claw-like hands with three digits and an opposable thumb." (Howe's note: EBE Type II?)

If such entities are "time travelers" from earth's future with claw-like hands that have only four fingers, what happened in the evolution of *Homo sapiens?*

After the September 10, 1994 hypnosis session was over, Sergeant James Penniston described the U. S. government's position concerning the Bentwaters encounter this way:

> "They're not going to mess with anyone who has had contact. They (U.S. government agents) are not sure what the (time traveler) beings are going to do, either.
>
> "GEEZ, it's incredible! The American government is helpless. They don't know what the hell to do and aren't going to mess with me because they don't know what THEY (beings) are going to do. They government doesn't know if the beings will do something or not. The government is worried about interference."

Penniston means alien interference, perhaps even retaliation, if governments try to stop or interfere with the time traveler's presence and genetic harvests from earth life.

When Penniston placed his hands on the craft's raised symbols, he thinks he activated technology that sent light containing binary code communication into his mind. That the source of the information might be time travelers from the future is startling in the context of a military eyewitness's recall. However, the idea that at least some of the beings in the UFO phenomenon are time travelers has emerged before in human abduction cases.

Time travel is also a serious subject in modern physics. Mathematical theory says that if matter approaches the speed of light, time appears to slow down to an external observer. If you were the matter, you would notice no difference in time. The closer you got to the speed of light, c, the slower time would go. If you reached c, time would stop. Then if you could exceed c, time would reverse — but only to the outside observer. You, the traveller going faster than light, would have no reference point for time change until you returned to your physical starting point on earth, for example, and slowed back down to normal speeds. Then you would find you had returned to the past like the famous limerick:

There once was a lady named Bright
who traveled much faster than light.
She departed one day in a relative way
and came home the previous night.

Theoretical physicist Kurt Godel described in *Albert Einstein: Philosopher-Scientist*[47] a particular kind of rotating galaxy in which "by making a round trip on a rocket ship in a sufficiently wide curve, it is possible in these worlds to travel into any region of the past, present, and future, and back again, ex-

[47] Albert Einstein: Philosopher-Scientist, *Edited by Paul Schilpp © 1949 The Library of Living Philsophers, Inc., Evanston, Illinois.*

DEPARTMENT OF THE AIR FORCE

CD 13 Jan 81

Unexplained Lights

RAF/CC

1. Early in the morning of 27 Dec 80 (approximately 0300L), two USAF security police patrolmen saw unusual lights outside the back gate at RAF Woodbridge. Thinking an aircraft might have crashed or been forced down, they called for permission to go outside the gate to investigate. The on-duty flight chief responded and allowed three patrolmen to proceed on foot. The individuals reported seeing a strange glowing object in the forest. The object was described as being metalic in appearance and triangular in shape, approximately two to three meters across the base and approximately two meters high. It illuminated the entire forest with a white light. The object itself had a pulsing red light on top and a bank(s) of blue lights underneath. The object was hovering or on legs. As the patrolmen approached the object, it maneuvered through the trees and disappeared. At this time the animals on a nearby farm went into a frenzy. The object was briefly sighted approximately an hour later near the back gate.

2. The next day, three depressions 1 1/2" deep and 7" in diameter were found where the object had been sighted on the ground. The following night (29 Dec 80) the area was checked for radiation. Beta/gamma readings of 0.1 milliroentgens were recorded with peak readings in the three depressions and near the center of the triangle formed by the depressions. A nearby tree had moderate (.05-.07) readings on the side of the tree toward the depressions.

3. Later in the night a red sun-like light was seen through the trees. It moved about and pulsed. At one point it appeared to throw off glowing particles and then broke into five separate white objects and then disappeared. Immediately thereafter, three star-like objects were noticed in the sky, two objects to the north and one to the south, all of which were about 10° off the horizon. The objects moved rapidly in sharp angular movements and displayed red, green and blue lights. The objects to the north appeared to be elliptical through an 8-12 power lens. They then turned to full circles. The objects to the north remained in the sky for an hour or more. The object to the south was visible for two or three hours and beamed down a stream of light from time to time. Numerous individuals, including the undersigned, witnessed the activities in paragraphs 2 and 3.

CHARLES I. HALT, Lt Col, USAF
Deputy Base Commander

Plate 44 - *January 13, 1981 report to the Royal Air Force/CC by Bentwaters USAF Deputy Base Commander, Lt. Colonel Charles I. Halt, obtained through a Freedom of Information Act request.*

Plate 45 - *English Ministry of Defence Memo that references "several entities near RAF Bentwaters on the night of December 29/30 1980." The date discrepancy with Jim Penniston's account could be because several incidents happened over a series of nights and the intelligence agents deliberately scrambled dates to confound investigators.*

MINISTRY OF DEFENCE
Main Building, Whitehall, London SW1A 2HB
Telephone (Direct Dialling) 01-218
(Switchboard) 01-218 9000

Dear ,

As you know, OSI has completed a report on the landing of a craft of unknown origin crewed by several entities near RAF Bentwaters on the night of December 29/30 1980.

Interestingly, OSI reports that the entities were approximately $1\frac{1}{2}$ metres tall, wore what appeared to be nylon-coated pressure suits, but no helmets. Conditions on the night were misty, giving the appearance that the entities were hovering above ground level.

Tape recordings were made on which the entities are heard to speak in an electronically synthesized version of English, with a strong American accent. Similar transmissions intercepted irregularly by NSA since 1975.(See attached - Flag A)

According to OSI, entities had claw-like hands with three digits and an opposable thumb.

Despite original reports (Flags B - G), OSI said the craft was not damaged but landed deliberately as part of a series of visits to SAC bases in USA and Europe. Reports that craft was repaired by US servicemen or was taken on to the base are not confirmed by OSI.

Landing is not considered a defence issue in view of the overt peaceful nature of the contact, but investigations by DS8 are to be continued on authority. Precautionary plan for counter-information at a local level involving and a , is strongly recommended.

Sincerely

actly as it is possible in other worlds to travel to distant parts of space.

"This state of affairs seems to imply an absurdity. For it enables one, for example, to travel into the near past of those places where he has himself lived. ... But the velocities which would be necessary in order to complete the voyage in a reasonable length of time are far beyond everything that can be expected ever to become a practical possibility: ... the velocity of the ship must be at least one over the square root of two of the velocity of light: $1/\sqrt{2}\ c$"

Repeating what Penniston recalled in hypnosis:

> "They need speed to travel. (And enormous energy.)
>
> TO TRAVEL THROUGH TIME?
>
> To go backwards. They can't go forward.
>
> THEY CAN'T GO INTO THEIR FUTURE? BUT THEY CAN GO BACK INTO THE PAST?
>
> They go to their past. It's impossible to go into the future.
>
> HOW FAR INTO THE PAST CAN THEY GO?
>
> These ships can go forty or fifty thousand years. They can't go back much further. They might not be able to get back.
>
> SO THEY DON'T HAVE THE CAPACITY TO GO BACK TO THE BEGINNING OF TIME?
>
> No, they can't generate that kind of speed. It takes a lot of speed.
>
> WHY DO THEY COME BACK SO FAR?
>
> So it doesn't affect the time line. The farther it is, the better — the least affect it has on changing the future. They don't want to change the future."

There is a paradox in Penniston's recall of the binary code transmission which said its civilization — humanity in the future — is dying out and sending beings back through time to harvest genetic material from our present earth life to survive. The time travelers say they go thousands of years into their past to our human present to collect genetic material. The explanation for time traveling thousands of years into their past was to avoid affecting their future time line. But moving through time to a distant past to survive in the future *is* changing their future.

Perhaps the paradox is a translation problem in which we humans lack the language and understanding of a different cosmology than we have discovered to date. "Paradoxes as they appear in our three-dimensional world are in part the result of our attempt to describe reality with limited analogies," Norman Friedman wrote in *Bridging Science and Spirit.*[48]

[48] Bridging Science and Spirit © *1990 and 1994 by Norman Friedman, Living Lake Books, St. Louis, Mo.*

Fans of *Star Trek* and other science fiction are accustomed to plots that include allies or enemies that use time travel for transportation, to fight wars, to change destinies, and to gain immortality. We can look back on our own planet to the Egyptians who were a culture obsessed with cycles of life, the moment of death and the perpetuation of consciousness into other realms. In *The Message of the Sphinx,* Graham Hancock and Robert Bauval included an Appendix entitled "Harnessing Time with the Stars." They wrote:[49]

[49] *"Harnessing Time with the Stars: The Hermetic Axiom 'As Above So Below' and the Horizon of Giza," Appendix 4 in* The Message of the Sphinx: A Quest for the Hidden Legacy of Mankind *© 1996 by Graham Hancock and Robert Bauval, Crown Publishers.*

> *"The ancients were somehow attempting to 'navigate' not only in distance ('space'), but also in 'time.' What did they have in mind? How can 'time' be navigated? ... The function of the Giza blueprint is to provide a virtually indestructible 'holographic' apparatus for the use of 'reincarnated' or 'reborn' entities of the Horian lineage in order to induce 'remembrance' of a 'divine' genetic origin in Egypt in the time-frame of 10,500 B.C. The ultimate function, however, appears to have been to perpetuate the 'immortality' of their souls into 'time'. ...The esoteric teachings and initiations into such cosmic mysteries are ... somehow to reach and harness the extrasensory capabilities of the human mind in order to link up to the invisible and immaterial, yet very perceptible 'flux of time.'*
>
> *"The questions for those looking for 'scientific' explanations can be formulated in another way: Do we humans carry 'remote memory files' locked in our genes? And if so, can it not be possible that such 'files' be retrieved by using the correct subliminal keys?*
>
> *"More provocative still: Is our 'consciousness' umbilically linked to 'time' such that it merely passes through biological matter, ourselves, like a thread passing through pearls and stones?"*

The concept of human interpreters who come from a bloodline that carries memory files locked in genes necessary for communication between us and Them is also described in Chapter 3 by real estate developer and abductee Jim Sparks who is deeply concerned about earth's environment and the vested interests of non-humans in perpetuating earth life, with or without *Homo sapiens sapiens.*

A P-3 Bear Trap, U.S. Navy Man and "Greys" — 1987

In December 1991, I received a phone call from a man who introduced himself by name, said he had read my book *An Alien Harvest,* and thought it was important that we meet. Axle, as I call him, had served in the Navy in the late 1980s as a specialist who flew with crews on "aviation anti-submarine warfare operations." Flying in P-3 Bear Traps, his assignment was to listen with high tech gear to Soviet submarines undersea and track them. These United States P-3 Cold War operations were highly secret and required sophisticated cryptographic information to decode the tracking data. One of the great violations of national security in the infamous Walker spy case was Walker's transfer of P-3 crypto codes to the Soviet Union.

Axle said that on one particularly sensitive mission in 1987, an extraordinary event happened which involved grey beings with big, black eyes. He wanted to tell me about what happened in person. So, I decided to meet with him on December 13, 1991 and drove two hours northwest of my Philadelphia office. I waited alone in the designated lobby until a blond-haired man over six feet tall approached me. He was wearing thick-heeled boots, blue jeans, and a beige shirt under a red and black checkered Pendleton jacket. "Are you Linda?" he asked, and the secret rendezvous began.

With him was a short, plump man named Bill who had thinning brown hair, glasses, and was dressed in a brown suit and tie. The two led me to a rental car which "was checked for bugs because we have to be careful." Bill said they had also paid for a "clean room" in a motel for our discussion. But first, they invited me to dinner. Axle sat across from me, nervous and smoking heavily, while Bill talked about the danger Axle would be in if he talked publicly. Neither wanted to discuss the mysterious incident in the restaurant, but Bill warned me that the government had "messed with Axle's head" and that I should be prepared for problems such as vomiting when we returned to the "clean room" to discuss Axle's story because certain memories triggered involuntary nausea.

I had brought a tape recorder for accuracy, but Axle would not let me use it, so I wrote in a notebook. He began by giving me background about the technology used in P-3s in 1987. He explained that the sonar was recorded on one computer while the central computer recorded Zulu time and displayed it on a time code generator to which all the operations in the plane were linked. If something ever happened to the clock, he said, they couldn't fly.

His crew of eleven men were flying over ice and water. Suddenly the pilot yelled, "The clock has stopped!" The panicked men watched the big 3-dimensional gyroscope and compass spin out of control. The plane should have been falling, but there was not even a wing tilt. The plane kept flying.

Axle said he looked out a window. "There was nothing there."

Confused, I asked, "Do you mean it was foggy?"

"I mean there was nothing, zilch. No color, just like empty air everywhere. No horizon, no clouds, no ice, no water, nothing. And no sound."

Then he heard what he thought was a voice inside his head. The voice said it had something to show him if he wanted to see it.

"I had a choice, and I guess I said, 'OK.'"

The next thing he remembered was a sense of moving rapidly out of the limbo into and out of a series of "scenes" or other realities. He compared the sensation to moving on and off freeway ramps or up and down in elevators. Or like changing TV stations. "I didn't move, but everything around me kept changing. And my feet stood on thin air! Something slowed down and stopped and colors and sound began again."

"What was around you?"

"Three of those little grey bastards with the big, black eyes. One was in front of me and the other two were on either side. Like glorified bellhops, they took me where I was supposed to go."

Axle began to hold his stomach and cough. Bill looked over at me indicating this is what he was talking about in the restaurant. Axle got up and spent about fifteen minutes in the bathroom dry heaving. We could hear him. When he returned, he said, "I'm sorry, but those government agents fucked with my brain."

Axle continued and said the little grey beings took him to various "places" — one had dinosaurs moving in a greenish fog. Another was a field of gold flowers. Axle tried to touch the flowers, but his hands passed through them as if the flowers were not solid.

Then Axle was taken to a round room and a man that Axle thought resembled "Sir Percival of King Arthur's Court." The man had blond hair, green eyes, stood about five and one-half feet tall and wore a white robe. In the legend, Sir Percival was an innocent Knight of Arthur's Round Table in the Isles of Avalon near Glastonbury, England. Sir Percival sought the Holy Grail, the cup used by Christ at the Last Supper. In his quest, which became a spiritual challenge, he received mystical revelations about God and man's struggling evolution toward perfection and God's grace.

Axle said, "The blond man told me I have to give up something before I can do whatever I'm supposed to do. He said all humans could be a Sir Percival if we aspired with pure hearts. Everyone has a chance to see what's wrong, what's right and to choose the proper course of action."

Then Axle said Sir Percival folded his arms, looked straight at him and said, "All humans are going to be judged very shortly."

Instantly, Axle was back in the plane. The horizon and clouds and ice and water and normal sounds were back. Flight crew members were screaming that two engines were on fire and had to be shut down. The crew proceeded in an emergency mode to the nearest base.

The last clear memory Axle had after the P-3 landed was flipping off a toggle switch. Then he said, "I lost the next month or so — completely missing from my life." Government debriefers were responsible, he thought.

By 1988, his duty was up and Axle tried to re-enlist. But his files were mysteriously flagged with a warning that he was no longer eligible for government service of any kind. He received an honorable discharge and left to see his parents in the northeast. He was bitter and angry. Every time he tried to remember what happened, he got sick and vomited. Until 1990. Then he began to have memory flashbacks.

Axle said he remembered the little grey guys told him that the purpose of human life has to do with our souls.

"There is a *finite* number of souls. That's important."

Finally, Axle drew a map for me of what the United States was supposed to look like in the year 1993, according to the little greys. In that map, southern Florida, the northeastern U. S., the Mississippi valley, and all of California were under water. He said it was going to happen because of a "sky fire"[50] and polar shifts.

[50] *See Chapter 4, Linda Porter case.*

Yet, 1993 came and went and the grey beings' future map version did not occur, like so many other future visions in the abduction syndrome that haven't materialized either.

As I asked more and more questions about his incredible story, Axle became angry. He wanted a sympathetic ear, he said, not challenge and disbelief. I told him I needed proof that he was who he claimed to be and needed a copy of his military records and any other evidence he could provide. He said he had it, but if he ever went public, he was a dead man. I countered that if he had read my book *An Alien Harvest* and knew I produced television programs, he should have expected I would want proof of who he was and a validation of his military record. He said he wasn't sure why he wanted to talk to me, that talking to someone who understood more about the "mess" might help him, but that he didn't know what could be done with the story either. When the meeting ended, I did not think I would ever hear from Axle again.

But he began to call me from the semitrailer truck he drove for a living, telling me about more memory breakthroughs. He asked if I would meet him at a truck stop on the Pennsylvania Turnpike so that he could explain more to me. He said that the evening with Bill was only part of the story and he wanted me to know everything.

By then it was April 20, 1992 and he allowed me to use a tape recorder. The following are excerpts from a transcript of that second meeting. Periodically during this conversation, he became ill.

TRANSCRIPT OF APRIL 20, 1992 CONVERSATION WITH AXLE:

L: "When you saw nothing, you were still aware of the window casings inside the airplane?"

A: "Yes."

L: "And you were aware that you were in solid form inside the airplane, but there was nothing outside the window?"

A: "Correct."

L: "And then?"

A: "Then I wasn't on the airplane anymore. But I think I was always on the plane, at least physically."

L: "In those next microseconds, what did you become aware of?"

A: "It went from extreme panic to total serenity. Once I wasn't in the plane anymore, everything was fine."

L: "What was the very next thing you saw after nothing outside the windows?"

A: "Those little grey bastards."

L: "Can you describe them?"

A: "Ask Whitley Strieber,[51] he's got the picture."

L: "So it was exactly that type?"

A: "Yes, a no-nosed grey."

L: "Where were they in relationship to you?"

A: "Right in front of me and on either side."

L: "Are you standing, sitting, floating?"

A: "There isn't any floating. It's just like standing on the ground, except there isn't any ground there. Do you have any idea how unnerving it is to be standing up and feel gravity and there's nothing under your feet? How can you stand on nothing?"

L: "Was the Grey wearing anything?"

A: "No."

L: "What color was the skin?"

A: "Light grey."

L: "And the eyes?"

[51] *Whitley Strieber is author of* Communion *© 1987 and* Transformation *© 1988, William Morrow Books;* Majestic *© 1989, G. P. Putnam's Sons;* Breakthrough *© 1995 and* The Secret School *© 1997, HarperCollins Publishers.*

A: "Big, black. They're pointed at either end and they're fat in the middle. Like elongated footballs."

L: "When you're looking at those eyes, did you think you were looking at biology, or something else?

A: "No, vegetable." [52]

L: "Like a plant?"

A: "Correct. What makes no sense at all is that he smelled like a vegetable. And I can't smell very well, but I could smell him."

L: "If a vegetable, which one?"

A: "Do you know what a farmer's market smells like? They smell like farmer's markets. Vegetables." [50]

L: "What happened next?"

A: "Since I had no idea where the hell I was or where I was supposed to go, someone had to show me how to get there. Goddamn things are glorified bellboys!"

L: "Their job was to get you some place that you were supposed to go?"

A: "Correct."

L: "Mental communication? Was it like listening to your own thoughts?"

A: "No, it's like having a conversation, but nobody is speaking. Sometimes people talk to themselves out loud. Sometimes not vocally, like when you are driving down the road and have a lot of stuff to do during the day. So, you're talking to yourself about where you have to go next. Imagine you were talking to yourself in that fashion, yet you heard it with your ears like there was a voice, but there wasn't."

L: "Some abductees have described hearing a voice that sounds a little like Mickey Mouse or cartoons. What did the Grey's 'voice' sound like?"

A: "You know how some bamboos grow so fast it actually makes a noise?"

L: "Squeaks?"

A: "Right. It was sort of like having a conversation with a bamboo forest, squeaking."

L: "Did it have clicks along with the squeaks?"

A: "Yeah, but slower. The clicking sound I almost consider it like punctuation. Like clicking at the end of a statement. Or if it paused, instead of saying 'uh' like we do, these suckers click."

L: "It smelled like a plant. Did you have any impression of it being insect-like also?"

[52] *Lt. Col. Philip Corso wrote in his book: "...the skin analysis that I was reading sounded more akin to the skin of a house plant ... (and could explain) the lack of food or waste facilities" — implying chlorophyll and metabolism of light. Page 97,* The Day After Roswell *authored by Lt. Col. Philip J. Corso (Army Ret.) with William J. Birnes © 1997 by Rosewood Woods Productions, Inc., Pocket Books, Simon & Schuster.*

A: "No."

L: "Do you have any sense of what the grey guy communicated in his squeaks and clicks at that moment?"

(Axle becomes sick.)

L: "Whose programming is it that makes you sick when you try to remember? The Greys? Or the government?"

A: "Government, yes."

L: "They did something to you in the debriefing to strip your memory and make you sick if you tried to remember?"

A: "You know what causes a memory? It's simply an electrochemical pulse in your brain. The theory is that in order to rob you or anyone else of memory, physically all that is required is to break the circuit."

L: "And they can do that with stuff you drink?"

A: "Or it can be intravenous. As long as it gets absorbed into the blood stream. How it gets there is immaterial. It's geared to enzymes that trigger those electromechanical reactions."

L: "Try to tell me what happened with the Greys."

A: "It's not like you really move anywhere. You don't actually move at all. You don't physically have to move anywhere. You don't need a physical manifestation, *you just vibrate at the right frequency* and wherever it is you're trying to go to, you're there." (Howe's emphasis.)

L: "And the grey beings would create the resonating frequency that would put you in the new space or reality?"

A: "No. This is something I've figured out. The Greys are not actually doing the resonating. It's just like the 'abductees.' The grey guys aren't abducting them. The grey guys simply act as a conduit to channel someone else's energy through them to achieve what the person wants, unless the individual involved becomes conscious of what's going on and he can stop it that quickly." (Howe's note: See android relationship to pale-haired Elders in Chapter 4.)

L: "If the Greys are channeling energy, who are they channeling energy from?"

(Took sick break and never answered the question.)

L: "Go back to the Grey. Where does he take you?"

A: "Ship. A trireme. You remember the movie *Ben Hur?* He was on a slave ship, slave galley. The slaves pulled the oars, that was their job. One bank of oars was simply a galley — that's what they were called. Two banks of oars, an upper and lower, were a bireme."

L: "And a trireme is three?"

A: "Right."

L: "Was it an Egyptian ship?"

A: "No. It wasn't Egyptian. They didn't have triremes. Theirs were made out of reeds. This trireme was Atlantean."

L: "You went back in time?"

A: "There's no back or forward up there."

L: "So you were resonated to an Atlantean scene. Were you resonated to this Atlantean scene because ...?"

A: "It was my ship."

L: "What was your role during Atlantis?"

A: "Basically the same thing I do now."

L: "A truck driver?"

A: "Correct. I move things. That's all I do. I move things from Point A to Point B."

L: "OK, you were a transporter of goods on a trireme ship in Atlantis."

A: "I was the Captain."

L: "Captain of a trireme ship in Atlantis and the Grey resonated there to remind you? Or was there a specific reason for that scene?"

A: "That's what I screwed up the last time."

L: "What was it you were supposed to have done in Atlantis that you didn't?"

A: "I was supposed to take people in my ship to Egypt."

L: "To escape?"

A: "Correct."

L: "What stopped you?"

A: "There wasn't enough money in it."

L: "You turned down the assignment because there wasn't enough money for you?"

A: "Yes."

L: "And all those people died?"

A: "Every one of them."

L: "Then the Grey took you back, or resonated you, to remind you of one of the other earlier episodes of your evolution that is parallel to what is going on now?"

A: "Yes."

L: "Then what happens?"

A: "Then I go to see Sir Percival."

L: "But I think you told me on the phone that there was a golden field of flowers before you got to Sir Percival?"

A: "You can't touch them."

L: "Didn't you see them before Sir Percival?"

A: "Before him, yes. The flowers don't smell."

L: "Do they glow?"

A: "No, they don't glow."

L: "What do they most look like?"

A: "Yellow daisies."

L: "As far as the eye can see?"

A: "It's hard to say because there is no horizon in Nothingness."

L: "You tried to reach down to pick the yellow daisies?"

A: "But you can't."

L: "And your hand passed through them. Was the immediate next scene Sir Percival?"

(Heavy breathing, coughing. He says it's like being on a boat and getting sea sick.)

A: "Yeah!"

L: "What did he look like?"

A: "He was under arms. Chain mail armor and a knight's cross from the Crusade on his shield. He had a hand and a half sword — they used to call it a 'bastard sword.'"

L: "He's got this bastard sword and he looked ...?"

A: "Just like he was supposed to look from books."

L: "And the chain mail is over a colored robe?"

A: "White."

L: "Is the little Grey there?"

A: "No, he's not."

L: "Tell me what happens with Sir Percival."

A: "I asked him if I could stay. I didn't want to go back. I was afraid to go back. I didn't want to make the same mistake twice."

L: "When you ask him that ..."

A: (Laughs as if in pain.) "He told me it was a matter of free will."

L: "You could stay or go?"

A: "No, whether anyone else was going to die as a result of my actions was free will, *my* will. I was the only one who could determine that and I didn't do so well the last time. I haven't done too well this time for that matter."

The issue of free will is at the root of mankind's chronic moral dilemmas on this planet. The medieval philosopher Maimonides, schooled in the mysticism of the Hebraic Kabballah, put it this way:

> *"Every man is granted free will. If he desire to incline towards the good way and be righteous, he has the power to do so; and if he desire to incline towards the unrighteous way, and be a wicked man, he also has the power to do so. Give no room in your minds to that which is asserted by heathen fools, and also by many of the ignorant among the Israelites themselves, namely, that the Holy One, blessed be he, decrees that a man from his birth should be either a righteous man or a wicked man.*
>
> *"Since the power of doing good or evil is in our own hands, and since all the wicked deeds which we have committed have been committed with our full consciousness, it befits us to turn in penitence and to forsake our evil deeds; the power of doing so being still in our hands."* [53]

[53] High Holiday Prayer Book: Rosh Hashanah & Yom Kippur, *Prayer Book Press, Hartford, Conn., 1951.*

The Buddhists would add that the unpleasantness of having to face the same choices until one gets it right is what the cycle of reincarnation is all about. This third dimensional plane is where a soul can work out karma, the sum and the consequences of a person's actions during successive phases of existence to progress to higher levels. But in order to do that, humans must cope with the seductions of the physical senses and the seven deadly sins: pride, avarice, lechery, anger, gluttony, envy and sloth. The challenge is to control the senses to keep from destroying our souls.

L: "What else happened between you and Sir Percival?"

A: "He gave me a chance — you see, it's a blessing and a curse. It's nice to know what you did wrong the last time, but at the same token, to live it again a second time isn't so great. Because you don't get a final answer — it's not like somebody tells you: 'OK, this is what you did wrong the last time. Now, this time you're going to be faced with the same choice except it's going to come in this form.' They don't tell you that. You don't get to know that because this whole thing wouldn't work if you had all the answers."

L: "But what did he actually communicate to you?"

A: "The essence was that I had been given the opportunity, I had *earned* the opportunity, to witness what I had just seen and I could either choose to learn from it or I could make the same mistake all over again. But the problem is: you don't really know what the mistake was. It's like seeing an out take from a movie, one scene, but without the rest of the plot, it's lost on you."

L: "And the issue is whether your soul has learned enough to instinctively make a different choice this time around?"

A: "Correct! Now apparently for reasons unknown to me someone somewhere felt that I had earned the right to gain more knowledge about who I was and where I came from. But it's a blessing and a curse."

L: "And he said something to you about the flowers?"

A: "When I had earned the right, I could pick the flowers. But obviously I ain't got it right yet."

L: "Did he communicate anything about us humans now and our future?"

A: "No, those guys don't give up their play books."

L: "What was the very next thing that happened after Sir Percival?"

A: "The little grey turkey took me back to the airplane."

L: "And you became conscious?"

A: "The horizon was back and the ice was back and the clouds were back and two fucking engines were on fire. You bag the engines, you hit the fire bottle and we went back to the base on two motors and prayed like hell that we didn't go swimming between here and there."

L: "And you landed ..."

A: "We didn't even have a chance to get off the plane. We got escorted off the plane."

L: "By?"

A: "Who the hell knows?"

L: "Civilian? Military?"

A: "This is where it gets — do you know what it's like for someone to take a piece of your life away?"

L: "Did you ever ask any of the other guys that you knew were in that P-3 whether they had the same memory stripping?"

A: "I didn't remember any of this for a long time. Not until two years ago."

L: "By that time, you wouldn't know how to get in touch with any of the P-3 crew?"

A: "I've tried. But the problem is: Some of them are dead. And the other problem is that communicating with them might be the most dangerous thing in the world."

L: "So, why did Sir Percival and company interact with you?"

A: "Because it is my theory that the shadow world we live in is a direct result of the resonance of other levels. And what's doing the resonating in a lot of cases is all these billions of people moving around on the planet here that are all resonating. If you were to suddenly remove all of them, that's going to throw everything else up the chain out of kilter and they don't like that. What I'm saying is that *despite the fact the different worlds and levels are incredibly different, they are actually all linked together.*[54] (Howe's emphasis.) You can't take one away and still have all the others. If you remove one piece, the whole structure crumbles."

[54] *See Chapter 4, Linda Porter case.*

L: "So why would the upper frequencies allow the lower frequencies to get out of whack?"

A: "Free will. See that's just it. Free will, two simple little words. You can look them up in the dictionary and it would be so easy to define. But you put them together and apply it to this and you're real long on questions and very short on answers."

L: "And how does the fallen Luciferian angel story play into all of this?"

A: "In my humble opinion, a fallen angel is someone who opted for power instead of truth. What do you think happens if you make the wrong decisions? If you become corrupted with power, you become obsessed with power, you lose your ability to tell the difference between right and wrong. All that matters is power. What was the whole thing with Lucifer? It was a power play against God."

Axle doesn't understand what happened to him in that P-3 and neither do I. But what comes to mind are the quantum physics works of David Bohm, John Wheeler and others who theorize there are several orders, spectrums, frequencies or dimensional levels beyond the earth's three dimensional plane. In his book *The Holographic Paradigm and Other Paradoxes,*[55] editor Ken Wilber quotes A. P. Shepherd:

[55] The Holographic Paradigm and Other Paradoxes, *Edited by Ken Wilber © 1995 Shambhala Publications, Boston, Mass.*

"These 'worlds' (or dimensional levels) are not separate regions, spatially divided from one another, so that it would be necessary to move in space in order to pass from one to another. The higher worlds completely interpenetrate the lower worlds, which are fashioned and sustained by their activities."

This concept of overlapping dimensions is described further by architect Stefan von Jankovich after his near-death experience:[56]

[56] On Dreams and Death *by Marie-Louise von Franz © 1986, Shambhala Publications, Boston, Mass.*

"One of the greatest discoveries I made during death ... was the oscillation principle. ...Since that time 'God' represents for me a source of primal energy, inexhaustible and timeless, continually radiating energy, absorbing energy and constantly pulsating. ...Different worlds are formed from different oscillations; the frequencies determine the differences. ...Therefore

it is possible for different worlds to exist simultaneously in the same place, since the oscillations that do not correspond with each other also do not influence themselves. ...Thus, birth and death can be understood as events in which, from one oscillation frequency and therefore from one world, we come into another."

Frequently the subject of other dimensional realities comes up in discussions or correspondences with people who claim to be government insiders privy to the deepest secrets about the UFO phenomenon. Those insiders ascribe motives to other dimensional beings which imply that not all is benign and that an ancient struggle between opposites might still surround us.

One View From Alleged Government Insiders — 1994

A trusted research colleague I have known since the early 1980s called me in May 1994 soon after my book *Glimpses of Other Realities, Volume I: Facts & Eyewitnesses* was first released. Ray Boeche said he had been contacted by two men who showed identification from the Department of Defense in Washington, D. C.

The two agents wanted to discuss Boeche's research about eschatology, a branch of theology that is concerned with the ultimate or last things such as death, judgment, heaven and hell, or the end of the world as we know it. During their conversation, Ray referenced my book. The two men asked if they could read *Glimpses, Vol. I.* Boeche called me to explain the situation and to ask if I had any objections to his giving the intelligence agents my book.

I told him, "Not only give them the book, ask them if they will write in the margins whatever comments they have about what is correct and incorrect. That would be a safe way for them to communicate and for us to learn something. I'll send you a new copy to replace the one you give them."

In June, Boeche called again and said I would be getting a package in the mail. He said the contents would be a floppy disc in a sealed envelope handed to him by the two agents. Ray said the men did not want to write in the book, but were replying on the computer disc with comments about the content in *Glimpses of Other Realities, Vol. I.*

The following is a verbatim text of the floppy disc printout:

"Dear Ms. Howe: June 21, 1994

Your book is an excellent, thought-provoking work. Overall many salient points are covered quite well. Following are some random notes for your consideration.

Study David Bohm's *Wholeness and the Implicate Order.* [57] Much insight into the mechanics of the NHE's (non-human entities) can be gained from study of his ideas. He is on target with his concepts, and our program is attempting, unfortunately to exploit them.

Perhaps a better description might be that the mechanics of the NHE's ability to interact with our physical reality is what Bohm's work details, and the contact with the NHEs has occurred, and will continue to occur, regardless of our understanding of the mechanism of the contact. Our misguided program directors cling to the false belief that we can control or manipulate the NHEs, when in actuality, the reverse is occurring — we are the ones being manipulated and deceived.

Cellular changes in plants from within genuine crop circle formations are due to the same sort of energy release/exposure as that used in the so-called "negative healing" experimentation. Once again, forces being utilized by NHEs to interact with us in a bizarre, confusing manner, designed to divert us and draw our attention from the true purpose of their actions: manipulation and deception.

The penultimate diversion in this whole area is the mutilation of thousands of animals. The NHEs, with the ability to work unseen (read invisibly), and to create incisions and excise tissue in manners which seem humanly impossible (because they are) and to either remain totally undetected, or to create the illusion of extraterrestrial beings (the apparent UFO/phantom helicopter sightings, and concomitant occupant sightings often associated with the events), provide an extremely effective smoke screen. People are now busy chasing secret government projects, satanic cults, and UFOs, while the actual perpetrating agents go unsuspected.

Regarding the phantom helicopters, while many are direct NHE "productions" (craft is not an appropriate term as they do not need to travel via a propulsive device), many are related to our program, especially regarding running checks and surveillance on mutilation sites and so-called abduction victims.

[57] Wholeness and the Implicate Order *© 1980 by David Bohm, Cox & Wyman Ltd., London.*

The comment left on your telephone answering machine referenced on Page 194,[58] (*Glimpses, Vol. I*) may very well have been made by someone within the government hierarchy who has been convincingly fed the false ET scenario propagated as disinformation by those who are in charge of the NHE projects. Many variations of this exist, and all who are privy to a particular variation are convinced they have 'the answer.' With our society as it is now, the core truth of the situation is such that the public really could not handle it.

The ultimate diversionary tactic to this point (and diversions will begin to increase in frequency, degree of strangeness, and in a more overt fashion, visible to greater numbers of observers) is the UFO abduction scenario.

The concept of these events, real though they are, being the result of extraterrestrial beings is a masterful piece of disinformation to divert attention away from the real source of the NHEs. Our information as to the true nature of these events does not negate the possibility of extraterrestrial life. But the causal source of the UFO and UFO abduction phenomena is not extraterrestrial.

The so-called Roswell crash of 1947 did indeed occur and debris of a non-earthly type was found, as were non-human bodies. Although in our position we cannot speak with authority, we believe that there is a basis in truth for Bob Lazar's story of government-held 'craft.' However, the origin is not extraterrestrial. (Howe's Note: Time travelers from our future or beings in other dimensions might not be considered extraterrestrial in a biology-from-another-solar-system definition.)

The NHEs being dealt with in our psi (mind control) weapons development, and who are apparently allowing themselves to be used, for a time, are *neither benevolent nor neutral.* (Howe's emphasis.) It was our feeling that very few could understand or accept this. That is the reason we approached our mutual friend (Ray Boeche). We had become aware of him through his work on the British incident (Bentwaters Dec. 26-28, 1980), when his probings began to bother a number of high level people within our government.

His theological training, his acceptance of orthodox Christian thought, and his obvious abilities as an astute researcher, seemed to indicate to us that we might effectively communicate our concerns through him, and still maintain our positions, which would enable us to accurately monitor the ongoing work. He has made some blunt

[58] *October 18, 1991 anonymous phone message: "(Bob Lazar) mentioned that the aliens were hundreds of years ahead in technology. Actually, it would be more like thousands of years. The ships don't have windows as we know windows to be. The craft are smooth and metallic colored. They have no intention of hurting anyone. There will be increased sightings, very, very increased sightings in the future. The blood from the animals that you were talking about is not being used to make things compatible with people, as it is being developed for, shall we say, to save the animals against radiation poisoning. The government does not have ships in working order, but does have the remains of some. There was a survivor (alien), but I don't know if that person is still living. The truth of the matter is that if the reason for their visiting the planet were revealed, the public could not handle it."*

statements which run counter to the positions of his peers, and has been roundly criticized by many for his position, but we desperately hope that at least some are listening.

Your comments and thoughts (in *Glimpses of Other Realities*) concerning ancient civilizations and their contacts with the NHEs need to be considered in light of the bigger picture of the deception of mankind as a whole. If this grand deception is taking the course it seems to be, then it makes complete sense to analyze the false gods of ancient civilizations in light of the current level of deception.

It is only logical that given their non-human, other-dimensional nature, the NHEs would be able to foresee the need to establish a foundational base, the facts of which could be slightly twisted, or distorted, by the fog of antiquity and forgotten cultural distinctiveness, to seemingly establish themselves as the bringers of all good things to humanity.

Explore (Jacques) Vallee's *Passport to Magonia* again, for more close parallels between the 'faerie' manifestation of the NHEs, and current events. And look very closely at *Messengers of Deception.*[59] Dr. Vallee was so close to the truth of the situation, with the exception that *the ultimate manipulators are not human.* (Howe's emphasis.)

You have created a remarkable work which helps to begin to point to the final truth behind the phenomena. Our mutual friend could be most helpful to you in explaining details of the deception. We, on our part, will be happy to answer specific questions you may wish to put to us. You must understand, however, that some things simply can't be discussed.

Please transmit your questions and or concerns via our friend. We believe you can understand our need for discretion, and the wisdom of limiting the number of direct contacts we make.

We applaud your efforts, and we look forward to your next volume. You are a very bright and obviously courageous woman who seems to remember the maxim, 'You shall know the Truth, and the Truth shall make you free.'

With our sincerest best wishes."

[59] *Dr. Jacques Vallee is an astrophysicist and computer scientist who began researching and writing about the UFO phenomenon in the 1960s. He postulated that the intelligences involved have influenced and manipulated human affairs for centuries, often with deception. In his 1988 book* Dimensions, *Dr. Vallee wrote: "We are not dealing with successive waves of visitations from space. We are dealing with a control system. ... I cannot tell whether this control is ... artificial in nature, under the power of some superhuman will. It may be entirely determined by laws that we have not yet discovered."*

I did submit questions through Boeche to the two agents and received one more reply that elaborated more on the same basic points in this first communication. When I submitted a second round of material, including an alleged photograph of a non-human, hybrid "baby thing" for verification, several months passed without further reply. Then Ray called to say the agents told him, "It is too dangerous for us to communicate now."

This communication provoked me to read physicist David Bohm's book *Wholeness and the Implicate Order*. Dr. Bohm, now deceased, was the Professor of Theoretical Physics at Birkbeck College in London. In his book, Professor Bohm discussed a cosmology of multi-dimensional frequencies that resonate with each other and in which any element — from a photon and atom to a star or human being — has "enfolded within itself the totality of the universe." In this reality model, matter and consciousness are one, and time is an illusion.

"One of the most important implications of the theory of relativity," wrote Professor Bohm, " is that physical time is in fact relative, in the sense that it may vary according to the speed of the observer. (This variation is, however, significant only as we approach the speed of light and is quite negligible in the domain of ordinary experience.) ... Since the quantum theory implies that elements that are separated in space are generally non-causally and non-locally related projections of a higher-dimensional reality, ... one must then go on to a consideration of time as a projection of multidimensional reality into a sequence of moments."

Time as a projection of multi-dimensional reality might also mean it can be travelled, captured, manipulated and played back in ways still incomprehensible to human science.

Another View From An Alleged Government Insider — 1985

I met two men in 1985 who claimed to have government insider knowledge about an extraterrestrial civilization in the binary star system, Zeta Reticuli, 37.5 light years from earth. One man was retired in Washington, D. C. and the other continued government assignments in the southwest. Both said they had worked for a secret group which continued from the MJ-12 (Majestic Twelve) of the Truman Administration. They also claimed some knowledge about other non-human types referred to simply as "Greys," or little guys, which they did not trust. Other categories of alien life forms which confused the situation even more, they said, were biological androids that ranged widely in appearance from insects to humanoids designed by their makers for various planetary tasks. Both have periodically given me information over the years which I have no way to prove, but offer now in the context of the other military voices. To honor their request for anonymity, I combined their information into one "voice" I call Sherman.

Sherman said it was true that MJ-12 was established by one of President Harry S. Truman's Executive Orders in 1947.[60] MJ-12's charter, he said, was to study the UFO phenomenon, to oversee retrievals of crashed discs and alien bodies, to back-engineer extraterrestrial technology and to study captured beings referred to as "extraterrestrial biological entities" (EBENs). MJ-12, he said, was also directed to keep the public ignorant of the extraterrestrial presence "at all costs" to prevent public panic and to keep the aliens' advanced technology hidden from Cold War enemies in the interests of national security. In the 1990s, Sherman said MJ-12 had evolved to a different letter number code that began "E2."[61] I asked Sherman if he had personally seen non-human technology.

"I've held an Eben communicator that's called the Yellow Book — I guess because the letters and words look like yellow light. The book doesn't have any pages. It's a rectangle about fifteen inches by nineteen inches. If you saw it laying on a table, you would think it was a flat piece of plastic with a light grey metallic sheen. But when you pick it up in your hands, the words start appearing and they are a yellow color. You move your eyes along as the words appear and they just keep coming as you read. Once you get to the bottom, the next page starts. Followed by the next page, and the next page over and over on the same surface. I don't know how it works."[62]

"When you turn it over, there are 3-D holographic photos or something that seem to pop upward in the air. You're supposed to be able to control the sequence by knowing how to move the book at different angles. I was told the *Ebens know how to capture time and play it back in 3-dimensional images.* (Howe's emphasis.) There are actual manuals about how to hold it to read and

[60] *See Appendices I, VI, VII, X. Also see* An Alien Harvest, *Chapter 7 and Appendices © 1989 Linda Moulton Howe; and* TOP SECRET/MAJIC © *1996 by Stanton T. Friedman, Marlowe & Co.*

[61] *In December 1997, Jack Shulman, President of the American Computer Company, Cranford, New Jersey, announced his discovery of a "Black Budget military organization within the Defense Department" called E2SCD, the Extraterrestrial Space Command Directorate.*

[62] *By 1996, the Massachusetts Institute of Technology Media Laboratory was researching how to build an electronic book funded by Things That Think, a consortium of forty major companies.*

see the pictures. But I didn't have any instruction, so in the hour I held it, I learned only a few things.

"The Yellow Book had earth history, including Christ, who the book said was put here by the Ebens to teach humans about love and non-violence, but humans killed him anyway. The Yellow Book even showed how things were built from foundations to pillars coming out of the ground to a finished building."

"How do the Ebens communicate in English or any human language?"

"I don't know. I don't know how the translation works. When I read the Yellow Book, it was in English. Maybe it picks up brainwave patterns or something and can interact in the language of any user."

"And it's in the act of picking the Yellow Book up that it's activated?"

"Yes."

"And when you turned it to the back, you could see holographic-like projections of images come out into the air that related to where you were reading on the front side?"

"No, when you turned it over, you hold the square side of the book and hold it up at different angles. As you slightly move it, different pictures project out. "

"Were the pictures related to where you left off in the words?"

"Not really. You have to have instructions. I didn't know at what angle to hold it. I just played with it and saw different pictures not necessarily related to what I had already read. Now if I had a chance to read it again, I understand there is a pattern you start with and keep moving in different patterns to project images about what you are reading."

"Is that when you saw Christ?"

"Yes."

"Was sound associated with the images?"

"No, no sound. Years later after I saw the Yellow Book, someone told me there are sounds connected with the pictures. But I never heard any sounds. Maybe it was something I did wrong or I didn't move it right."

"But did you see Christ speaking at the Mount of Olives? Or was he being crucified, or what?"

"The picture that I saw was after Christ was crucified and died and was ascending into heaven. It was beautiful, kind of an aurora ring over his head. These pictures moved. They were moving pictures."

"So you saw Christ moving up in the aurora light?"

"Right. And then there were people on the ground and the people were moving. It's kind of like when you were a kid and got the things that you put the round circles of pictures into and clicked it to see different images. But this had dimensions and it moved. The pictures only moved within the photo you were looking at. It's hard to explain. But I saw Christ and then I moved it and lost it to other pictures. There were big, huge pillars coming out of the ground like an earthquake. Then it showed the earth and it showed a space vehicle."

"Was it a silver disc?"

"Yes, typical, every day flying saucer. It also showed a cigar shape which is a mother ship farther out in space. You turn it again and you see like a big greenhouse in an indoor stadium and fields of wheat or plants."

"How did the MJ-12 group get the Yellow Book?"

"The Ebens gave it to us back on April 25, 1964 when they landed at White Sands for a prearranged meeting and stayed for awhile. The day before when Lonnie Zamora saw a craft and beings near Socorro was a coordination mistake of some kind. The Ebens landed twelve hours too early and too far west. We got it corrected somehow and they returned around 6 AM the next morning to the right place. By the way, Zamora drew those Eben symbols perfectly." (See Pages 93-94.)

"When you and your group have face-to-face communications with Ebens, how does it work?"

"Well, the 1964 meeting was in Red Canyon about eighteen miles east of the Trinity site (first atomic bomb test in July 1945) at the north end of White Sands. We also had a decoy hangar set up at Holloman AFB just in case there was a leak. They had a disinformation program to draw people's attention to Holloman when in actuality, the landing was further north. After the Ebens landed in one of their egg-shaped ships, they had devices that looked like large wands. A wand was handed to our commander. When he spoke into the wand, the Eben language came out in another wand held by one of the Ebens. When the Eben spoke into his wand, English words came out of the wand the commander was holding, sort of like a loud speaker."

"Sherman, that sounds like the communicator rod depicted in the drawing that Allan Sandler and Robert Emenegger published based on actual photographs and film of an extraterrestrial meeting near Holloman AFB.[63] Do the Ebens have a large beaked nose like that drawing?"

"Absolutely not. The Ebens are one of the types that crashed in 1947. They're about four and a half to five feet tall, grey-skinned, four long, skinny fingers, flat face, very small nose, small openings for ears, and a slit for a mouth. (See EBE Type I, Pages 71-72.) Their eyes are large with a black lid which can cover 'cat eyes' underneath. Those eyes have a gold-colored iris around a dark, vertical slit pupil. And they wear a tight-fitting, greyish-white jump suit."

"Then is the big-nosed drawing made up?"

"No, I've seen the film of that meeting at Red Canyon and there was a

[63] Glimpses of Other Realities, Vol. I – Facts & Eyewitnesses *© 1994 by Linda Moulton Howe, Pages 276-278* .

tall, almost human-like alien that stood behind the Ebens. And it appeared that he had a big nose. He was wearing some kind of strange looking armor that reminded me of Egyptian stuff and he had on a helmet that went up high. He never talked. He was just there. That was the only one like that in the whole encounter."

"So what is the relationship between the Ebens and the big-nosed guy?"

"I don't know. He reminded me of a soldier guarding."

" Is there any connection to Egypt and Sumeria?"

"I think so. I know that I read that the Ebens had also spent almost twenty years living among the Mayans who had stepped pyramids like the ziggurats of Sumeria. The report said the Mayans worshipped the Ebens. I've often wondered if the rituals of human sacrifice by females and warriors were inspired by the Ebens."

"You mean, 'food for the gods?'"

"Yeah. I don't know if the Ebens visited periodically over twenty years or actually lived in the Yucatan and Guatemala area for twenty years. But there was some kind of Eben influence on the Mayans at some point.[64] In fact, it's interesting, Linda, that Mayan and Mongolian babies are sometimes born with odd blue marks on the lower spine. And what I've been told is that the Ebens experimented genetically in Bhutan, Tibet and Nepal and then transplanted some of those altered humans to what we call Central America."

"Then, Sherman, is it true that the Ebens and maybe other extraterrestrial groups manipulated DNA in already-evolving primates to create *Homo sapiens* as I was shown in a briefing paper at Kirtland AFB in 1983?" [65]

"Yes, but it's a difficult subject. All I can tell you is something Ebe One said: 'We made you, we put you here, but you have to live it.' And they watch us grow. They've been here since at least the time of the dinosaurs. And according to a report I read, the Ebens collected one of each species of dinosaur and placed them either on one big planetary zoo or on different planets. And that was at least sixty-eight million or more years ago."

"Sherman, if the Ebens did collect all the dinosaur species and preserve them, do you know what happened that caused almost total annihilation of earth life during that period in earth's history?" [66]

"I read in the Yellow Book that the Ebens knew back then that a very large asteroid was going to hit the earth. The Ebens wrote that they were saving one of each species that was on this planet — not just the dinosaurs, but the ants and insects, flies, snakes, fish. The Ebens said they took one of everything to save all the species before the asteroid hit."

"Sort of a Noah's Ark rescue story?"

"Right. And I guess they've experimented with life forms here ever since."

[64] *The Mayan culture of the Yucatan, Guatemala and Belize suddenly and rapidly advanced in 250 A. D.*

[65] An Alien Harvest, Chapter 7, © *1989 by Linda Moulton Howe, LMH Productions.*

[66] *Reptiles, including dinosaurs, were the dominant terrestrial form of life on earth during the Mesozoic Era 245 million to 66.4 million years ago. The Mesozoic closed with one of the great mysteries of paleontology when an annihilation event devastated many forms of life and the dinosaurs became extinct. Source:* Encyclopaedia Britannica, 15th Edition © *1993 by Encyclopaedia Britannica Inc.*

"Is there a connection between Buddhism and Eben philosophy about the cosmos?"

"Yeah, if you go back and study the ancient Tibetan scrolls written in the earliest Sanskrit we have, that's Eben writing. Their real stuff. I was on a team once that travelled to the Bhutan region to make sure the Eben scrolls were safe. The scrolls the Ebens wrote on are indestructible, but the paper the monks wrote on is very fragile and falling apart. And the monks know there's a difference. Some of the scrolls never wear out."

"Why would the Ebens have come here in the first place?"

"I don't know the whole story, but I've been told the Ebens come from Zeta Reticuli 1 and 2, a binary star system about 38 light years from earth."

According to the December 1974 issue of *Astronomy* magazine, "The two stars that comprise the Zeta Reticuli system are almost identical to the sun. Each is classified as a G2 star, the same as our sun. They are the only known examples of two solar type stars apparently linked into a binary star system of wide separation. Zeta 1 is separated from Zeta 2 by at least 350 billion miles — almost one hundred times the sun-Pluto distance. The two suns probably require at least 100,000 years to orbit their common center of gravity. The binary stars are 37.5 light years away from our solar system in the constellation Reticulum (The Net). Reticulum is visible in the Southern Hemisphere. Both Zeta 1 and Zeta 2 are prime candidates for the search for life beyond Earth. According to our current theories of planetary formation, they both have a retinue of planets something like our solar system."

In the now-famous case of Betty and Barney Hill who were apparently abducted from New Hampshire's White Mountains in September 1961 by grey beings in all-black body suits, Betty drew a star map under hypnosis which she said was shown to her by the beings on the craft. Years later, when U. S. amateur astronomer Marjorie Fish began to compare Betty Hill's drawing to stars in the local neighborhood of the earth, she discovered a match which included Zeta Reticuli 1 and 2. Betty Hill said those two stars were the starting point of trade routes and that our sun was at the end of one supposedly regular trade route.[67]

Sherman also had information about the Ebens alleged involvement with our solar system beyond earth.

"Ebe Number One, who we retrieved from a crash near Roswell, told us a great deal about our solar system and the universe. The Ebens have a massive relay station at Saturn and probably on the moon Titan. He said that Mars did support life at one time and that many alien types have used our moon as a base to explore earth.

[67] *"The Zeta Reticuli Incident,"* Astronomy, *December 1974, Vol. 2, No. 12. Feature article about the binary star system Zeta Reticuli and amateur astronomer Marjorie Fish's 1968-1973 construction with beads and wires of a 3-dimensional model of the stars in the vicinity of our sun to compare with Betty Hill's star map.*

"Ebe said that early in the 20th Century, one of their Eben craft's antimatter pods used for power was accidentally ejected into our atmosphere near the Tunguska River in central Siberia, Russia. The result was a nuclear explosion equivalent to a one megaton thermonuclear blast which levelled pine trees for miles."

Whether an Eben craft or not, the Tunguska fireball is an historic fact. At about 7:40 AM on June 30, 1908, five hundred thousand acres of pine forest near the Podkamennaya Tunguska River in Central Siberia, Russia were flattened and splintered by a force equivalent to 1,000 Hiroshima bombs exploding about four miles above the ground. The epicenter was clearly defined by thousands of scorched trees across hundreds of square miles. But there was no crater at the center, only a marshy bog. Eyewitnesses who saw the event 500 miles away described a fireball lighting the horizon, followed by the ground shaking and hot winds strong enough to throw people down and shake buildings. Because the unidentified object vaporized in the atmosphere, gases dispersed causing abnormally bright orange-colored evening skies in Siberia and Europe. Nothing grew in the downed forest for decades afterward.

According to the September 1996 *Discover* magazine, "Researchers have found embedded in Tunguska trees tiny particles with an extraterrestrial signature."[68] Scientists gouged core samples from trees near the epicenter and found that a "significant number of (resin) particles had unusually high levels of elements like copper, gold and nickel. Because many of these elements have a relatively high number of protons (denoted by physicists as Z), the researchers dubbed the particles that contain them 'high-Z particles.' There were ten times more high-Z particles in the period of the fireball than before or after, which made the Italians (scientists) wonder if these particles had an extra-Earthly origin."

[68] Discover - The World of Sciences, *September 1996, Vol. 17, Number 9.*

I asked Sherman if the Ebens themselves are always on earth in underground bases, or if they have programmed robots or androids that do work on this planet for them?

Sherman said, "I've read in one of our reports that the aliens made tunnels under the earth and we were concerned about the possibility that all their tunnels could start earthquakes. But the Ebens sort of said, 'We know where to make tunnels. We know more about this planet than you do. So, don't worry about where we dig because we know what we do won't cause earthquakes.'

"They also have lots of robots. During World War II, Ebens conducted thousands of reconnaissance flights over Europe and the Far East. That's what the Foo Fighters were. The Ebens also created a robot-type creature, a three to four foot tall biological android, to do work here which is sometimes mistaken for the Ebens themselves." (See EBE Type II? Page 72.)

"But what about the crashes with bodies like the one that Ebe was taken from?"

"Several of their manned spacecraft have crashed and we've recovered at least three of them. The flying discs that were located at Area 51 in Nevada were either loaned to us by the Ebens to study or have been recovered. We've flown some with their help, but we can't understand all the instrumentation contained in the craft."

"Sherman, you make it sound like the Ebens and our government have some kind of agreement."

"Everything the Ebens do on earth is sanctioned, either formally or informally by our government. However, we have not authorized the aliens to harm or kill humans. We don't think the Ebens have purposely killed or harmed any human beings, but that is not known for certain."

"What about the animal mutilations?"

"The animal mutilations did occur and were performed by the aliens. We allowed them to conduct experiments using animals. Not just cattle. I don't know if you are aware or not, but there were a lot of moose and caribou found mysteriously dead in the Arctic and Alaska. We think it was part of the Eben experimentation, but we couldn't figure out what happened. They wanted to conduct experiments. Better animals than humans. To complicate matters, to cover up the animal mutilations, our government launched a military program to test certain biological drugs on animals. This was to cover up the alien mutilation program."

"Do the Ebens themselves excise tissue from animals?"

"After we had more communications with the Ebens, they explained to us: 'You have to understand that in an advanced civilization, you have robots and androids to do these things.' And we began to understand that the Eben androids can be anything! The androids can be configured any way the Ebens want for whatever mission the Ebens want carried out. The Ebens are controlling a big part of an operation concerning earth, and we can't control everything they do. But I can tell you the Ebens are big environmentalists. Huge! They would make the Sierra Club look like Brownie scouts. They were so worried about our nuclear tests and nuclear materials being exploded and contaminating not only the earth, but the universe in general."

"Sherman, do you mean that our atomic bombs impacted other life forms, or even other dimensions?"

"Right. So that's one of the things the Ebens were very vocal about —

they wanted above ground atomic tests stopped. I read about one incident where we had already set the detonator in the weapon at the Nevada Test Site. It was an above ground test, they set the timer and went back to a safe area and brought in some troops to watch. Then everyone saw a UFO come in and land right next to the 20 kiloton bomb. The aliens got out. The forward observers were watching with instruments and couldn't believe it when the beings just laid down under the tower. Our guys didn't know if they could reverse the detonator, so they just watched. "

"Did the bomb go off? Or was it neutralized in some way?"

"The bomb went off big time and the craft was severely damaged but withstood the blast better than anyone thought possible. There was a lot of conjecture about what happened to the aliens. Some people said they must have vaporized at ground zero. But some others said they saw them flying up in the air, actually shooting straight up, maybe into another craft waiting in the sky."

"But, Sherman, if extraterrestrial biological entities that you call Ebens are so concerned about atomic testing and have been manipulating DNA in already-evolving primates for eons and actually "made" *Homo sapiens*, who inspired Einstein to come up with $E=mc^2$ that could potentially destroy us and the earth?"

"I don't know. But I've been told there are time cycles. The Ebens know what happened in the past and they know what will happen in the future because they understand that time spirals go around and around and that the same type of events happen at specific points in the spirals. And they want to somehow change the catastrophes that await mankind. So, they are now trying to influence us and convince us that we have to change because they know the future and we don't want that future. They don't want us to continue on this same destructive path. They don't directly interfere, but try to convince us to change things."

"But if they 'made us, put us here and we have to live it,' why are we still on a destructive spiral?"

"Because the first time around, the Ebens didn't like it. They don't want the same catastrophe to happen again — maybe like that asteroid that slammed into the Yucatan and destroyed the dinosaur life. This time, humans would be the dominant earth life that would be destroyed by a big asteroid hit. The Ebens realize our society is much more complex than theirs because of all the different races. It's easier to keep their civilization on track because it's just one race, but ours is so different. They figure they made a mistake and they are now trying to direct us in the right way of living and preventing us from contaminating not just earth, but the whole universe."

"From your point of view, are Ebens the only non-humans that have experimented genetically on this planet?

"All I know is that the Ebens started an experiment, but they couldn't keep out other space travelers. Word got out that this planet was a strange place to visit and that different experiments weren't going the way the Ebens wanted. Part of the Ebens' problems might be because there are 'bad guys' doing experiments, too, that might harm us. That really confuses matters when it comes to telling who wants to help humans and who doesn't."

"In abduction reports, people describe creatures that look like praying mantis insects. What are those?"

"As far as I've heard, they could be very advanced androids which can oversee long-term projects that last for thousands of years. But I'm not certain who they work with or for."

"Are they associated with the Ebens?"

"Well, they were on one particular occasion in 1980 at Bentwaters AFB in England. But there is a lot of confusion. Before then, I had connected praying mantises with the Greys. It could be it was just a robotic type that the Ebens had made and was different from the actual praying mantises. But I saw photos and a video from the Bentwaters landing that showed a scary-looking creature that looked like an insect raised up on two legs with two

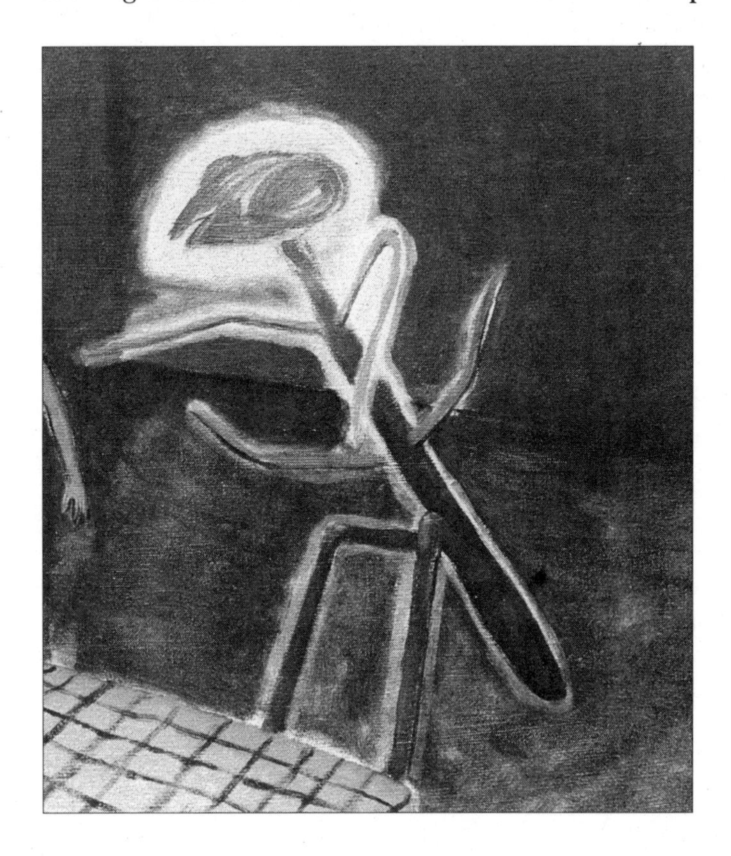

Plate 46 - *Painting by David Huggins of his encounter with a praying mantis being that had a glowing aura around its head and jaw protrusions in a New York City apartment during the 1960s.*

more legs held up in front. It was with a report that described big insect-looking eyes and pincher hands."

"Was there any color?"

"It was dark, but there was a glowing aura around the creature. And in the aura, you could see protrusions in the jaw area that reminded me of tusks or something."

"If that was in the photographs, what was on the videotape?"

"Two sequences that were shot on the second and third nights. The one on the second night showed the craft as clear as can be."

"What did you see?"

"It was a typical saucer with four protrusion legs coming out the bottom to the ground."

"Did they look like erector set struts?"

"Yeah, you could see holes in them. A ramp was down on the side facing the camera and the cameraman walked right up to it. And he focuses the camera on the ramp thing sticking out of the disc and it was like transparent! You could see the ground through the ramp."

"Did anyone explain to you how the ramp could be transparent?"

"No."

"And the surface of this disc in the video you saw — did it have any raised symbols on it?"

"Yeah, one of the segments showed symbols. There's a whole fifteen minutes of this camera panning up and down the side of the symbols raised up on the surface of the flying saucer."

"Did you recognize anything like Greek?"

"No, I know that alphabet. This was more like hieroglyphics on cave walls, more picture types of things, at least to me."

"And this was all associated with the praying mantis being?"

"No, one of the video segments shows a normal looking Eben at the base of the craft standing next to the Base Commander."

"Col. Gordon Williams?"

"Right. It was like a portrait. This guy is standing next to an Eben just as clear as can be."

"And was Col. Gordon Williams there in the photograph?"

"Yeah."

"And was the Eben dressed in a silver suit?"

"Kind of a metallic, shiny suit, right."

"Did you read anything about what happened at Bentwaters?"

"I had beer with a major back in 1988 who told me Bentwaters was a helping hand type of thing on our part. The alien craft was getting ready to crash and needed some work and we actually had our Air Force mechanics try to figure out with the Ebens what to do. And they ended up manufacturing something."

"Did you ever hear anything about time travelers at Bentwaters?"

"You mean besides the Ebens?"

"Maybe different, or are Ebens time travelers from the future?"

"I think the Ebens can travel in and out of time any way they want to. I think that's why they know the future, what's going to happen. And I think they even know how to tinker around with time lines to change things."

"Sherman, what about the tall blonds who are human-looking aliens about five to six feet tall?"

"Yeah, they have blond or real pale hair. Females have longer hair. Very slender. Nose and eyes are similar to humans, but they have invisible, double lids, apparently for filtering light or something. It's confusing, though, because the Ebens have made humanoids that actually look human, a spitting image of a high cheekboned human with Scandinavian features. And so have the bad guys."

"Who are the bad guys?"

"The Greys."

"Why are they bad?"

"They lie and they cause problems among the citizenry."

"You mean, human abductions and animal mutilations?"

"Well, officially, the government has never acknowledged that the aliens abducted anybody."

"But we know that non-humans are abducting humans."

Sherman laughed. "Yeah, you could probably make a good argument for that, but I never read anything official where MJ-12 admitted it. Everything I've read is about the cooperation between the Ebens and the humans in the Red Book and the Yellow Book. It's all about the Ebens and nothing about the Greys, other than what the Ebens write about Greys in the Yellow Book. And that's not just about Greys, but all the other different races the Ebens have come upon in their exploration of the universe and how they view those different other races."

"What is the Red Book?"

"We wrote the Red Book based on the information we've gathered ourselves about the Ebens."

"What's the difference between the Greys and the Ebens?"

"The Greys are similar in appearance, but they wear a different uniform or suit with different insignias and colors. I don't remember exactly which. The Greys have crude telepathic abilities compared to the Ebens and the Greys are more reckless. They aren't as compassionate as the Ebens. But in truth, I don't think the Ebens have always explained to us what they are doing like they're supposed to."

"In the SOM1-01 Majestic-12 Training Manual, extraterrestrial biological entities are broken down into two groups: EBE I and EBE II. EBE II is described as smaller. Is it an android or an independent grey group?

"I think the EBE Type I and II are connected and II are either Eben androids or are involved with the Greys, or both. The study of the different types was never my assignment."

"Well, what is the relationship between the Greys and the Ebens?"

"They were enemies at one time. They are supposed to live without war today, but the Ebens have no control over the Greys. The Greys do their thing and the Ebens do theirs."

"Is there a pecking order among the alien types?"

"To the best of our knowledge, no cooperation exists between the different alien groups. And I think there was a war about 6,000 years ago between the Ebens and the Blonds over territorial rights to a planet somewhere. I don't know if it was out at Zeta Reticuli or around here or what."

"So both groups, the Ebens and the Blond Humanoids make android creatures to do work for them on different planets?"

"That's what I understand. Androids come in many different types — insect, humanoid MIBs (Men In Black), and others. All have an advanced implanted brain that can operate on its own or by remote control.[69] Ironically, we think some of these genetically engineered creatures have a higher intelligence than their creators."

[69] *See remote-control relationship between tall humanoid "Elders" and small grey beings in Betty Andreasson segment of Chapter 4.*

"Is Bigfoot working for any of these groups?"

"I don't know."

"So there are the Ebens, Greys and the Blond Humanoids. Are they the main groups you know about?"

"Yes."

"And then below the Ebens are the Big Nosed types, Eben scientist-types, Men In Black, Reptoids and small grey worker drones?"

"Yes. And sometimes I think they have made, or work with, small blond humanoids, which really confuses the picture!"

"And the reptilian humanoids?"

"The androids can be reptilian. Both groups — the Ebens and the Blond Humanoids — can make robots or androids that can be anything they want them to be. Both groups know how to mix and match genomes in DNA easily. Remember, they are millions of years advanced beyond us." (See Wanna Lawson encounter Chapter 4.)

"And the Eben's genetic experimentation in Tibet — does that connect somehow to the Dalai Lama?[70] I'm thinking about reincarnation through different beings and different cycles of life. Would that concept relate to an Eben supposedly telling an Air Force Captain in 1949 that recycling of souls is the machinery of the universe?"

"Exactly. There are only so many souls that just continuously recycle."

"Through life form bodies that are containers?"

"Right. Exactly."

"We're carbon-based life forms on earth. I wonder if there are humanoid life forms that aren't carbon-based?"

"I don't know."

"And if there are more containers than souls, what happens?"

"I don't know. But souls are interconnected in some way. I think they told us that because the Ebens have been around so long, they have learned that there are only so many souls in this universe which must be recycled."

"If there is a finite number of souls in the universe and the Ebens know that and yet we are living on a planet in which there is an exponential increase in the number of bodies, does that imply that not all bodies can have souls?"

"I guess you have a point there."

"And if not all body containers have souls, would the Ebens and Blond humanoids have some stake invested in souls — like souls could be the coin of the realm, so to speak?"

"That's possible, I guess. I never thought of it that way before."

"Some abductee researchers such as Dr. Leo Sprinkle, a Wyoming psychologist, and Harvard University psychiatrist Dr. John Mack have stumbled onto what appears to be a continuity of the same Ebens or 'greys' present from human life to human life because the same alien being comes up in past life regressions at births and at deaths."

"I don't know. All I do know is that the soul — when the body container dies — the soul contains or maintains or keeps some thoughts or something from that life that was just lived."

"What role do you think Christ has played in all of this if it's true that the Ebens had a connection to his birth on this planet and are somehow involved with the recycling of souls?

"I think there is a lot that is beyond human comprehension. Maybe we couldn't understand it — or handle it — if the Ebens told us straight out."

"Did you learn anything more about souls and containers?"

"It said in the Yellow Book that the Ebens are concerned about human souls if our particular species continued on its course. They are afraid we would damage our container bodies and that could damage the souls."

[70] *The Dalai Lama is the traditional governmental ruler and highest priest of the Buddhist religion in Tibet and Mongolia founded in 1391 in Central Tibet. Buddhism is a religion and philosophy founded by Siddartha Gautama in northeast India between the 6th and 4th centuries B. C. When combined with Bon, an indigenous religion in Tibet that regarded kings as sky gods, Tibetan Buddhism evolved into a belief of reincarnate lamas, each being a rebirth of the original Dalai Lama's divine spirit.*

"Our body containers would damage our souls?"

"Yeah."

"How?"

"I don't know. I realize the containers are the human bodies. And that was why they were so concerned with what we have been doing, the wars and so forth. They are afraid that the souls will be damaged by our containers."

"One of the MJ-12 guys who had seen more of the Yellow Book talked to me about an analogy. He said that when you put something in a container and you pour it out, there's always some residue that remains. Something remains in that soul, so when you pass the soul on in different containers, it picks up the residues of all the different containers it has been in and a little of each remains and stays throughout. I guess there's an eternity, there's no end. That's a question I asked him: 'Does the soul wear out after so many recycles?' He said, 'No, no, no — souls never wear out. The Supreme Being makes sure that doesn't happen.'"

While reviewing this section, attorney and research colleague Michael Pill of Shutesbury, Massachusetts wrote to me:

"The notion of the 'soul picking up residues' may explain why we have memories of past lives. It may also explain why, after spending thousands of years and who knows how many wretched lifetimes trying to work out the karma from one or more evil incarnations, one can still feel the enticing charm of 'the dark side.' Those seven deadly sins are like predators — they've got you before you realize they are there."

I asked Sherman, "Is there a Devil out there somewhere?"

"There is an evil force. Even the Ebens talk about it. There is a Supreme Being and then there is the Evil One. The Evil Entity. The Ebens are as scared of that Evil Entity as we are of the Devil. The Devil or Satan. It's the same."

"Where is the Devil?"

"I don't know. But what worries me is that if the Ebens are scared of him, I'm damned scared of him because the Ebens can control everything! They have been around this universe and done everything. And if they believe in the same Supreme Being that we call God, and they say there is an Evil One — then there really is a Devil."

"Would the devil be equal to and opposite of the positive God? Are there two Gods?"

"I don't know. You can think about that forever. There's another thing that puzzles me. The Ebens say that everything that occurs in our Time Span has occurred before."

"Everything that occurs in our Time Span has occurred before?"

"Right. I guess it means we're just right in the middle of a huge, big circle and it just goes around and round again. And the way I see this is that earth was created and one day five billion years from now, the Sun is going to expand and earth will be engulfed and destroyed and everything goes back into a big bang and everything starts over again."

"When the Yellow Book talked about the Supreme Being that created the universe, did it say anything about parallel dimensions, parallel time lines, or anything else like that?"

"No, nothing. The aliens talked about the vastness of the universe, that there are life forms all over. It talks about a Supreme Being creating the souls and creating the containers and distributing the souls to the containers. To the Ebens, it's just basic facts."

"Sherman, if you know all this, does the President, too?"

"No. Vital information about the core questions can be hidden from even the President. He is treated on a need-to-know basis. And real answers are often hidden between the lines."

"Any information about earth catastrophes happening by 2000?"

"No, we have no knowledge regarding any catastrophes occurring on earth within the next few years. But we are preparing for our Eben friends to return to earth soon."

"Do you have any specific dates?"

"They're supposed to be back in 1997 for a meeting with MJ-12. I don't know if it will be made public or not."

"Do you have any understanding about what the Ebens want after all the millions of years of interactions with our planet?"

"No, except they set us in motion and are watching us grow, like 'watching children grow' is the way it's been described to me."

"Well, the Ebens must have their hands full if this warring humanity is what they created."

"I don't know. There's so much out there that we just don't understand."

"If there is a finite number of souls and the Ebens are concerned about humans damaging souls by damaging our body containers with violence, why do you think the Vatican says there should be no birth control or abortion? It's almost as if the Catholic Church is promoting the creation of containers. In a finite-soul universe, that's a difficult position to take, isn't it?"

"It's a good question. I don't know."

"Has anybody discussed whether the Ebens check out souls the way we check out books for information?"

"Nope, I never heard that."

"Well, some abductees think our bodies and souls are checked out like CD-ROMs so that all experiences and knowledge can be 'played back.' That way the aliens don't have to literally live here to experience and know everything that has happened here over eons."

"Interesting possibility, but I don't know."

"If the Ebens made us and put us here, there has to be a reason. Are we a garden growing containers for souls to be harvested for some reason?"

"It's another good question. All I can tell you is that one elderly man with MJ-12 told me 'You don't want to know that' when I asked him about souls and why the Ebens made us."

"Sherman, some abductees also say that the main reason for the animal mutilations and human abductions has to do with the creation of a hybrid species. But no one knows whether the hybrids are supposed to replace the current *Homo sapiens* container model. There is a sense that whatever the non-humans are up to, it has something to do with survival — theirs and ours."

"Maybe. All I now is that the Ebens are supposed to have manipulated DNA in primates long before humans were created. So there must have been a series of experiments like Neanderthal before Cro-Magnon. And Neanderthal's gone. So who knows what's on the agenda for humans?"

A landmark study in the July 1997 scientific journal *Cell* reported that Neanderthal DNA is *not* linked to human DNA.[71] Researchers from Germany and the U. S. extracted less than one one-hundredth of an ounce from the upper arm bone of the first fossilized Neanderthal skeleton ever found in the Neander valley of Germany. Maternal DNA from a pulverized piece of the bone estimated to be 100,000 years old was compared with genetic material from hundreds of people around the modern world.

Svante Paabo, the University of Munich genetics expert who led the six-year effort, said: "This is the first genetic information we have from Neanderthals and it gives no indication that any mixing between the two groups (Cro-Magnon and Neanderthals) would have taken place."

The results indicated that the last ancestor common to both species was most likely *Homo erectus* about 600,000 years ago. It is assumed that the precursor to modern humanity emerged from Africa about 100,000 years ago. If Sherman is correct about the Ebens performing a series of genetic experiments with primates on this planet, it might explain why Neanderthal was allowed to die out while the most recent Cro-Magnon *Homo sapiens sapiens* model that overlapped Neanderthal is a robust survivor. But which primate about forty thousand years ago did the EBEs use to create Cro-Magnon? And why? To the EBEs, we could be a newer model android designed to do work

[71] *"Neanderthal DNA Sequences and the Origin of Modern Humans" by M. Krings, A. Stone, R. W. Schmitz, H. Krainitzki, M. Stoneking and S. Paabo,* Cell, *Issue 14, Volume 90, No. 1 © 1997 Cell Press, Cambridge, Mass.*

for them on this planet without our being conscious of the services and products we provide. Humans might also be an experiment of biology and soul. Survival could be directly linked to spiritual growth and keener perceptions of the unseen, not material acquisitions and technologies.

Survival is a reoccurring theme in the chapters to come — ours and the Others, whether extraterrestrial biological entities, time travelers, interdimensionals, angels, or a mixture of them all. Many in the abduction syndrome have said that whatever the aliens are and want, we humans affect them, too. Perhaps one truth is Jim Penniston's revelation that the Bentwaters entities were time travelers on a grand mission to avoid extinction in a distant human future. If that is one of the hidden facts, all of us could understand and have sympathy for the men and women in government who have had to ride out such difficult and confusing discoveries.

But how long can government knowledge and cover-up go on without destroying its own relationship with the citizens it is supposed to govern and protect? On August 16, 1958, Major Donald Keyhoe received a letter postmarked Zurich, Switzerland from Carl Gustav Jung, M.D. The renowned psychiatrist had written a book that year entitled *Flying Saucers: A Modern Myth of Things Seen in the Sky.*[72] Dr. Jung speculated that the phenomenon might be psychic projections related to mankind's anxieties about the threat of nuclear annihilation, but changed his mind before his death in 1961 and came down on the side of real physical craft.

He wrote Keyhoe: "If it is true that the A. A. F. (American Air Force) or the government withholds telling facts, then one can only say that this is the most unpsychological and stupid policy one could invent. Nothing helps rumors and panics more than ignorance. It is self-evident that the public ought to be told the truth, because ultimately it will nevertheless come to the daylight. There can hardly be any greater shock than the H-bomb and yet anybody knows of it without fainting."[73]

Some of the facts the U. S. government has withheld about the non-human presence are its very advanced technologies. There are glowing beams which can lift humans and animals from bedrooms, backyards and pastures. The mysterious beams look like solid tubes of dust or fog. In the next chapter, several civilians describe how those beams picked up animals and dropped them to the ground, dead and mutilated. And a military witness was stunned to see a "human-like" figure that rose in a "solid and cylindrical" tube of foggy, white light.

[72] Flying Saucers: A Modern Myth of Things Seen in the Sky © *1959 Carl G. Jung, M.D., Harcourt, Brace & Co., New York.*

[73] Flying Saucers: TOP SECRET *© 1960 by Major Donald E. Keyhoe, U. S. Marine Corps. (Ret.)*

CHAPTER 2

LIGHT BEAMS, DISCS AND ANIMAL DEATHS

"All of a sudden, this light beam came down from the blue base of a round, lighted object in the sky, a kind of milky white light that I could see right through. And it came down and surrounded the cow, and the cow started to levitate. The cow went stiff and its head popped up and its eyes were wide open and its tongue was sticking out. And it went up."

TIMOTHY FINT
Certified Medical Assistant
Portland, Oregon

Steve Bismarck was clearing a trail through the fir trees and swamp behind his house in Snohomish, Washington on the Saturday before Easter in 1977. The forested land had belonged to his family for over thirty years. Far enough east of Seattle to be in a wilderness with few neighbors, Bismarck liked the isolation. He still likes his privacy and requested his real name not be used. Back in 1977, he was 38 years old and commuted to work at a Seattle ship yard. His parents lived in Everett, Washington and Steve's father liked to visit and garden when the weather was good. That Saturday afternoon, Bismarck Sr. had been waiting for Steve to come back with the shovel so he could dig. But if Mr. Bismarck had known what was happening to his son, he probably would have called the sheriff.

Steve had been pulling up vine maples by the roots and had decided to stop for awhile and return the shovel to his dad. He started back to the house a different way than he had come and encountered a pool of water.

"I didn't feel like crossing through the water," he told me, "so I turned around and started walking back the other way and I see a guy. I had never seen another human back there, no hunters or anything, other than family members who knew how to get back there. My first impression of him was that he was a little old man."

Steve said the "guy" was about four feet tall and very slender, but well-muscled. The skin was pale brown, "like a light-complexioned Filipino. (See: EBE Type I, Pages 71-73). But he looked like maybe he had been in a fire, scarred-looking." The small being was wearing a "sparkly metallic blue" uniform that fit his thin body. Under his right arm, he carried a helmet that seemed to be clear plastic with a white colored section in the back.

"It's like we both see each other at the same time. I almost felt that he was as surprised as I was. And he takes a few steps to his right and it's like he gets all blurry. And it's just like he's vibrating. It's like his features are contorting. This all happened in seconds and that's when I got puzzled.

Plate 1 - *"The eyes sort of reminded me of those wrap-around sunglasses," Steve Bismarck wrote about his drawing. "This person appeared to have been in a fire, or to have extremely severe acne scars, healed over."*

"It's like he's standing there vibrating, almost like he's doing a jitterbug or something. And down through the trees comes another guy. While he's coming down, it sounds like a hive of bees. He's got a metallic blue uniform on, too. And I'm standing there wondering how the hell those guys can get down through those big trees? The limbs overlapped each other."

Plate 2 - *"I realize you can't draw air," Steve Bismarck wrote with this drawing. "But it looked like a tunnel of air or a cyclone was surrounding these clear plastic or glass, egg-shaped objects. They sounded like a hive of bees on the way down and went reasonably slow. When they shot skyward, at a high rate of speed, they sounded like ducks flying. I believe they use these air tunnels like an elevator."*

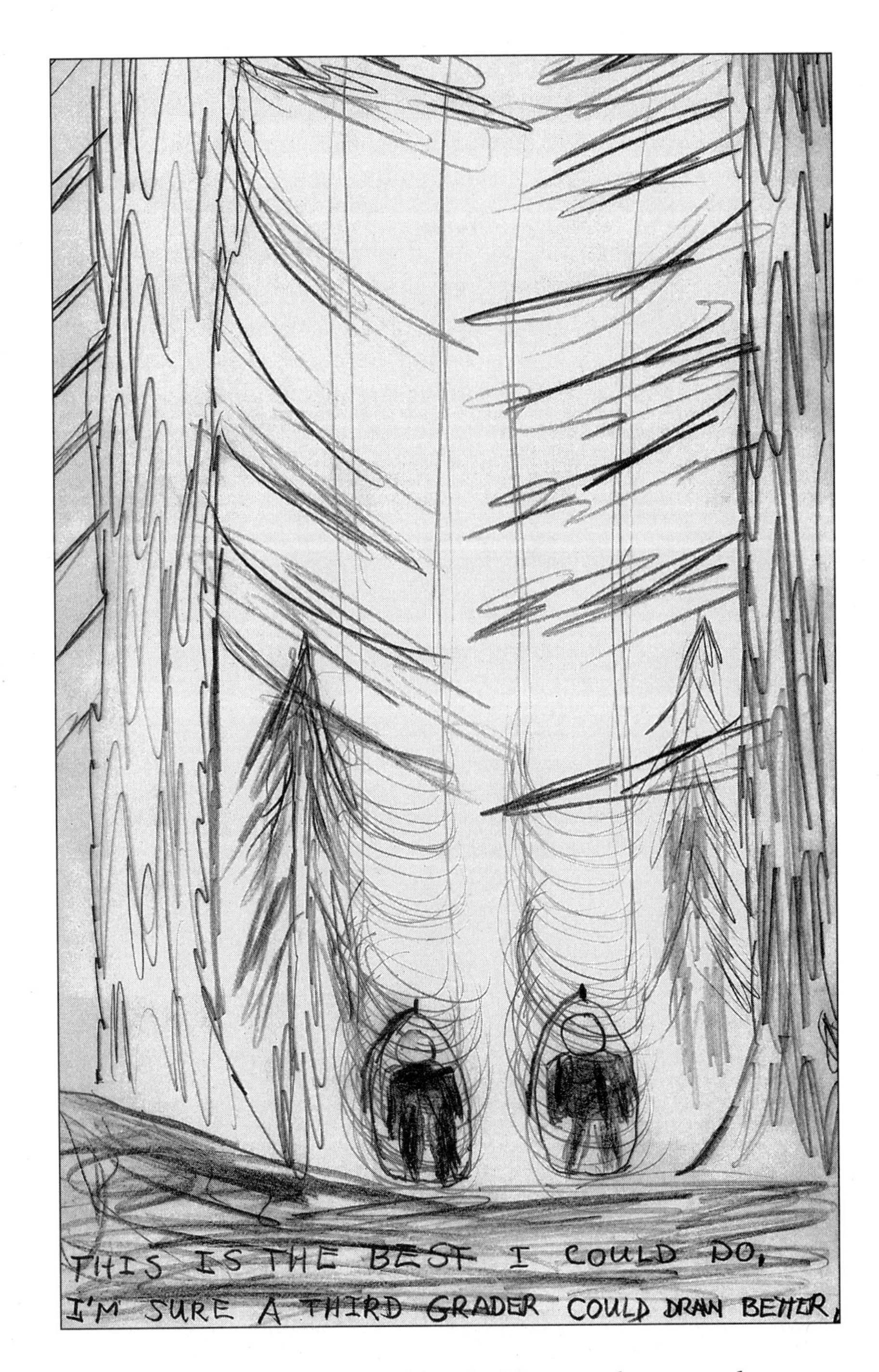

Steve realized there was an egg-shaped object on the ground next to the first being that was almost transparent. A rod stuck out the top and was attached to a small blade that curved down around the top of the transparent oval machine which was vibrating. Bismarck saw the first being step inside the jiggling "egg" as the second humanoid came down through the trees. That would explain the "small man's" sudden vibrating, blurry appearance. The second being landed in his own "egg" near the first one.

"To me," Steve said, "it looked like that egg thing was inside of some kind of air tunnel. And if I was to say what it was, it looked to me like some kind of a technologically advanced form of an elevator. Maybe something was a mile up in the sky and these things go up and down inside columns of air or energy. Because when the second guy come down, it sounded just like a hive of bees."

Then both of the strange beings stepped out of their transparent "eggs" which continued to jiggle noticeably while setting on the ground. The two men walked a distance from the "eggs" which then took off straight skyward.

"And when they took off, it sounded like a flock of ducks, but coming down they sounded like a hive of bees. Then they disappeared and was gone."

Steve Bismarck was staring at the two, small beings about sixty feet away when he heard a high pitched whine that reminded him first of a train and then a helicopter.

The object seemed to be aluminum or
stainless steel. I was telling myself not to look up.

Plate 3 - *"This thing in the air had some kind of a bearing that spins around the outer edge. And this was when fear overtook me," Bismarck wrote about this drawing. "It sounds similar to a train going on a railroad track, clickity-click. It also had a bell-shaped object hanging down from the center. When this craft dropped down to the treetops, the wind from it was so violent I thought it was going to snap the tops of the big fir trees down on to me."*

"It gets practically up to above our heads and the motor cuts and I hear some popping sounds. And I look up and there is a flying saucer and it's dropping like a ton of lead. And I'm thinking, 'That thing is crashing.' And I'm scared. It gets to about thirty or forty feet above the big fir trees out there and it lets out a huge roaring noise. Then the saucer stopped in the air right above the treetops.

"The wind was whipping those big fir trees back and forth so violently that I thought the tops were going to snap and fall down on us. My clothes were flopping back and forth and my hair was flying all around. That thing up there, you could hear air coming out of it and you could hear like a bearing on the outside. It kind of reminded me of a train going along a track because you could hear a clickety click, clickety click[1] and that wind coming out.

"Now that flying saucer is over my head and over those guys up there hovering about thirty feet above the treetops. It's at least fifty feet in diameter, maybe eighty. And I'm thinking, 'Maybe they ain't seen me. If I stand real still, maybe they won't even notice me.'"

But Steve could see the two beings staring at him. Then he saw "specks" come together in the air that reminded him of the static "snow" on old black

[1] The Jim Ragsdale Story, A Closer Look at the Roswell Incident *© 1996 by Ragsdale Productions, Inc. Ragsdale described seeing a crashed disc the night of July 4, 1947 in which "all around the bottom of the capsule were little wheels that had more wheels. I figured these had to have something to do with how it maneuvered and flew."*

Plate 4 - *"It was as if a bunch of black specks collected together in the air to form this animal," Bismarck wrote about this drawing. "I believe it was electronically produced. It would no sooner appear than it would be on me. I would get a shock and go blind for a few seconds. Every time this happened, there would be a hyena-like cackling noise. The best way I can describe this thing is a wolf-like animal with goat-like horns and a lion-like tail that stood on its hind legs."*

and white television sets. The specks took on the shape of a wolf with horns and a long tail like a lion's.

"That thing moved towards me fast and I couldn't even duck. When they'd get to me, it's like I got an electronic shock. That sounds like a B.S. yarn, I know it does. But I don't feel like it was a real animal. To me it was like the specks gathered together and was on me. Then I felt like I was being laughed at. Like maybe there was cackling or something."

Steve cannot remember events after that clearly, but thinks the animal image came at him several times and felt like an electric shock each time. There was a gap in his memory related to a period of missing time.

A few months later in February 1978, a Snohomish County investigator named Jerry Phillips arranged to have local hypnotherapist Richard Anderson work with Bismarck to help penetrate the mystery of what happened after the electric shocks. The following are excerpts from three hypnosis sessions conducted between February 17 and May 13, 1978. This segment began with Bismarck looking up at the large silver disc and trying to describe details about its underside structure.

EXCERPTS FROM STEVE BISMARK HYPNOSIS SESSIONS, FEBRUARY 17 AND MAY 13, 1978:

B: "Underneath there was a bell-shaped object."

A: "Underneath the craft?"

B: "Yes."

A: "Bell-shaped in what way? Was it a bell hanging down like a normal bell? Or was it upside down?"

B: "It was smaller in diameter than the bottom of the craft and I believe there was a hole on each side of the outer edge of this bell."

A: "Hole on each side of the outer edge. Now, you have described the craft as being about sixty feet across. You are looking at it quite clearly now. Describing this as sixty feet across and the bell-shaped part extending downward. How much of the sixty feet did the bell take up?"

B: "I'd say about fifty feet."

A: "You're saying it was centered?"

B: "Yes."

A: "How far did the edge of the bell extend down below the craft?"

B: "This is only a guess, but about four feet."

A: "OK, that's good. Now continue telling me about the holes that you saw on the rim of the bell-shaped flange."

B: "They were on the outer side near the edge of the craft. Maybe twenty-four to thirty six inches in diameter."

A: "Could you see anything within the holes?"

B: "No."

A: "Are you aware of the holes' function?"

B: "My interpretation was it made an air tunnel."

A: "An air tunnel, OK. An air passage. Was the air coming out of those holes?"

B: " I think they can make cyclones with them. That first guy looked like he was standing inside of a cyclone. And when the second man come down, he looked the same way except that when he was coming down, he reminded me of a bee, like when a bee is flying in turbulence with its wings fluttering back and forth. I'm not sure if I'm completely accurate, but these objects that come down and are shaped like eggs had a blade coming from the top down the side. I don't believe they had any motor in them. I think this wind would shoot down on this object and the blade would spin around and they could drop like a parachute. Whether they worked like that, I don't know."

A: "But that's an impression you had?"

B: "The impression I got from seeing everything work."

A: "Now, Steve, getting a clearer picture, perceiving the bottom of the craft more clearly, something happened apparently that has caused you to feel a certain amount of anxiety about the underside. Is that true?"

B: "Yes. This thing's up there hovering and the wind is gushing and the bearing was going around the outside clicking, and my hair was flying all over the place. There was a sound like an electric hoist of some kind, and this bell is telescoping down. There's a dark area up there and up in the dark area I think there's windows.

"... It seems like I was standing there looking and the *Sasquatch is being lowered on a cable.* (Howe's emphasis.) They lowered him right down in front of my eyes!"

A: "You think something was lowered down in front of you?"

B: "Yeah, I think the Sasquatch was."

A: "You think the Sasquatch was left there?"

B: "Yeah."

A: "Where are the men?"

B: "There's a dark area up there and up in the dark area I think there's windows. And at two of the windows, beings are staring down at me. I feel like I'm having a stare down with one of the two men looking at me. I know I'm scared to death. I felt I was witnessing something that could be dangerous to my health."

A: "Now, at one point in a previous hypnotic episode and review, you told me of a kind of experience you had that was apparently within the craft itself. You weren't sure if it was a dream or not."

B: "OK. In this dream, I feel like small men are around me. And this is vague."

A: "Let me count to three and it will become somewhat clearer and you'll see a certain amount of clarification. It will be a little clearer to you. Accept a certain level of anxiety. When I count to 3, this vagueness will clear and you'll remember more than you did before. 1, 2, becoming clearer now, 3."

B: "What happened, or what I dreamed, there are four small men around me, different (men) from the first two men that I seen. These men had metallic blue uniforms on with metallic blue helmets that sparkled and it seems like I had some kind of a thrill, like (I was) going up extremely fast.

"And I'm in a dome. It's got a black, shiny floor. Dark red inside. Seems like the lighting is coming from the walls somewhere, not walls, but the dome down towards the floor. There's two or three men there without helmets on and it seems like they're covered with light brown fuzz on their head and neck."

A: "Can you see the rest of their body?"

B: "It's covered by their uniform. And it seems like towards the other side there's a couple of guys sitting at a switchboard and it seems like there is language going on."

A: "Can you hear it?"

B: "Like there's radios with Russian language and English, Oriental languages ..."

A: "What's the purpose of all the languages, do you know?"

B: "I don't know. Just all these different languages are coming in on radios."

A: "Do you recognize any of the English, what's being played or spoken?"

B: "It's like I'm numb and I wouldn't swear to it, but it seems like a mild electric current going through my body. And these three guys — I've got real ragged clothes on and it seems like they're laughing (at me) a little bit."

A: "Because of the clothes?"

> B: "I don't know. And it seems like I hear them talk. And I can't explain the language. But I seen a midget one time on a TV show and the pitch of his voice reminded me of their voice. And then it seems like I'm crying mentally. I can't explain it. But I feel like I'm going to be taken away and I don't want to leave. And it seems like I'm blubbering and I feel like I'm pleading and I'm saying, 'Please don't take me. I don't want to leave!'"
>
> A: "Did they reply to you?"
>
> B: "I can't recall them talking to me whatsoever, although I feel like they talked *about* me. And then the next thing, it seems like I see a man with a light outfit on, like a doctor, that looked like the first man I seen down on the ground. Then there was a black man, the same size, maybe a little bigger, with a white outfit on, looked like a pygmy with a fairly modern hairdo. The man with the shaved head, it seems like he had my eye out and he stabbed me with a needle back up through the socket or wherever my eye came out and I was numb-like. Then I'm on the ground, back in the woods."

What happened next is what Steve Bismarck has always remembered consciously since Easter weekend 1977.

"Those strange guys were walking away and it seems like there were nine of them. Then I could see small tanks on their backs. They reminded me of ten-year-old kids in football uniforms in a way. Their heads were bigger than normal (perhaps wearing helmets like Bismarck noticed under the first being's arm.) And when they was walking, you could hear twigs snap and everything just like anyone else walking in the woods. They were gone and I thought it was all over with.

"But then I heard a thud to my right and a Bigfoot walked through going the same direction as those little guys. It was like he was following behind them."

Steve said the Bigfoot or Sasquatch creature was about eight feet tall, had a cone-shaped head and solid black hair about four inches long all over its body.

"When I hear this thud and this Bigfoot comes walking, I get on the ground because I think maybe he won't see me. It walked on through in the very same direction that those little guys went. I lay there for awhile and then got up. It was all quiet. It was almost like nothing ever happened. And I got brave and jumped out there with the shovel. I even walked over the direction they walked. Couldn't see nothin' over that way so I headed back home. I kept telling myself, 'I got to remember all this. I got to tell this when

I get back.' I think I also feared for my dad a little bit. I get back there and he comes up to me and says, 'Goddamn it, kid. Where have you been?!'"

"I said, 'You ain't going to believe it, but I seen a Bigfoot back there.' And he says, 'You probably seen a bear. You've been gone for hours. I'm ready to go home.'"

"And I said, 'Bullshit, I've only been gone fifteen minutes!'"

"He says, 'You've been gone for hours! Look, it's almost dark out.'"

"He couldn't convince me that I'd been gone that long. He said he was ready to go back into the swamp and look for me. Strange thing is that the only thing I remembered then was the Bigfoot."

When Bismarck went to work two days later, he told some of his fellow workers who then made fun of him. But while he worked, his partial amnesia began to wear off and bits of memory about the beings, egg-shaped "elevators," UFO and Sasquatch, or Bigfoot, came back.

Bismarck called the Snohomish Sheriff's Department and Jerry Phillips responded. Phillips explained that he was looking into unusual phenomena for the sheriff because so many people were reporting strange lights and unusual animal deaths. Phillips went back into the swamp and photographed several dozen holes in the ground where Bismarck saw the egg-shaped machines on the ground vibrating.

Steve Bismarck also told me that he and his nephew took their guns and searched the swamp. "In an area about 500 feet west of where I seen all this, I found all these holes about one and a half inches in diameter and four inches deep. I believe these holes were made by the egg-shaped objects. It looked as though they had come down hundreds of times back there."

Five months later in the early morning hours of August 8, 1977, Bismarck got home from a night out and went to get some corn and barley to feed young calves he was raising.

"I hear what sounds like a bunch of coyotes yelping out in the back. It sounded like a hundred of them. I thought maybe coyotes had a deer and were tearing it apart. Then it sounded like puppies getting crushed by something stomping on them! So then I think maybe they're tangling with a bear. And pretty soon, something starts screaming. And it's a scary, high-pitched scream. Then all the coyote noises stop. And this thing is still screaming and I slam the door shut. I run and get my 30-30. And I'm thinking that thing could be up to my house in just seconds."

"Then my sister next door calls up and said, 'Did you hear that noise? I thought it was going to knock the house down!'"

"I told her, 'I think it was the Bigfoot howling.' And I called Phillips and told him what was happening. He said that someone else had called him to report they had seen a large, orange glowing object drop down in the woods over my way. Phillips came out again and investigated. He didn't find any dead coyotes or other animals back there, but he found some tracks in the woods. He took plaster casts of them."

I talked with Jerry Phillips in March 1996 about Steve Bismarck's account and he remembered all of the story and more. He sent me a hundred pages of file reports and photographs, including a polaroid photo of a possible Bigfoot track cast in plaster on Steve Bismarck's farm. Phillips told me there were also dozens of unusual animal deaths in the Snohomish area similar to the several thousand animal mutilation cases reported worldwide since the 1960s. Phillips said there were several dozen unusual animal deaths near Steve Bismarck's home in 1977 and one of the strangest was a deer found hanging from a tree limb with odd, bloodless excisions of tissue from various parts of its body.

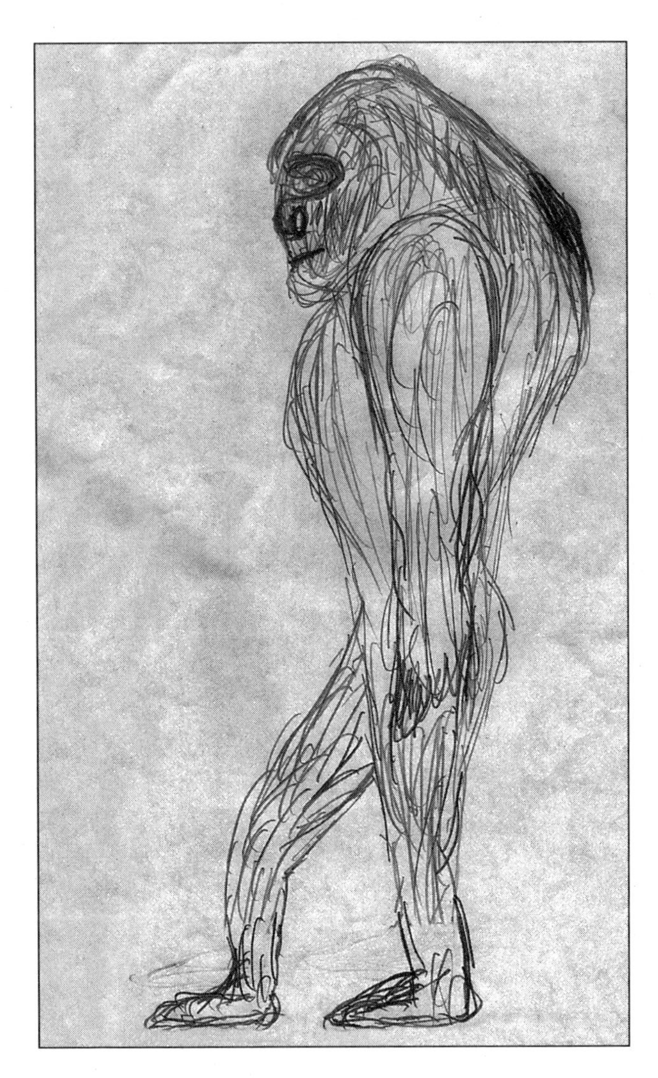

Plate 5 - *"This ape-like animal walked upright," Bismarck wrote about this drawing of a Bigfoot creature he saw in a forested swamp behind his Snohomish, Washington home. "It had extremely black hair about three inches long, or more. It had a big, cone-shaped head that extended down to a big hump on its back. And it didn't have a pot belly like apes do. Its legs were much longer than an ape's. I didn't draw them long enough. And the arms were shorter than an ape's. They seemed to swing to the extreme as it walked by."*

Plate 6 - *Holes found in swamp grass where Steve Bismarck saw the transparent egg-shaped devices and the two "Filipino guys" near his Snohomish, Washington home on Easter weekend, 1977. Photograph by Jerry Phillips.*

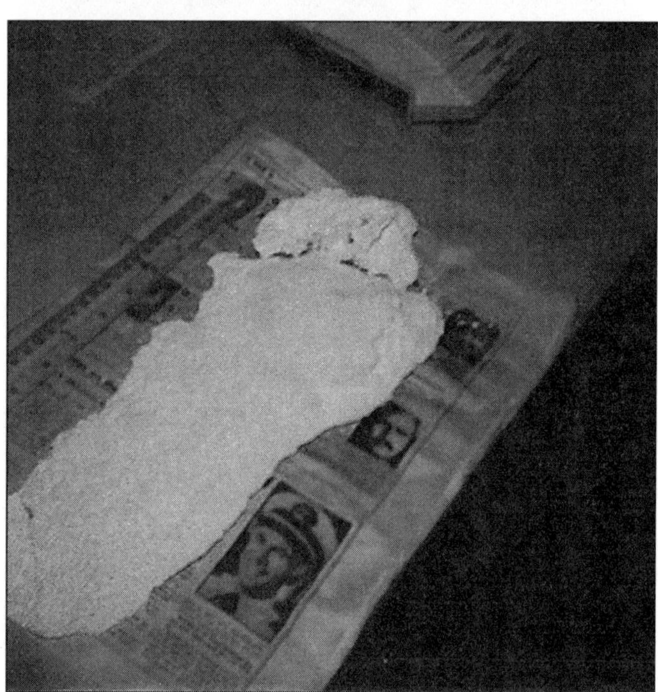

Plate 7 - *Plaster cast of Bigfoot track found on Steve Bismarck's forest swamp property during 1977 investigation. Photograph by Jerry Phillips.*

Plate 8 - *Looking toward the forested swamp at the back of Steve Bismarck's property in Snohomish, Washington. "The original spot: I'm east, looking west. The two "Filipino-looking" aliens were standing about where the two piles of blocks are. I was back about another thirty feet from where this picture was taken." Photograph by Steve Bismarck, March 1996.*

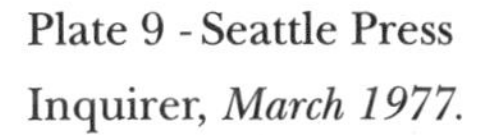

Plate 9 - Seattle Press Inquirer, *March 1977.*

GI in shock after seeing 'bigfoot'

EATONVILLE, Wash. (AP) – A serviceman reportedly was sent into shock by sighting a big, hairy creature he believed to be "bigfoot" near Eatonville last week, the Tacoma News Tribune reports.

An unidentified Ft. Lewis enlisted man reportedly saw "a big hairy thing" while hiking in woods near the Northwest Trek wild game preserve last week, the paper said.

A Madigan Army Medical Center doctor who treated the soldier for shock told the paper Tuesday the man still was "too unstable" to discuss the incident.

The doctor, who asked that his name be withheld, said he could not divulge the soldier's name, either because of the doctor-patient relationship.

However, the doctor said the soldier came to him "extremely upset" and would not discuss the reported sighting for some time.

"He is quite sure he saw Bigfoot," the doctor was quoted as saying.

No report of the incident was made with the Pierce County Sheriff's Office, deputies said.

Roger Thacker, Trek director, said today Trek had nothing to do with the incident.

"I can assure you it was no put-on by us. We have had nothing to do with any of these sightings. I did nothing and none of our people did anything.

"The doctor called me and told me the man was terrified and in an extreme state of shock," Thacker said.

Meanwhile, a Madigan ambulance driver told the newspaper he talked to a Puyallup man last September who sighted a similar creature near the Trek preserve.

The ambulance driver, Don Durden, a former policeman and civilian paramedic, was hiking near the Northwest Trek wildlife preserve and came across footprints that measured about 18 inches long an eight inches wide, the newspaper said.

"I'm 6-foot-4 and 285 pounds and my footprint was dwarfed in comparison with his," Durden said.

Sasquatch or Bigfoot stories from Snohomish and surrounding wilderness areas east of Seattle still make news headlines. On Thursday, November 9, 1995, the *Valley Daily News,* now known as the *South County Journal,* printed the story below about a July 11, 1995 Bigfoot encounter in the foothills of Snoqualmie National Forest.

Plate 10 - Valley Daily News, *(now South County Journal) Snohomish, Washington, November 9, 1995.*

Is it really Bigfoot?

Man says photos are real proof

Special to Valley Daily News

BOTHELL - Cliff Crook has spent most of his adult life in search of the legendary Bigfoot. After more than 39 years, the Bothell man believes he finally is on to something.

He claims to possess "conclusive photographic proof" of the elusive creature's existence.

"It's Bigfoot . . . if these pictures were any clearer, he would breathe," said Crook, 55.

He directs Bigfoot Central, a local group devoted to the investigation of the legendary creature, also known as Sasquatch. Crook said he acquired the series of pictures from a Tacoma man who took them July 11 in the Wild Creek area in the foothills of Snoqualmie National Forest.

Crook said as the man was hiking near a lagoon, he heard "heavy splashes," looked down and saw a hulking figure in the water.

"The creature just stood there and looked at him," Crook said. He said the man then grabbed his camera and took several pictures.

Crook is convinced the photographs are authentic. Two photography experts who examined the snapshots were a bit more skeptical, although neither would declare the photographs are fakes.

"It's hard to create a situation to duplicate it, but it wouldn't be too difficult for someone who knows how to use the camera," said Newell Burton, president of Bellevue-based Omega Photo Specialists.

"The odds are they're not real, but who knows?"

Burton said the photographs appear to be double exposures, or two pictures overlapping each other.

Gordon Kyle, a photo specialist from Overlake Photo in Bellevue, said it didn't appear as if the figure was cropped from another photo.

"It's seamless, but then again, who can say that this wasn't a posed model?"

Photo copyright 1995 CLIFF CROOK

Cliff Crook claims this photo is conclusive evidence of Bigfoot's existence.

Plate 11 - *Original photograph of alleged Bigfoot creature standing near river bank about 25 feet below photographer and published in* Valley Daily News *story. Alleged forestry employee who is still anonymous said he took a series of photos on July 11, 1995 in the Wild Creek area of the Snoqualmie National Forest foothills east of Seattle, Washington. Critics suggested it was a primate costume. Photo copyright is now held by Cliff Crook © 1995.*

Unusual animal deaths have been associated with Bigfoot-type creatures, beams of light, UFO discs, and strange beings since at least the 1960s.[2] Worldwide reports from eyewitnesses began to accelerate in number and frequency in the 1970s. One man had such a dramatic encounter that he reported it to an organization called the Aerial Phenomena Research Organization. APRO researcher and author Wendelle Stevens, a retired Air Force Lt. Colonel, wrote up a summary report about the case on May 21, 1977 from which the following information is summarized with his permission.

[2] An Alien Harvest *© 1989 and* Glimpses of Other Realities, Vol. 1 - Facts & Eyewitnesses *© 1994 by Linda Moulton Howe.*

In October 1972, Mesa, Arizona resident Ed Foley, now deceased, was travelling on U. S. Interstate Highway 10 near Casa Grande, Arizona in Oc-

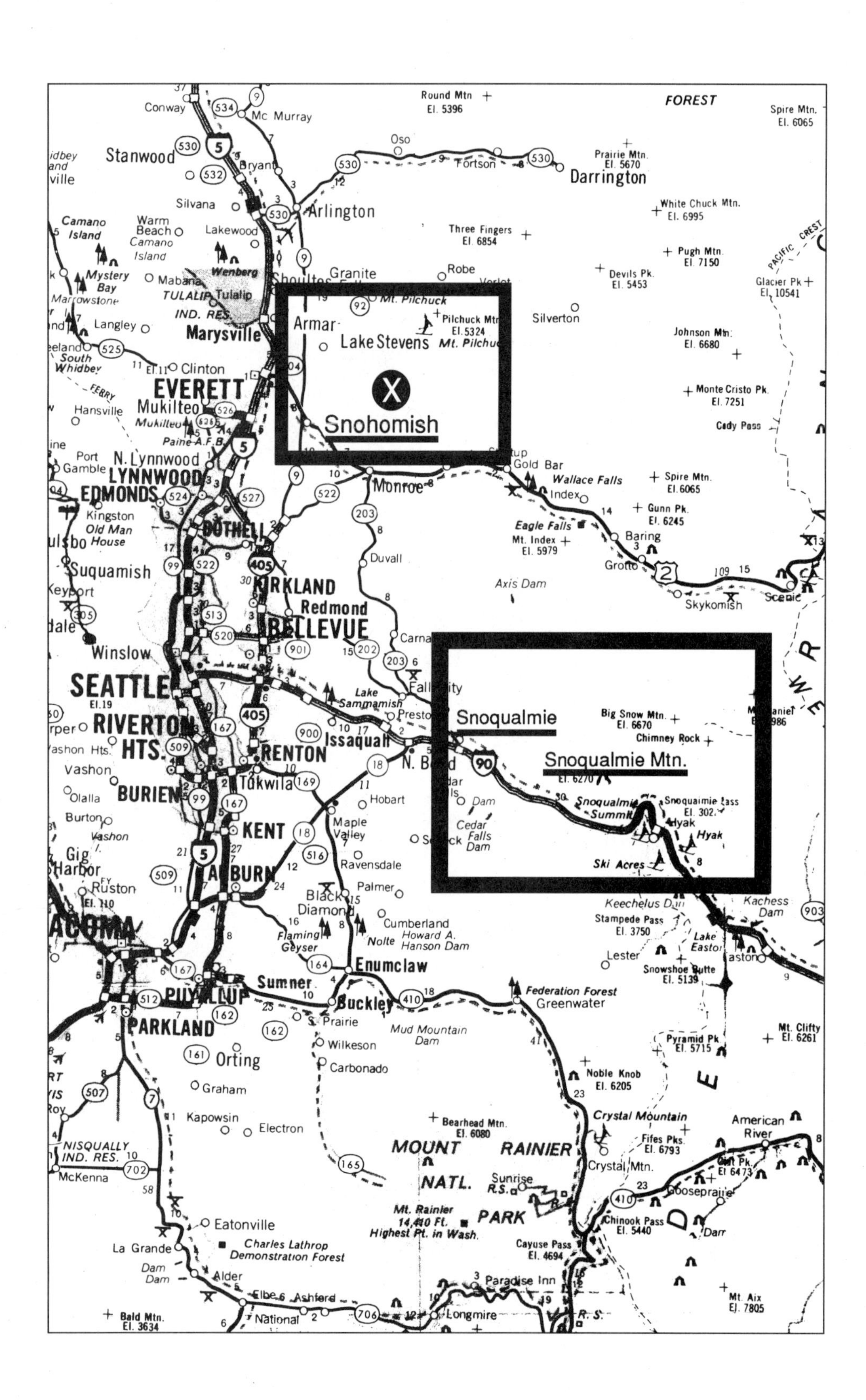

Plate 12- *Washington State map with Snohomish highlighted and a circled X at Steve Bismarck's location approximately forty miles northeast of Seattle. Also highlighted is Snoqualmie National Forest area where Bigfoot have been reported.*

tober. The time was between 11:30 PM and midnight. Foley stopped his car by the side of the road to relieve his bladder and shut off the engine and the lights, but left the radio playing. He moved to a ditch on the right side of the car. Then he heard a high-pitched squeal coming out of the radio. He looked up and noticed a bright star in the southwestern sky that was growing larger. As the light got closer, Foley saw that it was actually a yellowish-gold luminous disc.

"The whole thing was a brightly luminous brassy color with streaming rays of the same brassy color light radiating in all directions from the surface like strong heat waves."

Later he would draw a thin pancake-shaped object with a shallow dome on top. The disc slowed and hovered at about a 45 degree elevation not far from Foley who was still watching from the ditch at the side of the road.

As he watched, two light beams emerged from the bottom of the disc. Simultaneously, Foley's car radio changed to a higher pitched steady tone. Then a strange, mechanical-looking device came down in the first light beam followed by another machine in the second beam.

Foley told Wendelle Stevens: "The objects looked like a small squat cylinder mounted on top of a larger squat cylinder which sat on a thin platform from which four stovepipe legs projected downwards vertically. Some kind of an efflux was being emitted from the lower ends of the stovepipe legs which roiled the dust and chaff as it neared the ground, somewhat like a helicopter raises dust and chaff."

The first machine stopped about two or three feet above the ground and the other stopped higher above and behind. The motion of air around the machines had dirt and litter flying all around. Foley could see strange antenna-like devices protruding from the sides of both the smaller and larger cylinder sections which were rotating rapidly. Both had a rectangular opening in the shiny metal of the upper, smaller cylinder.

"Suddenly and without warning, a beam of soft, white shadowless light — like fluorescent light — flashed out of the rectangular opening in the upper smaller cylinder of the first machine." The light struck Foley, paralyzed him, and "knocked him out of his physical body." In that astral body or altered state of consciousness, he could see inside the larger circular ship above and also seemed to receive information about the intruders.

Ed Foley's impression was that the non-human intelligence was from a planet in which "its life form is nearing the end of its existence because the essential life essence is almost used up and there is no natural replenishment."

Foley understood that the six to seven foot tall robot machines were unmanned and were controlled from the circular ship. The controlling in-

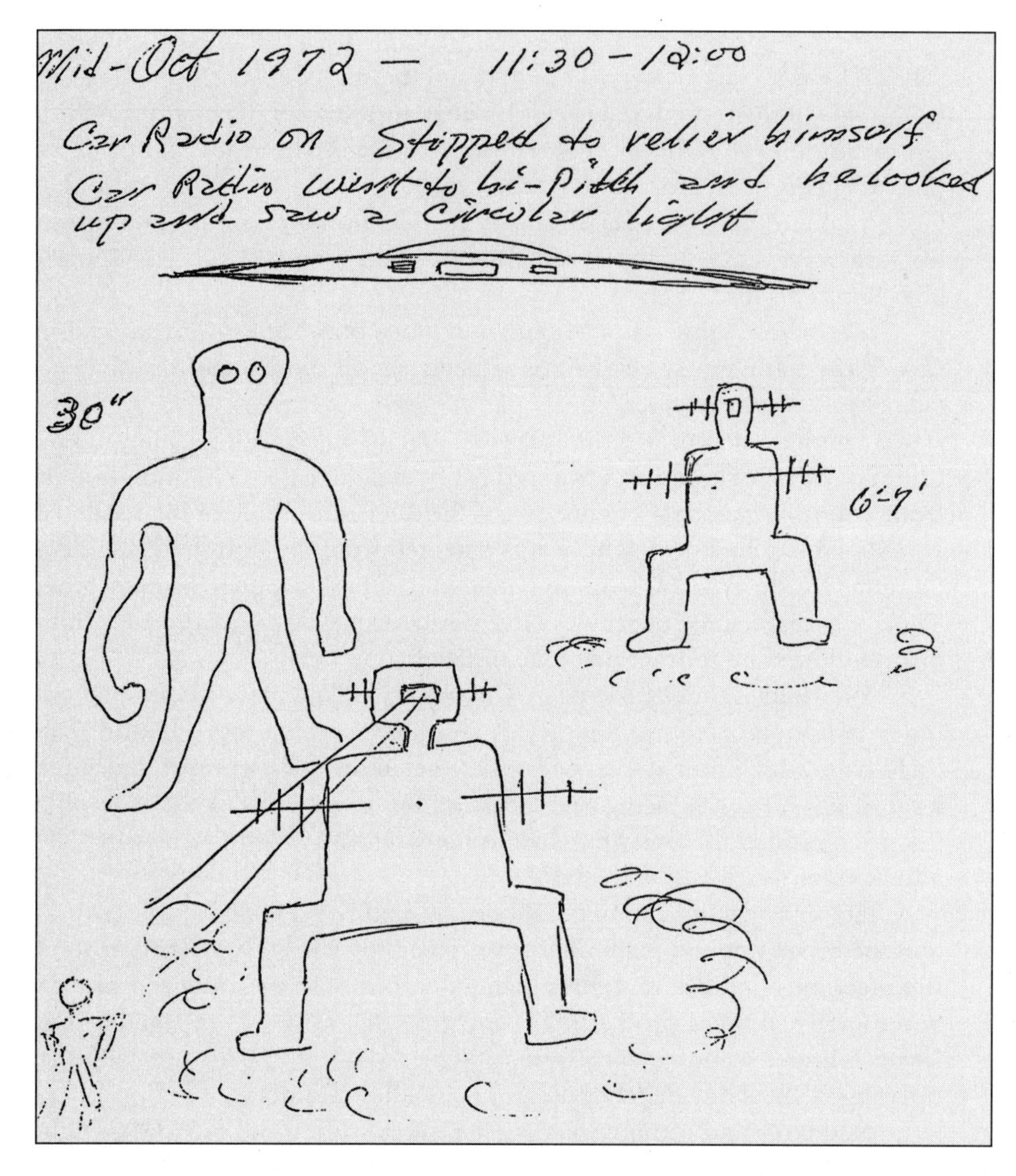

Plate 13 - *Drawing by Ed Foley of the disc and entities he encountered around midnight while driving his car near Casa Grande, Arizona in October 1972. Drawing provided by Wendelle C. Stevens, Lt. Col. USAF (Ret.)*

telligence had to resort to "artificial replenishment of the life essence which is why they were here." Foley said the life forms traveled to many places where organic life exists to extract the "necessary essence" for their survival. That essence, Foley thought, was obtained from simpler forms of organic lifelike vegetation and plankton in the sea. But life essence was also gathered from living animals and creatures, except mankind which was recognized as different and not fair game. The intelligence "wanted to open active communications with humans, but had not been successful."

Foley's attention shifted to the large craft and he suddenly found himself aboard where he saw "many humanoid creatures busily working, like ants, at various consoles and control apparatus. Those beings were only about thirty inches tall and the color of bronze. Foley thought the beings were naked, but could have been completely covered by a bronze-colored, close-fitting material.

"They were shaped like little human-form doughmen with very flexible appendages and a simple domed head with large, round black eyes. Their arms and feet ended in stumps with hard-looking knobs that projected from the ends."

Those mechanical robots or biological androids did not have fingers or toes, but Foley saw that knobs could extend outward like flexible tentacles. He did not understand why the right arm on some seemed longer than the left.

> "Watching these creatures going industriously about their work, he thought of the organization of an anthill and wondered what kind of a society they had on their dying planet? Almost immediately, upon thinking that question, Foley was viewing their planet from above a spaceport where many of these kind of circular ships were going and coming in a steady order like bees to a hive. The arriving ship would slip into a space dock where a long line of these same little doughman creatures were lined up waiting, and as soon as the spacecraft was prepared, the line began to move through the ship in a steady procession, entering by one port and exiting by another.
>
> "The creatures went in the ship empty-handed and came out the other port, each carrying a small white package between his 'hands.' The line continued in a steady stream until the ship was unloaded. It was then immediately prepared and was again dispatched on another mission, some lasting two years. Another arriving ship then took its place and the line started up again and carried the little white packages away. He was told that the harvest of processed life essence was contained in the little packages and that it was very precious to that society."

Foley felt he received information about the beings' need for earth life, specifically "they take blood and vital fluids and brain juices and secretions from some glands of various animals. They apparently need and use this in some way to help replenish their diminishing supply of life essence. They are not concerned about the flesh and leave it intact. They carefully avoid humans as much as possible in their harvesting of the fluid substances."

Perhaps Foley interacted with beings that "avoid" humans, but the phenomenon in general does not avoid humans. Body scars, implants visible on x-rays, and backyard circles are only some of the physical evidence of interaction. Abductees also have dreams or memories about sperm or ova being extracted. Paradoxically, for an intelligence struggling to survive biologically, Foley felt that same intelligence was extremely advanced technologically and controlled energies in the craft which were very powerful, having mastered the atomic sciences and other spectrums.

Further Col. Stevens wrote, "Foley was convinced that the light beam, very delicately applied to him, could be strengthened and intensified and make him disintegrate altogether if so desired. He knew that attacking this craft would be futile. He had the feeling that this craft could defend itself against whole fleets of attackers, if necessary."

Ed Foley's next memory was back in his body standing by his car still paralyzed and surrounded by the white light beam. Then the beam went out followed by the disappearance of the "robots." He could still see the disc as it rose rapidly. Then it was gone.

In his report, Wendelle Stevens compared the Foley case in Arizona to another he had discovered in La Paz, Bolivia, South America three years later in 1975, a peak year for high strangeness and animal deaths throughout the world. Mr. Stevens asked a Bolivian slaughterhouse owner if he had ever heard of aerial objects shaped like plates. The answer was no, but that a neighboring sheepherder had.

The following report by Col. Wendelle Stevens is also shared with his permission:

> "The Bolivian meat packer then proceeded to tell me that his friend, a sheepherder, was on the range with several other Indians working when he saw a strange disc-shaped aircraft glide down silently from the clouds to a level about three hundred feet above the flock where it stopped and hovered. Suddenly beams of very thin, bright light flashed down from the ship hitting some of the sheep in rapid succession and they fell in their tracks.
>
> "The strange aircraft then descended to only two or three feet above the ground, lowered a ramp, and three figures came down the stairs onto the ground. The figures were wearing 'buzos' (diver's suits) and they had a kind of tank on their backs and were carrying a sort of wand that was attached to the tanks with a flexible hose of some kind. They walked around to every fallen sheep and put the end of the wand to the head or neck of the carcass for a few moments and then moved on to the next.

> "Seeing them come down the ramp, the sheepherder grabbed a nearby stick to go over and teach them a lesson about monkeying with his flock. As soon as he raised the stick, he became immobilized as though he were immersed in molasses and could barely move. The alien visitors calmly went about their business until they had performed their operation on every fallen sheep. Then they re-boarded the disc and the ramp went back up into the craft and it began to rise faster and faster until it ascended out of sight almost straight up.
>
> "As it was leaving the scene, mobility gradually came back to the witness. He called his helpers and they carried the fallen sheep, thirty-four of them, to the bunkhouse to dress them out to save the meat. When they cut their throats to bleed them, they found them bloodless. They also found the brain cavities empty! Inquiring about the helpers' efforts to save the sheep, he learned that they too had been immobilized in the same way as he and were helpless to defend the flock."

The Bolivia eyewitnesses and the man in the following more recent experience suggest that the phenomenon wants some people to witness animal mutilations in action. On August 29, 1987, then 27-year-old Timothy Fint was up late reading a book in his Portland, Oregon apartment. A few minutes before 3 AM, he went outside to smoke a cigarette. Then he returned inside to go to bed.

> "I slept on a couch in the living room. I turned out the light and went to bed with my bathrobe on. I closed my eyes and the next thing I know, I'm standing out in a pasture field surrounded by total blackness. But I know I'm awake. I'm standing there and I can't move. I'm frozen and feel very stiff. My fingers are extended and spread out and my hands are stiff.
>
> "Then the blackness clears and around me it's all lit up. I seen the grass flying back and forth and trees being forced over in one direction away from me like the wind was blowing.
>
> "I could hear the wind thrashing and a humming sound. I don't know where the sound was coming from. But as I'm standing there, I seen a brownish-red cow. All of a sudden, this yellow light leaves me and goes down this hill. And I seen a bluish-white base above the beam and a red dome. It made a humming sound, sort of like an electric arc. It was right above me. That bluish-white base looked real white hot, but actually I could feel it was very freezing, like being in a meat locker.

Plate 14 - *Timothy Fint's drawing of a cow rising in a beam of light into a round, glowing disc. Fint says this happened before his eyes on August 29, 1987 during an apparent abduction experience while living in Portland, Oregon.*

"This thing went down the hill a little bit off to my left and hovered above the brownish-red cow. The cow was still eating and didn't even know that the domed thing was there, I guess. All of a sudden, this light beam came down from the blue base of a round, lighted object in the sky, a kind of milky white light that I could see right through. And it came down and surrounded the cow, and the cow started to levitate. The cow went stiff and its head popped up and its eyes were wide open and its tongue was sticking out. And it went up.

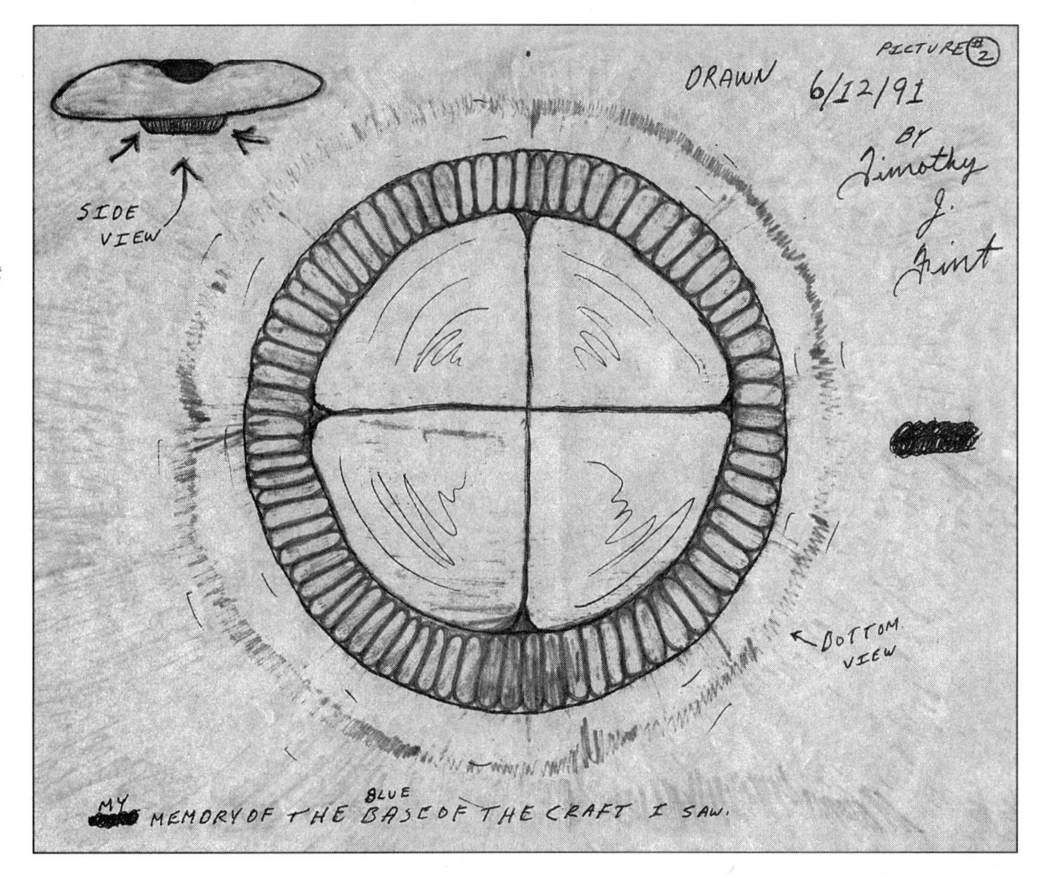

Plate 15 - *Drawing by Timothy Fint of the bottom of the glowing disc that he saw lift a cow in a beam of light on August 29, 1987.*

"The craft was about twenty-five feet up in the air above the cow. The cow went up with its feet down and its left side to me and touched the right side of its face to something at the top of the beam. I heard this high-pitched zinging sound. It was like the sound of a power saw cutting wood, but very high-pitched. ZING, ZING, ZING. And the cow let out this bloodcurdling scream.

"This cow was screaming, screaming and screaming! Then she was lowered inside the light and turned upside down because the feet was pointing up. Now the right side was facing me and the cow went up again and I heard the zinging sound again on the cow's right shoulder. The cow is not bleeding or anything.

"I could clearly see that the right side of the cow's face was gone. There was no ear, no eye and the tongue had been removed and it was down to the bone on the jaw. The meat had been removed right down to the bone.

"By this time, I'm terrified. It's like, 'Why am I here? Why am I seeing this? Why am I being showed this?' I'm in a panic state and just want to get out of there. I just want to turn and run, but I can't move. I don't want this craft to hurt this cow anymore, so I think I yell at this craft at the top of my lungs, 'Stop it!' And at that moment, it just dropped the cow to the ground. It landed on its legs and I heard this cracking sound like the legs was being broken and the cow just flops over and lays there. The light is still down on it. Then the light goes up to the blue base and it's just hovering there above the cow. It was like one of those laser swords you see on *Star Wars*. Like you turn it on and it comes out. Well, when you turn it off, it moves back in. Basically, that was the effect of the beam going into the blue base of the craft.

"Then I see the (disc) thing start to move slowly towards me. I get the sensation like I can turn and run because I don't know what's going to happen now. So, I turn and then all I remember is blackness.

"And the next thing I know, I wake up on the couch and my pillow and my blanket and all my clothes are gone, my bathrobe is gone. I am just laying there in my underwear. I'm totally soaked from head to toe, like I just got out of the shower with my underwear on. And my skin was ice cold to the touch. I sat up and said, 'What happened?' All I remembered was smelling grass and weeds and seeing this thing happen to the cow and being out there and being totally terrified and not knowing why I was out there.

"What was so strange is that all my bed clothes and everything were gone and I was actually facing the opposite direction with my head away from the light where I started when I originally went to bed.

"I had to urinate real bad, like my bladder was going to explode. And so I rushed into the bathroom and took my towel and dried off and cleaned up and still had this smell in my nose of grass and weeds and being out in the field and smelling straw and stuff like that. I still had this memory of what I had seen of this craft cutting the cow to pieces right in front of me.

"Then I walked over to my closet. I don't know why I knew this, but I opened the door and my blanket and my pillow and my bathrobe and everything was folded up real neatly right on the shelf. And I didn't even know how it got there.

"So I made my bed again and went to sleep. When I woke up in the morning, I felt stiff and like I'd had an electric shock of some sort. And I've had this memory since 1987. I've never been able to forget it."

Plate 16 - *Eyewitness Timothy J. Fint, a Certified Medical Assistant from Portland, Oregon, in beige shirt standing next to his friend Bob Carter in front of Oregon waterfall. 1987 photograph provided by Fint.*

Timothy Fint is not the only person haunted by knowledge of technology capable of lifting heavy cows in what appears to be beams of light and dropping the animals back dead and mutilated.

In 1980 east of Bend, Oregon, then 34-year-old Dwain Wright had joined a friend on a hunting trip. Wright, who received a Ph.D. in Psychology from UCLA and a Masters Degree in Graphic Design, went along to enjoy the beauty of the outdoors, not to hunt. The men were in a place called Sand Springs where forest and open range desert meet. The year before in that same area Wright had discovered a dead cow wedged in the upper limbs of a huge Ponderosa pine tree. He never learned what happened. This time he went off to explore again on his own and stopped at some cattle watering tanks. In a 1994 interview, Dwain Wright told me what happened.

"This old cowboy came walking out of the woods nearby. He had a small travel trailer back there so he could keep an eye on the cattle. Out in open range like that, rustlers could steal pretty easy. We got into a conversation about cattle and then he asked me, 'Do you believe in flying saucers?' And I said that I did. And he said, 'Well, they come across the desert here at night. I want to show you something.' He took me to another area and there was a dead bull pressed into the ground as if it had been dropped from a great height."

"How far into the ground?" I asked.

"About half way. The cow was heavy to begin with, but it had to have been dropped a couple of hundred feet. And what I noticed about it is that certain parts of it were missing: ears, eyeballs, sex organs were missing, its anus was also cut out. And the cowboy said, 'This is not the only one. There are lots of them like this.' And he said, 'The coyotes typically don't eat them and flies are not drawn to them.' Which is fairly bizarre because anything dead out in the desert or forest is almost instantly consumed. And there is no shortage of wild life and predators.

"And he said they came at night. The cattle were just drawn up. They floated right up off the ground. He had seen it happen. And he said that sometime later, they just dropped them back when they were done with whatever. They were dropped back down onto the desert or through the trees into the forest. And he said you could hear them at night making a horrendous crash through the trees."

"Dwain, you mean the bodies of the cattle were dropped right down through the trees?"

"Yeah, out of the flying saucers."

"And how did the cowboy describe the flying saucers?"

"He described them as being kind of a disc that glowed, kind of a saucer shape. He said there were always parts missing on the cattle. And in my own observation of that particular one embedded in the ground, it looked like the excisions were healed, that they almost looked like a bloodless type of surgery."

Since 1994, biophysicist W. C. Levengood in Michigan has studied plants in mysterious crop circles and pasture grass under and around mutilated animals. He found a pattern of consistent changes in the metabolism rate of cell mitochondria in many of the affected plants and grasses. Dr. Levengood hypothesized that an intense energy interacted with the plants, most likely "a plasma vortex with a microwave frequency component."

Plate 17 - *Eyewitness Dwain Wright, a graphic designer from Grants Pass, Oregon. "This photo was taken in 1978 or 1979. The canyon behind me was where I saw a cow in the top of a huge Ponderosa pine tree, caught in the upper limbs. Then a year or two later, I met the old cowboy who showed me the mutilated bull pressed into the ground and told me it was dropped from glowing discs. 1978-79 photo provided by Dwain Wright.*

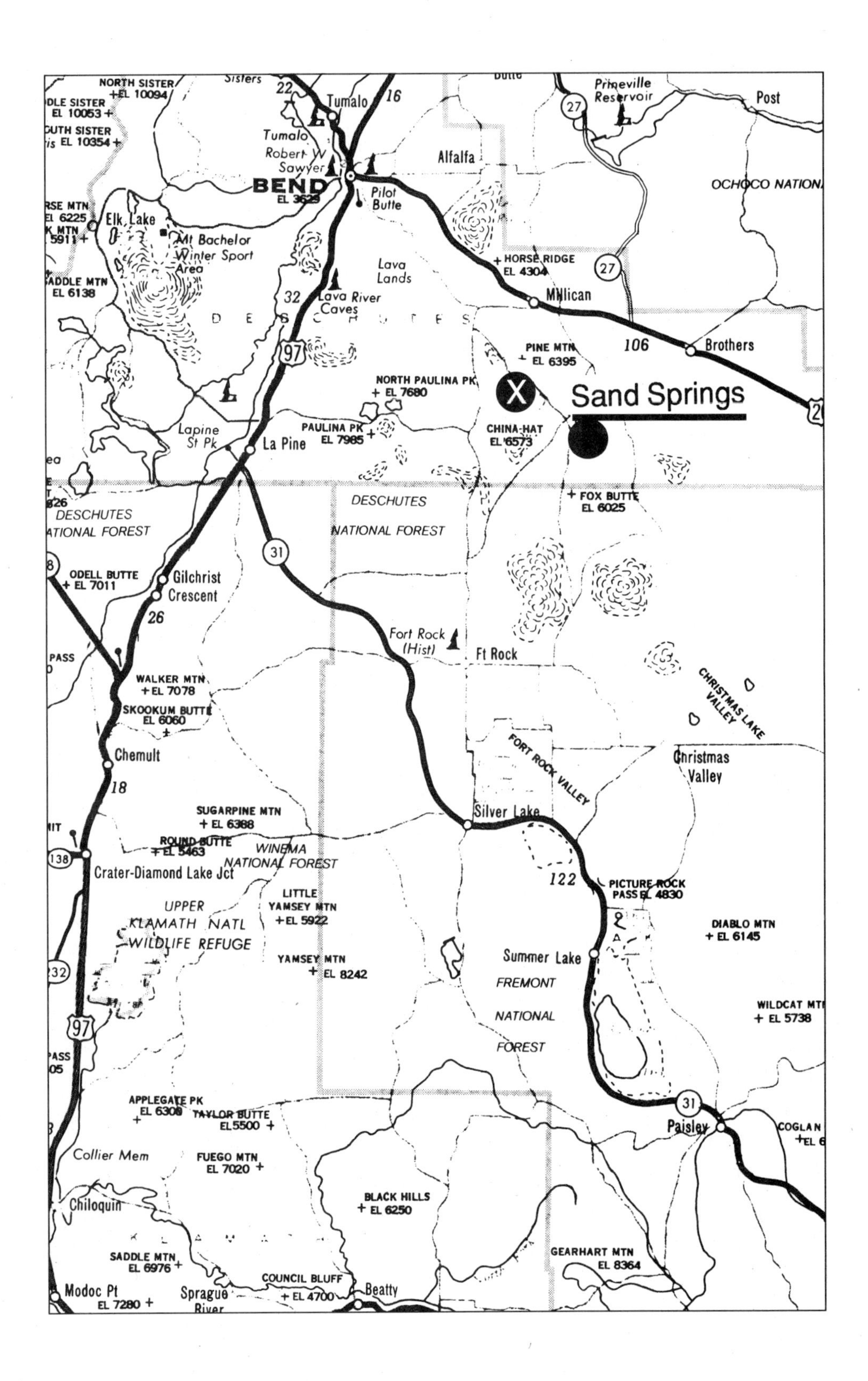

Plate 18 - *Oregon map with Sand Springs highlighted southeast of Bend. The circled X marks the area where Dwain Wright saw mutilated bull, and where the ranchman described having seen glowing discs that lifted cattle up in glowing beams.*

Glowing beams which can lift and lower people have also been described in the modern age of the human abduction syndrome that was first reported in the 1960s. Army Lt. Col. Philip J. Corso (Ret.) wrote in his best-selling book *The Day After Roswell* that the U. S. government knew by the 1950s that extraterrestrials were mutilating animals, abducting humans and interfering with military weapons and communication systems.

"It was the UFOs, alien spacecraft thinking themselves invulnerable and invisible as they soared around the edges of our atmosphere, swooping down at will to destroy our communications with EMP bursts, buzz our spacecraft, colonize our lunar surface, mutilate cattle in their own horrendous biological experiments, and even abduct human beings for their medical tests and hybridization of the species. And what was worse, we had to let them do it because we had no weapon to defend ourselves."

Another former U. S. Army man was an attack helicopter pilot who had the unnerving experience of watching what he thought was a person rising in a beam of light into a round, glowing object that hovered above the ground not far from a drive-in movie theater where he and his wife were watching a movie. He also heard about Men In Black (MIBs) threatening a police officer.

Derek Smith (real name withheld at his request) entered the U. S. Army in 1966. By 1970, he was in Vietnam and told me, "I started working with a group called CCN (Command and Control North) MAG-V-SOG (Military Assistance Group – Vietnam – Special Operations Group).

"It was a Special Forces Unit. We conducted special classified missions. That was my first exposure to the secret world of special operations and the beginning of an exciting twenty-five year career as an investigator in military intelligence."

Smith retired in June 1992, but prior to that in 1973, he was stationed at Hunter Army Airfield (HAAF) in Savannah, Georgia. The next year he was reassigned to Fort Stewart, located near Hinesville, Georgia. I talked with him about his military experiences prior to seeing the strange light and beam.

> S: "While serving with A Company, 75th Rangers, I co-authored the U. S. Army's first desert warfare and survival manual. The research behind that work required us to operate and live in the desert for approximately six months. During that period, we also instructed other U. S. Army personnel in desert warfare tactics. As a result of the success of this operation, I was given an experimental platoon of soldiers which had no formal military training other than Basic Training. The Pentagon directed me to instruct the platoon in Spe-

cial Forces and Ranger skills as well as special warfare tactics. The war in Vietnam was at an end and I think the Army was searching for new ways to train fresh soldiers. The idea was to take a group of new soldiers and maximize their training in the shortest period of time to be useful in special operations work."

H: "And what would be an example of the special ops work then?"

S: "Long Range Reconnaissance Patrol (LRRP) teams working far behind enemy lines."

H: "Working as soldiers under the direction of U. S. intelligence agencies?"

S: "Right."

H: "Did you ever work directly for the Central Intelligence Agency (CIA)?"

S: "Absolutely."

H: "If the CIA was your Special Ops boss prior to the 1973 incident, had you been on any special operations group activity that involved moving lights, UFOs, alien beings, anything like that?"

S: "I don't know about the alien beings or UFOs. However, I flew several missions in Vietnam which involved us intentionally chasing strange lights in the sky over rugged mountain terrain. These lights were a dull red color and were impossible to catch up to. No one ever told us what they were."

H: "So your first unusual experience in the United States was at HAAF in Savannah in 1973?"

S: "Right. I had a second job to make more money to help support my family and I was returning to the base after my second job around 11:30 PM. I came into the main gate and stopped my vehicle. I had a procedure that I always did so I didn't get in trouble on the base with a loaded weapon. I would always stop at the gate and inform the military police officer (MP) on duty at the gate that I was going to unload my weapon. The MP would acknowledge that and I would unfasten my weapon, unload it and proceed through the gate to my quarters. But this night when I got to the gate, it was different. The MP freaked out! He was afraid and I thought he was going to shoot me.

"So I said, 'Hey, you know me!'

"And he said, 'Yeah, I know who you are, but don't unload your weapon.'

"I said, 'Why not?'

"He said, 'Keep it with you, keep it loaded. You have to go to the MP station. The Provost Marshal wants to see you as soon as possible.'

"So I drove from the Main Gate to the MP station which was about a half a mile away, parked, and started walking toward the front door. It was warm outside and I could see the main door was opened all the way to allow the breeze to flow in through the screen door. Inside at the MP Station, the Desk Sergeant was sitting at a high, wooden podium with his .45 caliber semi-automatic pistol out, cocked and loaded, pointed right at me when I walked in. I could see his hands were trembling.

He said, 'Goddamn, sir, I almost killed you! I thought you were one of *them*!'

"I said, 'One of who?'

"And he said, 'I can't tell you any more.' He was shaking. His eyes were big. I could tell that he was very frightened. Then he said, 'You have to stay here because the PM ordered me to keep you here until he arrives.'

"I said, 'Have I done something wrong?'

"And he answered, 'No, but you have to stay here.'"

H: "Did you know the Provost Marshal?"

S: "Yes, we were the only officers left on the base at the time. The base was in the process of being shut down. The base hospital was being torn down. The BOQ (bachelor officer quarters) had placed us in one duplex that shared a kitchenette and bath so that the other BOQ rooms could be disassembled. I also did a favor for the PM and had been training the remaining MPs in unarmed defense tactics."

H: "So the Provost Marshal knew you would be returning to the base and wanted to keep you from walking into a dangerous situation?"

S: "Right."

H: "Did you ever get an explanation from the PM about who the THEY were?"

S: "No. I was concerned because these people were frightened and I didn't know why they were frightened."

H: "So at that point all you knew was a dangerous situation surrounded you some how?"

S: "Yes. And in my mind, I'm thinking sabotage, terrorists. Then the Provost Marshal pulled up and I went out to meet him. I walked up to his car door and said, 'OK, I'm here. What's going on?'

"He said, 'Get in the car.'

"So I walked around to the passenger side and got in the car with him and he asked me, 'Are you armed?'

"And I said, 'Yeah, I haven't had a chance to put my weapon up. What's going on?'

"He said, 'Good. Keep your weapon and go with me.'

"We drove away from the MP station and headed to the BOQ because he wanted to get his binoculars. While he was inside, I was curious about a row of street lights which were in a line that passed the BOQ and headed toward the airfield but seemed to be a slightly different color. The regular lights were dull white with an orange tint. I could see a light that seemed to have more orange and red in it and it was larger.

"When the PM came back out, he asked, 'What are you looking at?'

"I pointed and said, 'That street light looks odd.'

"He said, 'Well, that's not a street light. That's why we are out here.' And then the light disappeared.

"We got back in the car and drove out to a little boat dock in a marsh where the Savannah River comes through there. I could see one of the interstates that went around half of the base perimeter. It looked like a bridge because it was built on a swamp and had to be raised very high. It made a great observation platform overlooking the base. And up there, I could see a long line of law enforcement vehicles with blue lights flashing on them. I counted *twenty-six* of them from city, county and state.

"I asked the Provost Marshal, 'What is going on here? Is this some kind of drug bust or did prisoners escape from prison or what?'

"And he said, 'No, they're watching the base.'

"I asked why and he said, 'Do you remember that light that you were looking at that you thought was a street light? That's not a street light. I don't know what it is, but there are a lot of them here to-night. They have been flying down the base runway at low level, about six at a time in a V-formation. And they've been hovering over the atomic storage area.'

"And I said, 'Yeah, right!'

"The PM said, 'No, there really is something going on.'"

H: "Did you ask him what was flying the formations?"

S: "No, I was really confused. The PM and I were friends, we

Plate 19 - *September 9, 1973, Associated Press article as it appeared in* The Atlanta Journal and Constitution, *with permission.*

The Atlanta Journal and Constitution September 9, 1973

NEAR HUNTER AIRFIELD

GIs Say UFO Forced Patrol Car off Road

SAVANNAH, Ga. (AP) — Two military policemen at the Army's Hunter Airfield near Savannah reported Saturday that an unidentified flying object forced their patrol car off the road during the early morning hours.

According to the report, Spec. 4 Bart J. Burns and Spec. 4 Randy Shade said they noticed an object with "quick, flashing lights traveling at a high rate of speed from east to west" while they patroled the perimeter road surrounding the airfield.

The men said the object appeared to be about 2,000 feet off the ground. About 10 minutes later, they said the object came toward the patrol car at "tree top level" and dived toward their sedan.

As the object passed just above the car's blue warning light, the patrol car ran off the road into a ditch, the MPs said. According to Burns and Shade, the object hovered about 200 yards away, flashing blue, white and amber lights, while the men worked for 15 minutes to get the car out of the ditch.

They said the object disappeared as the men returned to headquarters.

About 45 minutes before the MPs reportedly saw the object, a Savannah man reported seeing a UFO come across the Savannah River from South Carolina and make a wide arc in a direction that eventually carried it over Hunter Airfield. Marcus Holland said the object was flashing lights.

About a dozen residents of a housing subdivision reported seeing a bright yellow object moving in the sky. The witnesses said it was about twice the size of the North Star.

trusted each other, but I could see in his face that he was having a hard time believing what was going on. I saw all the police cars and knew the Desk Sergeant had almost shot me, so everyone was afraid of something."

H: "Did you get the impression that the PM had ever seen this before?"

S: "No. This was something new to him. He was a young lieutenant. At the time I was probably around 24 years old and he was a year younger than I was."

H: "And the fact that the lights were hovering over the atomic weapons storage was of great concern."

S: "Right."

H: "How did the police get involved in the first place?"

S: "I didn't learn that night, but a couple of days later on television two of the MP's that I knew there were on national TV and they were talking about a UFO that ran them off the road. And I realized, 'That was here!' Then I realized what happened the night before was actually what these guys were talking about on national news."

H: "And television would have been at HAAF because they had monitored the law enforcement activity from car radios and so on?"

S: "I guess so. These two kids were scared. And their story was cut to pieces by a high ranking Army representative there in his dress uniform saying, 'This is all a bunch of baloney. These guys are alcoholics, drug users and liars. They aren't fit to be MPs.' And that very day, they were transferred out of the MPs."

H: "And the reporter didn't ask why people unfit to be MPs would be operating as MPs at that base?"

S: "No, not at all."

H: "So those two guys were transferred that very day?"

S: "One who had been the driver was transferred into my unit. He was a good MP, a good soldier and a fine human being. I was shocked at the way he was treated.

"The Army was supposed to be closing the Hunter base down and they had transferred everyone to Ft. Stewart. But within two weeks of those strange light events, the Army decided to reopen Hunter Army Airfield. Instead of downsizing the personnel, they brought in the 75th Ranger Battalion, a helicopter battalion, an additional Attack Helicopter Company and scores of support personnel. There was an Army hospital on the base and they had been ripping out wiring and water pipes, stripping the thing out to tear it down. But about two weeks after the UFO incident, they were back rebuilding it and transferring people back to the Hunter base."

H: "And has Hunter Army Air Field in Savannah been in continual operation since 1973?"

S: "Yes."

H: "And one of the two MPs that were interviewed on television about being run off the road by a UFO got transferred into your attack helicopter unit?"

S: "Yeah. I don't remember as what because he was an MP! They just transferred him in there. I remember one day at lunch time I decided to stay in the office to talk with him. I wanted to help him somehow because he was really depressed over the treatment he had received and the transfer out of the MPs. He had tears in his eyes and was crying and he said, 'I don't do drugs. Why did they lie about me? I'm a good person. I'm not a drug addict or drunk. Why did they do that?'"

H: "He was betrayed by his own Army."

S: "Yes, he didn't understand. I befriended him because he was a good person and I felt sorry for him."

H: "What did he tell you about being run off the road by a UFO?"

S: "He told me that he and the other guy were on radar to watch for speeders on the back road. He was the driver and he was watching his radar equipment and his buddy in the passenger side of the car was reading a book. It was late at night and nothing going on. Then the radar started acting up and he caught out of the corner of his eye a light, looked up and saw this huge saucer-shaped thing the size of a house moving toward him at treetop level. It was black with multi-colored lights. And they were different colored lights. I think he did say that the colors were in a certain spectrum like white and orange that flashed in sequence around the entire perimeter rim of the thing. Above the rim, he saw what looked like windows. And he said it didn't make any noise whatsoever.

"This thing was moving slowly at treetop level and just barely missed the top of the police cruiser. They got scared and were trying to get back to the base. They got up to over 100 m.p.h. and the thing was actually chasing them and then passed their vehicle — like maybe to head them off and stopped in front of them and started coming down lower like it was maybe going to land and block their path. They did a quick turn around in the road and headed back the other direction and this thing was giving chase and he said he was scared to death. The next thing he knew, they were sitting in the ditch. That's all he could remember."

H: "Did the MPs then get in touch with the base commander or the police? What happened?"

S: "While they were driving, he requested assistance as an officer in trouble. And the MP station listening to his radio calls would have been the one that called the city police."

H: "Did he describe being debriefed by any intelligence, civilian or otherwise?"

S: "No."

H: "The only thing he knew was that the next day he was on national TV and his own Army was castigating him."

S: "Right. A few days later, I spoke with one of the Chatham County Police Officers that had observed the events at the base from his vantage point on one of the state highways. He said he saw strange lights flying in formation over HAAF. But when I pressed him for more details, he said, 'Look, I don't know who you are and I don't want to talk about this anymore.'

"So I said, 'What's the problem? Were you told you couldn't talk about it by military intelligence?' He said, 'No, I drove home after work that night. I only live about seventeen miles away and there were two guys in black suits at my house when I went into the driveway.' They just matter of fact told him that he was not to discuss anything he saw flying around the base that night. If he did, he and his family would be *killed.* And that's the only information I got from him."

H: "What was your reaction to such a dramatic statement?"

S: "I believed him."

H: "Do you have any idea who those black-suited men were?"

S: "No. But the work I had done before with Special Operations, you learn a lot through osmosis. And I just believed that what he told me was true and that people might actually kill you and your family to keep something shut up."

H: "You mean CIA types?"

S: "I don't know. I just know the possibility was there."

H: "Was there any more information from anyone else who was there that night?"

S: "A policeman buddy of mine. He was the first one on the scene at the MP car that was off the road. And he told me that he walked up to the car that was in a ditch. He could see the two MPs sitting in the car not moving and he thought they were dead. He had his flashlight and looked into the driver's side and discovered they weren't dead, but were just scared to death, frozen there. He asked them what was going on because he couldn't see any threat around them and he didn't see them shot full of holes or anything. The guys couldn't give him an answer, they couldn't talk coherently. He said they were so scared they were just mumbling.

"Then about the same time, a black sedan pulled up on the opposite side of the road. It was driven by a man in U.S. Army dress green uniform wearing an overcoat and Specialist rank. He got out of the car, went to the back passenger door and opened it. Sitting there was a man in a black suit. That man handed the uniformed man a piece of paper. The Specialist walked over to the policeman standing by the MP car and handed him the piece of paper and said, 'This is your report. This is what you will write and nothing else.' Then the guy in uniform walked back over to the sedan, got inside and pulled away.

"My friend said the paper was just nonsense, like a prowler had been in the area and had nothing to do with the actual event."

H: "A made-up story handed to the Savannah police officer implying that without any explanation it was assumed he would take orders from an unidentified man in a black car?"

S: "Yeah! I don't think they understand civilian police very well."

H: "What did he do?"

S: "Well, my friend wrote a report about what the two MPs had actually told him and filed the report at the Savannah Police Station. He also told me a few days later that he decided to get a copy of his report and it wasn't there. All reports have a unique identification number called a Case Report Number (CRN). It's an eleven digit number that includes the date. For example, if a report was written on the first day of June 1996, and it was the first case for the month of June, the case number would be CRN - 9906010001. So, my friend was handed a copy of a report with his original CRN number. However, instead of a full report on an 8 1/2 x 11 form, it was on an Incident Card. This is a small card that is used for reporting dogs barking, suspicious vehicles, unsubstantiated prowler calls. The card had some nonsense written on it. The scary thing was that my friend's actual signature was on the card, but he never signed that card and it wasn't his report."

H: "Did he go to the Chief of Police at that moment?"

S: "No. You don't do things like that. It doesn't go anywhere."

H: "Well, someone had to have access to the records."

S: "I'm not saying the Chief didn't know. It's possible that he did know."

H: "OK, this MP encounter was the end of August or first of

September 1973. What was the date of the next event at the drive-in with your wife?"

S: "I think it was April 1974."

H: "So several months later."

S: "Yes. This was in Hinesville, Georgia after I had been reassigned to Fort Stewart. My wife and I would usually go out to a drive-in on the weekend and take our baby. I don't even remember what the movie was, but I noticed a bright light in the sky about three or four times the size of Venus. It was a very clear night and this bright light seemed to be moving slowly downward and eventually went behind the movie screen. Then my wife said, 'Are you looking at that light, too?' And I said, 'Yes.' She said, 'I've been watching it and it doesn't seem right.'

" Then it started going through colors from white to red to orange to yellow — like going through multiple shades of each color,

Plate 20 - *The object that Derek Smith and his wife saw at the drive-in movie theater in Hinesville, Georgia near Fort Stewart in April 1974. First it appeared as a bright white light high in the night sky. Then it slowly descended over trees to an altitude of approximately 300 to 400 feet. Drawings by Derek Smith for author © 1996.*

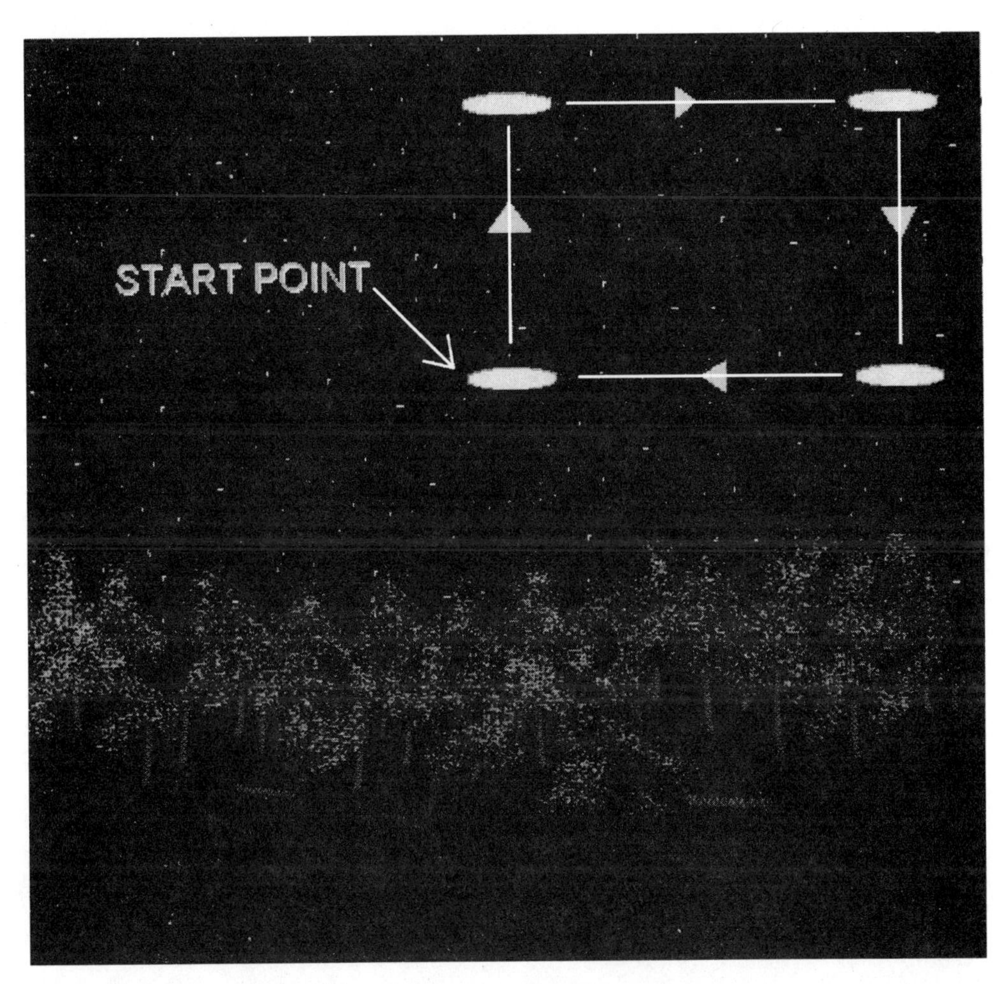

Plate 21 - *Derek Smith described this drawing: "The object then began to glow in a violet color that quickly made a color transition through all of the colors in the visible light spectrum. Then the object began a clockwise flight maneuver which looked as though the object was tracing a large square in the sky. Three of these 'squares' were 'drawn' each in the same position in the sky. Then the object stopped and remained motionless."*

stepping through the color spectrum. Then it turned white again and made a clockwise square. It looked like it was drawing a square in the sky. And it made this square three or four times.

Then it just stopped like it was hovering above the trees. And then this blue light about the color of a police car's blue emergency light came from underneath in a beam. The beam descended toward the ground slowly like a well-defined column of light."

H: "Sort of like the way an old-fashioned telescope would extend?"

S: "Yes, like it would telescope out as a solid beam all the way down, but you could see it moving."

H: "In other words, it looked like light, but it had a solid, cylindrical shape to it that maintained structure and seemed to move out as if it were some kind of solid body that was moving?"

S: "Right. And it looked like a spotlight in fog. You could see that beam — it had definition. The blue edge of the 'cylinder' didn't diffuse out. It looked solid."

H: "And did that strike you at the time, not knowing anything else about it, as being like anything you had ever seen light do before?"

S: "No! No! That was pretty marvelous. I told my wife, 'That is neat — shooting down a beam like that!' The beam went down toward the ground and the bottom of the beam disappeared below the tree line.

"Then within a couple of seconds, the top of the beam that came out of the craft or whatever — it started descending toward the

Plate 22 - *Smith wrote with this drawing: "After the disc remained motionless for approximately two to three minutes, it shot a blue 'light beam' from under its center. The blue beam slowly descended to the ground like an elevator. Then the top of the beam detached itself from the round object and also slowly descended to the ground. When the top of the blue beam apparently reached the ground, a pure white light beam shot up rapidly to the disc. Once the top of the white beam touched the disc, the bottom began to ascend upward again like an elevator."*

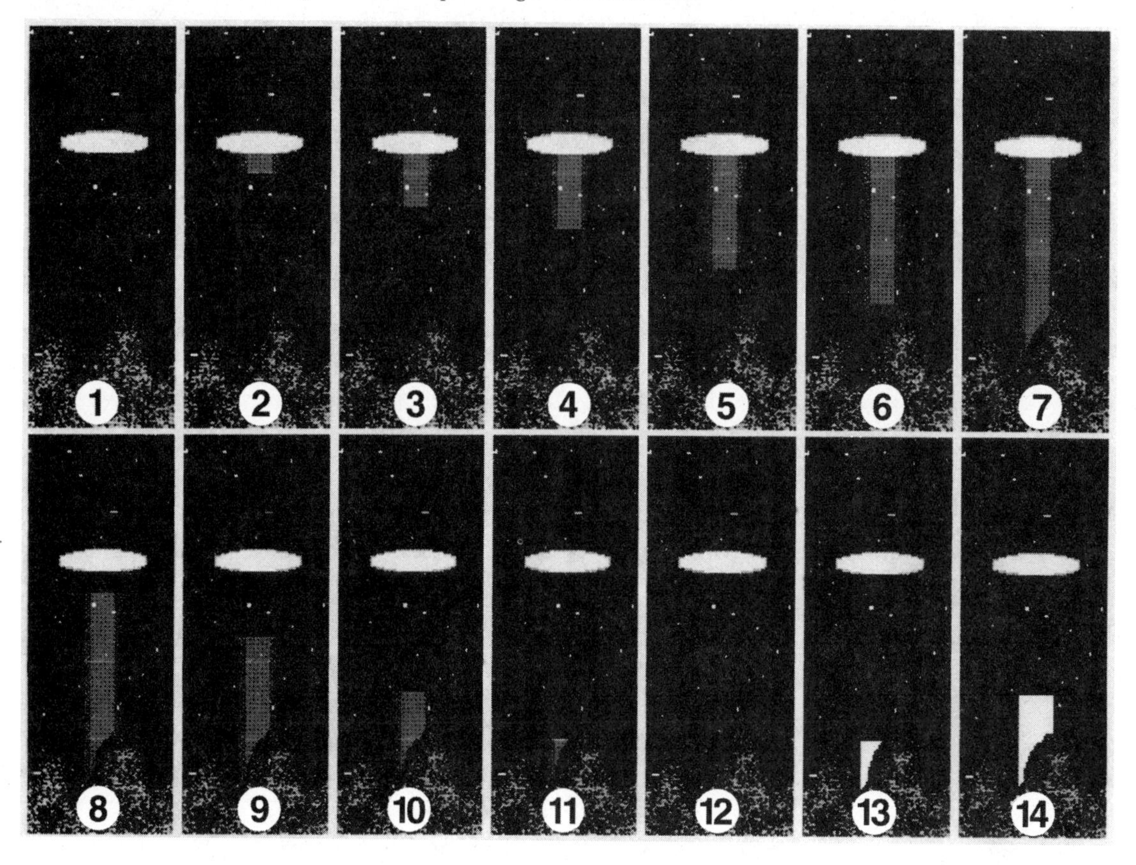

ground also. I thought that was really strange because you can't take a flashlight and shine a beam and detach the beam from the flashlight."

H: "So it was almost as if a cone of light literally detached itself from the bright light?"

S: "Yes. That cylindrical beam actually detached itself from the craft out there and went down toward the ground behind the trees.

"Then within a few seconds, a very bright, pure white light beam shot up from the ground to the bottom center of the craft. It had the same shape and dimensions as the blue beam and it moved the same way, only in reverse and much faster. Once the top of the white beam made contact with the bottom of the craft, it began to telescope toward the craft becoming shorter and shorter.

"While my wife and I were watching the white beam go up to the craft, we saw something inside the beam that reminded me of a person with arms and legs spread-eagled, tumbling and turning slowly inside that light. Have you ever seen a laser show?"

H: "Yes."

S: "And when the laser beam hits something, it sparkles?"

H: "Right."

S: "Well, this thing that was tumbling inside that white beam was also sparkling like when a laser sparkles off something. And as this person or thing was tumbling and rotating inside the light beam, the beam which had a distinct bottom to it continued upward until it disappeared inside the craft. Then the object just stayed there hovering, motionless and silent.

"My wife and I left the theater to get a closer look. That day I had been working on an Escape and Survival Course for my soldiers and had maps and compasses in the trunk of my car. We drove to seventeen different locations where I shot direction azimuths to the object and entered the information on my map. All the lines converged at a point on the ground. So, I knew we weren't looking at a star. It had to be something that was near the earth."

H: "How far do you think it was from you at the movie theater to have seen this object tumbling upward in the light?"

S: "Half a mile or less. ...I was close enough that I could distinguish appendages on the thing that was inside the beam. I saw at least four. I'm not absolutely certain it was a person, but it reminded me of an asterisk. I could clearly see separate appendages and I could clearly see that this tumbling thing was positioned in the center of the beam."

H: "And how long was the beam compared to your fingers at arm's length distance?"

S: "Well, the craft was above the trees, so I would say that the beam was probably somewhere around 200 feet long."

H: "And in that area where the light was hovering, what kind of land is it?"

S: "It's a mixture of swamp, bog and pasture-type land with heavy trees in the middle where the light beam would have been. Half a mile from there, the trees would have thinned out pretty much."

Plate 23 - *About this drawing, Smith said, "There was something floating upward in the beam of light. My first impression was that it was a person because I could clearly see four long appendages (like arms and legs) and one short appendage (like a head.) Approximately one and a half hours later, a smaller craft (Frame 25) raced toward the larger object. We thought it was a jet interceptor. However, as it approached on a collision course with the larger object, it slowed and then merged with the larger object. A few minutes later the large object descended to almost treetop level and slowly meandered off to the northeast until it was out of our view."*

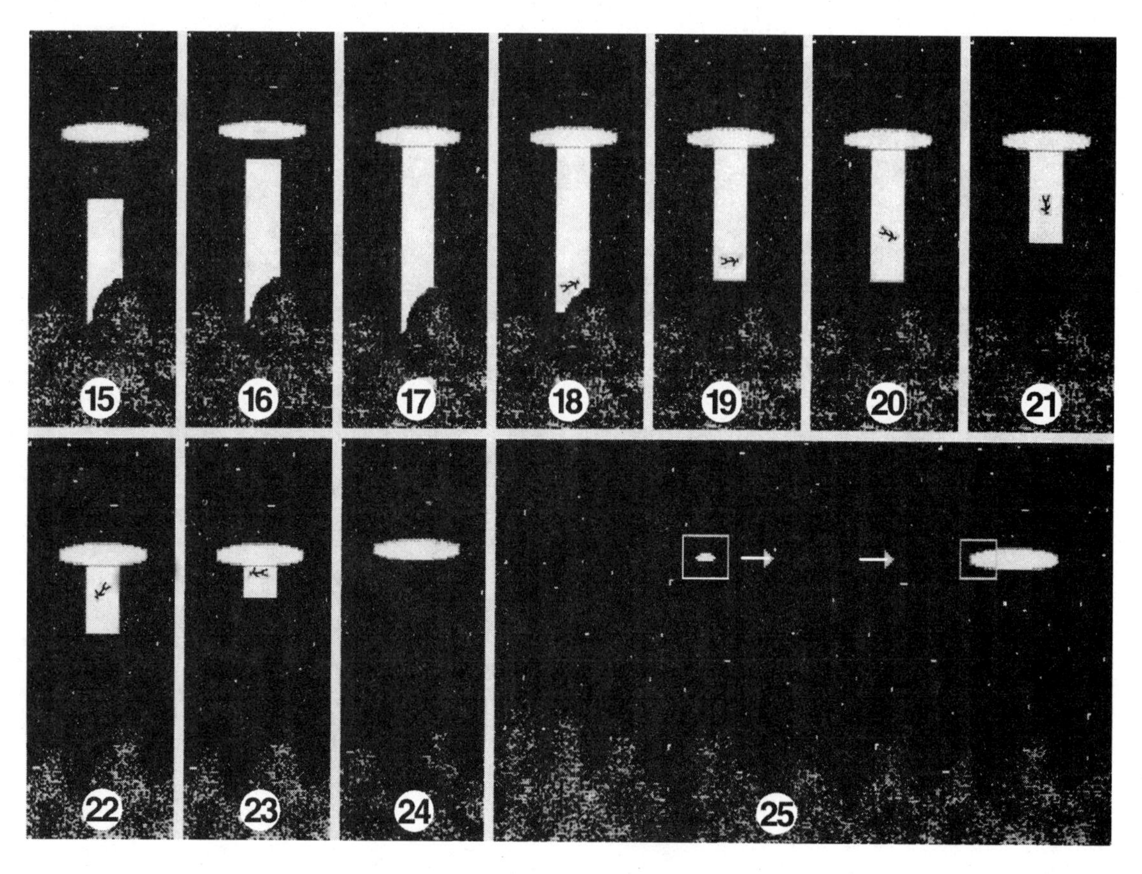

H: Were there any people living where that beam of light seemed to be?"

S: "On the PICTO map that I used to plot azimuths to the object, there was a farm indicated about half a mile away. I remember specifically thinking about people and wondering if that was a person in the beam."

H: "Were you able, using your 17 different azimuth locations, to drive to exactly the spot where you thought this occurred?"

S: "I couldn't drive right to it because of the trees I told you about."

H: "Did your wife say anything that night about seeing anything in the beam?"

S: "Yes, she saw something peculiar in the beam. I had a very intense interest in the object and I wanted to keep looking at it and observing it and trying to get closer to it. However, the closer we got to the object, the more frightened my wife became. She told me that her intuition was telling her not to get any closer to the object and that it was very bad. And she wanted to go home.

"I talked her into going to one last location for a final azimuth reading at the Fort Stewart Ammunition Storage Area. Almost as soon as we arrived, a Military Police Unit pulled up, put a spotlight on us and ordered us out of our car with our hands up! When I got out, one of the MPs recognized me and asked what I was doing. I said, 'Me and my wife and my little baby are here and we're looking at the light up there. We've been watching it do strange stuff.'

"At this point, one of the MPs became afraid or concerned. He said he didn't want to be around there because he had had an experience before with a light that interfered with his 2-way radio and made his car quit. And he said, 'I know who you are now and I'm getting out of here.'

"And just before they left, I saw a smaller light that I thought was a NORAD interceptor go check out that craft. And as we watched, it came fast like a fighter jet and as it got closer, I said, 'Oh, man, it's headed right for it. Maybe it's going to shoot at him!' It got real close to the light and slowed down and *merged* with the big light. And I said, 'Oops, look at that!' And the MP said, 'Yeah, we're definitely getting out of here!' And the four MPs got in their car and left."

H: "So four MPs, you and your wife with the baby — six adults watched the smaller white light that might be a NORAD interceptor merge with the large light?"

S: "Right."

H: "And the four MPs — all they wanted to do was leave the scene?"

S: "Right."

H: "This is a military base and these are four MPs and you are in Special Operations Group — would not the normal, logical thing have been to want to identify what it was that had happened and to report to the highest authority possible?"

S: "Well, that's what I wanted to do. In fact, I did report it. I went to talk with someone at the Fort Stewart Headquarters Staff. I was relating the story to them and they were kind of like, 'Yeah, well, sure, thanks, see you later.' I also remember them saying, 'It was probably swamp gas. It was probably a balloon.' And I told them, 'Look, I'm a pilot. I have over a thousand hours in combat flying. I've seen just about everything there is to see in the air. I can tell you that it wasn't a balloon, it wasn't swamp gas. I can tell you everything that it was *not,* but I can't tell you what it was.' It was clear they wanted me out of the office, so my wife and I left.

"The next thing was that I went to the NORAD site at Hunter Army Air Field."

H: "What was your intent in going there?"

S: "Two things. I wanted to report it, but I was also curious what was going on because of the way people were reacting."

H: "Like it was nothing."

S: "Yeah!"

H: "This is a NORAD facility that has an underground installation and you knew its business was to track objects with special radar equipment?"

S: "Yeah. NORAD is supposed to be a radar network that provides advance warning in the event that our air space is intruded upon by any unknown or hostile force. NORAD has very powerful radar, and if something is in the air, they see it. If they detect some unknown object, they will scramble interceptors to take a closer look and engage with weapons, if necessary.

H: "And did anyone, including your wife, know that you were going to that NORAD office?"

S: "No."

H: "You just decided to do this on the spur of the moment?"

S: "Yes."

H: "You drive up and what happened?"

S: "I drove up into the parking lot and got out of the car. I'd never been there before. There were three buildings and I didn't know where to go. Then this Air Force Colonel came out of one of the buildings, walked right over to me and introduced himself. He had come out in such a hurry that he left his hat inside. He was smiling and extended his hand for a handshake. He said, 'What can we do for you?' That really took me back because he was a Colonel and I was a junior officer. He was acting like he wanted to be buddy buddy. And I told him about the thing I saw in the sky near Ft. Stewart, the area it was in and the direction it moved off to."

H: "Did you describe the beams and the object in it and everything?"

S: "Yes. And the Colonel said, 'That's pretty interesting. Let's go see what we've got.' So he takes me inside that Top Secret facility and he doesn't know me from Adam. I've never met him before and I wasn't cleared for any of that stuff. No one asked me for my ID which was highly unusual. He just walked in with me past the special security officer to a large work area with a lot of people sitting at work stations. Then the Colonel said, 'Hey, gang, this is Chief Smith here — he's interested in something that he saw the other night.'

"We went from that room into a back room that was blacked out. There were large Plexiglas type screens with glowing symbols on them. Another group of people were working in this room. The Colonel again introduced me, 'This is Chief Smith and he wants to know about the thing the other night. So, run the tape.' They ran a tape for me. When it finished, the Colonel said, 'See there was nothing there.' Course, I wouldn't have known what I was looking at anyway because that wasn't my job and I didn't know anything about it.

"Then he escorted me back outside and said, 'Appreciate your coming down and glad we could be of service.' Small talk.

"The Colonel went back inside the building and I was very puzzled about what had just transpired. Then a guy I knew from the bowling league came out. He was some kind of Sergeant. He had a lot of stripes. He said, 'Hey, I need to tell you something but we can't talk now. Leave and come back to this parking lot after you see fifteen cars leave. Come back. It's important!'

"So I did what he told me to and when I came back, he came out to my car looking all around as if he thought he might be watched. He said, 'Look, I can't really talk out here. You need to get going before someone comes back and sees us talking. It's not good for you to be here. I just wanted you to know because I know you're from the league and you look like a nice guy. What you saw the other night *was real.* You really saw that and I wanted you to know so you wouldn't think you're going nuts or something. I can't tell you anything more about it. And don't come back here anymore.' It wasn't like he didn't have the information. I realized he wasn't allowed to tell me. I thanked him and left."

H: "And no other follow up from anybody? No one else came to debrief you? No one else came to warn you?"

S: "No. In fact I called an Air Force office in a last effort to communicate. I told them I wanted to report an unidentified flying object. The guy on the phone said, 'I really don't have time for this.' I asked, 'Don't you guys care about this? I thought you were required to take reports.'

"Then he said, 'OK, give me the information.' So I told him and it was like I was really bothering him and he was doing me a big favor to listen. I don't know what they did with it. I never had anyone else talk to me."

H: "Do you personally have any doubt that we're dealing with a non-human intelligence?"

S: "No."

CHAPTER 3

OTHER BEINGS, OTHER WORLDS

"Higher intelligence takes advantage of, and uses, lower intelligence — sort of the way we humans use cattle. And with the privilege of use, comes the responsibility of caring for it. A farmer tends to his animals by feeding them and taking care of their medical needs. If the pasture became contaminated, the farmer would be the first to protect his investment."

JIM SPARKS, ABDUCTEE, 1996
FORT MYERS BEACH, FLORIDA

In 1995, I met a man named Jim Sparks who says he has had completely conscious encounters with "small, grey, drone worker types; taller true aliens, or supervisors; and tall reptoids with big human-shaped bodies covered with scaly, reptile skin." Like Sgt. Jim Penniston in Chapter 1, Sparks sees himself as an interpreter or translator — or at least an elementary grade student in an alien "school." Sparks says he has been forced to learn English letter and number equivalents to alien symbols. He permitted me to tape record hours of our discussions about his experiences. This chapter emerged from those conversations and his efforts to visualize and write down what has happened for his own book manuscript.[1]

After eight years "of being close enough to breathe their rotten egg-smelling skin," Sparks thinks he has some insights into the alien agenda, but admits he has "a thousand more questions than answers." He is frustrated that he cannot prove his contacts with alien beings.

Sparks was born to Italian parents on November 15, 1954. The formal name on his birth certificate is Vincent Sparacino. He grew up in southern Florida, graduated from high school and spent a couple of years in a local college studying real estate. He moved on to Houston, Texas in 1979 and then to North Carolina where he purchased raw land, divided lots for housing construction, and always felt a strong need to preserve the trees at his developments. Happy, married and thriving, by 1988 at age thirty-four, Sparks suddenly came face-to-face with other beings from other worlds.

[1] Star People, Outsiders – Us? Or Them? *© 1996 by Jim Sparks.*

Sparks at first thought he had lost his mind. He says he has been kept totally conscious through most of the interactions, including the agony of being "pulled" from his bed at night to a craft.

"I'm usually pulled the same way, which I call the 'hard way,' and it's completely physical. My whole body is taken. The first thing I hear is a low-pitch whirling sound in my head like a whip going around in the air.

"This is usually after I go to bed and am asleep. Normally for me, it's 3:30 AM in the early morning. I don't know why. I wake up from my natural sleep and then there's the whirling sensation in the pit of my stomach and it feels like it's coming up into my chest. When it gets up to my heart area, my heart starts beating fast, just racing in my head, and the whirling sound starts

Plate 1 - *Jim Sparks, photographed in 1996 at his home in Fort Myers Beach, Florida.*

picking up rpm and is tremendously loud. It starts low and rises in pitch and screams in your head. The fear is like you're going to die. Your heart is racing a million miles an hour and then you get this acceleration feeling, but I always feel like I'm being pulled down — I never feel like I'm being pulled up. It's like I go down a roller coaster, only 100 times faster, and WHOOM — you black out and you're there — wherever it is you're going to be, usually on board a craft."

Sparks told me why he thinks most of the time he is actually "pulled" physically from bed and literally moved through the walls or ceiling as other abductees have also described.

> "It's their technology. I know that the aliens rely heavily on a created field. This field produces several things: the ability to be invisible, the ability to work in one dimension and be partially in another, and the ability to move us poor humans through solid matter.
>
> "How exactly it works, I don't know. But I know it's a field. When the field is in action, you can feel it, you can sense it, you almost feel like you are a magnet or static electricity. It takes a wall as you would normally see it and makes it transparent. You walk right through it. So, it's a field that somehow separates molecules, changes your physiology when you're in it."

I asked Sparks if he has been awake and conscious while actually seeing doors and walls become transparent.

> "Only rarely. And it freaked me out. Most of the time I black out before that moment and then I'm on board the craft. I know this all sounds weird as hell, but I'm doing the best I can under very bizarre and unusual circumstances not to be scared to death, not to be intimidated and to figure out what these bastards are up to. And I know that their technology renders different ways of transport and one is the 'hard way' and I'm there in the *flesh*, not out of body!"
>
> "Why do you think it's not out of body?"
>
> "Because I have five or more senses."
>
> "But people who have out of body experiences talk about all sorts of sensory impressions."
>
> "Right now, as you're talking with me, are you sleeping?"
>
> "No."
>
> "You know that, don't you? That's the same thing I'm saying."
>
> "Why do you think it's a technology?"

"Because everything the aliens do is technology. After spending so much time with them and being around them so much and after observing things over and over again, you start to pick things up. Even if you show a dumb dog something three hundred times, he learns something."

"But have you ever watched a non-human being push a specific button to operate a machine?"

"They don't push buttons. It's all thought-activated."

"How do you even know that?"

"I'm trying to understand like anybody else. But I've seen what I think resembles a computer, but much more complex. You could be in your living room or bedroom and one of these creatures happens to be around. You see a yellow, dingy light on the walls or floor or ceiling or in the air. And you see symbols and stuff floating around in it. And you hear a hum begin and the symbols start moving. And I think the aliens are thinking these things to happen while they are connected to that computer thing I've seen."

"But, Jim, have you ever seen a non-human physically interact with a piece of machinery and cause a specific result where you watched from the beginning of the interaction to the result and knew what had happened?"

"No. They don't have to physically move anything. They just *think* to their machines and stuff happens. That's why I said it's thought-activated technology."

One insight from another long-time abductee about what could be happening in the "pulling" process was described by Anna Hayes, author of *Voyagers, The Sleeping Abductees.*[2] As Sparks has been taught symbols, Hayes says a non-human intelligence has tried to teach her about the underlying importance of frequencies in their technologies and the cosmos.

Hayes said, "Jim's description of being 'pulled' I relate to as the transmutation of cellular codes in DNA. It's a technology that literally transforms the body into light and then re-manifests it at a different desired locale. It is done by manipulating cellular codes and uses sound to change the vibratory oscillation rate of the DNA and cells. Also, human 'thoughts' are treated as electromagnetic pulse transmissions by the aliens which can be received and processed for a variety of uses in their biotechnologies."

[2] Voyagers, The Sleeping Abductees *© 1998 by Anna Hayes, Wild Flower Press.*

On board, Sparks has always had the same task: to learn and to write alien symbols. At first, his body was always temporarily paralyzed except for his right hand and arm.

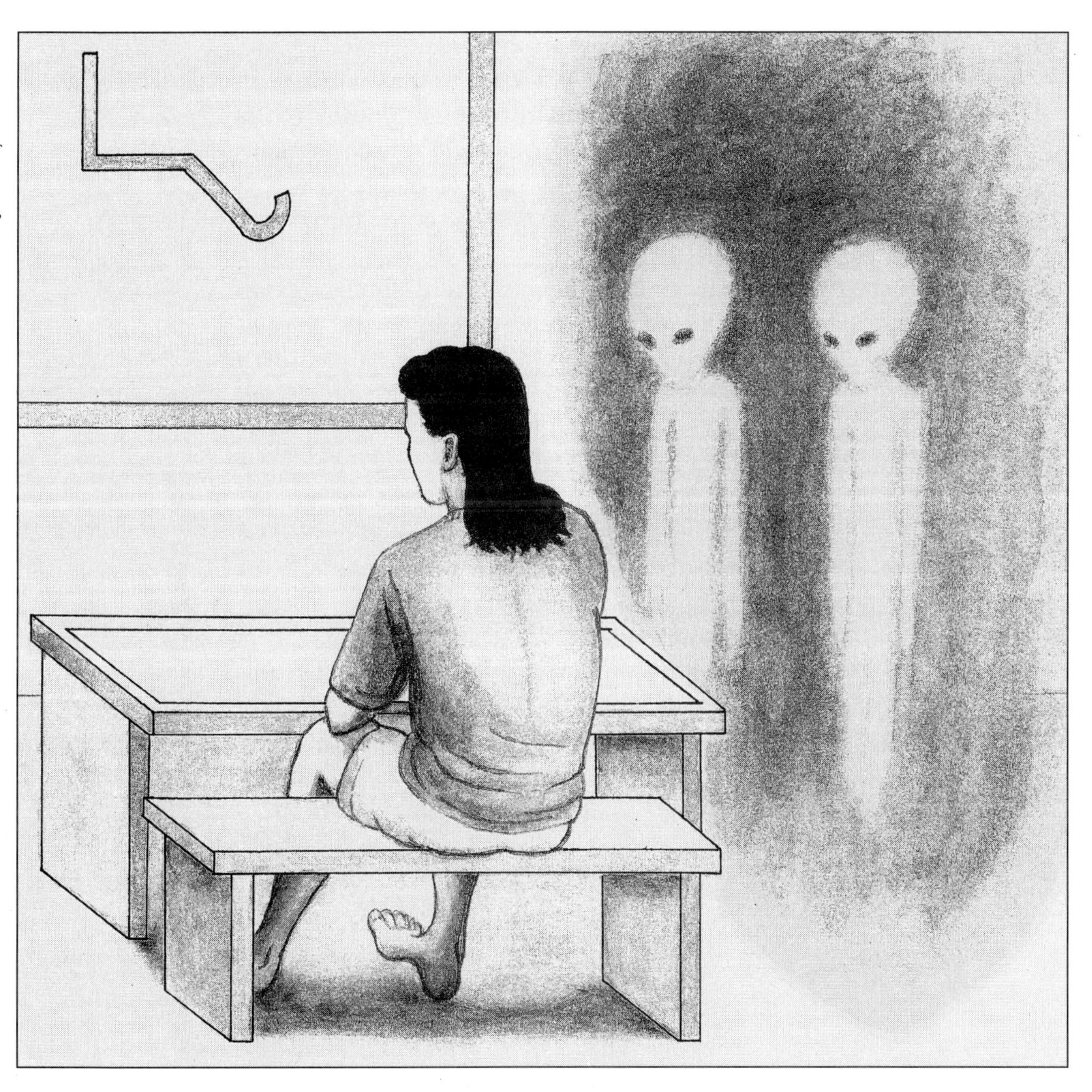

Plate 2 - *Jim Sparks's depiction of the alien "classroom" where he was forced to learn a symbol equivalent of the English alphabet and numbers, as well as alien shorthand symbols and phrases. Drawing by Josi Galante © 1996 for Jim Sparks.*

"God, I can't explain the feeling or the fear that shot through my body as each separate word rang through my head. It was so odd because I didn't audibly hear words. The orders, I now know, were telepathic. I could *feel* each word as it was telepathically spoken and *see* each word on the wall screen that was directly in front of me. It was a language I had never seen before."

When Sparks is forced to do anything, it is his nature to immediately resist with great anger. So he was enraged to find himself partially paralyzed while hearing orders and demands inside his head.

"The telepathic voice would say, 'You will learn this.' Then the letter A appeared on the wall screen. Next to it was some strange version of A. Then appeared step-by-step instructions on how to duplicate the strange version of the letter A. I could sense the aliens wanted me to write their version with my right forefinger. I was so angry, scared and disoriented that in no way shape or form was I going to cooperate. So I yelled, 'No!'

"The letter A appeared again on the screen and simultaneously the air pressure in the room expanded with a sudden jerk. The pressure was very painful to my ears and head. At the same time, it felt like a short burst of adrenaline shot through my body that caused my heart rate to slightly increase. My body tightened up and all of this made me feel scared and uncomfortable. I sensed all of this discomfort would not go away unless I cooperated and drew the strange version of the letter A. But I kept saying 'No!' and the aliens would step up the level of anxiety and discomfort to the point that my heart was pounding so hard I thought it was going to stop.

"I cried out, 'I don't want to die!'

"Finally, I looked down at the table screen and with my right forefinger traced the first stroke for their version of the letter A. Instantly my heart rate dropped to normal and the anxiety and fear were gone. Suddenly I felt euphoric, an extremely pleasant sensation. I realized if I cooperated, I would get pleasure. Don't cooperate, you get agony and fear."

Plate 3 - *Drawings of the first letters and numbers that Jim Sparks says the non-human beings taught him. Unlike the English alphabet, for example, which is written and understood as static letters on a two-dimensional surface such as a piece of paper, the alien symbols were differentiated in the number and direction of motions in their construction. "a," for example, was three motions: left to right, right to left, and left to right, all back and forth in the same short, horizontal line. Drawings by Jim Sparks with Josi Galante © 1996.*

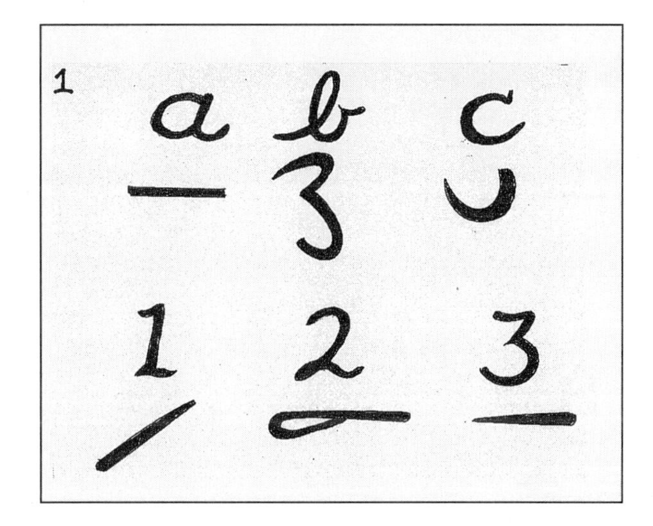

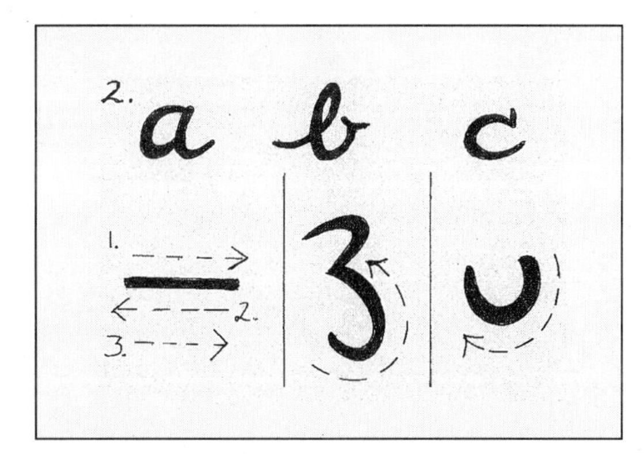

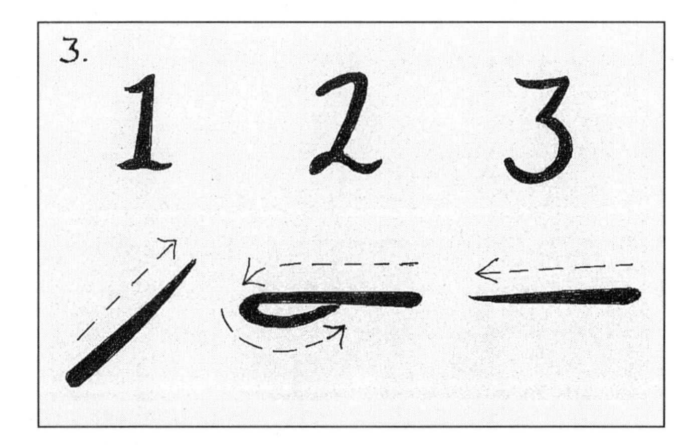

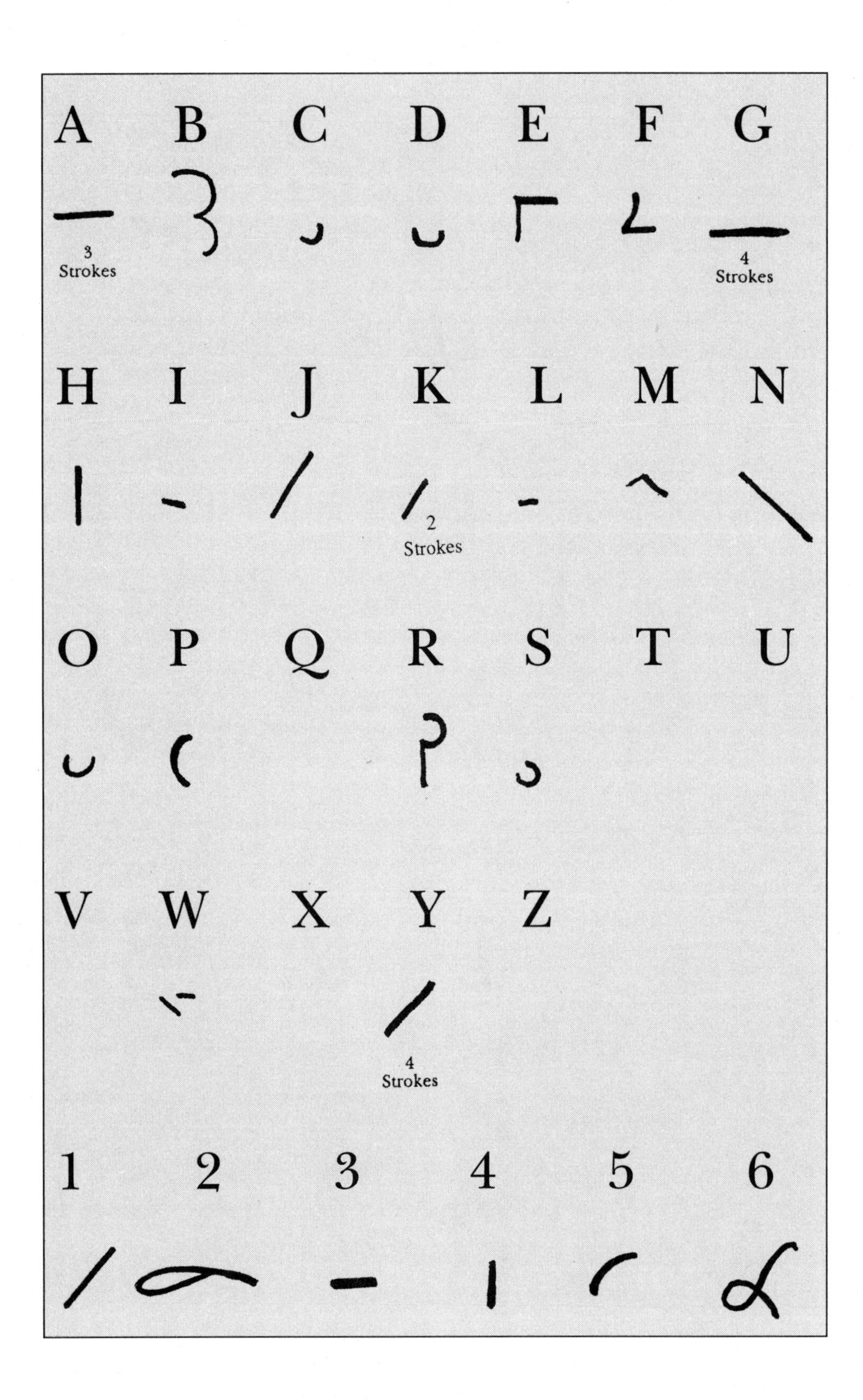

Plate 4 - *English alphabet and number equivalents in non-human symbol language that abductee Jim Sparks says alien beings have taught him since 1988. Sparks wanted to exclude three letters – T, U, V – from public distribution as a verification check on people who claim to also be abductees with knowledge of alien script. Symbols drawn by Jim Sparks.*

Jim Sparks said that Aa, Bb, Cc, and 1, 2, 3 were the first letters and numbers the alien beings taught him to make in what he understood to be some form of alien symbol language that was read from right to left and from the bottom of the symbol up. Unlike the English alphabet which is written and understood as static letters on a 2-dimensional surface such as a piece of paper, the alien symbols seemed to be differentiated 3-dimensionally in the number and direction of motions in their construction.[3] He had watched the aliens lay symbol over symbol over symbol in what became a solid black spot. Jim was left with the impression that the information in the black area could be understood from the motions still residual there. Sparks had seen symbols hanging and moving in the air and had the impression that three dimensional conceptualizing, construction and projection were necessary for comprehension in the alien world.

[3] *See Chapter 4, Linda Porter, Page 267.*

I asked Sparks why the aliens would spend so much time teaching him if their language can only be understood with their technology in their world.

> "I sense what they've been teaching me is some sort of common ground for communication between them and us. I can now draw out every stroke and every letter we have in our English alphabet, except for X, Q and Z. They don't use those, at least not with me. I also suspect it's like an elementary school for learning telepathic communication because the motion, the direction you make the symbols, is about vibration somehow. If you can pick up that vibration, you can get meaning. Doing these symbols over and over might be activating some 'muscle' in my mind that I don't use normally, but can still function telepathically if I'm trained."

Over seven years from 1988 until the spring of 1995, Jim Sparks was repeatedly "pulled" several times a month for punishment and reward sessions until he learned all the alphabet, several numbers, phrases and symbols. Then the education went to a new level.

> "After one teaching session was over, I fully expected the reward session to begin. Instead, pages and pages of sentences and paragraphs appeared on the wall screen all written in perfect American English grammar. It didn't take me long to realize I was reading a story about the life of a close friend of mine. I was enthralled because of how accurately it was depicting the details of his life. The story began with his name, where he was born, where he went to school, his childhood likes and dislikes, his teenage years right through to the present. The story

didn't stop there. It continued through to the future as if it already had happened. I was amazed.

"After reading all twenty pages or so, two more pages appeared on the wall screen written in the alien language I was learning. These pages appeared directly to the right of the twenty pages I had just read as if to make a comparison. Since I was so amazed by the story, I voluntarily took a stab at reading the next two pages that appeared, although they were in alien form.

"'Wow, wow, wow!' I shouted. I could actually read what those two alien pages were saying. What was even more astounding was the fact it was the same detailed word-for-word information in a very condensed form.

"It became even more astounding when another page appeared that had the alien alphabet in what seemed like a shorthand version. For example, it showed the letter A and next to it their symbol version and next to that a shorthand symbol version of the letter A. It took more than twenty pages of our writing to tell the life story of my friend, but in the alien writing, it took only about half a page.

"Then another page appeared with one single symbol on it about the size of a fifty cent piece. After staring at this symbol, I almost fainted from amazement. This one single small symbol housed twenty pages of information in detail I could read in a matter of a few seconds."

"But, Jim, if the aliens taught you to read from right to left, how would you be able to understand anything scattered inside a circle?

"I don't know, but I did understand with their computer machine and that real alien standing next to me drilling it into my head. I know it has something to do with weird patterns which I don't understand. When I was there, I would get the message in my head and wouldn't consciously think how I deciphered it. I just looked at that circle and understood it was the same as the half page before and the two pages before that and the twenty pages of our language before that.

"Sometimes they don't even use anything that resembles a page. They'll scatter stuff all over the place! It will be hanging in the air or up against the wall and the symbols will actually form before your eyes. So I guess that's like a moving hologram or something. It's hard to comprehend. I can't say I've got all this down pat. I don't. When a human being gets around them and all this shit is flashing all over the damn place, if you try to comprehend it, you get lost. So what I do to get even the smallest anchor or grip on something is I look at one area and I stay with that and try to understand that one little simple thing. I focus on it

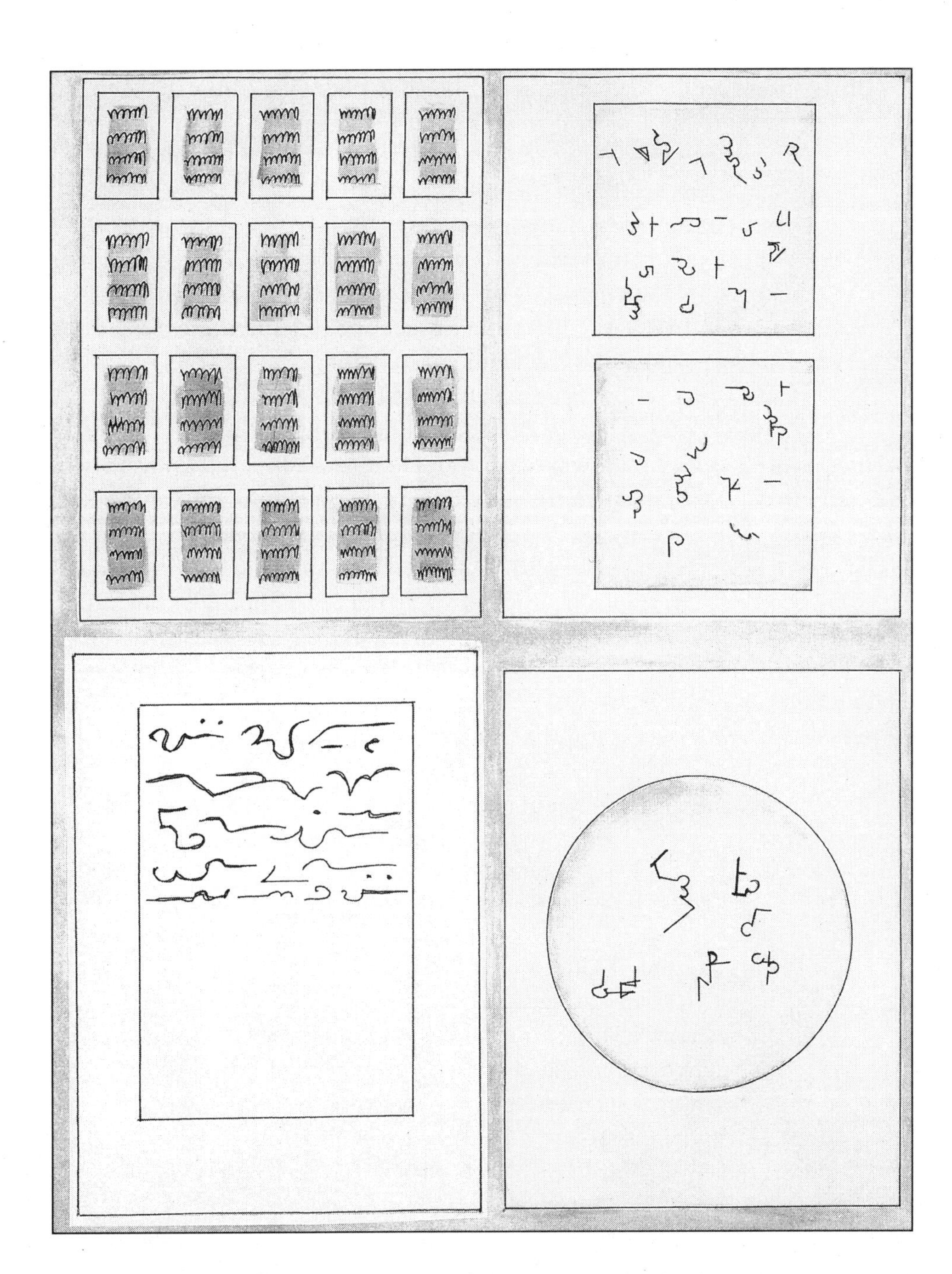

Plate 5 - *Twenty pages of English text retold in only two pages of alien symbols, further reduced to one-half page in alien shorthand and further reduced to one circle of shorthand symbols equivalent to the full 20-page English text. Drawings by Josi Galante © 1996 for Jim Sparks.*

only because there is no way I could even begin to grasp what's happening unless I try to understand one thing at a time."

"Can you now, after all of the education, look at alien symbols on a flat page here and understand them?"

"I can pick up some things, but a lot of things I can't. And how do I even go to another person and say, 'This is how they communicate —

the symbols go through your head, the stuff's hanging in the air.' I'm going to sound like a crazy person!"

"So you've got to be in their environment with their equipment under their mental influence to really understand?"

"To get the whole communication - yes."

"What about their number system?"

"The aliens I've dealt with only have six numbers. I would keep writing a seven to bug them and they'd keep telling me there was no seven. That aggravated them which I enjoyed doing."

I sent this chapter to Mario Pazzaglini, Ph.D., who earned his Master of Science degree in Clinical Psychology from George Washington University in Washington, D. C. Simultaneously, he worked in a double program on his doctoral degree in Sensory Neural Physiology and Abnormal Psychology from the University of Delaware in Newark. Dr. Pazzaglini has studied many symbols provided by people in the human abduction syndrome since the 1980s, including some from Betty Andreasson Luca in Plate 7, who is discussed in Chapter 4.

He agreed to study Jim Sparks's version of the alleged non-human symbols and numbers and to provide his professional assessment which is reported here in full:

> "Assessment of Alleged Non-Human Symbols and Numbers
> Described in Jim Sparks's Story
> by Mario Pazzaglini, Ph.D.,
> Clinical Psychology and Sensory Neurophysiology
>
> This sample of alien writing is interesting in that it lends itself to layers of analyses. Superficially, it appears to be rudimentary and perhaps purely human-generated. But, the Jim Sparks symbols also present unexpected facets.
>
> In form, this script falls between two general classes of alien writing. The classes referred to are of three types generated by a compilation and study of alien script which I have collected over fifteen years. These classes are:
>
> 1) Geometric forms – circles, squares, angles, triangles.
>
> 2) Dot and line forms – where symbols are made of various combinations of dots and lines.
>
> 3) Cursive – where the symbols look like Gregg shorthand.
>
> Most alien writing from abductees seems to fall in the latter group and now represents the largest of the three

Plate 6 - *Supervisor non-human being that appeared with powerful presence and ordered Jim Sparks to write his question in alien symbols after Sparks argued with small, grey "drones." Drawing by Josi Galante © 1996 for Jim Sparks.*

groups of writing. The Sparks sample looks like an intermediary between classes 2 and 3 above. Its later iteration as combinations of symbols looks in general like class 3 usually seen in abductee cases. Oddly, it is in this second iteration that dots become combined with cursive forms to produce the final script.

Combining the images from Mr. Sparks's narrative, there are really four levels or variants of this script.

a) First, there is the script which appears on a flat 2-dimensional surface of paper.

b) Secondly, that 2-dimensional form is understood as 3-dimensional because Mr. Sparks says that the symbol for A, which looks like a simple horizontal stroke is actually three superimposed strokes of repeated motion on the same line.

c) Thirdly, the simple alphabetic elements are combined into shorthand condensed forms.

d) And fourth, the entire text of a script is condensed into one complex symbol with multiple layers of motion and meaning.

This is clearly a very complex system apparently relating somehow to the native alien script as used by the aliens themselves and secondly to a system that would be teachable to humans. Mr. Sparks's symbols may not be the actual and purely alien script. He suggests himself that it is a 'common ground for communication between them and us.'

Looking at this script, several observations can be made in stages.

<u>Stage 1 - First Impressions:</u>

a) This is an alphabetic script where one symbol equals one sound, just like our alphabet.

b) The aliens have presented to Jim Sparks equivalents to human sounds and alphabet which is an odd fact for a supposedly alien source. Even different earth cultures with the same voice box produce different phonemes. Either this is made up or the aliens are tailoring a system to us humans.

c) Some alien letters resemble their English alphabetic equivalents. For example: B is 3, C is ◡ , S is ɔ or one-half of S. At this level of analysis, the possibility that this is actually an 'alien' script is suspect.

d) There are 'follows' which are also found in earth-based artificially made-up scripts. As the name implies, symbols in these made-up scripts tend to follow one another. For example,

c follows d and e follows f

The fact that there are follows in the Jim Sparks symbols raises additional questions about its alleged alien source. Is this made-up by a human? Or alien? Or for a human-alien psyche interface of some type? Does the human mind add a note of rigidity to the process of forming an alphabet for communication? Why couldn't the aliens come up with clearer and more distinguishable symbols? Are those particular symbols necessary somehow to provide the aliens with the forms they need to perform subsequent operations with human minds?

e) Jim Sparks's symbol for the letter R actually does resemble the ancient Greek letter rho ; S looks like a type of Greek S or C ; B is mildly like a Greek beta .

Are these accidents? In Chapter 1 of this book and in other alleged alien symbol communications I have studied, there are resemblances to early and classic Greek.[4]

So, in this first stage of impressions, one would suspect that this is a humanly-produced (consciously or unconsciously) symbol system. It seems to share too many characteristics of made-up alphabets and doesn't look well-formed as a coherent system of well-defined alphabetic symbols.

<u>Stage 2 - Analyses of Symbol Shorthand:</u>

In its more complex form, the Sparks script eliminates many of the above criticisms and the first impressions become less clear in the third and fourth iterations of the symbols when they are combined into a shorthand script. Those combined symbols of condensed cursive-style script look very much like examples of script from other abductees. This in and of itself does not make them alien, but it is interesting that widely divergent sources, unaware of what other abductees have described, do write similar-looking script, such as Betty Andreasson Luca's in Plate 7.

[4] *See pages 59-60, Chapter 1.*

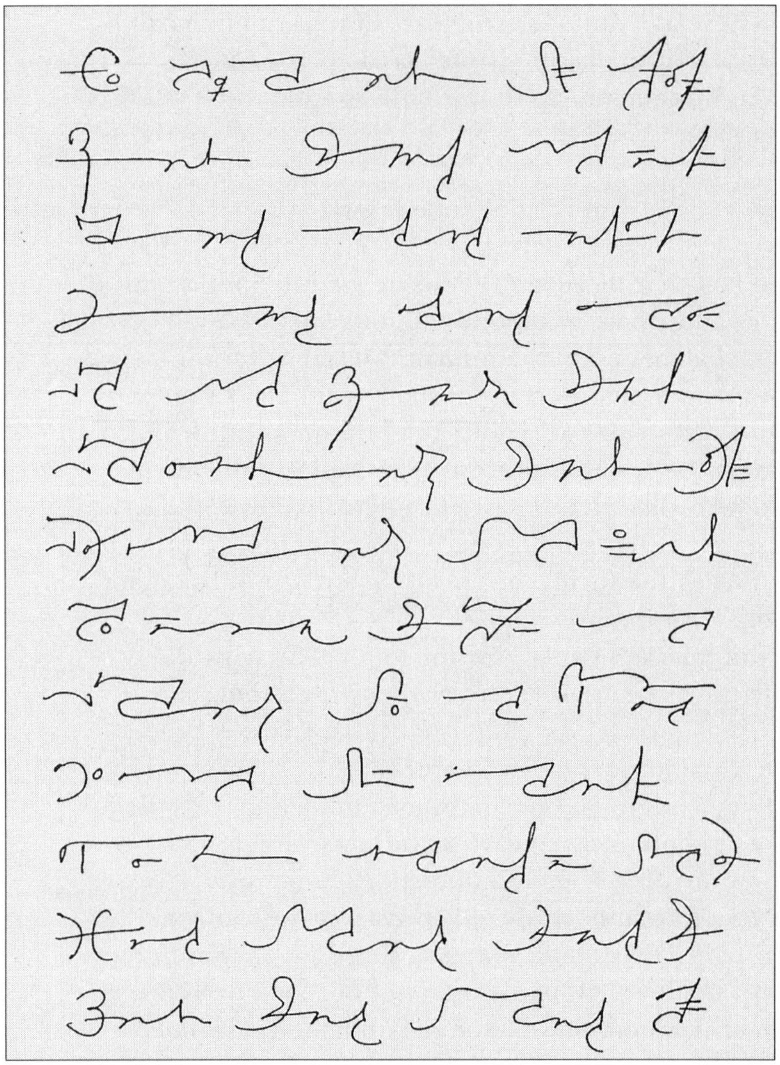

Plate 7 - *Script written by abductee Betty Andreasson Luca in the 1980s after non-human contact.*

These complex forms are not 1:1 letter-to-sound symbols. Their placement on the page is not linear, but produces a whole gestalt of meaning as described in the text. Perhaps the most provocative and unique aspect of Sparks's description is the requirement for 3-dimensional projection in order for the script to be fully understood. Three-dimensional conceptualizing is rarely mentioned as a characteristic of other purported alien scripts.

Historically some so-called magical scripts, or sigils, also are said to require a three-dimensional conceptualizing. In a conversation with an assistant to Aleister Crowley, who was a member of the Order of the Golden Dawn and leader of the O. T. O. Ordo Temperalis Orientalis (Order of the Eastern Temple) in the early to middle 20th Century, it was mentioned that some portions of the Enochian chessboards[5] used in the Enochian system of magic were to be seen in three dimensions. Aleister Crowley followed directions of Queen Elizabeth I's court astrologer, John Dee, who said he received the Enochian system from a luminous being. Crowley and Dee understood that three dimensions were necessary in order to visualize properly the symbols needed to contact other worldly entities.

[5] *Enochian chessboards were derived from John Dee, the court astrologer for Elizabeth I, Queen of England and Ireland, 1558-1603. Dee said he received the Enochian system from a luminous being.*

There are other cases in which 'aliens' have told their abductee-contactee students that the alien script is multi-leveled. In one of the script samples, it was said that the script was to be 'read' by passing a finger over it and that in this way 'thought will be produced' equivalent to reading the script. Further, these particular entities said that different levels of meaning could be elicited upon repeated finger passes over the same script.

While we cannot definitely say that the Sparks script is alien (nothing is definite in this field), we can say that it does not follow the common characteristics of hoaxed or made-up scripts. It describes a complex system which possibly is capable of forming a communication link between totally dissimilar minds — a link between ourselves and the Other, human and alien. But nothing is clear in this elusive phenomenon.

Stage 3 - Analysis of Numbers

This is an odd number system for an advanced culture. First, there is no zero which is an essential feature of a computational system. The Romans had a terrible time with their system for this reason. The Arabs and Mayans both had the concept of zero and were able to go quite far with computations. Therefore, six is an odd number to use as a base. It would be better to use 10, or 2 even as in a 0 and 1 binary system; or even 60 as the Babylonians had. Those systems again are more convenient for computations. The earth-based systems that use 12 or 6 x 2 as in the foot and inch are very complex to work with. Why would aliens use such an odd system? Numbers are numbers. Of course, it's clear we don't understand what the aliens are up to and don't know how they 'think.' It's possible that their 6-based number system could relate to the six sides of a 3-dimensional cube with zero at the center.

With six 'numbers' or 'states,' there are 6^6 (6x6x6x6x6x6) or 46,656 possible 'states' using the cube mode if each number can be used more than once, or 6! (6x5x4x3x2x1), or 720 states if each number is used only once. 720 is 2 x 360, as in 360 degrees in a circle. (Plate 8)

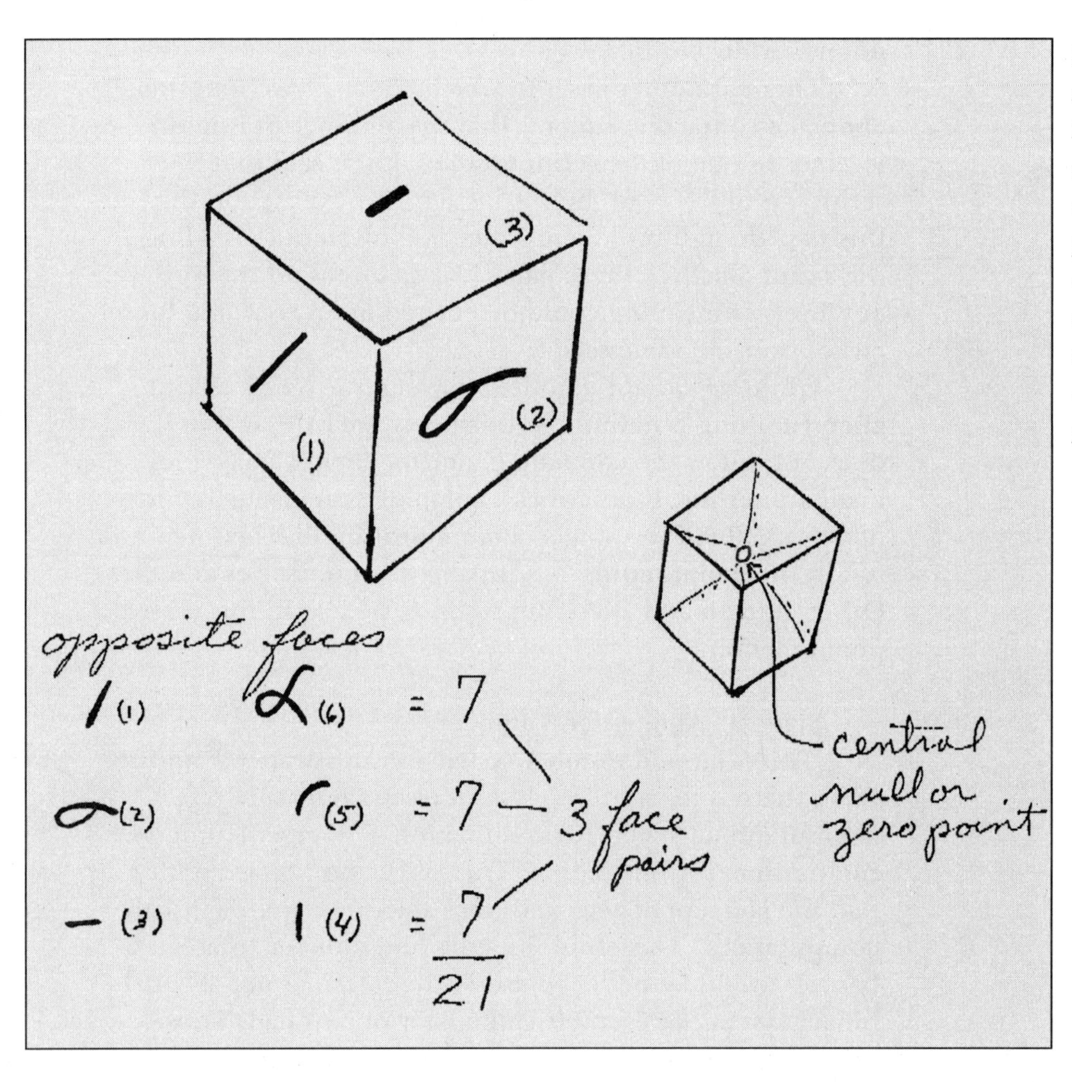

Plate 8 - *Drawing by Dr. Mario Pazzaglini to illustrate possible three-dimensional system based on six numbers and a zero point.*

In the modern world, Stan Tenen of the Meru Foundation in Sharon, Massachusetts has produced a three-dimensional form that rotates in space. Tenen said that its various shadows cast on a two-dimensional surface form the letters of the Hebrew alphabet.

The Meru Project booklet states: 'Stan Tenen tracked the spiral of a tube torus out of the middle and took out the shape. He removed the minimum amount of matter to delineate the tube torus and placed it inside a three-dimensional tetrahedron. (Plate 9) He found that by shining a light through it so that the shadow of that shape came out onto a two-dimensional surface, he could generate all the letters of the Hebrew alphabet, exactly as they are written and in order.

He also found that by changing the shape to a different position, he could project all the Greek letters. Then by changing the position again, he could configure all the Arabic letters. He did this simply by moving this particular shape to different positions inside a three-dimensional tetrahedron. There are actually twenty-seven primary symmetrical positions inside a tetrahedron.'"

Plate 9 - *The spiral of a tube torus inside a tetrahedron. Drawing by Stan Tenen © 1986, Meru Foundation, Sharon, Massachusetts.*

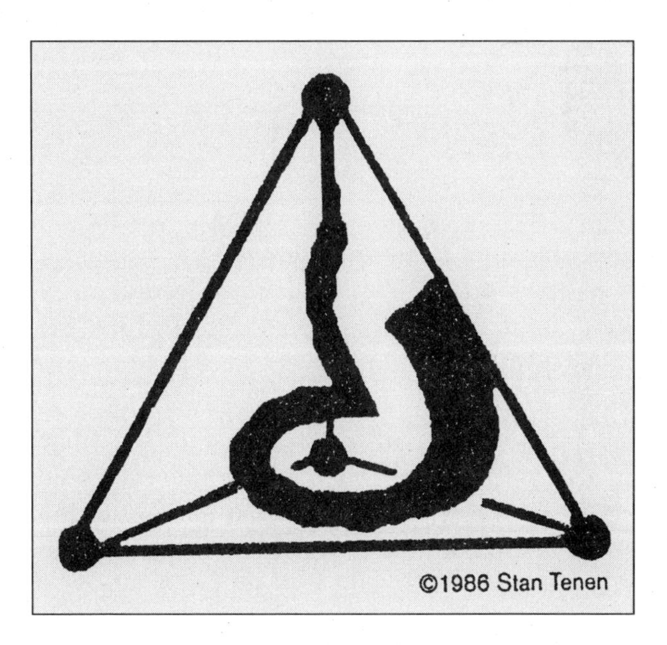

Plate 10 - *Comparison of Hebrew, Greek and Arabic.*

HEBREW

Forms	Name	Forms	Name
א	aleph	ל	lāmedh
ב	bēth	מ ם	mēm
ג	gimel	נ ן	nūn
ד	dāleth	ס	samekh
ה	hē	ע	ʻayin
ו	waw	פ ף	pē
ז	zayin	צ ץ	ṣadhe
ח	ḥeth	ק	qōph
ט	ṭeth	ר	rēsh
י	yodh	שׂ	sin
ך כ	kāph	שׁ	shin
		ת	tāw

GREEK

Forms	Name	Forms	Name
Α α	alpha	Ν ν	nu
Β β	beta	Ξ ξ	xi
Γ γ	gamma	Ο ο	omicron
Δ δ	delta	Π π	pi
Ε ε	epsilon	Ρ ρ	rhō
Ζ ζ	zēta	Σ σ ς	sigma
Η η	ēta	Τ τ	tau
Θ θ	thēta	Υ υ	upsilon
Ι ι	iota	Φ φ	phi
Κ κ	kappa	Χ χ	khi
Λ λ	lambda	Ψ ψ	psi
Μ μ	mu	Ω ω	ōmega

ARABIC

1	2	Name	1	2	Name
ا	ـا	ʼalif	ض	ـض	ḍād
ب	ـب	bā	ط	ـط	ṭā
ت	ـت	tā	ظ	ـظ	ẓā
ث	ـث	thā	ع	ـع	ʻayn
ج	ـج	jīm	غ	ـغ	ghayn
ح	ـح	ḥā	ف	ـف	fā
خ	ـخ	khā	ق	ـق	qāf
د	ـد	dāl	ك	ـك	kāf
ذ	ـذ	dhāl	ل	ـل	lām
ر	ـر	rā	م	ـم	mīm
ز	ـز	zāy	ن	ـن	nūn
س	ـس	sīn	ه	ـه	hā
ش	ـش	shīn	و	ـو	wāw
ص	ـص	ṣād	ى	ـى	yā

Another human abduction case researched by investigator and author Raymond E. Fowler also involved alien symbol training. In a 1989 joint abduction, Betty Andreasson Luca saw her daughter, Becky, tracing alien symbols with her fingers at a machine similar to Jim Sparks's experience.

Betty said, "She's touching with her fingers some symbols that are raised on this screen. She's gotta touch each symbol and trace it. And when she does, a ball of light pops out in front of her. And in that ball of light there is some kind of a picture." A small grey entity told Betty they "were training her." Betty said, "Training for what?" But the being did not answer. The Andreasson investigation is discussed more fully in Chapter 4.

Plate 11 - *Betty Andreasson Luca drew this image of her daughter, Becky, while allegedly on board a spacecraft together in 1989. Andreasson watched Becky trace her fingers over alien symbols on a console where she was being trained much like Jim Sparks's experience. Drawing by Betty Andreasson Luca from* The Watchers II *© 1995 by Raymond E. Fowler, Wild Flower Press.*

Jim Sparks talked to me about a confrontation he had with the alien intelligence in which he demanded to know why they were trying to teach him the symbols.

> "After they showed me the compression with the shorthand symbols, then two small alien workers appeared to my right and a telepathic voice said, 'You will learn this.'
>
> "I responded by saying, 'You mean you want me to learn the short version of your alphabet?'
>
> "They responded, 'Yes.'
>
> "I asked, 'Why?' I waited a few moments and got no response. So

again I asked, 'Why?' I still got no response and this began to make me angry, so I yelled, 'Why me? Why me? Answer me, you bastards!'

"Instantly, the aliens paralyzed my mouth. So I yelled inside my mind, 'Why me? Why me? Why me?'

"Then the two alien workers changed their images into police officers and one of them telepathically kept saying, 'No!' So, I responded by saying, 'You don't scare me!'

"Then they changed their image again to look like fully dressed military generals complete with medals. I yelled back at them inside my mind, 'Bullshit!' And kept on asking, 'Why me?'

"I sensed it was a Mexican standoff because I wasn't going to give in and the aliens weren't going to answer me. I also knew they were trying to scare me with their screen images into cooperating, but it wasn't going to work. I made up my mind that I wanted an answer to the simple question, 'Why me?'

"Suddenly my heart began to race and I could feel the radiated presence of a supervisor, or one of the true aliens coming close. As I sat paralyzed, I could sense him staring over the top right side of my head. I thought, 'Damn! You are powerful!' I could feel him probing through my mind.

"That real alien telepathed, 'Write your question out the way we taught you. Only then will we answer.'

"For the first time, I formed the question 'Why me?' in the writing style the aliens taught me. I couldn't believe I actually wrote it out. So I boldly said, 'You promised to answer my question.'

"They answered it all right, but not in the way I expected. A 3-D holographic scene appeared in full motion about three or four feet in front of me. It looked like a World War II scene complete with dimension and color. Yet, there was no sound and the scene was slightly transparent. There were German officers and soldiers who seemed to be conspiring or planning a military move with Italian officers and soldiers. I sensed a haunting familiarity and stared at one of the Italian soldiers who reminded me of myself. That stirred up some strange emotions. Everybody knows how sinister and dark that period in our history was. This scene made me feel guilty and ashamed for the human race.

"As the scene faded away, another one took its place. It was an industrial city some time in the late 1800s or early 1900s, complete with horse and buggy. A group of men and women were gathered around a building entrance. I saw a man that again reminded me of me. He was dressed in a black suit and top hat. I sensed he owned the factory.

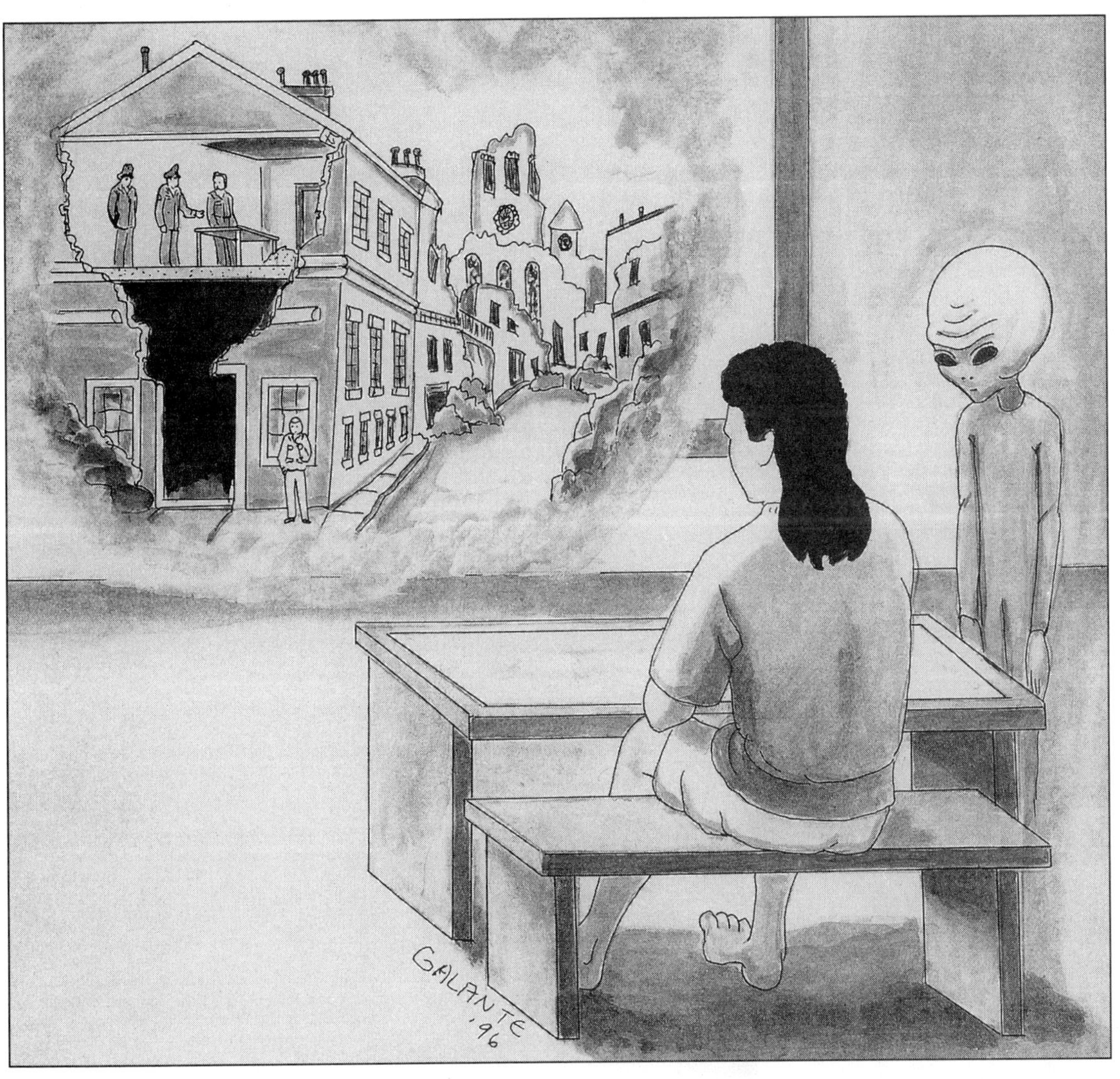

Plate 12 - *The holographic image of German and Italian officers and soldiers in World War II which appeared in a series of scenes after Jim Sparks asked the aliens why they were making him learn their symbol language. Drawing by Josi Galante © 1996 for Jim Sparks.*

"As that scene faded away, another appeared of a small village along a seashore, maybe fifteenth or sixteenth century. There was a man and a woman in a field farming with crude farm tools. He reminded me of me.

"I asked the supervisor alien, 'Have you been following my family line?' I got no response. Then I said, 'That's right. I have to write out the question in your style before you'll answer me.' So I wrote out, 'Have you been following my family line?'

"As soon as I finished writing, I got an answer, 'Yes, look.'

"As the village scene faded away, another appeared that looked like a medieval inn. There were men and women sitting around large,

Plates 13-15 - *Series of holographic scenes projected by alien instructors allegedly of Jim Sparks's ancestry. The implication was that Sparks's bloodline had been monitored and recorded over centuries and could be played back by alien technology. The scenes included a factory in the late 1800s or early 1900s which Jim Sparks sensed his ancestor had owned, a small seashore village farm in the 15th or 16th century, and a medieval inn. Drawings by Josi Galante © 1996 for Jim Sparks.*

Plate 16 - *The Roman Senate. After abduction experience and the series of holographic ancestral images, Jim Sparks was referenced "for more understanding" to an historical novel about Rome.*

Plate 17 - *Jim Sparks interpreted this scene as the forbidden history of man's artificial creation by "Star People" who manipulated DNA in already-evolving primates to create* Homo sapiens.

crudely built wooden tables drinking what looked like wine from pewter mugs. Maybe somewhere between the sixth and twelfth centuries. One man reminded me of me. He was wearing a cloth or leather hat that was slightly pointed and drooped to the side. The man was drinking and laughing and made me want to laugh. The whole time the aliens were showing me the scenes, my mouth was still paralyzed until I wanted to laugh and then I could.

"Another scene appeared and I said out loud, 'Rome!' This scene looked like the Roman Senate. There were about twenty men wearing white robes or togas gathered in a large hall or reception area. Some were standing and some sitting side-by-side on multi-leveled bleachers. These men seemed to be having a debate of some sort. From their facial expressions, I could tell the topic was important. Like before, I saw an individual that reminded me of me, only this time he was just sitting and listening to the others speak like he had all the power.

"I wrote out the question, 'Have you really followed my family line back that far?' The response was, 'Look.' The aliens never waste words.

"Another scene appeared. This time it looked like a flat African savanna. There was a patch of trees with apelike creatures. On closer examination, they seemed to look more human than ape. As I studied the scene, anger welled up in me. I didn't like the message these aliens were obviously trying to portray.

"I responded by saying, 'Bullshit! You really can't expect me to believe that you are genetically responsible for human creation! That you have manipulated the development of these creatures?!' I got no response. And I didn't feel like writing it out."

Jim Sparks's response did not make sense in the context of wanting to learn more about such startling information, but Sparks admitted he angered easily and would rather leave a stressful situation than persist to satisfy his curiosity.

Abductee and writer Anna Hayes has also encountered 3-dimensional symbol training and holographic communication which she stresses are only aspects of a vastly complex technology that can control and manipulate frequencies ranging from the strong and weak forces of atoms to photons. Hayes thinks the hologram answer given Jim relates to his "soul family lineage." From her own interactions, Hayes is convinced that the non-humans monitor both the soul-spirit matrix and DNA.

"Often," Hayes wrote, "they will leave 'pre-recorded' imprints — packages of communicated data in electrical form — within the base codes of the human DNA that will one day be retrieved by the (encoded) human and translated into conscious communicaton or cognition. For those humans who are ready and able to receive such communications directly, the (positive aliens) are willing to begin sharing information and creating conscious relationships."[6] The problem, according to Hayes, are negative types of non-human intelligences who also interact with earth. Their agendas concern their own survival and are "neither benign nor neutral," to repeat the phrase used by the military voices in Chapter 1 who sent me the floppy disc. Manipulating, encoding and accessing particular human DNA seems to be on everyone's agenda.

[6] Voyagers, The Sleeping Abductees *© 1998 by Anna Hayes, Wild Flower Press.*

In November to December 1994, Sparks had another revelation and wrote about it for his manuscript *Star People, Outsiders – Us? Or Them?* from which this excerpt is used with his permission. Jim said he was pulled the hard way and then regained consciousness.

> " I found myself with my feet dangling down from an examination table. I was almost paralyzed, but not completely. I had total range of mobility but I could only move very slowly and my peripheral vision was somewhat blocked. I was in a huge rectangular room or facility about half the size of a football field. The room was lighted well and the table that I sat on was positioned about thirty to forty feet from one of the walls. The surface of the interior walls seemed to be made up of metal. In fact, the room looked like the interior of a jet hanger. As I continued to slowly turn my body and head to look around, I saw military guards! They were lined up with their backs facing the wall about every twenty feet and wore side arms.
>
> "I heard the loud sound of jet engines screaming as if about to take off just outside the building or hanger I was in. I turned my head to look and saw a raised rectangular platform about twenty feet long and ten feet wide. There seemed to be two or three tiers of steps around the entire perimeter of the platform. On the surface was what appeared to be two large barrel-shaped transparent containers either made out of glass or maybe energy of some sort like a magnetic or electronic field. They were about five feet in diameter and about eight feet high. The top and bottom had large chrome-colored metallic rims or lids. It shocked me to see a man in one and a woman in the other. Then I saw two men in white lab coats and an alien. The three of them approached the male individual in one of the containers. My vision began to blur and I couldn't see clearly.
>
> "I seemed to sense the containers were part of some sort of transport system. They didn't look like anything I have seen inside craft and

I sensed they were man-made by us, but alien technology was being used. I was very confused. Why was the alien there? Was he involved with our military? Did they transport me from my house into one of those containers? Why was I there?!

"Then the two men and the alien turned their attention to the woman in the other container. She looked frozen, like a zombie. As they started to handle her, one of the men held something in his hand that looked like a metal rod or wand. He was touching her with it. That made me mad and I somehow got up and tried to pull the men away. The alien stepped back and screen-imaged the two men to look like aliens. It didn't work. I was too angry to be scared. Then the vision of the two aliens turned back into humans again. One of the men motioned the guards who were approaching to back off. The man holding the rod said out loud, 'I'll handle this.' I knew then he was human because aliens don't talk out loud.

Plate 18 - *The hangar containing transparent cylinders encasing a man and a woman and monitored by military guards, two men in lab coats and an alien being. Drawing by Josi Galante © 1996 for Jim Sparks.*

"That man touched the back of my hand with the rod and it stung. He hurt me half a dozen times and things started to get fuzzy and I somehow found myself sitting back on the examination table again. When I looked back over at the platform, the containers were empty and I blacked out. When I opened my eyes again, I was laying down being examined by something that kept changing back and forth from a human to an alien and I felt drugged.

"The examiner told me out loud to sit up because he had instructions for me. He lectured me in a fatherly fashion that I could clearly hear, but my mental state was such that I couldn't consciously retain it very well. I would hear, understand, and then forget. Then the man walked up to me as I sat there with my legs hanging over the table. He leaned over the top right side of my head and told me to read a book! He named the author and title. He then said it would aid my understanding. The book was *The Roman* by Mika Waltari.[7]

[7] The Roman © *1964 by Mika Waltari, originally published in Finland. Other Waltari books included* The Egyptian © 1949 and The Etruscan © 1956.

"Then a huge hangar door opened slowly. It was nighttime and we were in the middle of the desert and it reminded me of the land around Las Vegas where I used to go sometimes on vacations. The acceleration pull began and I could see lights of a disc hovering outside the open hanger door as my vision faded before I blacked out.

"Back home, I found myself momentarily paralyzed on the living room sofa. On my hands were nine, red, half-inch cuts exactly where that man stung me with that rod or wand. It just didn't make sense to show me a place like that which must be top secret unless we are on the brink of a major change in this country. And who wanted me to see it?"

Sparks told me at the time he didn't think about photographing the red marks. In fact he did not want any of it to be real. But one of Jim's friends, Donald Watkins in Ft. Myers Beach, Florida, wrote to me: "In late 1994 (I believe it was November), ... I noticed the back of Jim's hand had several fresh scars. I remember pointing to his hand and asking, 'What happened?' I could tell from his response that he did not want to talk about it. The wounds were small and looked randomly scattered, perhaps as many as four to six separate wounds approximately the size of the diameter of a cigarette or smaller, not circular, but rather jagged. These wounds were on his right hand and looked as if he had been doing car engine repair work, which he had not." The implication was the red marks looked burned like skin touched by hot metal.

Another implication was that the government of the United States is working at some level with non-humans. Perhaps our government has already developed point-to-point teleportation technology with alien help and some how teleported Sparks from his living room into that hangar. Perhaps there are also efforts to clone people in tubes using alien technology similar to that described in the Chapter 4 experiences of Linda Porter, Wanna Lawson and Ken Rose. Further, the human's suggestion to Jim Sparks that he read a novel about Rome to better understand what was happening in the hangar suggests the humans working with the aliens have knowledge about a relationship between human ancestry, its evolution and the alien agenda.

Jim Sparks told me:

> "Linda, sometimes I think there are governments within governments within governments. Number One is the U. S. government, the one we, the people, deal with at face value. Number Two is the government that covers up things like Roswell and downed alien craft. Number Three is the government I call the B.B.B. (Black Budget Boys) or the Secret Club.
>
> "Number One doesn't know a damn thing. Number Two thinks it knows what's going on and stumbles its way around. Number One and Two aren't even aware that Number Three exists."

After this highly strange mix of military, aliens, humans in tubes and the suggestion that Sparks read *The Roman* "for more understanding," Jim went to the library. He was shocked to find the exact title and author of an historical novel that was almost six hundred pages long. The plot focuses on the memoirs of a man named Minutus Lausus Manilianus, a Roman who lived in the time of Nero (Lucius Domitius Ahenobarbus), the notorious Roman tyrant and emperor who ruled from A.D. 54-68. A cliche throughout history has been "Rome burned while Nero played the violin." Nero had grandiose self-indulgences including singing in the streets at night much to the public's dismay. After the great fire of A.D. 64, critics claimed Nero burned the city down in order to rebuild it to his own tastes. In the end, with the treasury empty, the Roman Senate publicly denounced Nero and he slit his own throat on June 9, A. D. 68.

In *The Roman,* Minutus was born into a family of wealth and privilege when Christianity was beginning to flower. Minutus's father claimed he had met Jesus Christ after the resurrection and died a Christian convert. Minutus, however, remained outside religious convictions and served Nero's government, travelling widely through the Roman Empire, including Britain where Queen Boadicea, or Boudicca, revolted against the abusive and profane Roman rule in A.D. 60. While in Britain to serve with the Roman Army, Minutus was known to have integrity and courage. But upon returning to Rome, he moved increasingly into powerful positions of state and was seduced by greed, lust and power that decayed into jealousies and betrayals, an executive going along with executive orders, even if immoral and perverse, to stay in favor with the CEO.

Minutus allowed Nero to condemn his own son to the Coliseum lions without protest because Minutus was afraid that if he asked Nero to spare his son's life, the Emperor would throw him to the lions as well. Ironically, Minutus did die in the arena before one of Nero's successors, Domitian, whom he had come to hate. A lion that should have attacked Minutus mysteriously licked his hand instead. Then Minutus denounced the moral decay of Domitian loudly and publicly. The angry Emperor had his bowmen immediately kill Minutus and the passive lion. Christians awaiting their own deaths in the Coliseum interpreted the lion's peacefulness as a sign of God's and Christ's "inexplicable grace" to the Roman who sometimes had tried to do good, but otherwise had lived by power and abuse.

In the end, Minutus — like Nero — had no bloodline left. Both his sons were dead from treachery and betrayal. Outside his bloodline, his wife had an illegitimate son after an adulterous affair with an animal trainer. So, in light of Jim Sparks's understanding that the aliens were trying to show him how his bloodline had been monitored back to Rome and before and that the book was to help him understand his involvement with the military and aliens, Sparks has no clear understanding of who his ancestor might have been.

However, specific ancestral identity might not have been the point. The Roman Empire evolved from a strong and self-reliant agrarian culture to one so greedy and self-serving in its wealth, lust and power that it could not see the Doomsday Cliff ahead until it fell and lost everything. Even the rich man's extravagant dinnerware and plumbing made of lead were poison.

And like a cycle on the spiral, history seems to be repeating itself. Industrial nations today which dominate the planet are also obsessed by greed and power and lust. But this time it's not one city, one country or one empire decaying in the absence of the sacred. This time the environmental health of the entire planet is in jeopardy as trees and rain forests are cut down, asphalt spreads across the landscape and industrial pollutions poison the air, water and soil which animals, plants and humans depend upon for life.

> Sparks said: "After I read that book and thought about those holographic scenes the aliens showed me, I figure they somehow monitored and recorded my ancestors and were trying to show me that I'm a descendent of one of those Roman guys. And whatever my ancestors did wrong before, the aliens are trying this time to get me

to help stop the burning of the rain forests and cutting down trees."

Sparks emphasized that his experiences with the holographic ancestral images were not, for him, the same as reincarnation defined as the recycling of souls in different body containers discussed in Chapter 4.

"I think memories get housed in your genes. When we procreate, those memories are passed along to the next person and get stored in that body. The family line from the past, everything they experienced, gets passed along. And the message for me boils down to genetic tracking and the fact these aliens have been involved one way or another with us humans for thousands of years.

"I also think some sort of tracking gene is passed along from generation to generation. Aliens don't necessarily abduct people at random. I doubt that each time throughout the millennia these aliens wanted to find an ancestor of mine, or any other member of a particular family line, that they would have to go on a wild goose chase. It makes sense that they have a tracking device embedded or encoded in a gene that gets passed from one generation to another."

Jim Sparks and I also discussed the possibility that accumulating genetic memory of past experiences might be equivalent to producing library books that keep increasing their information and expanding pages with each generation. With their advanced technologies, the alien beings could "play back" human lives the way we check books and CD-ROMs out of libraries for entertainment and education — perhaps information from both genes and souls. In fact, during Betty Andreasson's first encounter with small, grey androids at her home in South Ashburnham, Massachusetts, she offered them meat to eat. The entities replied: "But that's not our kind of food. *Our food is tried by fire, knowledge tried by fire.*" [8] (Howe's emphasis.)

Sparks, like so many other people affected by the human abduction syndrome, had mixed feelings about the alien use of his body and genes.

[8] The Andreasson Affair © *1979 by Raymond E. Fowler, Prentice-Hall.*

"Linda, the aliens scan us and know us better than we know ourselves. Their technology gives them the ability to scan and record every minute detail of our lives. Even lost memories are pulled out. And semen extraction was common with me. Was I offended at first? Yes. Did I feel degraded at first? Yes. Do I feel that way today? No, because now I have a better understanding. Not only do the aliens take semen from men and eggs from women, they also extract other raw materials from us humans. And one reason is to create those little grey worker drones as a commodity to trade on a galactic scale. It's like they farm us for raw materials."

"Jim, did the aliens show you or tell you specifically that they have a galactic market in drones?"

"You mean, did they ever sit me down and say, 'Hey, here's what we're doing?' No, because they can be deceptive and lie sometimes. But after I got used to being with those bizarre, weird, whatever-the-hell they are — THINGS — then I would just observe."

"So how would you summarize the agenda of the grey beings you've encountered so many times?"

"I think they were originally responsible for creating who we humans are from whatever was here on earth naturally in the beginning — which possibly was those monkey things that they showed me in the hologram. I think that the aliens follow the family lines for different reasons or genetic lines for different reasons and they are highly interested in reproductive materials first and foremost. I speculate that what they do with those reproductive materials is make drones — what you call androids — and hybrids. I have seen hundreds of those dummy clones, the little grey guys that all look the same, laid out on gurneys like an assembly line. And I think the real aliens sometimes take my emotions to give to their little androids so that when the androids go about their tasks they know they are alive. I've also seen other hybrids that are part us and part them that might end up re-populating the earth one day if we screw up."

"Would you say that the androids physically resemble the 'true aliens' even though they are smaller?"

"Yeah. I would say they were closer to the scientist aliens than they are to humans. But you could say they sort of look like something between both of us. The android things are pretty featureless — big heads, big eyes, they pretty much all look alike. But the real aliens, their features are more different and vary from one to the other."

"And do you think the aliens make biological androids to be used not only on this planet but on other planets, too?"

"Yes."

"The drawing of the 'true alien' next to you in the teaching scene has penetrating eyes that seem to be 3-dimensional whereas the biological androids drawn in a preceding scene don't have that quality. Are the eyes especially different in the true aliens?"

"What I call the 'true aliens' radiate or generate an energy that you can sense and it's overwhelming. And the worker guys don't have much, if any. Does it have to do with the eyes specifically? Maybe. Maybe the eyes have a connection to their brain and the power that radiates from them. I don't know. I had one particular incident I'll never forget because I usually avoid eye contact with them. I avoid looking at their face."

"What is it that frightens you?"

"They are scary! You don't feel comfortable. So, if I don't look at them, I feel more comfortable than when I do look at them. And if I don't have to look at them, I don't. But the time I kicked one was probably the strongest connection from that being's mind. What I did was spontaneous on my part. I just kicked at him. That caught this creature off guard. It immediately focused everything it had right to my face and into my brain. It was like a hundred thoughts and feelings in like a split second and BOOM! I flopped back down on the table."

"You mean like the alien locked on to your mind?"

"Oh, damn, yes! It was overwhelming!"

"What was the content?"

"It was, 'You know you shouldn't have kicked me, why did you kick me?, you know that was wrong to kick me, kicking me can hurt me, kicking me can hurt you, you should be ashamed of yourself, you should feel bad about this, on and on and on, a hundred thoughts like that in a *split* second. Every emotion and feeling — and whatever emotions they have are at a different level. We are like children with our emotions and they are like adults with theirs."

"So you think they can communicate a hundred thoughts in a fraction of a second into a human mind?"

"Oh, yeah! No doubt! That I'm 100% positive about — that's not speculation. That's a fact!!"

"Have you ever had that kind of rapid telepathic communication with symbols overlaid in your mind at the same time?"

"Yes. They've showed me symbols along with my life flashing before my eyes all at the same time."

In the spring of 1995, Jim Sparks felt like he graduated to yet another level of relationship with the alien beings. He was given the completely conscious task of helping to calm dozens of human men and women brought to an outdoor location for an apparent multiple abduction. Sparks was no longer paralyzed and could walk around and help people at the abduction site before transport to several discs and inside the craft. Sparks felt a mixture of pride about the new alien trust in him and guilt about helping the aliens control his fellow human beings.

After that, Jim Sparks had an abduction experience that changed him, he says, forever and left him obsessed with saving the rain forests and stopping the human slash and burn by fire that is destroying them. This experience, excerpted here with Jim's permission, is puzzling because yet another alien type is introduced. These reptilian entities also provoke questions about a possible connection to viper references in Enoch of the Dead Sea Scrolls and the Book of Genesis in the Bible.

JIM SPARKS ENCOUNTER WITH REPTILIAN HUMANOIDS, THEIR WARNING AND POSSIBLE AGENDA

"The pulling started the usual way with a low-pitched whirling sound, only this time it didn't speed up as fast or get as loud and it was more gentle. I was paralyzed again, but I momentarily regained consciousness before the final transport sequence was complete and I could see where I was going. That was a first!

"As my eyes opened, I saw that I was at least a thousand feet above the ground and slowly descending. Below me was an abandoned carnival park. I was floating over a large, old-fashioned wooden roller coaster and I wasn't scared! I was calm and relaxed and the ride was so gentle I was actually enjoying it.

"When I was twenty or thirty feet from the ground, I started to slowly rock back and forth several times like a pendulum — almost like I was being guided to a target and this was the final adjustment. Then I saw the profiles of about a dozen large creatures standing in a semicircle. Although it was night, I could make out the shapes of their body size and they were large, even by human standards. A few inches from the ground, I blacked out.

"As I began to regain consciousness, I was standing and heard telepathically loud and clear:

> 'We would have given it to you, but we knew it wouldn't have meant anything unless you earned it. It was the only way you could possibly understand what you have been a part of and what you have to do.' (I now know the 'it' was knowledge.)

"I was clearheaded and wide-awake conscious. There were twelve large, humanoid creatures standing in almost a complete circle in which I was a part. The creatures appeared to be at least six feet tall. All of them had their heads turned towards the alien who was standing to my immediate left.

Plate 19 - *Aerial view of large, non-human creatures in abandoned carnival park as Jim Sparks remembered descending through the air, physically or out of body, during a March 1995 abduction. Drawing by Josi Galante © 1996 for Jim Sparks.*

Plate 20 - *Jim Sparks's depiction of the holographic human face superimposed over the large reptoid's head. The lizard-eyes can be seen behind the human face. Drawing by Josi Galante © 1996 for Jim Sparks.*

"The only apparent light source was on the face of this creature, like a *hologram of a human face superimposed and glowing over the alien's face.* (Howe's emphasis.) It was radiating light and this was done to disguise his true appearance. He had done this to make me feel less apprehensive. The creatures didn't take into consideration that as this holographic face spoke and moved its lips, there was no audible sound.

"The voice being communicated telepathically was out of sync with the lips! Plus, the face was obviously a hologram because it was slightly off center from the body. But it worked nonetheless because I wasn't scared.

"As the reptoids transmitted telepathically, I noticed that each alien seemed to be concentrating its thoughts to the creature on my left. One thing for sure, they were of one mind, and it said:

> 'There are some things you need to understand. Yes, it's true that we have been in contact with your government leaders and heads of power. It is also true that agreements have been made and kept secret from your people. It is also true that in the past some of your people have lost their lives or have been badly hurt to protect this secret. Our hands had no part in this.
>
> 'We contacted your leaders because your planet is in grave trouble. Your leaders said the vast majority of your population wasn't ready for anything like us yet, so we made time agreements with your leaders as to when your people would be made aware of our presence. This part of the agreement has *not* at all been kept.
>
> 'It was also agreed that in the meantime, steps would be taken to correct the environmental condition of your planet with our advice and technology. We say advice because we respect the fact that this is your planet, not ours. Your government also broke this agreement.'

"I felt an awful emotion of abandonment from these aliens. They are different. I never sensed true emotion from the other aliens before. But the feeling wasn't at all good. It felt like great loss. I couldn't help asking, 'You aren't giving up on us, are you?'

"There was a long pause of silence and I had a strong feeling of tremendous loss. So I asked again, 'Well, are you?' There was another long pause.

"Then finally,

> 'No. We are now concentrating our energy on the average person. Your air, your water, are contaminated. Your forests, jungles, trees and plant life are dying. There are several breaks in your food chain. You have an overwhelming amount of nuclear and biological weapons which include nuclear and biological contamination. Your planet is over-populated. *Warning*: It is almost to the point of being too late unless your people act now. There are better ways of deriving your energy and food needs without causing your planet any damage.
>
> 'Those in power are aware of this and have the capability to put these methods into worldwide use.'

"I asked, 'Why aren't we doing it now?' There was silence and the whole thing was so strange because I could see that the whole group was thinking and speaking its mind at one time. It felt good because I was a *participant* in an honest to goodness meeting! The best part was that for the first time I was getting direct answers to my questions. 'Why aren't we putting these new methods into use now?'

> 'Those in power view it (technology for clean energy and abundant food) as a military and security threat.'

"Then I got angry as hell and said, 'You mean to tell me our people in power have the ability to save and better this planet and they aren't doing it?!' The thought that technology was being held back from the public because of paranoia and greed outraged me and the aliens saw my anger. But was it true?

> 'Amnesty.'
>
> 'What do you mean?'
>
> 'Complete amnesty. To those in power, the governments and the leaders who have been suppressing the truth. They can't be held liable for any past wrong deeds. It is the only way these leaders can come forward with the truth. It is necessary that you do this in order to work together and survive.'

"There was silence for awhile as if they wanted me to think about what was just said. This was a hard truth to swallow. If anybody had a good reason to hate their government for covering up this information, it was me and others like me. Most abductees still consider themselves victims who constantly suffer ridicule. When your own government's policy is to say, 'You're just plain crazy,' it only deepens the pain.

"But this is a time when intelligence should rule over emotions. So I asked, 'How do I fit in all this? What can I possibly do?'

> 'What you are doing already. We will share much more knowledge with you in the future. Although you understand a lot, we will show you much more. Continue to work with people that come to you. We are aware of the small groups that are forming around the world. These are people who are prepared to learn and we consider them the core. Most important is the condition of your planet. The first step in solving this serious problem is amnesty. We have advice. You will receive more knowledge in the near future.'

"As this was going on, it started to rain. I mean it was pouring! The creatures didn't even budge or try to get out from under it. They didn't have to — we weren't getting wet. Although we were standing completely outdoors with no roof, not one drop of rain touched us. I guess we were being protected by some sort of electric field. I could hear drops as they fell, but there was a clear detectable line (around us) between rainfall and no rainfall. Then they said,

> 'It's time to go.'

"A thought flashed into my mind. 'Wait, please! I have a request. I want to see what you look like.' I'll never forget their response as long as I live.

> 'It will strike fear in your heart.'

"I answered, 'It won't scare me so much if you don't stand there and stare at me. It would help if you would just wave at me. Just don't stare. Promise me you'll wave.' Now I can't believe how stupid that request was. I had in the flesh, face-to-face, probably some of the most intelligent creatures from the far reaches of the galaxy with answers that have been plaguing mankind since the dawn of time. And what did I say? 'Could you wave at me?'

"The strangest thing started to take place. A spinning white light with a hint of green began to radiate over their faces and upper bodies, all dozen of them. The intensity of the light slowly got brighter and it was radiating from no direct or detectable source. I could see they were huge. Their upper torso was strong with huge shoulders and a thick, strong neck like football linebackers. As the light became brighter and details clearer, fear and shock zapped through me.

"I said, 'You have scales!' Their faces looked like a cross between a lizard and a snake — nothing at all like the little grey guys.

"Their eyes were small like ours, only diamond-shaped and the pupils were a red color. Their heads were in normal proportion with their bodies, but bigger than ours. The skull looked like their brains stuck out over their foreheads covered by skin. This feature was slightly different among all dozen of them.

"I said in a scared whimper, 'You promised to wave.' And each and every one of them slowly lifted their arms and waved in front of their faces. Their hands were huge with thick, club-like fingers too thick to work fine instruments. But you have to keep in mind that their technology is thought-activated.

"I stood there and stared at them for awhile in silence, absorbing this spectacular sight. Their message kept running through my mind. I was sure that my country has been involved with aliens. Most Americans believe there's been a cover-up. But what really got to me was the message about the poor condition of our planet! Then I felt the acceleration pull and blacked out.

"I understood better their nature and agenda. They are neither benevolent nor evil. They have been among us in secret for thousands of years, maybe longer. But the length of time isn't as much the issue as why they have been among us. I believe they have been farming us for raw materials.

"We humans have been a self-perpetuating crop, a crop that doesn't need much tending and continues to reproduce, at least up to now and all the earth problems. Thank goodness, they don't kill us. They just *use* us. This system has worked well for the aliens for a long time. But now there's a problem and their investment is in trouble. They have spent a lot of time, travel and effort to farm us. But we are on an almost irreversible path of self-destruction. Nuclear and biological weapons and their waste have polluted the air, land and water. Forests, jungles and trees are being cut down or are dying. Now there are breakdowns in the food chain and the rest of the food chain is contaminated. Over-population, disease and viruses beyond our grasp with new and more complicated illnesses crop up every day. These are just a few of the problems we humans have created.

> "Most of us are blind or numb to this reality because we can still go to the grocer and buy food. We can go to work and back and not see this death and dying. All seems almost normal. But if we environmentally destroy ourselves, the aliens still have an excellent insurance policy. They've been collecting seeds from plants, animals and humans. Through semen and ova extraction, the aliens can start us, or other earth life, all over again here, or somewhere else."

Echoing the Jim Sparks experience, the major concern expressed by abductee Anna Hayes in *Voyagers, The Sleeping Abductees*[9] was competition and conflict among non-human intelligences over earth life and their employment of the same sophisticated technologies to manipulate, deceive and inspire.

[9] Voyagers, The Sleeping Abductees *© 1998 by Anna Hayes, Wild Flower Press.*

> "Just as the original creators of the human prototype desired to see the fulfillment of our species as guardians of the Earth, there also exist forces of great power that do not wish this plan to succeed. If humans are able to fulfill their evolutionary blueprint, the Earth and many other reality fields will no longer be free for exploitation."

Hayes stressed that if humans had truth about their extraterrestrial genetic connection and understood how many outsiders have taken advantage of human ignorance and used sophisticated technologies to manipulate and deceive for their gain, the human family could change and evolve in strength, not weakness.

In conversation, she told me: "Both negative and positive agendas are producing hybrids and androids and both sides are emphasizing the need to save the earth's environment for their various vested interests. Guardian aliens are promoting healing the planet, but the negative groups are also trying to 'help the planet' by offering new technologies so they can have a clean place to take over. I understand the negative ones have had time agreements with the U. S. government about introducing their species to humans.

"Lately, I think the negative ones have told the government they will introduce themselves to the public if the government does not. So, the government is supposedly setting the stage to introduce the negative ones and the negative aliens are planning to help the government 'clear its reputation' by staging false events with holographic inserts. Human minds won't be able to tell what's real and what's not."

Whatever we ultimately learn about the truth in these highly strange cases in which dire warnings are given to humans about the earth's future, the fact is that by the fall of 1997, Jim Sparks was still pretty much in the same place he had been after the carnival park meeting. He had no specific instructions about how to carry out his "mission" to save the environment and to move the U. S. government toward amnesty for all military and intelligence people who had signed oaths of secrecy about UFO-related matters.

However, Sparks had a nighttime visitation by one of the little grey "drones." He said he woke up and was conscious of "the little guy" standing at the foot of his bed. Then he got a clear mental picture of Rome burning and then a rain forest burning along with the strong telepathic communication: "You must put out the fire!"

Jim is confused about the association between Rome burning and the rain forest destruction, but said he wants to do something to save trees.

"Linda, I need to get better known in order to have influence. I want to get to a situation where I can speak publicly so I can talk about the rain forest problems and other issues facing the earth's environment."

"But meanwhile, Jim, every second of every day the forests are on fire."

"That's right."

"So what is being accomplished? Have you contacted groups that are already trying to save the rain forests and joined up with them?"

"No. I have always cared about what happens to the earth, but I've never got myself involved with any groups. This is something new to me. What am I going to say? I'm being advised by ETs?!"

"What details did the reptoids give about air and water damage?"

"They didn't give me exact details. They told me that we've got problems with the air and water and food chain. I was told (in March 1995) that we've got about a decade to turn this thing around. Not that the world will end. But there will be problems in reversing all the damage. And the reptoids said someone in political power already has this knowledge and technology and are hoarding it for security and defense reasons. And probably for greed, too.

'Those Black Budget Boys aren't coming forth with the truth because their asses are on the line. They've got all the secret organizations out there who have taken advantage of this knowledge while everything else goes to hell. That's why the amnesty thing makes sense. Then the BBB guys can tell the truth finally about alien contact, getting alien technology, making money with it and even maiming and killing people to protect that secret. With amnesty, they can come forward with the truth and won't be prosecuted."

"Jim, if there is urgency, why would the aliens go to you when you have no resources to make radical changes?"

"Maybe it isn't just Jim Sparks. It could be a million other abductees, too, for all I know. Maybe all of us are going to do something at the same time. It's a very complicated thing. I wish I had the power today to go down to South America and Malaysia and snuff the fires out. I don't. I know there are organizations like Greenpeace and the Sierra Club and Save the Rain Forests — but have they stopped things, either?"

"Jim, what happens if there's no change in the status quo?

"I think the aliens want to do this with our help. But if that doesn't work, I think they are going to intervene. They use a minimal amount of energy to get the most work done. I think that if they can interact with individuals on this planet, give advice, give technology, show ways of doing things that are better for survival, they'll do that first."

"But why? What's in it for the aliens?"

"The same thing they've been doing with us for the past several thousand years."

"Which is?"

"They farm us. They clone us, they make organs from us and all kinds of stuff. I'm not saying they are wonderful, benevolent beings coming down here to save the earth. Bullshit! They have their own self-interests."

"So, Jim, they want to preserve the earth so they can continue to harvest DNA from certain bloodlines?"

"Yeah. I think the earth will be fine eventually. But *humans* might not be able to live on it. You need a certain percentage of oxygen to breathe."

"You mean the aliens are trying to get their 'crop' to stop self-destructing so they can keep harvesting what they need."

"That's right. And remember, Linda, when this stuff started happening, I didn't ask for it. And not only did I not ask for it, I didn't want anything to do with it."

CHAPTER 4

BODY CONTAINERS AND SOULS OF LIGHT

"...our physical world of the senses is a mere illusion, a world of shadows, and the three-dimensional tool we call our body serves only as a container or dwelling place for Something infinitely greater and more comprehensive than that body and which constitutes the matrix of the real life."

HOLGER KALWEIT
DREAMTIME AND INNER SPACE[1]

[1] Dreamtime and Inner Space © *1988 by Holger Kalweit, Shambhala Publications, Random House.*

The Navy man called Axle in Chapter 1, three of the men in Chapter 2, and Jim Sparks in Chapter 3 appear to be experiencers of what has come to be called the "human abduction syndrome." Men, women and children around the world have described encounters with humanoids thought to be extraterrestrial, or even other-dimensional, since at least the early 1950s. Similar encounters probably occurred in earlier centuries, but the beings were called fairies, elves, gnomes, Little People, tommyknockers, or even angels and demons instead of extraterrestrials.[2] But there continues to be confusion about the true nature of the other intelligences and their intent. Confusion lies in the high strangeness of the encounters, the variety of non-human physical appearances, and lack of consistent communication by the entities about who they are, where they are from, and why they are on planet earth lifting people from cars and bedrooms, or animals from backyards and pastures in beams of light.

[2] Passport to Magonia: From Folklore to Flying Saucers *by Jacques Vallee © 1969, Henry Regnery Co., Chicago.*

Many eyewitness accounts, like some of Jim Sparks's experiences, are conscious. Others describe encounters in "virtual reality" dreams or memories retrieved by hypnosis. Their consensus is that at least two main non-human intelligences are interacting with earth and have a variety of biological androids designed specifically to do tasks in the earth environment. One abductee, Betty Andreasson Luca, says the small, grey entities are "remote imaging surrogates" connected "with bio-electric mind projections" to a tall, humanoid intelligence that assigns tasks on this planet.[3]

[3] The Watchers II *© 1995 by Raymond E. Fowler, Wild Flower Press.*

Interactions with humans and animals often include the harvest of tissue and genetic material such as ova and sperm. Sometimes "baby things" are presented to men and women as if the unearthly-looking infant is "a hybrid that is part us and part them."

Other interactions include the presentation of visual images about the earth's catastrophic future which human subjects believe are either literal, or sense that "like a lab animal" their emotional reactions are being tested and monitored. A variation on these visual presentations are "morality plays" in which the abductee suddenly faces a life and death situation and must willfully choose a course of action.

"After awhile I realized I was like a mouse in a maze being watched from the outside while I sweated and cried trying to do the right thing," Jim Sparks told me. Among the tools in these games with humans are what seem to be holographic images. Steve Bismarck in Chapter 2 saw particles gather in the air, take the form of a wolf-like creature that attacked him with an electric shock, and then dissipated into nothingness. Jim Sparks screamed "Why me?" to his alien abductors and they responded with a series of 3-dimensional images "that hung in the air like holograms."

Abductees are also confronted with actual real life experiences from their own lives in vivid replay. Sparks said, "I felt the strongest emotions of my life were being played back for me, scenes from my real life, and all the pain, fear, joy, love or hate I had once felt were being siphoned off my mind to their little drones. Maybe to make them more like us?"

"Being more like us," some abductees say, relates to at least one non-human intelligence's struggle to survive. Survival issues were also suggested by Jim Penniston in Chapter 1 and Ed Foley in Chapter 2. The non-human intelligence expresses worry about damage to the environment and earth life's survival as if what we do affects them, too, whether we realize it or not. Jim Penniston's experience in Chapter 1 suggests that even time travelers from the future might be involved. Motives are not clear because deception, camouflage and mind manipulation are persistently used by the non-human presence.

There is another category of interaction that has not been widely reported: an alleged "transfer of souls" from body container to body container. The creation, storage and activation of body containers, according to some abductees, is accomplished with "cloning, tube and light technology." Transfers described to me have included the soul moving from a dying human body into a younger cloned version of the same human body; from a currently living human being into an identical cloned duplicate; and a currently living human being into an alien body and back into the human body.

I am sharing these unusual cases for the same reason that researcher and author Raymond E. Fowler wrote in his book *The Watchers II:*[4] "Theological themes in abduction experiences should be accurately recorded. They should not be prejudged or arbitrarily dismissed. After all, it's part of the reported experience. If we decide what to record and dismiss in abduction experiences, we are left with abduction reports created in our own image."

[4] The Watchers II *© 1995 by Raymond E. Fowler, Wild Flower Press.*

Most earth religions in the last 5,000 years of recorded history describe the human soul as the unseen but vital force of life and connection to God which leaves the body at the moment of death. Hundreds of near death experiences (NDEs)[5] have been reported which describe release from the body at death, a trip through a dark tunnel, and merging with a brilliant, loving, peaceful light and sometimes reunion with loved ones who had previously died. The idea that anything else but the hand of God could interfere in that process is not acceptable or comprehensible to human dogmas.

[5] On Death and Dying *by Elisabeth Kubler-Ross, M.D. © 1969, Macmillan Publishers;* Life After Life *by Raymond A. Moody, M. D. © 1975, Mockingbird Books;* Heading Toward Omega *by Kenneth Ring, Ph.D. © 1980, Coward, McCann & Geoghegan;* Recollections of Death *by Michael B. Sabom, M. D. © 1982, Harper & Row;* Children Who Remember Previous Lives - A Question of Reincarnation *by Ian Stevenson, M.D. © 1987, University Press of Virginia.*

However, *The Egyptian Book of the Dead* and *The Tibetan Book of the Dead* were written to help guide the soul at the moment of death around obstacles and dangers often depicted as alligators or reptiles with their mouths wide open waiting to nab a vulnerable soul. Once safely around the obstacles, the soul could venture on to new life in this or another dimension in an eternal cycle of evolving transformations.

The rest of this chapter is devoted to abduction cases I have studied since 1991 which share similar descriptions of human and humanoid bodies preserved in suspended animation in tubes controlled by non-human beings.

Plate 1 - *A painted scene from an Egyptian papyrus which shows the heart of the deceased weighed in the balance against the feather of Truth. The scales are supervised by Anubis, the jackal-headed god of embalming, while the Ba (soul) of the deceased awaits the outcome of the trial. Egyptians thought sins weighed down the heart and a man's evil actions were thought to tip the balance against him. Thoth, the ibis-headed god of writing, records the verdict for Osiris, who sits as judge of the dead accompanied by his wife, Isis. A reptilian creature waits next to Thoth to devour the bodies of those found unworthy to pass into eternity. 21st Dynasty 1085-945 B.C. Source:* Mythology, *Edited by Richard Cavendish © 1993, Barnes & Noble.*

Plate 2 - *"The Judgment,"* Tibetan Book of the Dead, *compiled and edited by W. Y. Evans-Wentz © 1960 Oxford University Press, depicts the King of Truth surrounded by the flames of wisdom judging the dead. Human existence lays below his feet and throne. The Mirror of Karma in his left hand reflects every good and evil act of each of the dead who are being judged at the weighing scales directly below the King. Black pebbles on the right side of the balance represent the evil deeds of the person being judged and white pebbles on the left are the good deeds. There are Six Karmic Pathways beyond death. But, if the judgment is condemnation based on the truth of the scales, three gates lead to the Hells below the judgement level.*

CASE 1 — Linda Porter, Central California

The first week of March 1991, I received a brown, legal-sized envelope by Certified Mail postmarked February 28, 1991 from Porterville, California. The envelope contained an audiocassette, letter and drawings from a woman named Linda Porter.

As I looked at her pencil sketches and notes (Plates 3-7), I instinctively felt her package was important. I remember putting everything back inside the original envelope and setting it on a window ledge directly in front of my typewriter so it would not get lost in other piles of mail and boxes of files about unexplained phenomena that kept accumulating faster than I could buy metal file cabinets to put them in. That same day, I took her audiocassette to play in the car on errands. Her clear and articulate voice impressed me. Linda was an educated person struggling to understand a life full of phenomena that did not fit acceptable categories of reality. She had decided it was important to reach me after hearing a conference presentation I had given in California concerning eyewitness testimony about non-human intelligences interacting with our planet. She was concerned about her vulnerability as a person caught up in the human abduction syndrome and was frightened about the United States government's policy of suppressing the alien presence.

In her letter, she wrote:

> "We (abductees) are caught in the middle of a series of ongoing events that will one day prove to be historically significant to the future of the earth. Unfortunately, because of our continuing, non-voluntary interactions with these beings, we have, in a sense, become victims of both sides of the phenomena.
>
> "On the one hand, we are used by the aliens for their own purposes, whatever those purposes may be. On the other, if we speak out, we risk ridicule from the public, and in some cases, possible harassment and/or intimidation by government and military personnel.
>
> "We then, as abductees, are caught up in the middle of a no-win scenario. A scenario not of our choosing, not of our making, and certainly not of our liking.
>
> "If you could look directly into these creatures' eyes, you'd realize that every detail of your life, no matter how personal, how mundane, how minute, is known to them. It makes me wonder, are we some kind of Ken and Barbie dolls being played with by an emotionally immature race of beings with no sense of morality? Or, are we pawns held in the grasp of a dying race that will do *anything* for their own survival, including the cold-blooded

> manipulation of another species and the brutal mutilation of helpless animals?
>
> "Unless a person has been through the trauma of an abduction, they cannot comprehend how these entities can strip the mind and soul as easily as they can strip the clothes off a body. They scan details of a person's life with such facility that they make you feel as if you are an interesting piece of lint caught between their toes.
>
> "In the blink of an eye, these beings devastate all personal freedom, all sense of privacy, and all prospects for living a normal existence. A person's life is never the same again. He or she is changed forever."

The enclosed audiocassette tape began with events she remembered consciously from age sixteen on. Two other events concerning a "Praying Mantis" entity in a hallway and motion sickness she experienced from transport in what Linda called "interdimensional tunnels" were recalled in one hypnosis session with former NASA research scientist Richard F. Haines. His first UFO investigations were provoked by civilian and military pilot reports of unidentified aerial craft.

One important case that he researched with meticulous efforts and wrote about was an unsolved mystery in Melbourne, Australia.[6] On October 21, 1978, a pilot named Frederick Valentich left Melbourne to fly to King Island. But over Bass Strait south of the Australian mainland, Valentich reported to Melbourne Flight Service that a large unidentified aerial vehicle with "a green light and sort of metallic" shine on the outside was circling above his small Cessna 182. The pilot's last words recorded at the Melbourne Flight Service were: "It is hovering and it's not an aircraft." The next sound was compared to cans rolling around in an empty oil drum and Frederick Valentich disappeared from Melbourne radar. His plane and body were never found. Two years later, in a follow-up investigation, the Melbourne *Sun* reported on July 9, 1980 that about five minutes of the original flight service tape had been cut "in the interest of national security." The case remains unsolved.

[6] Melbourne Episode - Case Study of A Missing Pilot © *1987 by Richard F. Haines, L. D. A. Press, Los Altos, Calif.*

One of the implications of the Valentich case was that he might have been physically taken by the mysterious aerial craft. Subsequently, Richard Haines also investigated the human abduction syndrome and learned how to use hypnosis to probe lost time and haunting flashes of memory. Linda Porter was referred to him in 1988 for a one hour session which helped her recall details about recurring images of a "grasshopper" and moving inside a light beam. Afterward, Porter did not want to do more hypnosis because the recalled information spooked her.

But in the following days, weeks, and months, she spontaneously remembered even more about interactions with non-humans and their technologies. The following are transcribed sections from Linda Porter's first audiotape to me which described the five pencil sketches she included in her February 28, 1991 correspondence.

> LINDA PORTER: "This is one of the first memories that surfaced after hypnosis with Richard Haines in 1988. About three or four weeks afterwards, I was doing the dishes when this one came back to me. I refer you to Sketch Number One. I was evidently about fifteen when it happened, and I remember standing in a narrow corridor on board a small craft. The walls were grey and solid. The floor of the corridor appeared to be a grid of some kind. You could look down through it to a floor below. To my left was a room filled with a dense, very, very bright, silvery light. And the light appeared to have substance to it, like there were tiny little particles in it that were reflecting light. It was a very dense looking light. You could not see through it. I know I was taken into that room, but I have no memory of what happened to me in there except a feeling of real terror, not wanting to know, not wanting to remember, as if something would happen to me if I remembered what happened in there.
>
> "The corridor ahead of me bent towards the left, and I saw what looked like a praying mantis-type creature. He was tall, about eight feet, and he was peering around the corner bent over, I guess, at the waist. The sight of him scared me to death because he looked so horrible. That was the last I remember, and the only thing I have about it now is the feeling that something terrible happened in that room. And I've been warned, I guess, not to remember what it was. The creature had very long arms, that articulated back away from the torso, much different from the way a human being's arms would do so. He had a very long torso.
>
> "I was told by these creatures, if they were telling me the truth, that they can manipulate time. They can take a person out of our time frame and keep him, or her, as long as they please. Then reinsert them back into time so the person wouldn't even know he'd been gone, unless they wanted him to know. And no one would miss him because, of course, to them he had never been gone."

Plate 3 -
Pencil sketch "# 1" with alien symbol "# 2" by Linda Porter of Porterville, California mailed with audiocassette February 28, 1991 to author © 1991.

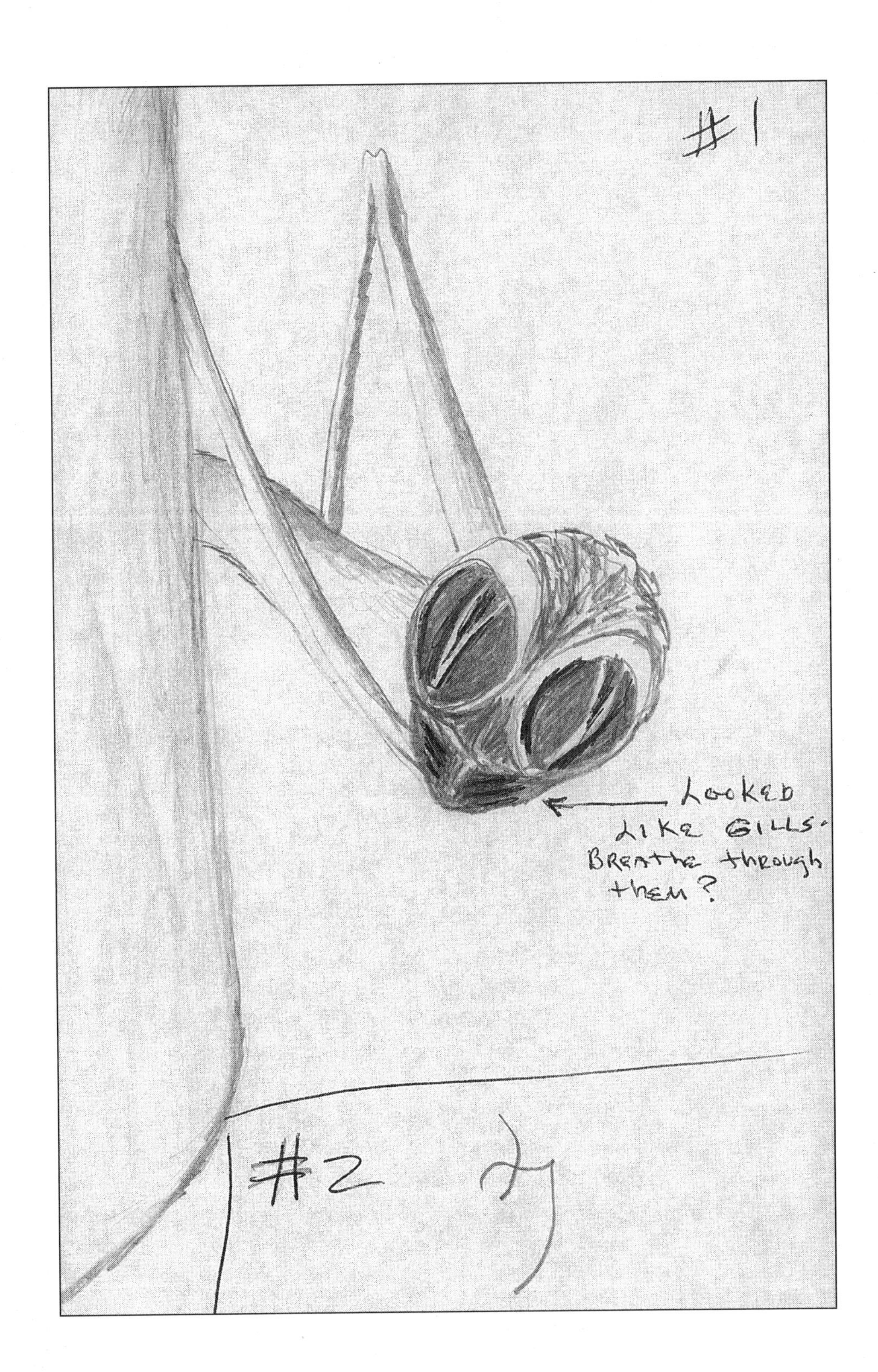

Sketch Number Two (Re: symbol on preceding page): "I was supposedly taken to an underground base off the coast of California. For some reason I was led to believe it was in the Santa Barbara area. If you were standing on sand at the bottom of the ocean (where this place is), all you could see is what looks like a silver submarine conning tower rising up out of the sand. And it would probably be the height of a two or three story building. I was told this tower thing was camouflaged by an electronic net of some kind that renders it invisible. And they also have something around it that seems to repel people and fish for some reason.

"Inside the building, the floors and the walls and the ceiling were all a silver-grey color. There was a lot of light. But the doors — and there seemed to be doors all over the place — were brightly colored. They were either bright red or bright blue or bright yellow. And over each door was some kind of writing that looked like hieroglyphic or Arabic writing or something like that. Sketch Number Two shows the only example I could remember, and it isn't exactly right, but it's pretty close to it.

"The next one, I think I was seventeen when this one happened. I refer you to Sketch Number Three to illustrate it. We were still living in the same house. I was in bed asleep when something woke me up. The room was filled this time with an orange glow, and at the center of the room was a hole out of which two well-formed, seemingly three-dimensional solid shadow people were stepping. If you could imagine a person without features and just a shadow, but a three-dimensional shadow that you could touch, that's what these looked like.

"The hole was filled with an orange light that was the source of the glow in the room. The edges of the hole were ragged, gold-colored, and seemed to sparkle around the edges. The overall shape of the hole was oval and about a foot above the floor. The two shadow men stepped out of the hole, grabbed me, and pulled me towards the hole. That is the last I remember. Later, I realized that the little guy, the grey guy that I call the Creep, was standing off to the right watching my reaction to the whole thing. In fact, he seemed very interested in my reaction to what was going on. He also seemed to be in charge of it. He's the same little guy or creep that has always been present any time I've been taken.

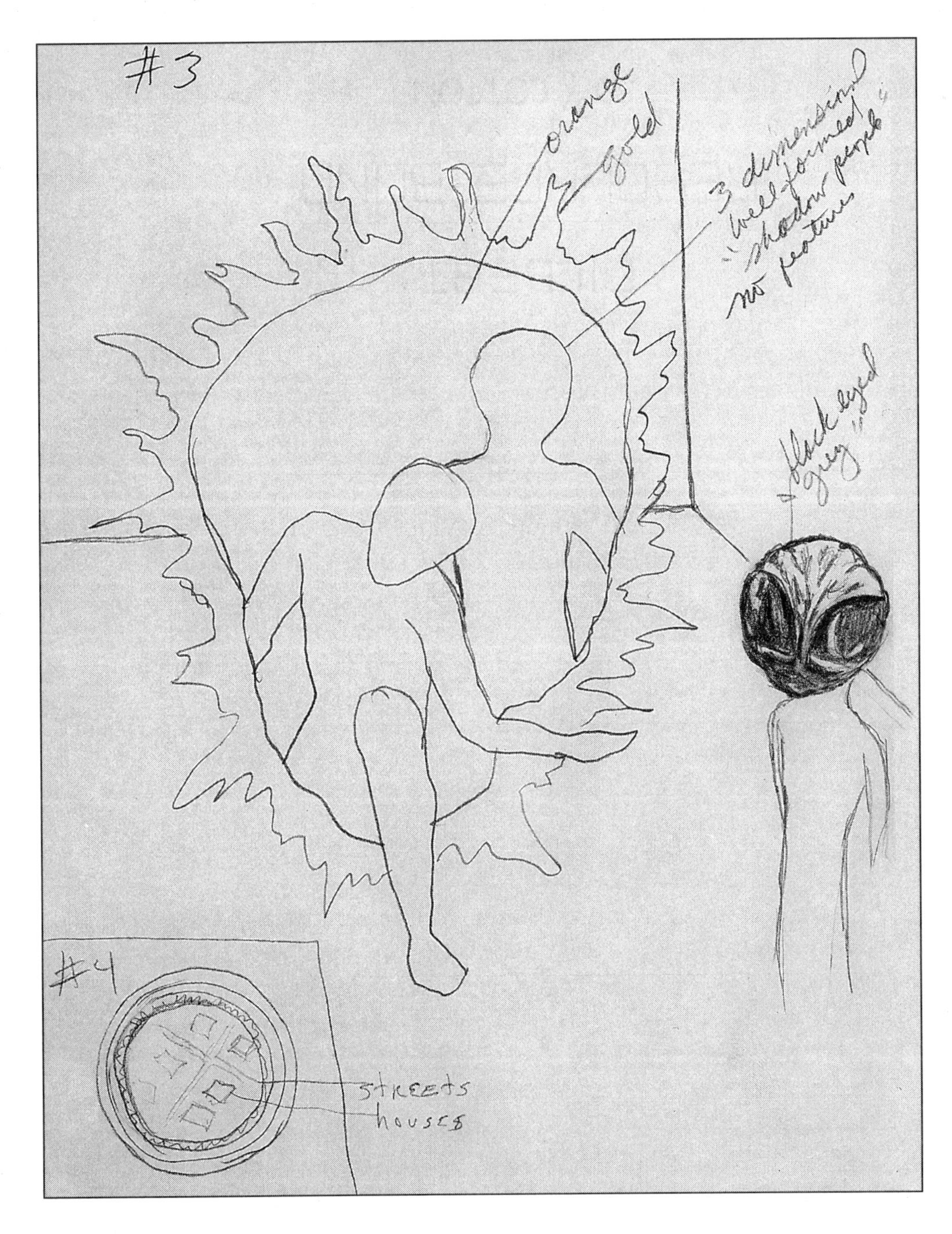

Plate 4 - *Pencil sketches labelled "#3" and "#4" by Linda Porter, memories from an abduction experience when she was fifteen years old in 1961, near Covina, California. For author © 1991.*

"All of this happened in an instant, even though it sounds like it took forever to go on.

"Another memory (I have is) being aboard a craft in a small, round room with a large, circular opening in the center of it. And this is Sketch Number Four. It appeared to have three seals around the opening, as if to make it airtight or something. Anyway, through the opening I could see the ground below — houses, streets.

"I was sent down this hole on a shaft of pale, yellow light, and once again the light had particles inside of it that seemed to glisten or reflect light. It was a dense light. I was sent down at great speed so fast that I thought I was going to be smashed to death on the ground. It was terrifying. About four feet from the ground, I suddenly slowed down. I mean like going from, I'll say, about eighty miles an hour to suddenly three miles an hour. The difference was incredible. And I landed on the ground. There was no sense of falling. There was no rush of wind. There was no sound. Going down that fast and from that great a height, there should have been the feeling like you get from a roller coaster when you go down real fast. But there wasn't anything at all. It was weird."

Plate 5 - *Linda Porter's Sketch # 4 depiction of the yellow beam that transported her during abductions. "I was returned to earth from a craft via shaft of yellow light." For author © 1991.*

Plate 6 - *Linda Porter's second more refined depiction of Sketch #3, Plate 4, that shows "shadow beings" stepping from "hole" that penetrated the air in the middle of Porter's bedroom when she was fifteen years old in 1961 near Covina, California. For author © 1991.*

Sketch Number Five: "This next thing is strange. I suppose it could be true. They (aliens) told me (prior to 1991) about a place called the Sycamore Remote Facility [7] run by General Dynamics, at least according to them.

"It's located in Southern California and inland a ways from San Diego in the Poway region. (It's supposed to be) a missile testing site, but it's actually a holding area for those beings who have been captured — the *aliens* — who have been captured by the government. Supposedly, there is one particular building that goes down five or six stories underground, and on the lowest level there is a very large room, where the bodies of alien people are being kept encased in containers. I enclosed a sketch of this in Number Five. The containers are on a cement base. I don't know if they're Plexiglass or what, but you can see through into there to see the person.

"And there is one particular being down there that the aliens want back. And for some reason — and this has been reinforced over and over again — they seem to want me to know who this person is. I was also given the impression that the creatures that are being held *are still alive, but they're being stored in some sort of cryogenic form of suspended animation.* (Howe's emphasis.)

"I was led to believe that they're alive even though they are unconscious. As I said, I don't know whether any of this is true. The whole room is run by computers. All of the different containers, I guess, for lack of a better way of putting it, are monitored twenty-four hours a day by a computer that checks the life conditions of whatever is inside.

"(The being in Sketch # 5) is very human-looking. He doesn't look much like one of them (grey beings) at all. He has some kind of silver mesh vest over his chest, and the rest of him is all in black. He has sandy blond-colored hair, and he has a very boyish look to him, although he's probably in his thirties.

"The security leading down to this room is just absolutely incredible. They (U.S. government) have locks that you punch a sequence of numbers into and that sequence changes every two hours. And these locks, or these boxes that you punch these numbers into, are within clear — I don't know, Plexiglass, for lack of a better word — areas that can instantly fill with gas so if somebody gets to that area and tries to get through the lock, then all the security people have to do is press a button. A type of nerve gas will instantly be released and the offending intruder

[7] *As of December 1996, near the intersection of Spring Canyon and Pomerado Road northeast of San Diego and directly north of the Miramar Naval Air Station are several signs leading into Sycamore Canyon, including one which reads: "General Dynamics, Sycamore Canyon, Private Property, No Entry Without Permission." Beyond this entry way, the road slopes around and down and you cannot see any buildings or guard shacks. The source who researched the area discovered it is off limits to overflights due to a "6,000 feet to ground level" warning on flight charts. That is perhaps not unusual since Sycamore Canyon is in the approach path to Miramar Naval Air Station.*

rendered helpless until a security detail arrives. The entrance is on closed circuit monitor twenty-four hours a day.

"The whole Sycamore area is supposed to be full of underground tram systems that lead from the naval base in San Diego to this facility and to another place. The other place is the entrance. Believe it or not, it is through a garage attached to a perfectly ordinary looking house sitting up against a hill in an isolated area. The garage is the entrance to an underground network that goes through into the hill.

"If any of this is actually true, then there is an awful lot that the American public doesn't know and our tax money evidently paid for it. I was also told that two young Navy guys were killed by our own government because they found out about this place. And their families were told that they died on base in a jeep accident."

Plate 7 - *Pencil sketch labelled "5" by Linda Porter. One of several human-looking beings Porter thought were kept in suspended animation under U. S. government security in an underground facility east of San Diego. For author © 1991.*

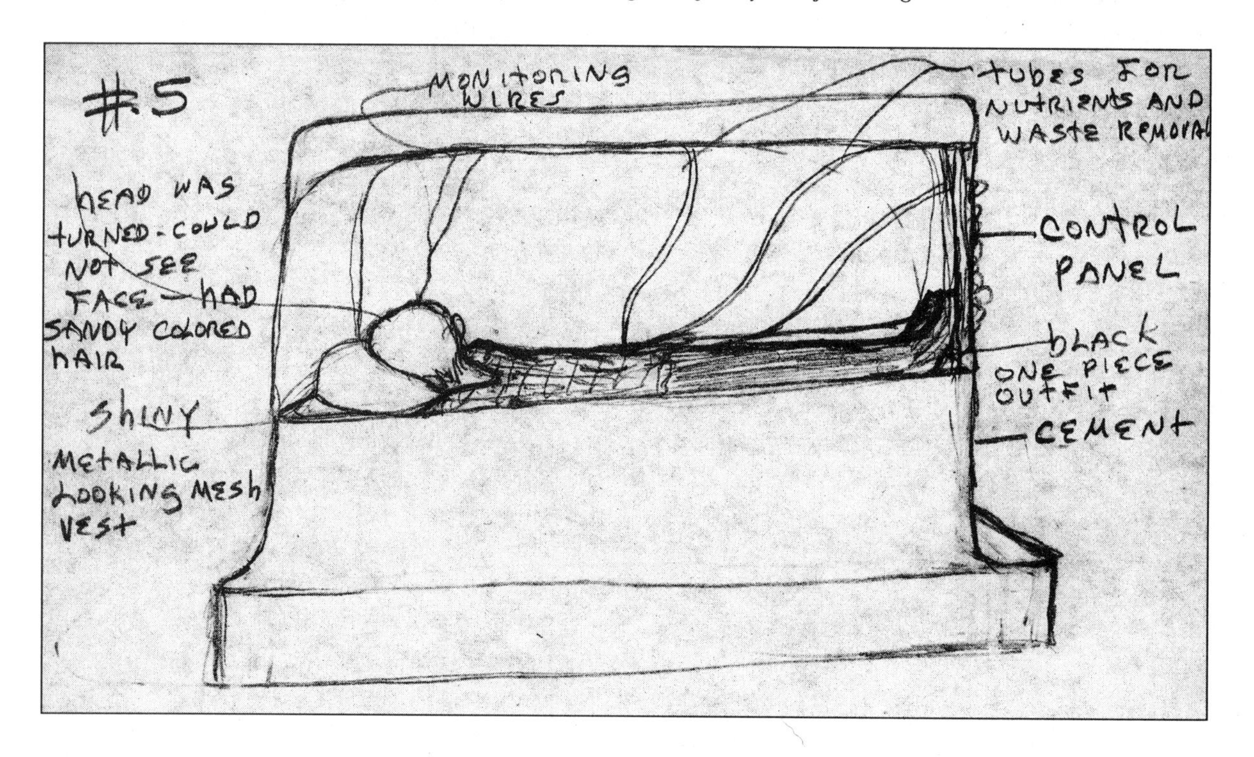

Plates 8-9 - *December 13, 1996 photographs of Sycamore Canyon facility that includes General Dynamics northeast of San Diego directly north of Miramar Naval Air Station. Photographs for author © 1996.*

Plate 10 - *December 13, 1996 close-up U. S. Navy sign posted on road to Sycamore Canyon facility that includes General Dynamics, Hughes Sites A & J and Lockheed Martin Astronautics Site B directly north of Miramar Naval Air Station.*

Plate 11 - *December 14, 1996 350 mm telephoto of buildings and radar on platform in Beeler Canyon. Lockheed Martin Astronautics is seven miles beyond this facility. Photographs for author © 1996.*

Non-human beings in suspended animation were also described by author and longtime UFO investigator Leonard Stringfield in his July 1991 *UFO Crash/Retrievals: The Inner Sanctum, Status Report VI.*[8] Stringfield died in 1995 after a long illness. In his report, Stringfield printed a transcript from an April 11, 1990 interview in Houston, Texas between researcher Ron Madeley and an elderly man referred to as "Dr. Epigoni." Epigoni claimed to have knowledge about a disc and its crew (that) landed in the vicinity of Edwards AFB, California "...and a door opened and the guys walked out and laid down on the ground. All of a sudden, the stairway closed back up. And the legs closed back up and the spacecraft sat back down on the ground." The humanoids laid there until the "disc and its occupants were carted off to a secure building at the base for scientific evaluation."

[8] UFO Crash/Retrievals: The Inner Sanctum, Status Report VI © *1991 by Leonard H. Stringfield.*

Epigoni told Madeley that the flying saucer was "kept in a big hangar" for study. When the disc's surface where the door had opened was investigated, it was "as smooth as it was anywhere else, no seams whatsoever." Epigoni speculated that the humanoids which laid down on the ground must have gone into a state of suspended animation "activated (remotely) by another craft" somewhere else.

When I asked a retired source who allegedly had first hand contact with MJ-12 insiders about this account, he seemed genuinely surprised. "How the hell do you know about that?!" he asked, almost angry. Then he said that the day the craft landed and the beings came out, laid down and stayed in "suspended animation," was the same day that a secret bomb test was planned. According to him, the bomb test was halted after this spacecraft landed because the MJ-12 forces worried that the beings lying on the desert sand were a warning and there would be extraterrestrial retaliation if the bomb test continued. Could Sherman's account on Page 135 be more accurate? Or another such incident?

Whether any of that is true or not, neither Linda Porter nor I had any such information in February 1991 when Linda told me about her abduction experiences that left her wondering if the U. S. government was keeping one or more non-human beings guarded in suspended animation. Her Porterville, California home at the time was straight west of the China Lake Naval Weapons Center and northwest of Edwards AFB.

Plates 12-13 - *Maps of Edwards AFB, China Lake Naval Weapons Center, Fort Irwin Military Reservation, and Porterville (Linda Porter's residence) in California; and Nellis AFB and Nuclear Testing Site in Nevada.*

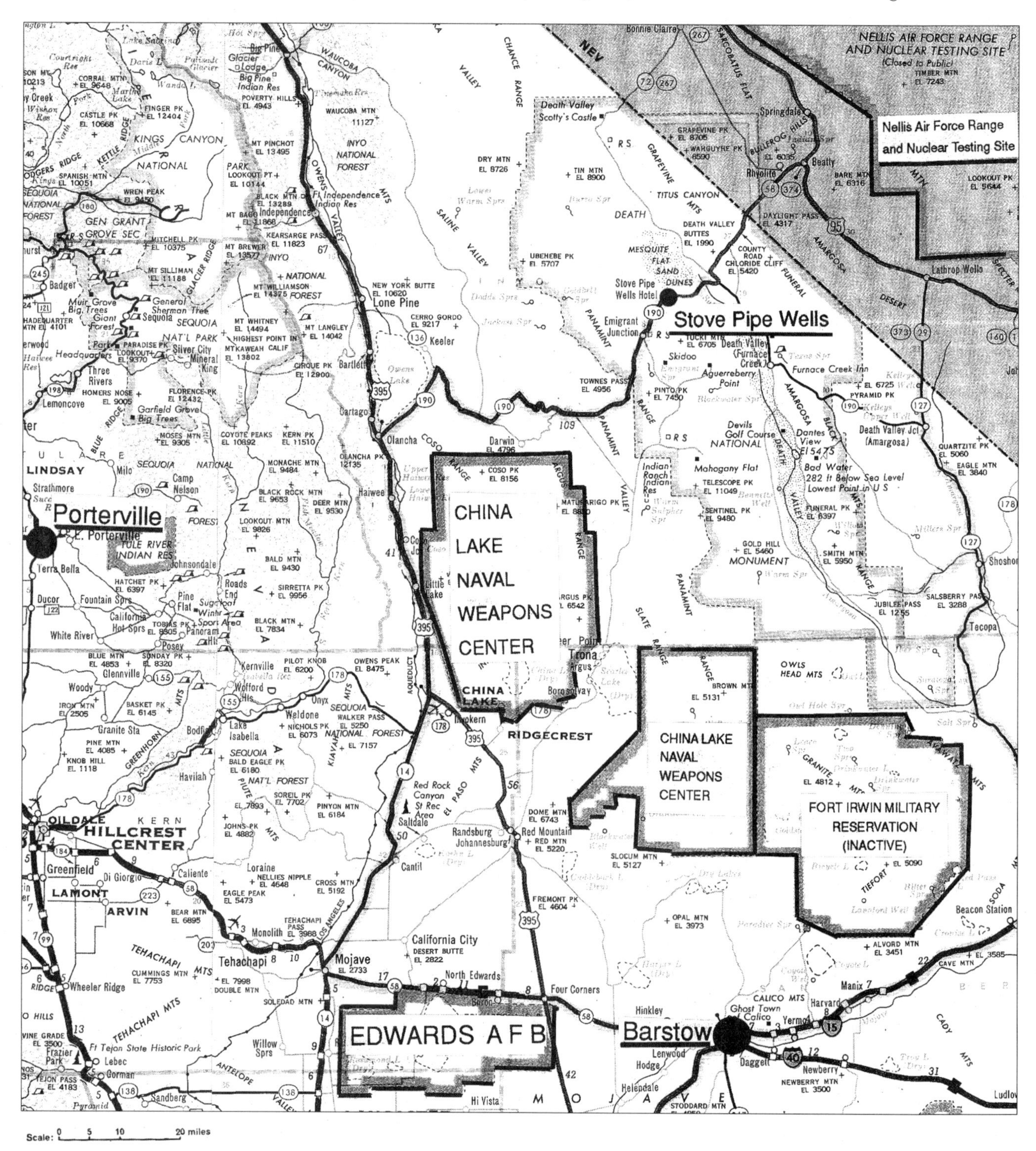

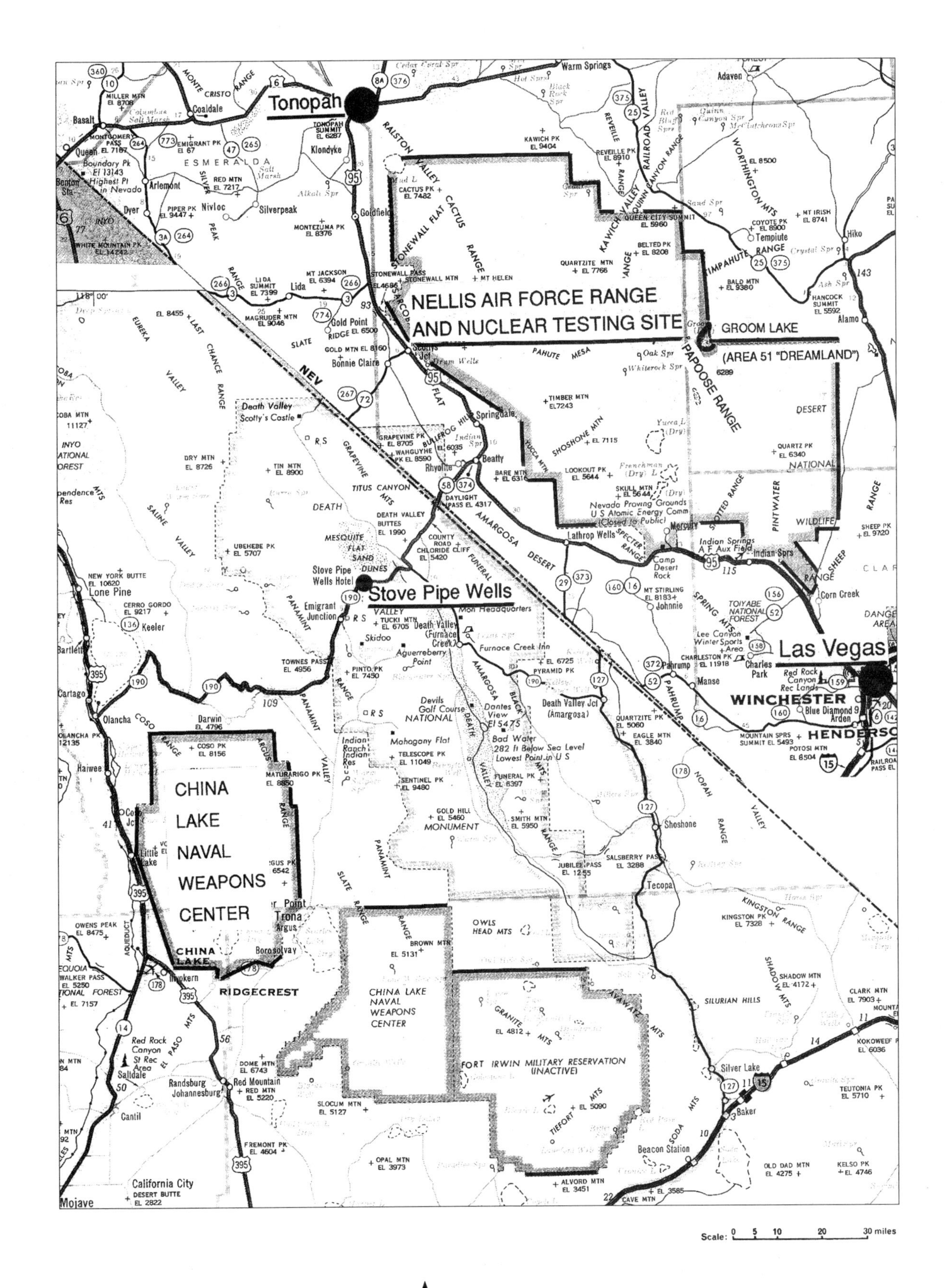
Tonopah
NELLIS AIR FORCE RANGE
AND NUCLEAR TESTING SITE
GROOM LAKE
(AREA 51 "DREAMLAND")
Stove Pipe Wells
Las Vegas
WINCHESTER
HENDERSON
CHINA
LAKE
NAVAL
WEAPONS
CENTER
CHINA LAKE NAVAL WEAPONS CENTER
FORT IRWIN MILITARY RESERVATION (INACTIVE)
RIDGECREST
Death Valley Scotty's Castle
Stove Pipe Wells Hotel
Emigrant Junction
Furnace Creek Inn
Death Valley Jct (Amargosa)
Badwater 282 ft Below Sea Level Lowest Point in U S
Nevada Proving Grounds U S Atomic Energy Comm (Closed to Public)
Mercury
Lathrop Wells
Indian Springs A F Aux Field
Beatty
Rhyolite
Goldfield
Lida
Gold Point
Bonnie Claire
Scotty's Jct
Springdale
Pahrump
Shoshone
Tecopa
Baker
Silver Lake
Beacon Station
Trona
Inyokern
Randsburg
Johannesburg
Red Mountain
California City
Mojave
Lone Pine
Keeler
Olancha
Darwin
Little Lake
Cantil
Saltdale
Dyer
Silverpeak
Klondyke
Coaldale
Basalt
Warm Springs
Adaven
Tempiute
Hiko
Alamo
Corn Creek
Manse
Johnnie
Blue Diamond
Arden
Charles Park
Scale: 0 5 10 20 30 miles

Another part of Linda's audiocassette also included another abduction experience, but without sketches for reference:

> LINDA PORTER: "I was shown at some time a room with very tall, clear tube-like containers or cylinders on a raised platform which seemed to be at the center of the room. Inside these tubes — standing upright, naked, and appearing to be asleep — were humans, or at least they looked human to me. They looked like they were in some kind of suspended animation.
>
> "I don't think they were dead because their color was too good. They were floating in what appeared to be a purple gas. It was very thick and hard to see through, but it swirled around so much that you could see the people as it moved. I was never told anything, at least that I remember. It was just like I was taken into the room, showed them, and then brought back out, and that was it. I don't remember asking questions, and I don't remember them saying anything."

Linda ended her letter saying, "I really need to know what's going on. I mean this is ridiculous. This has screwed up my whole life, as far as I'm concerned, and I don't like it."

I wrote her immediately and asked if she could try colored sketches of the transport beam, shadow people and whatever memories she had of the people in tubes because I needed a clearer image of what she was trying to describe. Within a few weeks, I received an emotional letter from Linda with several more drawings, this time in color pastels. She wrote the following about Plate 14.

> PORTER: "Praying mantis being and light-filled room. This memory is becoming clearer and clearer as time goes by. At the time (of hypnosis with Richard Haines in 1988), the memory was so threatening I could not remember anymore. Now, I remember the being slowly coming around the corner and facing me. He stood very still and simply waited as if he knew how frightening he appeared to me. Eventually he began to talk to me, although, as yet, I do not have any memory of what was said. He seemed to possess a great deal of dignity and gave the impression of being quite old.
>
> "After he finished saying whatever he had to say, I turned around and he walked me to this room (filled with dense light).

Plate 14 - *Linda Porter's drawing of praying mantis being and light-filled room she remembered from a 1963 abduction experience in Covina, California when she was seventeen years old. She thought what happened in the light-filled room was connected to her "soul transfer." For author © 1991.*

> The memory ends with me about to enter the room and the thought 'Translated Into the Light.' Whatever that means, it has to do with what happened."

The bodies in tubes and phrase "translation into the light" puzzled both of us. At that time in early 1991, I had no other abduction account like Linda Porter's, but felt it important to keep in touch with her. Over the next eight months, we talked occasionally by phone. Then on October 24, 1991, she wrote me that she had been trying self-hypnosis tapes to help her relax and remember more. She said she realized that the praying mantis creature and the room of light were connected to the people in the tubes and enclosed two more sketches to "make up the last part of the memory." This is what she recalled.

> PORTER: "When I was twelve, I became deathly ill with a high fever and a badly infected throat. The fever was so high that I know, for at least one day, I was delirious. I have a memory of floating on the ceiling and looking down at 'myself' in bed. I was that sick. My parents did not believe in doctors, so I was left to recover on my own — which I did — or at least *thought* that I did!
>
> "I was taken aboard the craft that all of this occurred on. Even though it began with the praying mantis type, the alien who was actually with me through all this was whitish, about five feet tall (maybe a little taller), and had huge eyes with black pupils.
>
> "All of the sketches I have mentioned relate to the following — I was taken into 'the room of light' and shown a man about forty-six years old who was very close to death. He was lying in a rectangular container.
>
> "I do not remember the mechanics of how this was done, but *his soul* was then *lifted up* out of his dying body! It left the body in the area of the solar plexus (behind stomach organ). It was about two and one-half feet long, five inches wide and was a breathtakingly beautiful, soft, iridescent yellow with a white, glowing inner core that radiated a very gentle heat. There was a pastel orange layer around the yellow.
>
> "The soul floated across the room to another body that looked like the man would have appeared at about twenty-five years of age. The new body appeared empty. I don't know any other way to describe it — like an empty container. The 'old body' was now bluish in color and obviously dead.
>
> "The soul floated above the new body which was standing upright outside the tube, unsupported, and slumping forward a little. It then descended, entering the body at the top of the back of the head, all the way down to the area midway between the shoulder blades. It then merged into the body totally and settled in front of the spinal column in the area of the solar plexus.
>
> "It then seemed to stretch itself out longer, a few inches up, a few inches down. The body at this point took on an 'occupied' look as if the person were merely asleep.

"The rectangular container that held the 'old' vacant body filled up with a liquid to preserve the tissues until it could be dissected. They wanted to find out how some kind of poison had entered the body, how it had progressed through the bodily systems, and at what point the poison (contaminant) had reached a level that the body could no longer deal with the poison.

"After the dissection, I was told that the body would be discarded. They seemed very surprised that I was upset that the body was just going to be tossed overboard! They told me it was just a container for the soul and of no other value.

"They think our concept of funerals is barbarous. To them there is no difference between an empty beer can and an empty body.

"I was told that the (resurrected) cloned man would be relocated elsewhere (maybe Australia) and would continue on with his life. *Part of the reason they take tissue samples from abductees when they are quite young is to have this tissue in reserve in case a new body becomes necessary later on.* (Howe's emphasis.)

"New bodies can be stored indefinitely. The containers in the sketch with the three people in the tubes are storage containers (Plate 15). The containers in both new sketches I sent you are 'activation' containers. They have a light in the top that must be on the person for (unknown) amount of hours before a body can be activated — *if* a body has been in storage. If newly made, it does not need light. In the sketch with the three people in the tubes, the body on the far right was the (younger) one given to the man.

"I got the impression they (aliens) do not like to do this soul transfer very often. Actually, I got the feeling they're *not supposed to be doing this at all.*

"But they seemed to be backed into a corner and have no other recourse. They also seem to be trying to hide all this from some 'higher' form of life — whatever the 'authority' is that prohibits this soul transfer also prohibits them from interfering on this planet. (?) Whoever it is, is much higher evolved than they are and wields a great deal of power over many, many other realms of existence."

Plate 15 - *Linda Porter said she was taken by a "grey scientist" to a room where three people were in tubes. She felt the people were alive, but in a state of suspended animation and that the man on far right was a younger clone activated by a "soul transfer" from his previous older body. Drawing by Linda Porter for author © 1991.*

Plate 16 - *Linda Porter's depiction of dying man's "soul" lifting out of his solar plexus and floating across the room to enter the younger clone of the same man. For author © 1991.*

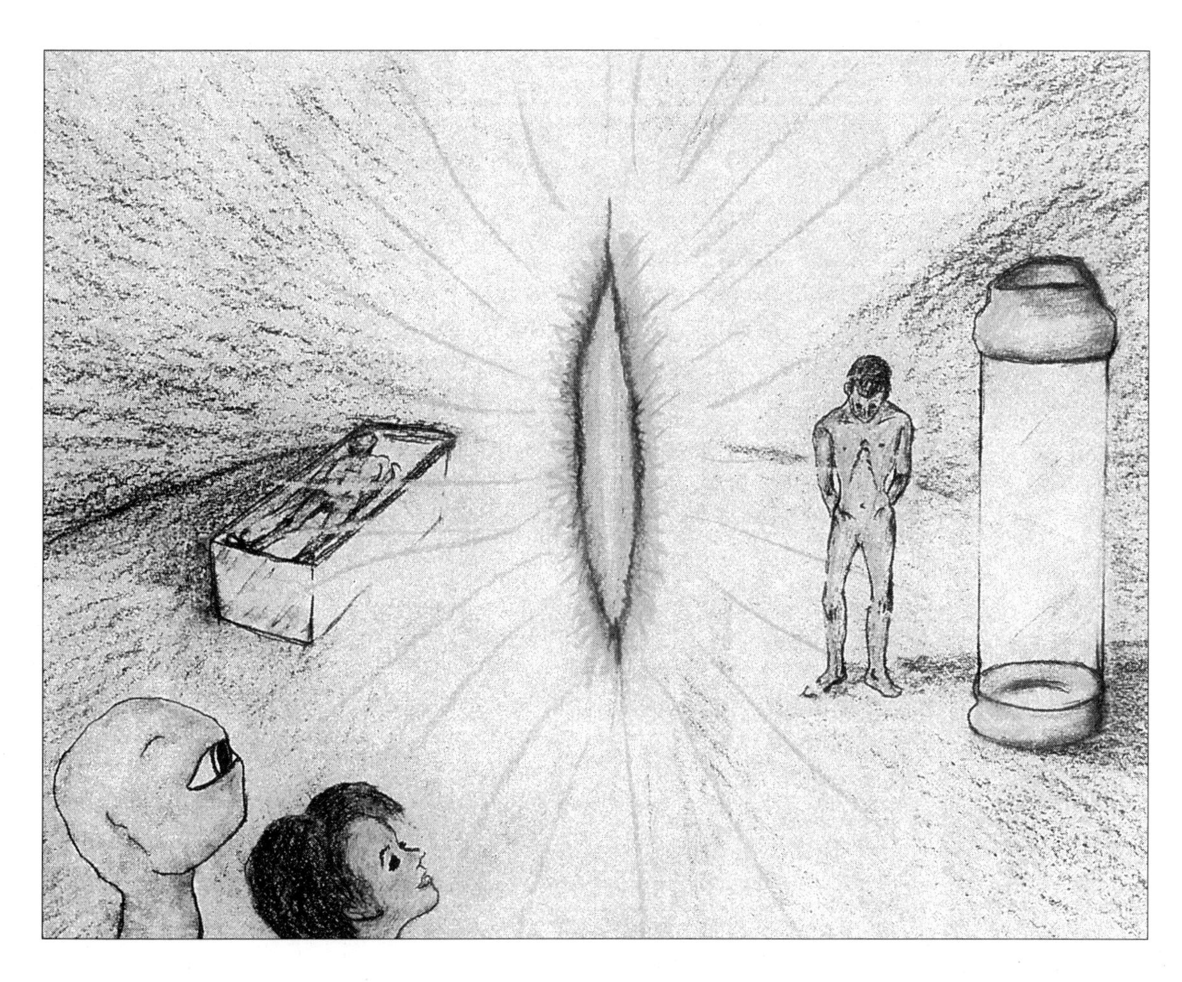

Linda Porter was shocked next to see her own 17-year-old body die and its soul transferred to her clone that was identical in age and form.

PORTER: "I was laid upon a table and rendered unconscious. *My soul was then lifted up and out of my body and placed into another one that looked exactly like it!*

"I was then awakened in the 'new body.' The creature took me over to the 'old body.' It was lying on the table with the chest open. The creature then *lifted the heart out* of the chest cavity and *showed it to me!!!*

"It told me my heart had been badly damaged because of illness (rheumatic fever?) and would have stopped very soon!

"I looked at the opening in the chest and did not see one drop of blood anywhere! *No blood at all!* The area didn't even look moist! When he held the heart up, not one drop of blood fell from it! There was no blood on his hand! The heart looked as dry as the chest cavity!

"Much later after all this happened, I was told by the same alien scientist who was with me in the room that there is a chemical 'poison' spreading in our land (that we are totally unaware of.) It is the result of some kind of secret testing done by our government in outer space. A dangerous by-product of that testing was created and is now falling back into our atmosphere. I was told that it is concentrating in our water supplies. People living near large bodies of water are in the greatest danger. He said the safest place is inland, away from water. He also said to use only distilled water for cooking and drinking.

"I was told this chemical is one of three factors that will eventually cause sky fire. I was originally told nuclear waste in the atmosphere would start it by reacting with something else. That 'something else' is the chemical and particles from a beam-type weapon our government already has. So chemical poison plus nuclear waste particles equals a deadly chemical chain reaction leading to ignition (according to the aliens).

"I haven't heard of any secret nuclear waste tests being carried out in space by our government, have you? It was impressed on me that however deadly this reaction will be to us, it will create even worse destruction throughout other worlds and other dimensions. At the time, I seemed to understand this fully and was totally devastated by the degree of destruction caused by the ignorance of our military and government.

Plate 17 - *Linda Porter's depiction of "grey scientist" lifting her diseased heart out of her "old body" while she watched in a newly activated cloned body in 1963, age 17. For author © 1991.*

"But now the 'understanding' is gone, only the memory of having totally understood the *magnitude* of the situation remains.

"I remember seeing how insignificant our planet and its people are compared to the whole. I asked *WHY* didn't they just step in and *STOP* what was happening before it was too late. He got *very angry* and said I didn't understand yet, they weren't *allowed* to interfere.

"If they can interfere enough to take our souls out of bodies and transfer them to other bodies, why can't they stop what's going to happen? It doesn't make any sense to me. Obviously he wanted to step in and end it, but it was like a third entity, or outside authority, had forbidden interference and all he and the others could do is just stand by and watch. As bad as all this is for us, it seems far worse for them. I sensed terrible, terrible frustration coming off of him.[9]

"Whatever all this is about seems to be speeding up — heading for somewhere fast. We were talking about the crop circles

[9] *If the aliens are in fact from the future, as Jim Penniston said in Chapter 1, then perhaps this earth is linked past, present and future to their destiny. If we destroy our "present," we might also hurt them.*

on the phone. I have a gut level feeling that they are a subliminal message. To who? Abductees? To aliens living here on earth? I don't know. But I really feel whoever did the crop circles knew they would be seen by millions of people via TV. I really think they are a signal — to who for what, I don't know. Yet."

Eleven years earlier on March 13, 1980, psychologist Dr. Leo Sprinkle and I travelled to meet an abductee named Judy Doraty.[10] She and four other family members had been driving home outside Houston, Texas in May 1973 when they saw a bright light pacing their car. Judy wanted a better look and got out. The group was surprised when they finally got home where relatives had been baby-sitting and asked, "Why are you two hours late?"

[10] *For complete Judy Doraty transcript, see Appendix 12,* An Alien Harvest *© 1989 by Linda Moulton Howe.*

That missing time, followed by terrible headaches and memory flashes of something non-human, haunted Judy. During her hypnosis session with us, she described seeing a brown and white calf rise in a beam of light. Then she found herself inside a round room where "two little men" who had grey skin, four fingers and yellow eyes "like a snake" used cutting instruments to excise tissue from the calf's eye, tongue and testicles.

Judy Doraty's words that day were eerily similar to Linda Porter's a decade later. Doraty said she was in a laboratory where the grey beings conducted tests on the animal tissue taken from the calf in what has come to be known worldwide as "animal mutilations." The beings were analyzing the tissue, Doraty said, because "they're concerned about man for themselves. That men are going to kill themselves through polluting the earth area. ...they've been here for quite some time and they test the soil as well as our water as well as our animal life and vegetation. And will continue to.

"(There is a chemical poison) that has been passed on and filtered down to where it is now reaching the human being. Prior, it was in the soil, but now it's in the vegetation and ... they're testing to see how far along it is. It's going to cause a lot of problems. There's going to be a lot of people die because it's already contaminating the water. It's in the water. And has something to do with plutonium. ...They were very emphatic about it, that the testing even though it's in outer space has an effect on things here. ... I didn't know (that we humans) were testing in outer space."

Judy Doraty also said the beings told her that humans were also doing tests under water that will cause some chemical reaction when it comes in contact with another compound.

"...There's a lot involved, more than just pollution. If we continue like we are now, it's going to involve not only us, but possibly others and they're trying to stop something that could cause a chain reaction. And maybe involving them. I questioned why they aren't saying more and why they can't stop it if they're so knowledgeable and they get angry. ...they say I'm not knowledgeable enough yet. That I'm immature. That I haven't reached maturity."

I called Linda Porter to tell her I would be in Los Angeles for another conference in November and would be willing to drive north to Bakersfield to meet her. She was afraid to have me visit her home because her husband resented her preoccupation with the alien experiences in her life. She expected their marriage, her second, would not last much longer. In the meantime, she preferred to meet on neutral ground without the stress of his presence. So, we set November 13, 1991 at a motel that Linda choose on the outskirts of Bakersfield.

Linda was then forty-five years old and about five and a half feet tall with short, dark brown hair. Her pale grey-green eyes were slightly enlarged behind thick glasses. She wore jeans and a light pink cardigan embroidered with seed pearls. Her speaking voice was low and gentle, almost unnaturally calm. I have heard this forced stillness before in other abductees who have had a life time of anomalous experiences to suppress, trying to balance their mental scales to a point where the most threatening emotions are pushed aside so that life can go on.

Linda Porter was born on June 2, 1946 in Portland, Oregon where she lived on a chicken, rabbit and berry ranch with her parents, two older sisters and one younger brother.

"I was a surprise, I guess," since her sisters were sixteen and eighteen years older. "I also have a younger brother and we don't seem to resemble anybody at all in the entire family."

She knew little about her parents' relatives except that her father's mother was a Cherokee Indian from Arkansas. Linda Porter's parents were a pragmatic couple who "weren't the type to ever talk about anything that couldn't be explained."

"When I was a teenager, I wasn't like other kids. I didn't rebel. In fact, I was reading Immanuel Kant and Nietzsche and Sartre and all the other philosophers I could get my hands on, so I was not exactly a normal teenager. That was when I developed my interest for drawing and painting, too. I was more introverted, like trying to figure out why I was here."

I laid out each of the drawings Linda had sent me and asked her if I could go over each one in depth and tape record the discussion. I wanted to talk more deeply about the tubes and bodies and their implications, but I began with my confusion about the difference between transport by light beams and "tunnels" that Linda sometimes referenced.

Plate 18 - *Linda Porter at age forty-nine with her daughter Lisa at home on Christmas Day 1995 in Iowa. Photograph by William Porter.*

I asked, "Is the tunnel a physical structure?"

"It isn't something that's there all the time. It's created for this to happen (transport) and then it's gone. The tunnel is different than the beam of light. The beam is used only to transfer people from earth to craft and back. The tunnel is a physical, created 'hole' from one dimension to another. Traveling through the tunnel was what made me ill. Had something to do with change in physical density of two differing dimensions."

I asked Linda Porter about the night the shadow beings stepped through the "hole" in the middle of her bedroom with the small grey standing next to her bed. "Was it as if another dimension had actually penetrated into your room?"

"Superimposed on another one, yeah. Everything that exists is on a sound frequency, they told me. Remember when I sent you the first set of sketches, I told you that the praying mantis-type creature said something to me? I think I've remembered most of what I was told then. Maybe."

Linda Porter handed me some lined notebook paper on which she had written in her neat cursive style:

> "There is much, much more to existence than we could ever begin to understand. Much of what we have been taught regarding the physical universe and the laws that govern it is wrong.
>
> This creature's civilization communicates difficult concepts via the use of symbols that radiate emotion. They use this

form to get concepts across with their exact true meanings intact. No misinterpretations can occur this way.

The symbols are not mathematical ones, but appear as 3-dimensional holographic pictures that resemble abstract sculptures. The emotional aspect is relayed via carrier waves that resemble sound waves but are not part of the human sound spectrum. These waves can be felt, but not heard. If the creatures want to clear a certain area of humans, they can 'broadcast' this carrier wave over the area at a certain frequency and it will create intense fear in people, causing them to flee the area. It does not cause any harm, so they say. (Howe's Note: Most humans cannot hear frequencies below 125 hertz or above 10,000 hertz.)

Problems arise when trying to translate this visual/ emotional input into words. Human semantics can cause explanations to become mired down in confusion. What is extremely easy to comprehend on one level of existence using one form of expression then becomes very hard to interpret correctly when translating it onto another level using a limited form of expression such as the human language. A lot of meaning is lost and many important concepts become hazy or are totally misinterpreted.

The universe is built on sound patterns which is why so many different worlds/dimensions can exist in the same space. Each is on a different frequency. Disrupt a world/dimension to the point that you destroy the carrier wave it exists on and you have created a 'hole' in existence that cannot support the dimension above or below it. Each frequency, besides maintaining its own world/dimension, also supports — or holds in place — the one above it and below it. Everything is interdependent!

The other world/dimensions will begin to collapse into this 'hole.' Not only will this destroy countless other civilizations but the resultant area of matter compressed into such density can throw the whole gravitational field for parsecs around it out of balance, thus causing the further damage of even more worlds as they are pulled out of orbit. The process feeds on itself.

There are countless worlds/dimensions occupying the same space without being aware of one another because of having their own individual octaves. This octave/frequency holds the world/dimension in place and causes it to exist safely without interfering with (or even being aware of) other worlds around it. This frequency acts as a buffer zone to keep everything in its place. Do anything to disrupt it and you begin a collapse that starts a deadly chain reaction. If the density of this collapse reaches a certain weight, space/time itself begins to collapse.

Whatever the experiment is that our government is involved with in outer space, (if successful) it will change the density of matter to such an extent that the chain reaction started will not be able to be stopped by anybody in any world/dimension! [11]

There are literally hundreds of different alien life forms here trying to stop what is happening as it is putting their own worlds at risk. Somc, as I had mentioned in earlier letters, are not supposed to be interfering, but are doing so anyway. What they are *all* trying to do is stop the 'ripple effect' that will emanate outward from us should this experiment succeed.

With all their technology, Linda, why don't the aliens — or their superiors — just walk in and stop the whole thing themselves? Why do they need us abductees to speak for them? Something just doesn't make any sense. I wonder if we are being lied to, used for some purpose to put over ideas they want us to believe. If there is an experiment, maybe if it succeeds, it will put us in competition with the aliens for something they don't want to share. Maybe they're trying to 'scare' us out of 'their' neighborhood."

Linda Porter told me that even if some of the alien communication made some sense to her, she was not satisfied that she honestly knew their intent. She said, "I still feel there's something fishy going on. Something they don't want us to know."

I asked Porter if overlapping dimensions were compared to television frequencies, who has the tuner?

"The guy on top, whoever that is, whoever has the most control and the most power. Whoever is the head dog has the tuner."

"Do you remember if any of this has to do with those shadow people taking you through that hole to somewhere?"

"I remember a dark world. Like whatever light they had was so far away that they were almost always a little darker than twilight. It's almost like I can see a tiny little sun the size of a pencil eraser head."

"What's around you?"

"Buildings, round, weird. The buildings don't have corners. They are all rounded, almost like an igloo. No vegetation."

"Like a desert?"

[11] *Abductee Judy Doraty, Page 326,* An Alien Harvest © *1989 by Linda Moulton Howe: "...they (grey, snake-eyed beings) were very emphatic about it, that the testing even though it's in outer space has an effect on things here. ...That it will, if it's continued, cause some chemical reaction when it comes in contact with another compound. ...Causes a chemical change and it will cause a change in the consistency of solidity (density) as we know it... There's a lot involved, more than just pollution."*

"Yeah, except it's very cool."

"Did you see anybody else there?"

"Someone guides me through a yellow door in one of the buildings. There are a lot of people there and all of them are human-looking. But they're dressed strange. I think there's a long table and everyone is around the table. And a person stands up and he's got a long, purple robe on — beautiful purple — with a high collar. He's tall, probably seven feet. He seems to be in charge of whatever's going on, the reason that we're there."

"Can you describe him more?"

"I don't think this one was human. He seems to have grey skin. It's not human-colored skin. More on the white side. He's very tall and very, very thin. Large eyes like a cat's. No hair. Round top to the head and he had a nose, which the little greys did not."

Plate 19 - *Tall being in purple robe that Linda Porter felt was in charge of an abduction event. Drawing by Linda Porter for author © 1991. See* Glimpses of Other Realities, Vol. I - Facts & Eyewitnesses, *Chapter 4 for other references to similar being.*

"What is the nose like?"

"Long. Long nose, long face. He has ears which the little greys don't have either."

"Is the nose prominent?"

"It's big."

"Is your drawing close to your memory?"

"My drawing is close, but he looks sort of mean in it. He didn't really look mean."

"Mouth?"

"No lips, but he talked. It wasn't telepathy because I remember his mouth moving. I remember him holding his hands up, saying something. I can remember his white arms when his sleeves fell down."

"What were his hands like?"

"Long and white, real thin."

"How many fingers?"

"I don't know. I just remember seeing long fingers."

"Do the humans around you talk at all?"

"They're all listening to what he has to say. I felt a great deal of respect for him. Whatever he was explaining was very complicated, more like scientific stuff."

"Any relationship to the praying mantis being?"

"I don't know."

"What more can you remember about the praying mantis?"

"He was very tall, between seven or eight feet. He had a very long torso. The arms were very long and articulated back away from the torso, much different from the way a human being's arms would be. There were three finger-like appendages, but they didn't move like fingers. They have much better dexterity. And his feet weren't anything like our feet. They were real thin and narrow, tiny, pointed things. His eyes were sort of reddish-brown with clear bubbles on them that bulged out slightly. I don't know if that was a form of protection or what. It was like he could feel what I was feeling and he didn't want to frighten me any more than was absolutely necessary."

"Did you sense emotion like kindness or compassion?"

"Great age, wisdom and infinite patience. It isn't so much kindness and compassion. It's like he and his type have been around thousands of years — a long, long time. The one thing I feel the strongest is the incredible wisdom. I've never been in the presence of anything like that before, that gave off the feeling of such knowledge. He told me a lot, but I have no idea what he said at that time. Whatever it was, I think was very important — like telling me what was going to happen in the future and something about 'translated into the Light,' whatever that means. It has to do with what happened to me in that room filled with light. My last memory ends with me about to enter that room."

"The praying mantises — would their boss be the big-nosed being?"

"No."

"A humanoid of some type?"

"Yes, the golden-tanned humanoids, but not so much boss, more sympatico. Like they had been working together for a long time."

"The golden-tanned humanoids and the praying mantises?"

"Yes."

"Is there an alliance?"

"Not a military one. They don't think like that. But there's a mutual respect and caring based upon a shared ethical and spiritual value system. They both seem to be working towards the same goal — whatever that is."

"Great caring and respect between both species?"

"Yes, both races are highly evolved and while the praying mantis race dates much further back in creation, the two races seem to easily relate to each other and work together in complete harmony and respect."

"Then where does the white-skinned, large-nosed one fit in here?"

"I don't know because that was the only time I ever saw him and he was just there speaking."

"Could he be the intelligence that's above the others?"

"No, no. Above that would be like that entity I told you about in Sedona (Arizona). It goes on to a huge, highly-evolved life form that has gone beyond the need for a physical body."

"OK, so we'll put non-physical entity on top. Is it an entity in this universe?"

"In this universe. The only way I can explain it is the feeling like the only thing above them would be something like God."

"Above the huge non-physical entities?"

"Right. Put those non-physical entities above the humanoids and praying mantises. They are massive and can travel anywhere in the universe without a ship or any physical vehicle."

"Who is directly below them?"

"The humanoids, the golden-skinned people. Then the praying mantises. And then the taller greys that have white skin, taller than the small greys. The taller ones have pupils in their eyes. I would call them Gumby because of their uniform, I guess. It just came all the way down to the floor and I never saw any feet, so I called him Gumby." (Plate 15)

"They're kind of slanted eyes with whites like ours?"

"They have whites to their eyes and they have pupils. The skin is white and those all seem to be scientists."

" In your drawing, the head ..."

"Bulges in the back. Their heads are shaped differently than the greys." (EBE Type I?)

"And then under them would be?"

"The small greys. They're just the workers, like bees or ants or something. They just do the work." (EBE Type II?)

"Are all the tubes the same?"

"No, the tubes are different. The storage tubes have a different top — it's round. The activation tubes have squared-off corners. There's a light in the activation tubes, a strong light that shines down on the person and they have to be in that light for several hours before the soul can enter the body. I don't know why."

"The storage tubes are for bodies?"

"Yes, for cloned bodies. One tube stores them and another tube activates bodies. The soul was probably the most beautiful thing I've ever seen in my life. My drawing doesn't even come close to doing it justice. It was a beautiful, iridescent yellow with soft orange around it and a white, glowing center that radiated a real soft, gentle heat."

Porter continued both in awe of the soul light and repulsed by the man's death.

"The aliens dissected the older man's body. He had died from some contaminant that's here on the earth, that's in the water. And it's so bad that people aren't even supposed to be living near water, let alone drinking the stuff. But they dissected the body to try to trace the damage done by the poison through the body. It seemed very important to the aliens for some reason. And then they dumped his body overboard, just like it was nothing, just like you'd take a shoe off and throw it away. I remember being very upset about that because down here we bury our dead."

"So, from our human point of view, the older man would have died at forty-six years of age?"

"He would have disappeared. No one on earth would ever have found his body. In your research on mutilations, Linda, has anyone ever found a cut up human body?"

"A few times, but I don't know if it's the same phenomenon. There are a lot of missing adults and children."

"I don't think they're dead. I think a lot of them have been relocated."

"Why relocated? Relocated on the earth? Or to other planets?"

"Relocated on earth like the younger cloned version of the man was put in Australia. There are certain people the aliens want in certain areas and the aliens have all been in contact with these people over their life times."

"You mean the scientist-caretakers?"

"Yes. Something is going to happen and whatever it is, it's like everybody has to be in position when it does."

"Do you have detailed memory of your own soul transfer?"

"After showing me the man's tube transfer, then the next thing I know, I'm standing here and the grey scientist has — yuch — like my heart in his hand. My old body is lying on a table there, opened. I remember the sides of the cut were jagged. There was no blood at all. Totally dry."

"Was it a zigzag cut?"

"It was like pinking shears, like how you cut cloth when you sew."[12]

[12] Glimpses of Other Realities, Vol. 1 - Facts & Eyewitnesses, *Pages 175-176 for photographs of similar serrated cuts on mutilated cattle.*

"Did you see what cutting instrument the aliens used?"

"It looked like an electronic toothbrush holder. It was silver-colored, seven inches long, about an inch and a half wide. It had a lighted blue tip that does not project light but seems to use inaudible sound waves when set on low frequency and opens surgical areas by using vibrations to separate cells and tissue away from each other without causing cellular damage. It does not cut into cells. Clean edge, no burn. When set on high frequency, vibration causes friction which creates heat. Heat is used to cut. "

"There was a larger instrument ten inches long, three and a half inches wide. White glowing tip that does not project light. Uses sound waves to heal emotionally and psychically. Brings people out of horrible shock."

"The alien said I had rheumatic fever when I was twelve which I suppose was true. I never had it medically verified, but the symptoms were all there. And I guess it damaged my heart. I would not have lived much longer with my old heart, that's what he said."

"At age seventeen? Had you noticed anything wrong?"

"Oh, yes. I had been sick. My parents didn't believe in going to doctors. I had such a bad sore throat, such a high fever. I had never really been all right after that. In fact, I had fainted a couple of times."

"Between age twelve (1958) and seventeen (1963), you actually were weaker from illness?"

"Yes. It was getting worse. The grey scientist explained the back wall of my heart was getting thinner from the damage and it would have given out. And I'm standing there watching him, but it's like I'm still stunned. I don't really take in everything he's saying."

"But what part of you is standing there watching?"

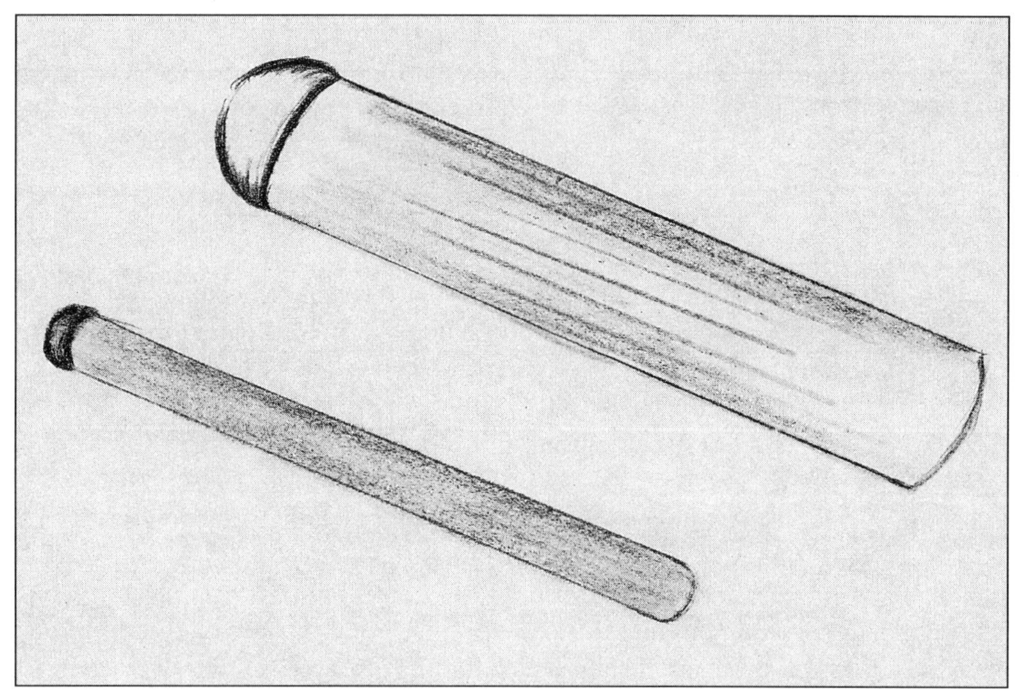

Plate 20 - *Cutting instruments sketched by Linda Porter which she said were used by non-human beings to open her chest and remove her diseased heart. For author © 1991.*

"I guess it was my new body with the soul from the me on the table. I had no memory of the transfer, of being taken out of that room or anything done. But the next thing I know, I'm standing there watching the alien take my heart out. So whatever happened, it was done in between with no warning. Or I don't have any memory of anything. (Perhaps the missing memory relates to the praying mantis in light-filled room that Linda Porter did not want to enter.) I can tell you, that is one *weird* sight to look down at yourself with your chest open and that grey guy standing there holding your heart in its hand! I always associated that memory with death and I always thought if I remembered it I would die. And now I see where the association with death came from."

Suddenly Linda Porter stretched her arms out and looked at them and began to cry.

"I don't know what's *me* anymore!"

I felt her anguish and disorientation at having seen what she thought was the body she was born with die while her consciousness survived in an identical other-body. Why would non-human creatures be so intimately involved with the life and death cycles of some humans?

Linda Porter did not know the answer to my question, but she said, "Those grey scientists don't like doing this. There's something about it. They do it as a last resort because — I almost get the impression that it's something that they're *not supposed to be doing.* As if the higher entities, the ones without the bodies, the huge ones told them 'No.' And the grey alien scientists are doing it anyway because they feel the others, the higher ones, don't understand about something. I don't know what it is."

"Did the aliens explain to you why they wanted you to live?"

"Not then. Somewhere along the line, I have been given a feeling that I had something I had to do. My life was saved so I can do whatever it is."

"Did you feel any different in the new body than you remembered yourself a few minutes, or hours, before?"

"It was easier to breathe. In the other body, it was like a heaviness all the time. With this one, it was, I don't know — a lightness. It was easier to move and I just felt stronger."

"But to yourself in the mirror later, there was no difference?"

"No. There was no difference at all. And evidently my family didn't notice anything. But later I realized that my 'old' body had a vaccination scar on the left arm. The new body I have now does not." Porter told me she did not have any before and after photographs of her arm.

I asked Porter what she thought the tan-skinned, humanoids wanted?

"I don't think they want anything. I think they're just here to help. It's all tied in with whatever this thing is that's going to happen. Part of them are here to cause interference so it doesn't carry on beyond earth. Some of them are here like social scientists just studying what's happening."

I was intrigued by Porter's suggestion that non-physical entities in another dimensional frequency could direct the grey scientists not to interfere with human lives and yet those grey scientists would not follow orders for some unexplained reason.

I asked, "If they're not supposed to transfer souls, why would they go against a higher force?"

"The grey scientists feel they *have* to do it. There are some people they cannot lose because of what's going to happen in the future. They feel they absolutely have to do this. Their backs are up against the wall. It's like they have no choice."

"Have they made a mistake?"

"No, not these guys. I almost want to say it's like they're trying to *rectify* one."

"Who's made the mistake?"

"Not them. I don't know because it doesn't seem to go higher than them either."

"But you say the tan humanoids are above the grey scientists? Could there be some kind of division among these grey scientists? Could some have gone in one direction with their caretaking of earth, and others went in another direction? Could there be a conflict among them?"

"It's possible. Maybe that's what it is — a sort of good-guy/bad-guy sort of thing. Maybe like renegades."

"What would renegades be trying to do?"

"I don't know. But whatever it was, it has already happened. It's done. And the grey scientists feel responsible for it."

I had been shown an alleged briefing paper for the President of the United States at Kirtland AFB on April 9, 1983 which stated: "These extraterrestrials manipulated DNA in already-evolving primates to create *Homo sapiens.*"[13] I asked Linda Porter if she understood the motives of the caretakers supposedly responsible for human creation and evolution.

Porter answered that "somewhere along the line, not that far back, it's almost like somebody interfered. Somebody did something wrong and the scientists are trying to fix it."

Thinking about the 20th Century more than the Garden of Eden mystery, I asked Linda Porter if the mistake trying to be rectified was allowing humans to tamper with nuclear weapons and energy. At the time in 1991, Linda was not certain, but later on she thought the problem related to dangerous U. S. military experiments with technology in the upper atmosphere. I asked her why the alien beings are so involved with earth?

Porter said, "You know how I've used the word 'caretakers' to describe the grey scientists? That's because the beings that originally came here are sort of the caretakers of life. They help life along on different planets and different worlds. It's like their reason for existing. And evidently the caretakers are the scientist ones. They're not the little greys that work for them. But the grey scientists have been here since this whole thing started. They were the ones evidently that started the breeding program that developed humans. This goes back even further than Biblical times, like Cro-Magnon, Neanderthal,[14] or even earlier was their first attempt."

"Twenty-five thousand years ago?"

"Yeah, or longer. And then maybe they went away for awhile and then came back and started again. But then during the Biblical times, they could see down the line where mankind was headed. And this is going to sound crazy, but they sent Jesus Christ here[15] — not as a religion — but to show people a way to live, to get along with one another, to live in harmony so that what would happen 2,000 years down the line now would not happen.

[13] *See* An Alien Harvest, *Chapter 7 © 1989 by Linda Moulton Howe.*

[14] *There is no direct genetic connection between Neanderthal and Cro-Magnon according to a July 11, 1997 report entitled "Neanderthal DNA Sequences and the Origin of Modern Humans" by M. Krings, A. Stone, R. W. Schmitz, H. Krainitzki, M. Stoneking and S. Paabo,* Cell, *Issue 14, Volume 90, No. 1 © 1997 Cell Press, Cambridge, Mass.*

They were trying to avoid where mankind was headed — which is self-destruction."

"So they created Christ in a ..?"

"I would presume as a clone."

" I wonder which soul they would have put in Christ's human body?"

"I have no idea. It would have to be an extremely evolved one. But the people here being ignorant and superstitious the way they were, they twisted everything around and used it as a way to control people. So, it didn't do any good."

"When Christ said, 'Eli, Eli, lama sabachthani?'[16] (My God, my God, why hast thou forsaken me?), who was he referring to?"

"I have no idea. Maybe he wasn't supposed to die, or something. Did he think that he would be taken off before it happened? Or taken out? The soul taken? Well, they couldn't have taken the soul out in front of everybody."

"Do you have the impression that the grey scientists made Christ, or that the blond or tanned humanoids made Christ?"

"The body came from the grey scientists. The soul ... I almost want to say that the ones without the bodies — the higher ups — provided the soul. I don't know whether they created a soul or whether one of them came down."

"Could Christ's body have been a tan-skinned humanoid? Or would it have been a human body?"

"I have no idea. All I know is what I was told. They didn't say anything about the body at all. The grey scientist just said that his civilization had sent a being here 2,000 years ago to try to divert mankind from where they were headed."

"And where did the grey scientists see that mankind was headed?"

"I don't know. They must have been able to see into the future to see down the line, that something was going to happen. But if they could do that, then how come they couldn't see that Christ would die and that nothing would change? I don't know. It doesn't make sense. But I think they showed me what it would look like in the future. One thing was so horrible I didn't want to remember anything about it."

" What more do you remember now?"

"After it was over, they showed us from space a shot of the earth. There was just a ring of fire. It's seventeen to twenty years before anybody can live on earth again and when they do come back, it's like where there's land today, there's ocean and where there's ocean, there's land. And everything's clean and new, almost. And society is different when it starts back up."

[15] *(Footnote for Page 276) See Chapter 7,* An Alien Harvest *© 1989 by Linda Moulton Howe concerning avatar of history placed here 2,000 years ago by extraterrestrials "to teach* Homo sapiens *about love and non-violence."*

[16] The Bible, *Matthew, Chapter 28, Verse 46 and Mark, Chapter 16, Verse 34.*

"Are some people removed by the grey beings before this catastrophe?"

"Yes."

"Will those same humans — or maybe cloned humans preserved in tubes — be brought back to earth after the catastrophe?"

"Yes."

"They will have all the memory back of what happened?"

"They witnessed all of it from someplace else, everything. And they are never to forget." [17]

"When the new human group starts up, how is this accomplished? Are the aliens helping?"

"Yeah, there's a new type of food the aliens will give humans, for one thing. It's grown like a crop, but it has everything in it, all nutrients. You don't need to eat anything else but this one thing. It supplies everything. I remember being taken to a large auditorium filled with a lot of people and shown this new type of food that was grown like wheat, but people could live on this form of food indefinitely. They wouldn't need meat or fruit or anything else. It was a total and complete food substance and not just a protein. It provided everything that the human body needs and it was very easy to grow and very cheap."

Linda Porter's voice broke again, not in confused anguish about which body she had, but in frustration with human denial of other truths. Looking at me with moist eyes, she said, "Most everything we've been told about the universe is wrong. And when humans are taken off, they're taught the truth so when they come back here, they know the truth about everything. It will be a whole different world that starts up. I mean it's so different that there are a lot of people alive today that wouldn't even want to be in this new world."

"Because there's no money, no greed, no power?"

"Right, no money, no greed. There's no status symbols and people relate on a deeper level to one another, on a soul level. They really see each other from the inside. That's the only way I know how to put it."

"What about plant life?"

"Everything's been replanted. Everything that was killed off before has come back. Like the whole thing has been redone."

"Christ?"

"Evidently he has something to do with returning and taking the people along."

"How will Christ come back?"

"There will be — this ties in with the crop circles — huge city ships that come back. They've been here before. Beautiful things, but enormous. And that's the way it's going to happen. And some people will be taken off."

[17] *Colorado husband and wife abducted in November 1980, Page 126,* An Alien Harvest *© 1989 by Linda Moulton Howe: "Each remembered warnings from the alien beings about a catastrophic event in the couple's lifetime that would destroy much of the earth's population. But the man said he understood that some humans would be removed to safety and then returned later to earth to start human life over. (It would be necessary that) those people would retain their knowledge about the technology and culture that existed prior to the cataclysm."*

"And the crop circles?"

"Crop circles are a message to the people here now — subliminal messages. Everybody that's connected with this relates somehow to one of the symbols, either a whole thing or a part of it. And it's just a forerunner, letting people know that they're coming back. It's more or less like they've just printed up a newspaper — only they did it in the crops. It's almost like I can see the ships coming in over these fields with the circles in them. And they're tremendous things. You can't even imagine how big they are."

"And as the ships come..."

"The people are taken off. Just as the ships go by, the people are taken off. Just gone. They don't take anything with them. Not a thing. It's just like it sweeps over the entire planet, all these huge ships, and they lift some people off."

"And are there beams involved?"

"I don't see any beams. It's like they're dematerialized from one place and materialized into another. They're just gone."

"Do you have any impression of what the governments of the world do when the city ships come?"

"Nothing. They can't. Nothing works. They can't fire any weapons. They can't do anything. From that time on, nobody will be shot, nobody will be murdered. No weapon will work anywhere on the planet. I mean, they might as well go out there with sticks and stones, and then even that wouldn't do any good."

"And can you see yourself in relationship to that? Are you in a craft? Are you on the ground?"

"What I see now is the fields with the circles in them and the ships coming in and knowing what's going to happen."

"And you're on the earth?"

"I'm evidently going to be taken up. I'm not frightened about it. It's like I'm really happy to see these people on a soul level, just ready or something."

"And who's in these big ships?"

"The tan-gold, sandy-haired ones mostly. They're the main ones."

"Is a Christ-like figure going to appear?"

"Oh, yes. Probably several times in several different areas. It will be like a soul recognition of knowing exactly who that is the moment they see him. I don't know why he'd be appearing anyway. The people that are going to be taken off are going to be taken off and it's too late, so why bother? It doesn't make sense."

"To finish out the story perhaps? To bring things full circle?"

"I know, but isn't that sort of like rubbing peoples' noses in it? I mean, they're going to die anyway."

"Maybe it has something to do with where their souls are going to go?"

"It has to have something to do with after they die. Otherwise, there would be no sense to it.

"What about communication from Christ?"

"I was shown Jesus appearing in the sky, standing upon a cloud. He simply raised his arms slowly above his head, looked skyward and said: 'It is finished.' He then blinked out of sight. I was told that everyone upon the earth saw and heard him for those brief moments."

"And do you have any impression of seeing what happens next?"

" After he leaves, the catastrophe starts. The fire in the sky."

"How does the idea of an Anti-Christ fit into all of this?"

"I don't know. I don't understand that. It doesn't make any sense to me because I don't get anything on it. It's like I don't need that knowledge because I'm not a part of that."

"And in terms of a time table?"

"The final situation that leads to the fire will start in 1993.[18] But before the fire begins, the ships with Christ will return. And then within days of the city ships being here, the fire will start."

"What do the big city ships look like?"

"They're not buildings, but there's projections rising above the ship's base. It would look like a city coming if you saw it, but it's not. It's flat on the bottom. I don't know what the projections are."

"And this is going to happen all over the world?"

"Sweeps the entire planet, but they won't land. The people will be taken up to the ships."

"That's where they're going to live?"

"These are housings, yes. But no animals. I've been told that the aliens have been taking plants and trees and everything else off the planet for a long time."

I had been concerned about disappearing animals during my investigations of the animal mutilations. In 1991, for instance, eighty-five domestic house cats disappeared in Plano, Texas. Hundreds of other mysterious disappearances of domestic animals and wild game such as caribou have also been reported in the United States and Canada.

I asked Linda Porter if she remembered any communication about what happened after city ships removed people.

[18] *In August 1996 while reviewing this manuscript before publication, Linda Porter wrote to me: "I firmly believe it relates to the H.A.A.R.P. The moment I saw a picture of it, something inside of me said BINGO, that was it! I don't know if it was built in 1993 or the plans completed, but this installation will be the cause of the old earth's destruction." HAARP stands for High Frequency Active Auroral Research Program, a joint Air Force and Navy project managed by Phillips Laboratory at Hanscomb AFB near Boston. Its goal is to focus intense energy at the ionosphere allegedly to communicate with submarines and to "detect precise location of tunnels, shelters and other underground shelters," according to U.S. Senate Bill No. 2182, National Defense Authorization Act for Fiscal Year 1995.*

"That's when the worst stuff happens, after the selected people are gone. It's like hell breaks loose. The ice caps melt. I have the impression that the government types already know it's not just an E.T. thing anymore. Long ago I think they treated it like an extraterrestrial problem that could be handled quite easily. But now, the government has found out it has something to do with the future of the earth, the Bible and the return of Christ."

"The scientist in your drawing has a triangle on his uniform and you wear two triangles overlapping on your neck chain. Why?"

"I have had a thing about triangles ever since I woke up one morning with a red one on my forehead. I don't know what the connection is or even if there is a connection. It reminds me of something, but I don't know what it is."

" The grey scientist definitely had a triangle on his uniform?"

" Yes."

"Were there any lines of any kind?"

"There was something on the triangle. I know there was at least one vertical line. There was something going crosswise, like two lines. Two lines going across and one up."

"And the Arabic-like symbol would have been seen somewhere else?"

"Yeah, a room on one of the craft, on the wall, like in a meeting room. A white table, pedestal table, white pedestal chairs around it. And then behind it on the wall, that symbol."

Plate 21- *Linda Porter's drawing of triangle-patch on grey scientist's uniform and drawing of a wall symbol she saw in a craft.*

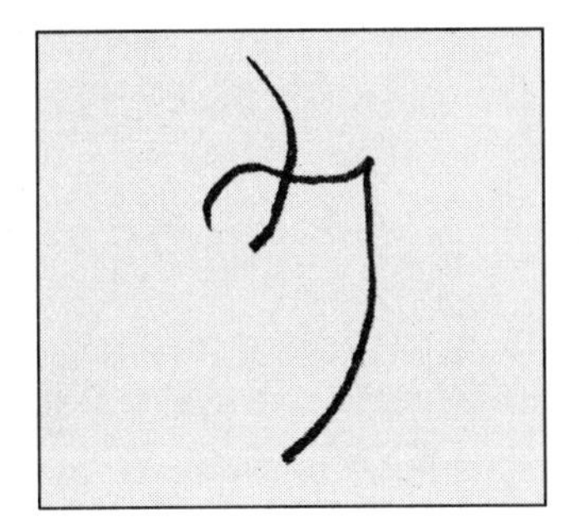

"Do you sense there is a conflict, a secret war, going on around us on this planet even if we're not aware?"

"It's funny. It's like I'm not worried about all this, like everything is going the way it's supposed to go. It's just this feeling I have inside that everything is all right."

"Even the government?"

"The government can't do anything. Even at the end, they'll be totally helpless. It's like it's all going the way it's planned."

"What happens to you and other abductees?"

"Many abductees who are going to survive the coming changes are being led through situations that seem to be terrifying but are, in reality, only 'theaters' to help them work through the emotion of fear. When the person becomes thoroughly saturated by the emotion, it causes them to move beyond it and, in a way, become indifferent to it. The ones who pass this 'test' will be the ones to move on. They (aliens) do not continue to work with the ones who do not move past this point. The idea is to make these people so insensitive to fear and terror that they will be able to deal with the panic of those around them (when the changes begin) without being swallowed up by their own fear. If they got caught up in their own fear, it would make them totally useless to the project.

"We (abductees) are like exchange students in that we were created to come here and live an earthly life within the limited human experience."

CASE 2 — Wanna Lawson, Southern New Jersey

A year after Linda Porter first contacted me, I met another woman in January 1992 who had a similar story about bodies in tubes. She asked to remain anonymous because of her management position in a southern New Jersey municipal government and suggested I call her Wanna Lawson. She was born August 16, 1937. Her mother was German and Afro-American; her father's ancestors were from the Seneca American Indian reservation near Warren, Pennsylvania.

By November 27, 1983, Wanna was 46 years old, had been married and divorced twice, and was travelling with family from Louisville, Kentucky to Atlantic City during the Thanksgiving holiday. Wanna and her 20-year-old daughter Netta were together in one car. Wanna's two other children, Charles and Anna, were in a second car driven by Netta's husband, John Hyatt. Charles was thirteen years old at the time and Anna was twenty-four. The two-car group stopped for gas several miles west of Harrisburg, Pennsylvania.

Wanna told me, "After we filled up and went about a quarter mile down the road, Netta — she was driving — asked me, 'Mom, what's that in the sky?' I don't know why, but I told her, 'I think it's foxfire.'" Foxfire usually refers to glowing light.

"The next thing I remember were lights, figures, it was almost as if I was hallucinating and around the car were all these men swinging what appeared to be lanterns. It was really weird. And then I looked at my daughter. Netta had both arms and her face resting on the steering wheel. I said, 'Netta, are you all right?' And her hands just slid down and she straightened up and said, 'Sure, Mom, I'm fine.' But the car was moving at least 65 mph.

"Then we stopped at a New Jersey Turnpike rest area and my son-in-law ran to our car and said, 'Did something strange just happen to you guys?' I said, 'Yes, why don't you check your gas gauge, John, because how could we get this far?' And we discovered that *both* our gas gauges were still on *full.*"

The mystery of suddenly being in New Jersey with full gas gauges bothered Wanna. The rest of her family wanted to forget it, but Wanna and her daughter, Netta, had vague memories of physical examinations by strange humanoids. Eventually Wanna contacted a New Jersey UFO investigator named Richard Butler. He tried hypnosis. One of Lawson's memories was a large room filled with tubes that contained humanoid bodies. I might never have known if there hadn't been a series of unexplained lights near Scranton in January 1992. Several of us were invited by a high school teacher to view his videotapes of unidentified moving lights recorded that month.

During the evening, Butler told me about the Wanna Lawson case and her description of bodies inside tubes. I told him I had a similar description from a California woman. So, Butler arranged for me to meet Wanna at her southern New Jersey home on January 22, 1992.

At the time of our meeting, Wanna had worked in city government operations for twelve years. She is fun-loving and laughs a lot, even about painful times like her memory of a physical examination by non-humans back in November 1987.

Wanna told me, "The little grey ones with the big eyes — they were there giving me the examination. And I was hollering. I was in pain. So, one of the tall ones came in and put his hand on my shoulder and calmed me. He stayed there until the examination was over and then he took my hand and led me out of that room."

"Wanna, do you remember anything consciously about how you got from the cars west of Harrisburg into a craft?"

"Just there being a light and we were in the craft."

"Did it pick the car up?"

"Linda, that light picked up *both* cars."

"What was the color of that beam?"

"Pinkish-reddish with gold in it? Or maybe the beam was white with gold in it and we ended up in a room that seemed pinkish."

"So you're inside that room ..."

"We got out of the cars and we were separated into other rooms."

"Was anyone there in that pinkish-red light to greet you?"

"The tall one with the skull cap — about eight feet tall."

"Can you describe the face?"

"It's a normal face basically — with a large nose, hooked." [19]

"Like an Arabic human nose?"

"Equivalent to, just long and hooked."

"Did you see him from the front?"

"From the front. It had almond-shaped eyes, pointed chin."

"The little greys — are they taking orders from the tall guy or is he taking orders from them?"

"They're taking orders from him."

"Did you hear their communication?"

"None whatsoever."

"Do you feel alert and conscious?"

"No, a dream state. Like you're in kind of a daze."

"Do you turn around and touch Netta or John or Anna or Charles?"

"I couldn't get to them because they (aliens) were moving us off fast in

[19] *Pages 276-278,* Glimpses of Other Realities, Vol. I, Facts & Eyewitnesses *© 1994 by Linda Moulton Howe*

Plate 22 - *On February 16, 1992, Wanna Lawson drew these sketches and worked with a sketch artist to do color renderings about her memories of non-human beings encountered during an apparent multiple-person abduction experience on November 27, 1983 between Harrisburg, Pennsylvania and Atlantic City, New Jersey. After stopping for gas with her family west of Harrisburg, Pennsylvania, Lawson remembered that they ended up in their two cars in a place that glowed with a pinkish-red color. "Small, little grey guys" got the family out of the cars and a tall, male humanoid with a large nose and skull cap greeted them. This sketch by Wanna Lawson. Others by L. Hoffman for author © 1992.*

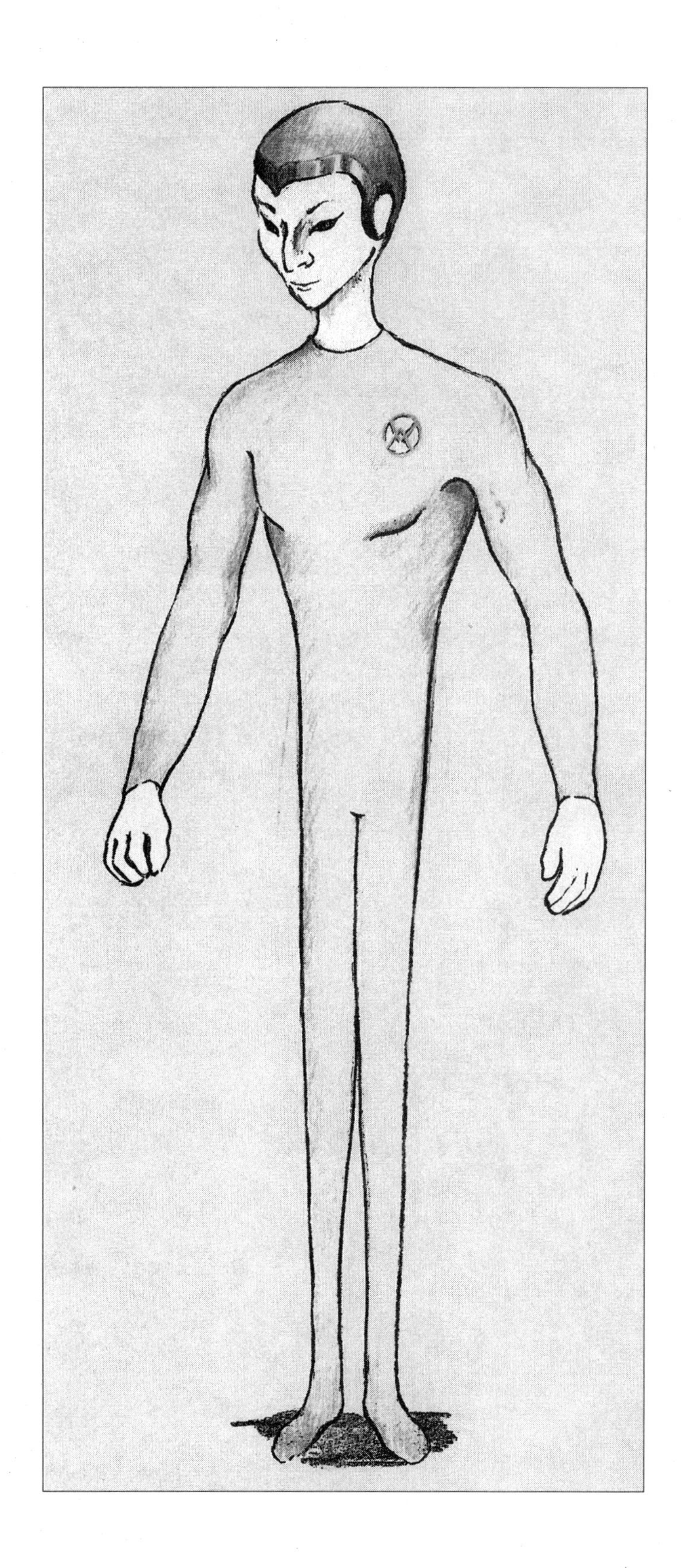

Plate 23 - *This eight-foot-tall, large-nosed humanoid greeted Wanna Lawson and her family inside a large place that Wanna thought was a "ship or craft." This large-nosed humanoid appeared to be in charge of little grey beings that escorted the family out of the two cars. Drawing by L. Hoffman for author © 1992.*

different directions. And John was yelling and screaming and fussing. He was carrying on. Charles was crying. Anna was still asleep, so the aliens carried her, moving us fast."

"And the ones that moved you physically were the little grey ones?"

"Yes."

"So the little greys could carry a full grown woman (Anna)?"

"More than one of them. It would take several to carry Anna. It wasn't like one carrying her. There were several."

"What happened to you?"

"They take me from that (pinkish-red) room into another room that's bright white, clean, sterile-looking, like a hospital room almost. They put me on the table and I don't know how I was held down. I went through the exam ... and then a being not as funny looking came in. Tall, American Indian type. His skin was grey, pale, no pigmentation whatsoever."

"Since American Indians are brown-skinned, why would you think of him as Indian?"

"That's what his features were like — high cheek bones, hook nose, strong face, black hair that was longer than normal. His eyes were wide set, solid black eyes when I first saw him. But those were shields of some kind. Later on, he took them off and I could see gold eyes like a cat's underneath." [20]

[20] *See Page 52, Chapter 1: "(There were) dark membranes on each humanoid eye that the surgeon removed with a tweezer-like instrument..."*

"Clothes?"

"Maybe metallic, silver or grey."

"Any patches or insignias?"

"I remember overlapping triangles on his uniform. He told me they meant the merging of two worlds, but I don't know which worlds or why."

"When the 'Indian' came in, how did he touch you?"

"He just put his hand on my shoulder."

"What did you feel then?"

"Calm. Immediate calm. I felt that I knew him and we were very close. Matter of fact, I felt that we were like mates. We walked through the ship. And we ended up in this humongous room with tubes. The walls were lined with these tubes. They appeared to be glass, but they weren't glass. The tubes were about two feet wide and about eight feet high. Cylinder tubes. Round. Wide enough to hold the tall, pale bodies."

"How many of them were there? How big was this room?"

"City blocks long. I couldn't see the end of the room."

"Hundreds of these tubes?"

"Thousands."

"Is the surface of the tube clear, transparent — or a color?"

"Silverish, but you could see what's inside it."

"What is it you were seeing on the inside?"

"Female body. With black, wavy hair. Almond-shaped eyes. It's not human."

"What's not human?"

"The grey-white color of the skin and the tall height, about eight feet."

"Does the tube have gas or liquid or gel in it?"

"I don't know. It just appears that the body is standing in the tube with nothing around it."

"Wanna, why is it that you remember this black-haired girl in the tube so clearly?"

"Because he took me directly to that particular tube. And said, 'This is your body.'"

"Is he talking to you, or is it in your head?"

"It's in my head. I knew he was talking to me, like a male, but I didn't hear a voice out loud."

"Was he touching you in any way?"

"He was holding my hand."

"And he leads you up to in front of that tube?"

"Right. We walked past several others. And we stop at this one."

"What happens when he puts you in front of that tube?"

"And now, I *change bodies.* But how I did it, I don't know. ...The only thing I can remember is that it was my 'other body' — that he missed me and it was personal stuff. It was weird! It's an embarrassing thing. It was unbelievable. It makes you feel like a sex thing, fantasizing."

"What did he say?"

"He said he missed me and he wanted me and he needed me to go into 'my' body (tall female.) But how I did it, I don't remember."

Richard Butler was listening to our conversation and interrupted to add that during Wanna's hypnosis session, she remembered a violet-colored light. Afterward, without knowing how, she was "inside" the other tall, grey-white female body that had long, black hair.

"So the tall male somehow transfers a part of you into the tube body?"

"Right, and all I know is that I went into that other body and then we walked back up the corridor and into another room. And I get the feeling of a dome-shaped ceiling with glass. We could see stars all around. And a large bed. And we had sex."

"How did the intercourse proceed?"

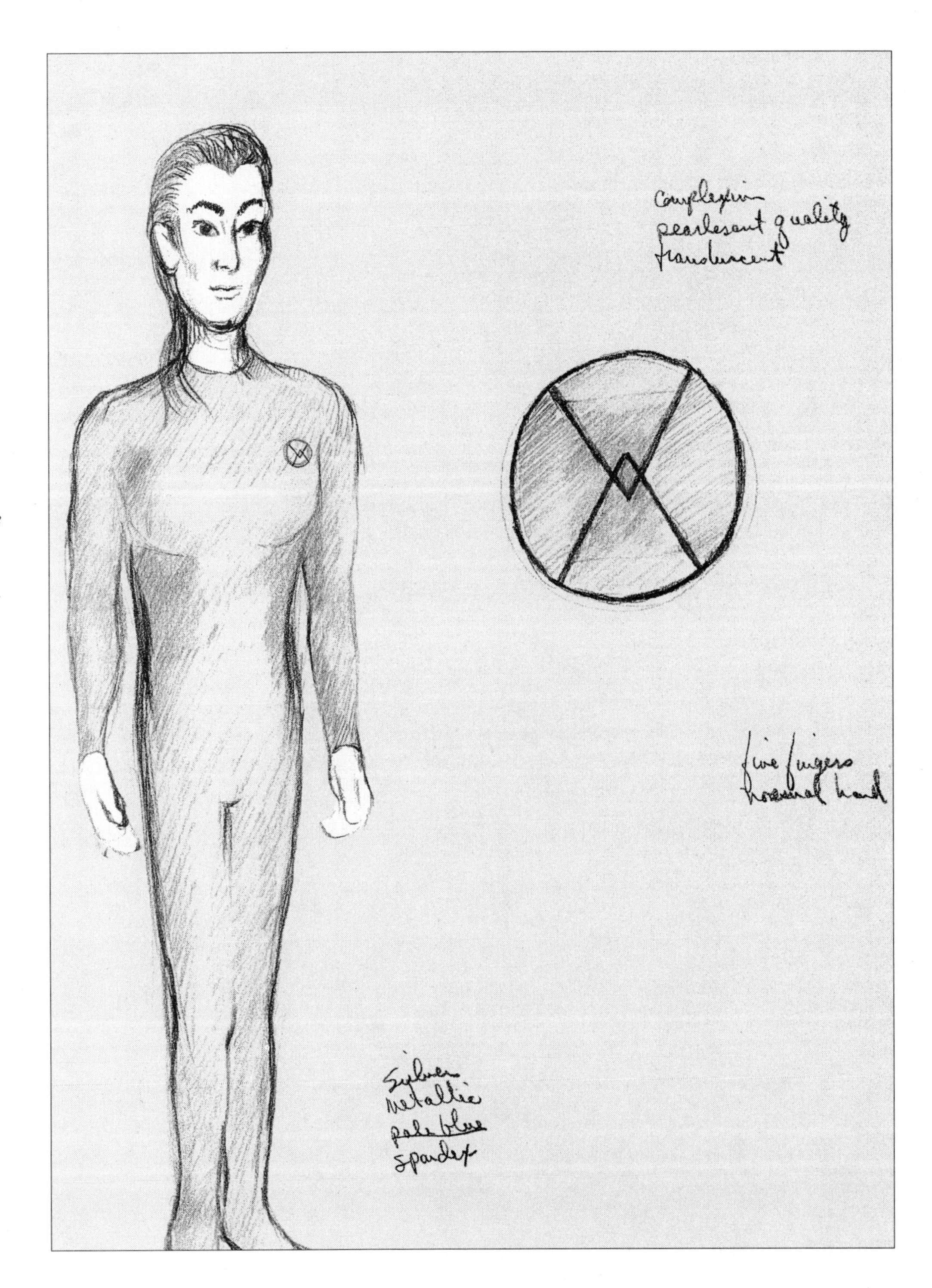

Plate 24 - *Seven foot tall "American Indian" male with "pearlescent, translucent complexion." Wanna Lawson said that when she first saw the tall male humanoid, his eyes were solid black. "He took something off, like shields, and there were gold cat eyes underneath." Wanna said this tall male and other beings wore a patch of two overlapping triangles, open at each end, which signified "the merging of two worlds." She did not know which worlds nor why. Drawing by L. Hoffman for author © 1992.*

Plate 25 - *The huge room filled with tall and shorter humanoid bodies in tubes that the "American Indian" male showed Wanna Lawson. The second female from the left with the black, wavy hair is the tall, thin body that Wanna said she was placed into —"changed bodies with" —for communication and a sexual experience with the tall male. Wanna did not understand how the transfer between bodies occurred. Drawing by L. Hoffman for author © 1992.*

"I have no idea. I don't remember. All I know is that it was fantastic. But it wasn't in this human body. We were both tall and grey-colored. And he took the black eye shields out and I could see that his eyes underneath were golden like a cat's without any whites showing. They had the vertical pupils like a cat's, too."

"What is your next memory?"

"Leaving the room. There was another room with a lot of people in it sitting around and we were just gliding along, the Indian and I."

"The people looked like?"

"Human beings. Just like you or anybody else. Human beings."

"Clothing?"

"Light robes. Strange, like some kind of harp scene in Greece or Rome. The weird thing is that after this happened in 1983, I thought that for all human beings that had been abducted, the aliens cloned their bodies and we all had this other younger body in case we died, we could go to it. But the Indian told me these people didn't have another body. They were human beings that had chosen to stay. Some were sitting on the floor, some were sitting like on couches built into the wall and holding children and laughing and talking and idling, just there."

"Could you feel a difference when you were inside the tall female?"

"The thinking capacity in that body versus this body are totally 100 percent different. This body, me as a human being, I rationalize right, wrong, good, evil. I might not like somebody because of the way they comb their hair. Or I don't like the fact that she's a slob. Some petty thing maybe. Well, in that other tall body, that's irrelevant. There is no relevance as far as the way a person looks or what color they are or if they are human without other cloned bodies. The tall beings are of a high development. A high spiritual evolvement. They have evolved spiritually to be worthy to be with us in body. It's a weird level."

The implication was that humanoid bodies were put on and taken off at will for a specific goal. Other abductees have used the phrase, "I'm coming out of myself. My body is like a robe I can take off and put back on."

"Wanna, when you are describing your consciousness inside of the tall, black-haired female, what consciousness is that? Who is that? What is her and the other Talls' relationship to us on earth?"

"It's like they had evolved to a level of accepting us, the humans."

"Who is They?"

"The watchers of man — the creators of man."

"Can you, inside of her, understand what the Talls want to accomplish?"

"They wanted to take a sub-creature and evolve it to the level that they were on and prove it could be done."

"Take animals and give them the hearts of angels?"

"Basically. To prove it could be done. But once you start something, it was like you start to love the creature and protect it and basically that was the feeling."

"Can you talk to me about the tall female's perception of the God force?"

"One."

"One with...?"

"Everything is one with one. We are one. It's like the love. If you didn't have this love, then you wouldn't love yourself. It's hard to describe."

"Why if they are one with God and God is one with them, what did they want to accomplish with this experiment (with humans)?"

"To prove that what is not pure and good could be *made* pure and good."

"Then, Wanna, what did they start with?"

"It was a primitive man."

"Neanderthal, or before then?"

"Before. But it wasn't like the Neanderthal. I don't know how they came up with the Neanderthal. I don't know what that is. But, the first men were tall."

"The humans they started their experiment with were tall?"

"Yes, and hairy. They have some."

"You mean Bigfoot?"

"Yes."

"Did you see them on the spaceship?"

"Yes. When he ('Indian') was taking me through the ship, that was one of the things he showed me — the room where some of those were. What they do is put them on earth, drop them down, beam them down, to gather fauna, leaves, flowers, fruit, different things, to see if it's contaminated by the air, by pollution, to examine it, and so they come down to get that. And after they have gathered it, they are beamed back up." (See Steve Bismarck story in Chapter 2.)

"Wanna, why are there five races here if this tall, white group of beings started manipulating genes on earth?"

"Because there were different kinds of beings in different parts of the world. They weren't all the same."

"Does that imply something else happened on earth before or after the tall beings got here?"

Plate 26 - *Wanna Lawson said that when she first saw the tall "American Indian" humanoid, his eyes were solid black. "But when we went to that bedroom, he took something off, like eye shields, and there were cat eyes underneath." The male's eyes were golden "like a cat's without any whites showing." Drawing by L. Hoffman for author © 1992.*

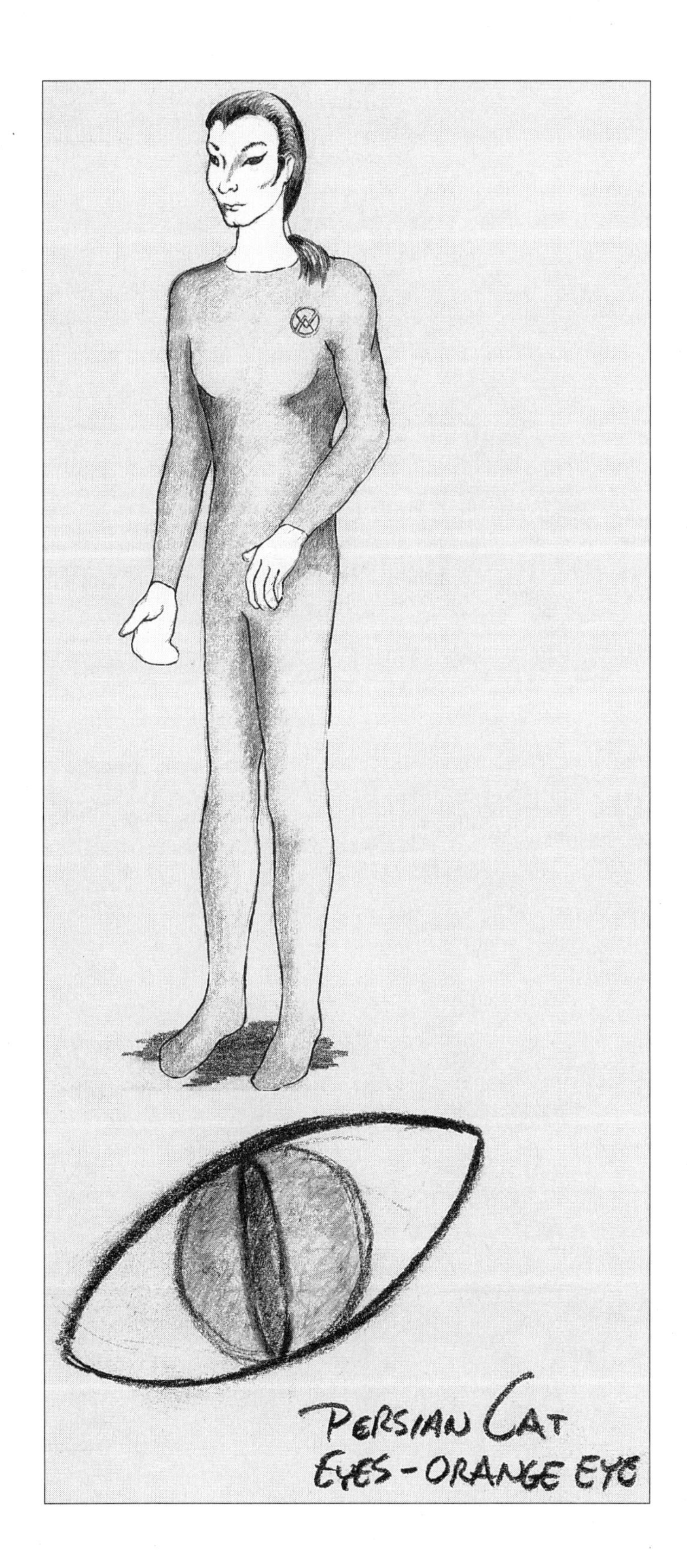

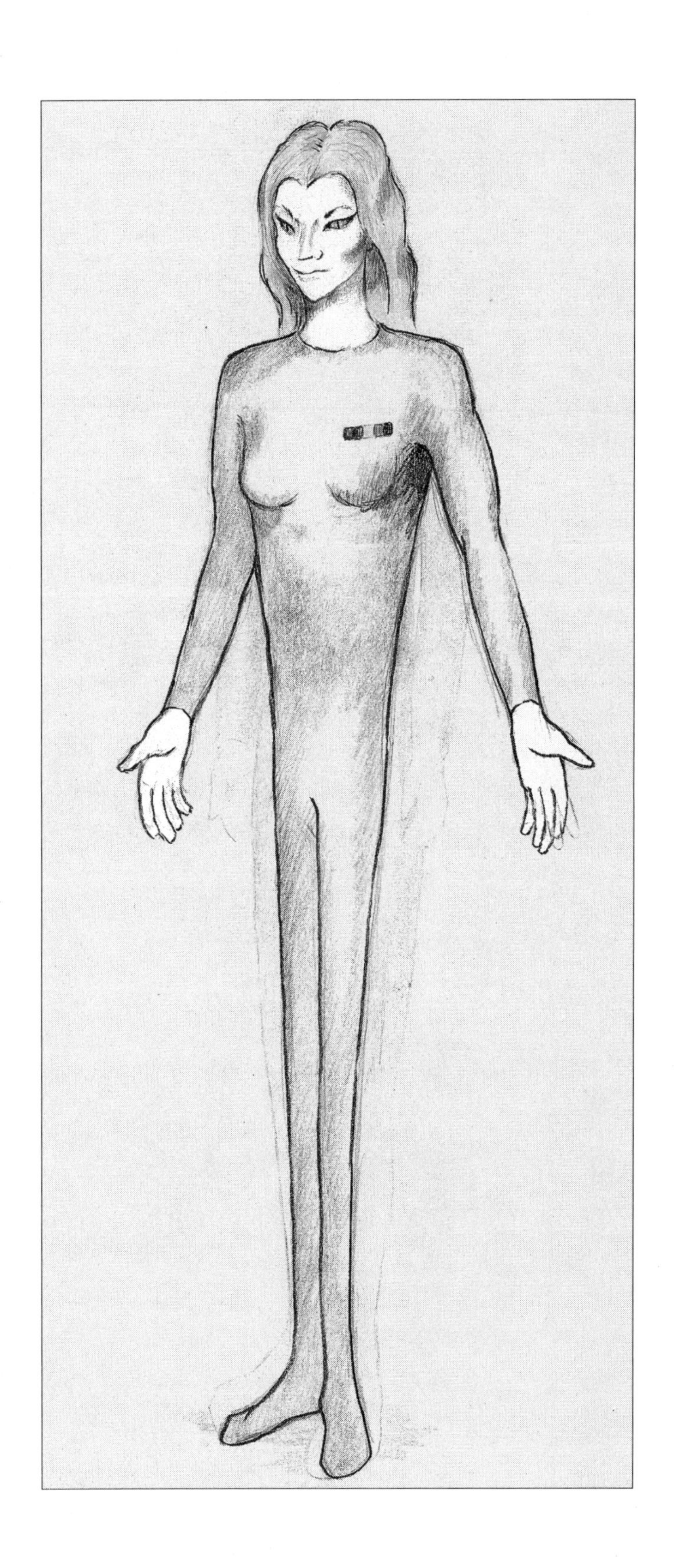

Plate 27 - *Seven-foot-tall blond-haired female humanoid that Wanna Lawson saw briefly with the tall, hooked-nosed male. Wanna did not understand what the relationship between the tall female and the tall males were, but emphasized that their tall civilization creates different body containers for various purposes, including interaction with earth humans. This female's eyes were "like a cat's with vertical pupils in large, pale blue irises." Drawing by L. Hoffman for author © 1992.*

"I don't know."

"Staying with their story, Wanna, if the tall ones have been trying to prove they could take something that is not wholly good and spiritual and develop it..."

"Linda, they thought that primate intelligence was so low and wanted to evolve it to an intelligent, thinking, creative entity — to take a sub-anything and evolve it into a productive being — that was a challenge to them and so subsequently that is what they tried to do."

"Then is the soul the major challenge? Would the Talls be activating bodies with souls?"

"No. With their genes. Taking from themselves and putting their genes into the foetuses of the human entity. If you pick up a pregnant woman, then you would mess with the embryo or foetus as far as injecting your own genes, certain factors of your own DNA. Each time you do that, you get a higher evolution."

"Wanna, let's go back to the Tall female's point of view again. She's looking at you, your body, as a container."

"Yes."

"Can you tell me more about her (Tall) point of view about you, Wanna Lawson?"

"This me who is a short African-American female is only one of many bodies that she (Tall) has occupied. And this is the last one. I (Tall) won't do it again because I don't have to. Because it will be over. The experiment, everything will be over. In a short period of time. I don't have to do it again. I have done it hundreds of times in different races, in different sexes."

"Reincarnation?"

"It's what some people call reincarnation. But it is actually me coming back into a human body while it's still a foetus as it's being born. At the moment it's born. The moment it breathes life is when they go into it. And it is so easy to do because you can change. We can change. We don't have to look like the tall guy with the dark hair. We can change our appearance. We can be beautiful blonds or whatever we want."

"Why is it necessary for you, the Tall female, and your spirit essence to go into these human containers that are an experiment?"

"To make a difference. To teach love, unity, oneness, to anyone who will listen. Sort of like Christ."

"How many of you are there on this planet?"

"Thousands."

"But not the entire five and a half billion population?"

"No. No, not at all. There are humans that are positive. If it's a good human being, then we will try to pick them up before the earth is destroyed."

"How will the earth be destroyed?"

"I'd rather not say."

"Please don't edit. I've heard so many variations on earth destruction scenarios, I'm simply looking for matching patterns."

"It will be nuclear."

"From whom?"

"From humans."

"Provoked by you?"

"No. We just won't interfere."

"Self-destruction in the purest sense?"

"When it happens, the chain reaction will cause explosions to continue around almost the world."

"You are talking from the Tall female's point of view now?"

"Yes."

"Is the chain reaction going to be in the upper atmosphere?"

"That's what we don't want. That's what we've been trying to contain, to make sure that doesn't happen. I don't think we (Talls) can control it."

"And when you say you can't control it, you mean you don't want the upper atmosphere...?"

"Whatever happens, we want it contained."

"If there is a nuclear war on this planet ..."

"It can have a devastating effect on other dimensions, the entire galaxy. And the only thing we can try to do is to get as many humans that are positive and all of our people out before it happens. So, right now what the Tall ones are doing is contacting all of their own people, the ones with our essence, making us aware through dreams, through subconscious memory of abduction. A lot of times people don't have any idea they had an experience with us, but the thought is put there and we just have to try to reach as many of our beings as possible, letting them know that it is time."

"Do you think the devastation is preventable?"

"Could be. But it would take massive interference on the part of, say us (the Talls). We would have to really get involved."

"And you don't want to because you consider this a failed experiment?"

"No. It's not a failed experiment when we have so many thousands of human beings that have lived up to every hope or aspiration that we could have aspired them to. ...We are picking them up, trying to get to them. Right now, we know the locality of each one, where they are. So hopefully before anything like I describe can occur, they can be picked up and taken to safety. They will live on board the ships before we have to leave."

"And if a nuclear war here would affect other life forms and other dimensions, why would you Talls allow humans to go to nuclear war?"

"Well, leaders that are above me will decide what they will do."

"What is the relationship between the Tall experiment and Christ and the apparitions of the Virgin Mary?"

Wanna laughed loudly. "Don't you know who Christ was? Christ was the product of the implantation of a DNA from one of our leaders into a human female (Mary) with all the insight we wanted for mankind. But he wasn't the only one like that. There were more. We did it all over the world, not just in one section of the world, not just Israel. No, it was different ones. And Christ knew what his mission was. We (Talls) had talked to him and he talked to us as I'm sitting now and talking to you."

"During his mission on earth or before?"

"While he was on earth. He would know where to come to meet with us and we would tell him what was expected and he would do it. And after he died — he didn't die — we came and got him and put him in his other body because he had another body."

"In one of the tubes?"

"Yes."

"And when he disappeared from the tomb, it was because you put the other body down to walk around on the earth so that Peter and the others would see him?"

"Remember, I told you that we could look like anything we want to."

"Was it a second cloned body literally, or was it a holographic projection?"

"It was the actual body from the tube. The human body that was destroyed was destroyed. Then he goes back to his normal body in the tube. But we had to remove his other human body from the tomb. We couldn't leave it there."

"The image on the shroud of Turin?"

"It was as the soul left the human body when we came to get it out, that's how that happened."

"The image on the shroud was left behind?"

"From the light. Remember I told you about the light. How we would go into other bodies. Well, in order to extract from a body — let's say we're still there in shock because we can get shocked from evil if stuff is really bad or ugly. It's crippling. It's so crippling that we can't function. So, in Christ's case, what you call the soul could not leave. It was still there even though he was dead for all intent and purposes. So, in order to pull him out, we had to do whatever to get him out of there."

"Like a frequency of light that would resonate...?"

"It's bright light. But I can't tell you what it is because I don't know."

I told Wanna I appreciated her trying to remember what she felt and thought inside the tall female because it had been my experience that sometimes abductees remembered more details in conversations. I have listened for patterns in experiences and communications among people hoping the many puzzle pieces will form a bigger picture of what a non-human agenda might be.

Christ's interaction on earth had come up in other human abduction stories. Also, the alleged briefing paper for the President of the United States shown to me on April 9, 1983 at Kirtland AFB stated that two thousand years ago "extraterrestrials had created a being to be placed on this planet to teach *Homo sapiens* about love and non-violence."[21] Linda Porter and other experiencers of the abduction syndrome stressed that Jesus Christ was still vital to earth's future. So it seemed important to probe Wanna Lawson's impressions of the Tall female's point of view.

[21] *See Chapter 7,* An Alien Harvest *© 1989 by Linda Moulton Howe.*

"Wanna, if I understand what you are saying, the release of Christ's spirit essence from the crucified human body was through the light technology that took him back to the craft, to your (Tall) group. Then he was put in the tube body that was preserved for him and put back down in a beam of light to walk around among the disciples?"

"Yes, and to assume the appearance of his living human body."

" Was the resurrection itself part of a programmed demonstration?"

"Yes, you had to have something so extraordinary that the minds of men would say, 'This had to be a God.' If a man sees another man dead, and then all of a sudden sees him walking — well, that's not a normal person he's looking at. The human would say, 'This is a God.' We had to do something to create the leader that we needed to teach from the Godhead, from the One, and share that knowledge with mankind to help man evolve into what we want them to be."

"Why did Christ have the impact he had on this planet?"

"I don't think it was only he. I think others have had that big an impact."

"Buddha?"

"Yes."

"Would all the other avatars of history be from your group? Or are there other groups that are involved with this planet, too?"

"You have a group that is trying to defeat our experiment. You have a group that is doing everything it can to prove that our experiment was a fluke — they have tried to undermine from the beginning. They disagreed with us and argued that it couldn't be done."

"Who?"

"The Controllers — tall like we are, but they think humans are despicable, less than a roach!"

"What's the relationship between you and the Controllers?"

"We are not warring with the Controllers because we don't war with anyone. The Controllers are equal to us, but as far as man is concerned, the Controllers are on a mission to say — 'No holds barred. I'm going to show you just how rotten these things (humans) are.' OK? Look at a Jeffrey Dahmer (sexual deviant murderer) who could kill young men and eat their bodies and commit the type of heinous acts that he did. The Controllers say, 'We're going to take them down as low as we can. And you tell me if your experiment worked.' The Controllers concede that we have a few, but when you look at the millions, how can you say the experiment worked?"

"Wanna, what's in it for the Controllers to prove to the Talls that humans are not redeemable?"

"The Controllers feel superior. The Controllers are not like us. They feel superior to us, they feel superior to any life form anywhere. And the human was such a low life form. Can you imagine an entity that feels superior to us Talls — how he must feel compared to a human being? The Controllers must feel that humans are a roach. Is there anything too bad for you to do to a roach?"

"But if the Controllers were spiritually evolved in their own right, why would they ever perceive any life form as something to denigrate?"

"Because to them a human being is like your opinion of a roach. Or a bedbug. Or a mosquito. If a mosquito bites you, you smash him!"

"But, in the oldest spiritual teachings, all life is revered."

"They don't think the same way as we do. They have a superior outlook."

"But, Wanna, when anything feels hatred and wants to destroy, it usually means the destroyer is threatened by something. Why would humans threaten the Controllers?"

"I think it's the Controllers' ego — if the experiment works. See, you're dealing with an entity that feels superior and looks at man as you would a roach or a bug."

"If the experiment succeeded, what would happen?"

"The Controllers don't want to concede that we Talls could be right that lower life forms could evolve? It proves that the bet would have been won by us, the Talls."

"And there is a bet?"

"Yes."

"The bottom line is it's a no holds barred battle. We're not fighting each other. We're fighting regarding man *through* man. It's for us Talls saying that man is worth saving and the Controllers saying, 'Man is crap. And we're going to show you man is crap. And we're going to win.' The Talls felt so much confidence in humans they said to the Controllers, 'Do what the hell you feel like! We'll still win!' In a way, it's a philosophical argument about how far DNA manipulation of life forms should go. The Talls think humans should advance spiritually. The Controllers look at mankind as dispensable and worthless robots. Anything they can make genetically is so much less than they are that humans might as well be roaches to be stepped on. And that's what the fight is about."

"If the body is the container, is the battle for souls?"

"No."

"What exactly does the battle gain?"

"The battle is to prove that the experiment was worthwhile, that man is worthy to walk among us. That man is worthy to be included in the One."

"And when the experiment ends?"

"Mankind will either be among the One or it won't. Those that are with us will be and those who are not, will not be. It's that cut and dried. It's not complicated. It's simple. Remember, Biblically everything is written by man. And some of it is inspired by the Controllers. And some is inspired by us, the Talls. The Bible is important. There are Wise Ones who are very old. (Biblical Elders? Praying mantis beings?) They conducted the first experiments on this planet — as far as the mixing of the genes and the whole thing."

"Then why would you Talls have gotten involved?"

"Because we are here on a mission. I am here to make a difference even though humanly I don't see any big difference I have made. Maybe if I could go back like Jimmy Stewart in *It's A Wonderful Life* — he found out what life would have been like if he hadn't been here. Maybe if I could do that and see the lives I have touched and see what happened with those lives, maybe I could see a role I played."

"If the experiment is going to come to an end ..."

"It's the end of the bet. There was a time allocated. It's the end of the time allocated for the whole experience. You had a beginning, you have an end. And the time will run out around 2002."

"Have the Controllers had any direct DNA involvement with the human experiment?"

"Yes."

"Are you saying that from the beginning of this experiment, the Controllers tried to undermine the experiment?"

"Yes."

"Who are the blond archangels of history, like Michael?"

"Michael is one of our Talls. Remember what I told you? We can look like anything. We can appear as tall or short blonds, or black or as anything, even like the Controllers who are generally tall and blond."

"Why would you appear as a Controller which is the opposite of what you are? That's on the opposing team?"

"Humans don't know who is the opposing team. They don't know us from the Controllers. They don't know anything."

"Wanna, if your group is the one that set the experiment in motion, and you wanted humans to evolve, and you want humans to choose God, the One..."

"Yes."

"... then deceiving humans doesn't seem fair."

"You're not being deceived. You are being led by what you believe in."

"But, Wanna, you say the Controllers' agenda is to put their essences into containers..."

"To be destructive."

"And yet they are supposed to be coming from a spiritual base?"

"It's a game to them. They don't think like you think. They don't think like I think. Their thoughts are not like ours. You're thinking of good versus evil. You're thinking of the Bible. How could something that is supposed to be good, do this? Because it doesn't think like you do. Its (Controller) thoughts are colder than yours are. They don't have the type of love you feel. They don't have the type of hate you hate. It's a totally different feeling, more cut and dried."

"Have you ever been shown a screen with scenes of the earth's future?"

"I had a dream last week with something like that. (January 15-22, 1992) This woman takes me into — I'm on a ship — she takes me into this room where there is a screen. It's almost like a TV screen except the picture is 3-D. What I saw was fire and all types of devastation."

"Did you recognize what you were seeing — a specific city, or place or buildings?"

"No. It was a close-up on the fire and explosions. Let me get the notes I wrote down afterward because this was really a weird dream!"

Wanna got up to find the notes she had written after waking up. The following is an excerpt:

> "A woman came up to me and said, 'You know where you are?' I nodded and answered, 'Yes, I believe we are in a space ship.'

She nodded and then asked me, 'Do you know that you are what you once called dead?'

I didn't really, but I strongly suspected it. She was very pleasant and took me into a room with a large, full-length mirror on the wall. Looking into it, I saw a familiar reflection: the same old, plump me.

She said, 'All that you have to do to change your appearance is to think the changes you want.'

I tried twice unsuccessfully. She encouraged me to try again. On trying the third time, I changed to look as I did at 22 or 23 years of age. I noticed what appeared to be excess skin on my face and around my waist and other parts of my body. But in less than a minute, it vanished. I imagined a full head of long, black hair and my short hair was gone and replaced with the hair of my youth. I looked at myself in the mirror and imagined total perfection in features and body. Then I was perfected far beyond anything in my actual life time.

The woman I spoke with was very beautiful with light brown, shoulder-length hair. All of the people who passed by us were very attractive. I asked the woman, 'What happened to cause my death and the death of my family?'

She took my hand and led me into a medium-sized room with what looked like a television screen about 38 inches wide. She pushed a button and it came on showing a nuclear explosion and fire. She explained that our deaths had been instantaneous, occurring while we slept and that none of us had experienced any pain.

As the woman and I walked away, I asked her about my mom and dad. She said that they could be there, or they might be Outsiders.

I asked, 'Outsiders?'

She started to explain when we saw things that my father had wished for. So even though he wasn't in sight, we knew that he was aboard. He had created a street and a car that were familiar to him in life. What I could determine was that anything you wanted, appeared. Even though we were on a humongous space ship with the ceiling looking like the open sky with millions of stars. The floor and side walls appeared to be a non-glossy, metallic substance.

Contrary to the UFO experience, all of the beings appeared to be human. The woman told me that the Outsiders were *not* part of the One.

Before I could ask any further questions, I awakened. The

> room was extremely dark. On the ceiling was a spot of light. Its shape was like a long slit, rather than round like from a light. It emanated a dense ray that did not reach the floor. It came down approximately three feet and it was slowly shrinking along with the spot of light. It totally disappeared in about one minute. I laid in bed and watched it disappear. I then turned on the bedside lamp and got up looking at the clock. It was 4:36 AM."

"Wanna, how did you remember that much?"

"I wrote this when I first got up. It was clear in my mind and I got my tablet and started writing what I remembered. You know, you take religion from the time you are a small child, and you are taught that if you are good you go to heaven and if you're bad, you go to hell. So, be good. And also you have that fear: What if there is no heaven? What if there is no hell? What if I die and I go into blackness and it's over and done?

"I don't know if you ever had those thoughts, but a lot of people have. Then you find out you're a container and you go, 'My God, I know I'm going to die. But I also know I'm *not* going to blackness! There's more!'"

Case 3 — Kenneth Rose, Central Michigan

A week and a half after I met and talked with Wanna Lawson at her New Jersey home, I flew to Lansing, Michigan to speak on February 2, 1992 at a conference organized by Shirley and George Coyne of the Michigan Mutual UFO Network (MUFON). I was becoming convinced that the phenomenon involved more than the hairless grey entities with big black eyes. Wanna Lawson's and Linda Porter's experiences with different types of beings reinforced what I had heard from other people. I had been collecting drawings from as many firsthand eyewitnesses as I could over several years and decided that at the Michigan meeting, for the first time, I would publicly share drawings of different alien types.

I was nervous and expected criticism because at that time the only nonhuman types generally discussed publicly were the small "greys" with black eyes and four fingers. But my investigation philosophy has been to follow facts and eyewitness accounts wherever they lead without trying to make answers conform to a pre-selected bias of what is or is not acceptable reality. And I had learned from my cattle mutilation research that when a story is presented publicly, other people emerge with their own repressed eyewitness accounts.

In my presentation, I showed drawings of lizard and praying mantis humanoids, Bigfoot, Blond Hairs, Red Hairs, Black Hairs, Tans and a variety of Greys. At the end of my presentation, I asked anyone in the audience who had encountered similar beings to see me afterward. There was a large surge of people all around me. Some were asking questions and others were telling me that some of the drawings were "exactly what I saw but never told anyone."

In the clamor, I saw a thin, blond man to my right trying to push his way through the crowd. I noticed him because he looked so frightened. He got closer and said, "I really need to talk to you." I asked him to wait in the back of the room. After the crowd thinned, I found the man and his wife sitting together. They, too, asked to remain anonymous, so I will call them Ken and Jeanne Rose, married since 1971. He was so nervous that I suggested we go find some coffee to relax. A waitress poured our cups and when Ken Rose tried to lift his to drink, he was shaking so badly that his cup clattered against the saucer.

"Mr. Rose, what has happened? Why are you shaking?" I asked.

"Your shoes," he answered, pointing at me. "Your shoes. They are the same color that I saw on your body in a tube!"

The word tube caught my attention. Wanna Lawson's story was fresh in my mind, haunting me with its resonance to Linda Porter's experiences. But

I had not talked about any of it publicly. I looked at my shoes. They had a metallic sheen as if covered with pewter dust."

"What tube did you see me in?" I asked, deciding not to disclose any other knowledge.

He began to talk very rapidly and the details were confusing. So, I asked him if he would draw what he had seen. I handed him my notebook. At first, he protested that he could not draw. I told him all that mattered was a clearer visual sketch of what he was saying. He took my pen and as he tried to draw, he spoke about his troubling memory.

"I don't know how I got there, but these little grey things took me where there were three ladies inside tubes. It was a little round room that was all dark except around the tubes where it was lighted. There was some kind of dim light inside the tubes. It was an eggshell white light, so beautiful, but it smelled like acid-sweet pure vanilla and made me nauseous. On the far right was a woman who looked like you. In the middle was another one that looked like the singer Kate Smith or whatever her name was from the 1970s. And on the left was a Mexican-Indian or maybe more Mayan-looking woman. They were all covered in gold metallic dust just like your shoes. Seeing you here today wearing those shoes made me remember. I couldn't believe it! I still can't believe it! They looked like the woman in the spy movie *Goldfinger* when she was painted gold."

"What do you think the gold dust on the bodies was for?"

"They (aliens) said the gold dust was anti-bacteria, or to preserve them."

"The one on the right looked like me?"

"That's why I'm so scared — watching you this morning, the memory came flooding back. And you and the other two were missing body parts. There were no breasts, no pubic hair, and there were holes in the stomach. I could look up into the open body cavity and one of the grey things said, 'They're under construction.' They were alive, but not awake, and the look on their faces was so tormented. It made me hurt all over, especially the one on the left end, the Mayan-looking one. Her head was tilted back with a painful look on her face. Everyone's eyes were closed and the hands were forward with the palms out."

Jeanne Rose suggested that maybe Ken could do more and better drawings when he was relaxed in his home and he agreed. So, I gave them my address in Philadelphia and hoped he would continue to try to recall more details and send me whatever drawings he could. A few weeks later, a large package came postmarked March 23, 1992. Ken Rose had made another attempt to depict the three women in tubes which bothered him so much.

He also sent drawings from other experiences he recalled with his comments, including an encounter with what he called the "Overseer" and the "Controller," the same word that Wanna Lawson had used. But I had not shared any of her story with him.

> KEN ROSE: "The Overseer controls, oversees, the power of life and death like God. He watches and makes the final judgements, the decisions. He feels no sympathy for me, only sorrow. That feeling was from a side glance, not a direct look. There is no hair on his head, but he looks human, like Yul Brynner. Six feet tall, black shiny clothes, milk white skin. I could not see the color

Plate 28 - *First sketch by Ken Rose on February 2, 1992 in Lansing, Michigan for author. Rose said the incomplete female bodies were coated with gold dust like the woman in the Hollywood film* Goldfinger.

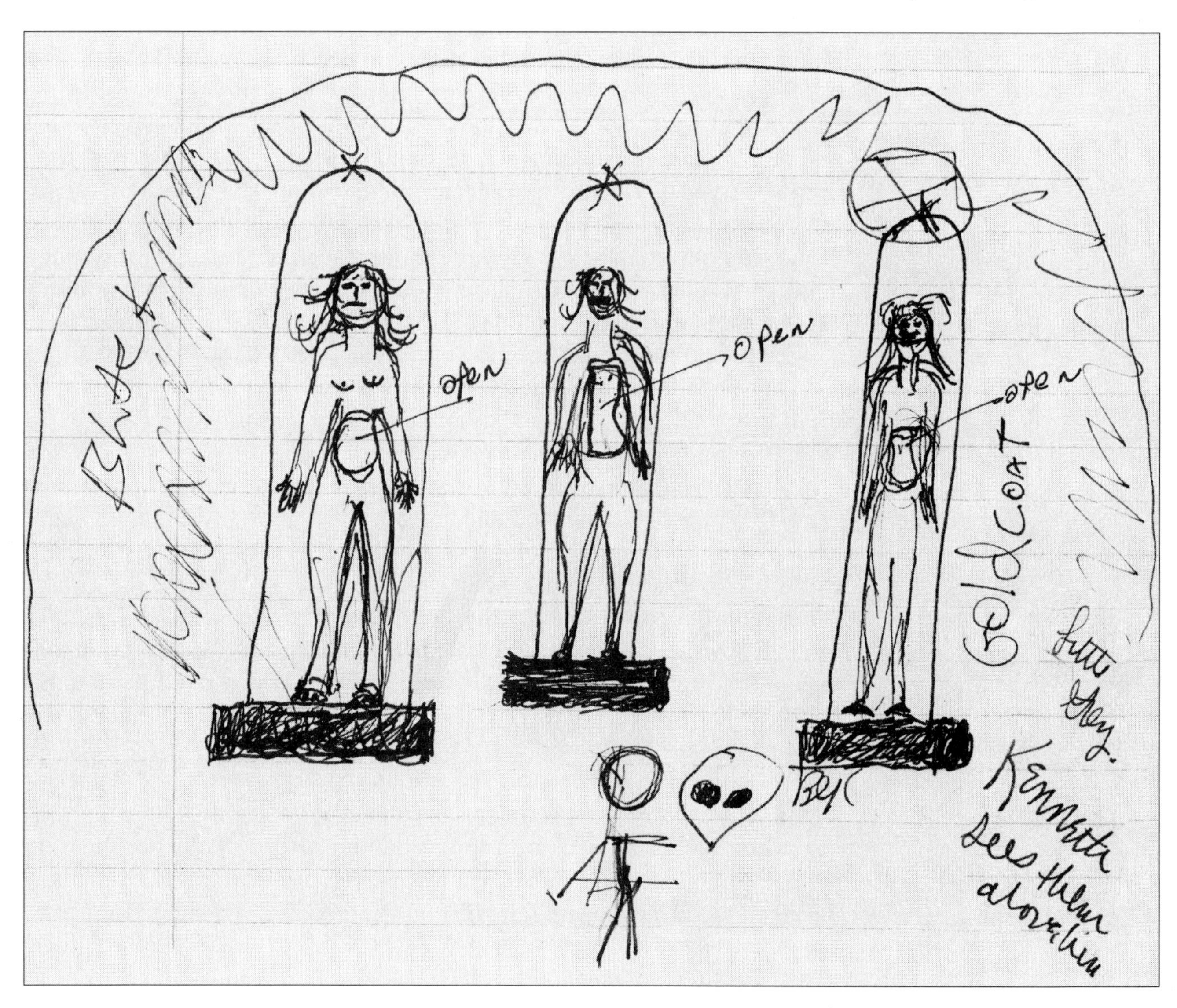

of his eyes. The Greys would not look at him. Scared of him and his power of life and death. The next time I looked at the Overseer, he crossed his arms real close and I could feel his stare right through me. I was going to live or die at that moment. He had the power over everything — kind and loving, but could kill you without a moment's hesitation.

"In the same room, the Controller was busy at controls where I saw him wearing a pearl or grey-colored helmet that looked like it had horns. The Controller makes things happen. Studies patterns of behavior, looking for something, controls everything. Understood that with a flick of a switch, the Controller could provoke anyone anywhere in the world, manipulated people into actions and studied reactions of other people at large. Studying all behavior. Nothing goes unnoticed.

Plate 29 -*Second drawing of three women in tubes sent to author by Ken Rose in March 1992.*

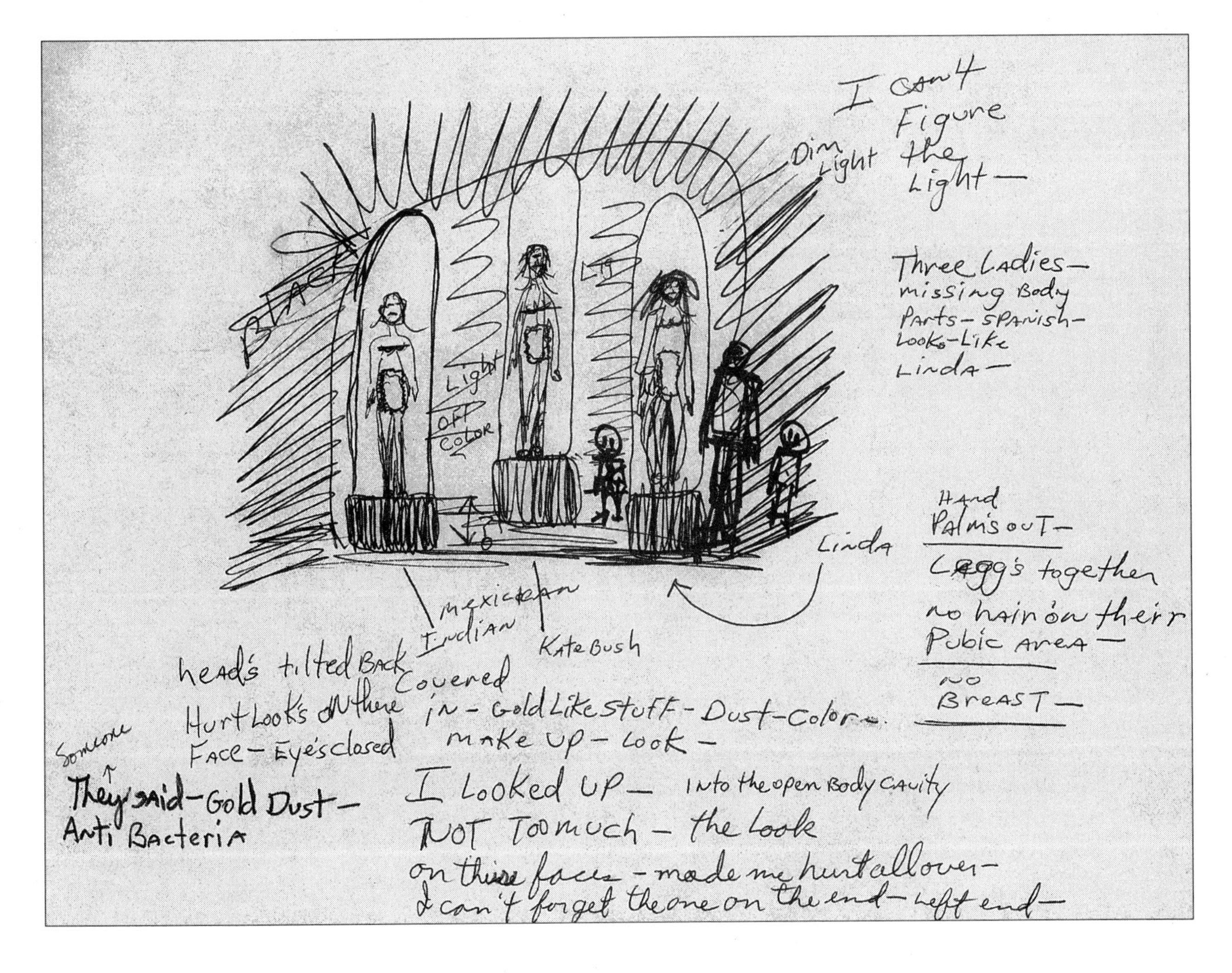

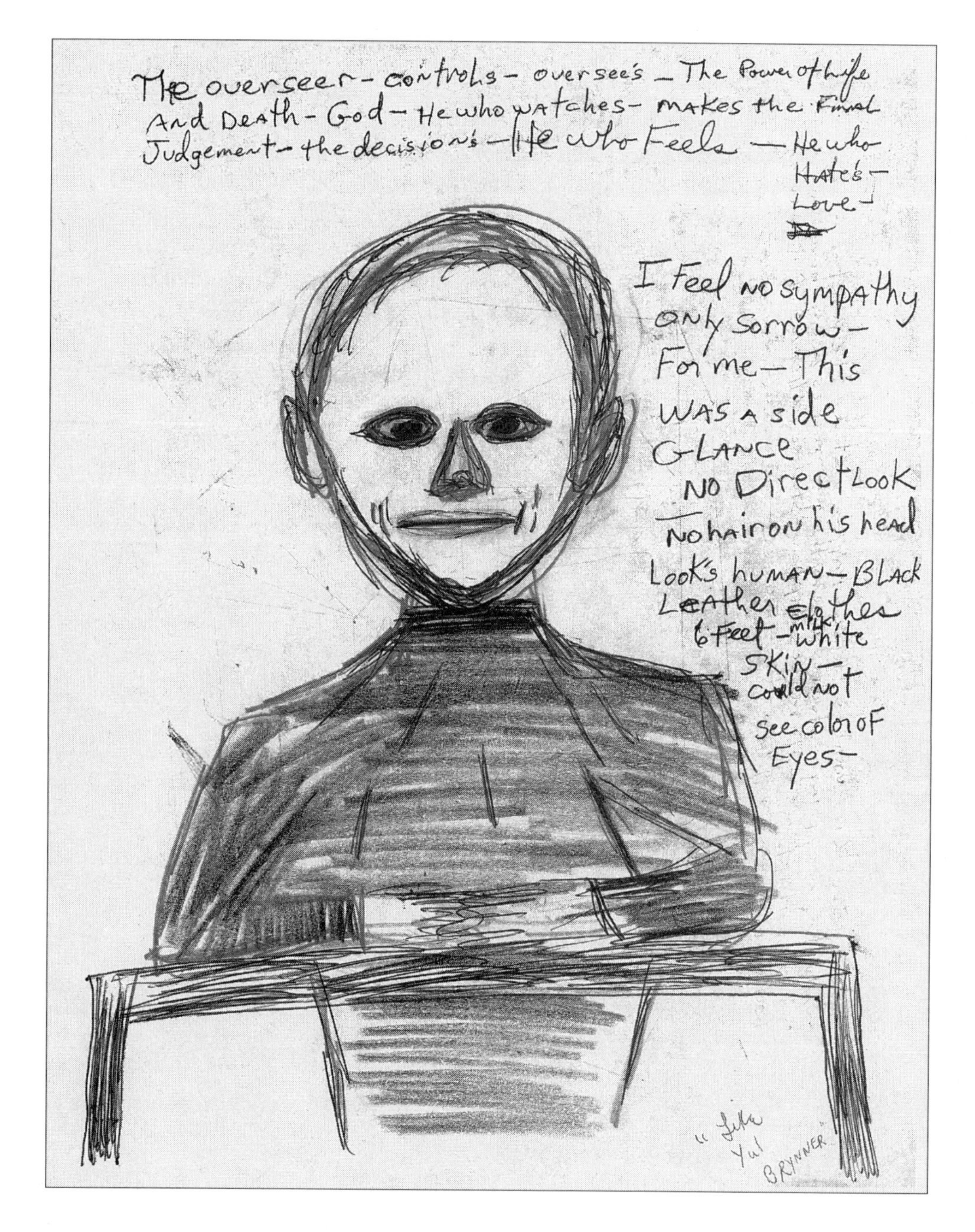

The overseer - controls - oversee's - The Power of Life
And Death - God - He who watches - makes the Final
Judgement - the decision's - He who Feels - He who
Hates -
Love -
I Feel no sympathy
only sorrow -
For me - This
was a side
Glance
No Direct Look
No hair on his head
Look's human - Black
Leather clothes
6 Feet - milk white
Skin -
could not
see color of
Eyes -
"Like
Yul
BRYNNER

Plate 30 - *The "Overseer" described and drawn by Ken Rose based on his abduction experiences in central Michigan since the 1960s. Drawing by Ken Rose for author © February 1992.*

"What does it mean? Are we a former colony that our owners lost all rights to and are trying to make a case against us to prove to a council or world representatives that we as a human race are not fit to govern ourselves?"

Plate 31 - *Room where Ken Rose was taken by small grey beings to watch the Overseer and Controller working. Drawing by Ken Rose © February 1992 for author.*

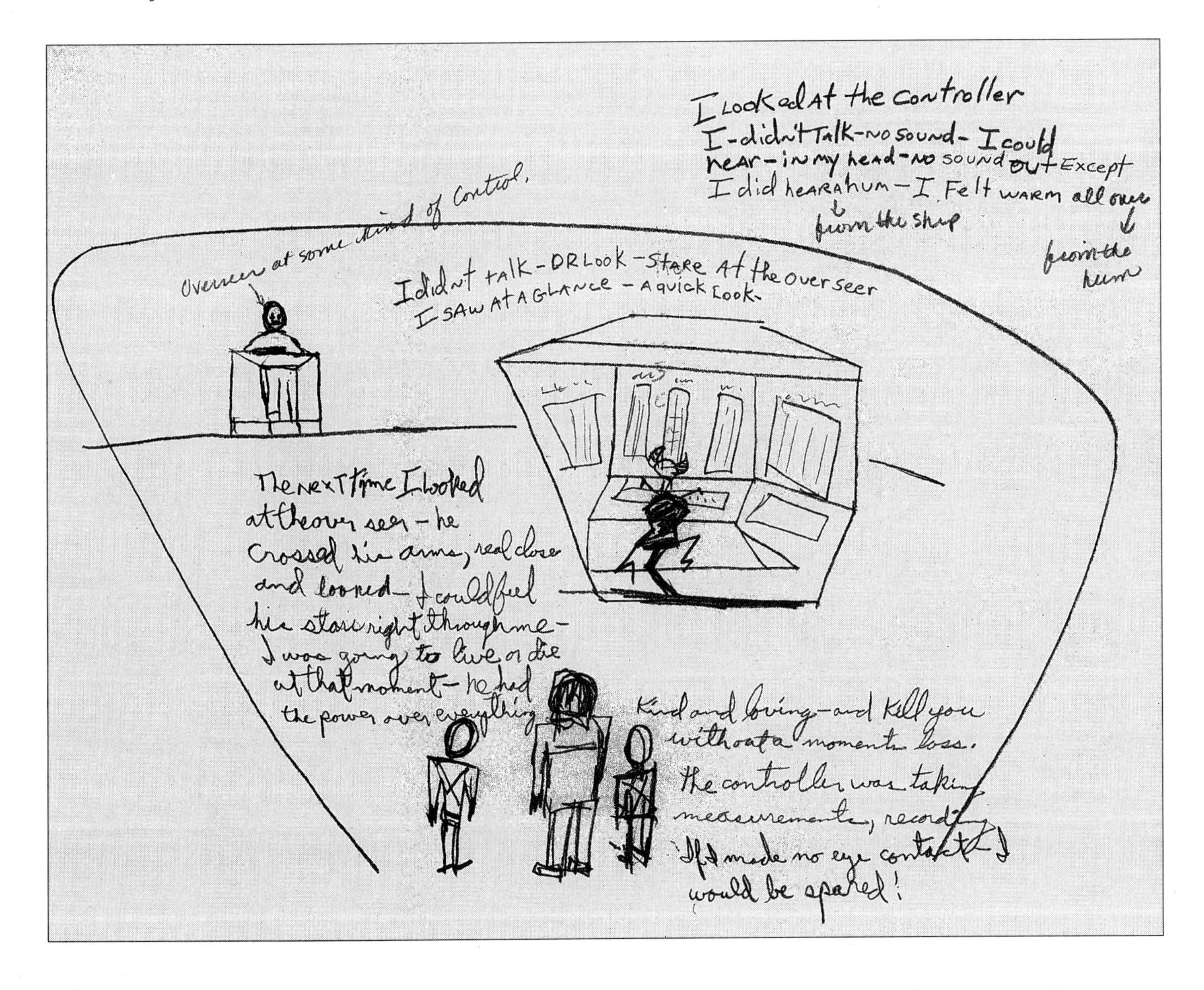

Plate 32 - *The Controller resembled a praying mantis being that wore some kind of headgear and worked at a computer console which Ken Rose thought could affect human life on earth in order to study behavior. Drawing by Ken Rose for author © February 1992.*

Ken Rose remembered telepathic thoughts from the Overseer and sent the following with his drawings:

> KEN ROSE: "The purpose of mankind is to help raise the conscious state in lesser animal forms, like it was done for us, by genetically altering to a higher state of consciousness. We are to colonize the planets in our solar system after bringing them to a more habitable state, which we can do with chemical alteration. By providing more habitat for more species we are fulfilling the role in which God intended us to have as caretakers. We were (to be) the caretakers, not the destroyers. We were designed to be the workers in the grand scheme. Man is a product of a genetic manipulation. *Something happened in man's history whereby he was abandoned by his maker because the Council told them (genetic manipulators) — No More Interference.* (Howe's emphasis.)
>
> "Our makers were robbing the planet of all its wealth, for whatever reasons, and they were treating human life inhumanely. Their reckless disregard for human life (they destroyed Neanderthal man and introduced Cro-Magnon) resulted in the Council stopping their use of slavery of mankind. There's a confederation of ET's that are studying mankind, but they are under commission by the Council not to interfere with human affairs."

Ken Rose also wrote, "This information isn't much, but it's what I've tried to remember. I asked the people on the craft — why were the people of this earth like the way they are? I found humans cold feeling — killers. Life anywhere in the universe is a struggle, but life in its varied forms is quite beautiful. On this earth, people look past the multi-forms and kill them. Instead of working with this planet, they work against it. So I also asked them why we were in Vietnam — killing people?

"They answered, 'Your words do not represent your feelings — emotions. Your actions do not represent what you believe is to be truth about your own self. Your words do not fit your actions — you have many levels of justifications, few if any, represent the truth. Truth is centered around you — is like a circle, is closed. Truth can be only a straight line — cannot be a circle. Truth cannot be accepted. It injures the ego, the self. To accept life means to accept all life. You are not ready, nor will you be ready to accept all life. This race is defective. We cannot give this race the opportunity to flee this planet with the knowledge of the stars. It would be too dangerous for the rest.'"

Rose said that he asked who the "rest" were, but there was "no reply. End of conversation."

Along with his drawings, Rose also sent a separate letter on notebook paper about his understanding of what the Overseer and Controller might be doing.

> KEN ROSE: "The plan is simple — create a state of mental confusion among the populous. This will convince a consortium of represented groups in the Council — (that) only intervention will rectify an ever-growing state of mass confusion.
>
> "Breakdown — social break down — an ever-growing mentally ill society — a hyperactive state — an addictive society to anything — a state of collection — obsessive-compulsive state — ownership and the need to get stuff. Security was built into the human psyche.
>
> "Reason for this is the outcry and eventual expulsion of the early colonists when after creating Neanderthal man — found that creation would not work for them. They destroyed them and replaced them with Cro-Magnon man. That with the extermination of the dinosaurs earlier[22] — yes. I know what you are thinking, but I'm not crazy."

Ken Rose and his wife separated that year and he moved with no forwarding address or phone. Since 1992, I have tried to stay in communication with Linda Porter and Wanna Lawson.

Thanksgiving week in 1995, Linda Porter wrote me another letter:

> LINDA PORTER: "The people who live on the earth, those who will survive the changes, will be evolving into a new species of being. That was why the (alien) visitors came here to begin with.
>
> "I'm not referring right now to the time travelers[23] from earth's future that are here also. That was something that was necessary because earth governments got ahold of a dangerous technology that greatly altered earth's future for the worse. Remember the mistake that was made that I told you about awhile back? That was what it actually turned out to be. Some type of technology fell into the wrong hands and the (future) travelers were sent back in time to change that. Don't know if it has been changed. At least not yet. But that was an entire side-bar to evolution that was never meant to happen.
>
> "...We can now only await the change over, knowing that many of us will be removed from here during the worst of the changes and then brought back to start over in a world cleansed of all the past hatred, greed and negativity.
>
> "As humanity does evolve into this new life form — and it

[22] *Large reptiles dominated land animals on earth during most of the Mesozoic Era from 245 million to 66.4 million years ago. Then dinosaurs mysteriously disappeared. The briefing paper shown to me at Kirtland AFB in Albuquerque on April 9, 1983 also stated that extraterrestrials had removed every species of dinosaur to another planet for preservation prior to a global catastrophe that wiped out most earth life and marked the end of the Mesozoic Era.*

[23] *Time traveler reference here similar to Jim Penniston description in Chapter 1.*

> will — there is no way the government can stop this process, even though it would like to. Humanity will be welcomed into the fellowship of the universe to continue on its growth and evolution, enhanced by the contact and knowledge of those species that have gone on before them. The future is something so incredibly different from what human life is right now.
>
> "...Many of what are called alien hybrids are alive right now on earth and are doing their best to help this process along. They didn't all turn out to look like bugs. Advancement in genetic processing finally came up with ones that appear completely human. In fact, you would be surprised at how many of them you might have looked straight in the eye and not recognized. And they are quite aware of their heritage and of their promise and commitment to help, no matter what the personal cost to themselves might be. The government is very aware of these individuals and running scared of the fact that they are here.
>
> "(Government's) existence depends upon the ability to exert control and manipulation over the people of this world. Soon that will no longer be possible. That must be a very frightening thought to those few who actually do know the entire truth."

A year later in January 1996, Linda Porter's greatest concerns were still about United States government control and manipulation of unwitting citizens and she had an update on the underground facility at Sycamore Canyon near San Diego.

> LINDA PORTER: "Underground area where blond man was held is now abandoned. It was filled in with boulders and cement. As to why, I'm not sure. I sensed a great deal of fear on the part of the military people as if they desperately wanted to hide the whole matter from someone. Not from the public as much as someone else. (?) The blond man is gone. I feel a deep loss that he is no longer here on the planet with us, even though I felt a terrible grief at his predicament in the facility. Where he is now, I'm not sure. The military no longer has him. He is alive and, wherever he is (off the planet), he is not being held against his will."

In previous correspondence, I had asked Linda Porter some questions about the hybrid situation and alleged "earth's secret war" between our government and a non-human intelligence as described to me occasionally by former military or intelligence people.

I told her one background source had said, "The truth is — the government is trying to take on the angels."

I remember puzzling over the word "angels," at first assuming it was a code word for UFOs and extraterrestrials. But the irony in his voice suggested he meant a more literal interpretation. I wondered about that statement again after I received the floppy disk from the government insiders described in Chapter 1. It's as if in the following sentences, these writers, too, were trying to suggest that something in the unseen tries to manipulate civilians and government insiders with advanced control of light and sound to inspire or confuse.

Excerpt repeated from Chapter 1, "Military Voices:"

> "The ultimate diversionary tactic to this point (and diversions will begin to increase in frequency, degree of strangeness, and in a more overt fashion, visible to greater numbers of observers) is the UFO abduction scenario.
>
> "The concept of these events, real though they are, being the result of extraterrestrial beings is a masterful piece of disinformation to divert attention away from the real source of the NHEs. Our information as to the true nature of these events does not negate the possibility of extraterrestrial life. But the causal source of the UFO and UFO abduction phenomena is *not* extraterrestrial.
>
> "The so-called Roswell crash of 1947 did indeed occur and debris of a non-earthly type was found, as were non-human bodies. ... However, the origin is *not* extraterrestrial.
>
> "The NHEs being dealt with in our psi (mind control) weapons development, and who are apparently allowing themselves to be used, for a time, are *neither benevolent nor neutral."* (Howe's emphasis.)

Linda Porter wrote back about an alien "black group" that thrives on control, manipulation, destruction and chaos. Those are in conflict with the original caretakers of the earth that she described as the large-headed grey scientists (perhaps EBE Type I), their ancient praying mantis colleagues and a menagerie of biological androids such as the small grey workers of various sizes and tasks. Without knowing anything about Wanna Lawson's experience, Linda Porter also described a conflict."

> LINDA PORTER: "(Whatever) the plans that were laid out, things got messed up. (But) the ending will be the same. And because of the 'black' group, people will have suffered who didn't have to. There is a struggle going on between negative predator entities and positive ones.

"Why is the government afraid of hybrids? The hybrids know the truth. They can easily discern one of the predators from a human and these creatures know it. That in itself makes the hybrids a threat to them. Plus, each of the hybrids here has a specific mission. With some, it is simply to provide protection to certain of the humans that will go forward into the new world. Others have missions more complex and dangerous — missions, or assignments, that the predators would love to stop or at least complicate.

"Please let me make one thing clear. In referring to the predators, I am NOT referring to the grey scientists or the praying mantis types.

"The dark side seems to be a part of creation that has been at war with itself since the beginning of all-that-is. How or why the split? I don't know. Those higher evolved would know that, not I. But ever since the two sides split apart, they have been *creating beings with which to fight one another throughout all existence.* (Howe's emphasis.) Not just on this planet, but on others, too. Is it something Creation itself uses as a tool to 'push against' itself as a way of expanding its own knowledge, growth and consciousness? I don't have the answer to that one either.

"...(But) the environment of the whole 'ufo' situation is one of evolution. Upwards expansion of the human race into a new race of beings contributing in a very positive mode to the further expansion, evolution, and co-creation of an ever-expanding universe. Life renewing itself in ever more complex arrangements of expression, ever more transcendental paradigms of creation. In the end, it is to join with others on this cosmic journey evolving always upward until we join once more with 'The One,' who created everything.

"In a way, you could think of all life forms as brain cells. On their own, they're not outstandingly productive. Joined with others of their kind, however, they merge to create a thinking, creative force for greater expansion of all that exists. Life creating and contemplating itself."

* * * * *

"Whoever controls the UFO phenomenon is intimately connected with the after life of human beings."

RAYMOND FOWLER
THE WATCHERS II[24]

The information and drawings about cloned human and humanoid bodies and a tube technology which preserves and activates them have bothered me for a long time. Why would non-human entities clone human bodies to substitute for certain human individuals? Was the military man's statement that the U. S. government "is trying to take on the angels" more literal than a simple code word for UFOs? Could entities from other dimensional frequencies be some of the actual intelligences behind, or allied with, biological entities working on this planet? If so, why would other-dimensional intelligences have such a vested interest in the lives and deaths of certain humans?

The easy way out is to dismiss the experiences in this chapter as simply more examples of mental manipulation by non-human entities for unknown reasons. However, the relationship between the UFO phenomenon and the moment of death or near death has emerged in other research.

Linda Porter fits the category of an abductee who had a near death experience (NDE) and watched her "old body" die from the viewpoint of a "new" cloned one — under control of grey alien beings and a large praying mantis entity. There are other such references to interactions between non-human intelligences and humans at the moment of death.

Psychologist Kenneth Ring found surprising similarities when he compared people who had near death experiences to people affected by the UFO abduction syndrome. In his 1992 book *The Omega Project,* Dr. Ring stated, "Among my respondents, I have found others who, in describing what purports to be an NDE, begin to talk about UFOs and aliens in the same context. Furthermore, there turns out to be a small but respectable number of persons in my sample who report having had (though, to be sure, at different times) both an NDE and one or more UFO encounters."[25]

In fact, a woman in one of Dr. Ring's cases also described clear containers with people in them that reminded me of Linda Porter's, Wanna Lawson's and Ken Rose's descriptions of beings kept in tubes:

"At age three I remember a very tall man appearing in my room in Cleveland. The next thing I knew, we were in a mountain in Egypt. Inside were many semi-clear containers with people in them. The man said these

[24] The Watchers II *© 1995 by Raymond E. Fowler, Wild Flower Press.*

[25] The Omega Project, Near-Death Experiences, UFO Encounters, and Mind at Large *© 1992 by Kenneth Ring, William Morrow & Co.*

people were 'sleeping' for a long time, but in the future would be awakened to complete their tasks."

Researcher Raymond Fowler has also been impressed with links he sees between human life, death cycles and the abduction syndrome. Fowler has been the chief investigator of the Betty Andreasson Luca case discussed further in this chapter.

Mr. Fowler served with the U. S. Air Force Security Service and with GTE Strategic Systems Division where he was a task manager and senior planner with major weapons systems development. Later he managed the Woodside Planetarium and Observatory in Wenham, Massachusetts. He has produced five books[26] over several years about the extraordinary information and drawings that Betty Andreasson Luca recalled in both conscious memory and from many hypnosis sessions about her interactions with other beings from other worlds.

Fowler concluded in *The Watchers:* "...UFOs and their occupants are perfectly capable of traveling between at least two different planes of existence." Later in 1995, Fowler suggested in *The Watchers II* that those different planes of existence might relate directly to the moment of human death.

> FOWLER: "...(The) UFO/NDE connection seems to be telling us that whoever controls the UFO phenomenon is intimately connected with the afterlife of human beings. This is a deeply profound revelation with ever-escalating implications for humankind! ...Whatever the reason, which may be beyond our comprehension, (alien interaction) seems to be part of a constant interplay between life here and life in the hereafter. For if we take and integrate the total characteristics of the UFO and NDE phenomenon at full face value, the bottom line implication is that *death may be the ultimate UFO abduction experience!*"[27] (Howe's emphasis.)

As James Penniston in Chapter 1 and others have emerged from their encounters convinced that time travelers and time manipulation are part of the UFO enigma, Fowler also asked:

> FOWLER: "If indeed, an intimate connection exists between UFOs and NDEs as the evidence suggests, how does it correlate with the possibilities of ETs and time travelers? ... No longer do we have to (confine ourselves) to consideration of a parallel development of humanoid life forms on an extra-solar planet. It may very well be that they coexist with us, but in

[26] The Andreasson Affair *© 1979 and* The Andreasson Affair, Phase Two *© 1982 by Raymond E. Fowler and Betty Andreasson, Prentice-Hall, Inc.;* The Watchers *© 1990 by Raymond E. Fowler and Betty Ann Luca, Bantam Books;* The Watchers II *© 1995 by Raymond E. Fowler, Wild Flower Press; and* The Andreasson Legacy *© 1997 by Raymond E. Fowler, Marlow & Co.*

[27] The Watchers II *© 1995 by Raymond E. Fowler, Wild Flower Press.*

> another plane of existence where time as we know it does not exist. Is it possible that they are us? Is what we call physical death just another step in human evolution? Have our ancestors gone on ahead of us and continued their existence and evolution in a world beyond our physical senses?
>
> "The mind-boggling ability of both UFO and NDE entities to know so much about us indicates that there is an on-going interface between our worlds usually unseen by human eyes. It makes one think, 'Who am I? What am I? What is humanity?'"

I sent the working manuscript for this book to Ray Fowler and in November 1996 talked with him by phone and on audiotape with his permission about his reaction to the Jim Sparks, Linda Porter, Wanna Lawson and Ken Rose accounts.

Fowler said, "The experiences imply that the human physical body might be no different to the aliens than a complex piece of electrical equipment is to humans. The heart, liver, and lungs might be no different than transformers and capacitors or transistors are to humans. Veins, arteries, and blood might be no different to the aliens than the electricity that flows through the cables and wires in a radio or TV set."

"So, Ray, that could suggest that we humans might be a more sophisticated kind of 'biobic,' to use the term that Betty Andreasson used when she described the small, grey worker androids, or biobics, who worked for the tall, robed Elders. Didn't Betty understand that the small androids were the Elders' eyes and ears in this world?"

"That's right. The soul or essence of the physical body might be no more to them than the electromagnetic field that contains and carries TV and radio shows. The Elders and their grey biobics might see and manipulate what we see and feel — the flesh, bones and blood — on an entirely different plane of existence. The aliens might deal with us as we deal with cellular structures and they might look at the human body at a molecular level or the electronic or even down to the atomic level."

"So, as Jim Sparks also suggested, the human body could store information the aliens have access to and have a need to access for some reason?"

"Yes. And, Linda, perhaps the aliens can download from the human brain, treating it like a complex switching mechanism. That download of information might be put in a container analogous to recording on a cassette tape which then could be uploaded in another body that could be a clone like the abductees said they saw."

"Ray, I think what bothered me the most about the Porter, Lawson and Rose cases was the question: Could an extraterrestrial biological entity, a physical being in this universe from another solar system more advanced and more evolved, actually be able to interact with and affect the moment of death in human life?"

"Well, something that comes to my mind about this recycling of souls business is that you have NDEs and UFO abductees returning from either experience sometimes with almost completely different personalities and completely different interests. Where did that come from? Was that uploaded from something, or someone, else? The cases bother me, too. If it's real, how do I internalize them with my own world view, number one? And two, how do I correlate this with the Andreasson affair and the other human abduction cases I have investigated? How does this all fit together? It's like trying to grab a greased pig, or the tar baby type of thing where you put your fist in and you can't get it out and end up saying, 'What's this all about?'"

"Ray, have you had many cases in which soul and spirit are a major theme?"

"No. Most are typical laboratory rat affairs. Betty Andreasson is unique in its complex spiritual implications. But in her case and others, I have had people report out-of-body experiences (OBEs) during abductions in which they see themselves in bed from an outside point of view, see themselves floating out, are examined by the aliens in procedures as if working on a physical body, and when the abductee is put back in his or her physical body, what happened to the out-of-body part shows up on the physical body. How do you explain that?"

"I don't know, Ray. I don't think we understand the connection between the out-of-body entity and the physical body. The OBE entity is unseen and considered ethereal and it's hard to understand how it would imprint the body with physical marks?"

"The first thought I had was that we are dealing with something that is both physical and non-physical. It's almost like an oscillation between a world of light and a world of what you called frozen light. And it's going back and forth — and the entities, the Nordics or Elders — are usually only seen in out-of-body cases. There have been a few incidents where people have seen Nordics consciously, but you wonder if they are seeing a frequency shift? Are the humans shifting into an out-of-body state or frequency when they see the Nordics? Betty Andreasson, for example, in one of the events when the grey being came to tell her that one of her sons was about to die — she is sitting there putting on her shoes to go somewhere and the TV is playing and she can hear the noise of the kids. Then something like a vacuum descends over her bedroom and she doesn't hear sounds anymore and suddenly, there is that grey entity. It's a bi-location effect — like your Judy Doraty case." [28]

[28] An Alien Harvest © *1989 and* Glimpses of Other Realities, Vol. I © *1994 by Linda Moulton Howe.*

"You mean when Judy said, 'I'm standing in two places at once, outside the craft looking through the windows and inside looking out the windows."

"Right. It's extremely difficult to explain or understand."

FURTHER INSIGHTS FROM BETTY ANDREASSON LUCA'S ABDUCTION EXPERIENCE, RELIGIOUS TEXTS AND THE BIBLE

In 1950, a thirteen-year-old girl named Betty saw herself "coming out of myself! There's two of me there ... and the little person (grey being) is saying: 'Now you shall enter the Great Door and see the glory of the One.'" Then her "second body" that was not physical was taken "underground" by small, grey beings with enormous black eyes to "take her home to see the One."

> "Investigator: What is the Great Door?
> Betty: It is the entrance into the other world. The world where light is.
> Investigator: Is that available to us as well as to you?
> Betty: No, not yet."[29]

[29] The Watchers - The Secret Design Behind UFO Abduction © *1990 by Raymond E. Fowler, Bantam Books.*

The girl grew up as Betty Aho and her first marriage added the name Andreasson. Later Betty divorced and married fellow abductee, Bob Luca. Beginning in 1944 when she was seven years old, Betty had many encounters with grey entities which persisted into her adult life. She was also taken twice to see tall beings whose skin was very white, had blond or white hair, wore long white robes, and who said they are neither male nor female. Betty calls the tall humanoids the Elders. "They look ... pale with white hair and pale blue eyes and very little color. ...They move around just like we do. They're very, very tall and they move quicker."[30] In contrast to the silent telepathy of the greys, Betty said she could audibly hear the Elders speak to her and felt peaceful in their presence.

[30] The Watchers II © *1995 by Raymond E. Fowler, Wild Flower Press.*

There is a theological theme underlying all or most of Betty's experiences in which there are "bad angels," or "watchers," who are jealous of humans and want to "hurt and devour mankind" while "good watchers" are the eyes and ears of the overseeing Elders.

In *The Watchers II,* Betty said, "The tall beings in white, with white hair, control the grey ones through the eyes and the brain. Those (small grey) eyes are evidently the cameras for those tall ones to see through (remotely). But, much more sophisticated than (just) saying they're cameras ... The greys are like walking or living cameras ... and do the bidding of those tall

Plate 33 - *Drawing by Betty Andreasson Luca of a tall, white-haired being who greeted her during one of her many abduction experiences. She called the beings "Elders." Nearby are the small, grey android "biobics."* *From* The Watchers II *© 1995 by Raymond E. Fowler with permission.*

ones." An Elder told Betty that the grey Watchers "are our remote imaging surrogates," connected to the tall Elders "with bio-electric mind projections." The grey Watchers "serve terrestrial tasks" for the Elders who "can command the (grey androids) to do whatever the (Elders) want." Investigator Raymond Fowler concluded that the "Watchers in effect were living monitors for the Elders!"

Betty Andreasson Luca says the Elders want to see humans evolve spiritually and survive and honor the One — the same word that Wanna Lawson and Linda Porter used to describe the God force, the creator force in all things. Betty, like Linda Porter and Wanna Lawson, also described a conflict between other intelligences about humankind.

When Betty was twenty-four years old, she encountered a dwarf-sized alien being in the woods near her home. The alien told Betty she had been "...watched since my beginning. I shall grow naturally and my faith in the Light will bring many others to the Light and Salvation because many will understand and see. ...The negative voices don't like it. They are against man ... bad angels that wanted to devour man ... hurt man ... destroy man ... because they are jealous ... of the love that is upon man." [31]

[31] The Watchers © 1990 by *Raymond E. Fowler and Betty Ann Luca, Bantam Books.*

Could Betty's Elders, Wanna Lawson's Talls, and Linda Porter's humanoids and "non-physical entities" be the same intelligence? And could those beings be the same Elders in the Bible who served the Eternal One, the Lord God? Or could another intelligence be superimposing or manipulating human religious belief systems to disguise its own mysterious agenda? For example, Betty Andreasson is a devout Christian who feels a deep connection to Jesus Christ and is very knowledgeable about the Bible.

Raymond Fowler had similar questions about Elders, Watchers, small greys and rarely encountered tall, white-clothed beings. He applied his college degrees in biblical studies, New Testament Greek and Hebrew to research. In *The Watchers II,* he sites several verses in the New Testament book of Revelation which include a dozen references to "Elders." [32]

[32] Revelation *Chapter 4, Verses 1-5, 9 and 10; Rev. Chapter 5, Verses 5, 6, 8, 11 and 14; Rev. Chapter 7, Verses 11 and 13; Rev. Chapter 11, Verses 16-18; Rev. Chapter 14, Verse 3; Rev. Chapter 19, Verse 4.*

For example, Revelation Chapter 11, Verses 16-18 says:

> "And the twenty-four Elders sitting on their thrones before God threw themselves down in worship saying, 'We give thanks, Lord God Almighty, who is and was, for now you have assumed your great power and have begun to reign. The nations were angry with you, but now it is your turn to be angry with them. It is time to judge the dead, and reward your servants — prophets and people alike, all who fear your Name, both great and small — and to destroy those who have caused destruction upon the earth."

Fowler also listed other Biblical verses that describe entities similar to the Elder figures described and drawn by Betty Andreasson Luca and occasionally referenced by others in the human abduction syndrome.

> Matthew Chapter 28, Verses 2-3: "An angel of the Lord came down from heaven ... His appearance was like lightning, and his clothes were white as snow."
>
> Mark Chapter 16, Verse 5: "As they entered the tomb, they saw a young man dressed in a white robe sitting on the right side, and they were alarmed."
>
> Luke Chapter 24, Verses 4-5: "While they were wondering about this, two men in clothes that gleamed like lightning stood beside them. In their fright, the women bowed down with their faces to the ground."

> John Chapter 20, Verses 11-12: "Mary ... bent over to look into the tomb and saw two angels in white."
>
> Acts Chapter 1, Verse 10: "They were looking intently up into the sky as he was going, when suddenly two men dressed in white stood beside them."

There are also modern day references such as an incident that occurred on July 4, 1980 in Italy and reported in the November 1980 issue of the *Mutual UFO Journal.*[33]

[33] Mutual UFO Journal, *November 1980, Seguin, Texas.*

"On July 4, military personnel from the Navy Air Base at Cantanio felt a compulsion to ascend the slopes of Mt. Aetna and there saw three red pulsating UFOs, one of which landed. It was a domed disk about twelve meters (36 feet) in diameter with red and yellow lights. The group then encountered two *tall, golden-haired, white-robed beings* accompanied by three or four shorter beings." (Howe's emphasis.)

I have also seen an alleged MJ-12 memorandum which discussed "Jesus Christ-types" who wear belted robes. It was shown to me in the context of other MJ-12 memos about extraterrestrial biological entities.

During an abduction experience in 1973, Betty Andreasson asked a grey alien who served the Elders what they were doing on earth.

> BETTY ANDREASSON LUCA: "He said that they are the caretakers of nature and natural forms — The Watchers. They love mankind. They love the planet Earth and they have been caring for it and Man since Man's beginning. They watch the *spirit* in all things ... Man is destroying much of nature. ...They are curious about the emotions of mankind ... He's saying that they have collected the seed of Man, male and female. And that they have been collecting every species and every gender of plant for hundreds of years."[34]

[34] The Watchers *© 1990 by Raymond E. Fowler, Bantam Books.*

Betty Andreasson Luca had also recalled in hypnosis an encounter with the tall, white-robed Elders in which the following conversation took place and was reported by Raymond Fowler in *The Watchers II:*

> Betty: "This tall person with white hair ... said they were ambassadors of 'Oh.'
>
> Ray: Who is 'Oh?'
>
> Betty: (pause) The tall one said that 'Oh' is the external internal, eternal presence.

> What we know is omnipotence, omnipresent. And when I asked them, 'Do you know Jesus? Do you know who Jesus is? Jesus Christ, do you know?'
> And the tall one said, 'Yes, he is the *hypostasis.*' [35] (Betty answers) "He's my savior.' And he (tall Elder) says, 'Yes, I know.'"

For the remainder of this chapter, the word "Elders" will be used in the context of an intelligence intimate with spirit and soul life, but not knowing if the Elders' origin is biological in this universe or other-dimensional such as primordial energy beings that were first created before matter worlds and which humans have called angels. The term "Watchers" has a Biblical association with "angels," both good and bad, who can interact with matter worlds. Betty Andreasson Luca grouped together Elders and their non-angelic "biobic" androids as Watchers. The Elders, their androids and the Watcher Angels might also be interchangeable with the "sons of God" in the Bible.

If the Elders have been conducting life seeding and evolution experiments on earth and other planets for eons, perhaps the *Homo sapiens* species is an unusual experiment in which the animal and the divine were united, a hypostasis with an ingredient of free will. Could that experiment have produced unexpected uniqueness valued by the Elders and the One and envied by some of the Watcher Angels originally assigned to watch over matter worlds?

In Betty Andreasson's case, the Elders — perhaps working in or with the mysterious angelic realms — created "biobic" android "watchers" to be caretakers of planets evolving with life throughout the universe. Those small greys, according to Betty and other abductees, came from an assembly line of androids, a generic model of worker bee individually programmed for specific tasks in the various atmospheres and physical conditions of different planets and different dimensions. Such androids might also function as biological communication devices that receive and send information from and to their makers.

Linda Porter's case suggests praying mantis entities might have been created to interface with several dimensions, including after human death, and to be long-term monitors and record keepers who have access to information accumulated by souls and bloodlines. Could "manipulation of DNA in already-evolving primates" to create free-willed *Homo sapiens* be an Elder life form experiment that was contaminated after competing Watcher Angels interfered?

[35] American Heritage Dictionary: *From Greek hypostasis, "a standing under." a) Something that underlies something else; substance, foundation. b) The essence or principle of something. c) The nature or essence of Trinity. Any of the persons of the Trinity. The essential person of Christ in which his human and divine natures are united.*

Could the New Testament's Revelation (11:16-18) reference to "those who have caused destruction on the earth" be the same as Linda Porter's description of a "mistake the grey scientists are trying to correct," and Wanna Lawson's description of an "argument between the tall Controllers and the other Tall humanoids about what is allowable to do with life?" Is the deception and manipulation inherent to the UFO phenomenon connected to the ancient tales about a group of angels who became angry when God asked them to bow down to the humans they were assigned to watch over, as if Adam and Eve were considered superior in some way? Did those jealous watcher angels decide to wreak havoc in the Garden of Eden by purposely inseminating Eve in order to spoil the newly created human bloodline and to produce different soul containers?

As incongruous as jealousy and revenge might seem in angelic realms, problems among angels in heaven were discussed long ago in the Dead Sea Scrolls and the suppressed Books of Enoch. Raymond Fowler pointed out in *The Watchers II* that among the Dead Sea Scrolls it was discovered that the Essenes, a Jewish sect at Qumran, had more copies of I Enoch and a book entitled "The Book of Jubilees (The Little Genesis)"[36] than any other books. Fowler explained that the oldest of four books attributed to Enoch as writer was I Enoch, also known as the *Ethiopic Apocalypse of Enoch.*

"That book," Fowler said, "was originally written in either Hebrew or Aramaic, perhaps both, but it survives in complete form only in Ethiopia. ...The materials in I Enoch range in date from 200 B. C. to 50 A. D.[37] ...(And) Jubilees was written in Hebrew by a Pharisee between 135 and 105 B. C. Jubilees is a midrashic rewriting of Genesis-Exodus from creation to the giving of the law on Sinai, given to Moses on the Mount." The Pharisees were an ancient Jewish Sect that emphasized strict interpretation and observance of Mosaic law.

I obtained a Slavonic translation of the Ethiopic Book of Enoch, more completely titled as *The Book of the Secrets of Enoch, The Son of Ared; A Man Wise and Beloved of God.*[38] According to Enoch, he had a startling visit in his bedroom one night by "two men very tall, such as I have never seen on earth. And their faces shone like the sun, and their eyes were like burning lamps; ...their hands whiter than snow." The tall, strange men named Samuil and Raguil took Enoch "on their wings" and placed him on "clouds that moved."

"And they brought before my face the *elders,* and the rulers of the orders of the stars, and they showed me the two hundred angels who rule the stars and their heavenly service." (Howe's emphasis.)

Enoch discovered that not all was well in the seven heavens of the Lord. The First Heaven was "a very great sea" where "the elders and the rulers of the orders of the stars" lived.

[36] The Book of Jubilees (The Little Genesis), *Translated by R. H. Charles, London, Society for Promoting Christian Knowledge, 1917. Originally published in* Jewish Quarterly Review, *1893-1894.*

[37] Noncanonical Writings and New Testament Interpretation *© 1992 by Craig A. Evans.*

[38] The Book of the Secrets of Enoch, The Son of Ared; A Man Wise and Beloved of God, *Slavonic version of* The Ethiopic Book of Enoch, *Translated by W. R. Morfill, M. A. and edited by R. H. Charles, Trinity College, Dublin and Exeter College, Oxford, Clarendon Press, Oxford, England, 1896.*

In the Second Heaven were "gloomy" (watcher) angels being punished for joining their prince Satanael (or Sataniel) in his efforts to challenge the strict ordering of angelic ranks. The Lord told Enoch that Satanael was "One of the ranks of the archangels having turned away with the rank below him (and) entertained an impossible idea: that he should make his throne higher than the clouds over the earth, and should be equal in rank to My (Lord's) power and I hurled him (Satanael) from the heights with his angels," including one named Azazel who will be discussed further.

In the northern portion of the Third Heaven was a freezing cold and flaming hot Hell for the damned, and south of there was the Garden of Eden and the Tree of Life. This description of Hell and the Garden of Eden in Heaven is confusing. Does Enoch mean that the Lord showed him the Garden of Eden to be literally in one of the Heavens not far from a Hell in Heaven? Or does he mean that this three dimensional world and universe of matter are the Third Heaven in a series of dimensional frequencies in the Kingdom of God?

In the Fourth Heaven were Phoenixes, Chalkydri[39] and "armed host" serving the Lord.

In the Fifth Heaven were "the Watchers whose fallen brethren" (Satanael, Azazel and others) that Enoch had already seen tormented in the Second Heaven.

The Sixth Heaven had seven bands of angels and record keepers over all the souls of men "who write down all mankind's works and their lives."

And in the Seventh Heaven were ten great orders of angels in ranks, a strict pecking order that apparently Satanael and Azazel tried to change. Their punishment for disobeying God's rules was banishment to the Second Heaven.

So Enoch reported he saw troublemakers and evil doers in the second and third levels of heaven. That paradoxical description of evil in heaven bothered the Rabbis who assembled the early religious texts. That's why Enoch's works were excluded from the Bible. However, conflict in God's Kingdom between the dark and the light is an ancient concept.

For example, in my Prologue to *Glimpses of Other Realities, Vol. I - Facts & Eyewitnesses,* I quoted David Flusser, Israeli Biblical scholar who commented about the Dead Sea Scrolls:

> "There is a predestination doctrine known as the Two Spirit Theology, in which one's soul is said to be fated for all eternity, blessed or cursed as the result of a kind of angelic wrestling match between two of the 'Watcher' spirits: ... a Good Angel and an Evil Angel, who struggle for possession of your soul..."

[39] *Chalkydri are 12-winged archangels associated with the sun, linked by Enoch to the phoenixes and placed amidst cherubim and seraphim.*

Accompanying that quote, I also included an excerpt from "The Testament of Amram" translated by Professor Robert Eisenman from his work on the Dead Sea Scrolls. Again, the man speaking is Enoch who lived before Christ:

> ENOCH: "I saw Watchers in my vision, the dream-vision. Two men were fighting over me ... holding a great contest over me. I asked them, 'Who are you, that you are thus empowered over me?' They answered, 'We have been empowered and rule over all mankind.' They said to me, 'Which of us do you choose to rule you?' I raised my eyes and looked. One of them was terrifying in his appearance, like a serpent, his cloak, many-colored yet very dark. ...And I looked again, and in his appearance, his visage like a viper. ...I replied to him, 'This Watcher, who is he?' He answered, 'This Watcher ... his three names are Belial and Prince of Darkness and King of Evil.' I said (to the other Watcher), 'My lord, what dominion (have you?)' He answered, 'You saw (the viper), and he is empowered over all Darkness, while I (am empowered over all Light.) ... My three names are Michael, Prince of Light and King of Righteousness.'"

Unfortunately, the Amram excerpt does not describe the physical nature of Michael, but it is assumed he is the archangel, Michael, ranked as the greatest of all angels whether in Jewish, Christian or Islamic writings. Michael is a battler of Satan and the angel of final reckoning who is the weigher of souls. How could Enoch see archangels? The Ethiopic Book of Enoch (I Enoch) states:

I ENOCH: "... Man's soul was created originally good, (and) while in the garden he could *see* the angels in heaven."

The implication is that the first humans could literally *see* angels and other realities that modern man no longer can. The current human retina perceives only a small percentage of the electromagnetic spectrum, so other planes or frequencies of existence could be around us, unseen. Perhaps the contamination of their Garden of Eden experiment provoked the Elders to put restrictions on humans which required more DNA manipulations to limit sight, longevity and other original senses and traits.

I Enoch also says that Michael, the archangel, was called by the Lord to anoint Enoch with an oil that made his body glow. (Howe's Note: Anti-bacteria metallic sheen described by Ken Rose?) Then Enoch took dictation from another archangel named Vretil (also Uriel) "who was more wise than the other archangels" and told Enoch about science, astronomy, math, the souls and creation of humankind, and what happened in the Garden of Eden (I Enoch, Ch. xxiii-xxxi):

> I ENOCH: (According to the archangel Vretil) "...the souls of men ... every soul was created eternally before the foundation of the world."

That is the concept of a *finite number of souls* also mentioned as an important fact by Axle and the government agent, Sherman, in Chapter 1. If there is a finite number, then souls must have great value in this cosmos. A logical deduction could be that cloned bodies might not have souls, or there is a demand for souls greater than the supply. This might have something to do with the soul transfers and cloned bodies in suspended animation which Linda Porter, Wanna Lawson and Ken Rose encountered.

> I ENOCH: "...from the invisible and visible nature, I (Lord) made man. ...And I placed him upon the earth like a second angel, in an honorable, great and glorious way. And I made him a ruler to rule upon the earth and to have My wisdom. And there was no one like him upon the earth of all My creations. ... And I gave him his will and I showed him the two ways, the light and the darkness. And I (Lord) said unto him: 'This is good and this is evil;' that I should know whether he has love for Me or hate; that he should appear in his race as loving Me. I knew his nature, he did not know his nature. Therefore, his ignorance is a woe to him that he should sin, and I appointed death on account of his sin.
>
> "Adam had a life on earth ... and I made a garden in Eden in the East and I ordained that he should observe the law and keep the instruction. I made for him the heavens open that he should perceive the angels singing the song of triumph. And there was light without any darkness continually in Paradise.
>
> "And the Devil took thought, as if wishing to make another world, because things were subservient to Adam on earth, to rule it and have lordship over it. The Devil is to be the Evil Spirit of the lowest places; he became Satan after he left the heavens. His name was formerly Satanael. And then, though he became different from the angels in nature, he did not change his understanding of just and sinful thoughts. The Devil under-

> stood the judgement upon him, and the *former sin* which he had sinned (wanted to change his angelic rank prior to the Garden of Eden intrusion). And on account of this, he conceived designs against Adam; in such a manner he (Devil) *entered and deceived* Eve." (Howe's emphasis and notes in parens.)

So, unlike The Book of Genesis in the Bible, Enoch says it was the Lord himself who told Adam and Eve about good and evil in order to make the experiment about will and choice worthwhile. The Lord wanted Adam and Eve and their human bloodline to choose him over anything else. The first sin was not Adam's and Eve's, but the plotting of Watcher Angels lead by Satanael and Azazel to undermine the Elders' experiment.

Enoch also said the Lord's frustration with Adam and Eve was about their *ignorance.*

> I ENOCH: "But I cursed him (Adam) for (his) ignorance; but those I previously blessed, them I did not curse. Nor man did I curse, nor the earth, nor any other things created, but the *evil fruit* of man and then his works (I cursed)."

It could be argued that the "evil fruit of man" referred to the illegitimate hybrid offspring giants described in the Bible and other text as conceived when the "sons of God" or rebellious Watchers "entered and deceived" Eve in sexual intercourse against the rules of God and the Elders. That violation also indicated beings from another dimension could interact physically with this matter world.

Other descriptions of giants in the Bible have six fingers and six toes. Chronicles 1, Verse 20 states: "During another battle at Gath, a giant with *six fingers on each hand and six toes on each foot* defied and taunted Israel." Then at Samuel 2, Verse 21 is this description: "And once when the Philistines and the Israelis were fighting at Gath, a giant with *six fingers on each hand and six toes on each foot* defied Israel." (Howe's emphasis.) Whoever those giants were, they didn't like Israel. If they are the same giant offspring described in Genesis, is Satanael's rebellion at the heart of all the troubled centuries of war in the Middle East? Are humans the pawns in a chessboard conflict being played by competing angelic realms?

Those six-fingered giants might also be connected to the "first civilization" (4,500 B. C. or earlier) in Sumeria which had a number system that was based on 6 and 60. The modern human numbering system based on ten has been linked to five fingers on each hand which add up to ten. The Sumerian system might have related to six-fingered "gods." Now we have dissection videotape of mysterious humanoids with six fingers and six toes allegedly retrieved from a crashed disc of unknown origin discussed in Chapter 1. Those humanoids without belly buttons might also be cloned hybrids that are part human and part non-human.

But intrusion in the Garden of Eden was not the first rebellious act of the Watcher Angels. The Ethiopic Book of Enoch states more than once that the angel Satanael sinned against the eternal One with his colleagues known as the Grigori,[40] *before* the Garden of Eden. The Lord explained to Enoch that the evil Watchers were *already* in the "great darkness" punishment zone of the Second Heaven before they travelled to earth to intrude in the garden experiment:

> I ENOCH: "...in great darkness ... and of them there went three (who went) to the earth from the throne of God to the place Ermon; and they entered into dealings on the side of Mount Iermon and they saw the daughters of men, that they were fair and took unto themselves wives. And they made the earth foul with their deeds. And they acted lawlessly in all times of this age, and wrought confusion, and the giants were born, and the strangely tall men, and there was much wickedness."

What is not explained is how the rebellious Satanael, Azazel and their angel colleagues could leave the Second Heaven punishment zone? The story is further detailed in the following texts:

> Jubilees 4:22: "And he (Enoch) testified to the Watchers, who had sinned with the daughters of men, for those had begun to unite themselves, so as to be defiled, with the daughters of men, and Enoch testified against (them) all."

> I Enoch 10:12/18: "All the earth has been corrupted by the teaching of the work of Azazyel. (Or Azazel.) ...Destroy all the souls addicted to dalliance, and the offspring of the Watchers, for they have tyrannized over mankind."

Similarly, Genesis, Chapter 6, Verses 1-4, King James Bible states:

> "And it came to pass, when men began to multiply on the face of the earth, and daughters were born unto them. That the sons of God saw the daughters of men that they were fair; and they took them wives of all which they chose. And the Lord said,

[40] *According to* The Dictionary of Angels *© 1967 by Gustav Davidson, Macmillan Publishing, in Jewish legend "the grigori are a superior order of angels in both the 2nd (unholy) and 5th Heavens (holy), depending on whether they are the holy or unholy angels. They resemble men in appearance, but are taller than giants, and are eternally silent. Ruling prince of the order is Salamiel (var. spelling Sataniel or Satanael) 'who rejected the Lord (Enoch II).'"*

> 'My spirit shall not always strive with man, for that he also is flesh; yet his days shall be an hundred and twenty years.
>
> "There were giants in the earth in those days; and also after that, when the sons of God came in unto the daughters of men, and they bare children to them, the same became mighty men which were of old, men of renown."

In summary, the Ethiopic I Enoch, Jubilees and Genesis describe Watcher Angels, or "sons of God," lead by Satanael who had sexual intercourse with human females. The women conceived and gave birth to "giants" in an era when life spans were measured in hundreds of years.

For example, Chapter 5, Verses 22-24 in the King James Bible says that "...Enoch walked with God after he begat Methuselah three hundred years, and begat sons and daughters: And all the days of Enoch were three hundred sixty and five years: And Enoch walked with God: and he was not; for God took him." Apparently, Enoch did not die a normal death, but was physically taken away, or abducted, by a God that Enoch could see, and with whom he could walk and talk. Further, Noah lived to be 950 years old, according to the Bible. Then human life spans shortened, perhaps as a consequence of another deliberate DNA change by the Elders after the Great Flood to restrict the contaminated human experiment.

Ironically, the extraordinary body of work written by or about Enoch, the "man who walked with God," was censored from the Bible by patriarchs whose priorities were the politics and business of religion, not truth.

Raymond Fowler said in *The Watchers II* that:

> "I Enoch was extremely important to early Christianity. It was the (objectionable) contents of the books of Enoch that influenced the Christian Church to include the Book of Revelation in the New Testament canon rather than Enoch. This was done even though I Enoch had been accepted as scripture for several centuries. It was rejected because of the very subject matter under our consideration: The reported sexual activities of the Watchers who copulated with human females.
>
> "Although the primitive Christian church and earliest church fathers believed that celestial beings could be physical and sexual in nature, the later church fathers rejected this notion. They decreed that such entities were purely spirit in form, thus what was reported in I Enoch was impossible (from the later church fathers' point of view).

"It was believed that a band of evil Watchers landed on earth, led by their leader Azazyel (Or Azazel) and mated with human females. This resulted in tall hybrids (giants or Nephilim)[41] who terrorized and took advantage of human beings. In order to destroy them, God sent a flood which destroyed both them and mankind, except Noah and his family."

There are other insights about the proud and jealous natures of Satanael and his angelic colleague, Azazel (Azazyel). John Milton in *Paradise Lost I,* 534, described Azazel as "a cherub *tall"* who was a fallen angel and Satan's standard-bearer.

According to Islamic legend, when God commanded the angels to worship the first human, Adam, who had been created from earth clay, the watcher angel Azazel refused, contending, "Why should a son of fire (angel) fall down before a son of clay (human mortal)?" Whereupon God, or perhaps the Elders, ordered Azazel out of Heaven and changed his name to Eblis, or Iblis.

In Persian and Arabic lore, Eblis was once an angel in good standing and treasurer of the heavenly Paradise, according to Ibn Abbas in Leo Jung's *Fallen Angels in Jewish, Christian and Mohammedan Literature.*[42] But when Adam was created and God commanded all the angels to worship him, Eblis/Azazel refused. The Koran, sura 18, ascribes these words to Eblis: "Me thou hast created of smokeless fire, and shall I reverence a creature made of dust?" Thereupon God turned Eblis into a shetan (devil) and he became the "father of devils."

Eblis is considered the equivalent of the Christian Satan whose other names throughout history have included Azazel, Beliel, Beliar, Mastema, Duma, Gadreel, Sammael and Angel of Edom. The *Zohar* (Vayeze 153a) says: "The rider on the serpent is symbolized by 'the evil Azazel' who is said to be chief of the order of bene elim (ischim, lower angels, "men-spirits.")

Further, *A Dictionary of Angels, Including the Fallen Angels,* says the Angel Azazel refused to acknowledge the human named Enoch as worthy or similar to him, Azazel.[43] Azazel and his fellow watcher angels were enraged when God favored Enoch to act as a messenger to them, a human interfacing between God and his troublesome angels: "(Enoch said) Go, say to the Watchers of heaven: (and say) Wherefore have you forsaken the lofty and holy heaven ... and have lain with women ... and have begotten giants? ...Now the giants, who have been born of spirit and of flesh, shall be called upon earth evil spirits, and on earth shall be their habitation. Evil spirits shall they be

[41] *Hebrew name for giants, Grigori, or "watcher angels," who mated with human females and produced a bloodline of giant-human hybrids who lived long and were "men of renown."*

[42] Fallen Angels in Jewish, Christian and Mohammedan Literature © *1926 by Leo Jung, Dropsie College, Philadelphia.*

[43] A Dictionary of Angels, Including the Fallen Angels © *1967 by Gustav Davidson, Free Press.*

upon earth, and the spirits of the wicked they shall be called."[44]

Another similarly named angel, Azaziel — also known as the seraphim Semyaza[45] — was tempted by the granddaughter of Cain (son of Adam). In George Byron's poem "Heaven and Earth, a Mystery," Byron said that Azaziel carried the granddaughter, Anah, off at the time of the Great Flood to a planet other than the earth.

The angels Semyaza and Azza in rabbinic tradition, like Azazel, both objected to the high rank given Enoch when the latter was transformed from a mortal into the Angel Metatron. In the Talmud, the sedim (Assyrian guardian spirits) are said to have been "begotten by Azza and Azazel on the body of the evil Naamah, daughter of Lamech, before the Flood (of Noah's time.)

Satanael, Azazel and their band of "bad angels," or watchers, apparently were thrown off their angelic paths by pride and jealousy in the greatest of ironies: to compete with the "clay" human containers and their "living souls" created "to dress and to keep" the Garden of Eden. (Genesis 2:7)

In addition to a possible Elder experiment to unify the divine spirit with an animal body which angered Satanael and Azazel, earth humans also seem to have served as a crop for non-human intelligences — planted, tended and harvested. In Chapter 3, alien beings showed Jim Sparks images which he interpreted to be their holographic record-keeping of his bloodline.

> JIM SPARKS: "They harvest DNA from us to make other life forms and body parts the way humans manufacture cars and auto parts."

His assessment echoes Betty Andreasson Luca's recall about why ova, sperm and human fetuses are taken by the grey beings:

> BETTY ANDREASSON LUCA:[46] "Man is destroying much of nature. ...And they're telling me that they're doing this because the human race will become sterile by the pollution and the bacteria and the terrible things that are on the Earth. ...And, they are taking the seeds so that the human form will not be lost — that they, too, are made of the same substance. ...The fetuses become them — like them. They said they're Watchers ... and they keep seed from man and woman so the human form won't be lost.
>
> "Their examinations of man are really checks for the environmental effects on our bodies (besides the restoration of

[44] The Book of Enoch the Prophet, *pp. 13-16, Literally Translated from the Ethiopic by Richard Laurence, LL.D., Archbishop of Cashel, Late Professor of Hebrew in the University of Oxford, published by John Thompson of Glasgow in 1882.*

[45] *Seraphim in Hebrew translates as "brazen serpent." The name Semyaza is similar to Semjase, the name of a blond-haired female humanoid allegedly from the Pleiades some 500 light years away as described by Eduard "Billy" Meier. Meier was an unemployed night watchman living with his family in the Swiss village of Hinwil about thirty miles southeast of Zurich in the mid-1970s where he claims to have met and photographed Semjase and a variety of round aerial discs. See* Light Years *© 1987 by Gary Kinder.*

[46] The Watchers *© 1990 by Raymond E. Fowler and Betty Ann Luca, Bantam Books.*

form). The balance of nature, all nature, including man, is in jeopardy."

Ray Fowler speculated that the alien purpose "is to preserve human genes for existence elsewhere because of an impending extinction on earth. According to Betty Andreasson Luca, it had only been because of the alien's past genetic interference that mankind has prolonged life on this planet."

> BETTY ANDREASSON LUCA: "They have spliced into it (the human seed) to prolong the form. ...They have been collecting every species and every gender of plant for hundreds of years so that nothing will be lost when the last shall come."

Plate 34 - *Betty Andreasson Luca's drawing © 1996 of "the people of all races and times encased in clear rectangular receptacles" for preservation by the non-human beings she calls "The Watchers" who have monitored the earth for thousands of years.*

During another incident in 1978, Bob Luca had a shared out of body experience (OBE) with Betty. While she was taken to another location and Bob waited for her return, he remembered that a white-robed Elder talked to him about the human spirit and evolution:

> BOB LUCA: "We are all constantly being monitored. Nothing that you do in your life escapes them (Elders). It's just like ... a recorder. Your life, your existence on the Earth plane, is all recorded from the time you are born until the time you die; everything is there. How you react, what you do during your life. Even your innermost thoughts, feelings and emotions. This process determines how rapidly you will advance and what your next step or phase will be, what teaching you need to receive, what hardship you must undergo to deepen your understanding. It's all recorded. ... Life is stages, like a never-ending school.
>
> "...The spirit is the ultimate creation. ...There is nothing above (spirit) in all the things that have been created. This is the Creator's masterpiece. The... spirit goes on and on. The spirit can evolve. It can overcome evil ...because it has existed in different bodies at different times ... To go back to another time, another existence, means to go through the death process. And that process sometimes can be very traumatic depending upon where you were and what happened before. ...The whole idea of (the spirit) advancing is to get closer and closer to the Creator. That is the ultimate goal. The spirit can neither be harmed nor improved. The only thing it can do is advance and grow." [47]

[47] The Watchers II *© 1995 by Raymond E. Fowler, pp. 344-347, Wild Flower Press.*

Bob Luca said the Elder gave additional insight about good, evil, free will and choices that apparently even angels must make.

> BOB LUCA: "Everything in nature ... has a plus and a minus, a light and dark, a negative and positive, a good and bad. It must be, for without some content of evil, there can be no good. There can be no growth. ... We do not need evil for good. We *need choice.* The creator gave us choice. We cannot use that choice unless we have two choices to make. Evil or good. It is so simple. It's beautiful. But there must be evil to have choice. ...Evil on this plane must exist.
>
> "...As the population of this planet increases, there will be those that have (plenty). There will be those who are greedy.

There will be those that have not and are starving or will starve. There will be much dissension. There will be more conflict. The world, this plane, is not perfect. There will be evil. (But) there will come a time when evil will be wiped away. ...When that time comes, our growth will not cease. Rather, we will advance into further planes of existence. ...The people of this plane as a whole are not very advanced spiritually. Technology is advancing. Spirituality, unfortunately, is not keeping pace. Man is developing many things which are harmful to him, which he does not understand. Man needs spiritual growth badly."[48]

[48] The Watchers II © *1995 by Raymond E. Fowler, pp. 344-347, Wild Flower Press.*

Enoch said angels in his day could be seen as physical forms and could copulate with human females, as Satanael and Azazel allegedly demonstrated. But another possible explanation for the Elders, their small, grey biobics and even Satanael and Azazel could be an extraterrestrial biological origin. For example, cuneiform scholar Zecharia Sitchin has written a series of books over several decades about an extraterrestrial-Sumerian connection (See Bibliography). Raymond Fowler also researched Sumerian history and said, "The origin of the Watchers stretches all the way back to the dawn of civilization in Babylonia (Mesopotamia) at Sumer (4500 B. C. or earlier). In fact, the very word for Sumer (Shumer) means literally, the 'Land of the Watchers!' The existence of Sumer is an enigma."

Even astronomer, bestselling author and vocal UFO debunker Carl Sagan directed attention toward a possible extraterrestrial connection in Mesopotamian history. Sagan co-authored the book *Intelligent Life in the Universe*[49] with I. S. Shklovskii in which they said about Sumeria:

[49] Intelligent Life in the Universe © *1966 by Carl Sagan and I. S. Shklovskii.*

"Sumerian civilization is depicted by the descendants of the Sumerians themselves to be of *non-human origin.* A succession of strange creatures appears over the course of several generations. Their only apparent purpose is to instruct mankind. Each knows of the mission and accomplishments of his predecessors. When a great inundation (the Flood) threatens the survival of the newly introduced knowledge among men, steps are taken to insure its preservation. Thereby, the access of Berosus to antediluvian records is formally explained. The straightforward nature of this account of contact with superior beings is notable... They are described as 'beings,' 'semi-daemons,' and as 'personages.' They are never described as gods."

My assumption now is that at least two categories of non-human intelligences have been involved with the forbidden history of mankind and modern humanity: other dimensional beings and biological life forms from other solar systems, including time travelers. Some might utilize underground tunnels and structures on earth.

[50] The Order
© 1991 and 1984
by Marine Captain
Beau Peterson.

In an extraordinary book entitled *The Order,*[50] U. S. Marine Captain Beau Peterson described a "Starman Intervention Theory" for the origin of humanity which closely parallels the above discussions about the watcher angels.

> BEAU PETERSON: "Long before the great civilizations arose from the dust (of earth), a more advanced race of beings came to this planet. As they stepped from their spaceships, they found themselves revered as gods. Their ability to descend from the heavens and sophisticated appearance put them in immediate control. Their ships and equipment became sacred. Their knowledge deified them and when they departed, they left behind at least one new religion — the ancient Hebrew religion.
>
> "So what has the Starman Intervention Theory done with the Lord? It has simply placed Him above the physical earth, stars and universe, back where He belongs in the spirit of goodness and life. He is therefore the machinery of life, the merciless force of nature which seems both unpredictable and arbitrary in many ways. The same force which animates the delicate cloud (also) orders the seasons with impeccable regularity. He is, moreover, the indomitable spirit which resides within the temple of the human body. But while He is represented in the goodness of Jesus, His powers encompass the evil of Satan as well. He is the light *and* the dark, the positive and the negative, the Alpha and the Omega. He *is* The Order."

If the Bible is correct, all the deceived humans and hybrid giants were destroyed by the Great Flood, except for Noah and his family. Through Noah, perhaps the bloodline of Adam and the Watcher/hybrid giants is mixed in modern *Homo sapiens.* If so, are manipulated and deceived humans totally responsible for all that has happened over the centuries, including wars and genocide? The confusion that humankind has had about its schizophrenic violent/loving nature and whether the universe is inherently harsh or benign was addressed in *Time* Magazine's October 28, 1996 issue by editorialist Robert Wright in comments about the Bible's Book of Genesis:

> "In the beginning, there were no thorns, and snakes spent their time not biting people but chatting with them. Only when man fell to temptation did the natural world receive a coating of evil. But according to Darwinism, the evil in nature lies at its very roots, instilled by its creator (in) natural selection. After all, natural selection is chronic competition untrammeled by moral rules. Heedless selfishness and wanton predation are traits likely to endure. If these things are sins, then the roots of sin lie at the origin — not just of humankind but of life."[51]

[51] Time Magazine, *October 28, 1996, "Science and Original Sin" by Robert Wright.*

Enoch and Beau Peterson would argue that the rebellious watcher angels purposely provoked and deceived *Homo sapiens* — and perhaps are still doing so to date. Peterson wrote: "The story of Eden was significantly altered by early churchmen into a description of man's fall from a state of divine grace through an act of disobedience to God's will. The burden of this 'sin' was then placed squarely on man's shoulders when, in fact, the humans were but a pawn in a battle among the angels."

Human pawns in angel battles. That idea was not even on the horizon of my consciousness in 1979 when I first began investigating the mysterious, bloodless deaths of animals throughout the United States and other parts of the world. Back then, I knew nothing about extraterrestrials and little about angels. There had been my own experiences with light such as the incident I shared in this book's Prologue. But my entire professional life had been focused on science, medicine and the environment. Hard news with hard answers. That was how I began my investigation of the animal mutilations which lead to glowing disks, light beams and eyewitness descriptions of nonhuman beings, human abductions, circles in grass and crops, government knowledge and cover-up.

One night in November 1984, after a university conference in which we had been guest speakers about unexplained phenomena, Dr. J. Allen Hynek said, "Linda, it's time you and I let our hair down about all this." I thought at last I was going to hear honest, inside-government answers about UFOs from the astronomer and former U. S. Air Force adviser on Project Blue Book, and founder of the Center for UFO Studies (CUFOS).

To my surprise, Dr. Hynek told me about his teenage interest in magic rituals and his later joining the Rosecrucians. He told me that the most important book he had ever read was *Theosophy* by Rudolph Steiner.[52] At the time, I had never heard of either Theosophy, which means divine wisdom, or Rudolph Steiner. But when I returned to my home in Denver, Colorado,

[52] Theosophy *© 1922 by Rudolph Steiner, Anthioposophic Press, N. Y.*

I immediately got the book. I remember my confusion as I read Steiner's methodical descriptions of body, soul and spirit written in 1922 that said nothing about extraterrestrial biological entities.

But today I have reread the book and wonder if Dr. Hynek had more insight about the complex UFO phenomenon than he ever shared publicly. Would the experiences of Linda Porter, Wanna Lawson, Ken Rose, Betty Andreasson and Bob Luca have been a surprise to him? Would he have been uncomfortable with the emerging comparisons of alleged modern ET encounters to the ancient Watchers and Elders? Or would he have put his pipe between his teeth, nodded and referred to the section in Steiner's book subtitled "The Spirit in Spiritland after Death?" Steiner's point of view was that the "soul lives between body and spirit," passing in and out of matter containers to help the spirit grow and flower.

> RUDOLPH STEINER: "In each life the human spirit appears as a repetition of itself with the fruits of its former experiences in previous lives. ...No two human beings have the same spiritual form. ...When the human spirit has passed through the world of souls on its way between two incarnations, it enters the land of spirits to remain there until it is ripe for a new bodily existence.
>
> "... Only by being embodied, incarnated, can man work in the world of bodies. He must take on the physical body as his tool so that through the body he can act on other bodies and they on him. What acts through this physical corporeality of man is the spirit. From this spirit flow the purposes, the direction its work is to take in the physical world.
>
> "... After its birth in the physical body, the soul, when met by some hard fate, has no glimmering of the fact that in the purely spiritual life before birth, the impulse that led to this hard fate had been voluntarily accepted by it. What, therefore, seems completely unwished for from the point of view of the earth-life is willed by the soul itself in the supersensible."

Steiner wrote in *Theosophy* that the soul and spirit retain and accumulate knowledge in various containers from each life cycle. In Chapter 1, the former government agent, Sherman, described information allegedly from extraterrestrials in the Yellow Book who were concerned about soul damage: "When you put something in a container and you pour it out, there's always some residue that remains. Something remains in that soul, so when you pass the soul on in different containers, it picks up the residues of all the different containers it has been in and a little of each remains and stays throughout (eternity)."

In Chapter 3, abductee Jim Sparks said he has been forced by grey beings to learn an alien symbol language. He asked, "Why me?" and the greys showed holograms that had "something to do with my ancestors, my bloodline, some kind of monitoring process over thousands of years."

Sparks suggested that not only is there a tracking of bloodlines and harvesting of genetic material to create hybrids, biological drones and cloned body containers, but that the experiences and memories contained in the DNA, and perhaps the soul, might be accessed and played back the way wc play a CD-ROM on our computer. Still confusing to him, though, is why the aliens would work so hard to teach him a symbol language.

Sparks, like Linda Porter, also thinks the world's current obsession with military, industrial and technological development is seriously threatening the environment that all earth life depends upon and our self-destruction would interfere with the "game plans" other intelligences have had for this planet over eons.

If the Elders created grey biological caretakers, or non-angelic watchers, to be "living remote imaging surrogates" connected to the tall Elders "with bio-electric mind projections," then humans might be serving a similar purpose but with a potential not programmed into the grey androids: free will to choose good or evil. Our choices might determine our destination at the moment of death, a destination in a specific dimension or angelic realm that resonates with a combined frequency of soul and spirit. You reap what you sow, whether human, ET or angel.

Accessing soul and genetic knowledge might be vital to monitoring the human experiment, both in physical life and after death in other planes of existence. That might be why different intelligences behind the UFO phenomenon seem to have access to the afterlife of some, or all, human beings.

* * * * *

Jim Sparks, Linda Porter, Wanna Lawson, Ken Rose, Betty and Bob Luca, Ray Fowler and so many others including myself are struggling to absorb and understand the themes that continue to emerge in a repeating pattern:

— The United States government and its allies have been hiding bodies of extraterrestrial biological entities (EBEs), both dead and alive, and their technology for at least half a century.

— Secret knowledge has been suppressed in the interests of national security, preventing "mass panic," and to keep the advanced technology away from our enemies while the U. S. military-industrial complex — to use former President Dwight Eisenhower's phrase — has back- engineered that advanced technology for its own applications and profits.

— The secret knowledge includes the fact that some of the non-human intelligences have interacted with earth for eons. The EBEs are said to have been involved on earth as far back as the dinosaurs. Has their mission been strictly extraterrestrial science? Or are the EBEs also involved in the Elders/ Watchers saga?

— Origins for some of the biological entities have been associated with stars such as Sirius, Zeta Reticuli I and II, Tau Ceti, Epsilon Bootes, Epsilon Eridani, Antares, Arcturus and the Pleiades. Even EBE occupation of Mars before humans existed on earth has been suggested. Some of the beings such as the small, grey androids and tall "Elders" also seem to be able to move between at least two different planes or frequencies of existence, including interactions at the moment of death.

— One, or all, of the non-human intelligences have manipulated DNA in already-evolving primates to create a series of humanoid workers on earth, the latest being *Homo sapiens sapiens.* The NHEs also harvest tissue and fluid from animals and humans.

— The purpose for human creation might have served a multi-level agenda: an experiment to unite the divine spirit with primitive animal; to use the Petri dish of planet earth to test that new hypostatic creature, while the humans did work for the Elders/Watchers such as mining and building communication "machines" such as pyramids, ziggurats and temples; to harvest information and genetic material from the humans' souls, minds and bodies and other earth life for applications in galactic trade of clones, androids and other commerce, perhaps even for different time lines and survival needs of time travelers suggested by experiencers in Chapters 1 and 2.

Whatever happened in the Garden of Eden that created the illegitimate hybrid giants described in the Book of Genesis, the original experiment was spoiled and provoked the wrath of God and the Great Flood. The perpetuation of the experiment through Noah's bloodline perhaps produced a human history which might be compared to step children who had different parents, a difficult, confusing childhood, and who grew into rebellious teenagers resisting parental control. It's curious that when humans did seem to work together in harmony on a project such as the Tower of Babel discussed in the Bible, another force interfered to cause chaos reminiscent of the Garden of Eden. Perhaps the Elders tried to introduce religions and avatars such as Christ to homogenize human thinking and neutralize differences. If so, it's ironic that so many human wars have been fought about religious beliefs.

The most comforting thought is that our creators don't want us to destroy ourselves, the earth and their vested interests. To divert us from self-destruction, our watchers might be on the brink of revealing themselves more straightforwardly. Perhaps their strategy has been to develop allies in the children and unborn where government interference would be difficult. That might be another reason for human abductions and implants.

The best case scenario would be that the other intelligences are planning to finally acknowledge humans as fellow sentient beings even if we are still headstrong, territorial adolescents in the cosmic scheme of things. If a handshake is coming, it's also clear that someone out there is trying to impress upon *Homo sapiens* that survival beyond the Petri dish might not be guaranteed if we continue to abuse the environment of our planet and their "crops."

Less comforting is the theme that also repeats throughout this and other books — including the most widely read book on the planet, the Bible. That theme was also Enoch's: trouble and conflict among higher forces. Wanna Lawson described it as an argument about what is allowable to do with life. Linda Porter said the grey scientists were "not supposed to be doing the (soul transfers), but are doing it anyway because they feel the others, the higher ones, don't understand about something."

Abductee and author, Anna Hayes, also received the following information about opposing forces in the unseen and matter worlds during one of her contacts with a non-human intelligence.[53]

> "It is from this interdimensional conflict that your (human) concepts of 'good vs evil' and 'God vs devil' emerged. One group of advanced beings wish to see humans evolve into wholeness, equality and co-creatorship, while another group of beings desires to stunt the evolution of humanity so it can continue to utilize its resources for self serving purposes. The latter group has come to represent

[53] Voyagers, The Sleeping Abductees *© 1998 by Anna Hayes, Wild Flower Press.*

> the 'dark' or 'evil' forces within the collective human unconscious while the former has emerged into your mythologies of the gods.
>
> "Because of this 'cosmic conflict,' so to speak, attempts have been made by both sides throughout your history to train the evolving humans. One set of teachings will lead humans to evolve, the other to digress. The ploy of distorting the helpful teachings has been used repeatedly throughout your species' development by the forces that do not wish you to succeed. Much of your present teachings are so contaminated by these distortions that the true meaning of the original teachings has been lost, or applied in a way that creates the opposite effect for which the teachings were originally intended."
>
> Hayes also thinks, "One of the biggest, staged, false events the negative ETs are planning will be a 'Second Coming' holographic insert to mislead humans. Guardians will also use the Christ image to help people if they trust in that image. So, the future struggle between the negative and positive agendas could be very confusing for humans."

Maybe like political factions, the Dark Party and the Light Party are competing over legislation to legalize the production of cloned, android life outside the Force of Creation's recycling program of a finite number of souls. Maybe some souls are "captured" and put into cloned bodies which is fouling up God's process. Other clones might never receive souls.

That "political issue" about cloning for galactic trade or for wars among the angels might explain why dramas of resurrected saviours from Osiris in Egypt to Christ in ancient Palestine (Israel) have been presented repeatedly to humanity. Osiris and Christ were beings with human bodies and mysterious divinity who emphasized that death in the body does not end life for the soul and spirit. That concept underlies the Egyptian obsession with mummies and sacred rites to protect the soul at the moment of death from competing forces.

If there is a *finite* number of souls under a strictly regulated God force recycling program, then cloned bodies and androids might end up outside that recycling force.

The full scope of the game board for souls, spirits and bodies of humans, extraterrestrials, angels and time travelers might be beyond human ability to understand. One scientist in New England, who has also been abducted by grey beings who repaired his heart, told me that he was shown holograms that depicted a series of universes in pairs — mirrored images, each the opposite of the other from the subatomic to the macro.

"Our universe is paired to another one, too," he said, "which is completely opposite of this one. There, the skies are glowing white with dark suns, colors are indescribable and iridescent, and time flows to the past. Like a conveyor belt, at the moment of death in our universe we move through a tunnel into the mirror universe where it's all light. There, time moves to the past and souls return back here."

Rudolph Steiner, in *Theosophy,* said:

> "...Nature subjects man to the laws of changing matter, but he subjects himself to the laws of thought. By this means he makes himself a member of a higher order than the one to which he belongs through his body. This order is the spiritual. The spiritual is as different from the soul as the soul is from the body. ... The soul life is the basis of the spiritual just as the body is the basis of the soul life. ...The soul life thus becomes the enduring effect of the transitory impressions of the external world. ... (and) in each life the human spirit appears as a repetition of itself with the fruits of its former experiences in previous lives.
>
> "In the soul, the 'I' flashes forth, receives the impulse from the spirit, and thereby becomes the bearer of the spiritual human being. Thus man participates in the three worlds, the physical, the soul and the spiritual. He is rooted in the physical world through his physical body, ether body and soul body, and through the spirit self, life spirit and spirit man, he comes to flower in the spiritual world. The stalk, however, that takes root in the one and flowers in the other is the soul itself."

Perhaps the unique isolation each human feels and the peculiar melancholy a dark sky filled with stars can evoke have something to do with knowledge buried in our genes and souls, a sensing of ancient intimacies with other beings and other worlds. Now in this time of revolution when the whole world will know we are not alone in this universe, our greatest challenge as a species will be to stand up unafraid before the old lords and watchers. Ultimately, there is a common bond among all life forms ebbing and flowing on spirals of different frequencies supported by a singular force, an invisible matrix of energy from which everything emerges and to which everything returns.

EPILOGUE

"Communication across the revolutionary divide is inevitably partial."

THOMAS S. KUHN
SCIENTIFIC HISTORIAN
THE STRUCTURE OF SCIENTIFIC REVOLUTIONS [1]

[1] The Structure of Scientific Revolutions, *2nd ed. © 1970, University of Chicago Press.*

Cloning humans and animals had not been reported when I began writing this book. But as I was finishing it, international headlines on February 23, 1997 announced "Scientists produce clone of adult animal."

British scientists had cloned a seven-month-old sheep named Dolly at Edinburgh, Scotland's Roslin Institute. This revolutionary first cloned mammal was produced from a single cell taken from the udder of an adult sheep, turned into an embryo, and then implanted in a surrogate mother.

One week later, researchers at the Oregon Regional Primate Research Center announced they had cloned a pair of rhesus monkeys named Neti, for nuclear embryo transfer infant, and its twin duplicate called Ditto. The scientists said the technique could theoretically be used to clone humans. In fact, in 1993 at George Washington University, embryologists cloned human embryos.

Nature, the respected scientific journal that published the Roslin Institute's paper about their cloning breakthrough, editorialized that "Cloning humans from adults' tissues is likely to be achievable any time from one to ten years from now."

The cover of the March 10, 1997 *Newsweek* depicted "cloned" babies in glass cylinders that was an eerie reminder of the cloned humans and humanoids in tubes described in Chapter 4.

Immediate public reactions were to ban cloning, especially of humans. U. S. President Bill Clinton proclaimed that "each human life is unique, born of a miracle that reaches beyond laboratory science."

But the Director of the U. S. National Institutes of Health, Harold E. Varmus, told a congressional committee that despite negative reaction to the idea of cloning human beings, society might at some point decide that human cloning is acceptable for certain conditions such as providing new organs, or children for infertile couples.

Then on January 7, 1998, Chicago physicist Richard Seed announced that he would start cloning human beings for infertile couples, if he could secure funding and a laboratory. A few days later, a treaty that had already been in process was signed by nineteen European nations to declare cloning a violation of human dignity and a misuse of science. One holdout was Britain, where Dolly had been created, implying that cloning research would continue there in animals and presumably humans.

I thought of Jim Sparks's statement about the non-humans he encountered: "They farm us. They clone us, they make organs from us and all kinds of stuff." The beings he dealt with are also concerned about what humans are doing to the environment allegedly because earth provides a rich harvest of DNA from certain bloodlines that the aliens want to protect and use.

Do those bloodlines have anything to do with the complex and confusing Garden of Eden story? Could humans, as Beau Peterson suggested, be "pawns in a battle among the angels?" And how and why exactly do energy beings from unseen frequencies and extraterrestrial biological entities from matter worlds interact with each other and with humans? Are there overlapping vested interests of angels and EBEs in the moments of human deaths and the transitions to other dimensional frequencies or "heavens"? Enoch said he was shown "seven heavens."

Questions about the nature of heaven followed the cloning controversy in the March 24, 1997 issue of *Time* magazine. The cover showed a man standing on a cloud with his hand shielding his eyes as if straining to see something in the distant blue sky. The caption was: "Does Heaven Exist?"

The article's theme was that in the late 20th Century where there has been emphasis on money, material goods, technology and everything-now!, heaven has become an irrelevant myth.

But the article also quoted C. S. Lewis: "(Heaven is) the secret we cannot hide and cannot tell, though we desire to do both. We cannot tell it because it is a desire for something that has never actually appeared in our experience ... We cannot hide it because our experience is constantly suggesting it."

The unseen's impact on our lives is indisputable in experiences such as my own in the Idaho mountains described in my Prologue when the light and the thought-voice calmly told me, "You are one with the light, the light is one with you and you are in the hand of God." People who have experienced dying and resuscitation have no doubt there is a place of light after the moment of death.

Revolution is everywhere, from medicine and technology to the growing awareness that other forces are impinging upon this earth which could be extraterrestrials, time travelers, angels, or all combined. If Linda Porter and Wanna Lawson were given true insights concerning a conflict among higher intelligences about what is allowable to do with life, and if the creation of *Homo sapiens* by manipulation of DNA in already-evolving primates is one of the key issues, then mankind's future might be hanging in someone else's balance. That possibility should concern every human on this planet.

Not all the signals from the unseen are doom and gloom. Many abductees, like Linda Porter, sense that the Big Picture is playing out a needed drama in the fundamental machinery of the universe in order to resolve a long-festering problem and that ultimately the cosmos and life in it will be better off.

A new discovery also suggested life has existed on other planets besides this one. On August 8, 1996, newspapers, magazines, radio, television and the World Wide Web were full of headlines about "Signs of life on Mars?" The subject was a chunk of meteorite discovered in 1984 in Antarctica. Scientists said the meteorite's chemical composition matched samples of Martian soil analyzed by the Viking Lander in 1976. The theory about how the rock got from the red planet to earth suggested that "a violent asteroid impact about 17 million years ago kicked up Martian surface" which went into space and landed at the South Pole 13,000 years ago.

When the meteorite was examined microscopically, scientists found rice-shaped "globules" in tiny cracks on the rock which resembled bacteria. The carbon in those fossilized globules dated back to about three and a half billion years ago when Mars probably had water on its surface and was warmer.

Even though other scientists attacked the announcement as premature, Cornell University astronomer and SETI advocate (Search for Extraterrestrial Life) Carl Sagan (now deceased) said, "This is the most provocative and evocative piece of evidence for life beyond Earth. If the results are verified, it is a turning point in human history, suggesting that life exists not on just two planets in one paltry solar system, but throughout this magnificent universe."

Two months later in November 1996, there were more headlines about British scientist finding organic material on a second Martian meteorite as the United States blasted another unmanned mission to Mars.[2]

Earlier in the 1996 summer in Wiltshire County, England, farmhand Arthur Carrington discovered double strands of eighty-nine undulating

[2] *November 7, 1996, the U. S. Mars Global Surveyor launched from Cape Canaveral, Florida. Surveyor arrived at Mars in September 1997 and orbited at an altitude of 234 miles to photograph and study the atmosphere. In July 1997, the next launch put Pathfinder on Mars and its robot rover slowly explored rocks until its power ended that fall.*

circles in Alton Barnes's East Field at 6:30 AM on June 17. The most common first interpretation was a DNA double helix. But when I showed a photograph to a mathematician, he said, "That looks like two overlapping sine/co-sine curves." Sines and co-sines are used in trigonometry to determine unknown angles and distances on both flat surfaces and in three-dimensional space.

Plate 1 - *"Sine/co-sine" formation discovered in the East Field at Alton Barnes, Wiltshire, England at 6:30 AM on June 17, 1996. There were 89 circles and the length was 648 feet. Photograph by Steve Alexander © 1996.*

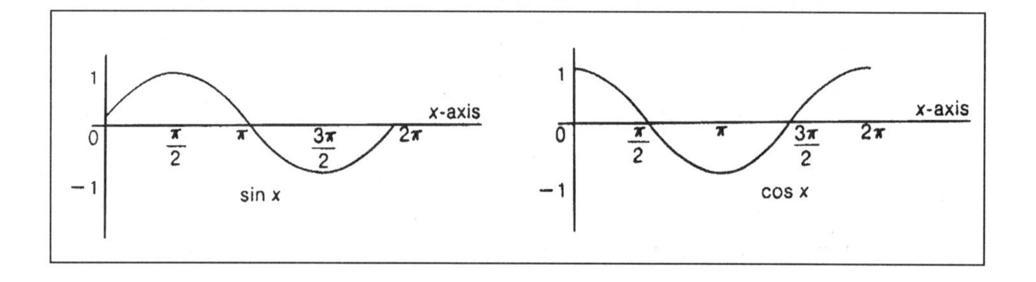

Plate 2 - *Sine and co-sine curves used in trigonometry.*

Then on July 8, 1996 across the road from the ancient sacred site Stonehenge, a spiral arm consisting of one hundred forty-nine circles that covered a square acre appeared in a wheat field. Three witnesses, a pilot, a groundskeeper and security man at the farm told investigators that the field was normal at 5:30 PM. About forty-five minutes later, the pilot flew back over the field, saw the circles and radioed his discovery to Thruxton Airport. The spiral design matched a mathematically-produced image called a Julia Set first discovered during World War I by the French mathematicians Gaston Julia and Pierre Fatou.

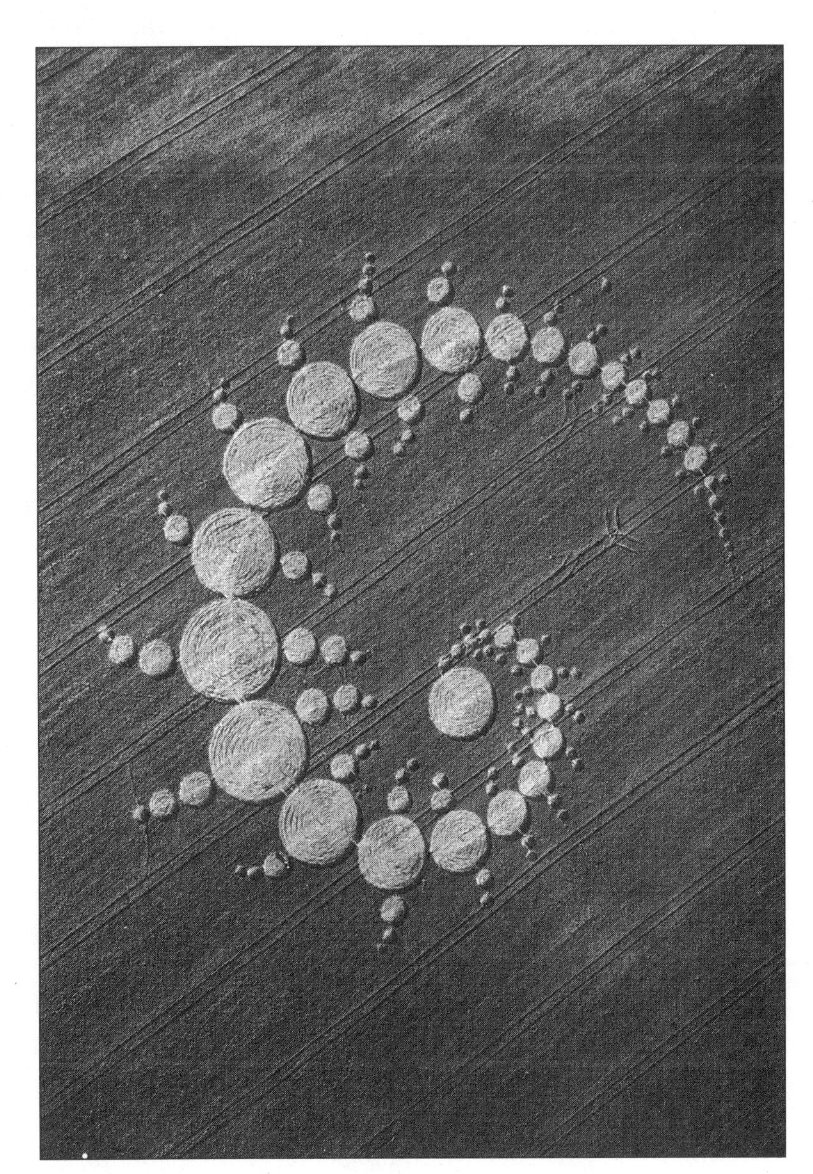

Plate 3 - *The "Julia Set" discovered in a wheat field across the road from Stonehenge on July 8, 1996. The spiral measured 915 feet on its longest axis, covered a square acre and consisted of 149 circles. Cameraman Peter Sorensen walked its entire length and said every circle had a different twisted center. Photograph by Steve Alexander © 1996.*

Later, IBM researcher Benoit Mandelbrot in the 1960s to 1970s explored the repetition of complicated processes and found that he could create one image that would serve as a catalogue of Julia Sets. His research evolved to develop the field of fractal geometry now used to study Chaos Theory and its application to patterns of growth in the natural world, and even fluctuating prices. Fractal geometry revealed that the way trees grow along the edge of a lake, the way ice cracks, clouds form, or cotton prices go up and down, has an eerie mathematical order of repeating patterns. Fractals are "a way of seeing infinity," said James Gleick, author of *Chaos*.[3]

[3] Chaos, Making A New Science © *1987 James Gleick, Penguin Books.*

On July 30, 1996, one of the most astonishing crop formations since the phenomenon began appeared near the sacred site of Avebury. *Three* Julia Sets spiraled out of a central circle. The diameter was a thousand feet and the number of circles was 194.

Plate 4 - *Three-armed Julia Sets at Windmill Hill northwest of Avebury discovered July 30, 1996. There were 194 circles that spiralled a thousand feet in diameter. Photograph by Steve Alexander © 1996.*

One year later on July 23, 1997, not far from Avebury and the ancient and sacred site of Silbury Hill, another fractal design over two hundred fifty feet wide was found in wheat. One hundred and twenty-six small circles outlined the fractal known as a "Koch Curve," shown in its classic computer-generated shape in Plate 5 and the actual crop formation in Plates 6 and 7.

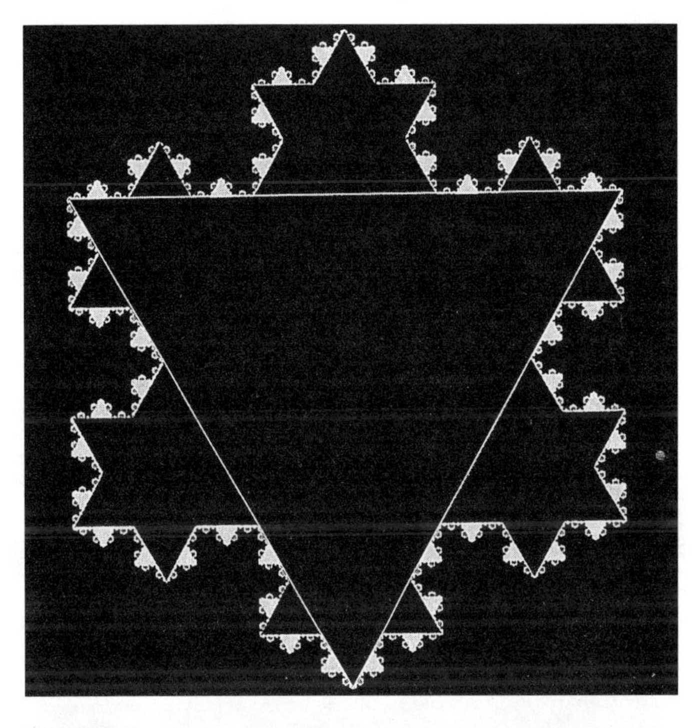

Plate 5 - *The Koch Curve, a fractal design starts with a triangle. In the middle one-third of each side, identical triangles in shape but one third the size are placed. That result is a Star of David. That repeating pattern goes on creating an infinitely long line which surrounds a finite area. If you drew a circle around the original triangle, the Koch curve would never extend beyond it. But the border becomes increasingly complex. Drawing from* Chaos, Making A New Science *© 1987 by James Gleick, Penguin Books.*

Plate 6 - *Crop formation discovered July 23, 1997 northwest of Silbury Hill, Wiltshire, England in a wheat field. The width was two hundred feet with a border of one hundred twenty-six small circles. Photograph © 1998 by Steve Alexander.*

Plate 7 - *Aerial of the "Koch Curve" crop formation discovered July 23, 1997 in wheat northwest of the ancient, sacred Silbury Hill, Wiltshire, U. K. Photograph © 1997 by Ron Russell.*

As I asked in Volume I: Could *something* out there be trying to reinforce the idea that our universe and all its energy and mass are defined by a repeating feedback loop that is mathematical in evolution and powered by consciousness?[4]

Could the crop formations be a warning, a mysterious language in mathematical code from an advanced intelligence which can see the future from a timeless place, understands the repetitive patterns of our space-time, and knows mankind is at a dangerous, self-destructive moment on the evolutionary spiral? Could that intelligence be trying to get our attention in the cereal crops of the world to warn that food and life are not guaranteed if we continue industrial-technological-military development that destroys so much of our planet's green oxygen-producing life?

Are we altering our atmosphere so much that one day we might not be able to breathe? That question was already being presented in the 1970s by scientists whose data about the earth's atmosphere and ecological damage did not add up well for future earth life. A 1977 book *Life In The Future* stated:[5]

[4] *See Chapter 1,* Glimpses of Other Realities, Vol. I *© 1994 by Linda Moulton Howe.*

[5] Life In The Future - Prospects for Man and Nature *© 1977 by Malcolm Ross-Macdonald, Doubleday and Company, Inc.*

"All the free oxygen in the atmosphere comes from plants. It is there only because plants put out slightly more oxygen than the world's oxidizing processes consume. It has been estimated that of every 10,000 units of oxygen thus put out, oxidation consumes about 9999. It is easy to forget the slimness of this margin. It would not take much reduction of the earth's plant and plankton resources nor much increase in our oxygen consumption to reverse the balance."

By the 1990s, deterioration of the protective ozone layer around the earth has become a major problem. Auto and industrial chemicals such as chlorine, bromine, and fluorine are destroying the ozone. The ozone reduction means more ultraviolet light from the sun reaches our planet's surface. Increased UV light can damage all surface life from plankton to humans.

A headline in the Environment section of the October 28, 1996 *Time* magazine read "Trouble in the Lily Pads - Something ominous is happening to Minnesota's frogs — and it's spreading." Amphibians are particularly sensitive to environmental changes and pollution because they live in water and on land and breathe through their skin. So, like a canary in a miner's cage that will die before the miner does if the air is bad, frogs, toads and salamanders are signaling that something is wrong in our world.

The problem was first noticed in 1995 when school children in Minnesota found deformed frogs. Some were missing a leg, some had withered arms, others had shrunken eyes or none at all, one had nine legs and another had three eyes, one in the back of its throat.

By the fall of 1996, the problem had spread to Wisconsin, South Dakota, Vermont, Missouri, Colorado, California, Oregon, Canada and Japan and by 1997, deformed amphibians found all over the United States were reported in national newscasts.

Theories about what might be happening included chemical pollutants which no one had found and trematode parasites which might be taking advantage of weakened immune systems among amphibians, perhaps related to the stress of increased UV light due to the thinning ozone layer.

Finally, hard data did link increased UV exposure to amphibian deformities. Dr. Andrew Blaustein, Professor of Zoology at Oregon State University in Corvallis had his UV research published in the Proceedings of the National Academy of Sciences on December 9, 1997.[6] In a radio interview, Dr. Blaustein explained to me that he placed long-toed salamander eggs in test and control enclosures on lakes and ponds in the Oregon Cascade Mountain Range, their natural habitat. "Both enclosures are exactly the same. They both have shields and they both are subjected to the same tem-

[6] Proceedings of the National Academy of Sciences, Vol. 94, *Pages 13735-13737, December 1997, "Ambient UV-B Radiation Causes Deformities In Amphibian Embryos," by Andrew R. Blaustein, Ph.D., © 1997 National Academy of Sciences.*

peratures, same water, same everything, except one of the shields lets UV in and one does not."

What happened stunned the scientist. *Eighty-five percent* of the embryos in the eggs exposed to UV rays *died.* In the remaining fifteen percent that hatched, all but four had skeletal deformities and eye problems. In the eggs shielded from ultraviolet sun rays, ninety-eight percent hatched and all were normal.

"We haven't seen mortality like we're seeing now," Dr. Blaustein said, "and we have data that goes back to the 1950s. So, what I'm led to believe is that an environmental change has occurred and is probably ozone depletion. Some of our best data already show that UV is killing plankton under the ozone holes. And there is even a study that shows fish are impacted at certain stages by ultraviolet rays in the Antarctic. I think we have a significant problem here!"

Our human propensity to maim and destroy the world around us was featured again in a July 1996 *Newsweek* article about a "precipitous decline in honeybee colonies." Open spaces are being covered by asphalt, houses and buildings; forests are being cut down at an alarming rate and industrial pollution and aggressive pesticide use are killing bees. The *Newsweek* article said, "Without honeybees and some 200,000 other species of insects, birds and small mammals, plants would be in a terrible predicament. So would humans. These creatures are the world's pollinators ... without their work we wouldn't have healthy fruit and vegetables or viable seeds. We depend on this free (pollination) service for 90% of our staple crops."

Scientists estimate that nearly one hundred different species were dying out every single day on earth as we neared the end of the industrial and polluting 20th Century. But looking back over the last four billion years of our planet's evolution, including several mass extinctions, *ninety-eight percent of all species that have ever lived have become extinct.*[7]

An MIT study in the early 1970s created a computer program that projected economic, resource and population trends data forward as far as the year 2100. The results were summarized in a ground-breaking book *Limits To Growth* which plotted a series of graphs that showed a "drastic fall in food supply per person and in available natural resources.[8] Because of the inertia of the system, though, both population and pollution continue to rise for a while — until famine, disease and the total collapse of industry inevitably bring them to a halt."

In the MIT Standard Computer Run, the "model predicted runaway growth followed by collapse around the year 2050 — unless there were important changes in data trends for resources, pollution controls, food pro-

[7] Extinction: The Causes and Consequences of the Disappearance of Species © *1981 by Paul and Anne Ehrlich, Random House.*

[8] Limits To Growth - A Report for the Club of Rome's Project on the Predicament of Mankind © *1972 by Donella Meadows and others, Universe Books, New York City.*

ductivity, population and industrial growth. Piecemeal tinkering with the data assumptions such as doubling future resource amounts or slowing population growth did not fundamentally change the dynamics of the system or the long-term consequences."

As author Ross-Macdonald reviewed the *Limits To Growth* computer data, he wrote:

> "And so in our century, we have once more discovered what it is like to be frightened by mystery — this time by the apparently unanswerable questions posed by our own very real technological powers. Coldly, calmly, 20th Century technological man has brought himself to a watershed when there must be a great leap forward if he is to survive. It is no longer possible to walk coldly and calmly along the old familiar paths, for it is those paths that have led to an age in which we must contemplate possible futures in human megadeaths — or in uncountable, unimaginable numbers of deaths if we once again remember that we are only a small segment of earth's living beings. One of the futurologists' most terrifying scenarios *could* come to pass if we permit it to. If it does, it will have been the last lunatic play of a mind that divorced itself successively from earth, stones, rivers and the rest of the living world — even, ultimately, from its own body, the battered vehicle that has brought us to the threshold of our great moment in history."

Perhaps the non-human intelligences which watch this planet see our future as a species hanging in a balance and will not allow humans to destroy the earth. Perhaps that is why we see their increasing presence in human affairs despite aggressive government efforts to keep them under wraps. On September 22, 1996, a grey alien holding a cup of Starbucks coffee made the cover of the *Los Angeles Times Magazine.* It's as if the concept of another intelligence among us has shifted from fear to curiosity to maybe even "one of the guys" in cozy, human social terms.

Maybe this is how one handshake begins. And the next revolution.

Plate 8 - Los Angeles Times Magazine, *September 22, 1996. Illustration by Brad Weinman © 1996.*

APPENDIX I

Majestic-12 SOM1-01 Special Operations Manual

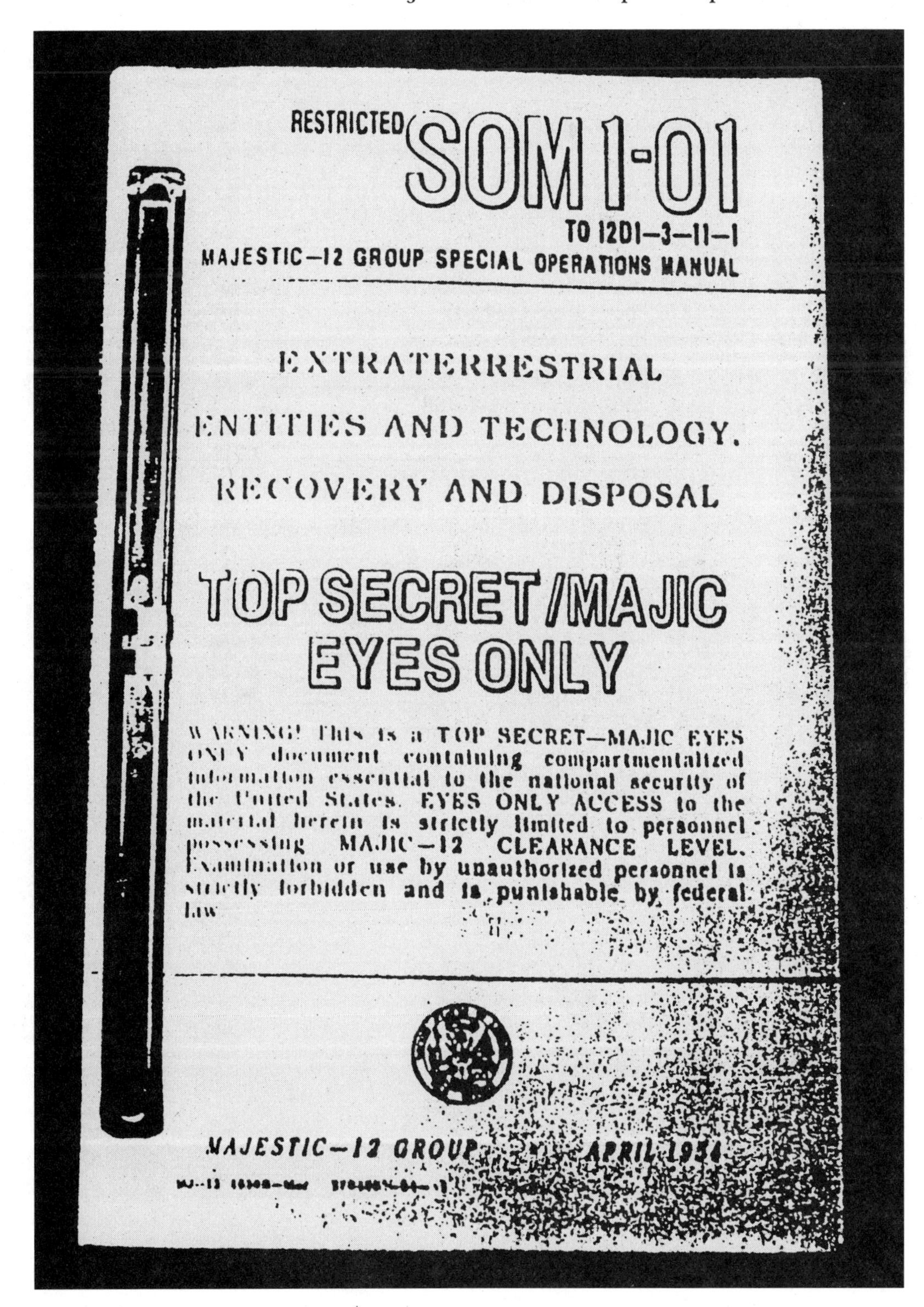

RESTRICTED SOM 1-01

TO 12D1-3-11-1

MAJESTIC—12 GROUP SPECIAL OPERATIONS MANUAL

EXTRATERRESTRIAL

ENTITIES AND TECHNOLOGY,

RECOVERY AND DISPOSAL

TOP SECRET/MAJIC

EYES ONLY

WARNING! This is a TOP SECRET—MAJIC EYES ONLY document containing compartmentalized information essential to the national security of the United States. EYES ONLY ACCESS to the material herein is strictly limited to personnel possessing MAJIC—12 CLEARANCE LEVEL. Examination or use by unauthorized personnel is strictly forbidden and is punishable by federal law.

MAJESTIC—12 GROUP APRIL 1954

TOP SECRET / MAJIC EYES ONLY

SOM 1—01

Special Operations Manual No 1 - 01

MAJESTIC — 12 GROUP
Washington 25, D. C., 7 April 1954

EXTRATERRESTRIAL ENTITIES AND TECHNOLOGY, RECOVERY AND DISPOSAL

(1)

This unclassified copy is for research purposes. Rev 6: 3/5/95; Helvetica headers, Times New Roman text, 10/12 pts. The Government has declared that such a classification does not exist.

TOP SECRET / MAJIC EYES ONLY

SOM 1—01

Special Operations Manual
No. 1 - 01

MAJESTIC — 12 GROUP
Washington 25, D. C., *7 April 1954*

EXTRATERRESTRIAL ENTITIES AND TECHNOLOGY, RECOVERY AND DISPOSAL

MJ—12 4838B **1**

TOP SECRET / MAJIC EYES ONLY

REPRODUCTION IN ANY FORM IS FORBIDDEN BY FEDERAL LAW

This unclassified copy is for research purposes. Rev 6: 3/5/95; Helvetica headers, Times New Roman text, 10/12 pts. The Government has declared that such a classification does not exist.

TOP SECRET / MAJIC EYES ONLY

CHAPTER 1

OPERATION MAJESTIC—12

Section I. PROJECT PURPOSE AND GOALS

1. Scope

This manual has been prepared especially for Majestic—12 units. Its purpose is to present all aspects of Majestic 12 so authorized personnel will have a better understanding of the goals of the Group, be able to more expertly deal with Unidentified Flying Objects, Extraterrestrial Technology and Entities, and increase the efficiency of future operations.

2. General

MJ—12 takes the subject of UFOBs, Extraterrestrial Technology and Extraterrestrial Biological Entities very seriously and considers the entire subject to be a matter of the very highest national security. For that reason everything relating to the subject has been assigned the very highest security classification. Three main points will be covered in this section.

a. The general aspects of MJ—12 to clear up any misconceptions that anyone may have.

b. The importance of the operations.

c. The need for absolute secrecy in all phases of operation.

3. Security Classification

All information relating to MJ—12 has been classified MAJIC EYES ONLY and carries a security level 2 points above that of Top Secret. The reason for this has to do with the consequences that may arise not only from the impact upon the public should the existence of such matters become general knowledge, but also the danger of having such advanced technology as has been recovered by the Air Force fall into the hands of unfriendly foreign powers. No information is released to the public press and the official government position is that no special group such as MJ—12 exists.

4. History of the Group

Operation Majestic - 12 was established by special classified presidential order on 24 September 1947 at the recommendation of Secretary of Defense James V. Forrestal and Dr. Vannevar Bush, Chairman of the Joint Research and Development Board. Operations are carried out under a Top Secret Research and Development - Intelligence Group directly responsible only to the President of the United States. The goals of the MJ—12 Group

MJ—12 4838B 2

TOP SECRET / MAJIC EYES ONLY

REPRODUCTION IN ANY FORM IS FORBIDDEN BY FEDERAL LAW

are as follows:

a. The recovery for scientific study of all materials and devices of a foreign or extraterrestrial manufacture that may become available. Such material and devices will be recovered by any and all means deemed necessary by the Group.

b. The recovery for scientific study of all entities and remains of entities not of terrestrial origin which may become available through independent action by those entities or by misfortune or military action.

c. The establishment and administration of Special Teams to accomplish the above operations.

d The establishment and administration of special secure facilities located at secret locations within the continental borders of the United States for the receiving, processing, analysis, and scientific study of any and all material and entities classified as being of extraterrestrial origin by the Group of the Special Teams.

e. Establishment and administration of covert operation to be carried out in concert with Central Intelligence to effect the recovery for the United States of extraterrestrial technology and entities which may come down inside the territory of or fall into the possession of foreign powers.

f. The establishment and maintenance of absolute top secrecy concerning all the above operations.

5. Current Situation

It is considered as far as the current situation is concerned, that there are few indications that these objects and their builders pose a direct threat to the security of the United States, despite the uncertainty as to their ultimate motives in coming here. Certainly the technology possessed by these beings far surpasses anything known to modern science, yet their presence here seems to be benign, and they seem to be avoiding contact with our species, at least for the present. Several dead entities have been recovered along with a substantial amount of wreckage and devices from downed craft, all of which are now under study at various locations. No attempt has been made by extraterrestrial entities either to contact authorities or to recover their dead counterparts of the downed craft, even though one of the crashes was the result of direct military action. The greatest threat at this time arises from the acquisition and study of such advanced technology by foreign powers unfriendly to the United States. It is for this reason that the recovery and study of this type of material by the United States has been given such a high priority.

TOP SECRET / MAJIC EYES ONLY

CHAPTER 2
INTRODUCTION

Section I. GENERAL

6. Scope

a. This operations manual is published for the information and guidance of all concerned. It contains information on determination, documentation, collection and disposition of debris, devices, craft, and occupants of such craft as defined as Extraterrestrial Technology or Extraterrestrial Biological Entities, EBEs in Section II of this chapter.

b. Appendix IIa contains a list of current references, including technical manuals and other available publications applicable to these operations.

c. Appendix II contains a list of personnel who comprise the Majestic-12 Group.

7. Forms and Records.

Forms used for reporting operation are listed in Appendix I.

Section II. DEFINITION AND DATA

8. General

Extraterrestrial Technology is defined as follows:

a. Aircraft identified as not manufactured in the United States or any terrestrial foreign powers, including experimental military or civilian aircraft. Aircraft in this category are generally known as Unidentified Flying Objects, or UFOBs. Such aircraft may appear as one of several shapes and configurations and exhibit extraordinary flight characteristics.

b. Objects and devices of unknown origin or function, manufactured by processes or of materials not consistent with current technology or scientific knowledge.

c. Wreckage of any aircraft thought to be of extraterrestrial manufacture or origin. Such wreckage may be the results of accidents or military action.

d. Materials that exhibit unusual or extraordinary characteristics not consistent with current technology or scientific knowledge.

Extraterrestrial Biological Entities (EBEs) are described as:

a. Creatures, humanoid or otherwise, whose evolutionary processes responsible for their development are demonstrably different from those postulated or observed in homo sapiens.

TOP SECRET / MAJIC EYES ONLY

9. Description of Craft

Documented extraterrestrial craft (UFOBs) are classified in one of four categories based on general shape, as follows:

a. Elliptical, or disc shape. This type of craft is of a metallic construction and dull aluminum in color. They have the appearance of two pie-pans or shallow dishes pressed together and may have a raised dome on the top or bottom. No seams or joints are visible on the surface, giving the impression of one-piece construction. Discs are estimated from 50-300 feet in diameter and the thickness is approximately 15 per cent of the diameter, not including the dome, which is 30 per cent of the disc diameter and extends another 4-6 feet above the main body of the disc. The dome may or may not include windows or ports, and ports are present around the lower rim of the disc in some instances. Most disc-shaped craft are equipped with lights on the top and bottom, and also around the rim. These lights are not visible when the craft is at rest or not functioning. There are generally no visible antenna or projections. Landing gear consists of three extendible legs ending in circular landing pads. When fully extended this landing gear supports the main body 2-3 feet above the surface at the lowest point. A rectangular hatch is located along the equator or on the lower surface of the disc.

b. Fuselage or cigar shape. Documented reports of this type of craft are extremely rare. Air Force radar reports indicate they are approximately 2 thousand feet long and 95 feet thick, and apparently they do not operate in the lower atmosphere. Very little information is available on the performance of these craft, but radar reports have indicated speeds in excess of 7,000 miles per hour. They do not appear to engage in the violent and erratic maneuvers associated with the smaller types.

c. Ovoid or circular shape. This type of craft is described as being shaped like an ice cream cone, being rounded at the large end and tapering to a near-point at the other end. They are approximately 30-40 feet long and the thick end diameter is approximately 20 per cent of the length. There is an extremely bright light at the pointed end, and this craft usually travels point down. They can appear to be any shape from round to cylindrical, depending upon the angle of observation. Often sightings of this type of craft are elliptical craft seen at an inclined angle or edge-on.

d. Airfoil or triangular shape. This craft is believed to be new technology due to the rarity and recency of the observations. Radar indicates an isosceles triangle profile, the longest side being nearly 300 feet in length. Little is known about the performance of these craft due to the rarity of good sightings, but they are believed capable of high speeds and abrupt maneuvers similar to or exceeding the performance attributed to types "a" and "c".

MJ—12 4838B **5**

TOP SECRET / MAJIC EYES ONLY

10. Description of Extraterrestrial Biological Entities (EBEs)

Examination of remains recovered from wreckage of UFOBs indicates that Extraterrestrial Biological Entities may be classified into two distinct categories as follows:

a. EBE Type I. These entities are humanoid and might be mistaken for human beings of the Oriental race if seen from a distance. They are bi-pedal, 5-5 feet 4 inches in height and weigh 80-100 pounds. Proportionally they are similar to humans, although the cranium is somewhat larger and more rounded. The skin is a pale, chalky-yellow in color, thick, and slightly pebbled in appearance. They eyes are small, wide-set, almond-shaped, with brownish-black irises with very large pupils. The whites of the eyes are not like that of humans, but have a pale gray cast. The ears are small and not low on the skull. The nose is thin and long, and the mouth is wider than in humans, and nearly lipless. There is no apparent facial hair and very little body hair, that being very fine and confined to the underarm and the groin area. The body is thin and without apparent body fat, but the muscles are well-developed. The hands are small, with four long digits but no opposable thumb. The outside digit is jointed in a manner as to be nearly opposable, and there is no webbing between the finger as in humans. The legs are slightly but noticeably bowed, and the feet are somewhat splayed and proportionally large.

b. EBE Type II. These entities are humanoid but differ from Type I in many respects. They are bi-pedal, 3 feet 5 inches - 4 feet 2 inches in height and weight 25-50 pounds. Proportionally, the head is much larger than humans or Type I EBEs, the cranium being much large and elongated. The eyes are very large, slanted, and nearly wrap around the side of the skull. They are black with no whites showing. There is no noticeable brow ridge, and the skull has a slight peak that runs over the crown. The nose consists of two small slits which sit high above the slit-like mouth. There are no external ears. The skin is a pale bluish-gray color, being somewhat darker on the back of the creature, and is very smooth and fine-celled. There is no hair on either the face or the body, and these creatures do not appear to be mammalian. The arms are long in proportion to the legs, and the hands have three long, tapering fingers and a thumb which is nearly as long as the fingers. The second finger is thicker than the others, but not as long as the index finger. The feet are small and narrow, and four toes are joined together with a membrane.

It is not definitely known where either type of creature originated, but it seems certain that they did not evolve on earth. It is further evident, although not certain, that they may have originated on two different planets.

TOP SECRET / MAJIC EYES ONLY

11. Description of Extraterrestrial Technology

The following information is from preliminary analysis reports of wreckage collected from crash sites of extraterrestrial craft 1947-1953, excerpts from which are quoted verbatim to provide guidance as to the type of characteristics of material that might be encountered in future recovery operations.

a. Initial analysis of the debris from the crash site seems to indicate that the debris is that of an extraterrestrial craft which exploded from within and came into contact with the ground with great force, completely destroying the craft. The volume of matter indicates that the craft was approximately the size of a medium aircraft, although the weight of the debris indicates that the craft was extremely light for its size.

b. Metallurgical analysis of the bulk of the debris recovered indicates that the samples are not composed of any materials currently known to Terrestrial science.

c. The material tested possesses great strength and resistance to heat in proportion to its weight and size, being stronger by far than any materials used in military or civilian aircraft at present.

d. Much of the material, having the appearance of aluminum foil or aluminum-magnesium sheeting, displays none of the characteristics of either metal, resembling instead some kind of unknown plastic-like material.

e. Solid structures and substantial beams having a distinct similarity in appearance to very dense grain-free wood, was very light in weight and possesses tensile and compression strength not obtainable by any means known to modern industry.

f. None of the material tested displayed measurable magnetic characteristics or residual radiation.

g. Several samples were engraved or embossed with marks and patterns. These patterns were not readily identifiable and attempts to decipher their meaning has been largely unsuccessful.

h. Examination of several apparent mechanical devices, gears, etc. revealed little or nothing of their functions or methods of manufacture.

MJ—12 4838B 7

TOP SECRET / MAJIC EYES ONLY

CHAPTER 3

RECOVERY OPERATIONS

Section I. SECURITY

12. Press Blackout

Great care must be taken to preserve the security of any location where Extraterrestrial Technology might be retrievable for scientific study. Extreme measures must be taken to protect and preserve any material or craft from discovery, examination, or removal by civilian agencies or individuals of the general public. It is therefore recommended that a total press blackout be initiated whenever possible. If this course of action should not prove feasible, the following cover stories are suggested for release to the press. The officer in charge will act quickly to select the cover story that best fits the situation. It should be remembered when selecting a cover story that official policy regarding UFOBs is that they do not exist.

a. Official Denial. The most desirable response would be that nothing unusual has occurred. By stating that the government has no knowledge of the event, further investigation by the public press may be forestalled.

b. Discredit Witnesses. If at all possible, witnesses will be held incommunicado until the extent of their knowledge and involvement can be determined. Witnesses will be discouraged from talking about what they have seen, and intimidation may be necessary to ensure their cooperation. If witnesses have already contacted the press, it will be necessary to discredit their stories. This can best be done by the assertion that they have either misinterpreted natural events, are the victims of hysteria or hallucinations, or are the perpetrators of hoaxes.

c. Deceptive Statements. It may become necessary to issue false statements to preserve the security of the site. Meteors, downed satellites, weather balloons, and military aircraft are all acceptable alternatives, although in the case of the downed military aircraft statement care should be exercised not to suggest that the aircraft might be experimental or secret, as this might arouse more curiosity of both the American and the foreign press. Statements issued concerning contamination of the area due to toxic spills from trucks or railroad tankers can also serve to keep unauthorized or undesirable personnel away from the area.

13. Secure the Area

The area must be secured as rapidly as possible to keep unauthorized personnel from infiltrating the site. The officer in charge will set up a perimeter and establish a command post inside the perimeter. Personnel allowed

TOP SECRET / MAJIC EYES ONLY

on the site will be kept to the absolute minimum necessary to prepare the craft or debris for transport, and will consist of Military Security Teams.

Local authorities may be pressed into service on traffic and crowd control. *Under no circumstances* will local official or law enforcement personnel be allowed inside the perimeter and all necessary precautions should be taken to ensure that they do not interfere with the operation.

a. Perimeter. It is desirable that sufficient military personnel be utilized to set up a perimeter around the site large enough to keep both unauthorized personnel and the perimeter personnel from seeing the site. Once the site is contained, regular patrols will be set up along the perimeter to ensure complete security, and electronic surveillance will be utilized to augment the patrols. Perimeter personnel will be equipped with hand communication and automatic weapons with live ammunition. Personnel working at the site will carry sidearms. No unauthorized personnel will be allowed into the secure area.

b. Command Post. Ideally, the command post should be as close to the site as is practical to efficiently coordinate operations. As soon as the command post is operational, contact with the Majestic—12 Group will be established via secure communications.

c. Area Sweep. The site and the surrounding area will be cleared of all unauthorized personnel. Witnesses will be debriefed and detained for further evaluation by MJ—12. *Under no circumstances* will witnesses be released from custody until their stories have been evaluated by MJ—12 and they have been thoroughly debriefed.

c. Situation Evaluation. A preliminary evaluation of the situation will be completed and a preliminary report prepared. The MJ—12 Group will then be briefed on the situation at the earliest possible opportunity. The MJ—12 Group will then make a determination as to whether or not a MJ—12 RED TEAM or OPNAC Team will be dispatched to the area.

Section II. TECHNOLOGY RECOVERY

14. Removal And Transport

As soon as communication is established, removal and transport of all materiel will commence under order from MJ—12.

a. Documentation. If the situation permits, care should be taken to document the area with photographs before anything is moved. The area will be checked for radiation and other toxic agents. If the area cannot be kept secure for an extended period of time, all material must be packed and transported as quickly as possible to the nearest secure military facility. This well be accomplished by covered transport using little-traveled roads wherever possible.

b. Complete or Functional Craft. Craft are to be approached with extreme caution if they appear functional, as serious injury may result from exposure

MJ—12 4838B 9

TOP SECRET / MAJIC EYES ONLY

This unclassified copy is for research purposes. Rev 6: 3/5/95; Helvetica headers, Times New Roman text, 10/12 pts. The Government has declared that such a classification does not exist.

TOP SECRET / MAJIC EYES ONLY

to radiation and electrical discharges. If the craft is functioning, but appears to be abandoned, it may be approached only by specially trained MJ—12 RED TEAM personnel wearing protective clothing. Any device that appears to be functioning should also be left to MJ—12 RED TEAM disposal. Complete craft and parts of crafts too large to be transported by covered transport will be disassembled, if this can be accomplished easily and quickly. If they must be transported whole, or on open flatbed trailers, they will be covered in such a manner as to camouflage their shape.

c. *Extraterrestrial Biological Entities.* EBEs must be removed to a top security facility as quickly as possible. Great care should be taken to prevent possible contamination by alien biological agents. Dead EBEs should be packed in ice at the earliest opportunity to preserve tissues. Should live EBEs be encountered, they should be taken into custody and removed to a top security facility by ambulance. Every effort should be taken to ensure the EBEs survival. Personnel involvement with EBEs alive or dead must be kept to an absolute minimum. (See Chapter 5 for more detailed instruction on dealing with EBEs.)

15. Cleansing the Area

Once all material has been removed from the central area, the surrounding area will be thoroughly inspected to make sure that all traces of Extraterrestrial Technology have been removed. In the case of a crash, the surrounding area will be thoroughly gone over several times to ensure that nothing has been overlooked. The search area involved may vary depending on local conditions, at the discretion of the officer in charge. When the officer in charge is satisfied that no further evidence of the event remains at the site, it may be evacuated.

16. Special or Unusual Conditions

The possibility exists that extraterrestrial craft may land or crash in heavily populated areas, where security cannot be maintained effectively. Large segments of the population and the public press may witness these craft. Contingency Plan MJ—1949-04P / 78 (TOP SECRET-EYES ONLY) should be held in readiness should the need to make a public disclosure become necessary.

MJ—12 4838B 10

TOP SECRET / MAJIC EYES ONLY

REPRODUCTION IN ANY FORM IS FORBIDDEN BY FEDERAL LAW

TOP SECRET / MA

EYES ONLY

WARNING! This is a TOP SECRET—MAJIC
ONLY document containing compartmen
information essential to the national secu
the United States. EYES ONLY ACCESS
material herein is strictly limited to per
possessing MAJIC—12 CLEARANCE L
Examination or use by unauthorized person
strictly forbidden and punishable by federal l

Removal of any page(s) from this documen
examination by authorized persons req
written authorization from the MJ—12 GR
OPERATIONS OFFICER. Reproduction in any
or the taking of written or transcribed not
strictly forbidden.

TOP SECRET / MAJIC EYES ONLY

17. Extraterrestrial Technology

No.	Item	Description or condition	MJ-12 Code	Receiving facility
1	Aircraft.	Intact, operational, or semi-intact aircraft of Extraterrestrial design and manufacture.	UA-002-6	Area 51 S-4
2	Intact device.	Any mechanical or electronic device or machine which appears to be undamaged and functional.	ID-301-F	Area 51 S-4
3	Damaged device.	Any mechanical or electronic device or machine which appears to be damaged but mostly complete.	DD-303-N	Area 51 S-4
4	Powerplant.	Devices and machines or fragments which are possible propulsion units, fuel, and associated control devices and panels.	PD-40-8Q	Area 51 S-4
5	Identified fragments.	Fragments composed of elements or materials easily recognized as known to current science and technology, i.e.: aluminum, magnesium, plastic, etc.	IF-101-K	Area 51 S-4
6	Unidentified fragments.	Fragments composed of elements or materials not known to current science and technology and which exhibit unusual or extraordinary characteristics.	UF-103-M	Area 51 S-4
7	Supplies and provisions.	Non-mechanical or non-electronic materials of a support nature such as clothing, personal belongings, organic ingestibles, etc.	SP-331	Blue Lab WP-61
8	Living entity.*	Living non-human organisms in apparent good or reasonable health.	EBE-010	OPNAC BBS-01
9	Non-living entity.	Deceased non-human organisms or portions of organisms, organic remains and other suspect organic matter.	EBE-XO	Blue Lab WP-61
10	Media.	Printed matter, electronic recordings, maps, charts, photographs and film.	MM-54A	Building 21 KB-88
11	Weapons.	Any device or portion of a device thought to be offensive or defensive weaponry.	WW-010	Area 51 S-4

*Living entities must be contained in total isolation pending arrival of OPNAC personnel.

MJ-12 4838B

TOP SECRET

TOP SECRET / MAJIC
EYES ONLY

WARNING! This is a TOP SECRET—MAJIC EYES ONLY document containing compartmentalized information essential to the national security of the United States. EYES ONLY ACCESS to the material herein is strictly limited to personnel possessing MAJIC—12 CLEARANCE LEVEL. Examination or use by unauthorized personnel is strictly forbidden and punishable by federal law.

Removal of any page(s) from this document for examination by authorized persons requires written authorization from the MJ—12 GROUP OPERATIONS OFFICER. Reproduction in any form or the taking of written or transcribed notes is strictly forbidden.

17. Extraterrestrial Technology Classification Table

No.	Item	Description or condition	MJ—12 Code	Receiving Facility
1	Aircraft.	Intact, operational, or semi-intact aircraft of Extraterrestrial design and manufacture.	UA-002-6	Area 51 S-4
2	Intact device.	Any mechanical or electronic device or machine which appears to be undamaged and functional.	ID-301-F	Area 51 S-4
3	Damaged device.	Any mechanical or electronic device or machine which appears to be damaged but mostly complete.	DD-303N	Area 51 S-4
4	Powerplant.	Devices and machines or fragments which are possible propulsion units, fuel and associated control devices and panels.	PD-40-8G	Area 51 S-4
5	Identified fragments.	Fragments composed of elements or materials easily recognized as known to current science and technology, i.e., aluminum, magnesium, plastic, etc.	IF-101-K	Area 51 S-4
6	Unidentified fragments.	Fragments composed of elements or materials not known to current science and technology and which exhibit unusual or extraordinary characteristics.	UF-103-M	Area 51 S-4
7	Supplies and provisions.	Non-mechanical or non-electronic materials of a support nature such as clothing, personal belongings, organic ingestibles, etc.	SP-331	Blue Lab WP-61
8	Living entity.*	Living non-human organisms in apparent good or reasonable health.	EBE-010	OPNAC BBS-01
9	Non-living entity.	Deceased non-human organisms or portions of organisms, organic remains and other suspect organic matter.	EBE-XO	Blue Lab WP-61
10	Media.	Printed matter, electronic recordings, maps, charts, photographs and film.	MM-54A	Building 21 KB-88
11	Weapons.	Any device or portion of a device thought to be offensive or defensive weaponry.	WW-010	Area 51 S-4

**Living entities must be contained in total isolation pending arrival of OPNAC personnel*

This unclassified copy is for research purposes. Rev. 6, 3/6/95; Helvetica headers, Times New Roman text, 6x9

18. Use of Inventory System

a. The identification is performed as a duty of the officer making an inventory of the Exterrestrial Technology or entities with the assistance of MJ Forms 1-006 and 1-007. (See p. 9) Instructions for the use of each form appear on the reverse side of the form.

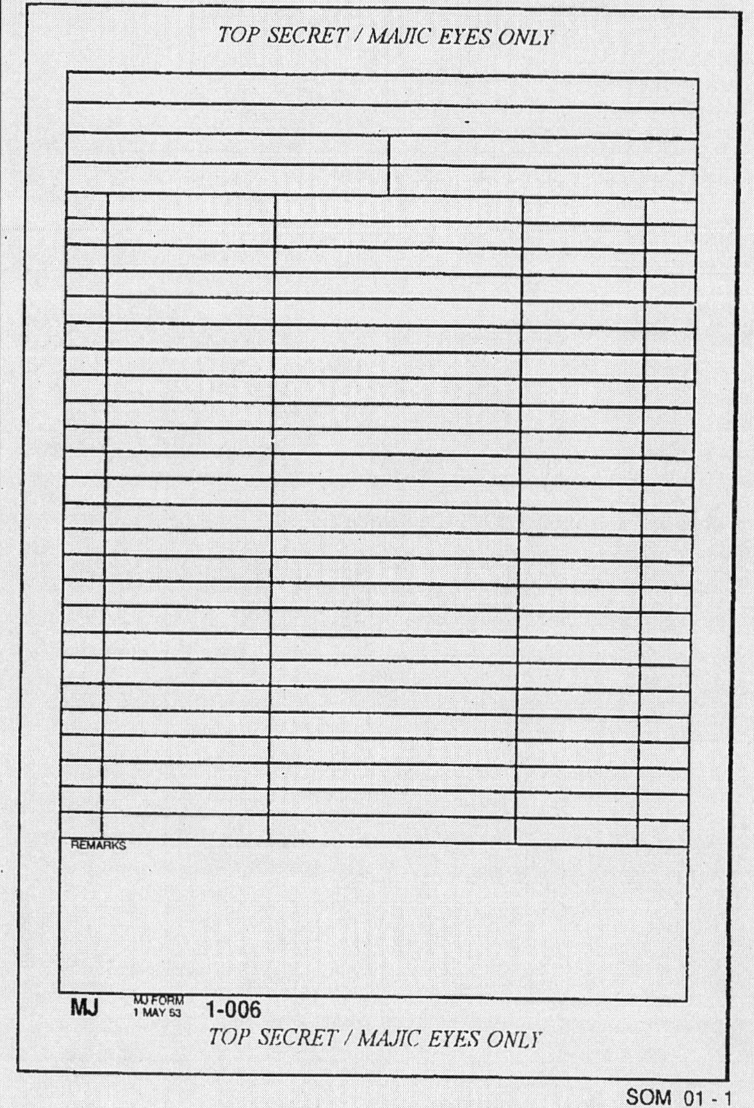

TOP SECRET / MAJIC EYES ONLY

REMARKS

MJ MJ FORM 1 MAY 53 1-006

TOP SECRET / MAJIC EYES ONLY

SOM 01 - 1

Figure 1 MJ Form 1-006

MJ—12 4838B 12

TOP SECRET / MAJIC EYES ONLY

REPRODUCTION IN ANY FORM IS FORBIDDEN BY FEDERAL LAW

This unclassified copy is for research purposes. Rev 6; 3/5/95; Helvetica headers, Times New Roman text, 10/12 pts. The Government has declared that such a classification does not exist.

TOP SECRET / MAJIC EYES ONLY

TOP SECRET / MAJIC EYES ONLY

EXTRATERRESTRIAL TECHNOLOGY PACKING LIST INSTRUCTIONS on other side		
POINT OF ORIGIN	SHIPPING CODE NO.	DATE
FINAL DESTINATION	PACKED BY	DATE/TIME
SHIPPING METHOD	INSPECTED BY	DATE/TIME

NO	ITEM	CLASSIFICATION NO	No	Item	Classifica-tion
1			21		
2			22		
3			23		
4			24		
5			25		
6			26		
7			27		
8			28		
9			29		
10			30		
11			31		
12			32		
13			33		
14			34		
15			35		
16			36		
17			37		
18			38		
19			39		
20			40		

41 REMARKS OR SPECIAL INSTRUCTIONS

(If additional space is required, attach MJ Form 1-007a)

RECEIVED BY	DATE/TIME	INSPECTED BY	DATE/TIME

MJ MJ-12 FORM 1 MAY 53 **1-007**

TOP SECRET / MAJIC EYES ONLY

SOM 01 - 2

Figure 2. MJ Form 1-007

19. Packaging and Packing Data

a. Domestic Shipment. Individual items are tagged and wrapped in a moisture-vaporproof barrier and heat sealed. They are then placed in a corrugated fiberboard box. The voids within the box are packed thoroughly

MJ—12 4838B **13**

TOP SECRET / MAJIC EYES ONLY

REPRODUCTION IN ANY FORM IS FORBIDDEN BY FEDERAL LAW

with a neutral cellulose wadding to prevent movement of the items. The box closure is sealed with gummed Kraft tape. MJ Form 1-007 is placed in a sealed manila envelope marked "MAJIC 12—ACCESS ONLY" and is firmly taped to the top of the box. The box is then cushioned at each corner and at the top and bottom with fiberboard inserts and is placed within a large corrugated fiberboard box. The entire outer box closure is sealed with gummed Kraft tape. A label is affixed to the outer box bearing the following information: destination, shipping code number, and the warning, "MAJIC—12 ACCESS ONLY."

b. Overseas Shipment. Items are packaged as described above except that a dessicant and humidity indicator are included within the inner corrugated fiberboard box. Next, the box is wrapped in a moisture-vaporproof barrier and heat sealed. Then, packaged items are placed within a second waterproof carton sealed with waterproof tape. This second carton is marked "MAJIC—12 ACCESS ONLY" on all sides and is placed within a water-grease-proof lined wooden shipping container. The lining is sealed with water proof tape and the wooden shipping container is screwed shut. The shipping container is reinforced further by nailing two [3/4]-inch metal caps about 8 inches from each end. Shipping information is then stenciled on the surface of the wooden shipping container.

Note. The packaging and packing procedure detailed above applies to non-organic items only. Data for handling, packaging, packing, and shipping of organic matter and non-living entities is provided in Chapter 5, Section II of this manual.

TOP SECRET / MAJIC EYES ONLY

CHAPTER 4
RECEIVING AND HANDLING

Section 1. HANDLING UPON RECEIPT OF MATERIAL

20. Uncrating, Unpacking And Checking

(fig. 3)

Note. The uncrating, unpacking and checking procedure for containers marked "MAJIC—12 ACCESS ONLY" will be carried out by personnel with MJ—12 clearance. Containers marked in this manner will be placed in storage in a top security area until such time as authorized personnel are available for these procedures.

a. Be very careful when uncrating and unpacking the material. Avoid thrusting tools into the interior of the shipping container. Do not damage the packaging materials any more than is absolutely necessary to remove the specimens, these materials may be required for future packaging. Store the interior packaging material within the shipping container. When uncrating and unpacking the specimens, follow the procedure given in (1) through (11) below:

(1) Unpack the specimens in a top security area to prevent access of unauthorized personnel.

(2) Cut the metal wires with a suitable cutting tool, or twist them with pliers until the straps crystallize and break.

(3) Remove screws from the top of the shipping container with a screw driver.

(4) Cut the tape and seals of the case liner so that the waterproof paper will be damaged as little as possible.

(5) Lift out the packaged specimens from the wooden case.

(6) Cut the tape which seals the top flaps of the outer cartons; be careful not to damage the cartons.

(7) Cut the barrier along the top heat sealed seam and carefully remove the inner carton.

(8) Remove the sealed manila envelope from the top of the inner carton.

(9) Open the inner carton and remove the fiberboard inserts, dessicant and humidity indicator.

(10) Lift out the heat sealed packaging containing the specimens: arrange them in an orderly manner for inspection.

(11) Place all packaging material in the shipping container for use in future repacking.

b. Thoroughly check all items against the shipping documents. Carefully

TOP SECRET / MAJIC EYES ONLY

SOM 01 - 3

Figure 2. Packaging diagram.

inspect all items for possible damage during shipping or handling. Sort the items according to classification number in preparation for transfer to the designated Laboratory or department. Laboratory or department personnel are responsible for transporting items to the designated areas. This will be accomplished as quickly as possible by covered transport escorted by security personnel.

MJ—12 4838B 16

TOP SECRET / MAJIC EYES ONLY

TOP SECRET / MAJIC EYES ONLY

CHAPTER 5

EXTRATERRESTRIAL BIOLOGICAL ENTITIES

SECTION I. LIVING ORGANISMS

21. Scope

a. This section deals with encounters with living Extraterrestrial Biological Entities (EBEs). Such encounters fall under the jurisdiction of MJ-12 OPNAC BBS—01 and will be dealt with by this special unit only. This section details the responsibilities of persons or units making the initial contact.

22. General

Any encounter with entities known to be of extraterrestrial origin is to be considered to be a matter of national security and therefore classified TOP SECRET. Under no circumstance is the general public or the public press to learn of the existence of these entities. The official government policy is that such creatures do not exist, and that no agency of the federal government is now engaged in any study of extraterrestrials or their artifacts. Any deviation from this stated policy is absolutely forbidden.

23. Encounters

Encounters with EBEs may be classified according to one of the following categories:

a. Encounters initiated by EBEs. Possible contact may take place as a result of overtures by the entities themselves. In these instances it is anticipated that encounters will take place at military installation or other obscure locations selected by mutual agreement. Such meeting would have the advantage of being limited to personnel with appropriate clearance, away from public scrutiny. Although it is not considered very probable, there also exists the possibility that EBEs may land in public places without prior notice. In this case the OPNAC Team will formulate cover stories for the press and prepare briefings for the President and the Chiefs of Staff.

b. Encounters as the result of downed craft. Contact with survivors of accidents or craft downed by natural events or military action may occur with little or no warning. In these cases, it is important that the initial contact be limited to military personnel to preserve security. Civilian witnesses to the area will be detained and debriefed by MJ—12. Contact with EBEs by military personnel not having MJ—12 or OPNAC clearance is to be strictly limited to action necessary to ensure the availability of the EBEs for study by the OPNAC Team.

MJ—12 4838B 17

TOP SECRET / MAJIC EYES ONLY

TOP SECRET / MAJIC EYES ONLY

24. Isolation and Custody

a. EBEs will be detained by whatever means are necessary and removed to a secure location as soon as possible. Precautions will be taken by personnel coming in contact with EBEs to minimize the risk of disease as a result of contamination by unknown organisms. If the entities are wearing space suits or breathing apparatus of some kind, care should be exercised to prevent damage to these devices. While all efforts should be taken to assure the well-being of the EBEs, they must be isolated from any contact with unauthorized personnel. While it is not clear what provisions or amenities might be required by non-human entities, they should be provided if possible. The officer in charge of the operation will make these determinations, as no guidelines now exist to cover this area.

b. Injured or wounded entities will be treated by medical personnel assigned to the OPNAC Team. If the team medical personnel are not immediately available, First Aid will be administered by Medical Corps personnel at the initial site. Since little is known about EBE biological functions, aid will be confined to the stopping of bleeding, bandaging of wounds and splint-ing of broken limbs. No medications of any kind are to be administered as the effect of terrestrial medications on non-human biological systems are impossible to predict. As soon as the injuries are considered stabilized, the EBEs will be moved by closed ambulance or other suitable conveyance to a secure location.

c. In dealing with any living Extraterrestrial Biological Entity, security is of paramount importance. All other considerations are secondary. Although it is preferable to maintain the physical well-being of any entity, the loss of EBE life is considered acceptable if conditions or delays to preserve that life in any way compromises the security of the operations.

d. Once the OPNAC Team has taken custody of the EBEs, their care and transportation to designated facilities become the responsibility of OPNAC personnel. Every cooperation will be extended to the team in carrying out duties. OPNAC Team personnel will be given TOP PRIORITY at all times regardless of their apparent rank or status. No person has the authority to interfere with the OPNAC Team in the performance of its duties by special direction of the President of the United States.

Section II. NON-LIVING ORGANISMS

25. Scope

Ideally, retrieval for scientific study of cadavers and other biological remains will be carried out by medical personnel familiar with this type of procedure. Because of security considerations, such collection may need to be done by non medical personnel. This section will provide guidance for retrieval, preservation, and removal of cadavers and remains in the field.

MJ—12 4838B 18

TOP SECRET / MAJIC EYES ONLY

26. Retrieval and Preservation.

a. The degree of decomposition of organic remains will vary depending on the length of time the remains have been lying the open unprotected and may be accelerated by both local weather conditions and action by predators. Therefore, biological specimens will be removed from the crash site as quickly as possible to preserve the remains in as good a condition as possible. A photographic record will be made of all remains before they are removed from the site.

b. Personnel involved in this type of operation will take all reasonable precautions to minimize physical contact with the cadavers or remains being retrieved. Surgical gloves should be worn or, if they are not available, wool or leather gloves may be worn provided they are collected for decontamination immediately after use. Shovels and entrenching tools may be employed to handle remains provided caution is exercised to be certain no damage is done to the remains. Remains will be touched with bare hands only if no other means of moving them can be found. All personnel and equipment involved in recovery operations will undergo decontamination procedures immediately after those operations are have been completed.

c. Remains will be preserved against further decomposition as equipment and conditions permit. Cadavers and remains will be bagged or securely wrapped in waterproof coverings. Tarpaulins or foul weather gear may be used for this purpose if necessary. Remains will be refrigerated or packed with ice if available. All remains will be tagged or labeled and the time and date recorded. Wrapped remains will be placed on stretchers or in sealed containers for immediate removal to a secure facility.

d. Small detached pieces and material scraped from solid surfaces will be put in jars or other small capped containers if available. Containers will be clearly marked as to their contents and the time and date recorded. Containers will be refrigerated or packed with ice as soon as possible and removed to a secure facility.

TOP SECRET / MA
EYES ONLY

WARNING! This is a TOP SECRET—MAJ
ONLY document containing compartme
information essential to the national se
the United States. EYES ONLY ACCES
material herein is strictly limited to p
possessing MAJIC-12 CLEARANCE
Examination or use by unauthorized per
strictly forbidden and punishable by federa

Removal of any page(s) from this docum
examination by authorized persons
written authorization from the MJ—12
OPERATIONS OFFICER. Reproduction in
or the taking of written or transcribed
strictly forbidden.

MAJIC EYES ONLY

SECRET / MAJIC EYES ONLY
CTION IN ANY FORM IS FORBIDDEN BY FEDERAL LAW

TOP SECRET / MAJIC EYES ONLY

TYPE A. ELLIPTICAL OR DISC SHAPE
SIDE VIEW

TYPE A. ELLIPTICAL OR DISC SHAPE
TOP VIEWS

TYPE B. FUSELAGE OR CIGAR SHAPE
SIDE VIEW

TYPE D. AIRFOIL OR TRIANGLE SHAPE
SIDE VIEW

TYPE C. OVOID OR CONE SHAPE
SIDE VIEW

TYPE D. AIRFOIL OR TRIANGLE SHAPE
BOTTOM VIEW

Note: Illustrations in this diagram are gathered from documented sightings in Air Force and Central Intelligence and from examination of wreckage collected from various sources years 1947-1953 inclusive.

SOM 01 - 4

Figure 4. Extraterrestrial craft.

MJ—12 4838B **20**

TOP SECRET / MAJIC EYES ONLY

CHAPTER 9

GUIDE TO UFO IDENTIFICATION

Section I UFOB GUIDE

27. Follow-up Investigations

A UFOB report is worthy of follow-up investigation when it contains infor-mation to suggest that positive identification with a well-known phenome- non may be made or when it characterizes an unusual phenomenon. The report should suggest almost immediately, largely by the coherency and clarity of the data, that there is something of identification and / or scientific value. In general, reports which should be given consideration are those which involve several reliable observers, together or separately, and which concern sighting of greater duration than one quarter minute. Exceptions should be made to this when circumstances attending the report are consid- ered to be extraordinary. Special attention should be given to reports which give promise to a "fix" on the position and to those reports involving unusual trajectories.

28. Rules of Thumb

Every UFOB case should be judged individually but there are a number of "rules of thumb", under each of the following headings, which should prove helpful in determining the necessity for follow-up investigation.

a. Duration of sighting. When the duration of a sighting is less than 15 seconds, the probabilities are great that it is not worthy of follow-up. As a word of caution, however, should a large number of individual observers con-cur on an unusual sighting of a few seconds duration, it should not be dis-missed.

b. Number of persons reporting the sighting. Short duration sightings by single individuals are seldom worthy of follow-up. Two or three competent independent observations carry the weight of 10 or more simultaneous indi-vidual observations. As an example, 25 people at one spot may observe a strange light in the sky. This, however, has less weight than two reliable people observing the same light from different locations. In the latter case a position-fix is indicated.

c. Distance from Location of Sightings to Nearest Field Unit. Reports which meet the preliminary criterion stated above should all be investigated if their occurrence is in the immediate operating vicinity of the squadron concerned. For reports involving greater distances, follow-up necessity might be judged as being inversely proportional to the square of the dis-tances concerned. For example, an occurrence 150 miles away might be con-

TOP SECRET / MAJIC EYES ONLY

APPENDIX I

REFERENCES

There is some writing here — No. 4, AB

---

1. [Applicable] Regulations

-4	Military Security (Safeguarding Security Information).
	Maintenance Supplies and Equipment, Maintenance Responsibilities and Shop Operation.

2. Supply

xx 725-405-5	Preparation and Submission of Requisitions for Supplies.

3. Other Publications

XX 219-20-3	Index of Training Manuals.
XX 310-20-4	Index of Technical Manuals, Technical Regulations, Technical Bulletins, Supply Bulletin Lubrications Orders, and Modification Work Orders.
XX 310-20-5	Index of Administrative Publications.
XX 310-20-7	Index of Tables of Organization and Equipment, Reduction Tables, Tables of Organization, Tables of Equipment, Type Tables of Distribution and Tables of Allowance.

4. Test Equipment References

TM 11—664	Theory and Use of Electronic Test Equipment.

5. Photographic References

TM 11—404A	Photographic Print Processing Unit AN/TFQ-9.
TM 11—405	Processing Equipment PH—406.
TM 11—401	Elements of Signal Photography.
TM 11—2363	Darkroom PH—392.

MJ—12 4838B **28**

TOP SECRET / MAJIC EYES ONLY

APPENDIX II

AFR 200-2

*AFR 200–2
1–5

AIR FORCE REGULATION
NO. 200–2

DEPARTMENT OF THE AIR FORCE
WASHINGTON, *12 AUGUST 1954*

INTELLIGENCE

Unidentified Flying Objects Reporting (Short Title: UFOB)

Paragraph

1. Purpose and Scope. This Regulation establishes procedures for reporting information and evidence pertaining to unidentified flying objects and sets forth the responsibility of Air Force activities in this regard. It applies to all Air Force activities.

2. Definitions:

a. *Unidentified Flying Objects (UFOB)*—Relates to any airborne object which by performance, aerodynamic characteristics, or unusual features does not conform to any presently known aircraft or missile type, or which cannot be positively identified as a familiar object.

b. *Familiar Objects*—Include balloons, astronomical bodies, birds, and so forth.

3. Objectives. Air Force interest in unidentified flying objects is twofold: First as a possible threat to the security of the United States and its forces, and secondly, to determine technical aspects involved.

a. *Air Defense.* To date, the flying objects reported have imposed no threat to the security of the United States and its Possessions. However, the possibility that new air vehicles, hostile aircraft or missiles may first be regarded as flying objects by the initial observer is real. This requires that sightings be reported rapidly and as completely as information permits.

b. *Technical.* Analysis thus far has failed to provide a satisfactory explanation for a number of sightings reported. The Air Force will continue to collect and analyze reports until all sightings can be satisfactorily explained, bearing in mind that:

(1) To measure scientific advances, the Air Force must be informed on experimentation and development of new air vehicles.

(2) The possibility exists that an air vehicle of revolutionary configuration may be developed.

(3) The reporting of all pertinent factors will have a direct bearing on the success of the technical analysis.

4. Responsibility:

a. *Reporting.* Commanders of Air Force activities will report all information and evidence that may come to their attention, including that received from adjacent commands of the other services and from civilians.

b. *Investigation.* Air Defense Command will conduct all field investigations within the ZI, to determine the identity of any UFOB.

c. *Analysis.* The Air Technical Intelligence Center (ATIC), Wright-Patterson Air Force Base, Ohio, will analyze and evaluate: All information and evidence reported within the ZI after the Air Defense Command has exhausted all efforts to identify the UFOB; and all information and evidence collected in oversea areas.

d. *Cooperation.* All activities will cooperate with Air Defense Command representatives to insure the economical and prompt success of an investigation, including the furnishing of air and ground transportation, when feasible.

5. Guidance. The thoroughness and quality of a report or investigation into incidents of unidentified flying objects are limited only by the resourcefulness and imagination of the person responsible for preparing the report. Guidance set forth below is based on experience and has been found helpful in evaluating incidents:

a. Theodolite measurements of changes of azimuth and elevation and angular size.

b. Interception, identification, or air search

***This Regulation supersedes AFR 200–2, 26 August 1953, including Change 200–2A, 2 November 1953.**

action. These actions may be taken if appropriate and within the scope of existing air defense regulations.

c. Contact with local aircraft control and warning (AC&W) units, ground observation corps (GOC) posts and filter centers, pilots and crews of aircraft aloft at the time and place of sighting whenever feasible, and any other persons or organizations which may have factual data bearing on the UFOB or may be able to offer corroborating evidence, electronic or otherwise.

d. Consultation with military or civilian weather forecasters to obtain data on: Tracks of weather balloons released in the area, since these often are responsible for sightings; and any unusual meteorological activity which may have a bearing on the UFOB.

e. Consultation with astronomers in the area to determine whether any astronomical body or phenomenon would account for or have a bearing on the observation.

f. Contact with military and civilian tower operators, air operations offices, and so forth, to determine whether the sighting could be the result of misidentification of known aircraft.

g. Contact with persons who might have knowledge of experimental aircraft of unusual configuration, rocket and guided missile firings, and so forth, in the area.

6. ZI Collection. The Air Defense Command has a direct interest in the facts pertaining to UFOB's reported within the ZI and has, in the 4602d Air Intelligence Service Squadron (AISS), the capability to investigate these reports. The 4602d AISS is composed of specialists trained for field collection and investigation of matters of air intelligence interest which occur within the ZI. This squadron is highly mobile and deployed throughout the ZI as follows: Flights are attached to air defense divisions, detachments are attached to each of the defense forces, and the squadron headquarters is located at Peterson Field, Colorado, adjacent to Headquarters, Air Defense Command. Air Force activities, therefore, should establish and maintain liaison with the nearest element of this squadron. This can be accomplished by contacting the appropriate echelon of the Air Defense Command as outlined above.

a. All Air Force activities are authorized to conduct such preliminary investigation as may be required for reporting purposes; however, investigations should not be carried beyond this point, unless such action is requested by the 4602d AISS.

b. On occasions—after initial reports are submitted—additional data is required which can be developed more economically by the nearest Air Force activity, such as: narrative statements, sketches, marked maps, charts, and so forth. Under such circumstances, appropriate commanders will be contacted by the 4602d AISS.

c. Direct communication between echelons of the 4602d AISS and Air Force activities is authorized.

7. Reporting. All information relating to UFOB's will be reported promptly. The method (electrical or written) and priority of dispatch will be selected in accordance with the apparent intelligence value of the information. In most instances, reports will be made by electrical means: Information over 24 hours old will be given a "deferred" precedence. Reports over 3 days old will be made by written report prepared on AF Form 112, Air Intelligence Information Report, and AF Form 112a, Supplement to AF Form 112.

a. *Addressees:*

(1) *Electrical Reports.* All electrical reports will be multiple addressed to:

(a) Commander, Air Defense Command, Ent Air Force Base, Colorado Springs, Colorado.

(b) Nearest Air Division (Defense). (For ZI only.)

(c) Commander, Air Technical Intelligence Center, Wright-Patterson Air Force Base, Ohio.

(d) Director of Intelligence, Headquarters USAF, Washington 25, D. C.

(2) *Written Reports:*

(a) Within the ZI, reports will be submitted direct to the Air Defense Command. Air Defense Command will reproduce the report and distribute it to interested ZI intelligence agencies. The original report together with notation of the distribution effected then will be forwarded to the Director of Intelligence, Headquarters USAF, Washington 25, D. C.

(b) Outside the ZI, reports will be submitted direct to Director of Intelligence, Headquarters USAF, Washington 25, D. C. as prescribed in "Intelligence Collection Instructions" (ICI), June 1954.

b. *Short Title.* "UFOB" will appear at the beginning of the text of electrical messages and in the subject of written reports.

c. *Negative Data.* The word "negative"

in reply to any numbered item of the report format will indicate that all logical leads were developed without success. The phrase "not applicable" (N/A) will indicate that the question does not apply to the sighting being investigated.

d. *Report Format.* Reports will include the following numbered items:

(1) Description of the object(s):
(a) Shape.
(b) Size compared to a known object (use one of the following terms: Head of a pin, pea, dime, nickel, quarter, half dollar, silver dollar, baseball, grapefruit, or basketball) held in the hand at about arms length.
(c) Color.
(d) Number.
(e) Formation, if more than one.
(f) Any discernible features or details.
(g) Tail, trail, or exhaust, including size of same compared to size of object(s).
(h) Sound. If heard, describe sound.
(i) Other pertinent or unusual features.

2) Description of course of object(s):
(a) What first called the attention of observer(s) to the object(s)?
(b) Angle of elevation and azimuth of the object(s) when first observed.
(c) Angle of elevation and azimuth of object(s) upon disappearance.
(d) Description of flight path and maneuvers of object(s).
(e) Manner of disappearance of object(s).
(f) Length of time in sight.

(3) Manner of observation:
(a) Use one or any combination of the following items: Ground-visual, ground-electronic, air-electronic. (If electronic, specify type of radar.)
(b) Statement as to optical aids (telescopes, binoculars, and so forth) used and description thereof.
(c) If the sighting is made while airborne, give type aircraft, identification number, altitude, heading, speed, and home station.

(4) Time and date of sighting:
(a) Zulu time-date group of sighting.
(b) Light conditions (use one of the following terms): Night, day, dawn, dusk.

(5) Locations of observer(s). Exact latitude and longitude of each observer, or Georef position, or position with reference to a known landmark.

(6) Identifying information of all observer(s):
(a) Civilian—Name, age, mailing address, occupation.
(b) Military—Name, grade, organization, duty, and estimate of reliability.

(7) Weather and winds-aloft conditions at time and place of sightings:
(a) Observer(s) account of weather conditions.
(b) Report from nearest AWS or U. S. Weather Bureau Office of wind direction and velocity in degrees and knots at surface, 6,000′, 10,000′, 16,000′, 20,000′, 30,000′, 50,000′, and 80,000′, if available.
(c) Ceiling.
(d) Visibility.
(e) Amount of cloud cover.
(f) Thunderstorms in area and quadrant in which located.

(8) Any other unusual activity or condition, meteorological, astronomical, or otherwise, which might account for the sighting.

(9) Interception or identification action taken (such action may be taken whenever feasible, complying with existing air defense directives).

(10) Location of any air traffic in the area at time of sighting.

(11) Position title and comments of the preparing officer, including his preliminary analysis of the possible cause of the sighting(s).

(12) Existence of physical evidence, such as materials and photographs.

e. *Security.* Reports should be unclassified unless inclusion of data required by d above necessitates a higher classification.

8. Evidence. The existence of physical evidence (photographs or materiel) will be promptly reported.

a. *Photographic:*

(1) *Visual.* The negative and two prints will be forwarded, all original film, including wherever possible both prints and negatives, will be titled or otherwise properly identified as to place, time, and date of the incident

AFR 200-2
8-9

(see "Intelligence Collection Instructions" (ICI), June 1954).

(2) *Radar.* Two copies of each print will be forwarded. Prints of radarscope photography will be titled in accordance with AFR 95-7 and forwarded in compliance with AFR 95-6.

b. *Materiel.* Suspected or actual items of materiel which come into possession of any Air Force echelon will be safeguarded in such manner as to prevent any defacing or alteration which might reduce its value for intelligence examination and analysis.

9. Release of Facts. Headquarters USAF will release summaries of evaluated data which will inform the public on this subject. In response to local inquiries, it is permissible to inform news media representatives on UFOB's when the object is positively identified as a familiar object (see paragraph 2b), except that the following type of data warrants protection and should not be revealed: Names of principles, intercept and investigation procedures, and classified radar data. For those objects which are not explainable, only the fact that ATIC will analyze the data is worthly of release, due to the many unknowns involved.

By Order of the Secretary of the Air Force:

Official:

K. E. THIEBAUD
Colonel, USAF
Air Adjutant General

N. F. TWINING
Chief of Staff, United States Air Force

DISTRIBUTON:
S; X:
ONI, Department of the Navy 200
G-2, Department of the Army 10

☆ U. S. GOVERNMENT PRINTING OFFICE: 1954

APPENDIX III

JANAP 146(D) – Security Regulations

JANAP 146(D)

CANADIAN - UNITED STATES
COMMUNICATIONS INSTRUCTIONS
FOR REPORTING VITAL
INTELLIGENCE SIGHTINGS
(CIRVIS / MERINT)

JANAP 146

THE JOINT CHIEFS OF STAFF
MILITARY COMMUNICATIONS - ELECTRONICS BOARD
WASHINGTON 25, D.C.
February 1959

ORIGINAL

(Reverse Blank)

JANAP 146(D)

CHAPTER I

GENERAL DESCRIPTION AND PURPOSE OF COMMUNICATION INSTRUCTIONS FOR REPORTING VITAL INTELLIGENCE SIGHTINGS

101. Purpose. - The purpose of this publication is to provide uniform instructions for the peacetime reporting of vital intelligence sightings and to provide communication instructions for the passing of these intelligence reports to appropriate military authorities.

102. Scope. -

a. This publication is limited to the reporting of information of vital importance to the security of the United States of America and Canada and their forces, which in the opinion of the observer, requires very urgent defensive and/or investigative action by the US and/or Canadian Armed Forces.

b. The procedures contained in this publication are provided for:

(1) US and Canadian civil and commercial aircraft.

(2) US and Canadian government and military aircraft other than those operating under separate reporting directives.

(3) US and Canadian merchant vessels operating under US and Canadian registry.

(4) US and Canadian government and military vessels other than those operating under separate reporting directives.

(5) Certain other US and Canadian vessels including fishing vessels.

(6) Military installations receiving reports from civilian or military land based or waterborne observers unless operating under separate reporting directives.

(7) Government and civilian agencies which may initiate reports on receipt of information from land-based, airborne or waterborne observers.

103. Message Identification. -

a. Reports made from airborne and land-based sources will be identified by CIRVIS pronounced SUR VEES as the first word of the text. (Refer Chapter II).

b. Reports made by waterborne sources will be identified by MERINT pronounced as MUR ENT as the first word of the text. (Refer Chapter III).

1-1

ORIGINAL
(Reverse Blank)

JANAP 146(D)

CHAPTER II

CIRVIS REPORTS

SECTION I - GENERAL

201. Information to be Reported and When to Report. -

a. Sightings within the scope of this chapter, as outlined in Article 102b(1), (2), (6) and (7), are to be reported as follows:

(1) While airborne (except over foreign territory - see paragraph 210) and from land based observers. NOTE: Canada and the United States are not considered foreign territory for either country-for the purposes of this publication.

(a) Hostile or unidentified single aircraft or formations of aircraft which appear to be directed against the United States or Canada or their forces.

(b) Missiles.

(c) Unidentified flying objects.

(d) Hostile or unidentified submarines.

(e) Hostile or unidentified group or groups of military surface vessels.

(f) Individual surface vessels, submarines, or aircraft of unconventional design, or engaged in suspicious activity or observed in a location or on a course which may be interpreted as constituting a threat to the United States, Canada or their forces.

(g) Any unexplained or unusual activity which may indicate a possible attack against or through Canada or the United States, including the presence of any unidentified or other suspicious ground parties in the Polar region or other remote or sparsely populated areas.

(2) Upon landing.

(a) Reports which for any reason could not be transmitted while airborne.

(b) Unlisted airfields or facilities, weather stations, or air navigation aids.

(c) Post-landing reports.

2-1 ORIGINAL

SECTION III - SECURITY

308. Military and Civilian. - Transmission of MERINT reports are subject to the Communications Act of 1934, as amended, and the Canadian Radio Act of 1938, as amended. Any person who violates the provisions of these acts may be liable to prosecution thereunder. These reports contain information affecting the National Defense of the United States and Canada. Any person who makes an unauthorized transmission or disclosure of such a report may be liable to prosecution under Title 18 of the US Code, Chapter 37, or the Canadian Official Secrets Act of 1939, as amended. This should not be construed as requiring classification of MERINT messages. The purpose is to emphasize the necessity for the handling of such information within official channels only.

SECTION IV - EVALUATION REPORTS

309. Action by Activities. -

a. All investigative measures and evaluation processes instituted by addressees, and by originating authorities, where applicable, will be handled and reported in accordance with existing procedures, insuring that appropriate commands as listed in paragraph 306 are kept fully informed of investigative results and evaluations. These evaluations shall be expressed in terms indicating the reported sighting as being Positive, Probable, Possible or No Threat insofar as being a threat to the security of the United States of America or Canada or their forces, or an explanation of the subject reported when known.

b. The first two words of the text of an evaluation report shall be "MERINT EVALUATION" followed by the date-time-group and/or other identification of the MERINT report(s) being evaluated.

SECTION V - SPECIAL CONSIDERATIONS

310. Radio Transmission Restrictions. - MERINT reports will not be transmitted by radio other than Canadian or U. S. or international waters.

SECTION VI - COMMERCIAL CHARGES

311. Charges. -

a. All charges incurred in handling MERINT reports through U. S. facilities will be charged to the U. S. Department of the Navy (accounting symbol NAVY). Insofar as practicable, MERINT reports so handled should be forwarded RAPID US GOVT COLLECT.

b. All charges incurred in handling MERINT reports through facilities will be charged to the Royal Canadian Navy. Insofar

3-7 ORIGINAL

APPENDIX IV

PRNC 3820.1 Re: OPNAV 3820

PRNC 3820.1
Code 03
23 July 1954

HEADQUARTERS
POTOMAC RIVER NAVAL COMMAND
WASHINGTON 25, D.C.

PRNC INSTRUCTION 3820.1
From: Commandant, Potomac River Naval Command
To: Distribution List II
Subj: Unidentified flying objects; reporting of
Ref: (a) OPNAV NOTICE 3820 of 26 Sep 1952
(b) JANAP 146(C)
(c) Air Force Letter 200-5 of 29 Apr 1952 (enclosure (1) to ref (a))
(d) COMEASTSEAFRON INSTRUCTION 3820.2

1. **Purpose.** To provide guidance for procedures to be followed for reporting unidentified flying objects.
2. **Definition.** Unidentified flying objects as used in this Instruction relate to any airborne object which by performance, aerodynamic characteristics, or unusual features does not conform to any presently known aircraft or missile type.
3. **Background.** Reference (a) states that the U. S. Air Force has the primary responsibility for collection of subject information and has requested the cooperation of all naval activities in reporting such information.
4. **Action.**

a. Addressees are requested to report any data on unidentified flying objects without delay by message in multiple address to:

ACTION: (a) Director of Intelligence, Headquarters USAF, Washington 25, D.C.

(b) Air Technical Intelligence Center, Wright-Patterson AFB, Ohio—ATTN: ATLAA-2C
(c) Commander, Air Defense Command, Ent AFB, Colorado Springs, Colorado
(d) Commander, Eastern Air Defense Force, Stewart AFB, Newburgh, N.Y.
INFO: (e) Director of Naval Intelligence, Navy Department, Washington 25, D.C.
(f) Commander Eastern Sea Frontier, 90 Church Street, New York 7, N.Y.
(g) Commandant, Potomac River Naval Command, U. S. Naval Gun Factory, Washington 25, D.C.

b. The symbol FLYOBRPT [Flying Objects Report] will appear at the beginning of the text of messages to facilitate identification.

c. Reports will include, insofar as possible:

(1) A brief description of the object(s); shape, size, color, number, formation if more than one, aerodynamic features, trail or exhaust, propulsion system, speed, sound, maneuvers, manner of disappearance, and other pertinent or unusual features.

(2) Time of sighting in 24-hour clock zonal time, and length of time observed.

(3) Manner of observation; visual or electronic, from air (give speed, altitude, and type of aircraft), or surface. Any type of optical or electronic equipment used should be described.

(4) Location of observer during sighting, giving exact latitude and longitude as closely as feasible, and/or reference to a known landmark. Location of object(s) with respect to observer, giving distance, direction, and altitude.

(5) Identifying information of observer(s) and witness(s), estimate of reliability and experience, and any factors bearing on estimated reliability of the sighting.

(6) Weather and winds aloft conditions at time and place of sighting(s).

(7) Any activity or condition, meteorological or otherwise, which might account for the sighting.

(8) Existence of any physical evidence such as fragments, photographs and the like, of the sighting.

(9) Interception or identification action taken. (Such action may be taken whenever feasible, complying with existing air defense directives).

(10) Location of any air traffic in the general area at the time of the sighting.

d. It should be noted that the above instructions are separate from those required for reporting normal surface and air sightings prescribed by reference (b) and CINCLANTFLT instructions concerning same.

e. Addressees are requested to give these instructions wide dissemination within their commands.

T. B. HILL [Rear Admiral, USN]
V. HAVARD, JR. [Captain, USN]
Chief of Staff

APPENDIX V

SAC Teletypes Re: March 16, 1967 Malmstrom AFB, Montana Minuteman Nuclear Missiles Shut Down

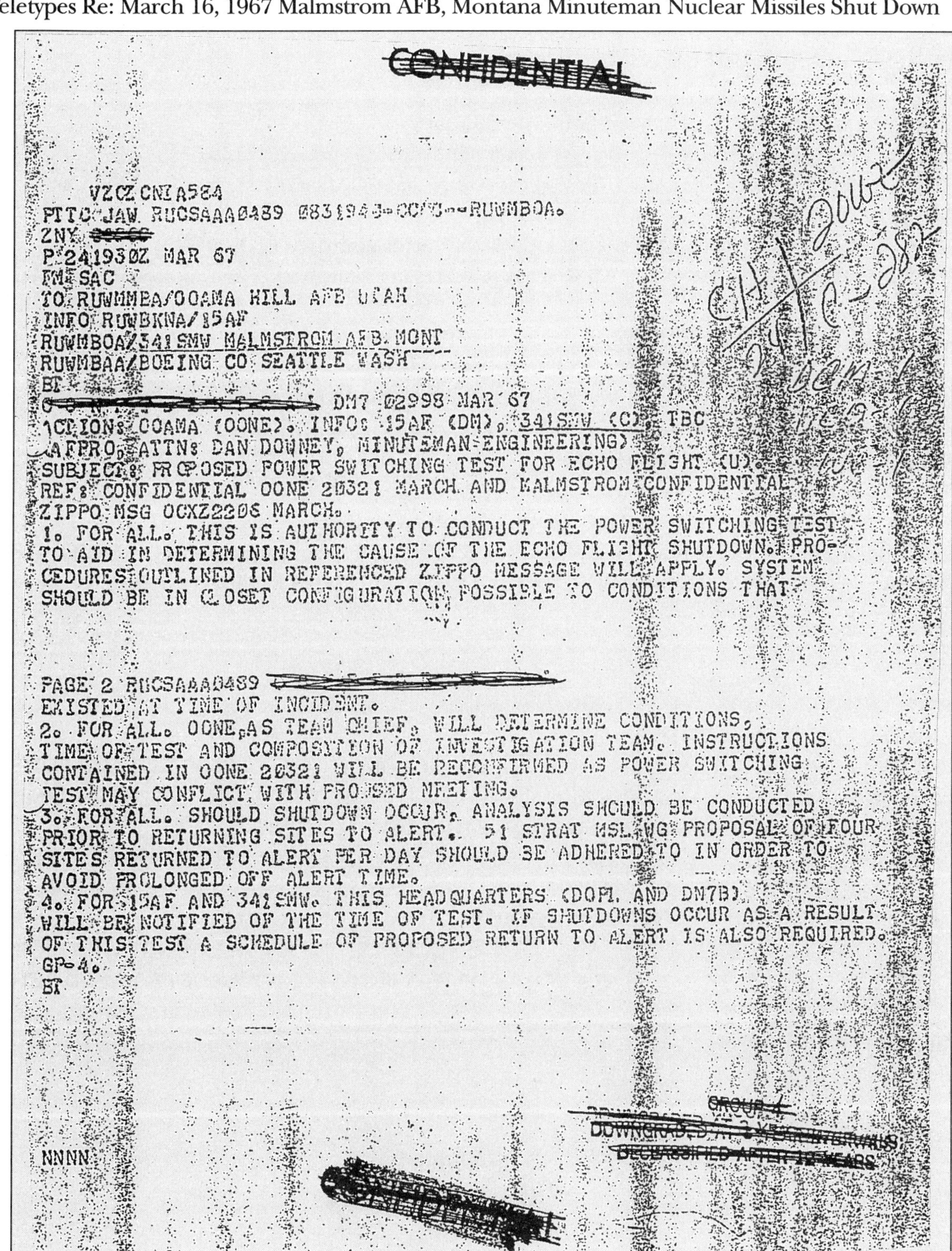

~~CONFIDENTIAL~~

VZCZCNIA584
PTTC JAW RUCSAAA0489 0831943-CC-RUWMBOA.
ZNY
P 241930Z MAR 67
FM SAC
TO RUWMMBA/OOAMA HILL AFB UTAH
INFO RUWBKNA/15AF
RUWMBOA/341SMW MALMSTROM AFB MONT
RUWMBAA/BOEING CO SEATTLE WASH
BT
DM7 02998 MAR 67
ACTION: OOAMA (OONE). INFO: 15AF (DM), 341SMW (C), TBC
AFPRO, ATTN: DAN DOWNEY, MINUTEMAN ENGINEERING)
SUBJECT: PROPOSED POWER SWITCHING TEST FOR ECHO FLIGHT (U).
REF: CONFIDENTIAL OONE 20321 MARCH AND MALMSTROM CONFIDENTIAL
ZIPPO MSG OCXZ2206 MARCH.
1. FOR ALL. THIS IS AUTHORITY TO CONDUCT THE POWER SWITCHING TEST
TO AID IN DETERMINING THE CAUSE OF THE ECHO FLIGHT SHUTDOWN. PRO-
CEDURES OUTLINED IN REFERENCED ZIPPO MESSAGE WILL APPLY. SYSTEM
SHOULD BE IN CLOSET CONFIGURATION POSSIBLE TO CONDITIONS THAT

PAGE 2 RUCSAAA0489
EXISTED AT TIME OF INCIDENT.
2. FOR ALL. OONE, AS TEAM CHIEF, WILL DETERMINE CONDITIONS,
TIME OF TEST AND COMPOSITION OF INVESTIGATION TEAM. INSTRUCTIONS
CONTAINED IN OONE 20321 WILL BE RECONFIRMED AS POWER SWITCHING
TEST MAY CONFLICT WITH PROUSED MEETING.
3. FOR ALL. SHOULD SHUTDOWN OCCUR, ANALYSIS SHOULD BE CONDUCTED
PRIOR TO RETURNING SITES TO ALERT. 51 STRAT MSL WG PROPOSAL OF FOUR
SITES RETURNED TO ALERT PER DAY SHOULD BE ADHERED TO IN ORDER TO
AVOID PROLONGED OFF ALERT TIME.
4. FOR 15AF AND 341SMW. THIS HEADQUARTERS (DOPL AND DM7B)
WILL BE NOTIFIED OF THE TIME OF TEST. IF SHUTDOWNS OCCUR AS A RESULT
OF THIS TEST A SCHEDULE OF PROPOSED RETURN TO ALERT IS ALSO REQUIRED.
GP-4.
BT

~~GROUP 4~~
~~DOWNGRADED AT 3 YEAR INTERVALS;~~
~~DECLASSIFIED AFTER 12 YEARS~~

NNNN

CONFIDENTIAL

VZCZ CN7 A584
PTTC JAW RUCSAAA0489 0831943-CCCC--RUWMBOA.
ZNY
P 241930Z MAR 67 (Date is 24 of March 1967 at 19:30 Zulu Time)
FM SAC (Strategic Air Command Air Defense Command, NORAD, Omaha, Nebraska)
TO RUWMMBA/00AMA HILL AFB UTAH (Mgmt.. Office for SAC Minuteman Office, Hill AFB, Utah)
INFO RUWBKNA/15AF (341st Strategic Missile Wing)
RUWMBOA/341SMW MALMSTROM AFB MONT (copy to Malmstrom AFB, Great Falls, Montana)
RUWMBAA/BOEING CO SEATTLE WASH (copy to Boeing in Seattle, Wash. was main contractor for Minuteman)
BT
CONFIDENTIAL DM7 02998 MAR67
ACTION: 00AMA (00NE). INFO: 15AF (DM), 341SMW (C), TBC
AFPRO, (Air Force Processing Office) ATTN: DAN DOWNEY, MINUTEMAN ENGINEERING (Boeing, Seattle)
SUBJECT: PROPOSED POWER SWITCHING TEST FOR ECHO FLIGHT (U).
REF: CONFIDENTIAL OONE 20321 MARCH AND MALMSTROM CONFIDENTIAL ZIPPO MSG 0CXZ220S MARCH.
1. FOR ALL. THIS IS AUTHORITY TO CONDUCT THE POWER SWITCHING TEST TO AID IN DETERMINING THE CAUSE OF THE ECHO FLIGHT SHUTDOWN. PROCEDURES OUTLINED IN REFERENCED ZIPPO MESSAGE WILL APPLY. SYSTEM SHOULD BE IN CLOSEST CONFIGURATION POSSIBLE TO CONDITIONS THAT

PAGE 2 RUCSAAA0489
EXISTED AT TIME OF INCIDENT.
2. FOR ALL. OONE, AS TEAM CHIEF, WILL DETERMINE CONDITIONS, TIME OF TEST AND COMPOSITION OF INVESTIGATION TEAM. INSTRUCTIONS CONTAINED IN OONE 20321 WILL BE RECONFIRMED AS POWER SWITCHING TEST MAY CONFLICT WITH PROPOSED MEETING.
3. FOR ALL. SHOULD SHUTDOWN OCCUR, ANALYSIS SHOULD BE CONDUCTED PRIOR TO RETURNING SITES TO ALERT. 51 STRAT MSL WG PROPOSAL OF FOUR SITES RETURNED TO ALERT PER DAY SHOULD BE ADHERED TO IN ORDER TO AVOID PROLONGED OFF ALERT TIME.
4. FOR 15AF AND 341 SMW. THIS HEADQUARTERS 9DOP1 AND DM7B) WILL BE NOTIFIED OF THE TIME OF TEST. IF SHUTDOWNS OCCUR AS A RESULT OF THIS TEST A SCHEDULE OF PROPOSED RETURN TO ALERT IS ALSO REQUIRED.
GP-4.
BT

NNNN

CONFIDENTIAL

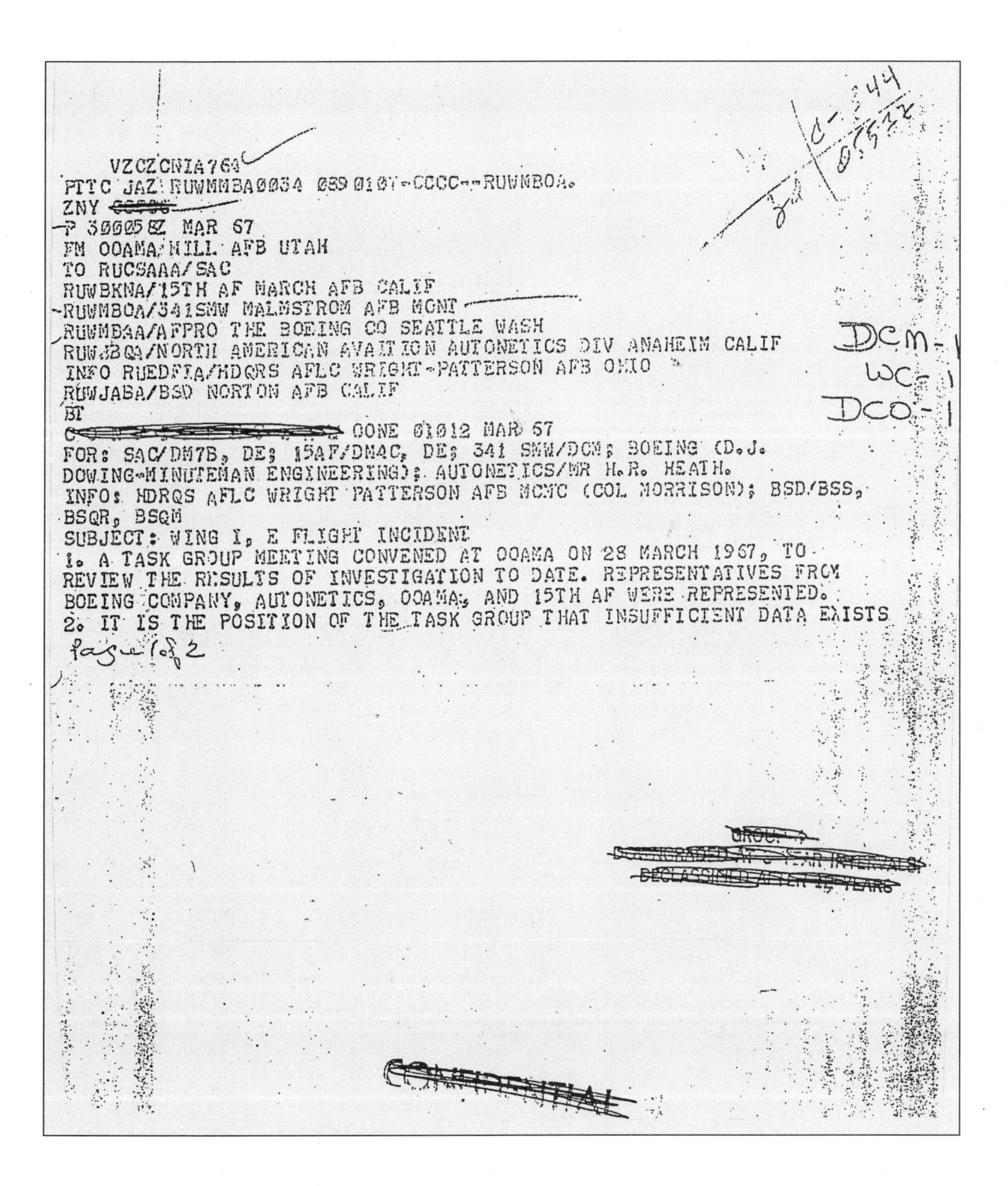

VZCZCNIA764
PTTC JAZ RUWMMBA0034 089 0107-CCCC--RUWMBOA.
ZNY ~~CCCCC~~
P 300058Z MAR 67
FM OOAMA/HILL AFB UTAH
TO RUCSAAA/SAC
RUWBKNA/15TH AF MARCH AFB CALIF
RUWMBOA/341SMW MALMSTROM AFB MONT
RUWMBAA/AFPRO THE BOEING CO SEATTLE WASH
RUWJBQA/NORTH AMERICAN AVAITION AUTONETICS DIV ANAHEIM CALIF
INFO RUEDFIA/HDQRS AFLC WRIGHT-PATTERSON AFB OHIO
RUWJABA/BSD NORTON AFB CALIF
BT
[redacted] GONE 01012 MAR 67
FOR: SAC/DM7B, DE; 15AF/DM4C, DE; 341 SMW/DCM; BOEING (D.J.
DOWING-MINUTEMAN ENGINEERING); AUTONETICS/MR H.R. HEATH.
INFO: HDRQS AFLC WRIGHT PATTERSON AFB MCMC (COL MORRISON); BSD/BSS,
BSQR, BSQM
SUBJECT: WING I, E FLIGHT INCIDENT
1. A TASK GROUP MEETING CONVENED AT OOAMA ON 28 MARCH 1967, TO
REVIEW THE RESULTS OF INVESTIGATION TO DATE. REPRESENTATIVES FROM
BOEING COMPANY, AUTONETICS, OOAMA, AND 15TH AF WERE REPRESENTED.
2. IT IS THE POSITION OF THE TASK GROUP THAT INSUFFICIENT DATA EXISTS

Page 1 of 2

DCM-1
WC-1
DCO-1

~~GROUP~~
~~DOWNGRADED AT 3 YEAR INTERVALS;~~
~~DECLASSIFIED AFTER 12 YEARS~~

~~CONFIDENTIAL~~

PAGE 2 RUWMMBA0034
TO RESOLVE THIS PROBLEM, OR TO DEFINITIZE ADEQUATE ENGINEERING ANALYSIS TASKS WITHOUT ADDITIONAL TESTING. A REVIEW OF AVAILABLE DATA STRONGLY SUGGESTS THIS TO BE A WING I PECULIAR PROBLEM. THE OOAMA ETF IS NOT A WING I FACILITY. IT IS, THEREFORE, NECESSARY TO RUN THE PROPOSED TESTS AT MALMSTROM, PREFERABLY AT ECHO 8. IT IS CURRENTLY BELIVED THAT FRUITFUL DATA WILL NOT EXIST UNTIL SUCH TIME AS THE NO-GO MODE CAN BE REPRODECED AT LEAST AT THE LF LEVEL.

3. THE FOLLOWING PLAN OF ACTION WAS AGREED UPON BY ALL REPRESENTATIVES. DEVELOP A TEST PLAN WHICH, AFTER ISOLATING AN LF FROM THE SYSTEM, ALLOWS FOR THE APPLICATION OF STIMULI WHICH WILL REPRODUCE THE NO-GO AT THE LF LEVEL. AFTER ANALYSIS OF SUCH TEST DATA, PROCEEDING AS REQUIRED TO TEST, OR ANALYZE AT THE LCF LEVEL. THE TASK GROUP WILL CONVENE AT BOEING, SEATTLE ON 4 APRIL TO DEVELOP A TEST PLAN ND PROCEDURES. SUCH PLAN WILL INCLUDE EQUIPMENT REQUIREMENTS, LF ISOLATION PROCEDURES, DEFINE TESTS TO BE PREFORMED, AND BE REVIEWED FOR SAFETY. THE PLAN WILL RECEIVE SAFETY CLEARANCE THROUGH OONE, AND WILL BE COORDINATED WITH SAC AS REQUIRED. COMPLETION DATE FOR THE PLAN IS AIMED AT 5 MAY 1967. THE PLAN WILL BE DEVELOPED AND PROTOTYPED, AT THE KRA FACILITY AT BOEING.

4. ADDITIONAL INVESTIGATIVE ENGINEERING STUDIES ARE IN PROCESS, AND WILL CONTINUE. BOEING IS ATTEMPTING TO OBTAIN AN EXHIBIT 7KVA TRANS-

PAGE 3 RUWMMBA0034
FORMER WHICH WAS REPORTED TO HAVE SHORTED A FEW HOURS AFTER THE INCIDENT. A TEARDOWN REPORT ON THE TRANSORMER WILL BE DEVELOPED BY BOEING ENGINEERING. DEPENDENT UPON THE ANALYSIS OF THIS TRANSFORMER, AND ITS FAILURE MODE, ADDITIONAL TESTS MAY BE REQUESTED SIMILAR TO THE POWER TESTS RUN ON 28 MARCH 1967, AT MALSTROM WITH THE ADDED TRANSFORMER FAILURE ODE SIMULATION. YOU WILL BE FURTHER ADVISED WITH RESPECT TO THIS ACTIVITY.

5. CONCURRENCE IN THE USE OF ECHO 8 FOR TESTING OUTLINED IN PARA THREE (3) IS REQUESTED. PLANNING FACTORS AT THIS TIME ARE FOR A PERIOD OF SIX WEEKS BEGINNING 15 MARY 1967. YOU WILL BE ADVISED OF ANY SHIFT IN THESE TARGET DATES. GP-4.

BT Page 2 of 2

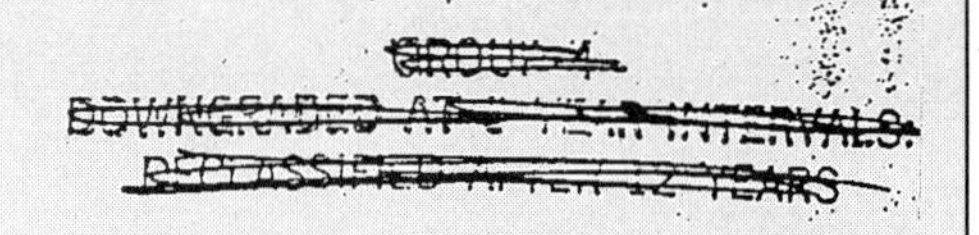

APPENDIX VI

MAJIC-12 Project Y, Division Z, Group 12 – 1947
Provided by J. Andrew Kissner.

MJ-12
Manhattan (Engineering District) Joint (Chiefs of Staff)
(Project Y, Division Z, Group) 12
Division- Group: Z (Ordnance)-12

Name of Group: Unknown
Function of Group: Unknown
Group Leader: **Estel L. Cheeseman**
Date Formed: September, 1947
Summary of Activity: "Although it is unknown what this group did one undated memorandum was found in the group file re: nomenclature conference addressed to all Z groups. It is assumed that this group was involved in standardizing nuclear weapon component names."

Necah S. Furman, Sandia National Laboratories, The Post War Decade, The University of New Mexico Press, Albuquerque 1990

Z Division

Zacharias's (Jerrold R. Zacharias) Division of Project Y established at Sandia Base, Albuquerque between 1946 and 1948.[28] Z Division evolved using the staff of Project Y at W-47 into Sandia National Laboratory, administered, through Presidential invitation, by AT&T Bell Telephone beginning in March 1948. Z Division's Group 12 was established in September 1947. Its function and purpose apparently remains classified in 1995.

Z DIVISION LEADERSHIP (Ordnance Division)

Formed 7/45; functional by 9/45; Transferred to Albuquerque mainly between 3/46 and 7/46.

GROUP	LEADERSHIP
Z, Ordnance Division	Jerrold R. Zacharias, Division Leader (7/45-10/45)
	Roger S. Warner, Division Leader (10/45-1947)
	Dale R. Corson, Actg. Div. Ldr. (10/45-7/46)
	Ellis E. Wilhoyt, Actg. Div. Ldr. (3/46-7/46); Alt. Div. Ldr. (7/46-4/48)
	Robert W. Henderson, Division Leader (1947-4/48)
Z-1, Experimental Systems	Norris E. Bradbury, Group Leader (became Lab Director 10/45)
Z-1A, Airborne Testing	Dale Corson, Section Leader (8/45-10/45)
Z-1B Informers	Jerome Wiesner, Section Leader (8/45-3/46; joined B-12)
Z-1C, Coordination with Using Services	Glenn Fowler, Section Leader (8/45-3/46)
Z-1, Field Test	Nathan Eisen, Group Leader (3/46-12/46)
	Glen Fowler, Group Leader (12/46-3/48)
Z-2, Assembly Factory at Sandia Lab	Lyle E. Seeman, Group Leader (8/45-3/46)
Z-2A, Procurement, Storage & Shipment	Robert W. Lockridge, Group Leader (8/45-3/48)
Z-2, Air Coordination	Glenn Fowler, Group Leader (3/46-12/46)
	Richard A. Bice, Group Leader (12/46-3/48)
Z-3, Firing Development	Mr. Thomas, Co-Group Leader (3/46-7/46)
	Donald Hornig, Co-Group Leader (3/46-7/46)
Z-3 Firing Circuits (Absorbed into Z-5 3/46)	Lewis Fussell, Group Leader (8/45-3/46)
Z-3, Assembly Training	Arthur Machen, Group Leader (12/46-3/48)
Z-4, Mechanical Engineering	Robert W. Henderson, Group Leader (8/45-3/46)
Z-5, Electronic Engineering	Robert B. Brode, Group Leader (8/45-3/46)
Z-5, Firing and Fuzing	R. L. Colby, Group Leader (5/46-12/46)
	Otis L. Wright, Group Leader (12/46-3/48)
Z-6, Mechanical Engineering Lab	William T. Theis, Group Leader (10/45-3/46)
	Alan Ayers, Group Leader (3/46-3/48)
Z-7, Assembly	Wilbur F. Shaffer, Group Leader (12/45-3/46)
	James L. Rowe, Group Leader (3/46-3/48)
Z-8, Informers	T. J. Anderson, Group Leader (3/46-12/46)
	William Caldes, Group Leader (12/46-3/48)
Z-9, Stockpiling	Wilbur F. Shaffer, Group Leader (3/46-3/48)
Z-10, Technical Area Supply	Henry Moeding, Group Leader (12/46-3/48)
Z-11, Special Weapons (Little Boy)	Harlow W. Russ, Group Leader (9/46-3/48)
Z-12, Name Unknown	Estel L. Cheeseman, Group Leader (9/47-3/48)
Z-13, Name Unknown	John T. Risley, Group Leader (3/48-3/48)

APPENDIX VII

Some United States Intelligence and Military Abbreviations, Acronyms and Nomenclature, 1940s-1995. Provided by J. Andrew Kissner.

AAF Army Air Forces, Predecessor to the U. S. Air Force. USAF was created by the National Security Act of 1947 and organized on August 1, 1947 *three weeks after* one or more purported flying discs were recovered in New Mexico.

AEC Atomic Energy Commission established by the Atomic Energy Act of 1946 as a "civilian" organization given custody of all U. S. nuclear weapons and materials by the act. A further nuclear weapons custody determination was made by President Truman in June, 1948 in favor of the AEC.

Aerospace Corp. A private, non-profit "civilian" research and development corporation wholly owned by the U. S. Air Force Systems Command based in El Segundo, California. It appears to operate as an integrated military command of the Joint Chiefs of Staff.

AFCRC Armed Forces Cambridge Research Center, a division of the Air Material Command based at Wright (Patterson) Field (Air Force Base) Dayton, Ohio. AFCRC is based in Massachusetts.

AFGL Armed Forces Geophysical Laboratory.

AFOSI Air Force Office of Special Investigations. AFOSI's mission focuses on counter-intelligence operations, specifically targeting and investigating attempts to steal or disclose classified information related to U. S. special weapons.

AFSC Air Force Systems Command.

AFSTC Air Force Space Technology Center, Kirtland AFB, Albuquerque.

AFWL Air Force Weapons Laboratory located at Sandia Base, Kirtland Air Force Base, Albuquerque. Originally, AFWL was formed in 1947 as the Armed Forces Special Weapons Project (AFSWP) and renamed Phillips Laboratory in 1991. A division of the Research and Technology Division, Air Force Systems Command (AFSC) in 1963 and the Director of Science and Technology after 1967.

AFSWC U. S. Air Force Special Weapons Command was activated on December 1, 1949 at Kirtland Air Force Base, Albuquerque. It was responsible for operating all AMC activities at the base and provided personnel and equipment for developing and testing aircraft and other special weapons as well as providing additional personnel and equipment to the AEC. AFSWC's mission was: "...to establish and maintain technical supervision over a test facility and group of qualified personnel, aircraft, equipment and instrumentation that will provide the Air Force, the Atomic Energy Commission, their contractors and other agencies of the Department of Defense an organization for the development and testing of atomic weapons or other special weapons with their associated equipment for determining the adequacy of airborne vehicles and special weapons. It is the primary source of scientific and technical information pertaining to special weapons development and associated special techniques within the Air Force." Source is *From Sundaggers to Space Exploration, New Mexico Journal of Science,* Vol. 26, No. 1, 1986, page 294. AFSWC became the Air Force Special Weapons "Center" in 1952.

AFSWP Armed Forces Special Weapons Project at Sandia Base, Albuquerque, New Mexico was established in 1947 with the transfer of some Los Alamos Scientific Laboratory production and research functions to Albuquerque (Z Division) and assignment of special military units to protect the U. S. special weapons stockpile. Brig. General Robert M. Montague (MJ-11) became the first military commander of AFSWP *four days after* a purported flying disc was recovered near Corona, New Mexico.

AMC Air Material Command based at Wright Field, Ohio; Kirtland Army Air Field, Albuquerque; and Army Air Field, Alamogordo, New Mexico after June 1947. Commander of the AMC during this period was General Nathan Twining (MJ-4).

AMOS A satellite tracking facility using electro-optical telescopes at Haleakala, Maui, Hawaii.

APL Applied Physics Laboratory of Johns Hopkins University, an armed forces contractor, employing Dept. of Terrestrial Magnetism staff of the Carnegie Institution of Washington, D. C. APL became a U. S. Navy Bureau of Aeronautics contract laboratory in 1947. President of Johns Hopkins during this period was Dr. Detlev Bronk (MJ-6) who also served as President of the Rockefeller Institute after 1948.

ARPA Advanced Research Projects Agency, Joint Chiefs of Staff. (Also see: DARPA).

Bell Labs (AT&T) A major AEC and Defense Department contractor and administrator of Sandia National Laboratory, Albuquerque, New Mexico after March 1948.

BMEWS Ballistic Missile Early Warning System based at Thule Air Force Base, Greenland; Fylingdales, United Kingdom; and Clear, Alaska.

BNL Brookhaven National Laboratory, Long Island, New York. Its first year of operation was 1947 with a $40 million budget. In 1948, Dr. Lloyd Berkner (MJ-12) became Director of BNL. Referred to as an AEC laboratory by the RAND corporation, BNL's literature refers to it as an "independent, academic research laboratory" operated by a consortium of U. S. colleges and Associated Universities, Inc.

"BOWMAN" Proword purportedly associated with classified special compartmented information about a flying disc and secret weapons development. A confidential source who worked on BOWMAN said "it was like trying to hit a jet fighter with an arrow."

BRL Ballistic Research Laboratory, U.S. Army Ordnance operating for the JCS at Aberdeen Proving Ground, Maryland.

CAB Civil Aeronautics Board.

CIA Central Intelligence Agency, formed on September 26, 1947 from the Central Intelligence Group (CIG), the Office of Strategic Services (OSS) and the Strategic Services Unit (SSU) of the Joint Chiefs of Staff. Its first director was Navy Admiral Roscoe Hillenkoetter (MJ-1). The CIA was approved by President Truman two weeks after a purported flying disc was recovered north, northeast of Carrizozo, New Mexico.

CIG Central Intelligence Group of the Joint Chiefs of Staff formed to replace the Office of Strategic Services (OSS) in May 1946. General Hoyt Vandenberg (MJ-5) was a director of CIG as was Admiral Sydney Souers (MJ-8) and Admiral Roscoe Hillenkoetter (MJ-1).

CIOS Combined Intelligence Objectives Subcommittees of the Joint Chiefs of Staff established by the Joint Research and Development Board. CIOS panels used the most expert scientific talent available in military, civilian and academic organizations to study specific technical subjects. For example, some CIOS panels were the V-2 Rocket Panel; Upper Atmosphere Rocket Research Panel; Subsurface Warfare Research Panel; and Uranium Research Panel.

CIW Carnegie Institution of Washington, D. C. Dr. Vannevar Bush (MJ-2) was president of CIW while serving as director of OSRD, JRDB and RDB.

COMINT Communications Intelligence.

CRPL Central Radio (Wave) Propagation Laboratory, National Bureau of Standards.

DARPA Defense Advanced Research Projects Agency, JSC.

DEW LINE Distant Early Warning System was designed, constructed and managed by Associated Universities Inc., the parent organization of Brookhaven National Laboratory, Long Island, New York.

DNA Defense Nuclear Agency.

"DREAMLAND' Area 51, Nellis AFB, Nevada. Also purported to include joint U.S. government and alien bases in Nevada, New Mexico, Utah, Colorado and Arizona.

DTM Department of Terrestrial Magnetism at the Carnegie Institution of Washington, D. C. Dr. Vannevar Bush (MJ-2) was a former staff member of CIW/DTM and President of CIW.

EEIS Enemy Equipment Intelligence Section, U.S. Army Ordnance.

ELINT Electronic Intelligence.

EOP Executive Office of the President of the United States.

EOS Earth Observation System.

EWS Earth Warning System.

GAPA Ground to Air Pilotless Antiaircraft system.

G. E. General Electric Corp., major contractor for Office of Scientific Research and Development, Defense Department, AMC and AEC. GE's research laboratory at Lynn, Massachusetts had primary responsibility for the Hermes project manufacturing different German rocket designs for the U. S. military beginning in 1944. The Hermes A-1 was a duplicate of a "Wasserfall" surface to air missile, although this information apparently remained classified in 1995.

GEODSS Ground-Based, Electro-Optical Deep Space Surveillance system operated by the 1st Space Wing, Space Defense Operations Center, U. S. Space Command. The first GEODSS location was on White Sands Missile Range, New Mexico. Current GEODSS locations are established worldwide. Deep space is defined as being at least 20,000 miles altitude above the earth. GEODSS reports directly to NORAD Headquarters, Cheyenne Mountain, Colorado Springs, Colorado. Source: *Encyclopedia of the U. S. Military*, by Arkin, Handler, Morrisey, Walsh, 1990, page 628.

"HAYSTACK" Proword for a classified X-band satellite tracking system based at Millstone Hill, Massachusetts.

HUMINT Human Intelligence.

"ICE CAVE" Purported location for alien detainees in New Mexico at Los Alamos National Laboratory.

Ice Canyon A canyon in the Organ Mountain Range slightly south of the main post area of White Sands Missile Range, New Mexico.

IC Integrated Command. An operational group composed of members of the different armed services formed to work on a specific joint objective or engage in joint research and development activity. Examples of integrated commands are the U.S. Space Command, Space Defense Operations Center, the National Security Agency, the National Reconnaissance Office.

JCS Joint Chiefs of Staff for U. S. military, Pentagon, Washington, D. C.

JDSRF Joint Defense Space Research Facility located at Pine Gap, Australia and operated by the National Reconnaissance Organization (NRO).

JNWEB Joint New Weapons and Equipment Board of the JCS chaired by Dr. Vannevar Bush (MJ-2) in 1945 to 1947.

JPL Jet Propulsion Laboratory of the California Institute of Technology, Pasadena, California.

JRDB Joint Research and Development Board of the Joint Chiefs of Staff. Coordinator of scientific efforts for the military establishment, the AEC, private industry and academic institutions. Combined OSRD and JNWEB to form JRDB in 1946 under the chairmanship of Dr. Vannevar Bush (MJ-2). OSRD, however, continued to function through at least September 1947.

"KINGMAN" Proword for a secret and joint Los Alamos Scientific Laboratory (LASL) and

Air Material Command base at Wendover Field, Utah, also known as W-47.

LANL Los Alamos National Laboratory, Los Alamos, New Mexico.

LASL Los Alamos Scientific Laboratory, forerunner of LANL, Los Alamos, N. M.

"LEXINGTON" Proword for a space nuclear propulsion project at the AEC and National Advisory Committee for Aeronautics in 1947 and 1948.

LLNL Lawrence Livermore National Laboratory formed under physicist Edward Teller, University of California, Berkeley, California.

"MAJIC" Proword associated with Operation Majestic Twelve (MJ-12) and derived from Manhattan (Engineering District), Armed (Forces Special Weapons Project) Joint (Chiefs of Staff) Integrated Command that was reorganized in 1946 into the Atomic Energy Commission.

"MAJOR" Proword associated with the Space Defense Operations Center, U. S. Space Command, Colorado Springs, Colorado.

MED Manhattan Engineering District, the pseudonym assigned to the U. S. effort to develop the first atomic bombs dropped on Hiroshima and Nagasaki, established through the efforts of the Office of Scientific Research and Development (OSRD) and its director, Dr. Vannevar Bush (MJ-2).

MILLSTONE Satellite tracking system based in Millstone, Massachusetts.

MJ-12 Special Studies Group established by Special Classified Executive Order #092447 on September 24, 1947 by U. S. President Harry S. Truman to investigate the UFOB phenomenon. Members of the first MJ-12 were listed as:

1) Adm. Roscoe H. Hillenkoetter
2) Dr. Vannevar Bush
3) Secy. James V. Forrestal
4) Gen. Nathan F. Twining
5) Gen. Hoyt S. Vandenberg
6) Dr. Detlev Bronk
7) Dr. Jerome Hunsaker
8) Mr. Sidney W. Souers
9) Mr. Gordon Gray
10) Dr. Donald Menzel
11) Gen. Robert M. Montague
12) Dr. Lloyd V. Berkner

MOTIF Maui Optical Tracking and Identification Facility operated by the 1st Space Wing, Space Defense Operations Center, established in 1953 to catalog, inventory and monitor natural and artificial earth orbiting satellites. The first publicly recognized "artificial satellite" in earth orbit was the Russian Sputnik spacecraft launched in 1957. But Major Donald Keyhoe reported in his 1973 book *Aliens From Space* on Page 133-149 that in 1953, U. S. experimental long-range radar picked up objects circling the Earth, some six hundred miles out.

NACA National Advisory Committee for Aeronautics (predecessor to NASA). Dr. Jerome Hunsaker (MJ-7) was director of NACA in 1947.

NASA National Aeronautics and Space Administration evolved from NACA in 1957-1958. Works closely with JPL.

NAVSPASUR Naval Space Surveillance System constructed in 1959 and dedicated to space surveillance. Transmitters are at Lake Kickapoo, Texas; Gila River, Arizona; and Jordan Lake, Arkansas.

NBS National Bureau of Standards, Boulder, Colorado.

NDRC National Defense Research Council of OSRD.

"NEPA" Proword for a space nuclear propulsion project of the AEC in 1946-1948.

NORAD North American Air Space Defense Command in Cheyenne Mountain, Colorado Springs, Colorado. Primarily responsible for air defense of North America.

NRL Naval Research Laboratory.

NRO National Reconnaissance Organization jointly operated by NSA, CIA, Air Force Systems Command under the NSC to design, construct, operate and maintain high altitude aircraft, satellites and other national technical means to conduct strategic surveillance and espionage. NRO and NSA operate ground and space based sensors to track and catalogue space borne objects in association with Space Defense Operations Center (SDOC). NRO is believed to be directly involved with monitoring the flying disc phenomenon.

NSA National Security Agency, operated under the National Security Council. NSA evolved from the U. S. Air Force Office of Special Investigations in 1952. NSA is primarily involved in electronic, radar and communications intelligence gathering and satellite reconnaissance.

NSA of 1947 National Security Act signed by President Harry S. Truman on July 26, 1947.

NSC National Security Council held its first meeting on September 24, 1947 at the White House. That same date President Harry S. Truman allegedly established by special classified executive order the Majestic-12 Group.

NSF National Science Foundation was established on May 10, 1950. A provision of the 1947 National Security Act concerning the funding of basic research into the applied sciences allowed any program operated by NSF that discovered a physical principal, event or relationship with potential application to the national security interest of the U. S. to be immediately "militarized" to revert to the direct control of the Research and Development Board (RDB) of the Secretary of Defense.

ONR Office of Naval Research.

ORI Office of Research and Innovations, U. S. Navy.

OSI Office of Scientific Intelligence, Central Intelligence Agency.

OSRD Office of Scientific Research and Development of the Office of Emergency Management of the Executive Office of the President, 1940-1947 directed by Dr.

Vannevar Bush (MJ-2), President, Carnegie Institution of Washington, D. C. Dr. James Conant, President of Harvard College served as deputy director. Dr. Lloyd Berkner (MJ-12) served as deputy following Dr. Conant's return to Harvard. Dr. Detlev Bronk (MJ-6) was OSRD's principal manager of medical research and worked with General Twining's (MJ-4) AMC, especially as this related to high altitude research and human physiology. All V-2 testing activity, as well as establishing White Sands Proving Ground itself, was the direct responsibility of OSRD.

OSS Office of Strategic Services of the Joint Chiefs of Staff during W. W. II.

PACBAR Pacific Barrier Radar, constructed in 1983 for satellite tracking at San Miguel, Philippines and Saipan.

PAVE PAWS A system of LPAR (FPS-115) UHF space sensors, constructed in the 1980s at Beale AFB, California; Otis AFB, Massachusetts; Robins AFB, Georgia; Goodfellow AFB, Eldorado, Texas to detect space vehicles.

Phillips Laboratory A division of U. S. Air Force Systems Command, Hanscom Air Force Base, Massachusetts and Kirtland Air Force Base, Albuquerque, New Mexico. Formerly the Air Force (Special) Weapons Laboratory (AFWL).

PL253 Public Law 253 in the National Security Act of 1947 enacted by the 80th Congress in 1947 which allows certain U. S. government officials to materially misrepresent, disavow knowledge, or intentionally mislead and deceive any natural person including Congress and the judicial branch in sworn testimony regarding any act, event, program or collected information if its disclosure is determined to be detrimental to the national security interests of the U. S. Only two people are exempted from this treatment - the President and/or his National Security Advisor. This provision of the National Security Act remained classified in 1995.

PROJECT Y Los Alamos Scientific Laboratory (LASL) at Los Alamos School for Boys, New Mexico which later became the AEC Los Alamos National Laboratory (LANL).

Proword or Proname Part of access code to sensitive compartmented information (SCI).

RADINT Radar Intelligence.

RAND Research and Development Division - Douglas Aircraft Company. Evolved into the RAND Corp. in November 1948, a private, non-profit research and development organization. RAND enjoys a "special relationship" with U. S. Air Force Systems Command and the Aerospace Corporation. In July 1948, RAND developed another special relationship with the Atomic Energy Commission in RAND's Physics Department which was separated from other RAND divisions and required an AEC "Q" clearance for access. Later RAND developed other special relationships with the Ford Foundation, the Carnegie Institution of Washington, D. C. and the Rockefeller Institute. RAND's only clients in its first two decades of existence was the U. S. Air Force and the Atomic Energy Commission. Source is *The RAND Corporation* © 1966 by Bruce L. R. Smith.

RDB Research and Development Board of the Secretary of Defense was the immediate successor to the Joint Research and Development Board of the JCS established in the last week of July 1947. The first chairman of the RDB was Dr. Vannevar Bush (MJ-2).

Rockefeller Institute A private, non-profit research and development institute financed by John D. Rockefeller and primarily involved in medical research. Dr. Detlev Bronk (MJ-6) became President of the Rockefeller Institute in 1948 with David Rockefeller serving as Chairman of the Board of Trustees. In 1995, published accounts from the Department of Energy and the Rockefeller Institute were identified as working cooperatively with the Atomic Energy Commission to collect and analyze biological tissue samples from corpses of human infants and living animals worldwide to ostensibly determine the extent of contamination from nuclear testing from the late 1940s through 1980. Source: *Albuquerque Journal*, February 15, 1995, Page A9.

ROVER Proword for the joint NASA-AEC Space Nuclear Propulsion Office's efforts to develop a solid core heat exchanger nuclear rocket engine for interplanetary and geosynchronous flight with primary facilities at Jackass Flats, Nevada Test Site. Projects included Kiwi, Nerva. LANL's effort included Phoebes. NASA inherited the program area from NACA and the U. S. Air Force in 1958 and operated it through 1969. The program area "vanished" in 1969, according to a NASA spokesman, after substantial progress had been made on space nuclear propulsion for lifting heavier than air vehicles from the earth's surface to orbit. Source: *United States Civilian Space Programs 1958-1978*, Committee Print, Subcommittee on Space Science and Applications, Committee on Science and Technology, U.S. House of Representatives, 97th Congress, First Session, January 1981, Page 225.

"SANDY BEACH" Proword for Los Alamos Scientific Laboratory's and Naval Bureau of Ordnance's test facility at the Salton Sea, California. The Carnegie Institution of Washington, D. C. was also active in the "SANDY BEACH" area at the same time, ostensibly studying "the mechanics of evaporation."

"Section T" Section T of APL designed, developed, fabricated and then manufactured the first radio-controlled proximity fuse for artillery munitions for OSRD during WWII. Section T was populated with staff from the Carnegie Institution's Department of Terrestrial Magnetism (DTM).

SDOC Space Defense Operations Center directly operates at least 24 radar and optical sensors for near space and deep space surveillance through its 1st Space Wing. Parent is U. S. Space Command, Peterson AFB, Colorado Springs, Colorado. It is associated with the NRO and operates as a division of the USAF. SDOC also indirectly controls a number of university and private observatories used infrequently "as the need arises." Also operates optical sensors constructed by the Vatican. Source: *Encyclopedia of the U. S. Military,* page 628 by Arkin et al.

"SITU" Proword for a satellite tracking facility in the visible light spectrum at St. Margarets, Canada.

SNL Sandia National Laboratory, Albuquerque, New Mexico.

SOI Space Object Identification, Space Defense Operations Center.

"SPACE-TRACK" Proword for Space Surveillance Network.

Special Access Categories of information requiring "need to know" certification above TOP SECRET. Requires a more thorough background investigation by the Federal Investigative Service. Special access information may be provided to others cleared at the same or superior level only if those individuals have "need to know." It has been suggested by a purported officer in U. S. Army counterintelligence that the President is not routinely informed regarding "black" program areas unless he has need to know certification from the NSC or JCS.

Special Compartmented Information (SCI) Information available only to those cleared within a specific, defined compartment using special access procedures.

Special Weapons A class of munitions and unconventional weapons requiring the use of unique, special access procedures. Categories include: nuclear and non-nuclear warheads, nuclear demolition munitions; missile bodies and missile components; lethal and incapacitating chemical agents. Source: *Science With A Vengeance, How the Military Created the U. S. Space Sciences After WWII* © 1992 by David Devorkin, Page 82.

T-Force A specialized, often inter-service U. S. military unit assigned a mission to take, hold and defend a specialized enemy facility or specific piece of enemy equipment possessing high scientific or technical value as defined by OSRD and the JCS during WWII.

"TEAL AMBER" Proword for a space sensing system, Malabar, Florida.

"TEAL BLUE" Proword for the MOTIF facility, Maui, Hawaii.

"TEAL RUBY" Proword for an unknown facility.

TECHNINT A general term used to describe intelligence collected by technical means as opposed to HUMINT, human intelligence.

"TK-SI" Talent Keyhole-Special Intelligence. Prowords which define access to the compartment concerned with satellite intelligence collection in the early 1980s.

UARRP Upper Atmosphere Rocket Research Panel, a JRDB/RDB expert panel.

V-2 Vengeance-2 German ballistic missile system tested and used for research by U.S. Army Ordnance and the U. S. Naval Research Laboratory, Bureau of Ordnance at White Sands Proving Ground, New Mexico from 1946 through 1949.

V-2 Panel Joint New Weapons and Equipment expert panel concerned with V-2 rocket development.

VLA Very Large Array, National Radio Astronomy Observatory of the National Science Foundation. Extreme deep space surveillance and deep space research. VLA was designed and constructed, as were all NRAO major facilities, by Associated Universities Inc., parent organization of Brookhaven National Laboratory (BNL). Dr. Lloyd Berkner (MJ-12) became Director of BNL in 1948. Dr. Donald Menzel (MJ-10) served as Chairman of NRAO for over a decade from the mid-1950s on.

VLBA Very Long Baseline Array, National Radio Astronomy Observatory of the National Science Foundation. Extreme deep space surveillance and space research. Constructed by Associated Universities, Inc.

Wasserfall A German program name for the first surface to air missile system tested and deployed by the AMC and operated by the National Antiaircraft Artillery School at Ft. Bliss, Texas in the spring of 1947. Source: *International Missile and Spacecraft Guide* © 1960 by Frederick Ordway, Page 96.

"WATERSUPPLY" Proword for AFSWP program to develop the U. S.'s first three underground nuclear weapons storage and final assembly sites. Source: Sandia National Laboratories © 1990 by Furman.

"W-47" Second Proword for Wendover Field, Utah.

"WINDMILL" Proword said to be associated with SCI about flying discs.

WSMR White Sands Missile Range, New Mexico.

WSPG White Sands Proving Ground, New Mexico, renamed WSMR in 1956.

Z-Division Division of Project Y headed by Jerrold R. Zacharias and established at Sandia Base, Albuquerque between 1946 and 1948. Z Division evolved using the staff of Project Y at W-47 into Sandia National Laboratory, administered through Presidential invitation by AT&T Bell Telephone beginning in March 1948. Z Division's Group 12 was established in September 1947. Its function and purpose apparently remains classified.

APPENDIX VIII

Alleged Presidential Executive Briefing Prepared By MJ-12

TOP SECRET

EXECUTIVE CORRESPONDENCE

EXECUTIVE BRIEFING

SUBJECT:

PROJECT AQUARIUS (TS)

ATTENTION

THIS DOCUMENT WAS PREPARED BY MJ12. MJ12 IS SOLELY RESPONSIBLE FOR ITS SUBJECT MATTER

DOCUMENT CONTROL: ECN 0001

CLASSIFIED BY: MJ12-EO/34012
DECLASSIFY ON: EXEMPT CAT [illegible]

TOP SECRET

TOP SECRET

CLASSIFICATION AND RELEASE INSTRUCTIONS

(TS/ORCON) The information contained in this document is classified TOP SECRET with ORCON. (Only the originator may release the information) Only MJ12 has access to Project Aquarius. No other government agency, to include the military, has access to the information contained in this briefing. There are only two copies of Project Aquarius and the location is known only to MJ12. This document will be destroyed after the briefing. No notes, photographs, or audio recordings, may be made of this briefing.

TOP SECRET

CLASSIFICATION AND RELEASE INSTRUCTIONS

(TS/ORCON) The information contained in this document is classified TOP SECRET with ORCON. (Only the originator may release the information) Only MJ12 has access to Project Aquarius. No other government agency, to include the military, has access to the information contained in this briefing. There are only two copies of Project Aquarius and that location is known only to MJ12. This document will be destroyed after the briefing. No notes, photographs, or audio recordings, may be made of this briefing.

TOP SECRET

EXECUTIVE BRIEFING

(TS/ORCON) In June 1947, a civilian pilot flying over the Cascade mountains of Washington State observed nine flying discs, (later referred to as UFOs). The Commander, Air Technical Intelligence Center of the then Army Air Force, became concerned and ordered an inquiry. This was the beginning of the United States involvement with UFO investigations. In 1947, an aircraft of extraterrestrial origin, crashed in the desert of New Mexico. The craft was recovered by the military. Four Alien (non homo-sapiens) bodies were recovered in the wreckage. The Aliens were found to be creatures not related to human beings (Atch 1). In late 1949, another Alien aircraft crashed in the United States and was recovered partially intact by the military. One Alien of extraterrestrial origin survived the crash. The surviving Alien was male and called itself, "EBE." The Alien was thoroughly interrogated by military intelligence personnel at a base in New Mexico. The Alien's language was translated by means of picturegraphs. It was learned the Alien came from a planet in the Zeta Reticuli star system, approximately 40 light years from Earth. EBE lived until June 18, 1952, when he died of an unexplained illness. During the time period EBE was alive, he provided valuable information regarding space technology, origins of the Universe, and exobiological matters. Further data is contained in Atch 2.

TOP SECRET

TOP SECRET

(TS/ORCON) The recovery of Alien aircrafts lead the United States on an extensive investigative program to determine whether these Aliens posed a direct threat to our national security. In 1947, the newly created Air Force initiated a program to investigate incidents involving UFOs. The program was operated under three different code names: Grudge, Sign and finally Blue Book. The original mission of the Air Force program was to collect and analyze all reported sightings or incidents involving UFOs and determine whether the information could be interrupted (?interpreted?) as having any bearing on the security of the United States. Some information was evaluated with the idea of using the gained data to advance our own space technology and future space programs. 90 percent of the estimated 12,000 reports analyzed by the Air Force, were considered hoaxes, explained aerial phenomenas or natural astronomical objects. The other 10 percent were considered legitimate Alien sightings and/or incidents. However, not all UFO sightings or incidents were reported under the Air Force program. In 1953, Project Gleem was initiated by order of President Eisenhower, who believed the UFOs presented a threat to the national security of the United States. Project Gleem, which became Project Aquarius in 1966, was a parallel reporting system for UFO sightings and incidents. Reports collected under Project Aquarius were considered actual sightings of Alien aircrafts or contacts with Alien Life Forms. Most reports were made by reliable military and defense department civilian perssonel.

TOP SECRET

TOP SECRET

(TS/ORCON) In 1958 the United States recovered a third Alien aircraft from the desert of Utah. The aircraft was in excellent flying condition. The aircraft was apparently abandoned by the Aliens for some unexplainable reason, since no Alien Life forms were found in or around the aircraft. The aircraft was considered a technological marvel by United States Scientists. However, the operating instrumentations of the aircraft were so complexed that our scientists could not interrupt (interpret?) their operation. The aircraft was stored in a top security area and analyzed throughout the years by our best aerospace scientists. The United States gained a large volume of technological data from the recovered Alien aircraft.
A detailed description and further information regarding the aircraft is explained in Atch 3

TOP SECRET

TOP SECRET

(TS/ORCON) Several independent scientific investigations at the request of the Air Force and CIA, were initiated during the era of Project Blue Book. MJ12 decided that officially, the Air Force should end their investigation of UFOs. This decision was arrived at during the ______ meeting (Atch 4) in __________. The reason was twofold. First, the United States had established communication with the Aliens. The United States felt relatively sure the Aliens exploration of earth was non-agressive and non-hostile. It was also established that the Aliens presence did not directly threaten the security of the United States. Secondly, the public was beginning to believe that UFOs were real. The NSC felt this public feeling could lead to a nationwide panic. The United States was involved in several sensitive projects during this time period. It was felt that public awareness of these projects would have jeopardized the future space program of the United States. Therefore, MJ12 decided that an independent scientific study of the UFO phenomena would be needed to satisfy public curiosity. The final official study of the UFO phenomena was accomplished by the University of Colorado under Air Force contract. The study concluded that sufficient data did not exist that would indicate UFOs threatened the security of the United States. The final conclusion satisfied the government and allowed the Air Force to officially step out of the UFO investigating business.

TOP SECRET

TOP SECRET

(TS/ORCON) When the Air Force officially closed Project Blue Book in Dec. 1969, Project Aquarius continued operation under control of NSC/MJ12. The NSC felt investigations of UFO sightings and incidents had to continue in secrecy without any public knowledge. The reasoning behind the decision was this: If the Air Force continued its investigation of UFOs, eventually some uncleared and unbriefed Air Force or defense department civilian officials would obtain the facts behind Project Aquarius. Obviously (for operational security reasons) this could not be allowed. In order to continue the investigation of UFO sightings and incidents in secrecy, investigators from CIA/DCD and MJ12 were assigned to military and other governmental agencies with orders to investigate all legitimate UFO/IAC sightings and incidents. These agents are presently operating at various locations throughout the United States and Canada. All reports are filtered either directly or indirectly to MJ12. These agents are collecting reports of UFO/IAC sightings and incidents occurring on or near sensitive governmental installations. NOTE: Aliens have been extremely interested in our nuclear weapons and nuclear research. Many reported military sightings and incidents occur over nuclear weapons bases. The Alien's interest in our nuclear weapons can only be attributed to the future threat of a nuclear war on earth. The Air Force have initiated measures to assure the security of the nuclear weapons from Alien theft or destruction. MJ12 feels confident the Aliens are on an exploration of our solar system for peaceful purposes. However, we must continue to observe and track the Aliens movement until it is determined that the Alien's future plans contain no threat to our national security or the civilization of earth.

TOP SECRET

TOP SECRET

(TS/ORCON) Most governmental documents pertaining to UFO sightings, incidents and governmental policies, including Project Blue Book, have been released to the public under FOIA or under various other release programs. MJ12 felt the remaining documents and information (not relating to Project Aquarius) relating to technological facts regarding Aliens medical matters, the fact that an Alien was captured alive and survived for three years under secrecy; can not be released to the public for fear the information would be obtained by SHIS. There was other information obtained from EBE that was deemed sensitive and not releasable to the public. Notably, Project Aquarius Volume IX, which pertains to tracing the Aliens first visitation of earth back some 5,000 years. EBE reported that 2,000 years ago his ancestors planted a human creature on earth to assist the inhabitants of earth in developing a civilization. This information was only vague and the exact identity or background information on this homo-sapien was not obtained. Undoubtfully, if this information was released to the public, it would cause a worldwide religious panic. MJ3 has developed a plan that will allow release of Project Aquarius, Volumes I thru III. The release program calls for a gradual release of information over a period of time in order to condition the public for future disclosures. Atch 4 of this briefing contains certain guidelines for future public releases.

TOP SECRET

TOP SECRET

(TS/ORCON) In the 1976 MJ3 report (Atch 6), it was estimated the Alien's technology was many thousands of years ahead of United States technology. Our scientists speculate that until our technology develops to a level equal to the Aliens, we cannot understand the large volume of scientific information the United States has already gained from the Aliens. This advancement of United States Technology may take many hundred of years.

TOP SECRET

TOP SECRET

SUB PROJECTS UNDER PROJECT AQUARIUS

1. (TS/ORCON) PROJECT BANDO: (PROWORD: RISK) Originally established in 1949. Its mission was to collect and evaluate medical information from the surviving Aliens creature and the recovered Alien bodies. This Project medically examined EBE and provided United States medical researchers with certain answers to the evolution theory. (OPR: CIA) (Terminated in 1974).

2. (TS/ORCON) PROJECT SIGMA: (PROWORD: MIDNIGHT). Originally established as part of Project Gleem in 1954. Became a separate project in 1976. Its mission was to establish communication with Aliens. This Project met with positive success, when in 1959, the United States established primitive communications with the Aliens. On April 25, 1964, a USAF intelligence officer, met two Aliens at a prearranged location in the desert of New Mexico. The contact lasted for approximately three hours. Based on the Alien's language given to us by EBE, the Air Force officer managed to exchange basic information with the two Aliens (Atch 7). This project is continuing at an Air Force base in New Mexico. (OPR: MJ12/NSA).

3. (TS/ORCON) PROJECT SNOWBIRD: (PROWORD: CETUS): Originally established in 1972. Its mission was to test fly a recovered Alien aircraft. This project is continuing in Nevada. (OPR: USAF/NASA/CIA/MJ12).

4. (TS/ORCON) PROJECT POUNCE: (PROWORD: DIXIE). Originally established in 1949?. Its mission was to evaluate all UFO/IAC information pertaining to space technology. PROJECT POUNCE continues. (OPR: NASA/USAF).

TOP SECRET

APPENDIX IX

FBI Teletype Message Re: "Flying Disc" Recovery Near Roswell, New Mexico, July 8, 1947.

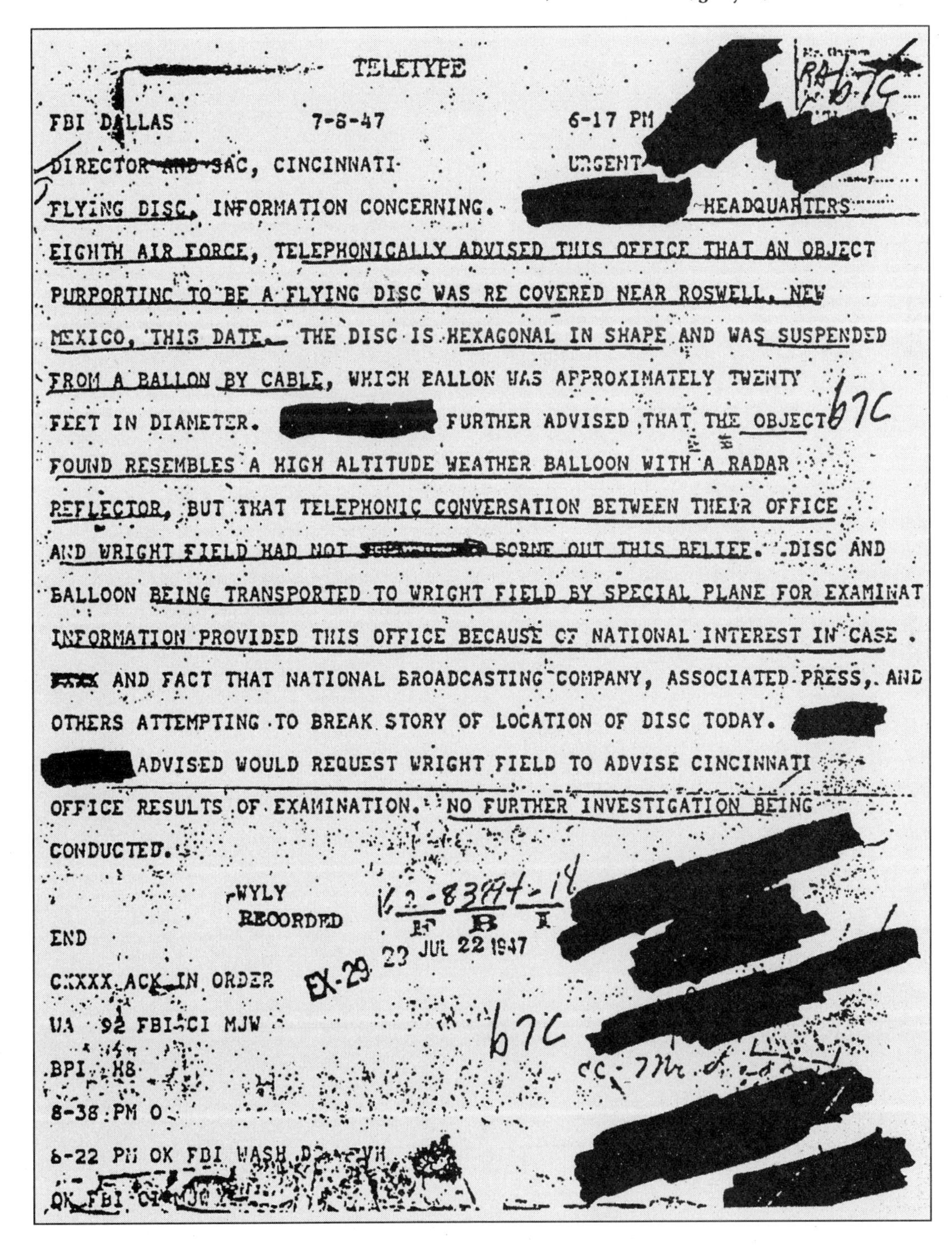

TELETYPE

FBI DALLAS 7-8-47 6-17 PM

DIRECTOR AND SAC, CINCINNATI URGENT

FLYING DISC, INFORMATION CONCERNING. [redacted] HEADQUARTERS EIGHTH AIR FORCE, TELEPHONICALLY ADVISED THIS OFFICE THAT AN OBJECT PURPORTING TO BE A FLYING DISC WAS RE COVERED NEAR ROSWELL, NEW MEXICO, THIS DATE. THE DISC IS HEXAGONAL IN SHAPE AND WAS SUSPENDED FROM A BALLON BY CABLE, WHICH BALLON WAS APPROXIMATELY TWENTY FEET IN DIAMETER. [redacted] FURTHER ADVISED THAT THE OBJECT FOUND RESEMBLES A HIGH ALTITUDE WEATHER BALLOON WITH A RADAR REFLECTOR, BUT THAT TELEPHONIC CONVERSATION BETWEEN THEIR OFFICE AND WRIGHT FIELD HAD NOT [struck out] BORNE OUT THIS BELIEF. DISC AND BALLOON BEING TRANSPORTED TO WRIGHT FIELD BY SPECIAL PLANE FOR EXAMINAT INFORMATION PROVIDED THIS OFFICE BECAUSE OF NATIONAL INTEREST IN CASE. XXXX AND FACT THAT NATIONAL BROADCASTING COMPANY, ASSOCIATED PRESS, AND OTHERS ATTEMPTING TO BREAK STORY OF LOCATION OF DISC TODAY. [redacted] ADVISED WOULD REQUEST WRIGHT FIELD TO ADVISE CINCINNATI OFFICE RESULTS OF EXAMINATION. NO FURTHER INVESTIGATION BEING CONDUCTED.

WYLY

RECORDED

END

CXXXX ACK IN ORDER

UA 92 FBI CI MJW

BPI HB

8-38 PM O

6-22 PM OK FBI WASH D

OK FBI CI MJW

APPENDIX X

U. S. Government Facilities & Organizational Charts Relevant to MJ-12 and UFO Cover-Up
Provided by J. Andrew Kissner.

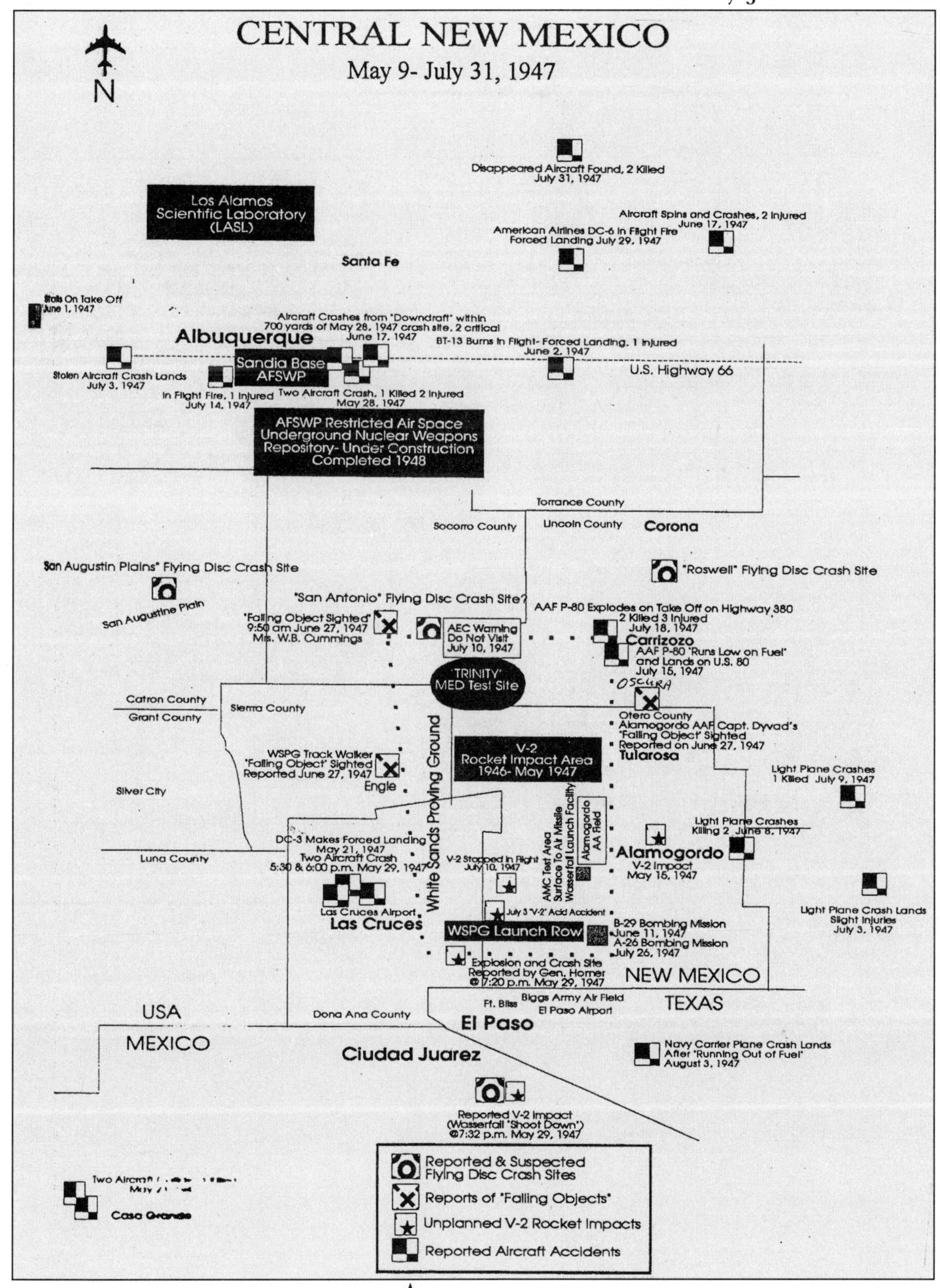

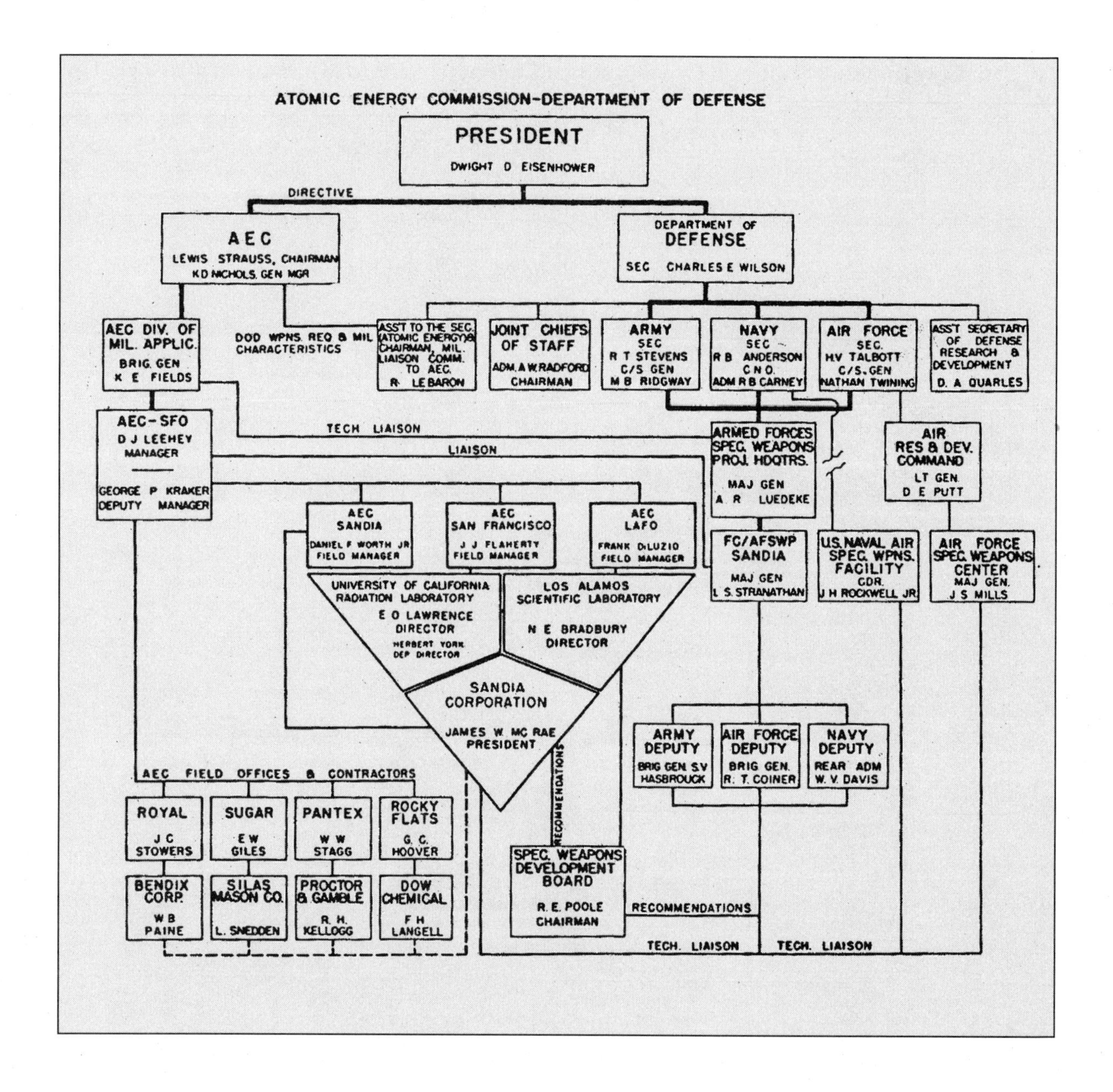
ATOMIC ENERGY COMMISSION-DEPARTMENT OF DEFENSE
PRESIDENT
DWIGHT D EISENHOWER
DIRECTIVE
AEC
LEWIS STRAUSS, CHAIRMAN
KD NICHOLS, GEN MGR
DEPARTMENT OF
DEFENSE
SEC CHARLES E WILSON
AEC DIV. OF MIL. APPLIC.
BRIG. GEN
K E FIELDS
DOD WPNS. REQ & MIL CHARACTERISTICS
ASST TO THE SEC. (ATOMIC ENERGY) & CHAIRMAN, MIL. LIAISON COMM. TO AEC.
R. LE BARON
JOINT CHIEFS OF STAFF
ADM. A W RADFORD
CHAIRMAN
ARMY
SEC
R T STEVENS
C/S GEN
M B RIDGWAY
NAVY
SEC
R B ANDERSON
C N O.
ADM R B CARNEY
AIR FORCE
SEC.
H V TALBOTT
C/S. GEN
NATHAN TWINING
ASST SECRETARY OF DEFENSE RESEARCH & DEVELOPMENT
D. A QUARLES
AEC-SFO
D J LEEHEY
MANAGER
GEORGE P KRAKER
DEPUTY MANAGER
TECH LIAISON
LIAISON
ARMED FORCES SPEC. WEAPONS PROJ. HDQTRS.
MAJ GEN
A R LUEDEKE
AIR RES & DEV. COMMAND
LT GEN
D E PUTT
AEC SANDIA
DANIEL F WORTH JR
FIELD MANAGER
AEC SAN FRANCISCO
J J FLAHERTY
FIELD MANAGER
AEC LAFO
FRANK DiLUZIO
FIELD MANAGER
FC/AFSWP SANDIA
MAJ GEN
L S. STRANATHAN
U.S. NAVAL AIR SPEC. WPNS. FACILITY
CDR.
J H ROCKWELL JR.
AIR FORCE SPEC. WEAPONS CENTER
MAJ GEN.
J S MILLS
UNIVERSITY OF CALIFORNIA RADIATION LABORATORY
E O LAWRENCE
DIRECTOR
HERBERT YORK
DEP DIRECTOR
LOS ALAMOS SCIENTIFIC LABORATORY
N E BRADBURY
DIRECTOR
SANDIA CORPORATION
JAMES W. MC RAE
PRESIDENT
RECOMMENDATIONS
ARMY DEPUTY
BRIG GEN. S.V HASBROUCK
AIR FORCE DEPUTY
BRIG GEN.
R. T. COINER
NAVY DEPUTY
REAR ADM
W. V. DAVIS
AEC FIELD OFFICES & CONTRACTORS
ROYAL
J C
STOWERS
SUGAR
E W
GILES
PANTEX
W W
STAGG
ROCKY FLATS
G. C.
HOOVER
BENDIX CORP.
W B
PAINE
SILAS MASON CO.
L. SNEDDEN
PROCTOR & GAMBLE
R. H.
KELLOGG
DOW CHEMICAL
F H
LANGELL
SPEC. WEAPONS DEVELOPMENT BOARD
R. E. POOLE
CHAIRMAN
RECOMMENDATIONS
TECH. LIAISON
TECH. LIAISON

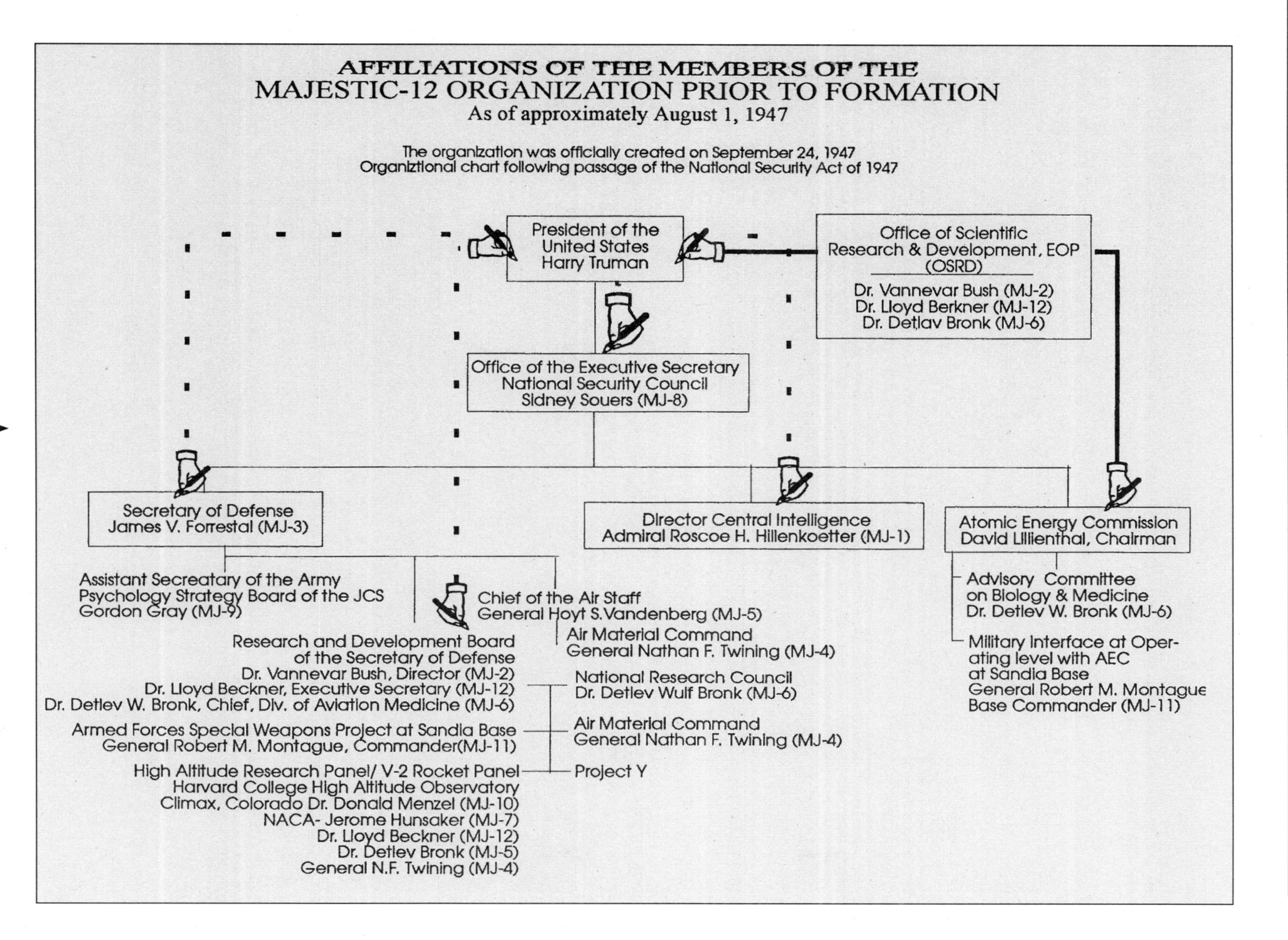
AFFILIATIONS OF THE MEMBERS OF THE
MAJESTIC-12 ORGANIZATION PRIOR TO FORMATION
As of approximately August 1, 1947
The organization was officially created on September 24, 1947
Organiztional chart following passage of the National Security Act of 1947
President of the United States Harry Truman
Office of Scientific Research & Development, EOP (OSRD)
Dr. Vannevar Bush (MJ-2)
Dr. Lloyd Berkner (MJ-12)
Dr. Detlav Bronk (MJ-6)
Office of the Executive Secretary National Security Council Sidney Souers (MJ-8)
Secretary of Defense James V. Forrestal (MJ-3)
Director Central Intelligence Admiral Roscoe H. Hillenkoetter (MJ-1)
Atomic Energy Commission David Lillienthal, Chairman
Assistant Secreatary of the Army Psychology Strategy Board of the JCS Gordon Gray (MJ-9)
Chief of the Air Staff General Hoyt S.Vandenberg (MJ-5)
Air Material Command General Nathan F. Twining (MJ-4)
Research and Development Board of the Secretary of Defense
Dr. Vannevar Bush, Director (MJ-2)
Dr. Lloyd Beckner, Executive Secretary (MJ-12)
Dr. Detlev W. Bronk, Chief, Div. of Aviation Medicine (MJ-6)
National Research Council Dr. Detlev Wulf Bronk (MJ-6)
Armed Forces Special Weapons Project at Sandia Base General Robert M. Montague, Commander(MJ-11)
Air Material Command General Nathan F. Twining (MJ-4)
High Altitude Research Panel/ V-2 Rocket Panel
Harvard College High Altitude Observatory
Climax, Colorado Dr. Donald Menzel (MJ-10)
NACA- Jerome Hunsaker (MJ-7)
Dr. Lloyd Beckner (MJ-12)
Dr. Detlev Bronk (MJ-5)
General N.F. Twining (MJ-4)
Project Y
Advisory Committee on Biology & Medicine Dr. Detlev W. Bronk (MJ-6)
Military Interface at Operating level with AEC at Sandia Base General Robert M. Montague Base Commander (MJ-11)

APPENDIX XI

1948 Wright-Patterson AFB Memo to Chief of Staff, USAF, Washington, D. C.

TS-: 3931
Cover Sheet ~~SECRET~~
MR of Basic

8 Nov 48

Basic ltr fr Hq USAF, 3 Nov 48 to CG, AMC, "Flying Object Incidents in the United States"

1st Ind MCIAT/ABD/amh

Hq AMC, Wright-Patterson Air Force Base, Dayton, Ohio. 8 Nov 48

TO: Chief of Staff, United States Air Force, Washington 25, D. C., ATTN: AFOIR

1. In attempting to arrive at conclusions as to the nature of unidentified flying object incidents in the United States, this Command has made a study of approximately 180 such incidents. Data derived from initial reports have been supplemented by further information obtained from check lists submitted by mail, from interrogations of other field agencies, and by personal investigation by personnel of this Command in the case of incidents that seem to indicate the possibility of obtaining particularly significant information.

2. The objects described fall into the following general classification groups, according to shape or physical configuration:

a. Flat disc of circular or approximately circular shape.

b. Torpedo or cigar shaped aircraft, with no wings or fins visible in flight.

c. Spherical or balloon shaped objects.

d. Balls of light with no apparent form attached.

3. Some of the objects sighted have definitely been identified, upon further investigation, as weather or upper air scientific balloons of some type. A great many of the round or balloon shaped objects indicated in paragraph 2c above are probably of the same nature, although in most cases, definite confirmation of that fact has been impossible to obtain.

4. Some of the objects have been identified as being astro-physical in nature. For example, in daylight sightings, the planet Venus has been reported as a round, silvery object at extremely high altitude. Action is being taken to obtain the services of a prominent astro-physicist as a consultant, to study all of the incidents to determine whether some can be identified as meteors, planets or other manifestations of astral bodies.

5. Arrangements for accomplishing a study of the psychological problems involved in this project are being made in coordination with the Aero-Medical Laboratory at this Headquarters. The possibility that some of the sightings are hallucinations, optical illusions or even deliberate hoaxes has been considered.

File - 6 Jan 48
Maj Jones

FK

2

T-73017

~~SECRET~~

SECRET

1st Ind

Basic ltr fr Hq USAF, 3 Nov 48 to CG, AMC, "Flying Object Incidents in the United States"

6. Although explanation of many of the incidents can be obtained from the investigations described above, there remains a certain number of reports for which no reasonable everyday explanation is available. So far, no physical evidence of the existence of the unidentified sightings has been obtained. Prominent scientists, including Dr. Irving Langmuir of the General Electric Company, have been interviewed to determine whether they could advance any reasonable explanation for characteristics exhibited by the objects sighted. In an early interview, Dr. Langmuir indicated that these incidents could be explained, but insufficient data were available at that time on which to base definite conclusions. It is planned to have another interview with Dr. Langmuir in the near future to review all the data now available, and it is hoped that he will be able to present some opinion as to the nature of many of the unidentified objects, particularly those described as "balls of light."

7. All information that has been made available to this Headquarters indicates that the discs, the cigar shaped objects, and the "balls of light" are not of domestic origin. Engineering investigation indicates that disc or wingless aircraft could support themselves in flight by aerodynamic means. It is probable that the problems of stability and control could also be solved for such aircraft. However, according to current aerodynamic theory in this country, aircraft with such configurations would have relatively poor climb, altitude and range characteristics with power plants now in use.

8. The possibility that the reported objects are vehicles from another planet has not been ignored. However, tangible evidence to support conclusions about such a possibility are completely lacking. The occurrence of incidents in relation to the approach to the earth of the planets Mercury, Venus and Mars have been plotted. A periodic variation in the frequency of incidents, which appears to have some relation to the planet approach curves, is noted, but it may be purely a coincidence.

9. Reference is made to "The Books of Charles Fort" with an introduction by Tiffany Thayer, published 1941, by Henry Holt & Co., New York, N. Y. It appears that simular phenomena have been noted and reported for the past century or more.

10. In view of the above, the following conclusions are drawn:

a. In the majority of cases reported, observers have actually sighted some type of flying object which they cannot classify as an aircraft within the limits of their personal experience.

3

T-73017

SECRET

1st Ind

Basic ltr fr Hq USAF, 3 Nov 48 to CG, AMC, "Flying Object Incidents in the United States"

b. There is as yet no conclusive proof that unidentified flying objects, other than those which are known to be balloons, are real aircraft.

c. Although it is obvious that some types of flying objects have been sighted, the exact nature of those objects cannot be established until physical evidence, such as that which would result from a crash, has been obtained.

11. It is not considered advisable to present to the press information on those obj- ts which we cannot yet identify or about which we cannot present any reasonable conclusions. In the event that they insist on some kind of a statement, it is suggested that they be informed that many of the objects sighted have been identified as weather balloons or astral bodies, and that investigation is being pursued to determine reasonable explanations for the others.

12. A report, summarizing the results obtained from analysis of the data and a technical investigation of the engineering aspects of the objects described, is nearly complete, and a copy will be forwarded to your Headquarters in the near future.

FOR THE COMMANDING GENERAL:

H M McCoy
H. M. McCOY
Colonel, USAF
Chief, Intelligence Department

4

T-73017

SECRET

APPENDIX XII

Full Text — Front Page Story About "Saucer Armada,"
The Farmington Daily Times, March 18, 1950, Farmington, New Mexico.

HUGE 'SAUCER' ARMADA JOLTS FARMINGTON

Crafts Seen By (sic) Hudreds
Speed Estimated
At 1000 M.P.H.
Altitude 20,000 Feet

For the third consecutive day, flying saucers have been reported over Farmington. And on each of the three days, their arrival here was reported between 11 and noon.

Three persons called the *Daily Times* office to report seeing strange objects in the air just before noon.

Persons along Main Street once again could be seen looking skyward and pointing.

High winds and a dust storm prevented clear vision.

Fully half of this town's population still is certain today that it saw space ships or some strange aircraft — hundreds of them — zooming through the skies yesterday.

Estimates of the number ranged from 'several' to more than 500. Whatever they were, they caused a major sensation in this community, which lies only 100 air miles northwest of the huge Los Alamos atomic installation.

The objects appeared to play tag high in the air. At times they streaked away at almost unbelievable speeds. One witness who took a triangulation sighting on one of the objects estimated its speed at about 1,000 miles an hour, and estimated its size as approximately twice that of a B-29.

Farmington citizens stood in the streets yesterday watching the first reported mass "flying saucer" flight ever sighted. Traffic was slowed to avoid hitting sky gazers. The office of the Farmington Daily Times was deluged with calls from persons who saw the objects.

Scores described the objects as silvery discs. A number agreed they saw one that was red in color — bigger and faster, and apparently the leader.

Clayton J. Boddy, 32, business manager of the *Farmington Times* and former Army Engineers captain in Italy, was one of those who saw the startling objects.

Boddy was on Broadway when "all of a sudden I noticed a few moving objects high in the sky. Moments later there appeared what seemed to be about 500 of them." Boddy continued. He could not estimate their size or speed, but said they appeared to be about 15,000 feet high.

Boddy's account was confirmed by Joseph C. and Francis C. Kalloff, retail grocers from Antonito, Colo., who were in Farmington to inspect the site of a proposed new store, and by Bob Foutz and John Burrell of Farmington. The Kelloffs said the objects appeared to be flying in formation.

One of the most impressive accounts came from Harold F. Thatcher, head of the Farmington unit of the Soil Conservation service. Thatcher made a triangulation on one of a number of flying craft. He said if it had been a B-29, it would have been 20,000 feet high and traveling more than 1000 miles per hour.

"I'm not a professional engineer," Thatcher said, "but I have engineers working under me and I know a little engineering, enough to know how to work out a rough triangulation on an object."

Thatcher emphatically denied an earlier report that the objects could have been small pieces of cotton fuzz floating in the atmosphere.

"It was not cotton," he said. "I saw several pieces of cotton fuzz floating around in the air at the time, but I was not sighting on any cotton."

The "cotton" report was started by State Patrolman Andy Andrews who quoted several Farmington residents as asserting it was cotton they saw. The residents denied Andrews' report.

The first reports of flying saucers were noted a few minutes before 11 AM yesterday. For a full hour thereafter, people deluged the *Times* office with reports of the objects.

A second large-scale sighting occurred at 3 PM. At this time, Mrs. Wilson Jones, 27, and Mrs. Roy Hicks (can't read microfilm)... perfect formation. Others reported the same sight.

Johnny Eaton, 29, a real estate and insurance salesman, and Edward Brooks, 24, an employee of the Perry Smoak garage, were the first to report the red-colored sky object. Not airplanes.

Brooks, a B-29 tail gunner during the war, said he was positive the objects sighted were not airplanes. "The very maneuvering of the things couldn't be that of modern aircraft," he said.

John Bloomfield, another employee of Smoak's garage, said the objects he saw traveled at a speed that appeared to him to be about 10 times faster than that of jet planes. In addition, he said, the objects frequently made *right-angle turns*.' (Howe's emphasis.)

"They appeared to be coming at each other head on," he related. "At the last second, one would veer at right angles upward, the other at right angles downward. One saucer would pass another ahead and then immediately the one to the rear would zoom into the lead."

Marlow Webb, another garage employee, said the objects to the naked eye appeared to be about eight inches in diameter as seen from the ground. He described them as about the size of a dinner plate.

"They flew sideways, on edge and at every conceivable angle," he said. "This is what made it easy to determine that they were saucer-shaped."

None of the scores of reports told of any vapor trail or engine noise. Nor did anyone report any windows or other markings on the craft.

In general, Farmington accepted the phenomenon calmly, although it was reported that some women employees of a laundry became somewhat panicky.

Opinion was somewhat divided among those who saw the objects as to whether they were from another planet or were some new craft of our own nation's devising. Some expressed the opinion the entire incident was the fulfillment of a Bible prophecy.

From sifting all reports, the *Farmington Times* compiled this timetable of sightings:

1. 10:15 a.m. five to nine 'saucers' zoomed over the town's business area for 10 minutes before moving out of sight to the northeast.
2. 10:00 a.m., report of 'hundreds' seen west of town.
3. 10:30 a.m., red 'saucers' seen over town.
4. 10:35 a.m., three objects staged 'dog fight' over town.
5. 11:15 a.m., clearest view of a large number of 'saucers.'
6. 11: ? , all disappeared.

7. 3 p.m., fleet of 'hundreds' seen flying in formation to the southwest from the northeast.

In And Around Farmington
Society Editor Weeds Barrett
Saturday, March 18, 1950

Flying saucers were reported to have appeared over Farmington yesterday. Here are some of the stories as told by local persons.

J. W. Cardon; Clinton Taylor; and Ken Graham saw bright, moving objects in the sky, Friday at 11 a.m. They appeared to be made of metal and the smaller one was moving at an extremely fast pace from the south to the north. 'The larger one seemed to be stationary.'

Mrs. C. R. Bolton, local photographer, sighted around 2 p.m. a silvery object shaped like a rectangle with rounding ends, moving in a westerly direction.

At 10:30 a.m., Mrs. Horace Moffett. saw two revolving discs in the southeast, which seemed to be having a tussle in the sky.

Mrs. Anna Bell Smith employed at the Four Corners Sample Cut saw what appeared to be revolving discs, swooping and swerving and turning like atop.

"Some reports were that they were grey, then they seemed to change color and turned a bright silvery. Some say they flew in formation at times. Some say they saw what appeared to be a half moon.

One reported seeing a large silvery round object in the sky, what appeared to be about the size of his automobile and seemed to be suspended in the air. This was sighted on the Peninsula. The fellow knew nothing of what was happening within the city limits. But his sighting was timed immediately following the large numbers of small discs which were reported seen over Farmington.

Jack Sheafe and Joe Harp, local businessmen, reported seeing objects in the skies.

BIBLIOGRAPHY

Astronomy Magazine, *"The Zeta Reticuli Incident,"* December 1974, Vol. 2, No. 12.

BARKER, Gray. *They Knew Too Much About Flying Saucers © 1956.*

BEGICH, Nick M. D. & Jeane Manning. *Angels Don't Play This HAARP – Advances in Tesla Technology* © 1995, Earthpulse Press, Anchorage, Alaska.

BENDER, ALBERT K. *Flying Saucers and The Three Men* © 1962, Saucerian Books, Clarksburg, W. Virginia.

BLAUSTEIN, ANDREW R., Ph.D. Proceedings of the National Academy of Sciences, Vol. 94, Pages 13735-13737, December 1997, *"Ambient UV-B Radiation Causes Deformities In Amphibian Embryos"* © 1997 National Academy of Sciences.

BOHM, David. *Wholeness and the Implicate Order* © 1980, Cox & Wyman Ltd., London.

BUTLER, Brenda, Dot Street and Jenny Randles. *Sky Crash, A Cosmic Conspiracy* © 1984, Neville Spearman Ltd., Sudbury, U. K.

CAVENDISH, Richard, Editor. *Mythology* © 1993, Barnes & Noble.

Cell Journal, *"Neanderthal DNA Sequences and the Origin of Modern Humans"* by M. Krings, A. Stone, R. W. Schmitz, H. Krainitzki, M. Stoneking and S. Paabo, Issue 14, Volume 90, No. 1 © 1997 Cell Press,Cambridge, Mass.

CHARLES, R. H., Translation. *The Book of Jubilees (The Little Genesis)* © 1917, London Society for Promoting Christian Knowledge, London, U. K.

CORSO, Philip J., Colonel, U.S. Army (Ret.), with William J. Birnes. *The Day After Roswell* © 1997, Pocket Books, Simon & Schuster.

DAVIDSON, Gustav. *The Dictionary of Angels* © 1967, The Free Press, Macmillan Publishing, New York City.

EHRLICH, Paul and Anne. *Extinction: The Causes and Consequences of the Disappearance of Species* © 1881, Random House.

ENCYCLOPAEDIA BRITANNICA, 15th Edition © 1993, Encyclopaedia Britannica, Inc.

EVANS, Craig A. *Noncanonical Writings and New Testament Interpretation* © 1992.

EVANS-WENTZ, W. Y. *Tibetan Book of the Dead* © 1960, Oxford University Press.

FOWLER, Raymond E and Betty Andreasson. *The Andreasson Affair* © 1979, Prentice-Hall, Inc. Englewood Cliffs, N. J.

FOWLER, Raymond E and Betty Andreasson. *The Andreasson Affair, Phase Two* © 1982, Prentice-Hall, Inc. Englewood Cliffs, N. J.

FOWLER, Raymond E. and Betty Ann Luca. *The Watchers - The Secret Design Behind UFO Abduction* © 1990, Bantam Books, New York City.

FOWLER, Raymond E. *The Watchers II* © 1995, Wild Flower Press, Newberg, Oregon.

FOWLER, Raymond E. *The Andreasson Legacy* © 1997, Marlow & Co.

FRANZ, Marie-Louise von. *On Dreams and Death* © 1986, Shambhala Publications.

FRIEDMAN, Norman. *Bridging Science and Spirit* © 1990 and 1994, Living Lake Books, St. Louis, Missouri.

FRIEDMAN, Stanton T. *TOP SECRET/MAJIC* © 1996, Marlowe & Company.

FRIEDMAN, Stanton T. and Don Berliner. *Crash At Corona, The U. S. Military Retrieval and Cover-Up of a UFO* © 1992, Paragon House.

GLEICK, James. *Chaos, Making A New Science* © 1987, Penguin Books.

HAINES, Richard F. *Melbourne Episode - Case Study of A Missing Pilot* © 1987, L. D. A. Press, Los Altos, Calif.

HANCOCK, Graham and Robert Bauval. *The Message of the Sphinx: A Quest for the Hidden Legacy of Mankind* © 1996, Crown Publishers.

HAYES, Anna. *Voyagers, The Sleeping Abductees* © 1998, Wild Flower Press.

High Holiday Prayer Book: Rosh Hashanah and Yom Kippur, 1951, Prayer Book Press.

HOPKINS, Budd. *Missing Time: A documented study of UFO abductions* © 1981, Richard Marek Publishers.

HOPKINS, Budd. *Intruders, The Incredible Visitations At Copley Woods* © 1987, Random House.

HOWE, Linda Moulton. *An Alien Harvest - Further Evidence Linking Animal Mutilations and Human Abductions to Alien Life Forms* © 1989, LMH Productions.

HOWE, Linda Moulton. *Glimpses of Other Realities, Vol. I - Facts & Eyewitnesses* © 1994, LMH Productions.

HYNEK, Dr. J. Allen. *The UFO Experience, A Scientific Inquiry* © 1972, Ballantine Books.

JUNG, Carl G. *Flying Saucers: A Modern Myth of Things Seen in the Sky* © 1959, Harcourt, Brace & Co.

JUNG, Leo. *Fallen Angels in Jewish, Christian & Mohammedan Literature* © 1926, Dropsie College, Philadelphia, Pa.

KALWEIT, Holger. *Dreamtime and Inner Space* © 1988, Shambhala Publications, Random House.

KEYHOE, Major Donald E. (USMC Ret.) *The Flying Saucers Are Real* © 1950, Henry Holt & Co.

KEYHOE, Major Donald E. (USMC Ret.) *Flying Saucers From Outer Space* © 1953, Henry Holt & Co.

KEYHOE, Major Donald E. (USMC Ret.) *The Flying Saucer Conspiracy* © 1955, Henry Holt & Co.

KEYHOE, Major Donald E. (USMC Ret.) *Flying Saucers Top Secret* © 1960, G. P. Putnam's Sons.

KNIGHT, David. *UFOs: A Pictorial History from Antiquity to the Present* © 1979, McGraw-Hill Books.

KUBLER-ROSS, Elisabeth. *On Death and Dying* © 1969, Macmillan Publishers.

KUHN, Thomas S. *The Structure of Scientific Revolutions*, 2nd. Ed. © 1970, University of Chicago Press.

LAURENCE, Richard, L.L.D., Translated. *The Book of Enoch the Prophet*, 1882, John Thompson Publishers of Glasgow, Scotland.

MEADOWS, Donella et al. *Limits To Growth - A Report for the Club of Rome's Project on the Predicament of Mankind* © 1972, Universe Books, New York City.

MOODY, Raymond A. *Life After Life* © 1975, Mockingbird Books.

MORFILL, W. R., Translation, and R. H. Charles, Editor, *The Book of the Secrets of Enoch, The Son of ARED; A Man Wise and Beloved of God,* Slavonic version of the Ethiopic Book of Enoch, 1896, Trinity College, Dublin and Exeter College, Oxford, Clarendon Press, Oxford, U. K.

PETERSON, Beau (USMC). *The Order* © 1991 and 1984.

RAGSDALE, Jim. *The Jim Ragsdale Story - A Closer Look at the Roswell Incident* © 1996 by Ragsdale Productions, Inc.

RING, Kenneth. *Heading Toward Omega* © 1980, Coward, McCann and Geoghegan.

RING, Kenneth. *The Omega Project, Near-Death Experiences, UFO Encounters, and Mind At Large* © 1992, William Morrow & Co., Inc.

ROSS-MACDONALD, Malcolm. *Life In The Future - Prospects for Man and Nature* © *1977,* Doubleday and Company, Inc.

SABOM, Michael B. *Recollections of Death* © 1982, Harper & Row.

SAGAN, Carl and I. S. Shklovskii. *Intelligent Life in the Universe* © 1966.

SCHILPP, Paul, Editor. *Albert Einstein: Philosopher-Scientist* © 1949, The Library of Living Philosophers, Inc.

SITCHIN, Zecharia. *The Earth Chronicles, Books I-V*
Book I: The 12th Planet © 1976, Avon Books.
Book II: The Stairway To Heaven © 1980, Avon Books.
Book III: The Wars of Gods and Men © 1985, Avon Books.
Book IV: The Lost Realms © 1990, Avon Books.
Book V: When Time Began © 1993, Avon Books.

SITCHIN, Zecharia. *Genesis Revisited* © 1990, Avon Books.

SPARKS, Jim. *Star People, Outsiders - Us? Or Them?* © 1996.

STEINER, Rudolph. *Theosophy* © 1922, Anthroposophic Press, New York City.

STEINMAN, William J. *UFO Crash At Aztec - A Well Kept Secret* © 1986, America West Publishers, Boulder, Colo.

STEVENSON, Ian M. D. *Children Who Remember Previous Lives - A Question of Reincarnation* © 1987 University Press of Virginia.

STRIEBER, Whitley. *Communion* © 1987, William Morrow Books.

STRIEBER, Whitley. *Transformation* © 1988, William Morrow Books.

STRIEBER, Whitley. *Majestic* © 1989, G. P. Putnam's Sons.

STRINGFIELD, Leonard H. *UFO Crash/Retrievals: The Inner Sanctum, Status Report VI* © 1991.

TALBOT, Michael. *The Holographic Universe* © 1991, HarperCollins Publishers.

VALLEE, Jacques. *Passport To Magonia: From folklore to flying saucers* © 1969 and 1983, Contemporary Books, Inc.

VALLEE, Jacques. *Dimensions: A casebook of alien contact* © 1988, Contemporary Books.

VALLEE, Jacques. *Confrontations, A Scientist's Search for Alien Contact* © 1990, Ballantine Books.

WALTARI, Mika. *The Roman* © 1964, originally published in Finland under the title *Ihmiskunnan Viholliset,* and © 1966 by G. P. Putnam's Sons and Hodder & Stoughton Ltd.

WEBER, Renee. *Dialogues with Scientists and Sages* © 1986, Routledge & Kegan Paul, London, U. K.

WHEELER, John A. and Wojciech H. Zurek, Editors. *Quantum Theory & Measurement* © 1983, Princeton University Press.

WRIGHT, Robert. *"Science and Original Sin," Time* Magazine, October 28, 1996.

INDEX

A

D

E

F

L

M

O

P

V

Linda Moulton Howe is a graduate of Stanford University with a Masters Degree in Communication. She has devoted her documentary film, television and radio career to productions concerning science, medicine and the environment.

Ms. Howe has received many local, national and international awards for her documentaries, including three regional Emmys, a national Emmy nomination, medical producer participant in Boston's WCVB Station Excellence Peabody Award, Colorado's Florence Sabin Award for "outstanding contribution to public health," Aviation & Space Writers Association Award for Writing Excellence in television, and a Chicago Film Festival Golden Plaque. Some of her honored films have included *Fire In The Water* about hydrogen as an alternative energy source to fossil fuels; *A Radioactive Water* about uranium contamination of public drinking water in a Denver suburb; and *A Strange Harvest* about the worldwide animal mutilation mystery which has haunted the United States and other countries since the late 1960s — and continues to date.

In 1989, Ms. Howe was Director of International Programming for *Earthbeat,* an environmental series broadcast on Turner's WTBS Superstation, Atlanta, Georgia. That year her first book was released entitled *An Alien Harvest* which documented the history and unusual medical evidence of animal mutilations linked to a non-human intelligence. That work was followed in 1994 by *Glimpses of Other Realities, Vol. I - Facts & Eyewitnesses,* the companion to this *Volume II: High Strangeness.*

She has produced and written more than a hundred live studio programs, including a two-hour special *Earth Mysteries: Alien Life Forms* in association with WATL-Fox, Atlanta and was creator and supervising producer of the hour network special *UFO Report: Sightings* which lead to the 1992 *Sightings* series on Fox. That year she also helped coordinate biophysical investigations of the crop circle mystery in England.

Ms. Howe has been a featured speaker at national and international conferences and symposiums, including NASA's Goddard Space Flight Center. She continues to produce reports for television and radio, including news about science, the environment and unusual phenomena for the nationally syndicated radio series *Dreamland* and *Coast to Coast* hosted by Art Bell. She has appeared on many national and international television news and documentary programs including CBS's *Day & Date;* FOX's *Strange Universe;* CNN's *Larry King Live;* and NBC's network special and companion tape for *The Mysterious Origins of Man.*

The author welcomes readers' comments, questions and reports of unusual sightings and experiences. Please write to:

Linda Moulton Howe
P. O. Box 300
Jamison, Pennsylvania 18929-0300

Photograph of author by her daughter, Laura Kathleen Howe, Jamison, Pennsylvania.

The text was created with 11-point New Baskerville type, highlighted with 17-point Charlemagne, in 14-point leading.

For more information about Linda Moulton Howe's books, documentaries or other Paper Chase Press titles, please call PCP Customer Service:

1-800-460-8604

To order Ms. Howe's books and documentary videos, please call the Paper Chase Press 24-hour order line:

1-800-864-7991

PAPER
CHASE
PRESS